ISBN 978-0-260-52449-2
PIBN 10270769

THE

NEW ENGLAND

HISTORICAL AND GENEALOGICAL

REGISTER

1906

VOLUME LX.

BOSTON
PUBLISHED BY THE SOCIETY
1906

680032

INDEX OF SUBJECTS.

James L. Rogers

NEW-ENGLAND
HISTORICAL AND GENEALOGICAL REGISTER.

JANUARY, 1906.

JAMES SWIFT ROGERS, A.B.

By Almon Danforth Hodges, Jr., A.M.

It was a heroic deed, undertaken with no desire of reward or hope of glory, but simply for the purpose of saving the lives of two unknown black men. Planned on the spur of the moment, and executed at once in the face of what seemed to others certain death, it was successful through its brilliant audacity. So far as I can learn, it was never alluded to afterwards by the man who performed it, and only after his death were the details made public.

The First South Carolina Volunteers — the first slave regiment mustered into the service of the United States during the late civil war — was on duty at Port Royal Ferry in South Carolina. Port Royal Island was held by the United States troops with headquarters at Beaufort, while the main land was occupied by the Confederate forces. Before the war the main thoroughfare between Beaufort and Charleston had been the Shell Road, of which the ferry across the Coosaw River formed a part. At the ferry the road projected on each side as a causeway into the river, ending in a wharf or pier for the use of the ferry-boat. The ferry had been abolished by the war, the piers were in damaged condition, and the river-channel formed a barrier between the opposing picket lines. Occasionally at night scouting parties in boats ventured across the river, but these adventures were difficult and dangerous. To cross by day was simply to invite sure death or captivity.

Early one morning two dusky forms amid the piles at the end of the opposite causeway were descried by some of the Union pickets. Their frantic signals indicated that they were fugitive slaves, anxious to pass the barrier between slavery and freedom and unable to swim across the stream; but their case seemed hopeless, and while some watched for developments, the rest went about their allotted duties. Suddenly there appeared on the river a dug-out, propelled boldly towards the further side by a Federal officer, who calmly paddled up to the causeway, took the fugitives on board and began the return journey. When the canoe had reached mid-stream, it was discovered by the enemy and saluted with a storm of bullets. These, however, failed to reach their mark, and the boat, continuing steadily on its course, gained its haven in safety. Evidently a passage in broad daylight was considered such an impossibility by the Confederate pickets that they had ceased their vigils for a moment, and this exact moment was seized by the daring officer for his chivalrous deed.

To do such an act for the benefit of another without reference to the possible cost to himself, and to do it in a simple, unostentatious manner, was characteristic of James Swift Rogers. He was then a captain, and in the abundant vigor of youthful manhood. He was full of life and full of the joy of living. There were loving parents and friends awaiting his return to his home and his college. Above all, there was one who had agreed to keep herself only unto him so long as both should live. The future held out the brightest allurements, and there was so much to live for. Yet when a call for help came, his helping hand was at once extended in complete forgetfulness of self. And as it was then, so it was throughout his life. Quiet, self-sacrificing friendship was inborn in him. Perhaps he inherited it from his Quaker ancestors.

John[2] Rogers of Marshfield, whose father bore the same name, joined the Quakers about 1660 and suffered accordingly, as is set forth in the Scituate Friends' Records. He and his descendants for five generations persisted in the faith. His son Thomas[3] and his grandson John[4] were born, married and died in this same town of Marshfield. Stephen[5] Rogers, of the next generation, moved to Danby, Vermont, and there his son Aaron[6] Rogers was born, married Dinah Folger, and had by her twelve children. Aaron's eighth child, Elisha Folger[7] Rogers, was born June 20, 1813, married December 12, 1835, Elizabeth Mitchell, and had, at Danby, two children: Jethro Folger[8] Rogers, born in 1836, who died in infancy; and James Swift[8] Rogers, born March 28, 1840, the subject of this sketch. *

While a young child, James Swift Rogers was taken by his parents to New York City; and thence, when he was about nine or ten years of age, to Worcester, Mass., where his uncle Dr. Seth Rogers had a successful sanatorium. Here, at his first coming, he met two persons whose idealizing influences began at once and lasted through life: — the girl who became his wife; and the clergyman who modified his theological creed, intensified his convictions regarding right and wrong, increased his hatred of slavery, became his captain and then his colonel during the civil war, and was his friend always.

Rogers entered Harvard College in 1861. The bugles of war were then calling men to arms. His parents were Quakers and strongly opposed to fighting, and he had been bred in this faith; but when the chance offered for striking a blow at slavery, he joined the army. He enlisted in Company C, 51st Massachusetts Volun-

* For a more complete record of this family, see John Rogers of Marshfield and Some of his Descendants. By Josiah H. Drummond, 1898.

teers, his friend and mentor Thomas Wentworth Higginson being captain, and became corporal and sergeant. When his captain was made colonel of the First South Carolina Volunteers, he took the commission of captain in this regiment.* To join this regiment of black soldiers required considerable moral courage. There was, among the officers and soldiers of the North, a strong prejudice against the experiment of enlisting the slaves. It was not believed, except by a few, that these blacks would have the courage to face their former masters; to arm them was considered unwise, and to associate with them as their officers was thought degrading. Moreover, the Confederate authorities had declared that these troops would be regarded as outside of the ordinary rules of warfare, would be shot or hung when captured. But all these considerations were to him only stronger demands for his help, and he acted promptly and cheerfully in response. How well he performed his duties, how readily he adapted himself to the requirements of a difficult position, how efficient he was in training and leading his men whom he inspired with respect and affection for himself — this his commanding officer told at his funeral.

Edward Earle was a prominent citizen of Worcester, of which city he became mayor. He and his wife, Ann Barker Buffum, were members of the Society of Friends. Both were strong characters and maintained stoutly their religious tenets, which included hatred of slavery, and also of war. Their only child was Anne Buffum Earle. That the man who was to marry their daughter should become a soldier was to them a sorrow, which became an unbearable pain when he transferred from a nine-months' regiment to one enlisted for three years. So they applied for his discharge to the commanding general at Port Royal, who promptly declined to release "the best captain" of the regiment, but offered instead to promote him to be major. Then they appealed to the Governor of Massachusetts, and to the authorities at Washington. So resolute and persistent were their efforts, backed by all the influence they could command, that they finally obtained positive orders from the War Department, in compliance with which Captain Rogers was obliged to resign; and late in the year 1863 he returned to his studies at Harvard, where he was graduated in 1865.

For the graduating class at Harvard the college course terminates practically with Class Day. As a loyal member of his class, Rogers could not leave Cambridge until after that day. But at the earliest possible moment—the 26th day of June—he married his long-chosen wife, and the bridal journey lasted until Commencement Day, when he returned to Harvard to receive his degree of A.B.

After graduation, Rogers resided in Worcester, where he engaged in business, and where his three children were born. These were:—Edward Earle Rogers, the "Class Baby," that is, the first-

* See Army Life in a Black Regiment. By Thomas Wentworth Higginson, late Colonel 1st South Carolina Volunteers, 1870.

born child of any graduated member of a class at Harvard, who was born May 3, 1866, and died October 1, 1884; Eliot Folger Rogers, born July 28, 1868, a brilliant scholar, who was graduated at Harvard in 1890, receiving there the degrees of A.B., A.M., and Ph.D., and also a Fellowship, studied at Göttingen University in Germany, and died October 2, 1895, just after beginning his duties as Instructor in Chemistry at Harvard; and Annie Rogers, born March 3, 1872, who married on June 6, 1895, Charles Davison Knowlton, M.D., and is now living in Boston.

In 1878, Mr. Rogers moved to Red Rock, Pennsylvania, and for some years was engaged in oil-producing in Pennsylvania, New York and Kentucky. In 1882 he went to Rockport, Massachusetts, where he was in the employ of the Rockport Granite Company. In 1889 he went to Saratoga Springs, New York, and thence in 1893 to Chicago, in both places superintending the erection of gas-generating plants, having patented many devices relating to fuel gas. In 1899 he came to Boston, where he and his wife made their home with their married daughter. Here he became connected with the Boston Book Company, and was manager of *The Green Bag*, a periodical devoted to legal matters.

Being a man of superabundant vigor and endowed with sturdy health, having inherited from his ancestors of five generations those principles of love of righteousness, abhorrence of injustice, and duty towards one's neighbor which are typified by the name of Friend, which is the proper designation of the Quaker, he was always taking upon himself some work of kindness and usefulness in addition to his business duties. While living in Worcester he joined the Worcester Agricultural Society, the Worcester Horticultural Society, the Worcester County Mechanics Association (he was skilled in the use of tools), and the Grand Army of the Republic; was commissioned Justice of the Peace, and elected member of the Common Council; was made a trustee of the Worcester County Institution for Savings, and Treasurer of the Lyceum and Natural History Association. In Pennsylvania he joined the Masons and the A. O. U. W., and served on the School Board of Foster Township. While in Rockport he was member of the School Board and joined the Military Order of the Loyal Legion. In Chicago he was connected with the city Civil Service Commission. Notable for its judicious and generous helpfulness was his work for the Associated Charities, in aiding the needy, encouraging the weak and, if need be, reproving the wayward.

While in college he was awarded a prize for excellence in reading, and his ability in this direction was afterwards utilized by giving public readings in Massachusetts, Pennsylvania and New York. He was an occasional contributor to periodical publications, and in 1884 wrote for the benefit of the Grand Army a military drama entitled "Our Regiment," which was acted by several posts. In

1903 he met Major Caleb Huse, formerly of the United States Army, who in 1861 cast his fortunes with the South, and had been sent to Europe as Purchasing Agent by the Confederate Government. Mr. Rogers persuaded the major to write out some of his interesting experiences, and published them in 1904, under the title of "The Supplies for the Confederate Army; how they were obtained in Europe and how paid for."

When living in Chicago, Mr. Rogers became interested in the study of genealogy, and with his usual energy undertook to compile the histories of all the Rogers families in the United States—a tremendous task, as he was well aware. He printed in the REGISTER of January, 1901, a brief account of Hope Rogers of Connecticut and his descendants. In 1902 he published James Rogers of New London, Conn., and his Descendants. Two years later he carried through the press The Rogerenes, some hitherto unpublished annals belonging to the Colonial History of Connecticut, a book whose publication must have been postponed indefinitely without his generous aid. Working diligently, he accumulated the most valuable collection of facts extant concerning many families of his name. His manuscripts, neatly arranged and excellently indexed, have been given by his widow, in accordance with his expressed desire, to this Society.

He joined the New England Historic Genealogical Society in 1899, and at once became one of its most valued members, being a frequent donor to the library and serving most efficiently on many committees. In January, 1905, he was elected a member of the Council, and held this position at the time of his death.

His end came suddenly, as he had always hoped. On a Thursday afternoon, with but slight warning, and at the end of a busy day, he was unexpectedly stricken down. That evening the operation for appendicitis was performed, but too late. He evidently was aware that the summons had come, and at intervals jotted down generous and kindly directions for the disposal of material not fully covered by his will. Through his thoughtfulness at this time, our Society has received the valuable gift of his genealogical collections. On Sunday, April 9, 1905, his life of usefulness was quietly ended.

No account of this man's life could be complete without reference to her whose silent influence was so strong and so helpful during forty years of married happiness. Her unvarying steadiness of character, her unfaltering cheerfulness and unfailing love carried them both safely through the tragedies of life, mitigating the sorrows and enhancing the joys which come to mortals. Thrice death struck at those dearest to her—her children and her husband—while to the outside world she maintained her sweet serenity and her faith. If her heart was broken, she gave no sign and made no complaint. Yet three months after her husband's death, on July 1, 1905, she followed him across the silent river.

INSCRIPTIONS FROM GRAVESTONES IN CHRIST CHURCH, NORWICH, CONN.

Communicated by GEORGE S. PORTER, Esq., of Norwich.

CHRIST CHURCH (Episcopal) of Norwich, Conn., was organized in 1747, and its earliest house of worship was opened two years later. The present, and fourth, church building of the society occupies the site of the first, and stands on a lot on Washington street which was donated by Capt. Benajah Bushnell nearly one hundred and sixty years ago. The churchyard is preserved, but the head and foot stones which formerly indicated the graves of departed members were long since removed and placed in the cellar of the church, where they are cemented into the walls and flooring. This underground room is dark and gloomy, and searchers have difficulty in deciphering the inscriptions, all of which are here reproduced.

Here lies the | Body of Jonathan | Son to Mr. Caleb Ar- | nold & Ann his wife | He was drowned | April ye 29th 1769, | in the 6th year of his | age.

In Memory of | Benaiah Bufhnell Esq | who departed this life | (in hopes of a better) | Janry. 27th A:D: 1762 | in the 8Jft Year | of his Age.

In Memory of Mrs. | Hannah: Confort of Mr. | Benajah Bufhnell & Daught | to John Griswold Esqr | late of lime Decs. who | Departed this life in hope | of A Better, on the 10th day of | Augs. 1772 in ye 49th year | of her Age.

Sacred | to the memory of | Jabez Bushnell, | who died | Augt. 10th 1820 | aged 38.

In Memory of | Mrs. Sarah, wife to | Mr. Samuel Brown, | who died March | 12th 1795, in the | 95th Year of | her age.

In | Memory of | Miss Hannah Bushnell | who died | March 19, 1825, | aged 87 years.

In memory of | Jabez Bushnell | who died | Novr 18th 1810 | aged 66 years.

In memory of | Lydia Bushnell, | Wife of Jabez | Bushnell, who died | April 2d 1814, | aged 53 years.

In memory of Mrs. | Zeruiah Relict to | Benajah Bufhnell Efq. decd. | who departed this life | March 15th 1770 in the | 84th year of her Age.

In memory of Mifs | Nancy M. Cartey who | died Auft. 1ft 1791 | in in ye 25th year | of her age.

Mrs. Prudence | Bufhnell

In memory of | Capt. Richard | Bufhnell he de | parted this life | June 5th 1784 | in ye, 74th year | of his Age.

In Memory of | Sarah the wife of | Capt. John Coluer | who died auguft ye Jft | 1757 in ye 63rd year | of her age

In memory of | Mrs. Phebe Culver, | Wife of | Capt. Stephen Culver, | who died | October 8th 1805, | aged 56 years.

In memory of Mrs. | Hannah Davison, | wife of Mr. | Baizillai Davi-ſon | who died Nov. 1ſt | 1799, aged 58 years.

In memory of | Capt. William Daviſon, | who, much lamented, | died with the | yellow fever on the | 30th of July 1803, | aged 40 years.

Albertus | Sirant | Destouches Eſqr.

In Memory of | Saumille daught. | to Exeter & han- | nah Dobe who | died augſt. 29th | 1786 in her | 2d year.

In | Memory of | Mr. Brazilla Davison, | who died | May 22, 1828, | aged 90 years.

Here lies the mortal | part of Mrs. Sally Daviſon | the beloved con-ſort of | Mr. William Daviſon & | daught. to Capt. Eliſha | Edgerton & Mrs. Eliſabeth | his wife, who died may 24th | 1793, in ye 27th Year of her age

. Alſo Gurdon their ſon died | June 13th 1793, aged 6 weeks

In memory of | Mr. | Bentley Faulknor, | who died | March 6th 1776, | aged 40 years.

In Memory of | Mr. Bently | Faulkner, | Son of Mr. Bently and | Mrs. Mehitabel | Faulkner, who died | Sept. 21ſt 1789 in ye, | 17th Year of his age.

In Memory of Mr. | Bently Faulkner | who departed this | Life March 5th 1776, | Aged 42 years.

In memory of | Miſs Hannah Faulknor, | daughter of | Mr. Bentley Faulknor, | who died Sept. 14th | 1800, aged 29 years.

In memory of | Mrs. Mehitabel, | relict of Mr. | Bentley Faulknor, | who died | Oct. 16th 1821, | aged 83 years.

Mrs. Mary I. Fitch | Wife of | Stephen Fitch Esq. | Died | Sept. 27, 1837, | in her 42nd year.

Anne Grifte | J759

In Memory of | George ye Son of | Thomas & Anne Grifte | who falling through | the Ice, was Drowned | Decemr: J3th 1757, | Aged 25 Years & 7 Days.

In memory of Mr. | Thomas Grift who | departed this life | Auguſt 16th 1782 | in ye 82d Year | of his Age.

Here Lies the Body of | Mrs. Alice Hall | the wife of Mr. | Daniel Hall, | who departed this life | March ye 3d 1757 | in the 63d year | of her age.

Elizabeth | Hamilton, 1765.

Sacred | to the memory of | Mr. Solomon Hamilton, | Who died June 23d 1798 | aged 87 years.

Alſo of Solomon, ſon of | Mr. and Mrs. Hamilton, | who died in England | Feby 17th 1763, in the 25th | year of his age.

Sacred | to the memory of | Mrs. Zerviah conſort of | Mr. Solomon Hamilton, | who died July 18th 1782, | aged 69 years.

Alſo of John ſon of | Mr. and Mrs. Hamilton | who died on the coaſt | of England Sep 22d 1763 | in the 24th year of his age.

In Memorie of | Mrs. Zerviah Holden, | wife of Mr. Phinehas | Holden & Daughter of | Mr. Benajah & Mrs. Zerviah | Bushnell, died Augt. 23d | 1786, Aged 65 Years.

Sacred | to | the memory | of | Zerviah Tyler, | daughter of | James & Zerviah | Huntington, | who died | At Springfield, Massts: | Nov. 18, 1832, | Aged 19.

In memory of Capt. Allen | Ingraham, who was loſt | at ſea Sept. 1785, in ye | 43d. Year of his age.

Alſo died Mary daught to | Capt. Allen Ingraham and | Mrs. Lydia his wife decm 31st | 1792, in ye, 19th Year of her age

Miſs Sally Ingraham

In memory of Mrs. Ann | Johnson conſort of Capt. | Samuel Johnſon and only | daughr. of Evan Malborn | Esqr. who departed this | life Decr. 12th 1786 in ye | 47th Year of her age.

In Memory [broken] | Capt. Samuel Jo[broken] | of New port, depa[broken] | January 12th A. D. 1782 [broken] | of his Ag[broken]

In Memory [broken] | Elizabeth Joh[broken] | Daughter of Capt. Sam[broken] | Ann Johnso[broken] | Life

In Memory of Mrs. | Eliſabeth conſort to | Mr. Robart Lanceſter, | who departed this | life in hopes of a better | March 24th 1782, in ye | 76th year of her Age.

This monument is | erected by the family | of Zabdiel Rogers | in token of respect to | the memory of | Mercy Lanceſter, | who died Dec. 8th 1807, | aged 65 years.

In Memory of Mr. | Robert Lancaſter, who | departed this Life in hopes | of a better April 4th 1770 | Aged 70 years.

In Memory of Bela Leffingwell | who died at Charleston, South | Carolina, July 27th 1796, in | the 31ſt year of his age.

Alſo here are deposited the | bodies of Prudence & Eunice | Leffingwell. Prudence died | Novr. 18th 1795, in the 27th | year of her age. | Eunice died Septr. 26th 1796, | in the 22d year of her age.

Lucy, widow of Bela Leffingwell, | died Dec. 19, 1856, aged 91.

Sacred | to the memory of Mrs. | Charity Leffingwell, | Relict of Mr. | Matthew Leffingwell, | who died | July 15th, 1809, | aged 73 years.

Sacred | to the memory of | Harriet H. | the beloved child of | Bela & Lucy | Leffingwell, who died | July 31ſt, 1811, | aged 17 years.

In memory of Mrs. | Mary Leffingwell, | Wife of Mr. | Matthew Leffingwell, | who died July 6th 1813, | aged 49 years.

Also | of Simeon Leffingwell | their son, who was lost | at Sea March 4th | aged 22 .

This monument | is erected to the memory | of | Mr. Mathew Leffingwell | who departed this life | June the 29th AD. 17[broken]

In Memory of Capt. | Solomon Malbone late | of New port in the | State of RhodIſland | who died Auguſt | 24th 1787 in ye, 76th | year of his age.

In memory of two infants, | twin daughters of Eliſha H. | & Sally Mansfield, Lucy | H. died March 29th, 1819, AE | 8 weeks & 1 day. Lydia D. died | April 4th 1819, AE 9 weeks.

Mr. | John | Nichols.

In memory of | Samuel Noyes, ſon | of William Noyes, | who died July 24th | 1781, in the 33d year | of his age.

In memory of | Ephraim ſon of | Mr. Ephraim & | Mrs. Prudence | Punderſon, who | died ſept. 12th 1785, | aged 11 Months.

Hannah Louisa, | daughter of | Roswell & Eunice | Roath. died | June 25, 1822,

In memory of | George ſon to | Mr. James & | Mrs. Sophia | Rogers, died | march 10th 1796, | aged 9 M

Sacred | to the memory of | Mrs. Sophia, conſort of | Mr. James Rogers Junr | who died Octor. 9th 1796, | in the 29th year | of her age.

Mr. | Ephraim | Smith

In Memory of three ſons of Mr. William | & Mrs. Sybel Stephens |

Caleb Cooley Stephens died Janr. 10th | 1784, aged 18 days. | William Stephens Jur. died march | 18th 1785, aged 7 weeks & 3 days | William Stephens 3d died march 4th | 1787 in his 2d year.

Sacred | to the memory of | Elizabeth Tisdale, | consort of Doct. Nathan Tisdale, | and daughter of the late | Rev. John Tyler, who died | Dec. 22, 1824, in the 43 | year of her age.

Also | Sacred | to the memory of | Doct. Nathan Tisdale, | who died | July 15, 1830,

Here Lies Inter'd the | remains of Mifs Betfey | Tracy. Daughter to Capt. | Ifaac Tracy & Mrs. | Elifabeth his wife | fhe Departed this | Life march 9th 1782 | Aged 19 years.

Mrs. | Emma Tyler.

Here lie interred | The earthly remains of | Mrs. Hannah, | relict of the late | Rev. John Tyler, | who departed this life | Jan. 19, 1826, | in the 75 year of her age.

Here were deposited | the remains of John Tyler, fon | of the Rev. John Tyler, & of | Hannah Tyler his wife, who | died July 30, 1784, in the 12th | year of his age.

Alfo in memory of John Tyler, | 2d fon of this name of the Rev. | John Tyler & of Hannah Tyler | his wife, who died at the ifland of Martinico, Aug. 19, 1802, in | the 18th year of his age.

Here lie interred | the earthly remains of | The Rev. John Tyler | For 54 years Rector of Christs | Church in this city. Having | faithfully fulfilled his ministry, | He was ready to be dissolved | and to be with Christ. | His soul took its flight | from this vale of misery, | Jan. 20, 1823, in the 81 | year of his age.

Here are deposited | the remains of | Miss Mary Tyler, | daughter of the Rev. | John Tyler & Mrs. | Hannah his wife, | who died March 17th AD. 1806, Aged 28 years.

In M[broken]ory of | [broken]Y Ren[broken] | to [broken] Van Mair [broken]ne | [broken] departed this life September | 2Jft J783, in the 64 Year of her age.*

In memory of | Miss | Abby Warren, | daughter of | Lemuel & Abigail | Warren, died | Oct. 6, 1833, | Aged 68.

In memory of | Mrs. Abigail Warren, | wife of Mr. Lemuel | Warren who departed | this life Oct. 27th AD. | 1808, Aged 67 years.

Also | In memory of Mr. Dan | iel Warren who died in | Auzoays, west indies | April 14th AD 1790, Aged | 22 years.

In memory of | Miss Hannah Warren, | who died May 29, | 1827, aged 56.

In memory of | Mr. Lemuel Warren, | who departed this | life Oct. 10, 1812, in | the 79 year of his age.

In memory of | Miss | Lydia Warren, | daughter of | Lemuel & Abigail | Warren, died | March 15, 1835, | Aged 73..

In memory of Capt. | William Wattles, | who departed this | life April 18th AD. | 1787 in the 48th | year of his age.

In memory of Mr. | Elifha fon to Mr. | Zephaniah & Mrs. | Lydia Whipple | who died Janr. 24th | 1789, in ye, 17th | Year of his age.

Here were deposited | the remains of Capt. | Solomon Whipple, | who died fept. 4th 1801, | in ye, 30th year of his age.

Also, | In memory of Bufhnell | Whipple, who was | drowned at Sea Augft. 1785 | in ye 17th year of his age.

* This stone is in the churchyard.

EPHRAIM DARWIN OF GUILFORD, CONN., AND HIS DESCENDANTS.

Compiled by Hon. RALPH D. SMYTH, and communicated by Dr. BERNARD C. STEINER.

1. EPHRAIM[1] DARWIN was admitted a planter at Guilford, Dec. 11, 1672, and had his portion of land out of the third division, according to his list of estate. He had probably been in Guilford for several years. The rocks at the head of Fair Street, Guilford, were long called Ephraim's rocks, after him. He married first, June 10, 1678, Elizabeth, daughter of Richard Goodrich; and married second, Rachel ———. He died in Sept., 1725. The name was sometimes spelled Durren. His list in 1716 was £29.

Children:

1. i. DANIEL,[2] b. Sept. 15, 1680; d. Sept. 9, 1682.
2. ii. SAMUEL, b. Jan. 24, 1683-4.
iii. RACHEL, b. Nov. 11, 1685; d. Nov. 9, 1691.
3. iv. JOSEPH, b. Feb. 9, 1687-8.
4. v. EBENEZER, b. Apr. 9, 1691; removed to Greenwich, and Salem, N. J.
5. vi. DANIEL, b. May 6, 1694; d. Dec., 1756.

2. SAMUEL[2] DARWIN (*Ephraim*[1]), married first, Jan. 5, 1710, Sarah, daughter of James Hill, who died Dec. 4, 1711; and married second, in Dec., 1713, Abigail Benham of Wallingford. His list in 1716 was £32. 16. 0., and his home lot of 3 acres was assessed at £3.

Children:

i. SARAH,[3] b. July 5, 1715.
ii. ELIZABETH, b. Nov. 5, 1718.
iii. DINAH, b. Oct. 17, 1720.
iv. SAMUEL, b. Mch. 20, 1723.
v. THANKFUL, b. Jan. 9, 1726.
vi. EPHRAIM, b. Mch. 6, 1729.

3. JOSEPH[2] DARWIN (*Ephraim*[1]), of Wallingford in 1722, had a list of £36. 14. 0. at Guilford in 1716, but no home lot. He married, Dec. 18, 1711, Anna, daughter of William Parent.

Children:

i. ELIZABETH,[3] or ISABEL, b. Sept. 26, 1712.
5. ii. JOSEPH, b. Dec. 19, 1715.

4. DANIEL[2] DARWIN (*Ephraim*[1]), of Branford, married, Aug. 10, 1720, Abigail Champion of Lyme.

Children:

i. MARY,[3] b. Oct. 21, 1721.
6. ii. DANIEL, b. Jan. 31, 1726.
iii. ABIGAIL, b. Aug. 29, 1730.
iv. STEPHEN, b. Apr. 16, 1733.
v. EBENEZER, b. Apr. 24, 1740; m. July 13, 1761, Dinah Thorp of North Haven, and had *Jonathan Champion*,[4] b. Apr. 4, 1763.
vi. NOAH, b. Apr. 16, 1743; d. June 14, 1764.

5. JOSEPH[3] DARWIN, JR. (*Joseph*,[2] *Ephraim*[1]), of Woodberry, Branford, and North Branford, married Elizabeth ———.

Children:

i. ETHAN.[4]

ii. UZZIEL.
iii. IRA.
iv. ADAH, d. Nov. 21, 1767, at Branford.
v. SUBMIT, twin, b. Aug. 9, 1754.
vi. LUCINA, twin, b. Aug. 9, 1754.

6. DANIEL[3] DARWIN, JR. (*Daniel*,[2] *Ephraim*[1]), married, Feb. 8, 1748, Susannah Adkins, and lived at Branford.

Children:

i. SARA,[4] b. Sept. 30, 1752.
ii. JOSIAH, b. Apr, 26, 1755; d. Jan. 4, 1756.
iii. DANIEL, b. Dec. 8, 1756.
iv. ANNA, b. Sept. 21, 1759.
v. MICHAEL, b. July 5, 1761.
vi. SIMEON, b. July 23, 1763.
vii. HULDAH, b. Aug. 12, 1765.

MR. PATRICK FALCONER OF NEWARK, N. J., AND HIS DESCENDANTS.

Compiled by Hon. RALPH D. SMYTH and communicated by Dr. BERNARD C. STEINER.

1. PATRICK[1] FALCONER came to America, probably from Scotland, about 1684. He is said, in his epitaph written by his friend the Rev. Abraham Pierson, Jr., to have "suffered much for Christ," but when and where does not appear. It has been conjectured, however, that it was in Scotland, during the religious difficulties of that period.

In "The Model of Government of the province of East New Jersey in America and encouragement of such as design to be concerned there," published in Edinburg in 1685, reprinted in Whitehead's "East Jersey," is a letter from Patrick Faulkner to Maurice Trent, dated "Elizabeth Town, East Jersey, 28th October, 1684." This is among "letters to different individuals in Europe (Scotland) from sundry individuals in America." The letter was written shortly after his arrival, and praises the country highly. He also speaks of having travelled through Maryland and Pennsylvania. Where Mr. Falconer spent the three or four intermediate years after the date of this letter does not appear. In 1688, Patrick Falconer, then of Woodbridge, was administrator of Robert Adam. The next year, 1689, he was at New Haven, where he married Hannah, daughter of Governor William Jones and grand-daughter of Governor Eaton. They were both about 30 years of age at that time.

Patrick Falconer could not have remained long at New Haven, for June 20, 1690, he was at Newark, New Jersey, administrator on the estate of Samuel Kitchel, who left a will dated Feb. 11, 1683, but whose wife Grace, named as executrix, had died before him; and he appears as a witness to the will of David Ogden, Dec. 26, 1691, but when the will was proved, Feb. 27, 1691-2, "Patrick Falconer being deceased," the other witness testified alone. He was called "merchant." On his gravestone in the old burying-ground is this inscription: "Here lyeth the body of Patrick Falconer, who died January 27th, 1691/2, aged 33 years." In his will, recorded in Trenton, New Jersey, he provided that his daughter,

Hannah, be maintained till she arrive at the age of eighteen, and then that she should have fifty pounds in money; his wife, Hannah, was to enjoy the whole estate in any part of Europe, New England, New Jersey, or elsewhere, and to be sole executrix with power to sell, etc.; his honored father Wm. Jones, and his loving brother John Jones to be overseers, and his "brother James Falconer to be the overseer to take care to preserve what I have in Europe for my wife and child," also James Emmett to be overseer to assist in settling accounts in New York, Long Island, New Jersey, or elsewhere west of the Hudson River.

Sometime subsequent to Patrick Falconer's death, a John Falconer of London gave a power of attorney to David Falconer to act and do for him in East Jersey as a proprietor, but there is no evidence that either of these were relatives of Patrick.

It appears that Mrs. Hannah Falconer sold her interest in her husband's property and returned to New Haven, where she was in 1695. Subsequently she married James Clark of Stratford, and removed to that place.

Children:

i. HANNAH,[2] b. 1690, probably at Newark; m. Aug. 2, 1710, Dea. Seth Morse of Dedham, and had *Ruth*, who m. Samuel Lee.

2. ii. PATRICK, b. Aug. 12, 1692, at New Haven (posthumous); d. July, 1735. He lived at Guilford, where he was listed for £21 and a horse, in 1716.

2. PATRICK[2] FALCONER, JR. (*Patrick*[1]) married, in 1722, Deliverance, daughter of Thomas Cooke, Jr. Prior to July, 1737, she married second, —— Hill, and died Feb. 12, 1781.

Children:

i. HANNAH,[3] b. Aug. 23, 1723; m. Mch. 6, 1745, Charles Miller of Durham.

ii. SARAH, b. Mch. 15, 1727; d. single, Sept. 24, 1797.

iii. MARY, b. Apr. 11, 1729; m. Nov. 20, 1755, Simeon Norton.

3. iv. CHARLES, b. May 11, 1731; d. Oct. 18, 1803.

v. REBECCA, b. Jan. 13, 1734; d. single, Feb. 9, 1816.

3. CHARLES[3] FALCONER, or FAULKNER (*Patrick*,[2] *Patrick*[1]), of Guilford, served in the French and Indian war and in the Revolution. He married first, Jan. 6, 1760, Hannah Morse, who died Apr. 30, 1765; and married second, Mch. 4, 1767, Mary Bly of Middletown, who died Feb. 28, 1810.

Children by first wife:

i. BENONI,[4] b. July 1, 1760; d. July 16, 1760.

ii. HANNAH, b. Sept. 3, 1761.

iii. MARY, b. July 10, 1763; d. July 10, 1768.

iv. CHARLES, b. Oct. 13, 1764; d. Oct. 15, 1769.

Children by second wife:

v. PATRICK, b. Nov. 30, 1767; d. 1817; m. Prudence, dau. of John Goldsmith, and removed to Middletown, N. Y.

vi. MARY, b. Jan. 26, 1771; d. Apr. 8, 1791.

4. vii. CHARLES, b. Mch. 20, 1773; d. at Philadelphia, 1835.

viii. FRIEND LYMAN, b. Feb. 15, 1777; went West.

ix. SALLY, b. 1779; lived in Branford.

4. CHARLES[4] FAULKNER, JR. (*Charles*,[3] *Patrick*,[2] *Patrick*[1]), married, May 1, 1800, Clarinda Stone, who died Aug. 30, 1868.

Children:

i. CHARLES,[5] b. Feb. 28, 1801; d. Mch., 1802.

ii. CHARLES HAND, b. Apr. 15, 1803; d. Sept. 16, 1842; lived in Buenos Ayres, and Georgetown, S. C.; m. (1) Ann Edwards Roberts, who was b. Feb., 1811, and d. Feb. 1, 1833; m. (2) Feb., 1840, Martha Folk of Georgetown, S. C. Children by first wife: *William Roberts*[6] and *Christina.*

iii. MARY ANN, b. Jan. 3, 1807; m. May 4, 1833, Joel Stone of Guilford.

iv. WILLIAM, b. Dec. 27, 1808; m. (1) Oct. 15, 1829, Frances H. Lord of Norwich, who was b. Sept. 5, 1805, and d. Apr. 20, 1848; m. (2) March 27, 1850, Mary G., dau. of Pitman Stowe of Hartford. Children by first wife: *Francis*[6] *William, George Lord, Caroline Pierson,* and *Ella*; child by second wife: *Charles Pitman.*

PASSENGER LISTS TO AMERICA.

Communicated by GERALD FOTHERGILL, Esq., of New Wandsworth, London, England.

IT was formerly the duty of an official to keep a strict account of all persons leaving the shores of England or Ireland, and this was no doubt at all times carried out in a more or less perfect way.

As regards England, these were all burnt by a fire at the Custom House, London. In some few cases, however, duplicates had been made for various official reasons, and these were printed, so far as then discovered, by Hotten.*

In making researches among the British Archives, I have discovered others. One series of these has been printed and is called a "List of Emigrant Ministers to America." Others I hope to print from time to time in the pages of the REGISTER.

The following are lists of passengers who left Ireland between the years 1805–1806, and contained in a British Museum Manuscript numbered Add. 35932.

The following is an example of a list, affidavit and certificate, showing that some trouble was taken in making the records:

Thomas Ryan	Patrick Ryan
John Cronnan	Mich[l] Enright
John Daly	Pat Hennesy

Edward Kellerman maketh oath that the above is a true list and description of the passengers engaged to go in the Ship *Numa* to America, and that not any of them is or are atrificers, artisans, manufacturers, seamen or seafaring men, and that he will not take any other passengers but those expressed in the above list, and that this list is a duplicate of the original one transmitted to the Lord Lieutenant and Council save and except six of the passengers mentioned therein who are not to proceed.

Sworn before the Custom House, Limerick, 2 Ap[l]., 1803. } EDW[d] KELLERAN.

I certify that I have personally examined the Men in the above List and that to the best of my knowledge I do believe they are of the occupation above discribed. Limerick, 3 Ap[l]., 1803.

WM. PAYNE, Brig[r] Gen[l].

* "The Original Lists" of Emigrants to America, 1600–1700, edited by John Camden Hotten. New York, 1874.

A List of Passengers who have sailed on board the *Mars* for America from Dublin, 29 March, 1803.

Wm Ford	gent	Robert Gibson	American merchant
John Morris	servant	——— Teeling	clerk
Wm Sherlock	merchant	James Murphy	labourer
Hugh Jackson	"	John Hobleton	"

A List of Passengers on the Ship *Portland* for Charlestown, 29 Mch., 1803.

Charles Adams	age	48	farmer of	Limerick
Margt Adams his wife	"	39		"
Ric O'Carroll	"	22	"	Bolinbroke
Danl O'Carroll	"	20	"	"
Thos Egan	"	29	writing clerk	Limerick
Martin Corry	"	58	labourer	"
John Connery	"	29	"	"
Mary Egan	"	60		
Eliza Corry	"	33		
Mary Connory	"	24		
Mary Egan junr	"	27		
Betty Fitzpatrick	"	26		
Michl Quillan	"	48	gent	
Mary Quinlan	"	46		
Mary Quinlan junr	"	13		
Thos O'Duyer	"	22	gent	
Michl O'Donnovan	"	26	"	"
John Mullins	"	26	labourer	"
James Meehan	"	26	"	Clare
Patk Kernan	"	24	"	"
Terence Murray	"	18	"	"
Patrick Magrath	"	21	"	"
Andrew Lee	"	26	"	Caperas
Ric Ennery	"	19	writing clerk	Limerick
Hugh Morgan	"	22	labourer	"
James Kerly	"	37	farmer	Ballyhoben
John Walsh	"	27	labourer	Limerick
Ann Considen	"	22		"
John Cummins	"	21	"	Claraline co. Tippy
Wm O'Brien	"	26		Thomas Town
Margaret Fehilly	"	24	"	Limerick
Margt Hayes	"	18		"
Mary Callaghan	"	14		"
Joseph Fihilly		7		
Michl Fihilly		5		
John Fihilly		3		
Mary Fihilly		2		

A List of Passengers on the Ship *Eagle* for New York, 29 Mch., 1803.

Alex Radcliffe	age	23	farmer	Ballyroney
John Menter	"	28	labourer	Belfast
Wm Calvert	"	33	"	Killeagh
Ann Calvert	"	24	spinster	"
James Bryson	"	27	farmer	Kilrock
Peter Leonard	"	28	"	Hillsboro

Wm Logan	age 36	labourer	Dromore
Thos Bain	" 18	farmer	Dounpatrick
Joseph Webb	" 25	labourer	Cockslem
Wm Wilson	" 22	"	Derrylea
Margt Wilson	" 20	spinster	"
Wm Kineard	" 52	farmer	"
Robt Kineard	" 18	labourer	"
Wm Hancock	" 19	"	"
Thos Wilson	" 23	"	Armagh
James Diennen	" 19	"	Dovehill
John English	" 40		Tynan
Isabella English	" 32		"
Wm Kerr	" 18	"	"
James Lister	" 20	"	"
George Lister	" 25		"
John Graham	" 24	"	"
Thos Spratt	" 50	farmer	Clough
John Browne	" 24	"	Saintfield
Saml Campbell	" 18	labourer	Banbridge
Charles Martin	" 20	farmer	Ballymoney
Robert Halridge	" 16	clerk	"
Robt Eakin	" 38	farmer	Coleraine
Wm Rafield	" 23	"	Ballymena
Wm Woods	" 27	labourer	Sea Patrick
Neha Kidd	" 20	"	Keady
John Shields	" 20	farmer	"
John Cully	" 24	"	"
David Clement	" 22	"	"
Andrew Clement	" 20	"	"
Wm McAlister	" 20	"	Ballycaste

A List of Passengers on the Ship *Susan* for New York from Dublin, 5 Apl., 1803.

John Dornan	age 43	bookseller	Dublin
Mrs Mary Dornan	" 40	spinster	"
Three small children			
Mrs Frances Russel	age 40	grocer	Dublin
Mrs Annie Russel	" 38	spinster	Louth
Three small children			
John Midleton	age 29	merchant	Louth
James Erwin	" 28	physician	"
Wm Erwin	" 26	"	"
Chas Rivington	" 25	merchant	New York
Robert Noble	" 60	"	"
Mrs Nelly Welch	" 31	spinster	Wexford
Miss MaryAnn Finly	" 21	"	Meath
James Truer	" 22	farmer	County Meath
Thomas Fitzgerald	" 23	"	County Wexford
James Byrne	" 19	"	County Meath
John Byrne	" 21	"	" "
Wm Finly	" 18		County Wexford
James Kelly	" 24		" "
John Riley	" 31		" "
James Kelly	" 25		" "

A List of Passengers to go on board the American Brig *Neptune*, Seth Stevens Master, for Newcastle and Philadelphia, burthen per admeasurement 117 tons, at Warren Point, Newry, 29 Mch., 1803.

John Grimes	labourer	aged 28	Susan Dene	spinster	aged 18
Agnes "	his wife	" 26	David Gallon	farmer	" 40
James Crummy	farmer	" 45	John Henry	ditto	" 40
Agnes "	his wife	" 30	Hanna "	his wife	" 30
Mary "	their daughter	" 15	Nancy "	their daughter	" 13
Sarah "	ditto	" 12	James "	their son	" 11
James "	their son	" 6	William Countes	labourer	" 26
David	ditto	" 4	Mary Countes	his wife	" 21

List of Passengers to proceed by the American Ship *Rachel*, Benjamin Hale, Master, to New York from Sligo, 15 Apl., 1803.

Robert Ormsby	clerk	Owen McGowan	labourer
James Gillan	farmer	Fred^{k} Corry	"
John Read	clerk	Pat Gilmartin	"
James Henderson	clerk	Pat Gilan	
Peter McGowan	schoolmaster	Pat Foley	
Chas Armstrong	clerk	Pat Feeny	
Lau^{ce} Christian	labourer	Mich^{l} Horan	
Patt "	"	John Farrel	
James Donald	"	John Commins	
Wm Corry	"	Danl Gilmartin	
Danl McGowan	"		

List of Passengers on board the Ship *Margaret*, Thomas Marsh, Master, bound for New York, from Newry, 18 Apl., 1803.

Eliz Brothers		aged 44	Hugh Alexander	labourer	aged 29	
Mary "		" 19	Jane "		aged 22	his family
Saml "	labourer	" 12	Jane "		" 3	his family
James "		" 10	Sarah "		" 2	his family
William "		" 7	Robert Goocy	farmer	aged 20	
M Ann Anderson		" 30	Samuel Douglas	"	" 18	
Mat^{u} Doubly		" 12	Thomas Haxten	labourer	" 19	
James Farrell		" 3	John Rolston	"	" 27	
James Harkness	labourer	" 40	Ann Beard		" 24	
Jane "	his family	aged 36	Ann Beard		" 2	
Thos "	his family	" 12	James McClean	farmer	" 60	
Margt "	his family	" 10	Eliz McClean		" 60	
Sarah "	his family	" 10	David McClean	labourer	" 24	
Abigal "	his family	" 8	John "	"	" 22	
Robt "	his family	" 6	George "	"	" 28	
James "	his family	" 4	William Riddle	"	" 19	
Eliz Story		aged 47	Samuel Magil	"	" 21	
Ben Story	farmer	" 18	Samuel Magil	"	" 39	
Ann Story		" 16	Biddy Enery	"	" 35	

List of passengers intending to go from Belfast to Philadelphia in the Ship *Edward*, from Belfast, 19 Apl., 1803.

James Greg	farmer	age 46	James Fox	labourer	aged 40
Thomas Greg	"	" 13	Ja. Mooney	"	" 16

John Greg	farmer	age 19	James Towel	labourer	aged 22
Thomas Fleming	labourer	" 19	James Burns	"	" 20
Hugh Porter	"	" 24	Robt Labody	gent	" 32
John Martin	"	" 21	Hers McCullough	farmer	" 27
Alexr McMeekin	"	" 21	Wm Scott	"	" 22
Adm Dunn	farmer	" 30	James Kirkman	"	" 40
Thomas Monks	farmer	" 60	Wm Bingham	"	" 40
Robert Monks	"	" 22	James Bingham	"	" 14
Joseph Monks	"	" 20	John Norris	labourer	" 16
Thomas Monks	"	" 17	Hugh Murphy	"	" 18
John Smith	labourer	" 20	Edwd Wilson	gent	" 18
Hu McBride	"	" 26	Ardsal Hanlay	laborer	" 22
W "	"	" 25	James Read	"	" 23
W Dawson	"	" 28	Jos Haddock	"	" 27
Jno Craven	"	" 25			

A List of Passengers who intend going to Newcastle, Wilmington and Philadelphia in the Ship *Pennsylvania,* Elhana Bray, Master, from Londonderry, 16 Apl., 1803.

Patrick Lealer	aged 50	of Shabane	labourer
Robert Donaldson	" 46	"	"
Bell Donaldson	" 36	"	spinster
Mary "	" 24		"
Jane "	" 25	"	"
Mary "	" 20	Clanely	"
Nancy Maxwell	" 30	"	"
Robert "	" 10	"	labourer
Nash Donald	" 26		"
Patrick Donal	" 50		"
Margaret Steel	" 26	"	spinster
Peter Derin	" 56	"	labourer
James McGonagal	" 26	Tulerman	"
Charles Canney	" 28	"	"
Richard Dougherty	" 36	"	"
Margaret Heaton	" 28		spinster
Patrick McCallen	" 33	"	labourer
Hugh Breeson	" 40	"	"
Mary O'Donnell	" 25	Strabane	spinster
Samuel Gilmour	" 20	Sr Johnston	*spinster*
Ann Gilmour	" 15	"	"
Jas Elgin	" 10	"	labourer
James Boyd	" 26	"	"
William Oliver	" 26	Sr Johnstown	"
Thomas Wilson	" 25	"	"
Nancy Wilson	" 26	"	spinster
Nancy Wilson junr	" 24	"	"
Jas Wilson	" 20	Muff	labourer
John Wilson	" 56	"	"
Saml "	" 45	"	"
Eleanor "	" 36	Newton Limavady	spinster
John Moore	" 22	" "	farmer
Bridget Dever	" 55	" "	spinster

John Lewis	aged 33	Newton Limavada		labourer
Fanny Lewis	" 70	"	"	spinster
Fanny Lewis junr	" 15	"	"	"
And^w Lewis	" 20	"	"	labourer
Susan "	" 36	"	"	spinster
George "	" 33	"	"	labourer
James Stewart	" 25	Dungiven		"
Ja^s King	" 45	"		"
Willm McBride	" 50	"		
Will Parker	" 61	"		
Alex^r Houston	" 45			
Francis "	" 20	"		"
John Brigham	" 26	"		farmer
Jane "	" 25	Ballyshannon		spinster
Eliz Brigham	" 26	"		"
Ezek^l Brigham	" 25	"		labourer
David Brigham	" 22			"
Wm White	" 18	"		"
Ja^s Mitchell	" 22	Derry		
Fra^s Dormet	" 20	"		
Wm Montgomery	" 22	"		"
May "	" 41	"		spinster
Saml "	" 12	"		labourer
Rebecca Montgomery	10	Ballendreat		spinster
Robert Little	" 26	"		labourer
John Little	" 24	"		"
Math^w Armstrong	" 23			"
Ja^s Todd	" 20	"		

[To be continued.]

STEPHEN BURTON OF BRISTOL, R. I., AND SOME OF HIS DESCENDANTS.

By Miss Susan A. Smith, of Dorchester, Mass.

1. Stephen[1] Burton, although spoken of as a wealthy and highly educated man, always holding prominent office, and active in the public interest, has left very little of himself upon record. Savage says he was "probably son of Thomas." In Mr. Waters's "Gleanings," Vol. 1, page 319, is the will of Margaret Prescott of the Parish of St. Thomas the Apostle, London, widow, dated Nov. 1, 1639, proved Jan. 3, 1639–40, in which she mentions her "son-in-law Stephen Burton and my daughter Martha his wife," but no connection between this Stephen and the Thomas named by Savage, or the Stephen of this article, has been proved.

The first evidence found of the presence of Stephen[1] in Boston was in 1670, when he was witness to a deed. In 1673, John Cranston, of Newport, R. I., sold land in Boston, bequeathed to him by the will of William Brenton of Rhode Island, to "Stephen Burton of London Junior, merchant, now resident of New England," and from that time, for over ten years, he had interests in Boston.

In 1680, Stephen Burton joined with "John Walley, Nathaniel Byfield and Nathaniel Oliver, men of large estate," in the purchase, from Plymouth Colony, of Mount Hope, the seat of the Great Sachem, Phillip, which has been called the "reward" to the Colony for the memorable conquest, but evidently he did not immediately take up his residence at Mount Hope, for in 1681 he was constable at Boston.

Oct. 28, 1681, at the sitting of Plymouth Colony Court, at the request of the four purchasers of Mount Hope, it was granted that it should be a town, to be called "Bristoll," and the first "Recorder" of the new township was Stephen Burton. Any one who examines the first book of Deeds at Taunton, kept by him as Recorder,* cannot fail to notice the beautiful handwriting and the scholarly elegance of its arrangement.

In 1689, "Lieut." Burton was one of the selectmen "to wait on court," and he was also one of the Town Council "to join with the Commission officers by way of ordering concerns in exegencies relating to militia affairs." He was one of the first Deputies from Bristol to the General Court, and served five times, 1685, '86, '89, '90, and '92.

In 1690 he was appointed by Plymouth Court to look after the "revenues and Customs" of Bristol County, and "to give despatches to vessels and see that Acts of Navigation be observed and render account," but in 1692 complaint was made that Stephen Burton neglected his duties, because of "head trouble," and his death is recorded July 22, 1693. It is said that he resided on Burton Street in Bristol, and that the house was destroyed by the British in 1777.

He married first, Abigail, daughter of Gov. William and Martha Brenton of Rhode Island, who died at Bristol in 1684; and married second, Sept. 4, 1684, Elizabeth, only daughter of Gov. Josiah and Penelope (Pelham) Winslow, who died at Pembroke, Mass., July 11, 1735, and whose grave-stone is in an excellent state of preservation.

Children by first wife, born in Boston:

i. STEPHEN,[2] b. Aug. 8, 1677.
ii. A DAUGHTER, b. Oct. 16, 1680.

Children by second wife, born in Bristol:

iii. PENELOPE, b. Aug. 8, 1686.
2. iv. THOMAS, b. Mar. 16, 1692-3.
v. ELIZABETH, who never married, and of whom marvellous stories are told of the elegance of her personal belongings, one tradition being that she had a "quart measure of jewels," and many magnificent dresses. An elegant dower-chest stood in the Burton house at Pembroke as late as 1810, when it was sold.

2. THOMAS[2] BURTON (*Stephen*[1]) settled in Pembroke, Mass., where he was town clerk and schoolmaster many years.

In Middlesex Co. Deeds, Vol. 28, fol. 229, is a transfer dated Aug. 6, 1728, of "Thomas Burton and Elizabeth Junior of Plymouth County," to "Nathaniel Cotton of Bristol County Clerk" of a tract of land at "Natticut" on the Merrimac River, being "three fourths of one sixteenth of ten thousand acres, derived from our honored father Stephen Burton deceased," who purchased it from "Mr. John Cranston of Neport R. I., who had it from William Brenton Esq., as see his last will and testament." In this document

* The office of Recorder at that time included "Clerk of the Peace," "Clerk of Common Pleas," and the duties now performed by the Registers of Deeds and of Probate.

both Elizabeth the widow of Stephen,[1] and Alice the wife of Thomas,[2] resign dower.

In 1730 it was voted in Duxbury that Thomas Burton should keep their school, provided "he shall tarry in said town and not remove out of it"; but about that time he purchased a large estate in Center Pembroke, where he ever after lived. His family Bible is now in possession of Mrs. Henry Bosworth of Pembroke, whose husband is a descendant.

Thomas[2] married, May 10, 1722, Alice, born Apr. 15, 1697, daughter of Elisha and Elizabeth (Wiswell) Wadsworth. He died Oct. 22, 1779, aged 87 years, and she died June 9, 1791, aged 95 years. (Gravestones at Pembroke.)

Children:

i. MARTHA,[3] b. June 19, 1723; d. Sept., 1723.
ii. PENELOPE, b. Oct. 27, 1724; m. Oct. 23, 1751, Seth, son of Lieut. Samuel and Susanna Jacob.
iii. ELEANOR, b. May 4, 1728; d. Oct. 27, 1751; m. Feb. 5, 1746-7, Nathaniel, son of Hudson and Abigail (Keen ?) Bishop of Pembroke. Children: 1. *Nathaniel*, b. Oct. 14, 1747; m. June 6, 1779, Abigail Bearse. 2. *Eliphalet*, b. Sept. 23, 1751; m. May 16, 1776, Elizabeth Tubbs.
iv. ELIZABETH, b. May 9, 1737; m. May 14, 1766, Daniel, b. July 8, 1739, son of Elisha and Elizabeth (Lincoln) Bonney. He d. Aug. 13, 1813, aged 74 yrs., and she d. May 17, 1807, aged 70 yrs. No children.

A DORCHESTER RELIGIOUS SOCIETY OF YOUNG MEN.

Communicated by ALBERT MATTHEWS, A.B., of Boston.

ON December 25, 1698, there was formed at Dorchester a "Society of Young Men mutually joining together in the Service of God." The Society apparently had no distinctive name, and, though it seems to have existed for a century and a half, there appear to be no allusions to it in the histories of Dorchester. There are, however, three sources of information in regard to the Society. In 1779 there was printed at Boston, "Early Piety recommended. A Sermon, Preached Lord's-day Evening, February 1st, 1778, to Two Religious Societies of Young Men in Dorchester. By Moses Everett, A.M., Pastor of the Church in that Place. Published at the Request of the Societies and others." In the course of this sermon Mr. Everett says:

> It is a happy consideration, that amidst all the degeneracy of the times, the ancient religious Societies of *young Men*, are upheld among us. That there are still so many who are willing to own a regard for the interests of religion, while it is so generally disregarded and contemned by the youth. Such societies, are indeed worthy a particular share in the affection of all good men. . . . They are honorable. . . . They are greatly ornamental to religion . . . and tend much to the advancement of its dignity and interests (p. 24).

These words are of too general a nature to be of much value, and the fact, as stated on the title-page, that this sermon was preached to *two* societies, rather intensifies than clears up our ignorance. But in 1799 there was printed at Charlestown "A Discourse, Addressed to the Religious Society of Young Men in Dorchester, on the Termination of One Hundred Years from the Time of its Establishment. By the Rev. Thaddeus Mason Harris." The Introduction to this discourse is as follows:

ON December 25, 1698, a number of young persons, actuated by a love for religion, and a desire to assist and promote each other's advancement in the offices of piety, agreed upon 'a private weekly meeting, for religious exercise, and the good improvement of the evening of the LORD'S day.'

ABOUT eleven years after, as the members had become numerous, and it was inconvenient to assemble in one place, it was deemed advisable to divide; and one branch of the society continued to meet in the south part of the town, and the other in the north.

THE society is composed of serious and well disposed youths, who continue members till they form family connections, or leave the town. There is no recollection of a single instance of the expulsion of an individual for ill conduct, or of any one having desired to leave the society from dislike. The utmost harmony and fraternal affection have prevailed in their meetings: and the institution has been promotive of the happiest effects in encouraging and assisting youthful piety and practical godliness.

THAT a society constituted of persons whose dispositions and principles are apt to be mutable, and easily affected and estranged by the dissipations of early life, should have been zealously supported *through a whole century*, is a circumstance which must forcibly excite our admiration. On the termination of this period, the young men of the elder branch of the society requested that a discourse might be delivered to them in public, to commemorate the establishment of the Institution, and to further its views. In compliance with this request the following was written and delivered, and to gratify the society it is now published (pp. 3, 4).*

Our third source of information is a manuscript written on parchment now owned by Mr. Charles J. Means of Boston, a son of the late Rev. James H. Means of Dorchester — the successor of the Rev. John Codman. This parchment, which could not have been written earlier than 1707, contains the Articles agreed upon December 25, 1698, and the names of about three hundred and fifty members, many of them autograph signatures.† It is printed at the end of this paper.

But while our knowledge of this particular Society is meagre, it may not be without interest to give an outline of the causes which led to its inception, especially as this will show that other similar societies existed in this neighborhood early in the eighteenth century. The scandals, both public and private, which characterized the reigns of Charles II. and James II. were a cause of shame to many Englishmen, and became so notorious that a reaction set in after the Revolution. In 1895 Miss Mary Bateman wrote:

In the reign of William and Mary the rise of a number of voluntary associations, with moral, religious, or philanthropic aims, expressed the widespread desire for social reform. It is true that in 1689, as in 1642, social reform was not made a party cry; but the cordial reception given to the Prince of Orange, especially in the city of London, was partly due to the belief that the social disorders of the last two reigns would be suppressed. The city authorities

* In an Appendix (pp. 19-24), Mr. Harris says that "An account of the societies of young men in England, with rules and directions for their use, may be found in Baxter's Practical Works, Vol. iv;" quotes some rules for such a society from *A Help to National Reformation;* and gives some extracts from "a little book, published about the beginning of the present century, entitled 'Private meetings animated and regulated,' . . . which may serve to shew the *original* plan and design of such institutions." The last I have not seen. My attention was called by Mr. William P. Greenlaw to the two sermons quoted in the text. Copies of both, owned by the Dorchester Antiquarian and Historical Society, are deposited in the library of the New England Historic Genealogical Society, and are bound in Volume viii of a series labelled "Historical Discourses, Dorchester."

† I am indebted to Mr. William B. Trask, to Mr. Henry E. Woods, and to Mr. Henry H. Edes, for aid in deciphering some of the names on the parchment.

combined with their Whiggism the Puritan horror of profanation of the Sabbath, cursing and drunkenness, and they knew that they had William's sympathy in these matters. The first sign of a change in the policy of the Government was given in a letter sent by William to the bishops, 1689, ordering them publicly to preach against the keeping of courtezans, swearing, etc., and to put the ecclesiastical laws in execution without any indulgence. The next was given in a letter of Mary, written in the absence of the king, to the Justices of the Peace in Middlesex, July 9th, 1691, which recommended the execution of the laws "against profaning the Lord's Day, drunkenness, profane swearing and cursing, and all other lewd, enormous, and disorderly practices" which had universally spread themselves by the neglect and connivance of the magistrates. Any officer of justice guilty of these offences or negligent in punishing them was to be punished himself as an example.

On the whole, however, it was not through Court influence that progress was made in the reform of manners. It was from the people, not from the Government, that the movement of social reform came. The work which Cromwell had given to his major-generals was now taken up by voluntary associations. The title "Society for the Reformation of Manners" was first used in 1692,* when five or six private gentlemen of the Church of England, with the help of the Queen, banded themselves together to inform against all persons who broke the penal laws. To prevent the charge of covetousness, the societies paid over the fines to charities, and took a subscription from their members to pay the expenses of prosecutions. In 1698 the societies received a stimulus from a proclamation against vice and impiety in all classes issued by William III. The spread of vice was ascribed to the magistrates' neglect to enforce the laws, and the judges of assize and justices of the peace were ordered to read the proclamation before giving the charge, and all ministers of religion were to read it four times a year after divine service.†

* For this statement, Miss Bateman refers to Coke's *Detection* (iii. 66) and Wilson's *De Foe* (i. 279). But neither Coke nor Wilson says that the *title* was used in 1692: merely that the Societies arose in or about that year. The earliest use of that exact title I have found is in a pamphlet called *Proposals for a National Reformation of Manners, Humbly offered to the Consideration of our Magistrates & Clergy. To which is added, I. The Instrument for Reformation. II. An Account of several Murders, &c. and particularly A Bloody Slaughter-House discover'd in Rosemary-lane, by some of the Society for Reformation, . . . As also The Black Roll, Containing the Names and Crimes of several hundred Persons, who have been prosecuted by the Society*, London, 1694. This was licensed February 12, 1693–4, and was "Published by the Society for Reformation." To the sermons preached before the Societies, there was frequently added an "Account [for the preceding year] of the Progress made in the Cities of London and Wesminster, and Places adjacent, by the Societies for Promoting Reformation of Manners." The first of these accounts was the "Black Roll" printed in the above pamphlet of 1692. Later they appeared as broadsides under the title of *Black List*, and in the British Museum are copies of the Sixth (1701), the Eighth (1703), the Tenth (1705), the Thirteenth (1708), the Fourteenth (1709), and the Fifteenth (1710). From them it seems probable that the Societies were officially organized in 1694, and presumably their title dates from that year.

The earliest allusion I have found to the originators of the Societies is in a pamphlet entitled *A Vindication of an Undertaking of Certain Gentlemen, In Order to the Suppressing of Debauchery and Profaneness*, printed in London in 1692, of which there is a copy in the Boston Athenæum. Though published anonymously, it was written by Edward Fowler, Bishop of Gloucester, who says:

"But to come to the Business of these Papers: Certain pious Gentlemen, all of the Church of *England*, laying greatly to heart *these* things, resolved to make Tryal, whether any thing could be done towards giving a Check to DEBAUCHERY and PROFANENESS; and joyntly agreed upon this following Method for the Reforming of Offenders in those *Two* most scandalous Instances, by due Course of Law" (p. 6).

The title later used is not found in this pamphlet, but in the Preface the author asks: "*But how can Zeal for so good a thing as Reformation of our Manners, be ever* Ill-timed?" (p. iv.) There are in the British Museum two copies of this pamphlet, one with the title as given above, the other entitled *A Vindication Of a Late Undertaking of Certain Gentlemen*, &c., London, 1692.

† In H. D. Traill's *Social England* (1895), iv. 592, 593. See also Sir W. Besant, *London in the Time of the Stuarts* (1903), pp. 355–358; Besant, *London in the Eighteenth Century* (1903), p. 158; R. Coke, *A Detection of the Court and State of England* (1719), iii, 66; J. P. Malcolm, *Anecdotes of the Manners and Customs of London from the Roman Invasion to the Year 1700* (1811), pp. 182–185; J. P. Malcolm, *Anecdotes of the Manners and Customs of London during the Eighteenth Century* (1810), i. 93–96; W. Wilson, *Memoirs of the Life and Times of De Foe* (1830), i. 286–302, ii. 84–90.

Most of the societies organized late in the seventeenth century had for their object the suppression of immoralities of various kinds and the prosecution of the offenders. After enumerating the duties of about a dozen of these, the writer of a pamphlet published in London in 1699 goes on to say:

Besides those above-mentioned, there are about *Nine and Thirty Religious Societies* of another kind, in and about *London* and *Westminster*, which are propagated into other Parts of the Nation; as *Nottingham*, *Gloucester*, *&c.*, and even into *Ireland*, where they have been for some Months since spreading in divers *Towns* and *Cities* of that Kingdom; as *Kilkenny*, *Drogheda*, *Monmouth*, *&c.* especially in *Dublin*, where there are about *Ten* of these *Societies*, which are promoted by the *Bishops*, and *inferior Clergy* there. These *Persons* meet often to *Pray*, *Sing Psalms*, and *Read* the *Holy Scriptures* together, and to *Reprove*, *Exhort*, and *Edifie* one another by their *Religious Conferences*. They moreover carry on at their Meetings, Designs of *Charity*, of different kinds; such as Relieving the *Wants* of *Poor House-keepers*, maintaining their *Children* at *School*, setting of *Prisoners* at *Liberty*, supporting of *Lectures* and *daily Prayers* in our *Churches*. These are the SOCIETIES which our late *Gracious Queen*, as the Learned *Bishop* that hath writ her LIFE tells us,* took so great *Satisfaction* in, that She inquired *often* and *much* about them, and was *glad* they went on and prevailed; which, thanks be to GOD, they *continue* to do; as the Reverend Mr. *Woodward*, who hath obliged the World with a very particular Account of the *Rise* and *Progress* of them, hath lately acquainted us.† And these likewise are SOCIETIES that have proved so exceedingly *Serviceable* in the Work of REFORMATION, that they may be reckoned a chief *Support* to it, as our late *Great Primate* Arch-Bishop *Tillotson* declar'd, upon several Occasions, after he had

* Gilbert Burnet's *Essay on the Memory of the late Queen*, published in 1695. There is a copy in the Harvard College Library.

† The Rev. Josiah Woodward preached a sermon before the Societies on December 28, 1696. There is a copy in the Harvard College Library. In the Epistle Prefatory we read:

"*And therefore it cannot but be matter of great Joy to all good People to hear of your successful Progress in this your* pious Enterprize. *What exalted Praises will they offer to God, when they hear of your Order, Courage, and Unanimity in a Work of such absolute Necessity; and when they understand that* Thousands *have been brought by your means to legal Punishment, for their abominable Enormities; and that Multitudes of scandalous Houses . . . have been suppress'd by you; and that* public Vice and Profaneness *is manifestly check'd, and in a way to be rooted out by your exemplary Diligence, Zeal, and Expence in this great Undertaking? As it is more particularly related in an* Account of the Rise and Progress of the Religious Societies of Young Men, *lately published*" (pp. vii. viii).

The title of Woodward's pamphlet is, *An Account of the Rise and Progress of the Religious Societies in the City of London, &c. And of the Endeavours for Reformation of Manners Which have been made therein.* No copy of the first edition is known to me, but according to Arber's *Term Catalogues* (ii. 600) it was published in November, 1696, under the title of *An Earnest Admonition to All; but especially to Young Persons, to turn to God by speedy repentance and reformation. Being the substance of six Sermons. . . . To which is added, An Account of the Rise and Progress of the Religious Societies of Young Men, and of the Societies for Reformation.* In the British Museum are copies of the second (1698), the third (1701), and the fourth (1712) editions. The following extracts, pertinent to our subject, are taken from the second edition:

"IT is now about twenty years ago, that several young Men of the *Church of England*, in the Cities of *London* and *Westminster*, were about the same time touch'd with a very affecting sense of their Sins, and began to apply themselves, in a very serious manner, to *Religious Thoughts and Purposes*" (p. 31).

"INSOMUCH, that there are now near twenty *Societies* of various *Qualities* and *Functions*, formed in a Subordination and Correspondency one with another, and engaged in this Christian Design in and about this *City* and *Suburbs*: All which have their set Hours and Places of meeting, to direct, support, and execute this their undertaking.

"IN this Number of *Societies for Reformation* here given, I do not include any of the thirty two *Religious Societies* before mentioned. For tho they all agree in the love of Virtue, and dislike of Vice, yet their first and more direct Design of Association seems to be distinguish'd thus. In that the *Societies for Reformation* bent their utmost Endeavours from the first to suppress *publick Vice*; whilst the *Religious Societies* endeavour'd chiefly to promote *Religion* in their own Breasts, tho they have since been eminently instrumental in the Publick Reformation" (pp. 83, 84).

examined their *Orders*, and inquired into their *Lives, That he thought they were to the Church of England.**

That a movement which met with such an impetus in England should have extended its influence to the American colonies, is what one would naturally expect. In a pamphlet published in London in 1705, we read:

A Reverend Divine, who hath been lately in our Northern Plantation in *America*, by the Encouragement of divers of our Bishops, for the Propagation of Christianity there, order'd a whole Impression of the *Account of the Societies*† to be Printed off, and sent thither, for the promoting a *Reformation*, by these Methods, in those Parts of the World. And this Reverend Person the last Month told me, that he thinks they have since made a more remarkable *Reformation* there, than in either of Her Majesty's Kingdoms.‡

Some contemporary letters written by an unknown New Englander are fortunately preserved. In the pamphlet which has just been cited will be found the following extracts:

From *New England* we are told, That great Care hath been there taken of late for the Punishment of *Vice* and *Prophaneness* by the Methods that are here us'd; and a Gentleman in that Country, in his Letter bearing date *April* 10. 1702. informs us, That several Societies are formed in *Boston*, and he thinks that in a little time he shall acquaint us of others set up in other Parts of that Country.§

A Gentleman in *New-England*, in a Letter dated *October* 8. 1704. writes to his Correspondent in *London in* the following Words: *The* Societies *lately erected for the Service of Religion in* London, *and in some other Parts of* Europe, *have by their laudable Example had an Influence upon a Country as far distant from them as* New-England *in* America. *And we thought it might be some Satisfaction to you and other good Men with you, to have a summary Account of the Good which is daily doing among us, in Imitation of the Example that you have given us. We shall accordingly inform you, that a Number of Gentlemen who make the best Figure in this Place, did a few Months ago establish a* voluntary Conversation *once in a Fortnight. The Gentlemen of the* Society for Propagation of Religion *have already had a sensible Blessing of God upon their Consultations and Undertakings. They have sent into every Town of the Provinces Treatises to animate the* Observation of the Lord's Day. *They have conveyed unto such People among our selves as frequently and prophanely absent themselves from the* Publick Worship of God, *a Sheet of* Considerations *to reclaim them from that Prophanity. They compiled and emitted an* Abstract of Laws *against all punishable Wickedness, and armed the Officers in the several Parts of the Province therewithal. They are now endeavouring to introduce more Religion into our Sea-faring Tribe, and Season our Vessels with better Orders than have been generally practised. These are but some of the good Things which they have done in a very little while. We*

* *An Account of the Societies for Reformation of Manners, in London and Westminster, And other Parts of the Kingdom*, London, 1699, pp. 15, 16. In the British Museum Catalogue and elsewhere this pamphlet, of which two editions appeared in 1699, is attributed to Woodward: but the allusion to Woodward quoted in the text shows that he could not have been its author. There is a copy of the pamphlet in the Boston Athenæum and in the Harvard College Library. In a sermon preached before the Societies on June 27, 1698, the Rev. Thomas Jekill referred in the Epistle Dedicatory to "*the several Accounts that have been given of your Affairs in Print; first by the Right Reverend Bishop of* Gloucester, *and since by the Reverend Mr.* Woodward, *and some others.*" The first allusion is of course to Edward Fowler's *Vindication* (1692), already quoted in a note on page 32, while the second allusion is to the pamphlet by Woodward mentioned in the last note.

† Presumably the *Account* published in 1699. There are in the British Museum a pamphlet published in London about 1700 called *A Short Account of the Several Kinds of Societies, set up of late Years, for the promoting of God's Worship, for the Reformation of Manners*, etc.; and a pamphlet published at Edinburgh in 1700 by Sir Francis Grant Lord Cullen, entitled *A Brief Account, of the Nature, Rise, and Progress of the Societies, for Reformation of Manners, &c., in England and Ireland: with a Preface Exhorting to the Use of such Societies in Scotland.*

‡ *An Account of the Progress of the Reformation of Manners, in England, Scotland, and Ireland, And other Parts of Europe and America*, thirteenth edition, London, 1705, p. 4. There is a copy of this pamphlet in the Harvard College Library.

§ *Ibid.* p. 9.

shall supersede the mention of the rest, with one comprehensive Service they produced in Boston, *our chief Town, a* Society for the Suppression of Disorders; *many good Offices have been done for the Town in a little while by that Society; they Printed a Sheet of Methods and Motives for such Societies; the Sheet they scattered throughout these Colonies. In many Towns they have erected such Societies, and conformed unto the Advice that have been set before them. In these Towns the Ministers and the Societies, with which they have accomodated themselves, to be admirable Engines for the maintaining and promoting all good Order among their People. We receive Letters from divers Quarters wherein they do even with some Rapture give Thanks to God for the Advantage they have already received by these Societies. They generally carry on their Design with Prudence and Silence, and great Modesty, but with wondrous Efficacy. We confess we owe unto you the Relation, because we are beholding to you for the Example that hath been followed in our feeble Essays to do what we can for the Advancement of the Greatest Interest. May the God of all Grace prosper all your and our Essays thus to do what Good we can.**

In another pamphlet, published in London in 1706, we get a few more letters written by the same person. Some extracts follow.

A Reverend Divine of *New-England* in his Letter dated from *Boston* the 23d of *November* 1705, says thus: Sir, *It was but Yesterday that your letter to our worthy Friend Mr.——— arrived; however, we were not willing to miss this Opportunity of returning you our hearty Thanks for your grateful Communications, and of letting you know, that we take every Opportunity of returning greatest Thanks to the God of Heaven, for disposing and assisting so many (as we perceive by your Letters) unto such noble Methods of being Serviceable.*

And because you may expect something of that also, we will go on where we left off in the Account we formerly gave you of our Proceedings in those best Intentions, the Reformation of Manners, and the Propagating of Christian Knowledge and Goodness.

Our Societies for the suppression of Disorders, increase and prosper in this Town; there are two more such Societies added unto the former; There are also Religious Societies without Number in this Country that meet at proper Times, to pray together, and repeat Sermons, and forward one another in the Fear of God.

In some Towns of this Country, the Ministers who furnish themselves with a Society for the Suppression of Disorders, hardly find any notorious Disorders to be suppressed: but then their Societies are helpful unto them in doing abundance of Good for the Advancement of serious Religion in the Neighbourhood, and to make their Ministry much more Profitable in the Weekly Exercise of it.†

Lastly, a Gentleman writes from *New-England*, in his Letter of the 20th of *November* 1705. *To gratifie your Desires to know what Progress we make here in our Societies, I make bold to add a Line or two to certify, That in* Boston *the Societies for suppressing Disorders (of which mention was made in my former Letters) are upheld, and two other Societies of the same Nature erected. All which are spirited to be active, according to their Abilities and Influence, to promote Virtue, and discountenance and suppress Vice. And not only in* Boston *are such good Things done, and doing, but in many Places in the Province besides. Omitting many other things that might be enumerated as to other Places, I shall sum up in short, an Account of what hath been done in a Town called* Taunton, *through the rich Mercy of God: The Reverend Mr. ———,‡ Minister there, having seen some Printed Accounts of the Methods for Reformation in* Old England, *in imitation thereof (after earnest Prayers to God for Success) obtained of several Inhabitants of the Place (that were noted for Sobriety and Zeal against Sin) to meet with him once in each Month, to consult what might be done to promote a Reformation of Disorders there. And after a Day improved in Fasting and Prayer together,*

* *Ibid.* pp. 11, 12.

† *A Help to a National Reformation. Containing an Abstract of the Penal-Laws against Prophaneness and Vice. . . . To which is added, An Account of the Progress of the Reformation of Manners in England and Ireland, and other parts of the World.* Fifth edition, London, 1706, pp. 13, 14. There is a copy in the Boston Public Library. There is in the British Museum a copy of the first edition, printed in 1700.

‡ The pamphlet from which this is taken formerly belonged to the New England Library collected by the Rev. Thomas Prince and now in the Boston Public Library. It contains notes in the handwriting of Prince himself, and at the bottom of p. 15 is written: "[* i e ye Rev mr *Samuel Danforth*]."

they first attempted to reduce the Heads of Families to set up Family Worship; and God gave them great Success; So that most of the Families in the large Towns hearkened to their Exhortations and Reproofs; and set upon the Practice of Family Prayer Morning and Evening; every day having heard and read some Accounts of the Religious Societies of Young Men in London, *they were encouraged to endeavour the like among them. And beyond their Expectation (God working with them) prevailed with the greatest part of the Youth to form themselves into Societies for Religious Exercises, signing some good Rules to be observed by them therein, much like the Orders of the Societies of the Young Men in* London, *The good Effect whereof was the putting an End to and utter Banishment of their former disorderly and profane Meetings to Drink, &c. and to the great Grief of Godly Minds.*

There is also something done in the Town (and in some others) towards the founding of a School, by getting Lands granted and laid out by the Inhabitants for the particular Design of upholding a School. And whereas some Prints from Old-England *certify us, That the Inferior Clergy are advised to meet together often, and consult how to promote* Reformation.* *In like manner some Essays are made, that Neighbouring Ministers in this Province might uphold some stated Meetings, to consider of what they may do for the same End.*

Now, Sir, our Imitation of the pious Zeal of godly Men in Old-England, *is a sufficient Testimony of our Approbation of what is doing there. And blessed be God that there is a great Number in this Province, who daily pray to God for the Prosperity of* Old-England: *And especially that Religion in the Power and Life of it may Flourish there.*†

These letters and extracts give us an interesting glimpse into the moral and social life of New England two centuries ago. For half a century or more the English Societies continued their activities.‡ How long the movement lasted in New England is not known to the present writer, and it is hoped that the facts now given will lead to further discoveries in the same direction. In 1895 the Rev. Francis E. Clark wrote:

> But the most remarkable example of Endeavorers before the Endeavor Society is found in a short-lived movement which began nearly two centuries ago in the churches of Massachusetts.§

Mr. Clark then goes on to describe and to quote from a pamphlet printed by Cotton Mather at Boston in 1724 and entitled, "Religious Societies. Proposals For the Revival of Dying Religion, By Well-Ordered Societies For that Purpose. With a brief Discourse, Offered unto a Religious Society, on the First Day of their Meeting." Mather makes a passing allusion to the societies which have been considered in this paper, but does

* *Cf.* p. 33, *ante*.

† *A Help to a National Reformation*, pp. 14–16.

‡ Some of those who preached to the Societies were Dissenters, but most of them were of the Church of England. The sermons were at first quarterly, but later became annual. The libraries of Boston and Cambridge contain the following sermons: Josiah Woodward (1696), Lilly Butler (1697), John Woodhouse (1697), John Russell (1697), Samuel Bradford (1697), Samuel Wesley (1698), William Hayley (1698), Edward Fowler (1699), Gilbert Burnet (1700), St. George Ashe (1717), Edward Gibson (1724), Edward Chandler (1725), Thomas Green (1727), Richard Smalbroke (1728), Thomas Leavesley (1730), Francis Hare (1731), James Knight (1733), Arthur Bedford (1734), Edward Cobden (1736), Samuel Smith (1739). The British Museum contains some of the above sermons and also the following: William Bisset (1704), Samuel Wright (1715), John Leng (1718), Moses Lowman (1720), William Butler (1722), John Wynne (1726), Robert Drew (1735), Samuel Say (1736), William Simpson (1738), Samuel Chandler (1738). There is also in the British Museum *A Sermon Preached before the Former Societies for Reformation of Manners: To which is added, An Abridgment of the forty-second Account of their Progress made in the Cities of London and Westminster, and Places adjacent, for promoting a Reformation of Manners. Whereunto is subjoined, A Declaration from the present society*, London, 1760. This pamphlet ends as follows: "Justice Hall in the Old Bailey April the 21st 1760. where the Society meet every Monday Evening at 6 o'Clock. FINIS" (p. 36). Finally, several other pamphlets relating to the Societies will be found in the British Museum.

§ *World Wide Endeavor*, p. 43. My attention was called to this passage and to Mather's tract by the Rev. William H. Cobb, librarian of the Congregational Library, which owns a copy of the tract.

not add to our information. The societies to which attention has been called existed a quarter of a century or so before the appearance of Mather's pamphlet, and it is clear that the evolution of the Christian Endeavor Society is to be traced to them rather than to Mather's pamphlet.

The document mentioned at the beginning of this paper follows.

Articles covenanted and agreed upon this 25th day of December in the Year of our Lord God one Thoufand fix Hundred and ninety eight. between us who are hereunto fubfcribed, being a Society of Young Men mutually joining together in the Service of God, in the 11th Year of the Reign of our fovereign Lord William the third, by the Grace of God, of Great Britain, France and Ireland, King, Defender of the Faith &c.

Whereas the eternal Jehovah hath in his free Love made Man a reafonable and rational Creature, and hath given to us a Law to regulate and order our Lives by, It fhould be the great Care and Concernment of all Men in general, and of thofe that live under the Light, Power, Means and Gospel of an almighty and alsufficient Saviour, in a very singular and particular Manner, for to walk and order their Lives and Converfations according to their Faith and Belief, as the holy Spirit of God in his holy Word fhall guide and direct in fuch Ways, Means, Methods, and Inftitutions, as may increafe their Love to, and Faith, and Hope, and Truft in God, and prove beneficial unto their own precious and immortal Souls, as well as Joy and Comfort unto all the Godly: and an example unto all ungodly Sinners. And fince that the blefsed and eternal God hath declared in his holy Word that he defires not the Death of Sinners; and that where but two or three are gathered together in His Name, that there He will be in the midft of them and blefs them; and that he loves them that love him and they that seek him early fhall find him: and fince that God hás appeared and made known his Spirit and Power wonderfully upon the enlivening, enlightening, comforting, converting and confirming fundry, in the former and prefent Generation, and make them great Blefsings unto his Church and People, by and through the Means of godly and pious Societies and Converfations. We following their Example, and trufting alone for Help and Afsistance from God; do jointly and feverally confent and agree unto thefe Articles following, viz, I) First, That upon every Sabbath Day Evening, as many of us as are well, and in Health; except that fome unavoidable Accident happen, will come at the Place and Time appointed for the carrying on of our Exercife; and continue two Hours, or thereabouts in our Service. II) Secondly. That when we are met together, our Service is to begin, first, with Prayer; Secondly, a Psalm to be fung at the Appointment of him that first began the Exercife. Thirdly, if the Time be not far fpent a godly sermon is to be read. Lastly, We will conclude with Prayer.—In the Year of Our Lord and Saviour one Thoufand feven Hundred and feven. January the 25th. It was agreed upon by the whole Society, that they would meet once in a Month a Thursday Night: and the Exercife to be carried on in Prayer; and a Psalm to be fung at laft.—And alfo it was agreed upon, that if any Perfon belonging unto our Society doth not attend at the Place appointed for the carrying on of our Exercife, he is to declare his Reafon for the same. III) Thirdly, All fhall equally take their Turns in carrying on the Exercife as their Names are annexed; and that if any one defires to be excufed, he fhall get another of the Society to take his Turn in carrying on of the Exercife, and it fhall be reputed and reckoned, that he who of right fhould have done it, hath taken his Turn. IV) Fourthly. That whatfoever Slips or Miftakes happen from any perfon, while in Prayer, or any other Exercife, there fhall be nothing faid, nor any Motions made, that may any ways impofe upon, or make the Perfon an Object of Laughter; but all are in Love and Friendfhip to bear with the Miftakes one of another: for no man is able to ftand upon his own Strength, and God may let the ablest fall into grofse Errors. V) Fifthly. No Perfon belonging unto our Society, fhall at any Time, make known unto any others, any of the Slips or Miftakes of any of the Society, but all our Actions fhall be kept fecret unto ourfelves, least through the Subtilty of Satan much Mifchief be incurred thereby. VI) Sixthly. No fcandalous Perfon fhall be admitted into our Society; nor any other Perfon if they will not confent unto thefe our Articles, after they have been with us one or two Nights for a Tryal. VII) Seventhly. No Perfon fhall break off from us, and leave our Society, after their Names are annexed, except that first he declares his Reafon for the fame, unto our Satisfaction; provided he be not disabled by Distemperature of Body, or be by Providence removed away from us. VIII) Eighthly and Lastly. If it fo happen, which God forbid, that any of our Society fall into grofs and fcandilous Sins, whereby the Ways of Religion and Godlinefs are fcandalized and reproached; or if any, after their Hands are annexed, break and violate thefe our Articles, for the firft Offence they shall be reproved, and if they ftill continue refractory, for the fecond Offence fhall be under fharp Admonition, and for a third Offence fhall be totally expelled our Society. Amen.

[1st Column]
*Bernard Capen
*Jabez Searle
*Hopestill Clap
*Jofhua Wight
*William Spoul
*Thomas Evans
*Ifaac How
*John Stiles
*Hopeftill Capen
*Matthias Evans
*Samuel Tolman
*Daniel Tolman
*James White
*Abraham How
*John Henfhaw
*Richard Field
*Ebenezer Paul
*John Tolman
*John White
*William Trefcot
*John Capen
*Edward Capen
*Samuel Hall
*Ebenezer Withington
*John Danforth
*Jofeph Topliff
*Samuel Withington
*Jofeph Payson
*John Withington
*Samuel Capen
*Preserved Capen
*Ebenezer Hemmenway
*John Smith
*William Withington
*Ebenezer Topliff
*Abijah Baker
*Nathaniel Topliff
*Nathaniel Tolman
*Jacob Eliot
*Thomas Hall
*Benjamin Stuart
*Jonathan Capen
*David Tolman
*Ephraim Payfon
*Henry Payson
*Confider Leeds
[2nd Column]
*John Capen
*Edward Payson
*John Blake
*Jofiah Blake
*George Payson
*Stephen Williams
*Richard Hall
*Jonathan Payson
*Jofeph Weeks
*Purchafe Capen
*John Tolman
Thomas Randal
*Samuel Capen
*Ebenezer Weeks
*John Robinfon
*Aquilla Tolman
*Henry Leadbetter
*John White
*Jonas Tolman
Jofeph Viles
*James Trott
James Andrews
Richard Smith
Benjamin Smith
*Hopeftill Withington
*Ebenezer Bird
Samuel Hayward
*Naphthali Pierce
Samuel How
*Jofhua Severs
*Thomas How
*John Clap
*Matthias Evans
*Edward White
*James Baker
*Timothy Fofter
Daniel Tolman
*Elijah Tolman
*David Trott
Johnfon Tolman
Abijah White
Ebenezer Tolman
*Samuel Hall
*Defire Tolman
*Thomas Fofter
*Thomas Baker
[3rd column]
Thomas Clap
Joseph How
Ebenezer Topliff
*Samuel Withington
Elijah Baker
Ebenezer Ball
*Samuel Sever
*James How
*William Tolman
*Stephen Jones
Jofiah Tolman
John Evans
*Robert Capen

*John Spur
George Baker
*Robert Larmon
*Thomas Kilton
William Marion
Ambrose Talbut
*Solomon Kilton
Ifaac Humphry
Samuel Dinfman
Samuel Capen
Samuel Topliff
*John Robinfon
*Ebenezer Pierce
Bernard Capen
Benjamin Badcock
Job Staples
Simeon Tupper
Jonathan Payson
*Joseph Weeks
Benjamin Lyon
Jonathan Davenport
Benjamin Talbut
*Joseph Trefcott
*John Foster
Thomas Leeds
Jonathan Trefcot
Abraham Wheeler
Samuel How
John Tolman
Jofeph Capen
Samuel Pierce
Paul Hall
*Edward Breck
[4th column]
Jonathan Leeds
Ezekiel Tolman
Samuel Tolman
Ebenezer Blake
Hopeftill Hall
Alexander Glover
John Pierce
Elijah Tolman
Jonas Tolman
John How
Edward Glover
*Joseph Turner
Ebenezer Jones
Ebenezer Tolman
Thomas Davenport
*Ambrose Davenport
*Abraham How
John Baker jun^r^
Abijah White jun^r^
Samuel Henfhaw
Jofeph Badcock
Samuel Jones
Samuel Withington, 3^d^
Richard Hall jun^r^
Jonathan Pierce
Defire Tolman
Ebenezer Davenport
Jofeph Davenport
*Joseph Blake
Henry Morts
William King jun^r^
John Henfhaw
*Benjamin Dickerman
Increafe Toleman
Joseph Clap Junr
Jonathan Blake
*Jofhua Williams
Jofhua Wales
Edward Fofter
Seth Blake
Ebenezer Withington
Ebenezer Capen
Stephen Jones
Samuel Adams
George Vose
James Pierce
[5th column]
Nathaniel Swift
James Blake jun^r^
Ifaac How
[From here on the names are autographs.]
Daniel Wiswall
Philip Withington
Jofeph Lovel
*Isaac Dauenport
Thomas Phillips
George Minot
Nathaniel Glover
Thomas Baker
Peter Niles
Mather Withington
Nathaniel Topliff
George Davenport
Pelatiah hall
Lemuel Crane
William Vose jun^r^
Samuel Davenport
Joseph Weeks Withington
Reuben Torrey
Edward Robinfon
James Lewis
Thomas Tolman
Jonathan Wiswall
Lemuel Pierce
Thomas Pierce
Ebenezer Pierce
Edward Prefton
John Preston jun
*Daniel Bird
William Pierce
George Reading
George Payson
*David Pratt
James Tileston
Daniel Withington
Samuel Capen
John Lemest
Stephen Hearsey
Jonathan Leeds
Phinehas Withington
Geo Manning
Ebenezer ——
Stephen Evans
Edwd W Baxter
[6th column]
Michal Shaller
John How

Samuel Pierce Jun
*Eliakim Buckman
George Stand
Samuel Wheeler
Lewis Withington
John Robinson
Benjamin Jacobs
Samuel Glover
William Wales
Ephraim Dauenport
Jonas Tolman
John Tolman
Ezekiel Tolman
James Holden
William Tolman
Enos Withington
George How
Sam[l] Topliff jun[r]
Elisha Tolman
Abraham How Jun[r]
John Davenport
John White jun[r]
Lemuel Tolman
Rufus Kilton
Eben[r] Tolman 3[d]
Samuel Clap 3[d]
Nathaniel Tolman
John Dickerman
Benjamin Pierce Ju[r]
Enos Blake Ju[r]
Daniel Davenport
Nathaniel Minott
Samuel White
Moses Tolman
Tho[s] I. Tolman
[7th column]
Alexander Leeds
John Ayres
Andrew Mackintosh
Abraham Wheeler
Edmund Smith
Joseph Arnold
John Leeds J[r]
Ebenezer Tileston
Stephen Tolman
Isaac Howe Jun[r]
James Leeds
W[m] Holden Jun[r]
John Peirce
Henry Withington
Nath[l] Swift Jun
Jofeph Howe
Samuel Howe Jun[r]
Jeremiah Evans
Jonathan Pierce
Joseph Tolmans
Sherod Man
SamuelHaws
Joseph Howe
Samuel Thacher
Edward Foster
Phinehas Withington
Samuel B. Pierce
William Swift
John Foster
David Peirce
John Smith
Edward Moies
Jofeph Foard
Charles Foard
Stillman Lothrop
Isaac Clapp
Tim[y] Foster
Lewis Pierce
[8th column]
John C Philipes
James Withington
William Richardson
Thomas Tolman
Henry Lyon
Isaac Davenport
Joseph Foster
Jacob Howe
William Jacobs
Ezekiel Thayer
Atwood Litchfield
Sam[l] H. Tolman
——————— 1809 [in pencil]
James Clap
Leonard Withington
Samuel Page
Richard Coun
Peter Blake
Elijah I Jones
John Seaverns
Paul Perry
William S. Williams
Jeremiah S B Blake
Josiah Codding
Cyrhas Houghton
John Tolman Jun[r]
W[m] Hammond
Eben[r] W Withington
Seth Tillson
Fisher Holmes
1834
Daniel Leeds
John C. Clapp
Caleb Hill
Edward Jones J[r]
George Leeds
James C. Sharp
W[m] R. Bradford
David Baker
[9th column]
Josiah Davenport
James Semple
Seth H. Ford
Benjamin Farington
William Adams
Elbridge G M[c]Elroy
Theodore Cary
Eliphalet Stone
Charles B. Adams
Edw Lemist
William L Wilcox
Henry H. Penniman
N N Gleason
James O. Clapp

[*Filed*]
Young Mens names

A LIST OF MARRIAGES BY REV. SAMUEL NILES OF BRAINTREE, MASS., 1739–1762, NOT ENTERED ON TOWN RECORDS.

Copied from the Church records by EDWARD EVARTS JACKSON, Esq., of Braintree.

REV. SAMUEL NILES was ordained pastor of the Second Church [now First] in Braintree, Mass., May 23, 1711. According to a record which he kept, he administered the ordinance of the Lord's Supper 301 times, baptized about 1200 persons, and received 312 to full communion in his church. He continued to preach, without a colleague, till the last Sabbath of his life, and died on his birthday, May 1, 1762, aged 88 years.

1739.	May	31.	James Thayer and Esther Wales.
	Oct.	11.	Samuel Arnold and Bethiah Wild.
	Nov.	28.	Isaac Mors and Elizabeth Turner.
1740.	Jan.	1.	Benjamin Hunt and Sarah Arnold.
		3.	Moses Nash and Ann White.
	Feb.	28.	John Hunt and Ruth Whitmarsh.
	Mar.	20.	Zachariah Thayer and Lydia Pray.
1741.	June	11.	Thomas Thayer and Lydia Allen.
	July	30.	William White and Sarah Allen.
	Sept.	24.	Nathaniel Thayer and Mrs. Sarah Allen.
1742.	Jan.	14.	Abraham Thayer and Sarah Hunt.
		28.	Joseph Ludden and Elizabeth Wild.
	Mar.	11.	James Hollis and Elizabeth Thayer.
	Aug.	19.	Nathaniel Moseley and Sarah Capen.
1743.	Jan.	4.	William Linfield, Jr. and Sarah Thayer.
		6.	Joseph Brackett and Mary Nightengale.
	Mar.	10.	Benjamin Ludden and Joanna Wales.
	Apr.	8.	Benjamin Veazie and Mary Thayer.
	Dec.	23.	Lemuel Thayer and Ann Curtis.
1744.	Jan.	4.	Samuel Blancher and Mary Whitmarsh.
		18.	Benjamin Clark and Bethiah Shaw.
	Mar.	15.	James Faxon and Relief Thayer.
	Apr.	12.	Joseph Field and Abigail Newcomb.
	July	19.	Ephraim Hunt and Miriam Spear.
	Sept.	6.	Josiah White and Sarah Holbrook.
	Dec.	13.	Nathaniel Wales and Anna Wild.
1745.	Feb.	14.	John Thayer, Jr., and Abigail Thayer.
	Apr.	24.	Abijah Neal and Lydia Spear.
	May	16.	Humphrey Burrill and Hannah Thayer.
	Aug.	8.	Elijah Thayer and Margaret Tower.
	Nov.	7.	Benjamin Ludden, Jr., and Esther Capen.
		13.	Obadiah Thayer and Dorothy Hollis.
			William Wild and Deborah Allen.
1746.	Jan.	15.	Richard Hayden and Mary Hobart.
			Isaac Copeland and Lydia Thayer.
		30.	Edward Faxon and Hannah Blancher.
		31.	John Wild and Anna Thayer.
	Feb.	20.	Caleb Thayer and Abigail Faxon.

	Mar.	6.	Ichabod Holbrook and Hannah Hayden.
	June	12.	Elijah Veazie and Ann Trask.
		16.	James Packard and Mary Thayer.
	July	10.	Joseph Arnold and Mary Butts.
	Sept.	28.	Thomas Faxon and Elizabeth Hobart.
	Nov.	17.	Nathaniel Wales and Sarah Hayward.
1747.	Jan.	1.	Eliphalet Sawen and Rachel Thayer.
		8.	Samuel Noyes and Jane Copeland.
			William Whitmarsh and Elizabeth Hayden.
	Apr.	2.	Enoch Hunt and Susanna Hobart.
		23.	John Thayer and Ann Hunt.
	Aug.	22.	Benjamin Foster and Ruth Thayer.
	Oct.	15.	Benjamin White and Marcy Thayer.
	Nov.	9.	James Nash and Margaret Tomson.
		19.	David Vinton and Ruth Dorman.
		20.	Jonathan Thayer and Dorcas Hayden.
	Dec.	10.	Benjamin Hayden and Mary Wild.
			Thomas French and Silence Wild.
1748.	Jan.	14.	Micah Thayer and Mehitable French.
	May	24.	James Denton and Mary Hobart.
	Oct.	25.	Uriah Thayer and Deborah Copeland.
	Dec.	6.	James Thayer and Deborah Arnold.
1749.	Mar.	2.	John Sozin (?) and Deborah Ludden.
	Apr.	12.	Elisha Faxon and Sarah Allen.
	May	11.	Ephraim Willis and Ann Ludden.
	July	11.	Abijah Allen and Ruth Penniman.
	Aug.	24.	Thomas Faxon and Joanna Allen.
			David Linsfield and Hannah Vinton.
	Sept.	14.	Samuel Tucker and Elizabeth Hayward.
	Dec.	21.	Gideon French and Elizabeth Thayer.
1750.	Oct.	11.	Ephraim Hunt, Jr., and Delight Mann.
		18.	Seth Mann and Elizabeth Dyer.
	Nov.	13.	Capt. John Thayer and wid. Elizabeth Hayden.
	Dec.	6.	Seth Turner and Rebecca Vinton.
			Nehemiah French and Joanna Whitmarsh.
1751.	Jan.	10.	Obediah Thayer and Joanna Thayer.
	July	4.	Daniel Pratt and Sarah Nash.
		18.	Oliver Sawyer and Sarah Bowditch.
	Aug.	7.	Moses Littlefield and Mary Mann.
	Oct.	17.	Abiah Thayer and Elizabeth Hunt.
1752.	Jan.	1.	Richard Thayer and Susanna Wild.
	Mar.	19.	John Slone and Deborah Spear.
		24.	Hezekiah Ludden and Mehitable Thayer.
	Apr.	25.	Edward Chipman* and Margaret Dyer.
	Dec.	7.	Elisha Niles and Anna Wild.
		28.	Elijah Faxon and Beulah Wild.
1753.	Jan.	6.	Jacob Copeland and Abigail Daget [Daggett].
		19.	Nathaniel Glover and Mary Field.
	Feb.	15.	Nathaniel Ludden and Anna French.
	Mar.	8.	Joseph Winchester and Mary Rawson.
	May	17.	Samuel Ward and Elizabeth Holbrook.
	June	1.	Isaac Lufkin and Dorothy Ludden.

* Should be Edward Chessman.

	June	28.	William Salisbury and Elizabeth Beal.
	Oct.	30.	Luke Lambert and Rachel ———
	Nov.	1.	Azariah Faxon and Dorcas Penniman.
		16.	Thomas Carsnan (?) and Sarah Jones.
		30.	Jesse Wild and Judith Thayer.
	Dec.	12.	Thomas Kingman and Susanna Copeland.
		27.	Micah Wild and Rachel Hobart.
1754.	Jan.	24.	Israel Eaton and Jerusha Rawson.
		31.	Joseph Porter and Hannah Ripley.
	Apr.	4.	Nathaniel Curtis and Elizabeth Copeland.
	June	20.	Christopher Capen and Abigail Thayer.
	Sept.	2.	John Stevens and Lydia Webb.
		23.	Joseph Thayer and Zilpah Lane.
	Sept.	28.	Boylston Adams and Molly Allen.
	Oct.	24.	Recompense Wadsworth and Hannah Paine.
	Dec.	10.	Nathaniel Belcher and Lydia Brackett.
1755.	May	2.	Enoch Hayden and Amy Thayer.
		12.	Benjamin Miller and Mary Arnold.
	July	24.	Nathaniel Niles and Mary Clark.
	Sept.	11.	Richard Thayer and Esther French.
	Dec.	16.	Randal Wild and Jerusha Thayer.
1756.	Feb.	5.	Winter Bowson and Rebecca Capen.
	Mar.	28.	Elisha French and Mary Ludden.
	Aug.	12.	Moses French and Elizabeth Hobart.
	Sept.	2.	David French and Mehitable Pratt.
	Nov.	18.	Josiah Hayden and Rehumah Thayer.
			Caleb Hayden and Mary D. Gipson.
		25.	Silas Wild and Ruth Thayer.
	Dec.	9.	Elisha Thatcher and Abigail Webb.
1757.	Feb.	24.	Joseph Curtis and Betty Newcomb.
	May	5.	Gideon Thayer and Zipporah Curtis.
	July	7.	Daniel Hayden and Miriam Hunt.
			Micah Wild and Deborah Hollis.
1758.	Feb.	14.	Moses Jones and Sarah Thayer.
	Mar.	28.	Samuel Pratt and Nabbe Hobart.
	Apr.	20.	Nathaniel Capen and Deborah Curtis.
	Oct.	19.	Josiah Lincoln of Hingham and Mollie Holbrook.
	Nov.	23.	Joseph Wild and Rachel Hollis.
1759.	Apr.	19.	John Trask and Mary Miriam.
			Joseph Larel (?) [Lovell] and Susanna Thayer.
1760.	Apr.	24.	Caleb Bagley of Scituate and Phillippa Peaks.
	Apr.	31.	Aaron Renough of Weymouth and Hannah Niles.
	June	12.	Rev. Jonathan Mills and Mrs. Hepzibah French.
	Nov.	13.	David Holbrook and Mary Jones.
		27.	Ezra Penniman and Eunice Thayer.
1761.	Mar.	5.	Samuel French and Elizabeth Allen.
		12.	Richard Hayden and Mary Jordan.
	Apr.	30.	Benjamin Veazie and Abigail Brackett.
	May	28.	Thomas Vinton, Jr., and Jemima Mills.
	June	18.	Nehemiah Blancher and Mrs. Mary Hayden.
	Nov.	19.	Peleg Hersey of Hingham and Lucy Holbrook.
		27.	Israel Peaks and Alice Howland.
	Dec.	3.	John Curtis and Abigail Thayer.
1762.	Feb.	10.	Abel Thayer and Dorothy Curtis.

A REVOLUTIONARY ROLL.

Communicated by Alfred Cass, Esq., of Germantown, Penn.

The following roll of soldiers in the Revolution was the property of Capt. Enoch Page of Nottingham, N. H., and is now owned by his granddaughter Miss Hannah F. J. Kinsman of Cornville, Me.

Cambreg June 13 1775 A return of Capt. Willam Hdſon Ballerds Companey Jn Col. James Frys Regement

---

	Menſ Names	*There Ages*	*Where they Belong*	*When Entered*	*When Entered the Servis*
Serg	William Lowell	37	Almsbury	April 19	April 20
Serg	Samuell Huntoon	25	Kinstown	may 5	may 10
Serg	theophils Colby	27	South hampton	Deto 11	Deto 25
Corp	Job Hasket	31	hampton fawls	Deto 8	Deto 12
	Stephen Bartlet	20	Almsbury	April 19	April 20
	Joseph Worker	40	porchmouth	may 3	may 6
	Nemier osgood	20	Almsbury	April 19	April 20
	Stephen Lowell	21	Deto	Deto 19	Deto 20
	Ephrim Colins	19	Deto	Deto 19	Deto 20
	Jehieha lord march	18	Deto	may 1	may 4
	moses magoon	20	Brintwood	Deto 9	Deto 10
	Jonathan young	19	Kingstown	Deto 8	Deto 10
	Banjmin Clough	18	Deto	Deto 6	Deto 10
	Banjmin quinby	18	poplin	Deto 8	Deto 10
	Calib gording	21	Kingston	Deto 8	Deto 12
	Jonathan hoyt	18	poplin	Deto 8	Deto 10
	William Evans	22	Kingston	Deto 11	Deto 12
	Joseph Sewell	17	South hamton	Deto 11	Deto 15
	Jacob flandars	17	Deto	Deto 11	Deto 15
	Jabez Dow	27	Kensington	Deto 13	Deto 19
	Danil Daverson	23	hampton fawls	Deto 15	Deto 19
	melcher word	36	Deto	Deto 15	Deto 19
	John Rolins	24	Deto	Deto 16	Deto 19
	Jacob Bag Currier	21	Almsbry	may 1	June 4
	John Row	24	porthmouth	Deto 3	April 6 [*sic*]
	peter Kittredge	22	audover	June 3	June 3
	Samuel Lankerster	21	South hampton	Deto 8	Deto 8
	Stephen Ladlaw	23	Kena Back	may 2	may 4
fifer	John grenwood	16	Boston	Deto 14	absent
	train of artlry				
	Samuell Blasdel	19	Amsbury	April 19	April 20
	Zaceheus Clough	21	poplin	may 9	may 10
	Moses gary	22	Deto	Deto 9	may 10
	Daniel gilman	20	Deto	Deto 9	Deto 10
	Samuel quinby	17	Kingſtown	June 12	June 8 [*sic*]
	Jeremiah Dudly	20	Dto	Dto 12	Dto 8 [*sic*]

ANDREW N. ADAMS.

By Erastus Hibbard Phelps, Esq., of Fair Haven, Vt.

Andrew N. Adams was born in Fair Haven, Vermont, January 6, 1830, and died in his native town, March 13, 1905. He was the son of Joseph and Stella (Miller) Adams. The ancestors of his father, who was born in Londonderry, New Hampshire, Feb. 14, 1802, were Scotch, and came to this country from the north of Ireland with the Scotch-Irish Colony that settled in Londonderry in 1721. Although called Scotch-Irish because they came from Ireland, these early settlers of Londonderry were of Scotch lineage pure and simple, and being rigid Protestants of the Presbyterian faith they tolerated no mixture with the Celts, and disliked being called Irish.

The parents of Joseph Adams immigrated to Whitehall, New York, in 1806, and in 1823 he married Stella, daughter of Capt. William and Paulina (Phelps) Miller. Capt. Miller was a native of Pittsfield, Massachusetts, and settled in Hampton in 1786, where he reared a large family of children, the eldest being the Rev. William Miller, widely known as a student of prophesy, and founder of the sect known as Second Adventists.

The subject of this sketch was the fourth child of Joseph Adams and Stella Miller. His preparatory school training was obtained in the common schools of Fair Haven, and at the Green Mountain Liberal Institute, South Woodstock, Vermont. Later, he was a student at the Theological Seminary at Meadville, Pennsylvania, graduating, however, at the Harvard Divinity School in 1855, in the same class with George Hughes Hepworth.

Immediately after his graduation, on August 1, 1855, he was married to Angie Margaret Phelps, of Orwell, Vermont, and at once entered upon his chosen profession, becoming pastor of the First Parish Church in Needham, Massachusetts, where he was ordained Nov. 21, 1855. In 1857 he removed to Franklin, Massachusetts, and became pastor of the First Universalist Church of that place, where he remained until the summer of 1860, when he resigned, and returned to Fair Haven, Vermont, to assist his father in a rapidly growing mercantile business. In 1869 he engaged, in company with his father and brother-in-law, David B. Colton, in sawing and manufacturing marble, and in this business he was interested at Fair Haven, and afterward at Belden's, Vermont, until a few years before his death.

He was always deeply interested in the welfare of his native town, and was at times justice of the peace and town treasurer, was an active member of the school board for many years, was principal director of the public library, was for twenty-five years trustee of the Rutland County Grammar School, at Castleton, Vermont, and at the time of his death was president of the board of trustees.

At the death of his father, he was made a director in the First National Bank of Fair Haven, which position he resigned a few years before his death.

In 1884–5 he represented his town in the State Legislature, and in 1888–9 he was a member of the State Senate, and occupied a very prominent position as a member of the joint committee on education. In 1870 he wrote and published a History of Fair Haven, a book of 516 pages, which is a most exhaustive history of the town from its settlement. He was for a number of years a contributing member of the Rutland County Historical Society—in fact it may be said that he was the leading spirit of that body.

Although for many years engaged in active business, Mr. Adams was by nature a student and a man of letters. In the latter part of his life he was deeply interested in genealogical subjects, and devoted years of study and labor to a history of the Adams family.

He first published, in 1894, a history of the descendants of James and William Adams of Londonderry (now Derry), New Hampshire. This included his own immediate branch of the Adams family. In 1898 he published a genealogical history of Henry Adams of Braintree, and John Adams of Cambridge, Massachusetts, a book of over 1200 pages with numerous illustrations. This book was the result of a great amount of patient, persistent, and painstaking work, and the author in his preface says it was "undertaken at first in intervals of leisure for the sake of the knowledge to be derived, and prosecuted later in order that others might have the benefit of the compilation, in a succinct and accessible form, of valuable records and material drawn from many and widely scattered sources."

This was followed, in 1900, with a history of Robert Adams of Newbury, Massachusetts, and his descendants, a book of 560 pages. At the beginning of this volume, in his address "To the Reader," the author speaks of other branches of the Adams family, notably "William of Ipswich," "John of Plymouth," "George of Watertown," as well as several other first-comers in Massachusetts, Connecticut, Maine, and New Hampshire. The author announces that he has compiled extensive lists of all these families, which could be published for the benefit of others if there were sufficient interest among the living descendants to warrant the labor and expense.

Sufficient encouragement having been given, in November, 1904, Mr. Adams issued an announcement "To the Descendants of William Adams, a first settler in Ipswich, Mass.," that the collation of the genealogical records of this great branch of the Adams family in America was approaching completion, and would be published early in the ensuing spring or summer. It was estimated that the material in hand would make a book of 600 pages.

Mr. Adams did not live to see the book published, but he left a voluminous mass of material relating to the subject, which has been given to the New England Historic Genealogical Society, where it will be preserved and can be consulted. He was elected a member of the Society in 1895.

Besides his historical and genealogical works, Mr. Adams was the author of numerous essays and addresses on educational and kindred subjects. He was deeply interested in scientific subjects, especially in geology, and among his published papers was one of exceeding interest on "The Geology of Vermont as developed along the Western border in the oldest fossilifirous rocks of the Continent."

His death is a serious loss to his family and the town in which he had resided so many years, and in whose interests he was always so deeply concerned. His widow and three married daughters survive him. The daughters are: Alice A., wife of Horace B. Ellis of Castleton, Vermont; Annie E., wife of George B. Jermyn of Scranton, Pennsylvania; and Stella M., wife of John T. Powell of Fair Haven, Vermont.

His large and valuable library has been presented to the town of Fair Haven, and will occupy a separate department in the Carnegie library building which is about to be erected.

Mr. Adams was, withal, a man of rare qualities of mind and heart, a man of refined and cultivated tastes, of broad and liberal views, a thoroughly honest and progressive citizen, a true and loyal friend.

From the great number of letters of sympathy received by the family from friends and acquaintances scattered throughout the whole country, the following extracts furnish ample evidence of the high esteem in which he was held even by those who were not fully in accord with his peculiar views. A prominent Congregational clergyman writes: "I was always drawn to Mr. Adams, not on account of kindred beliefs, but our spirits seemed to be kindred. If we could not agree in our conclusions we could, and I think did, agree in our desire to know the truth and conform our lives to its behests. I suppose that when we stand within the glory of the heavenly light, we shall find that the earthly views of all of us were inadequate, and perhaps in large part mistaken; and that they served their ends only by furnishing us hints and clues to the reality which is greater and more glorious than we can now conceive." Another letter from a lawyer, many years younger than Mr. Adams, says: "I always had great admiration for his character and intelligence. I don't think any one man has exerted greater influence on myself than Andrew N. Adams. He said to me once, several years ago, that whether or not he should have a personal, individual existence after this life he had no satisfactory evidence; but that it did not trouble him, for he knew he should continue to live after death in the influence and example of his life, — that that was the best part of man, and that could not die. So that while he could not say that he believed in the life everlasting as expressed in the creed, using those words as commonly understood, he did believe that what we love most in the life of our friends is everlasting; and his hope was that his influence and example might be such that he could wish it to continue forever. It seems to me that these words were an expression of the character of the man." Another clergyman, whose religious belief was in sympathy with that of Mr. Adams, writes: "His was truly a long, honorable and useful career, — not alone to his family and friends, but to the world. The principles of independent religious thought that he so faithfully lived and taught have helped to leaven the liberal thought of the world. A man so intellectually aggressive is not circumscribed in his influence by the 'pent up Utica' of town or state. But, alas, the dearest of earthly ties must be broken! Nothing earthly is permanent. Spirit, — spirit divine, spirit only is substantial, immortal. This is our comfort, that the reality, the divine essence within us that constitutes selfhood, cannot, like the body, die."

THOMAS TREADWELL OF IPSWICH, MASS., AND SOME OF HIS DESCENDANTS.*

By William A. Robbins, LL.B., of Brooklyn, N. Y.

1. Thomas[1] Treadwell† appears to have settled first at Dorchester, Mass., where his proportion of land on the Neck (sometimes called Lud-

* The author is indebted to Prof. George A. Treadwell of New York City for liberal assistance, and to Mrs. George H. Treadwell (Connecticut branch) and Mr. Smith R. Treadwell of Baltimore, Md., for much valuable data.

If sufficient encouragement be given, an extended genealogy will be published in book form, containing an account of all the descendants of Thomas and Edward Treadwell down to about 1900, the lines of daughters, where they have married, being carried one generation. In such a work it is proposed to present a great deal of collateral matter not here given, such as biography, copies of documents, including photographic copies of the original wills of Thomas Treadwell and his wife, fac-similes of early signatures, together with references and authorities, and exhaustive indices. The material for this is now well in hand.

† The earliest mention in this country of the name Tre(a)dwell found by the author is that of Thomas, in the records of Dorchester, Mass., under date of 18 Mar., 1637. Felt, however, in his History of Ipswich, Essex, and Hamilton, Mass., page 12, mentions a Mr. Treadwell as a settler in Ipswich, in 1635; but that Mr. Treadwell was probably no other than this Thomas. Neither Savage nor Pope refers to any other Treadwell for the year 1635.

Both Felt and Savage mention a John Treadwell in Ipswich in 1638; but Pope omits him, and the author has never been able to find the original record upon which to base such a claim. In 1637, an Edward Treadwell first appears in this country on the Ipswich records. Later, he settled on Long Island, New York, where he died, leaving two sons from whom have sprung the Connecticut and Long Island Tre(a)dwells, a very numerous and widely scattered family. The aforesaid Thomas and Edward were probably brothers; but no other evidence for this statement has been discovered than this contemporaneous residence in Ipswich.

In Hotten's "Original Lists" we find that on 28 July, 1635, Thomas Tredwell, a smith, Mary Tredwell, each aged 30 years, and Thomas Tredwell, aged one year, embarked from London in the *Hopewell*, with certificate from the minister of St. Giles Cripplegate, but an examination of the records at St. Giles Cripplegate, made in 1889 by Mr. Benjamin F. Treadwell, failed to disclose the Tre(a)dwell name.

low's Neck) was, 18 Mar., 1637, "3 acres, 3 goods, 20 rodes," and of other land, "3 acres, 3 goods, 26 rodes"; but prior to 23 Apr., 1638, he had moved to Ipswich, Mass., on which date he sold his Dorchester holdings (Boston Rec. Com. Report, No. 4, pp. 31, 34).

His wife was probably Mary Taylor, sister of Samuel Taylor who died in Ipswich, in June, 1695.

In his will, Thomas[1] Treadwell mentions "my sister Bachellor," and the inventory of his estate refers to "Bro. Bacheller." The names of Thomas[1] Treadwell and his wife appear several times in the inventory of the estate of Henry Bacheller who died in Ipswich, 3 Feb., 1678.

Theophilus Wilson in his will, 1690, mentions Nathaniel[2] Treadwell as his "cozzen;" and John Giddings, in a deposition made in 1664, recites a like relationship between Nathaniel[2] Treadwell and Thomas Wilson. Thomas[1] Treadwell was admitted freeman, 7 Sept., 1638. Subsequently, he served on several juries in Essex Co. He died in Ipswich, 8 June, 1671 (will dated 1 June, 1671, probated at Ipswich, 26 Sept., 1671, in Essex Co. Probate, 28115), and his wife died in Ipswich, 1 Dec., 1685 (will dated, 28 Oct., 1682, probated at Ipswich, 20 Apr., 1686, in Essex Co. Probate, 28102).

Children, all born in Ipswich excepting Thomas,[2] who was probably born in England:

2. i. THOMAS.[2]
ii. MARY, b. 29 Sept., 1636; living, 4. Oct., 1695; m. in Ipswich, Mass., in 1659, John Gaines, probably a shoemaker, who d. Sept., 1688; lived in Ipswich. Children: 1. *Mary.* 2. *Martha.* 3. *John.* 4. *Sarah.* 5. *Abigail.* 6. *Elizabeth.* 7. *Abyell.* 8. *Esther.*
3. iii. NATHANIEL.
iv. ESTHER, b. 21 Mch., 1640-1; d. in Ipswich, 4 Jan., 1730; m. in Ipswich, 8 Oct., 1665, Daniel, b. 1642, d. 29 May, 1695, son of Daniel and Abigail (Andrews) Hovey. Children: 1. *Daniel.* 2. *Nathaniel.* 3. *Abigail.* 4. *Thomas.* 5. *John.* 6. *Mary.* 7. *Ebenezer.* 8. *Mercy.* 9. *Ebenezer (?).*
v. MARTHA, b. 16 Mch., 1642-3; d. in Ipswich, 3 Mch., 1738; m. in Ipswich, 19 Feb., 1664-5, Robert, b. about 1641, d. in Ipswich, about 1713, son of Robert and Hannah (Jordan) Cross of Ipswich; lived in Ipswich. Children: 1. *Robert.* 2. *Thomas.* 3. *Martha.* 4. *Abyell.* 5. *Stephen.* 6. *Mary(?).*

2. THOMAS[2] TREADWELL (*Thomas*[1]), born probably in England about 1634, living 8 Jan., 1712, but may have died in 1718, married in Ipswich, Mass., 16 Mch., 1664/5, Sarah, born 22 June, 1640, living Mch., 1708, daughter of William and Joanna (Bartlett) Titcomb of Newbury, Mass. He was made freeman, 24 May, 1682. His estate was divided among his children during his life time.

Children, born in Ipswich:

4. i. THOMAS.[3]
ii. ELISHA, a tanner; went to Canada on a military expedition soon after Mar., 1689-90, where he died intestate, before 31 Mch., 1691; unmarried.
5. iii. JOHN.
iv. SARAH, b. 10 Jan., 1672-3; d. 5 Aug., 1738; m. 5 Jan., 1693, Jacob, a widower, b. in Ipswich, 3 Aug., 1662, d. Nov., 1705, son of Jacob and Elizabeth Perkins. He was a weaver and farmer, and a sergeant in the militia. Children: 1. *Elisha.* 2. *Sarah.* 3. *Mary.* 4. *Hannah.* 5. *Judith.*
v. MARY, b. 9 Aug., 1675; d. probably before 28 Oct., 1682.
vi. ANN, b. 16 Aug., 1679; d. 16 Apr., 1682.

3\. NATHANIEL[2] TREADWELL (*Thomas*[1]), born 13 Mch., 1637–8, died in Ipswich, Mass., 11 Jan., 1726–7, married first in Ipswich, 19 June, 1661, Abigail, who died 16 June, 1677, daughter of Thomas and Abigail (Warner) Wells of Ipswich; married second, in Ipswich, 25 Mch., 1677–8, Rebecca, born 1 Apr., 1656, living 14 July, 1715, daughter of William and Elizabeth (Stevens) Titcomb of Newbury, Mass., and half sister of the wife of his brother Thomas Treadwell; and probably married third, Anne ——, who died in Ipswich, 17 May, 1733. He took the freeman's oath, 10 Apr., 1683. He was the administrator of the estate of his "brother-in-law" Henry Bachelder. The estate of Nathaniel[2] was divided among his children during his life time.

Children by first wife, probably all born in Ipswich:

i. ABIGAIL,[3] b. 2 Feb., 1662–3; living 28 Oct., 1682.
ii. MARY, b. 22 Oct., 1665; living 14 July, 1715; m. in Salem, Mass., 28 Jan., 1684, Samuel, b. in Salem, 23 Jan., 1657, d. 6 Jan., 1723–4, son of Robert and Sarah Stone of Salem; lived in Salem. Children: 1. *Samuel.* 2. *Robert.* 3. *Elizabeth.* 4. *Katherine.* 5. *Mary.* 6. *Sarah.*
iii. NATHANIEL, b. 15 Jan., 1667–8; d. in Ipswich, 3 June, 1672.
iv. HANNAH, b. 7 Feb., 1669–70; d. in Ipswich, 23 Oct., 1733; m. in Ipswich, 22 May, 1690, John, Jr., b. 11 Mch., 1667–8, d. Mch., 1717–8, son of Lieut. John and Sarah (Woodman) Adams of Ipswich. He was a miller, residing in Ipswich. Children: 1. *Hannah.* 2. *Sarah.* 3. *Abigail.* 4. *John.* 5. *Mary.* 6. *Priscilla.*
v. THOMAS, b. 25 May, 1672; d. in Ipswich, 11 July, 1672.
vi. SARAH, b. 15 Aug., 1674; living 30 June, 1729; m. about 1694, Dea. Joseph, b. in Newbury, Mass., 11 Oct., 1669, d. 18 Oct., 1732, son of Joshua and Sarah (Sawyer) Brown of Newbury, Mass. He was a trader, and resided in Newbury and Amesbury, Mass. Children: 1. ——. 2. ——. 3. ——. 4. *Nathaniel.* 5. *Joshua.* 6. *Simeon.*
6\. vii. NATHANIEL.

Children by second wife, probably all born in Ipswich:

viii. ELIZABETH, b. 18 Jan., 1678–9; living 14 July, 1715, before which date she m. —— Sawyer.
ix. CHARLES, living 1747; m. in Hampton Falls, N. H., 1 Jan., 1723, Sarah, widow of Joseph Swett of Hampton Falls. She d. between 17 Dec., 1743, and 30 Oct., 1745. He lived in Wells, Me., and Hampton Falls, N. H., and was probably the father of the *John*, a cordwainer, of Hampton Falls, who was farmed out as a pauper, 15 Apr., 1771.
7\. x. SAMUEL.
8\. xi. THOMAS.
xii. REBECCA, b. 8 Apr., 1686; d. probably before 14 July, 1715.
xiii. ANN, living 14 July, 1715. Did she m. (intention published in Ipswich, 29 Nov., 1729) John Johnson, Jr., of Ipswich?
xiv. ABIGAIL, living 14 July, 1715. Did she m. (intention published in Ipswich, 4 Aug., 1738) Henry Morris of Ipswich, she then being of Amesbury, Mass.? He was a fisherman, and with wife Abigail was living in Amesbury, 20 Nov., 1745.
xv. MARTHA, living 1740; m. in Wells, Me., 1 June, 1715, Nathaniel, b. probably in Wells, 17 Sept., 1692, living 21 Jan., 1744, son of Nathaniel and Patience Clark of Wells. He was a yeoman, and resided in Wells. Children: 1. *Samuel.* 2. *Nathaniel.* 3. *Mary.* 4. *Benjamin.* 5. *Isaac.* 6. *Sarah.* 7. *Patience.* 8. *Susanna.* 9. *Abigail.* 10. *Adam.* 11. *Seth.*

4\. THOMAS[3] TREADWELL (*Thomas,*[2] *Thomas*[1]), born in Ipswich, Mass., 3 Mch., 1665–6, died in Ipswich, 13 Jan., 1743–4, married first,

Mary ———; and married second, before 19 May, 1693, Frances, born 3 Nov., 1670, died in Ipswich, Oct., 1744, daughter of William and (? Ruth) Sawyer of Newbury, Mass. He was a shoemaker, and designated "Jr.", 1689–1712.

Child by first wife:

i. MARY,[4] b. in Ipswich, 8 June, 1691; d. probably unmarried, after 12 July, 1760.

Children by second wife:

ii. HANNAH, b. about 1694; living 4 Mch., 1728-9; intention of m. published in Ipswich, 29 Dec., 1716, to John, b. 12 May, 1692, probably the same who was drowned on Canso Bank, 7 Apr., 1737, son of John and Martha (Cheney) Leighton. Children: 1. *John.* 2. *Daniel.* 3. *William.* 4. *Thomas.* 5. *Hannah.* 6. *Samuel.* 7. *Ezekiel.* 8. *Martha.* 9. *Sarah.* 10. *Francis.*

9. iii. THOMAS.

5. JOHN[3] TREADWELL (*Thomas,*[2] *Thomas*[1]), born in Ipswich, Mass., 28 Nov., 1670, died in Ipswich, 16 Dec., 1727, married Mary, born about 1680, died in Ipswich, 23 Oct., 1756, daughter of Philip and Elizabeth (Herrick) Fowler of Ipswich.

Children, all born in Ipswich, except possibly Martha:

i. ELIZABETH,[4] b. in Ipswich, 16 July, 1699; d. 6 Nov., 1779; m. intention published in Ipswich, 23 June, 1723, to Mager Gould of Ipswich, a fisherman, who was bapt. 19 July, 1724, and d. about 1781. Children: 1. *John.* 2. *William.* 3. *John.* 4. *Mager.* 5. *Elisha.* 6. *Elizabeth.*

ii. SARAH, b. 12 June, 1701; d. young.

iii. MARY, b. 13 Mch., 1702–3; supposed to have been living 28 Nov., 1787; m. intention published in Ipswich, 19 May, 1722, to Richard Shatchwell of Ipswich, who d., probably in Ipswich, 28 May, 1772. Children: 1. *Mary.* 2. *Sarah.* 3. *Richard.* 4. *John.* 5. *Daniel.* 6. *Sarah.* 7. *Mary.* 8. *Lucy.*

iv. MARTHA, b. 1705; d. in Ipswich, 27 Oct., 1727.

10. v. JOHN.

vi. ELISHA, b. 24 May, 1710; d. in Ipswich, 24 Sept. 1732; a farmer; unmarried.

11. vii. JONATHAN.

viii. SARAH, b. 8 Mch., 1718-9; living, 15 Nov., 1740; m. in Ipswich, 29 Sept., 1737, Dr. Abraham, a widower, of Hampton, N. H., b. 28 Aug. 1707, living 15 Nov., 1740, son of John and Abiah (Marston) Green; lived in Stratham, N. H. Did they have a daughter, *Sarah?*

6. NATHANIEL[3] TREADWELL (*Nathaniel,*[2] *Thomas*[1]), born in Ipswich, Mass., 13 June, 1677, died in Ipswich, 17 Aug., 1723, married, before 1698, Hannah ———, who died, probably in Ipswich, 17 Apr., 1745, as the third wife of Ensign George Hart of Ipswich, to whom her intention of marriage was published in Ipswich, 4 Apr., 1724. Nathaniel[3] was designated "Jr.", 1720–1723.

Children, born in Ipswich:

12. i. JACOB.[4]

13. ii. NATHANIEL.

14. iii. CHARLES.

iv. NATHAN, b. 7 Mch., 1707–8; d. young.

v. HANNAH, b. 25 Sept., 1709; d., probably in Ipswich, 18 Aug., 1750; m. 23 May, 1728, John, b. 22 Jan., 1707, d. 11 July, 1768, son of John and Mercy (Adams) Smith, who m. (2) Susannah How, widow. He was a lieutenant. Children: 1. *John.* 2. *Hannah.* 3. *Mercy.* 4. *Sarah.* 5. *Charles.* 6. *Cheney.* 7. *John.* 8. *Abigail.* 9. *Eunice.* 10. *Aaron.* 11. *Josiah.* 12. *Samuel.*

vi. NATHAN, b. 7 Oct., 1711; d. probably before 7 Mch., 1723.
15. vii. JABEZ.

7. SAMUEL[3] TREADWELL (*Nathaniel*,[2] *Thomas*[1]), born probably before 1687, died between 24 Nov., 1744, and 30 Sept., 1772, married before 6 Aug., 1718, Mary, living 11 Jan., 1727–8, died probably before 14 June, 1734, daughter of Jonathan and (? Mary) Hammond of Wells, Me. He was deacon of the First Church at Wells, Me., and served on several trial juries in York County, Me.

Child, born in Wells, Me.:

16. i. SAMUEL.[4]

8. THOMAS[3] TREADWELL (*Nathaniel*,[2] *Thomas*[1]), born in Ipswich, Mass., 8 Apr., 1686, died in Ipswich, suddenly, 17 Feb., 1743–4, married (intention published in Ipswich, 18 Mch., 1715–6) Sarah, born 24 May, 1695, died probably in Ipswich, 2 Jan., 1764, daughter of William and Mary (Lowden) Goodhue. He was designated "Jr.," 1719–40.

Children, born in Ipswich:

17. i. JOSEPH.[4]
ii. SARAH, bapt. in Ipswich, 18 Sept., 1720; living 21 Apr., 1769; m. (intention published in Ipswich, 17 Aug., 1738) Samuel, Jr., b. 19 Jan. 1710–11, d. in Ipswich, 26 Aug., 1757, son of Samuel and Mary (Burley) Adams of Ipswich. Children: 1. *Sarah.* 2. *Samuel.*
iii. ELIZABETH, bapt. in Ipswich, 1 Apr. 1722: d., probably in Ipswich, 23 July, 1778; m. (int. published in Ipswich, 3 June, 1750) Aaron Caldwell, a widower, b. 18 Apr., 1721, d. before 21 Sept., 1765, son of John and Elizabeth (Lull) Caldwell. Children: 1. *Elizabeth.* 2 *Moses.* 3. *Stephen.* 4. *Mary.*
iv. MARY, bapt. in Ipswich, 19 June, 1726.
v. MARY, bapt. in Ipswich, 21 Dec. 1727; living, unmarried, 21 Apr., 1769. Was she the Mary who d. in Ipswich, 20 Nov., 1798, "one of the poor"?
18. vi. THOMAS.

9. THOMAS[4] TREADWELL (*Thomas*,[3] *Thomas*,[2] *Thomas*[1]), who died between 4 Oct., 1758, and 4 Apr., 1760, married first (intention published in Ipswich, 29 Oct., 1726), Sarah, baptized 12 Aug., 1705, died in Ipswich, 4 June, 1729, daughter of Beamsley and Hannah (Glazier) Perkins of Ipswich; and married second, in Ipswich, 16 May, 1734, Hepzibah, born in Rowley, Mass., 13 June, 1700, died between 24 Oct., 1765, and 29 May, 1778, daughter of John and Dorcas Hobson, and widow of Jeremiah Dow of Ipswich. He was a cordwainer, and later a farmer, and was designated "3rd" in 1742. He resided in Ipswich and Littleton, Mass.

Child by first wife:

i. SARAH,[5] b. in Ipswich, 25 May, 1729; d. in Ipswich, 13 June, 1729.

Children by second wife:

ii. SARAH, bapt. in Ipswich, 23 Feb., 1734–5; d. in Ipswich, 1 Aug., 1738.
iii. HANNAH, bapt. in Ipswich, 7 Nov., 1736; m. in Littleton, Mass., 5 Oct., 1757, Eliphalet Densmore of Littleton; lived in Littleton, Mass., and Washington, N. H. Children: 1. *John.* 2. *William.* 3. *Hannah.* 4. *Dorcas.* 5. *Moses.* 6. *Thomas.* 7. *Eliphalet.* 8. *Lydia.* 9. *Asa.* 10. *Daniel.* 11. *William.* 12. *Sarah.*
19. iv. SAMUEL.
v. JOHN, b. in Ipswich, 9 Mch., 1738; d. in Ipswich, 27 Mch., 1739.

vi. JOHN, bapt. in Ipswich, 17 Mch., 1740-1; d. between Nov., 1759, and 27 Feb., 1760, probably at Crown Point, N. Y.; served in the expedition against Crown Point.
vii. SARAH, bapt. in Ipswich, 3 Apr., 1743; d. in Littleton, Mass., 30 Mch., 1788.
20. viii. THOMAS.
ix. MARY, b. between 1737 and 24 Oct., 1758.

10. JOHN[4] TREADWELL (*John,*[3] *Thomas,*[2] *Thomas*[1]), born in Ipswich, Mass., 24 Sept., 1707, died 29 Apr., 1782, married first, 9 Oct., 1728, Hannah, born probably in 1704, died in Ipswich, 24 Sept., 1747, daughter of Thomas and Sarah (Langley) Boardman of Ipswich; and married second (intention published in Ipswich, 19 Mch., 1747-8), Priscilla, born 8 Mch., 1723, d. probably in Salem, Mass., 3 July, 1803, daughter of Thomas and Priscilla (Appleton) Burnam.

Children by first wife, all born in Ipswich:

i. JOHN,[5] bapt. 21 Sept., 1729; d. in Ipswich, 17 Mch., 1737.
ii. MARTHA, bapt. 13 Feb., 1731; d. in Ipswich, 15 Mch., 1737.
iii. ELISHA, bapt., 7 Apr., 1734; d. in Ipswich, 17 Mch., 1737-8.
iv. WILLIAM, bapt. 20 June, 1736; d. in Ipswich, 20 Mch., 1737-8.
21. v. JOHN.
vi. MARTHA, bapt. 9 Aug., 1741; d. probably in Ipswich, 2 Nov., 1818; m. (int. published in Ipswich and Rowley, Mass., 12 Oct., 1765) Joseph Jewett of Rowley, b. 14 May, 1739, d. (? 1) Aug., 1774. Children: 1. *George*. 2. *Joseph*. 3. *John*. 4. *David*. 5. *Hannah*.
vii. MARGARET, bapt. 10 Apr., 1743; d. in Ipswich, 19 Apr., 1743.
viii. MARGARET, bapt. 26 Feb., 1743-4; d. probably before 1756.
ix. SARAH, bapt. 3 Feb., 1744-5; d. probably in Ipswich, 10 Dec., 1829; m. (int. published in Ipswich, 22 June, 1765) Joseph, b. Ipswich, 23 Dec., 1739, d. 20 Mch., 1776, son of Joseph and Sarah (Lord) Willcomb. He was a sea captain, residing in Ipswich. Children: 1. *Sarah*. 2. *Joseph*. 3. *William*. 4. *Mary*. 5. *Hannah*.

Children by second wife, all born in Ipswich

x. PRISCILLA, bapt. 5 Mch., 1748-9; d. in Ipswich, 9 Jan., 1786; m. 12 Mch., 1772, Nathaniel, b. probably in Ipswich, 20 Mch., 1747, d. probably in Ipswich, 30 June or 1 July, 1807, son of Peletiah and Jane (Farley) Kinsman of Ipswich. He was a sea captain, and resided in Ipswich. Children: 1. *Nathaniel*. 2. *Hannah*. 3. *Priscilla*. 4. *Michael*. 5. *Michael*. 6. *Priscilla*.
xi HANNAH, bapt. 22 Sept., 1751; d. 18 Jan., 1776; m. in Ipswich, 13 Apr., 1773, Francis, Jr., b. 28 Dec., 1752, d. suddenly, 28 Feb., 1799, son of Joseph and Mary (Eveleth) Rust of Ipswich. He married twice after the death of his wife Hannah. Children: 1. *Joseph*. 2. *Hannah* (?).
22. xii. ELISHA.
xiii. MARY, b. 16 Jan., 1753; d. probably before 9 Mch., 1782.
xiv. MARGARET, b. 4 Jan., 1756; d. in Ipswich, 19 Feb., 1786; unmarried.
xv. ELIZABETH, b. 17 July, 1760; living, 9 Mch., 1798; m. in Ipswich, 6 Oct., 1785, Jeremiah, b. 19 Apr., 1762, d. at Point Petre, Guadaloupe, W. I., 14 Aug., 1807, son of Daniel and Hannah (Giddings) Goodhue. Children: 1. *Jeremiah*. 2. *Elizabeth*. 3. *Daniel Treadwell*. 4. *Priscilla*. 5. *John*. 6. *Hannah*. 7. *Mary Treadwell*. 8. *Perley Putnam*.
xvi. WILLIAM, bapt. 8 Feb., 1767; d. probably before 9 Mch., 1782.

11. JONATHAN[4] TREADWELL (*John,*[3] *Thomas,*[2] *Thomas*[1]), born in Ipswich, Mass., 31 May, 1713, died probably in 1760, married in Wenham, Mass., 29 Nov., 1738, Ruth, born in Wenham, 23 Dec., 1716, daughter of Stephen and Ruth Patch of Wenham. She probably

married second (intention published in Ipswich, 31 Dec., 1762), Joseph Whipple. Jonathan[4] was a joiner by trade, and resided in Ipswich.

Children:

i. MARTHA,[5] b. in Topsfield, Mass., 25 Mch., 1740; d. probably in Ipswich, 29 Apr., 1820; m. (int. published in Ipswich, 13, in Wenham, Mass., 16 July, 1757) Jeremiah Shatswell of Wenham, probably son of Jonathan and Mary (Burnham) Shatswell of Ipswich. Children: 1. *Jonathan.* 2. *Jeremiah* (?).

ii. RUTH, b. in Ipswich, 13 July, 1742; d. in Rowley, Mass., 16 Mch., 1749.

iii. MARY, b. in Ipswich, 4 Apr., 1746; d. probably in Rowley, 5 Sept., 1747.

iv. MARY, bapt. in Rowley, 12 Feb., 1748; probably m. in Ipswich, 22 Nov., 1770, Jesse Dutton of Beverly, Mass.

v. RUTH, bapt. in Ipswich, 6 Oct., 1751; buried in church yard several miles west of Odessa, Canada; m. in Ipswich, 13 July, 1769, John Parrott of Beverly, Mass., who was b. about 1745, and is buried beside his wife. He was a sea captain; and served in the Revolution; resided in Beverly, Mass., till about 1780, when he moved somewhere about 40 to 60 miles from Boston, Mass., and finally settled near Odessa, Canada, with his brother James, who served on the British side in the Revolution. Children: 1. *John.* 2. *Sarah.* 3. *Elizabeth.* 4. *Mary.* 5. *Patty.* 6. *Jonathan.* 7. *James.*

12. JACOB[4] TREADWELL (*Nathaniel,*[3] *Nathaniel,*[2] *Thomas*[1]), born in Ipswich, Mass., 24 Jan., 1698–9, died 17 Apr., 1770, probably in Portsmouth, N. H., married in Portsmouth, in Nov., 1721, Sarah, died in Portsmouth, 16 Mch., 1770, in her 68th year, daughter of William and Anna (Carter) Cotton, Jr., of Portsmouth, N. H., and probably widow of Henry Nicholson. He was a tailor, and later a tanner, residing in Portsmouth, N. H. Was he the "Mr. Treadwell" on the tax list of New Castle, N. H., for the year 1720?

Children (the *N. H. Gazette* states there were eighteen, but the record of only the following nine has been found):

i. ANNA,[5] d. suddenly, buried 11 Dec., 1806, aged 84 years; m. before 1760, Capt. Thomas, lost at sea, going from Portsmouth to Boston, before 16 Nov., 1768, son of Capt. Thomas and Sarah (Cotton) Walden of Portsmouth. He was a mariner. Children: 1. *Jacob.* 2. *Anna.* 3. *Thomas.* 4. *Sarah.*

ii. ELIZABETH, living 28 May, 1771; m. in Middleton, Mass., 10 Nov., 1766, Jotham Blanchard, who was living in 1781. He was a merchant, styled "captain," and lived in Portsmouth and Peterboro', N. H. Children: 1. *John.* 2. *Sarah.* 3. *Elizabeth.* 4. *Rebecca.* 5. *Mary* (?).

23. iii. WILLIAM EARL.

24. iv. NATHANIEL.

v. DANIEL, b. 1734; d. 1760; graduated at Harvard College, 1754; Professor of Mathematics and Natural Philosophy at Kings (now Columbia) College.

vi. SARAH, living 13 Mch., 1773; m. in Portsmouth, N. H., 8 Nov., 1762, Joshua Wingate, d. in Halifax, Nova Scotia, in 1806, aged 68 yrs., son of Dr. John and Martha (Wingate) Weekes of Greenland, N. H. He graduated at Harvard College, 1758; was a minister and a loyalist during the Revolution, for which he was driven from his parish; resided in Marblehead, Mass., and Halifax, Nova Scotia. Children: 1. *Elizabeth.* 2. *Martha W.* 3. *Joshua Wingate.* 4. *Helen* (*Hannah*?). 5. *John.* 6. *Sarah W.* 7. *C. W.* 8. *Foster.* 9. *James.*

25. vii. SAMUEL.

viii. JOHN, d. June, 1759, aged 13 yrs.
ix. GEORGE, bapt. in Portsmouth, 19 June, 1748.

13. NATHANIEL[4] TREADWELL (*Nathaniel,[3] Nathaniel,[2] Thomas*[1]), born in Ipswich, Mass., 10 Sept., 1700, died in Ipswich, 31 Jan., or 1 Feb., 1777, married first (intention published in Ipswich, 29 May, 1725), Mercy, born 11 Apr., 1705, died in Ipswich, 1 Jan., 1747–8, daughter of John and Mercy (Adams) Smith; and married second (intention published in Ipswich, 28 July, 1750), Hannah, who died in Ipswich, 6 July, 1792, aged 87 years, probably daughter of Zerubbabel and Mary Endicott. Nathaniel[4] probably intended to marry (intention published in Ipswich, 17 Apr., 1725) Margaret, probably the daughter of Jeremiah and Susanna Dow, who was born in Ipswich, 4 Dec., 1707. He was a captain in the militia, and styled "gentleman," but familiarly known as "Landlord Treadwell" through keeping the Inn at Ipswich. His wife Hannah was known as "Landlady Treadwell."

Children:

i. NATHANIEL,[5] bapt. in Ipswich, 26 June, 1726; d. in Ipswich, 2 July, 1726.
ii. NATHANIEL, bapt. in Ipswich, 14 Sept., 1729; d. in Ipswich, 25 Apr., 1730.
iii. NATHANIEL, bapt. in Ipswich, 27 Aug., 1732; d. probably, Aug., 1747.
26. iv. JACOB.
*v. HANNAH, bapt. in Ipswich, 21 May, 1738.
vi. MERCY, bapt. in Ipswich, 25 Apr., 1741; m. (int. published in Ipswich, 15 Apr., 1763) Samuel Fellows of Gloucester, Mass. Children: 1. *Nathaniel Treadwell.* 2. *Samuel.*
27. vii. AARON.
28. viii. MOSES.

14. CHARLES[4] TREADWELL (*Nathaniel,[3] Nathaniel,[2] Thomas*[1]), born in Ipswich, May, 1705, died in New Castle, N. H., 26 Nov., 1793, married first, about 1727 or '28, Mary, born in New Castle, 8 Oct., 1711, died in New Castle, 6 May, 1783, daughter of William and Lydia Kelly of New Castle; and married second, in Portsmouth, N. H., 2 Jan., 1786, Mrs. Phebe Dennett of Portsmouth, who was buried 28 Oct., 1805, aged 83 years. He was a hairdresser, and later a shopkeeper or merchant, and lived in New Castle and Portsmouth, N. H.

Children:

i. WILLIAM,[5] b. 10 Nov., 1729; d. young.
29. ii. NATHANIEL.
iii. WILLIAM, b. 30 July, 1733; d. probably before Sept., 1783.
iv. HANNAH, b. in Portsmouth, 24 Aug., 1734; d. 20 Jan., 1832; m. 2 Nov., 1758, Ammi Ruhamah, b. in No. Yarmouth, Me., 15 Mch., 1735, d. suddenly, 8 Dec., 1820, son of Rev. Ammi Ruhamah and Dorothy (Bradbury) Cutter of No. Yarmouth. He was a graduate of Harvard College, 1752; a physician; Surgeon General in the French and Indian War, 1756–7; and resided in Portsmouth, N. H. Children: 1. *Mary.* 2. *Hannah.* 3. *Elizabeth.* 4. *Charles.* 5. *Dorothy.* 6. *Daniel.* 7. *William.* 8. *Jacob.* 9. *Nathaniel.* 10. *Sarah Ann.*
30. v. JACOB.
vi. MARY, b. 3 Jan., 1738; d. young.
vii. MARY, b. 20 Sept., 1740; d. probably before Sept., 1783.
viii. SARAH, b. 23 Dec., 1744; d. probably before Sept., 1783.
ix. LYDIA, b. 12 Jan., 1746; d. 21 May, 1759.

[To be continued.]

REMONSTRANCE AGAINST SETTLING A MINISTER AT SOUTH HAMPTON, NEW HAMPSHIRE.

Copied from the original paper by JOHN FRENCH JOHNSON, Esq., of Amesbury, Mass.

Sept. 7. 1742,

To the Associated ministers of the neighboring Towns mett at the new township of South Hampton, the following considirations are offered as Reasons why a great number of Inhabitants now falling in sd' town can not joyn with othere in their designs, and also why we think the present affair of setling a Minister there should be deferred, viz:—

1st because the affair of the Line is yet under debate and we know not whether we shall belong to sd' place, and that if we should expend for this purpose, or bring ourselves under obligations it may be lost as to us or Inswearing to ourselves & descendents.

2nd, That if we were disposed yet the difficulty of attending here for us and especially for here three quarters of the year is such that we see no possibility of it.

3rd, That in case ever the line be established as now run we intend God willing to accomidate ourselves better in a Meeting house & shall endeavor all we can to be set oft for this end, and then as to the present design of this dayi ntended by some we desent. first because the first meeting that voted this obtained partly by chance & partly as we judge unfairly. second that this last meetiug was not agreeable to a former vote in this place with respect to the notifying meetings & not all as we understand at all warned of this. third we have proposed some things which we think Reasonable at present which have not been Regarded by them and finally that if all within the bounds of sd' Town should appear at a legal meeting and matters fairly tryed we are fully perswaded there is a majority with us against them.

Benjamin Brown
Nathaniel Maxfield
Jonathan Brown
Benjamin Brown Jr.
George Maxfield
David Goodwin
George [illegible]
Jonathan Watson
Henry Hoyt.
Jonathan Sands
David Goodwin
Benjamin Baker
Jothan Grifen
Caleb Hobs
Benjamin Kimball
Thomas Fowler (D his mark)
John Sargent
Jacob Colby
Abraham Merrill
William Sargent

Samuel French
Aaron Currier
Samuel Goodwin
James George
Philip Challis
David [illegible]
Amos Page
Robert Worthen
Jonathan Kimball
Samuel Smith
Jacob Smith
David Colby
Thomas Green
Roger Eastman
Thomas Carter
John Carter
Samuel Carter
Jacob Carter
Nathaniel Ash
Jacob Morss
Zaccheris Colby.

CHURCH OF ST. LAWRENCE, READING.

CAVERSHAM, FROM READING.

THE FORBURY PARK, READING.

OUR ENGLISH PARENT TOWNS.

READING.*

By Oscar Fay Adams, Esq., of Boston.

The borough and market town of Reading cannot point with certainty to the period of its origin. It was in existence when the Danes came up the Kennet and made the spot their headquarters in 871, but history does not go further back. In Domesday Book it is mentioned as Radynges. From the thirteenth to the sixteenth centuries parliaments were occasionally held here, and in the Civil War it surrendered to the Parliament forces under Essex in 1643.

The Massachusetts town, incorporated May 29, 1644, named in honor of the Radynges of Domesday, remains a quiet rural community, and the Pennsylvania Reading, surrounded by its cordon of hills in the heart of Berks County, though founded a century after the New England town, bears in population and importance far greater resemblance to the mother town across the sea. In Vermont is found another Reading, chartered July 6, 1761, and there are Readings in Illinois, Iowa, Kansas, Michigan, Missouri, Nebraska, New York, and Ohio. The Massachusetts locality, originally styled Lynn Village, was named Reading in honor of the early home of some of its first settlers.

The English town is situated on the Kennet, near its junction with the Thames, the two branches of the former stream being here spanned by four bridges, while an iron suspension bridge crosses the Thames on the eastern side of the town. A water route to the Severn is afforded by the Kennet and Avon Canal. A business-like air is everywhere apparent, and a live business town one soon finds Reading to be. Biscuit making heads the list of its industries, the biscuit factory of Huntley and Palmer being the largest in the kingdom, for Reading biscuits are as widely famous as Pears Soap. In the suburbs are seed farms covering more than three thousand acres, and "Sutton's Seeds" have carried the name of Reading around the world.

In 1121, Henry I. founded here a Benedictine monastery which speedily became one of the most powerful in England. Its abbots were mitred and kept their seats in Parliament until, at the word of Henry VIII., abbots and abbeys ceased to be. Hugh Farrington,

* Population, 72,214 (1901); 36 miles from London (Paddington terminus of Great Western Railway), 43 miles from London (Waterloo terminus of South Western Railway), 63 miles from London (Charing Cross terminus of South Eastern Railway). Parish Churches: St. Giles, register from 1564, living, a *vicarage*; St. Mary, register from 1538, living, a *rectory*; St. Lawrence, register from 16[illegible]5, living, a *vicarage*; Grey Friars; Holy Trinity; St. John the Evangelist; St. Stephen; Christ; All Saints; St. Saviour; etc. Other churches and chapels: 4 Congregational; 5 Baptist; 3 Wesleyan; 2 Primitive Methodist; Presbyterian; Unitarian; Roman Catholic; Friends. Schools: Free Grammar; Kendrick; Blue Coat; Green; National; Board; Science and Art; University Extension. Four weekly papers. Corporation: high steward, mayor, ten aldermen, thirty councillors.

the last abbot, refusing either to yield up his convent or acknowledge the monarch's supremacy, was, with two of his monks, summarily hanged, drawn and quartered before the gate of his own abbey, thus furnishing to all concerned an object lesson of a kind that the king was not at all averse to giving. Somewhere within the abbey Henry I. was buried; and before its high altar, long years after, were wedded John of Gaunt and Blanche of Lancaster. After the suppression of the abbey, it was converted into a palace which was demolished in the Civil War. The great gateway, carefully restored in 1861, yet stands, forming a portion of the assize courts, a public thoroughfare passing beneath its hugh arch.

To the east of the gate is a long row of stone residences, and immediately beyond these is the greater part of the abbey ruins; lofty, shapeless masses of flint and rubble, covering several acres. Except in the case of the chapter house and the great hall where parliaments were held, the original purpose of the separate portions, muffled now in ivy, cannot be definitely settled. To the north of the gateway some lesser fragments of the abbey are to be seen in the small park known as The Forbury, once the outer court of the abbey. The park is a pleasant spot but far too small, an objection that can scarcely be urged against the memorial in the Forbury to the Berkshire soldiers killed in the Afghan wars—an immense cast-iron lion on a pedestal. The material does not commend itself strongly to lovers of art, but the lion is certainly ferocious of aspect. Overlooking the park is a Roman Catholic church designed by Welby Pugin, a rather lifeless copy of Norman models.

The four ancient churches of Reading are those of Saint Giles, in Southampton Street, consisting of nave, aisles, choir, porch and west tower, the latter sustaining a slender stone spire; Grey Friars, in part a restoration, in part a rebuilding of the church of the Grey Friars monastery; Saint Mary; and Saint Lawrence. The church of Saint Mary, erected in 1551 from the ruins of a nunnery founded by Elfrida in repentance for the murder of Edward the Martyr, has an open timbered roof, and in outline displays nave, choir, gabled south aisle, north transept, and western pinnacled tower. It has a large churchyard with modern churchyard cross, and faces an open area called The Butts, which is adorned by a huge fountain. The church of Saint Lawrence, in the market place, shows a mixture of the work of the First and Third Pointed periods, and contains several interesting monuments and brasses. It consists of nave, north gabled aisle, chantry chapel, choir, south porch, and west tower with tall pinnacles. Its west window is a memorial to Archbishop Laud, a native of Reading, and in the choir is a window to the memory of Charles Lamb.

In Friar Street, next north of Saint Lawrence, are the municipal buildings, of red and black brick, erected in 1875 and 1882, the earlier part designed by the architect Waterhouse. They include a Town Hall, council chamber, free library, museum, and government art schools. Other buildings of importance are the Royal Assembly Room in Friar Street, Royal County Theatre, Berkshire Hospital, and the immense and gloomy prison made famous by Oscar Wilde's powerful "Ballad of Reading Gaol." In Erleigh Street is the Free Grammar School, an ancient foundation occupying modern structures. Archbishop Laud was once a pupil here. In the shadow of the tall clock-tower of the Municipal Building is a marble statue of Queen Victoria, and in Broad Street may be seen a bronze statue of the late Mr. Palmer, exhibiting that eminent biscuit maker in a standing posture and of heroic size, holding in his right hand a silk hat and a partially opened umbrella. It was placed in position some years before the death of its subject, and probably afforded him keener satisfaction than it did his fellow citizens. So far as the writer is aware, it furnishes the only instance of the appearance of the umbrella as a monumental adjunct.

On the Oxfordshire side of the Thames is the village suburb of Caversham; not far to the southward is the village of Shiplake, in whose parish church the poet Tennyson was married, while at Bradfield, a few miles to the west of Reading, is the College of Saint Andrew, founded in 1850 and now accommodating over 300 pupils.

NOTES.

To evade the ship money tax, already referred to in notes by me upon other of the English Parent Towns, a large emigration had set into New England. In the spring of 1638 a band of emigrants was formed in the neighboring parts of the counties of Berks, Wilts, Hampshire, and Oxford. Reading is about fifty miles north from Southampton; and Gloucestershire and Dorset on the west, and Sussex and Surrey on the east, were the bounds of the country in which dwelt the little band who sailed from Southampton, 24 April, 1638.

"The List of the names of the passengers intended for New-England, in the good shipp, the Confidence of London, of 200 tonnes, John Jobson Mr and thus by virtue of Lord Treasurers warrant of the 11th of April, 1638." (REGISTER, ii, 109.) At the head of the list was the family of Walter Haynes, linen draper, who settled in Sudbury, Mass., and who came from Sutton Mandeville, Wilts, ten miles southwest of Salisbury. (REGISTER, xxxix, 263; xlvii, 72.)

John Blanford, John Riddet, and Richard Bidcombe, three servants, are supposed to have come from the same place. Unfortunately the parish register does not begin till 1654.

Peter Noyes, yeoman, was from Penton Mewsey, Hampshire, three miles north-west from Andover. John Bent, husbandman, was also from this parish, or rather the adjoining part called Penton Grafton. (REGISTER, xxxii, 407; xlviii, 288.) Nicholas Guy, of Watertown, Mass., carpenter, came from Upton Gray, Hampshire, three miles south-west from Odiham, and five south-east of Basingstoke, both places being identified with the Dummer family who had come a few years before. Roger Porter, husbandman, of Watertown, came from Long Sutton, Hampshire, two and a-half miles south of Odiham. John Sanders, husbandman, of Newbury. Mass., came from Landford, ten miles south-east from Salisbury, but he later returned to England, and was at Wick farm in Downton, Wilts. He married Hester, daughter of John Rolfe of Newbury, who was a fellow passenger, coming from Melchet Park, Whiteparish, Wilts, seven miles south-east from Salisbury.

Thomas Goodenow came from Shaftesbury, on the borders of Dorset, but a few miles south-west of Semley, Wilts, where his brother John came from, and near to Dunhead, Wilts, where Edmund Goodenow came from.

Edmund and William Kerley, of Sudbury, husbandmen, were from Ashmore, Dorset, five miles south-east of Shaftesbury and on the Wiltshire border.

John Stephens, of Newbury, husbandman, was from Caversham, Oxfordshire, just across the Thames from Reading. With him was his brother William. The family is an old one there, and attained some prominence in later days. In the 17th century they held the farm of "Aldwinn's Tenants," and in the last century Mr. John Stephens of Caversham Rise was a benefactor to the poor, by a bequest. In the parish church of St. Peter (originally Norman) the east window is a memorial to him.

Thomas Jones, tailor, of Caversham, Oxfordshire, aged 36 years, with his wife Ann and four children, came to New England in 1638. He was not the Thomas Jones of Dorchester, as the latter was here in 1635. He was the father of Abraham Jones of Hull, who in 1658 sold to Daniel Cushing land in the plain neck, Hingham, given to him by his father Thomas Jones. (Suffolk Co. Deeds, iv, 129.) Abraham Jones in 1657 had seven sons, Benjamin, Thomas, Abraham, Josiah, Joseph, John, and Ephraim. (History of Hingham, ii, 386.) The land was granted by the town to Samuel Ward in 1637, and by him transferred to Thomas Jones in 1638. (Suffolk Co. Deeds, iv, 279.)

Robert Jones appeared in Hingham in 1637. It is probable he was a relative of Thomas; if not, he came from the same vicinity in England. 4 Dec., 1646, "Elizabeth Curtes & Jane Curtes granted unto Robert Jones of Hingham theire father in law a lre of Attur[r] to aske &c: of the executo[rs] of the last will &c of Jane Alexand[r] late of Reading in Oxfordshire deceased theire severall & respective Legacies given them by the last will & testament of the said Jane Alexand[r] theire grandmother & of the Receipt &c: also to compound &c: & to appeare &c: thereto required &c: & generally to doe all thing[s]. witnes their hand & seales." (Aspinwall's Notarial Records, p. 41.)

Another settler was John Benson, who also came from Caversham. He was of an old Oxfordshire family and was married in Caversham church, where at least one of his children was baptized.

On the Thames, four and a half miles north-east of Reading, is Shiplake, whence came the widow Martha Wilder and her daughter Mary to join other children in New England. Joseph Parker, tanner, came from Newbury, England. At his death he had an estate in England, some of which was at Romsey, Hampshire, seven miles north-west from Southampton. From Romsey also came Richard Bidgood, of Boston.

Sarah Osgood and four children came from Wherwell, four miles south-east of Andover in Hampshire. (REGISTER, xx, 24.)

Samuel Sewall had relatives in the Dummer family living at Romsey, and he also owned land at Lee (Sewall's Diary, Vol. 1), which is in Romsey Extra, and (1880) includes the farms of Henry Swanton and Thomas Wiltshire.

The will of Joan Alexander, of Swallowfield, six miles south-east from Reading, was probated in 1629; Henry Alexander of Reading, in 1625; and Augustin Alexander of Reading, 1636. Richard Curtis of Reading, probated 1639.

Thomas Collier, born in England in 1622, married, 30 Dec., 1647, Jane Curtis. Robert Jones, in his will in 1688, mentions his daughter Jane Collier.

21 Dec., 1649, "Thomas Collier of Hull husband of Jane the daughter of Curtes late of Reading in Berkshire did constitute John Curtes his brother in lawe his true & lawfull Atturney granting him power &c: to aske &c: of the Executo[rs] of Jane Alexander late of Reading aforesaid all such Legacie &c: as was bequeathed to the s[d] Jane his wife by the last will of the s[d] Jane her grandmother & of the receipt to give acquitance &c: also to compound &c: & to appeare in any court &c: there to doe say sue &c: wth power to substitute &c: ratifying &c." (Aspinwall's Notarial Records, p. 240–1.) Thomas Collier died in 1691, leaving wife Jane and five children.

John Cogswell, Jun., of Ipswich, Mass., in a letter from London, dated 30 Mch., 1653, speaks of his cousin Stevens. (REGISTER, xv, 177.) In Massachusetts Archives, xxxix, 506, the name is given as Roger Stevens of Redding, Co. Berks. Roger Stephens married, 29 July, 1640, Martha Blowers, at St. Mary's, Reading.

Waters's "Gleanings," i, 46, gives a reference to the will of Francis Phips, the elder, of Reading, Eng. The will, proved in 1668, mentions his son Constantine, who was baptized 9 Nov., 1656, at St. Mary's, Reading, died 9 Oct.,

1723, and was buried 15 Oct., 1723, at White Waltham, Berks, ten miles east of Reading. This Constantine was Lord Chancellor of Ireland, and father of William who married a daughter of the 3d Earl of Anglesey, and grandfather of Constantine, Baron Mulgrave.

The first Constantine has been frequently spoken of, erroneously, as a son of Sir William Phips, governor of Massachusetts. The latter was a son of James Phips, a gunsmith from Bristol, Eng., where there were others of the name. Francis Phips was not the only one of the name in Reading, Eng., as there were, contemporary with him, Thomas and John Phips, tallow chandlers.

Augustine Clement, painter, of Dorchester, came from Reading, Eng. He had property at Wokingham (not Wockington, as given by Pope), which is seven miles south-east from Reading. The property was then (1638) in the possession of his sister-in-law Margaret Mathew. Another sister, Anne Clement, was living at Shinfield, Berks, four miles south of Reading. The parish registers of Wokingham begin in 1674, and of Shinfield in 1649.

In 1635, on the same ship with Clement, came Sampson Salter, fisherman, who was from Caversham, and went to Newport, R. I.

Of the early settlers at Reading, Mass., the only one who seems to have been connected with Reading, Eng., is John Damon, who is said to have been baptized in the church of St. Lawrence, Reading, 25 June, 1620, and settled at Reading, Mass., in 1644, the date of its incorporation.

The records of Reading, Eng., are preserved in its town hall, and they are ancient and numerous. Besides ancient deeds, accounts of the Treasurers, etc., there are some twenty-three folio volumes, making up a "Corporation Diary" covering two centuries, the annals of the town from 1622–1822, an interesting period. Of this material, four volumes have been printed by the borough, to the year 1654.

The Church wardens' accounts of St. Mary, Reading, 1550–1662, and its Registers, 1538–1812, have been published. A History of St. Lawrence, Reading, has also been printed. WALTER KENDALL WATKINS.

RECORDS OF THE SECOND CHURCH OF SCITUATE, NOW THE FIRST UNITARIAN CHURCH OF NORWELL, MASS.

Communicated by WILFORD JACOB LITCHFIELD, M.S., of Southbridge, Mass.

[Continued from Vol. 59, page 392.]

1747

Nathanael Eells fon of North Eells and Ruth his wife was born Jan: 1st 1746/7———And Baptifed Jan: 18.——

William Turner Son of Charls & Unice, was baptifed Jan: 25th 1746/7.

Mary Clap daughter of Natll & Defire was baptifed Jan: 25th 1746/7

Elifabeth Curtice of Samll & Rachel was baptifed Feb: 15. 1746/7

Sarah Riply daughter of Jofhua Riply and ——— his wife was Baptifed Feb: 22 1746/7

Temperance Fofter daughter of Elifhah & Temperance his wife was baptifed march 29. 1747.

Hannah Brigs daughter of James Briggs & Hannah his wife was Baptifed march 29. 1747

Content Barker daughter of Barnabas Barker & his wife ——— was baptized April 5th 1747.

Lufanna [or Lufanda] Perry daughter of Jofeph Perry & his wife was bapt April 26 1747.

Elisabeth Turner of Benj[m] & Mercy was baptised May 17th 1747.
Sarah Bryant of Thom[s] & Sarah was baptised may [? 17] 1747.
Deborah Jacob daughter of Deacon Joseph Jacob & Mary his wife was Baptized May 24. 1747
Deborah Torry of Cap[t] Caleb Torry & mary his wife was baptised may 31. 1747.
Ruth Vinal daughter of John & Mary, was baptised June 7th 1747
Joseph Eells Son of John & Abiah Eells was baptised June 21st 1747.
Abigail Wilson daughter of W[m] & Mary wilson was baptised June 21st 1747
John Right Son of Mercy Right was baptised June 21st 1747.
Luce Cushing daughter of the Honourable John Cushing Esq[r] And Mary his wife was Baptised June 28th 1747.
John Woodart son of James & Sarah was baptised June 28th 1747.
{ Luke Palmer an Jnfant Child of Joseph and Jane Palmer being sick with the throat trouble was baptised Jn private June 30th 1747.
Roland Turner & Anna Turner Twinn children of Abial and Elisabeth Turner were baptised July 5th 1747
Robert Cushing Son of John Cusshing jun[r] and deborah his wife was baptised July 5th 1747.
{ Iuly 7th 1747. J baptised two Children of Joshua & Lydia Palmer. they being dangerously Sick. the name of the one was Lydya the name of the Other was ———
Anna Hatch daughter of Nehemiah Hatch and Mary, was baptized July 19th 1747
Lydia Copeland daughter of Joseph & Elisabeth was baptised July 26th 1747.
Mercy Tolman daughter of Elisha & Miriam, was baptised Aug[t] 2[d] 1747.
Charls Samson had a child baptised by the Revd M[r] Bryant of Braintree, on the 9th of Auguft 1747.
William Lincoln Son of Jsaack & Abigail was baptised Aug[t] 30th 1747.
Nehemiah Randal Son of Gershom & Elisabeth was baptised Sep[t] 6. 1747.
Iacob Stetson Son of Matthew & Hannah was baptised Sep[t] 27th 1747.
Calvin Curtis, Son of Elisha & Sarah was baptised Sep[t] 27. 1747.
Susannah Randal daughter of Perez and Sarah was baptised Sep[t] 27. 1747.
Gershom Bowker Son of Lazarus & Abigail was baptised Oct: 4th 1747.
Deborah Bowker daughter of John & Ann was baptised Oct: 4th 1747.
Lydia Randal daughter of Elisha & Zeporah was baptised oct: 11. 1747.
Luce Turner daughter of Hawkins & ——— was baptised Oct 11. 1747.
Joshua Turner Son of Jsrael & Deborah was baptized Oct: 25. 1747
Eunice Stetson daugher of George & Eunice was baptised oct: 25 1747
Elizabeth Tolman daughter of Joseph & Mary was baptised Nov: 8. 1747.
Mary Church daughter of Thomas and Mary; was baptised Nov: 29 1747.

The whole number of the baptised this year is 42.

1748

Sarah Wheelwright daughter of John & Sarah, was baptised Ian: 10. 1747/8.

Lucrefia Gilkie, daughter of James and Grace was baptifed Jan: 24. 1747/8.

Lydia Collomar daughter of Thomas Collomar & Hannah his wife was baptifed Feb: 14. 1747/8

Amos Curtice Son of Amos & Mary was baptifed Feb. 14. 1747/8

Martha Farrow daughter of Thomas & Jemimah, was baptifed Feb: 14. 1747/8

Iacob Lincoln Son of Jsaac & Abigail was baptifed March 6th 1747/8.

Margret Briggs daughter of John And Abigail Brigs was baptized March 27. 1748

Eunice James daughter of John and Prudence was baptized April 3, 1748.

Ann Bryant of Peleg & Mary was Baptifed April 3d 1748.

Samuel Stockbridge Son of Samll & Sarah was baptized April. 17. 1748.

Lydiah Tower of Jonathan & Lydia was baptifed April 17th 1748.

Bathfheba Damon daughter of Dauniel & Judith, was baptized May 1st 1748.

Stephen Silvefter fon of Nehemiah & ——— his wife was baptized may 8th 1748.

Jsrael Silvefter Son of Jsrael and his wife was baptifed May 8. 1748.

Abigail Bryant daughter of Samll Bryant and mary his wife was baptifed May 8. 1748.

Deborah Man an Jnfant of Jofiah & Mary Man was baptifed in private, being fick. may 13·

Mary Palmer of Jofehp [*sic*] & Jane his wife was Baptifed may 15th 1748.

Jofhua Bowker Son of Bemjm [*sic*] and Hannah was Baptifed May 22. 1748.

Iune 4th 1748. J baptifed an Jnfant child of Jonathan & Elifabeth Elems which child died Jun 6th

{ June 7th J baptized, Abigail Bryant an Jnfant Child of Benjmin Bryant and his Wife ———

Thomas Cufhing Son of Jofeph and Lydia, was baptized June 26. 1748

Lufannah Prouty daughter of William and his wife was baptifed June 26. 1748

Abigail Cufhing daughter of the honourable John Cufhing, Efqr, & Mary his wife, was baptifed July 3d 1748.

Lurania Silvefter daughter of Elifha Silvefter an[d] ——— his wife was baptifed July 3d 1748.

Job Curtice Son of Samuel & Rachel was baptifed July 10th 1748.

Adult. Sarah Hooper a young woman Living with Mr Samll Stockbridge was baptized July 10. 1748

Hannah Stetfon, daughter of Gidion Stetfon & ——— his wife baptized July 24

Jsaac Dammon Son of Jsaack & Lydya was Baptifed July 24, 1748.

Elifabeth, daughter of Cefar a negro Servant or Slave, to Capt Torry, and Sarah his wife, a free Jndian woman was baptized Augt 28· 1748.

Defire Stoddard daughter of Benjm Stoddard & his wife, ——— was baptifed Augt 28. 1748.

Abigail Standly daughter of Jabez & Abigail Standly was baptifed Sept 11. 1748.

{ Bartlet Bowker an Jnfant Son of Lazarus Bowker was baptifed in Private, Sept 12, 1748.

Sarah Cole daughter of James Cole & Sarah his wife was baptifed Sep^t 25. 1748.

Jsaack Buck, son of Jsaac & mary was baptifed Sep^t 25. 1748

Molly Stetfon daughter of Jofeph Stetfon & ——— his wife was baptifed Sep^t 25 1748

{ Samuel Eells Son of North & Ruth Eells was baptifed Sept 26 1748 in private, being fick & not Likely to Live

Nathanael Jacob Son of Deacon Jofeph Jacob & ——— his wife was bap^d Oct 9th

Jofeph Neal son of Job & his wife was baptifed Oct: 9th 1748.

Macael Hatch Son of Michael & his wife Oct: 23. 1748

Sufanna Clap of Nath^ll & defire his wife was baptifed Oct: 30th 1748

{ Defire Elmes daughter of Jonathan Elmes & ——— his wife an Jnfant was baptifed in Private oct: 31. 1748

Luce Jacob daughter of Jofhua & Mary was baptifed Nov: 13. 1748.

Hannah Silvefter daughter of W^m and Mary was baptifed nov: 20. 1748

Luce Cufhing daughter of James Cufhing jun^r & his wife baptifed Nov: 27. 1748.

Huldah Lambert of John Lambert & his wife, baptifed Nov: 27. 1748.

Sarah Briggs, of James & Hannah was baptifed Dec: 11. 1748.

{ Lydia Barrel, daughter of William Barrel, & Lydia his wife deceafed was baptized in private Dec: 16. 1748

Seth Turner fon of Jeffe & Lydia was baptifed Dec: 18. 1748.

Bartlet Bowker of John Bowker and his wife was baptifed Dec. 25 1748.

The whole number of the baptifed this year amounts to 50.

1749

Sufanna Brooks daughter of Wm Willian [*sic*] Brook[s] & his wife ——— was Baptized Jan 22 1748/9.

Deborah Cufhing daughter of John Cufhing & Deborah was baptifed Jan: 29 1748/9.

Samuel Bryant Son of Sam^ll Bryant Junr & Mary his wife was baptifed march 5.

Adult. Sarah houfe Daughter of David Houfe deceafed was baptifed March 5. 1748/9

Molly northy Hatch daughter of nehemiah Hatch was baptifed by m^r Bourn march 19.

Sarah Fofter daughter of Elifha Fofter & his wife ——— was baptifed April 2^d 1749

Luther Curtice Son of Elifha Curtice & his wife was baptized April 9th 1749.

John Dwelly Son of Jofeph Dwelly deceafed and Mary his widow was baptized April 9th 1749

Rachel wade, daughter of Jofeph & Rachel was baptized April 9th 1749

Robert Randal Son of Perez & Sarah Randal was baptized April 9th 1749.

Hannah Clap daughter of Jofeph Clap and ——— his wife, was baptifed April. 23. 1749

Mary Man daughter of Jofiah man and Mary his wife was baptifed April 23. 1749

Margret Briggs daughter of John & Abigail was baptifed may 14th 1749

Thomas Cufhing Son of Deacon Jofeph Cufhing jun^r & Lydia his wife was baptifed June 4th 1749

Margret Bowker daughter of Benj^m and Hannah was baptifed June 4th 1749.

Calvin Turner Son of Jonathan and Abigail was baptifed July 2nd 1749

Barne Wade & Zebulon Wade Children of Zebulon wade and his wife were baptized in private July 19th [?] 1749.

Adult Mary Turner wife of Nat^ll Turner was baptized July 23 1749.

Elijah Turner fon of Nathan^ll & Mary was baptized July 23. 1749

Betty Woodart daughter of James woodart his wife deceafed was baptized July 23 1749.

Efter [Esther] Tower daughter of Benj^m & his wife —— of Abbinton was baptized Aug 6th 1743.

Jofeph Copeland, fon of Jofeph & Elizabeth was Baptized Sept 3^d 1749

Adult Philifs a Negro Slave to Dr Otis was baptifed Sept 3^d 1749

Olive & Betty, & Ruben three Children of the above named Philis were Baptised Sept 3^d 1749

{ Thankfull Eells, daughter of North Eells, & Ruth, his wife, was Baptifed In private about five of the Clock in the morning, and died between Twelve and one of the Clock Oct: 8 1749.

Zechariah Dam̄on Son of Zechariah Dammon, and Anna Lenthall his wife, was baptized Oct: 15th 1749

Rhoda Bryant daughter of Peleg & Mary was baptifed December 3^d 1749

Lydia James daughter of John James & Prudence his wife was baptifed Dec: 31. 1749

The whole number of the baptifed this year amounts to 31.

1750.

Iacob Turner Son of Jsrael & Deborah was baptized March 25. 1750.

Lydia Stockbridge of Sam^ll & Sarah was baptifed April 1st 1750.

Demmick Bowker of Lazarus & Abigail was baptifed April 1st 1750.

BathSheba Barker of Barnabas & Mary was Baptifed April 15th 1750

Samuel Dammon of Daniel & Sarah was Baptifed April 15th 1750.

Luscenda Stetfon of Jofhua & Lillis was baptized April 29. 1750

Nathanael Jacob, Son of Deacon Jofeph Jacob & mary his wife was baptifed May 6th 1750

Luther Stetfon fon of Job & Mary was baptifed may 6th 1750.

Silva Church daughter of Jofeph, & Grace his Widow was baptized May 6th 1750.

Adult Philis a Negro Servant to Deacon Jofeph Cufhing was baptized June 3^d 1750.

Caleb Cufhing fon of Jofeph & Lydia was baptifed July 1st 1750.

Sufanna Man daughter of Jofiah man & —— his wife was baptifed July 8th 1750.

Sufannah Randal daughter of Benja^m Randal jun^r & Hannah his wife was baptized July 15th 1750.

Nathanael Silvefter Son of Nehemiah & Mehitable was Baptifed July 29. 1750

Anna Wade daughter of Zebulon Wade and —— his wife was Baptifed Augt 5th 1750.

Samuel Curtice Son of Sam^ll: & Rachel was baptifed Augt 12th 1750.

At a Meeting of the 2^d. Church of Christ in Scituate on ye 11th. Day of Oct^o 1750 being the first Chh. Meeting after the Death of the Revd Mr Eells. S^d Church chose ye Revd Mr Shearj^a. Bourn Moderator of the S^d

Meeting and after Prayer to God for his presence & Direction S^d Church chose Joseph Cushing Junr Clerk of S^d Church during the prefent Vacancy.

Sarah Buck Daughter of Isaac Buck Iun^r and Mary his wife was Baptised September ye 2^d 1750 by Mr Lewis.

Charles Tolman Son of Elisha and Miriam Tolman and James Gilkey Son of James and Grace Gilkey were Baptised September ye 9th 1750 by Mr Niles.

Barker Cushing Son of Mr John Cushing Iun^r and Deborah his Wife and Bailey Randall Son of Perez and Sarah Randall and William Son of Sambo a free Negro and Martha his Wife an Jndian were all Baptised October ye 14th 1750 by Mr Anger [Angier].

Joseph Tolman Son of Joseph and Mary Tolman was Baptised Oct^o ye 28th 1750 by Mr Nath^ll Eells of Stonington

Abigail Eells Daughter of John and Abiah Eells was Baptised November ye 4th 1750 by Mr Edward Eells.

Jra Bryant Son of Samuel Bryant Iun^r and Mary his Wife was Baptised November ye 4th 1750 by Mr Edwd Eells

Sarah Cushing Daughter of James Cushing Junr & Mary his Wife was Baptised Novemb: ye 4th 1750 by Mr Edwd Eells

Ruth Dammon, Joanna Dammon, and Leafa Dammon Daughters of Joseph and Joanna Dammon were Baptised November ye 4th 1750 by Mr Edwd Eells of Middletown

Steel Foster Son of Capt Joseph Foster and Abigail his Wife was Baptised Ianuary ye 6th 1750 by Mr Gay

Thankful Eells Daughter of North Eells and Ruth his Wife was Baptised January ye 20th 1750 by Mr Wales of marshfield.

Abigail Clap Daughter of Nathan^ll Clap Esqr and Desire his Wife, was Baptized February ye 10th 1750/1 by Mr Bourn.

Nathaniel Dammon Son of Zachariah Dammon Junr and Anna Lenthal his Wife Was Baptized February ye 24th 1750/1 by Mr Bafs.

Bethiah Turner Daughter of Abiel Turner and Elizabeth his Wife and George Stetson Son of George and Unice Stetson his wife and Lucy Brigs Daughter of James Briggs Junr and Hannah his Wife and Mary Stetson Daughter of Gideon Stetson were all Baptized June ye 2^d 1751 by Mr Edward Eells of Middletown.

Iane Palmer Daughter of Joseph Palmer and Jane his Wife and James Cole Son of James Cole and Lucy Stodder Daughter of Benjamin Stodder Iun^r were all Baptised June ye 2^d 1751 by the Revd Mr Edward Eells of Middletown.

Nathaniel Cushing Son of Joseph Cushing Iun^r and Lydia his Wife ——— and Seth Turner Son of Jonathan Turner & Abigail his Wife, and John Briggs Son of John Briggs and Abigail his wife and Lucy Bowker Daughter of John Bowker and Ann his Wife were all Baptised June ye 23^d 1751 by the Revd Mr Gay.

James Briant Son of Peleg Briant and Mary his Wife and James Barrel Son of James Barrel and Deborah his Wife were both Baptised June ye 30th 1751 by Mr Bourn.

[This concludes the baptisms of the "Rev. Nathaniel Eells book," so-called. The entries from the death of Rev. Mr. Eells were made, undoubtedly, by Joseph Cushing.]

THE BRISTOL BRANCH OF THE FINNEY FAMILY.*

By Franklin C. Clark, M.D., of Providence, R. I.

This family appears to have come from England before 1639, and consisted of a mother, a daughter, Catherine, and two sons, Robert and John.

"Mother Finney" died in Plymouth, Apr. 22, 1650, "aged upwards of 80" years.

Children:

i. Catherine,[1] m. Gabriel Fallowell, who d. Dec. 28, 1667, aged 83; d. June 7, 1673. Children: 1. *John*, m. ——; d. before 1649. 2. *Ann*, m. Thomas Pope of Plymouth, who d. July 28, 1637; d. in May, 1646.

ii. Robert, b. about 1608; m. Sept. 1, 1641, Phebe Ripley, who was b. 1619, and d. Oct. 9, 1710, in her 92d yr.; d. Jan. 7, 1687-8; resided in Plymouth; was granted land in 1641; a freeman in 1648; an exciseman and juryman; deacon of the church from 1669 till his death; and deputy from Plymouth to the General Court, 1657-60, '62-4, '69, '71-2. Having no issue, he willed his property in Plymouth to his two nephews, Robert and Josiah, the sons of his brother John; and in 1689 they petitioned the Court for the lands left them by their uncle Robert.

1. iii. John, called "John the Pilgrim."

1. John[1] Finney married first Christiana, or Christian, who died in Plymouth, Sept. 9, 1649; married second, June 10, 1650, Abigail, daughter of Thomas Bishop and widow of Henry Coggin, who died May 6, 1653; and married third, June 26, 1654, Elizabeth Bailey, who was buried in Bristol, Feb. 9, 1683-4. He received a grant of land in Plymouth in 1639, and again in 1640 and 1641; was made freeman in 1644; was an exciseman from 1646 to 1648; and served on several juries. With his son John, Jr., he was admitted a freeman of Barnstable, May 29, 1670, where John, Jr., finally settled. He was at one time a resident of Scituate, Mass.; and later joined the company which settled Bristol, in 1680; but in 1682 he sold his interest in the Mount Hope lands, at Bristol, to his son Jonathan. From 1682 no record of him appears till 1702, when he seems to have removed to Swansea, Mass. He probably died not long after, as a deed was executed by him at that time to which he signed with a mark.

Children by first wife, born in Plymouth:

i. John,[2] b. Dec. 24, 1638; the founder of the Barnstable line.

ii. Thomas, b. about 1648; d. in 1653.

Children by third wife, born in Barnstable:

2. iii. Jonathan, b. Aug. 14, 1655.

iv. Robert, b. Aug. 13, 1656; removed with his brother Josiah to Plymouth; afterwards joined the ill-fated expedition to Canada under Phips, in which he lost his life in 1690. His will is dated July 23, 1690.

v. Hannah, b. Sept. 2, 1657; m. (1) in 1677, Dea. Ephraim, b. Jan. 27, 1648, d. Feb. 18, 1732, son of Ephraim and Ann (Cooper) Morton of Plymouth; m. (2) John Cooke of Kingston, Mass., by

* The earliest records show the spelling of the name as *Finney*, and the Plymouth and Bristol lines, with but a single exception, have retained this spelling. The Barnstable line, however, from the first adopted that of *Phinney*. There was another family, settled in Connecticut, of the name of *Pinney*, which should not be confounded with the Barnstable Phinneys some of whom removed to that State.

whom no issue. Children: 1. *Hannah*, b. 1677; m. Benjamin Morton. 2. *Ephraim*, b. 1678; m. ———. 3. *John*, b. 1680; m. Reliance (or Rebecca), dau. of his uncle John Phinney of Barnstable. 4. *Joseph*, b. 1683; m. ———. 5. *Ebenezer*, b. 1685; m. ———.

vi. ELIZABETH, b. Mch. 15, 1659; probably m. Dec. 19, 1773, Haile, b. about 1753, son of Benjamin and Mary (Haile) Barton of Warren, R. I. Children: 1. *Molly*, b. Aug. 21, 1774. 2. *Rose*, b. Sept. 30, 1775. 3. *Elizabeth*, b. June 23, 1777.

vii. JOSIAH, b. Jan. 11, 1661; settled in Plymouth, Mass., and founded a large family.

3. viii. JEREMIAH, b. Aug. 15, 1662.

4. ix. JOSHUA, b. Dec., 1665.

2. JONATHAN[2] FINNEY (*John*[1]), born Aug. 14, 1655, in Barnstable, Mass.; married, intention Oct. 18, 1682, Joanna, born in 1669, died Nov. 30, 1739, at Bristol, daughter of John and Elizabeth Kinnicutt of Bristol. He was one of the first settlers of Bristol, and made freeman in 1680. He died in Swansea, Mass, in May, 1728. His descendants spell the name *Phinney*.

Children:

i. JOANNA,[3] b. Nov. 30, 1683; m. ——— Clark.

5. ii. JONATHAN, b. Nov. 3, 1686.

iii. MEHETABEL, bapt. Jan. 19, 1688-9.

iv. ELIZABETH, bapt. in 1695; d. June 30, 1730; m. ——— Bradford.

v. LYDIA, bapt. in 1695; m. Hopestill Cotton.

vi. MARY, bapt. in 1695.

6. vii. EBENEZER, bapt. Apr. 23, 1699.

viii. HANNAH, bapt. Sept. 1, 1700; d. June 30, 1730.

3. JEREMIAH[2] FINNEY (*John*[1]), born Aug. 15, 1662, in Barnstable, Mass.; married, Jan. 7, 1684, Esther, born in 1664, died Apr. 11, 1743, in Bristol, daughter of Thomas and Mary Lewis of Bristol. He was made freeman of Bristol, with his father, in 1680. He was a shipmaster, and died in Bristol, Feb. 18, 1748.

Children:

i. JEREMIAH,[3] b. 1684; d. young.

ii. MARY, b. Mch. 26, 1686; m. ———.

iii. HANNAH, b. Jan. 14, 1687-8; m. Jan. 14, 1706-7, Thomas, b. 1680, d. Apr. 18, 1754 or '5, son of Thomas and Hannah (James) Diamant, or Diman. The family removed from Long Island to Bristol in 1712. She d. Dec. 22, 1744, in Bristol. Children, the first four born on Long Island: 1. *James*, b. Nov., 1707; d. Oct. 8, 1788. 2. *John*, b. about 1709. 3. *Rebecca*. 4. *Jeremiah*, b. 1710; d. Nov. 10, 1798. 5. *Jonathan*, b. 1712; d. Feb. 25, 1797. 6. *Phebe*, b. 1717; d. Sept. 14, 1790. 7. *Lucretia*, b. 1719; d. Jan. 31, 1797. 8. *Daniel*, b. Dec. 16, 1797.

iv. MEHITABLE, b. May 8, 1687; m. ———.

v. JOHN, b. Aug. 3, 1690; d. young.

vi. REBECCA, b. Feb. 24, 1691-2; probably m. Mch. 11, 1716, Samuel Harris of Swansea, Mass.

vii. ESTHER, b. May 4, 1693; m., int. Oct. 31, 1719, Joseph Joy of Rehoboth, Mass., who d. 1754; d. in Bristol, May 26, 1754. Children: 1. *Esther*, b. 1720; d. Aug. 2, 1747. 2. *Joseph*, b. June 25, 1725. 3. *A child*, b. 1726; d. July, 1734.

viii. DEBORAH, bapt. Oct. 20, 1695.

7. ix. JOHN, b. Apr. 13, 1696.

x. ABIGAIL, b. Apr. 17, 1697.

8. xi. JEREMIAH, bapt. Sept. 7, 1700.

4. JOSHUA[2] FINNEY (*John*[1]), born Dec. 1665, in Barnstable, Mass., married, intention May 31, 1688, Mercy Watts of Bristol, who died Feb. 12, 1724. He removed, with his father, to Bristol in 1680, where he was made freeman a little later. All his children were born in Bristol. He finally removed to Swansea, Mass., where he died Sept. 7, 1714.

Children:

9. i. JOSHUA,[3] b. May 7, 1689.
ii. ELIZABETH, b. Sept. 25, 1691 or '92; d. Sept. 19, 1701.
iii. MARY, b. Apr. 12, 1694.
10. iv. JOHN, b. Aug. 15, 1696. He is known as Dr. John, and removed to Lebanon, Conn.
11. v. Samuel, b. May 20, 1699.
12. vi. JOSIAH, b. July 26, 1701.
vii. ELIZABETH, b. May 1, 1707; m. Nov. 4, 1733, Nathan Luther of Swansea, Mass. One child, *Huldah*, b. Jan. 12, 1743.

5. JONATHAN[3] PHINNEY (*Jonathan*,[2] *John*[1]), born Nov. 3, 1686, in Swansea, Mass., married, May 6, 1730, Mercy Read, born in 1706, died Nov., 1767. He was a farmer, and resided in that part of Swansea which lies just to the east of Warren. He was a mariner before he became a farmer, and died in Swansea, Nov. 26, 1736. After his death, his widow married second, Benjamin Smith.

Children:

i. HANNAH,[4] b. June 17, 1731; m. 1747, Richard, son of Barnard Haile of Warren; d. May 27, 1797, in Warren. Children: 1. *Hannah*, b. May 31, 1748. 2. *Anne*, b. Oct. 28, 1751. 3. *Jonathan*, b. Mch. 22, 1753. 4. *Barnard*, b. Aug. 4, 1755. 5. *Richard*, b. Apr. 11, 1758. 6. *John*, b. Aug. 11, 1760. 7. *Elizabeth*, b. Sept. 25, 1765. 8. *Samuel*, b. Sept. 5, 1770.
ii. JONATHAN, b. Apr., 1733; d. May, 1733.
iii. JONATHAN, b. Aug. 4, 1734; d. Sep. 2, 1739.
13. iv. ELISHA, b. Mch. 30, 1737, a posthumous child.

6. EBENEZER[3] FINNEY (*Jonathan*,[2] *John*[1]), born Apr. 23, 1699, in Swansea, Mass., married, intention May 28, 1726, Jane, born in 1692, daughter of Thomas and Jane (Nelson) Faunce of Plymouth, Mass. He resided in Bristol for a time, and then seems to have lived in Easton, Norton, and Plymouth, finally dying in Middleborough, Mass. It is possible that he married, as a first wife, in Norton, Abigail, daughter of Sylvanus Campell.

Child:

i. NELSON,[4] b. July 8, 1728; d. Aug. 23, 1730.

7. JOHN[3] FINNEY, (*Jeremiah*,[2] *John*[1]), born Apr. 13, 1696, married Mary, daughter of Sylvanus and Mary Campbell of Norton, Mass. He purchased land there in conjunction with his cousin Ebenezer, who also, at least for a time, resided in Norton. John is styled a cordwainer or shoemaker. He came to Norton about 1717, and removed to Easton about 1766. He probably died in Kingston, Mass., Oct. 11, 1787.

8. JEREMIAH[3] FINNEY (*Jeremiah*,[2] *John*[1]), born in 1700, married, intention May 17, 1727, Elizabeth, born Dec. 14, 1706, died Nov. 8, 1760, in Bristol, daughter of Thomas and Elizabeth Bristow of Bristol. He was a shipmaster, resided in Bristol, and died Oct. 21, 1759.

Children;

14. i. JOSIAH,[4] b. July 1, 1728.
ii. A CHILD, d. Feb. 27, 1730.
iii. ELIZABETH, b. in 1731; d. May, 14, 1759.
15. iv. JEREMIAH, b. Mch. 19, 1732-3.
16. v. THOMAS, b. Nov. 16, 1737.
vi. MARY, b. Nov. 14, 1742; m. 1765, as his second wife, Corban, b. in 1732, son of John and Dorcas (Corban) Barnes of Plymouth, Mass. Children: 1. *Mary*, b. 1766; m. Sept. 16, 1795, Eleazer Holmes. 2. *Rebecca*, b. 1768. 3. *Betsy*, b. 1771; m. (1) Thomas Davie; m. (2) —— Leucas; m. (3) —— Mayhew. 4. *Charlotte*, b. 1774; m. Stephen Harlow. 5. *Corban*, b. 1778. 6. *Patty*, b. 1781; m. Ansel Holmes. 7. *Deborah*, b. 1785; m. Alden Leucas. 8. *Abigail*, b. 1789; m (1) William Keene; m. (2) Isaiah Carver.
vii. ESTHER, b. Nov. 14, 1744, d. Mch. 26, 1745.

9. JOSHUA[3] FINNEY (*Joshua*,[2] *John*[1]), born May 7, 1689, in Bristol, married Martha Carter, who was born in 1671, and died May 14, 1751. He resided at first in Swansea, and afterwards purchased land in Lebanon, Conn., in 1726, removing thither with his family about 1750. Two of his brothers, John and Josiah, removed to Litchfield Co., Conn. He was a farmer, and died after 1750.

Children:

17. i. WILLIAM,[4] b. May 10, 1715.
ii. JOSHUA, b. May 11, d. Nov, 29, 1716.
iii. MARY (or MERCY), b. July 5, 1718; m. Mch. 14, 1733-4, Joseph Mann; d. before 1743.
iv. MARTHA, b. Mch. 4, 1719-20.
18. v. JOHN, b. June 2, 1721.
19. vi. OLIVER, b. Nov. 11, 1728.

10. JOHN[3] FINNEY (*Joshua*,[2] *John*[1]), born Aug. 15, 1696, in Bristol, married, Sept. 14, 1716, Ann Toogood of Swansea, Mass., who died Aug. 11, 1776. He removed first to Norton, Mass., then purchased land in Lebanon, Conn., in 1728 or '29. He also owned land in Kent, Conn. He appears to have been a physician, though in deeds he is called "blacksmith." At one time he was a resident of Swansea. He died June 6, 1773, in Lebanon, Conn.

Children, born in Swansea:

i. JOEL,[4] b. Feb. 24, 1716-7.
20. ii. JOHN, b. Oct. 14, 1718.
21. iii. NATHANIEL, b. Jan. 3, 1720-1; went to Nova Scotia.
iv. JOSHUA, b. Feb. 24, 1723-4.
v. ANN, b. Apr. 30, 1727.
vi. MERCY, b. Jan. 1, 1729-30; m. Dec. 21, 1752, Reuben Sacket of East Greenwich, now Warren, Conn.
22. vii. DAVID, b. Aug. 24, 1732.
viii. MARTHA, b. and d. June 12, 1735.
23. ix. JABEZ, b. Nov. 21, 1737.

11. SAMUEL[3] FINNEY (*Joshua*,[2] *John*[1]), born May 20, 1699, in Bristol, married, Mch. 12, 1726-7, Elizabeth, daughter of John Wood of Warwick, R. I., and widow of Thomas Tibbitts. He removed to Warwick about 1726, where he died in 1765. He was a blacksmith.

Children:

i. BENJAMIN,[4] b. July 26, d. Aug. 5, 1727.
ii. MERCY, b. Mch. 25, 1732; m. Dec. 21, 1752, Reuben ——, of Warren, Conn.; removed in June, 1765, after her father's death, to Little Compton, R. I.

12. JOSIAH[3] FINNEY (*Joshua,*[2] *John*[1]), born July 26, 1701, in Bristol, married, Jan. 1, 1723–4, Elizabeth Mann, who died in 1775. He was in Lebanon, Conn., in 1750, where he early purchased land. He was one of the earliest settlers of Warren, Conn. His will was proved Aug. 22, 1774.

Children, born in Swansea:

i. ELIZABETH,[4] b. Jan. 19, 1723–4.
ii. JOSIAH, b. Jan. 27, 1725–6; d. Sept., 1726.
24. iii. JOSIAH, b. Feb. 24, 1727–8.
iv. KEZIAH, b. Mch. 5, 1730.
v. LYDIA, b. Mch. 6, 1732; d. before 1771.
25. vi. DAVID, b. June 21, 1734.
26. vii. JONATHAN, b. June 1, 1736.

13. ELISHA[4] PHINNEY (*Jonathan,*[3] *Jonathan,*[2] *John*[1]), born Mch. 30, 1737, married first, May 5, 1763, Jemima, born in Newport, R. I., in 1742, died in Warren, R. I., Feb. 12, 1764, daughter of John and Hannah (Claggett) Treadwell; and married second, in 1766, Rebecca, born Feb. 11, 1740, d. Oct. 28, 1818, daughter of Henry and Rachel (Whittaker) Peck of Rehoboth, Mass. He was made freeman of Warren in 1760, was a farmer, and died Jan. 18, 1815.

Child by first wife:

i. JONATHAN,[5] b. Jan. 30, 1764; d. Oct. 11, 1779.

Children by second wife:

ii. AARON, b. Apr. 24, 1767; d. in 1787, abroad.
27. iii. DANIEL, b. Sept. 14, 1768.
28. iv. BENJAMIN, b. Oct. 8, 1771.
v. JEMIMA, b. Mch. 29, 1773; m. Hezekiah Kingsley of Swansea. Children: 1. *Nathan.* 2. *Elisha.* 3. *Luther.* 4. *Henry Peck.*
vi. ELISHA PECK, b. Oct. 31, 1774; m. Dec. 14, 1806, Lydia, b. Jan. 27, 1782, d. Oct. 17, 1857, dau. of David and Rebecca (Brightman) Barton of Freetown, Mass. He resided in Swansea and Warren, was a farmer, and d. Apr. 14, 1854. No issue.
vii. REBECCA, b. Sept. 22, 1777; m. in 1797, Capt. William, b. May 5, 1776, son of Thomas and Phebe (Throop) Champlin of Bristol, R. I.; d. Mch, 8, 1858. Children: 1. *John Bowman,* b. May 29, 1798. 2. *William,* b. May 16. 1800; m. Eliza K. Phinney. (See 27, ii.) 3. *Julia Ann,* b. Apr. 21, 1802; d. Dec. 13, 1891; m. —— Hodges. 4. *Charlotte,* b. Jan 11, 1805; d. Apr. 4, 1893; m. prob. —— Barney. 5. *Mary.* 6. *Elisha* (?).
viii. HANNAH, b. Oct. 11, 1779; m. (1) —— Corban; m. (2) Dea. —— Bruce of New York.
ix. NATHAN, b. Oct. 5, 1782; d. Jan. 3, 1802, abroad.

14. JOSIAH[4] FINNEY (*Jeremiah,*[3] *Jeremiah,*[2] *John*[1]), born July 5, 1728, in Bristol, married first, May 19, 1751, Mary, born Dec. 3, 1732, died Sept. 18, 1760, daughter of Allen and Hannah (Church) Carey of Bristol; and married second, Sept. 16, 1761, Martha, born in 1739, died May 22, 1823, daughter of James and Martha (Giddings) Gibbs. He was a farmer, and resided in Bristol, R. I., where he was at one time postmaster. He died July 23, 1804, in Bristol.

Children by first wife:

i. JEREMIAH,[5] bapt. Feb. 4, 1753; d. at sea, July 25, 1773.
ii. ELIZABETH, bapt. Dec. 8, 1754; d. Sept. 21, 1756.
iii. ALLEN, bapt. Mch. 20, 1757; d. July 31, 1758.
iv. MOLLY, bapt. June 10, 1759.

Children by second wife:

v. MARTHA, bapt. Aug. 29, 1762; m. 1783, John, b. June 13, 1760, d. Oct. 4, 1813, son of Nathaniel and Sarah (Little) Fales of Bristol; d. Apr. 13, 1843, in Providence, R. I. Children: 1. *Charlotte*, b. Jan. 5, 1784; d. Dec. 12, 1848. 2. *Fidelia*, b. Jan. 27, 1785; d. July 14, 1822. 3. *Timothy*, b. July 23, 1788. 4. *James Gibbs*, b. Oct. 10, 1789; d. Oct. 21, 1790. 5. *James*, b. July 20, 1791. 6. *Betsey Paine*, b. Mch. 29, 1792. 7. *Abby Finney*, b. Mch. 23, 1794. 8. *Nancy Church*, b. Mch. 23, 1796. 9. *Joseph Jackson*, b. Apr. 10, 1798; d. May 9, 1799. 10. *Henry DeWolf*, b. Feb. 8, 1800; d. Mch. 30, 1801. 11. *Martha Gibbs*, b. Mch. 10, 1802.

vi. CHARLOTTE, b. Feb. 10, 1764; m. June 1, 1784, William, b. Dec. 19, 1762, d. Apr. 19, 1829, son of Mark Anthony and Abigail (Potter) DeWolf of Bristol, R. I.; d. Apr. 15, 1829, in Bristol. Children: 1. *Henry*, b. Mch. 21, 1785; d. Oct. 18, 1857. 2. *William*, b. Dec. 8, 1788; d. Oct. 12, 1830. 3. *Charlotte*, b. June 17, 1793; d. Apr. 22, 1885; unmarried. 4. *Maria*, b. Oct. 26, 1795; d. Dec. 16, 1890; m. —— Rogers. 5. *Abigail*, b. Apr. 18, 1798; d. Apr. 22, 1817; m. —— Davis.

vii. SARAH, b. 1767; m. Nov. 15, 1789, Capt. Hezekiah, bapt. May 12, 1763, d. at sea, Sept. 15, 1795, son of Hezekiah and Ann Usher of Bristol, R. I.; d. May 4, 1820, in Bristol. Children: 1. *Ann Frances*, bapt. May 24, 1795. 2. *George Fenno*, bapt. May 24, 1795; m. his cousin Abby French. 3. *Hezekiah*, bapt. May 24, 1795; d. Feb. 5, 1796.

viii. THOMAS GIBBS, b. 1768; d. at sea, Oct. 4, 1787.

ix. GEORGE, b. 1770; d. at sea, May 9, 1792; unmarried.

x. SUSANNA, bapt. July, 1772: m. June 23, 1811, Capt. Oliver, b. in 1775, d. probably Jan. 8, 1814, son of Richard and Mary Fitch of Norwich, Conn.; d. Jan. 8, 1848, in Bristol.

xi. ANN (or NANCY), b. Sept. 19, 1773; d. Dec. 17, 1839; unmarried.

xii. ELIZABETH, bapt. June 18, 1780.

xiii. RUTH THURSTON, bapt. Oct. 9, 1781; m. June 16, 1811, Elkanah, b. 1782, d. Sept. 22, 1856, son of Elkanah French; d. Feb. 4, 1858. Children: 1. *Emily F(inney*, probably). 2. *Abby Finney*, m. her cousin George F. Usher. 3. *A child*, b. Nov., d. Dec. 25, 1818.

xiv. ABIGAIL (?), b. 1776, d. Oct. 16, 1796, in Bristol.

15. JEREMIAH[4] FINNEY (*Jeremiah*,[3] *Jeremiah*,[2] *John*[1]), born Mch. 19, 1732–3, in Bristol, married first, Deborah ———, born in 1740, died Nov. 9, 1791; and married second, Apr. 14, 1792, Mary, born in 1747, died Sept. 20, 1821, daughter of Samuel Coy. He was a shipmaster. In the Revolutionary War he served as private, in 1778, in Col. Nathan Miller's regiment, of Rhode Island. (See MSS. in the State House, Providence, Vol. IV, p. 43.) He died July 17, 1807, in Bristol.

Children by first wife:

i. THOMAS,[5] b. 1758; d. Mch. 8, 1760.

29. ii. LORING, b. 1761.

iii. ELIZABETH, b. 1763; m. Feb. 26, 1803, Isaac Lafayette, son of Richard and Lydia Newton of Wrentham, Mass.

iv. DEBORAH, b. 1766; m. Dec. 22, 1785, Lucius Rhodes.

v. REBECCA, b. 1768; m. Nov. 10, 1785, Capt. Jesse, son of Ichabod and Sylvia Davis of Freetown, Mass., who d. before 1843; d. June 2, 1843. Children: 1. *Polly*, b. June 7, 1786. 2. *Lucinda*, b. Mch. 23, 1790. 3. *Anthony*, b. Oct. 9, 1794. 4. *David*, b. July 9, 1798; d. Jan. 27, 1830. 5. *Amanda*, b. May 6, 1802. 6. *John Jeremiah Finney*, b. Dec. 4. 1808; d. Sept. 16, 1841.

vi. MARY, b. 1770; m. Apr. 24, 1788, Capt. Parker, b. Apr. 26, 1765, d. Feb. 26, 1839, in Providence. R. I., son of Ezekiel and Hannah (Parker) Clark of Rochester, Mass.; d. Mch. 28, 1835, in Providence, R. I. Children: 1. *Henry Finney*, b. Jan. 1, 1790; m. Sept. 20, 1815,

Alice, dau. of Edward and Alice (Dexter) Taylor; d. June 20, 1820, in Indiana. Issue. 2. *George Gibbs*, b. Oct. 1792; m. (1) Mch. 30, 1818, Anne Eliza Wescott; m. (2) Nov. 4, 1833, Mary Dring Bolles; d. Oct. 31, 1869; issue. 3. *Mary*, b. Feb., d. July 25, 1794.

30. vii. JOHN, bapt. Sept. 26, 1773.

viii. JEREMIAH, b. 1774; d. Jan. 1, 1799.

ix. HANNAH, b. 1776; m. Nov. 5, 1795, Elisha, b. Apr. 26, 1766, d. Nov. 21, 1822, son of Peter and Abigail (Briggs) Carpenter of Norton, Mass.; d. June 30, 1805, in Warren, R. I. Children: 1. *Mary*, b. Mch. 24, 1798; m. ——— White. 2. *Louisa*, b. Nov. 28, 1799; m. ——— Howard.

[To be concluded.]

RECORDS OF THE CHURCH IN VERNON, CONN.

1762–1824.

Communicated by Miss MARY KINGSBURY TALCOTT, of Hartford, Conn.

From the manuscript copy owned by the Connecticut Society of Colonial Dames.

[Continued from Vol. 59, page 416.]

Anno Dom

Anno Dom[i] 1808.

Jan[y] 22. An infant child of Sam[l] Lyman.
Jan[y] 30. The 2nd infant child of Samuel Lyman
Feb[y] 9. The 3[d] infant child of Sam[l] Lyman.— 16. An infant child of Aaron Eaton.— 25. Daniel Skinner aged 80 years.
May 23. Efther Talcott aged.
June 24. A daughter of Isaac King aged about 3 years.
Sep[t]. 2. The wife of Roger Loomis aged 74.— 29. Rofanna M[c]Lean aged 19.
Oct[r] 1. Reuben Smith, son of Eben[r] Hunt aged 3 years.
Nov[br] 3. Afahel Root, aged 82 years & 6 months.

Anno Dom[i] 1809.

Jan[y] 13. Horace Grant, son of Warham Grant, aged 1 [yrs] 9 [moths].— 25. A child of Ezekiel Olcott Ju[r] aged 2 years.
May 18. An infant child of Ashur Isham.
June 24. An infant child of Alpheus Chapman.— 29. John Dart, aged 87.
July 20. John Sparks, aged 77.
Aug[t] 22. Cap[t] Ezekiel Olcott aged 74.
Nov[br] 25. The wife of Francis Grant aged —
Decem[br] 11. An infant child of Alex[dr] M[c]Lean.— 20. Edward son of Brent Paine aged 5. months.

Anno Dom[i] 1810.

Jan[y] 8. An infant child of Eben[r] Kellogg Jun[r].
March 28. Asahel Webster aged 71.
June 3. Elijah Tucker aged 73.
Aug[t] 15. John Worburton aged 38.
Sep[t] 3. The wife of Dea[n] Benj[n] Talcott, aged 80.

ADom[i] 1811.

Feb[y] 4. An infant child of Eben[r] Kellogg Jn[r].— 21. Stephen Johns, aged 31 years.

March 2. Widow Mary King, relict of Dea^n^ S. King ag^d^ 91.—5. The wife of Josiah Jones, aged 30 years.—24. A child of Reuben Sage Jn^r^ aged about 18 mon^ths^.—30. Roxy, the wife of Francis M^c^Lean, aged 31. years.
Apriel 13. Deacon Benjamin Talcott, aged 86 years.
May 16. The wife of Jonathan Chapman aged 75.
June 3. A child of Thaddeus Fitch aged about 24 y^rs^.—19. The widow Wyles, aged 87 years.
July 18. A son of Elijah Paine, aged about 2½ y^ears^.
Augt 9. Joseph Hyde, aged 69. years.
Octr 2. James Tudor, son of Dea^n^ Saml Talcott aged about 2 months.—9. Patience 2^d^ wife of Joseph Loomis, aged 35. y^rs^.—27. John Pain, aged 71.
Nov^br^ 17. Milo Landfear in ye 3^d^ year of his age. A child who lived with Capt Roberts.
Decem^br^ 16. Twin infant children of Ruffel King.

Anno Dom^l^ 1812.

Apriel 1. Elisabeth, wife of Phinehas Chapman, ag^d^ 60.
May 2. A son of Elijah Lee, aged about 4 months.
May 10. Ebenezer Kellogg J^r^ Efq^r^ aged 47 years 6m. 19 ^days^.—26. Roger Dart Doct^r^ aged 54 years.
July 14. Anna, daughter of Roswel Smith aged 10 y^rs^
Augt 25. Betsey Rogers, daughter of Leonard Rogers aged 27.
Octr 8. The second wife of Reuben Skinner, ag^d^
Nov^br^ 2. A child of Levi Dart Ju^r^ aged about 2 weeks.—8. An infant child of Alderman.—29. A tw^in^ infant child of Erastus Hunt.
Decem. 5. The other twin infant child of Erastus Hunt.

ADom^l^ 1813.

Jany 20. Harriet an infant child of Darius Hunt.
March 22. Eunice daughter of Brento^n^ Paine aged about 8 months.—28. An infant child of Ralph Eaton.
Apriel 3. Brento^n^ Paine, in the 36th year of his age.—4. Sophia Sage, daughter of Reube^n^ Sage, aged 25.—5. Jerusha, wife of Darius Hunt, aged 36.
Apreil 10th Elijah Paine, aged 38 years.
May 26. Deacon Samuel Talcott, aged 56.
July 10. An infant child of Eli Hammond.
Augt 10. Olive, the wife of Eli Hammond, aged 42 years.
Octr 4. A child of Solomon Carpenter aged about 2 years.—18. A child of Daniel M^c^Kinney aged about 2 y^rs^.
Decem^br^ 19. Jonathan Chapman, aged 84 years.

ADom^l^ 1814.

Feby A child of ——— Westons.
Apriel 2. Anna, second wife of Francis Grant, ag^d^ 27.
July 3. Anna, wife of John Walker, aged 60.—5. The wife of Capt Alex^dr^ M^c^Kinney, aged 69 y^rs^ 11 ^months^.
Augt 9. Betty wife of Alexander McLean, aged 41.—10. Reuben Sage, very suddenly, aged 66.—11. Jonathan Smith, aged 92.—12. A child of Chester Fitch, aged 8 months.—15. A daughter of Joshua Pearl Jn^r^ aged 3 years.—24. Allice, The wife of Oliver Dart aged 22 yr^s^
Sep^t^ 30. A child of John Cady, aged 16 months.

Octr 1. Martin Kellogg, aged 22 years & 11 mon^ths^.— 6. The widow Wilson, aged 53 years.— 11. A little Girl of John Cady, aged about 3 years.— 29. Jabez Cheesebrough, aged 58.

Anno Domi 1815.

Feby 21. A female child of Erastus Hunt, aged about ten months.
March 5. Susannah, 2^d^ wife of Elijah King aged 64.— 15. David Dorchester aged about 40.
June 8. A child of Oliver Dart, aged 2 years & 10 mos
Septr 5. David Smith aged near 87.— 17. Eunice [Smith] relict of David Smith, aged 80.
Nov^br^ 7. Mary wife of Elijah Skinner Junr aged 42.— 20. Julius Skinner, aged 29.

Anno Domini, 1816.

Jany 20. Orinda, daughter of Daniel Kellogg, in the 20th year of her age.
— 24. Chloe, the wife of Col^l^ Oliver King, aged 65 years.
Feb. 20. Betsey the wife of Peter Dobson, aged 24.
March 6. James Thrall, aged 70 years.
March 18. Ruth Cone, daughter of Daniel Cone, ag^d^ 33.— 25. The wife of Ebenezer Bevins aged 52.
Apriel 16. Thaddeus Fitch, aged 54.
July 1. Seth Baker, aged 83.
Augt 11. An infant child of Fredirack Walker.
Octr 23. James Cady, son of Amos Cady, ag^d^ 23.

Anno Dom^i^ 1817.

Jany 27. Joshua Pearl Ju^r^, aged 38.
Feby 11. Roger Loomis, aged 84.— 13. Lemuel King Ju^r^ aged 20 years.
—27. Widow Rebecca Dorchester, aged 84.
March 15. Lydia, wife of Capt C. Roberts, aged 61.
June 10. Widow Kezia Allis, aged 86.— 15. Sally, the wife of Elam Tuttle, ag^d^ 45.— 18. A child of Isaac Brunson, ag^d^ about 2 years.— 20. The wife of Henry White, aged 57.— 25. The wife of Ozias Grant, aged 77.
July 17. Electa, wife of Elisha Grant, aged 36.— Widow Hannah Loomis aged.
June 10th A child of Lyman Ransom aged 6 Days.
Sept. 3. Revd Ebenezer Kellogg aged 80 years.— 4. Lora child of Erastus McKinney aged 2 years.
Oct. 11. Elisha child of David Jackson aged 15 months.— 29. Anna, Daughter of Jacob Talcott aged 19 years.

Anno Domini 1818.

Jany 9th Thomas Johns aged 72 years.— 29. Sally child of Justus Talcott Ju^r^ age 11 months.
March 11th Capt Oliver Hunt, aged 55 years.— 21st An infant daughter of Jemerson Cheesebrough aged two days.
April 16th Abigail wife of Daniel Bramau, belonged at E. Hampton Mass, aged 74.
May 3rd Isabella Columbus Thompson aged 15, daughter of ———.— 11th Deborah wife of Joshua Pearl aged 63.
July 6th Oliver King Esqr. aged 70.— 28th Rachel Hunt (suddenly) aged 53.
Sept. 5th Nancy wife of John A. Hall aged 41.

Octr 8th Doct. Lester Fuller aged 24, Buried in Hampton, his native place.

AD. 1819.

Jany 8th An infant child of Joel King.
Feb. 6th Widow Fitch aged 85.—A child of Joel Robbins aged 3 months.
March 13th Thomas Chapman aged 68.— 25th Alexander McKinney aged 81.—An infant child of Anson Rogers.
May —. Mary Baker aged 76.— 22nd Bellows Newton aged 16.
July 2. Harriet H. daughter of Asbur Huntington aged two years.— 24. Eunice, daughter of Warren McKinney aged two years.— 27th An infant daughter of David Jackson aged 16 months.
Sept. 17th Tide, (Negro) aged.— 17. Lorana Grant aged 37.
Oct. 18th Child of Ashur Huntington aged 14 months.
Dec. 29th Leander, infant son of Obadiah K. Smith, aet — weeks.

1820

April 1. Widow Rebecca Chapman aged 69.
May 3rd William Cone infant son of John Abbot aged —.
June 12th Ruth daughter of [John] Alderman, aged 5 years.— 21st Hannah Goodrich aged Supposed Age 100.
July 11th Calista, child of Asa Cone aged 2 years.— 20th Jared Parker son of Eliphalet Parker aged 9 years.— 24th An infant child of Erastus McKinney.
Oct. —. Hannah wife of Benjamin Talcott, Aged.
Nov. 2nd Daniel Root aged.— 5th Pamela wife of Ephraim Tucker aged 49.
Dec. 17th Polly wife of Gordon Smith aged 34.

1821

Jany 30. Ezekiel Olcott, Aged 44 years.
March Daughter of Erastus McCollum Aged 15 months.
April An infant child of Eliphalet Bingham.— 23. Olive Talcott daughter of Jacob Talcott, Aet. 13 years.
June 1st Wareham Grant Aet 56 years.— 8. Abijah Johns Jun. Aet. 33 years.
July 16. Abigail Daniels Aet. 80 years.
October 4th Mary Corning Aet. 61 years.

1822

Jany 3rd Abijah Johns Aet. 80 years.— 9th Percy Hammond Aet. 49 years, wife of Eli Hammond.
Feb. 11th Cyrenius Edwin son of John Lucas, 1 year.
March 3rd Ruth King aged 55 years.—Child of David Jackson aged—.
April 5th Everline Daughter of Ansel House aged 11 years.— 7th Clarrissa Daughter of Ralph Eaton 1 year.
May 1st Rachel Talcott Relict of Mr Caleb Talcott aged 79 years.— 18th Abigail Hyde Relict of Mr Joseph Hyde aged 77 years.— 29th Johanna McLean Relict of Capt Alexander McLean aged 75 years.
June 8th Caleb Merrick Aged 55 years.—Mr Roswell Smith aged 53 years.—Infant child of M^{r}. John Clark.
July 18th Jimeson Chesebrough Aged 42 years.— 28th Ebenezer Nash Esq. aged 52 years.
August 7th Samuel Root Aged 71 years.

Sept. 9th Olive Abbot Relict of Col. Joseph Abbot Aged 84 years.
Oct 22d Frederick Walker aged 31 years.
Nov. 6th Fila Thrall Daughter of Mr Joel Thrall aged 17 years.—30th Capt Ozias Bissell aged about 92 years.
Dec. 22d Elisha Chesebrough aged 40 years.

1823.

Jan 23d Lucy Aurelia Daughter of Mr Phineas Chapman Jur aged 2 years.—29th. Fanny Alderman Aged 22 years, Daughter of Mr John Alderman.
Feb 16th Sarah Talcott Relict of Dean Samuel Talcott Aged 58 years.
March 2d George Chapman Aged 9 years Son of Mr John Chapman.—31st Mr Jonas Sparks aged 53 years.
April 15th Fanny Hacket about 18 years.
May 8th Reuben Skinner aged 72 years.—22 Ozias Grant Aged 90 years.
July 21. Nathan Corning aged 62 years.
August 29. Child of Varnie Parkerson Æ about 14 Months.
Sept. 4th Daughter of Samuel Cooley from N. York aged about 2 years.—11. Child of Benjn I. Godfrey about —.
Oct. 1st Eldad Skiuner Aged 54 years —9. Royal Talcott Aged 26 years.—22. Clarrissa Potter Aged 30 years, wife of Warterman Potter of Southbridge Mass, in Vernon on a visit.—26. Phineas Chapman Aged 76 years.
Nov. 29. Sarah Welles aged 60 years, Wife of Thomas Welles.

1824.

Feb 14th Jeremiah Perrin aged about 59 years.
March 31st Lydia Ladd aged 63 years.
April 2d Richard Harris Huntley Æt 78 years.
May 12th Hervey N. Cunningham Aged 22 years.
June 29th Sophia Amelia aged 4 years, Daughter of Reuben Sage.

THE PERSONS UNDERWRITTEN WERE MARRIED Pr ME, EBENr KELLOGG.

AD 1762.

Decembr 9th John Daniels & Abigail King.

AD 1763.

April 23. Brenton Paine & Hannah Hills.—item, Saml Blackmer & Abigail Brunſon.

AD 1764.

June 25. Daniel Orſborn & Hannah Ely.
July 10. John Paine & Damaris Hills.
Septbr 18. Reuben Searl & Mercy Allis.
Novbr 15. Eliſha Crane & Lydia Owen.
Decembr 13. Thomas Biſhop & Phebe Tucker.

AD 1765.

May 2. Moſes Thrall & Lucy Hills.

AD 1766.

May 28. Gideon King & Charity Tucker.
Augt 7. John Craw & Almy Hitchcock.
Octbr 16. Daniel Badger & Lucretia Johns.
Novbr 5. Ebenezer Baker & Sarah King.

AD 1767.

Ap^{l} 2. Abial Holt & Eunice Marſhal.— 9. Simeon Lynn & Martha Brunſon.— 21. James Thrall & Mary Welch.
May 6. Saml Hills & Suſanna Naſh.
July 29. Fenn Johnſon & Rebecca Biſhop.

AD 1768.

Ap^{l} 21. Elijah Brunſon & Abijail Wright.
Nov^{br} 17. Zadoc How & Rachel King.
Decem^{br} 22. Alexander McLean & Joanna Smith.

AD 1769.

Feby 1. John Hodge & Hannah Allis.
Augt 17. Juſtie Lomis & Sarah Hitchcock.
Sep^{t} 7. Edward Paine & Bette King

AD 1770.

July 12. Thomas Chapman & Rebecca Darte.
Decem^{br} 20. David Dorcheſter & Suſanna McLean.

AD 1771.

Feb 14. Sherabiah Ballard & Sarah Emerſon.
Ap^{l} 2. Lemmie Thrall & Lydia King.

AD 1772.

Jan^{r} 23. John Hall & Eunice Dorcheſter.— 30. Nathl Walker & Mary Allis.
Octo^{r} 15. Reuben King & Suſanna Millard.— 22. Cornelius Smith & Rhoda Johns.
Nov^{br} 12. James Nooney & Sarah King.
Decem^{br} 17. Reuben Tucker & Martha Carrier.

AD 1773.

Ap^{l} 6. John Tucker & Miriam Smith.
Augt 12. Elihu Jones & Lydia Bliſh.
Nov^{b} 11. Reuben Skinner & Margeret M^{c}ray.— 17. Daniel Reed & Sarah Brown.
Decem^{br} 23. Stephen King & Eliſabeth Darte.

AD 1774.

Apriel 21. Abel West & Hannah Chapman.
July 14. Ephraim Ladd & Lois Chapman.
Sep^{t} 1. Barzillai Little & Bette Bliſh.

AD 1775.

Augt 3. Daniel Cone & Kezia Chapman.
Sep^{t} 21. David King & Eunice Darte.
Decem^{br} 28. Gurdon Fowler & Mary Chapman.

Anno Dom^{i} 1776.

July 4. Eleazer Piney & Eunice King.
Nov^{br} 7. Timothy Benton & Mehitable White.— 14. Theophilus Bawldwin & Elſe Morris.

Anno Domi 1777.

March 6. Ezekiel Ladd & Sybel Lomis.

AD 1778.

Jany 8. Hugh Johns & Bettee Miller.
March 5. Solomon Loomis & Mary Chapman.
Apriel 2. Ephraim Webſter & Prudence Smith.— 27. Nathan Chapman & Lois Ely.
May 7. Hezekiah Loomis & Lydia Dorcheſter.
June 11. Ehen^r Walker and Sarah Allis.

Anno Domini 1779.

January 7th David Crane and Jeruſha Smith.— 21. Phinehas Jones & Olive Wentworth.— 25. Thomas Evans & Anna Reed.
Nov. 11. Daniel Root & Lydia Whitnee.

Anno Dom^l 1780.

Feb^r 24. Charles King & Ruth Darte.
May 4. David Ladd & Lucy Rogers.
June 1. Rufus Safford & Mary Anders.

Anno Domi 1781.

March 22. Solomon Gilman & Priſsilla Loomis.
Augt 16. Iſrael Strong & Mary Brunſon.
Sep^t 12. Ebenezer Darte and Dorcas Olcott.

1782.

Feb. 18. Daniel Root & Mary Smith.
March 21. Samuel King & Bettee Jones.
June 6. Nathaniel Kingſbury & Sarah Dorcheſter.— 13. Joſeph Loomis and Lois Pain.
July 4. Isaac Brunſon and Rachel Reed.

Anno Dom^l 1783.

Jany 9. Samuel Loomis and Jennet Walker.— 30. Joſeph Darte and Sybil Ladd.
Feb. 6. Theophilus Griſwold & Eliſabeth Talcott.
May 1. John Walker & Anna King.
Octr 16. Phinehas Chapman & Eliſabeth Johns.— 30. Daniel Carpenter & Hulda Leonard.
Nov^{br} 26. Joiiah Whitney & Mary Loomis.
Decem^{br} 11. Jonathan Skinner and Peggy Simons.

1784.

Jany 1. Elijah Loomis and Rachel Chapman.— 1. Benjamin Pickitt and Eſther Chapman.
Mar^h 18. Hoſea Brownſon and Anna Phelps.
May 13. Aaron Farmer and Sarah Darte.
June 24. Daniel Dorcheſter and Sarah Keney.
July 15. John Daniels & Eſther Dike.
Augt 3. John Stiles & Jemima Allis.
Nov^{br} 25. Daniel Fitch and Anna McRay.
Decem^{br} 9. Jonathan Fowler and Sarah Peck.— 22. John Skinner, & Cleopatria Kilbourn.

1785.

June 16. Juſtus Talcott, & Sarah Johns.
Nov^{br} 21. Leverett Millard & Lydia Skinner.
Decem^{br} 21. Stephen Dorman & Roxana Grover.

1786.

Ap[l] 13. David Carpenter & Martha Brunſon.
May 25. Oliver Hunt, & Jeruſha Simons.
June 14. Roſwell Loomis & Sarah Evens.
July 6. Jabez Brownſon and Mirilla Phelps.
Octob[r] 5. Joſeph Peck, and Anna Skinner.— 12. Elnathan Grant, & Roxy Fitch.— 19. Moſes Evens & Eliſabeth Carpenter.
Nov. 9. Jonathan Skinner & Thankful Fitch.— 30. William Pain, & Lucy Darte.

1787.

Jan[y] 31. John Olcott & Patty Talcott.
Feb[r] 7. Salma Rider, and Abigail Root.
June 7. Reuben Reynold and Abigail Lord.
Nov[r] 1. Jacob Strong & Eliſabeth Loomis.
Decem[br] 27. Guſtavus Kilbourn & Bettee Skinner.

1788.

Feb[y] 13. Benjamin Plumley & Anna Fitch.— 18. Sylby Geer & Jane M[c]Ray.
March 24. Alexander Kinny J[r] & Roxy Talcott.
May 29. Calvin M[c]Ray, & Eliſabeth Kinney.
Sep[t] 9. Levi Darte, and Oren Smith.
Nov. 27. Thaddeus Fitch & Rebeckah Webſter.
Decem 3. Samuel Howard and Rachel Talcott.

1789.

April 2. Ranfford Webſter & Tryphena Vaun.— 9. John Church Hutchins & Irena Chapman.
June 4. Allen Brunſon, & Myrinda Kenny.
July 2. Luke Loomis & Ruth Loomis.— 16. William Thrall & Orel Grant.
Nov[b] 26. Phinehas Talcott & Hannah Kellogg.
Decem 20. Dorman Drake, & Deſire Simons.

ADom[l] 1790.

Oct[r] 7. John Tucker & Ruth Benjamin.
Nov. 11. Roſwell Smith & Hannah Kingſberry.— 21. Charles Welles & Polly Hitchcock.— 23. Hab Wyles and Eunice Root.
Decem[br] 16. Abial Grant to Elſe King.—item, Lemuel King to Jane Brounſon.

1791.

Feb. 10. Solomon Queavy to Charity Simons.
March 10. George Caſe to Bethſaida King.
May 11. David Smith to Olive Talcott.
July 14. Charles Kibbe to Deborah Pain.
Oct[r] 12. John Olcott to Betty Smith.

A.D. 1792.

Feb. 2. Thomas Morehouse to Eunice Pain.— 16. Roſwell Craw to Polly Strong.
May 6. Doct[r] Elijah Fitch Reed to Hannah McLean.
Sep[t] 20. Reuben Carpenter to Miriam Darte.
Octo[r] 11. Richard Ingerſol to Auzabah Darte.— 25. Converſe Fitch to Aruma Grant.

Anno Dom[l] 1793.

Aug[t] 1. Joel Rockwell to Widow Lucy Ladd.
Oct[r] 3. Caleb Talcott to Lydia Baker.— 31. Phinehas Grover to Lovice Fuller.

[To be continued.]

GENEALOGIES IN PREPARATION.

THIS list is based upon returns made to the New England Historic Genealogical Society by the various compilers.

The families are printed in capitals, the progenitors in italics, and the compilers and their addresses in Roman.

ABBOTT.—*George of Rowley, Mass.*, by Maj. L. A. Abbott, U. S. A., Washington, D. C.

ALDEN.—*John of Duxbury, Mass.*, by Mrs. Harriet C. Fielding, 30 Winans St., East Orange, N. J.; by Mrs. Charles L. Alden, 75 Harvard St., Dorchester, Mass.; and by Henry Shaw, 200 Bradstreet Ave., Beachmont, Mass.

ALDRICH.—*George of Mendon, Mass.*, by Marcus M. Aldrich, Box 114, Mendon, Mass.

ALLEN.—*Samuel of Windsor, Conn., Ethan of Vermont fame, and fifty other Allen lines*, by Orrin P. Allen, Palmer, Mass.

ALLEN.—*Roger of New Haven, Conn.*, by George P. Allen, Box 84, North Woodbury, Conn., and Carlos P. Darling, Lawrenceville, Pa.

ALLEN.—*Timothy of Grandvill, N. Y.*, by A. E. Allen, 2034 Jackson Blvd., Chicago, Ill.

ALVORD.—*Alexander of Northampton, Mass.*, by Samuel Morgan Alvord, 252 Ashley St., Hartford, Conn.

AMES (see EAMES).—*William of Braintree, Mass.*, by Azel Ames, M.D., 24 Yale Ave., Wakefield, Mass.

ANDREWS.—*John of Wales, Maine*, by C. L. Andrews, Augusta, Me.

ANDRUSS.—*Timothy of Newark, N. J.* (?), by Geo. H. Andruss, 2437 Warring St., Berkeley, Cal.

ARMSTRONG.—*David of Delaware Co., Ohio*, by James R. Clark, Maunie, Ill.

ARNER.—*Heinrich of Butler Co., Pa.*, by G. Louis Arner, Jefferson, Ohio.

ASHLEY.—*Thomas, John, Enoch, Elkanah, Elisha, Isaac, and William, of Poultney, Vt.*, by Burton J. Ashley, 6515 Normal Ave., Chicago, Ill.

AXTELL.—*All lines*, by Cyrus R. Axtell, Grafton, Mass.

BABCOCK.—*Rev. William Smyth of Barrington, N. H.*, by Mrs. Elisabeth Mathews-Richardson, Lock Box 113, Danielson, Conn.

BACON.—*Michael of Dedham, Mass.*, by Leon Brooks Bacon, 1131 Williamson Bldg., Cleveland, Ohio; and William F. Bacon, Medford, Mass.

BAILEY.—*Richard of Middletown or Haddam, Conn.*, by T. O. Bailey, Station B, Cleveland, Ohio.

BAKER.—*Anthony of Nova Scotia* (?), by Ellis B. Baker, 448 George St., New Haven, Conn.

BANCROFT.—*Thomas of Lynnfield, Mass.*, by John M. Bancroft, Bloomfield, N. J.

BARBOUR.—*George of Medfield, Mass.*, by Edmund Dana Barbour, 610 Sears Bldg., Boston, Mass.

BARBOUR.—*John of Portland, Maine*, by Mrs. Caroline T. Barbour, 49 Neal St., Portland, Me.

BARD.—*Peter of Montpelier, France*, by William Nelson, Paterson, N. J.

BARDWELL.—*Robert of Hatfield, Mass.*, by Arthur F. Bardwell, 37 Woodside Terrace, Springfield, Mass.

BARKER.—*Ephraim of Pomfret, Conn.*, by James C. Parshall, 209 Tallman St., Syracuse, N. Y.

BARNES.—*Thomas of Middletown, Conn.*, by Trescott C. Barnes, Pleasant Valley, Conn.

BARNS.—*Dea. Benjamin of Branford, Conn.*, by Byron Barnes Horton, Sheffield, Penn.

BARRETT.—*Thomas of Chelmsford, Mass.*, by Joseph Hartwell Barrett, Loveland, Ohio; and Harold L. Barrett, 649 Centre St., Jamaica Plain, Mass.

BARRON.—*Ellis of Watertown, Mass.*, by John B. Brainerd, M.D., 18 Huntington Ave., Boston, Mass.

BARTON.—*William of Hibernia, N. J.*, by William E. Barton, 228 North Oak Park Avenue, Oak Park, Ill.

BASYE.—*All lines*, by I. Walter Basye, Bowling Green, Pike Co., Mo.

BATES.—*Jacob of Dudley, Mass.*, by Wilford J. Litchfield, Southbridge, Mass.

BAXTER.—*Baxters of America*, by Rev. Anson Titus, 10 Raymond Ave., Somerville, Mass.

BEACH.—*John of Connecticut*, by Fred H. Beach, Dover, N. J.

BEACH.—*Noah of Hanover, N. J.*, by W. Beach Plume, 16 Hawthorne St., Orange, N. J.

BEAMAN.—*Gamaliel of Dorchester, Mass.*, by Emily B. Wooden, 29 St. Clair St., Rochester, N. Y.

BEANE.—*Lewis of York, Maine*, by Charles A. Beane, 213 Commercial St., Portland, Me.

BECKWITH.—*Matthew of Lyme, Conn.*, by A. C. Beckwith, Elkhorn, Wis., and Edward Seymour Beckwith, Elkhorn, Wis.

BEEBE.—*John of Broughton, England*, by Wm. A. Eardley, 466 State St., Brooklyn, N. Y.

BEECHER.—*Isaac of New Haven, Conn.*, by Mrs. A. H. McGraw, 456 Russell Ave., Cleveland, Ohio.

BEEDE.—*Eli of Kingston, N. H.*, by George F. Beede, Fremont, N. H.

BELL.—*Alexander of London, England*, by Alexander Graham Bell, 1331 Connecticut Ave., Washington, D. C.

BENNETT.—*Arthur of Newmarket, N. H.*, by Mary Bennett Morse, 24 Park St., Haverhill, Mass.

BENNETT.—*Samuel of Providence, R. I.*, by Robert R. Bennett, 1717 T St., N. W., Washington, D. C.

BETTS.—*Azor of Annapolis Co., N. S.*, by L. N. and Mrs. J. G. Nichols, Snyder Hill, Ithaca, N. Y.

BILLING.—*Roger of Quincy, Mass.*, by C. Billings, Billingsbridge, Ontario, Canada.

BISHOP.—*John of Guilford, Conn., Thomas of Ipswich, Mass., and James of New Haven, Conn.*, by William Whitney Cone, Brandsville, Mo., and George A. Root, Topeka, Kas.

BISSELL.—*Benjamin of Hebron, Conn.*, by F. Clarence Bissell, Box 309, Willimantic, Conn.

BLAKE.—*John of Middletown, Conn.*, by George M. Blake, 403 East State St., Rockford, Ill.

BLANCHARD.—*Blanchards of America*, by Mrs. Louise (Blanchard) Bethune, 215 Franklin St., Buffalo, N. Y.

BLOSSOM.—*Thomas of Plymouth, Mass.*, by Edwin Stockin, Watertown, Mass.

BOND.—*Nicholas of Hampton, N. H.*, by Arthur Thomas Bond, 16 Central St., Boston, Mass.

BORST.—*Martines*, by George Thurston Waterman, Albany, N. Y.

BOSWORTH.—*Edward of England*, by Mrs. Mary Bosworth Clarke, 143 Napier Place, Richmond Hill, N. Y.

BOURNE.—*Richard of Lynn, Mass.*, by Henry Herbert Smythe, Falmouth, Mass.

BOWERS.—*George of Scituate, Mass.*, by Dwight E. Bowers, Box 595, New Haven, Conn.

BOWLES.—*John of Roxbury, Mass., Thomas of Maryland, and others of Virginia*, by Thomas M. Farquhar, S. W. Cor. 19th and Ellsworth Sts., Philadelphia, Pa.

BOWMAN.—*Nathaniel of Cambridge, Mass.*, by John Elliot Bowman, 79 Elm St., Quincy, Mass.

BRACKEN.—*William of Newcastle Co., Delaware*, by Dr. H. M. Bracken, 1010 Fourth St., S. E., Minneapolis, Minn.

BRACKETT.—*Samuel of Berwick, Maine*, by Charles A. Beane, Portland, Me.

BRADLEY.—*Daniel of Essex Co., Mass.*, by Mrs. Edward McClure Peters, 11 West 8th St., N. Y. City.

BRAINERD.—*Daniel of Haddam, Conn.*, by Lucy A. Brainard, 4 Atwood St., Hartford, Conn.

BRAY.—*Aaron of Newburyport, Mass.*, by Smith Adams, Milltown, Me.

BRECKENRIDGE.—*Alexander of Augusta Co., Va.*, by Wm. C. and Mrs. James M. Breckenridge, 12th and Spruce Sts., St. Louis, Mo.

BRETT.—*William of Bridgewater, Mass.*, by Mrs. Lucy G. Belcher Goodenow, 212 Riverbank Court, Cambridge, Mass.

BREWSTER.—*William of Plymouth, Mass.*, by Mrs. Lucy Hall Greenlaw, Sudbury, Mass; and Miss Emma C. Brewster Jones, 4146 Floral Ave., Norwood, Cincinnati, Ohio.

BRISTOL.—*Henry of New Haven, Conn.*, by Mrs. R. D. Bristol, 307 West 98th St., N. Y. City.

BROWN.—*Francis, Joseph, and Samuel*, by Smith Adams, Milltown, Me.

BUCKLAND.—*William of East Hartford, Conn.*, by Frank Gardner, 119 South 4th St., Sunbury, Pa.

BUCKNAM.—*William of Malden, Mass.*, by W. F. Bucknam, Ayer, Mass.

BULL.—*William of Hamptonburgh, N. Y.*, by Stevenson H. Walsh, 411 Walnut St., Philadelphia, Pa.

BURLEY, or BURLEIGH.—*Giles of Ipswich, Mass.*, by Charles Burleigh, M.D., Malden, Mass.

BURLINGAME.—*Roger of Providence, R. I.*, by Mary Stevens Ghastin, 2297 North Hermitage Ave., Chicago, Ill.

BURTON.—*John of Salem, Mass.*, by Mrs. William Roome, Butler, N. J.

BURTON.—*Samuel of Middletown, Conn.*, by George L. Burton, 87 Church St., New Haven, Conn.

BUTLER.—*Lt. John of Framingham, Mass.*, by Albert N. Butler, 43 King St., Ashtabula, Ohio.

BUTLER.—*Richard of Hartford, Conn.*, by Mrs. Laura Butler Taylor, 2935 Bismarck Ave., Louisville, Ky.

BUTTERFIELD.—*Benjamin of Chelmsford, Mass.*, by A. A. Butterfield, Jacksonville, Vt.

BYRNE.—*Daniel of Jones' Creek, Delaware*, by Dr. Wm. A. Macy, Kings Park, Long Island, N. Y.

CADLE.—*Henry of Gloucestershire, England*, by Henry Cadle, Bethany, Mo.

CADY.—*Nicholas of Groton, Mass.*, by Orrin P. Allen, Palmer, Mass.

CAPEN.—*Bernard of Dorchester, Mass.*, by Walter Nelson Capen, 17 Battery Place, N. Y. City.

CAREW.—*Thomas of Braintree and Boston, Mass.*, by James Sheldon, 69 Wall St., N. Y. City.

CARNEY.—*Mark*, by Sydney H. Carney, Jr., M.D., 14 West 130th St., N. Y. City.

CARTER.—*Rev. Thomas of Woburn, Mass.*, by Prof. Howard Williston Carter, Norfolk, Conn.

CARY.—*Jeremiah of Winstead, Conn.*, by Mrs. James W. Cary, 22 Magazine St., Cambridge, Mass.

CARY.—*John of Bridgewater, Mass.*, by Dr. Murray Edward Poole, Ithaca, N. Y.; and Mrs. Lucy G. Belcher Goodenow, 212 Riverbank Court, Cambridge, Mass.

CASE.—*All lines in U. S. prior to 1800*, by Dr. Erastus E. Case, 902 Main St., Hartford, Conn.

CASE.—*John of Simsbury, Conn.*, by Willard E. Case, Auburn, N. Y.; and C. V. Case, Lock Box 883, Ashtabula, Ohio.

CASTOR.—*John George of Oxford Township, Phila. Co., Pa.*, by Rev. William Reese Scott, Christ Church Rectory, Media, near Phila., Pa.; and Richard A. Martin, 145 West 82 St., N. Y. City.

CATE.—*James of Portsmouth, N. H.*, by M. Ray Sanborn, Yale University Library, New Haven, Conn.

CAUFFMAN.—*Isaac*, by Harry Shelmire Hopper, 400 Chestnut St., Philadelphia, Pa.

CHACE (see CHASE).—*Holder of East Claridon, Ohio*, by C. V. Case, Lock Box 883, Ashtabula, Ohio.

CHAMBERLAIN.—*Edmund of Woodstock, Conn.*, by Geo. W. Chamberlain, 1 Summer St., Weymouth, Mass. Also at work on the following: *Henry of Hull, Mass.; Jacob of Revere, Mass.; John of Bloomsburg, Pa.; Richard of Sudbury, Mass.; Robert of Concord, Penn.; Thomas of Chelmsford, Mass.; Thomas of Maryland; William of Billerica, Mass.; William of St. Peter's Parish, Va.*

CHANDLER.—*Roger of Concord, Mass.*, by Charles H. Chandler, Ripon, Wis.

CHAPMAN.—*Robert, Jr., of Saybrook, Conn.*, by Rev. William Durant, Saratoga Springs, N. Y.

CHASE (see CHACE).—*William of Yarmouth, Mass.*, by William A. Eardeley, 466 State St., Brooklyn, N. Y.

CHATFIELD.—*George of Killingworth, Conn.*, by Edward C. Chatfield, 613 Fulton St., Minneapolis, Minn.

CHITTERBUCK.—*Of Berkeley and King Stanley, Gloucestershire, England*, by W. P. W. Phillimore, 124 Chancery Lane, London, W. C., England.

CLARK.—*Elijah of Center Village, Ohio*, by James R. Clark, Maunie, Ill.

Clark.—*Richard of Exeter, N. H.*, by Guy Scoby Rix, Concord, N. H.

Claypoole.—*Norton of Kent Co., Delaware*, by Edward A. Claypool, 309 Bush Temple, Chicago, Ill.

Clement.—*Jan of Schenectady, or New Utrecht, or Flatbush, N. Y.*, by Lewis H. Clement, 2461 Glenwood Ave., Toledo, Ohio.

Cobb.—*David of Boston, Mass.*, by Rev. Edward Porter Little, 310 N. 6th St., Hannibal, Mo.

Cobb.—*John of Taunton, Mass., or Barrington, R. I.*, by Mrs. Mary L. Alden, Troy, N. Y.

Coffee.—*James of Gloucester Co., N. J.*, by Harry Shelmire Hopper, 400 Chestnut St., Philadelphia, Pa.

Coggeshall.—*All lines*, by Thelwell Coggeshall, Girard College, Philadelphia, Pa.

Colby.—*Zaccheus of Amesbury, Mass.*, by Mrs. Florence Danforth Stamp, Adams Basin, Monroe Co., N. Y.

Cole.—*James of Plymouth, Mass.*, by Ernest B. Cole, 1922 Broadway, Indianapolis, Ind.

Coles.—*Robert of Warwick, R. I.* (?), by H. R. R. Coles, 30 Broad St., N. Y. City.

Colesworthy.—*Gilbert of Boston, Mass.*, by Wm. G. Colesworthy, 66 Cornhill, Boston, Mass.

Collins.—*Tillinghast of Philadelphia, Pa., and William of Gloucester, N. J.*, by Harry Shelmire Hopper, 400 Chestnut St., Philadelphia, Pa.

Colver.—*Edward of Groton, Conn.*, by Frederic L. Colver, 143 Fifth Ave., N. Y.

Comstock.—*Samuel of Providence, R. I.*, by G. S. Comstock, Mechanicsburg, Pa.

Congdon.—*Benjamin of Kings Town, R. I.*, by G. E. Congdon, Waterman, Ill.

Cony.—*Nathaniel of Stoughton(?), Mass.*, by Mrs. Lucy G. Belcher Goodenow, 212 Riverbank Court, Cambridge, Mass.

Cook.—*Peter of Philadelphia, Pa.*, by Allen M. Cook, 96 Boush St., Norfolk, Va.; and Albert Cook Myers, Kennett Square, Chester Co., Pa.

Coombs.—*Allister of New Meadow, Brunswick, Me.; Anthony of Rochester, Mass.; John of Bellingham, Mass.; Jonathan of East Woodstock, Vt.; William of Warren, Mass.; Moses Newell of Newark, N. J.; Hiram M. of Thetford, Vt.; Jonathan of Islesboro', Me.; also families in Virginia and Kentucky*, by Rev. Chas. N. Sinnett, Box 205, Edmore, N. D.

Cosgrove.—*William of Hanover township, Morris Co., N. J.*, by L. N. and Mrs. J. G. Nichols, Snyder Hill, Ithaca, N. Y.

Cotton.—*William of Portsmouth, N. H.*, by Frank E. Cotton, 48 Glen St., Malden, Mass.

Cowen.—*John of Scituate, Mass.*, by Wilford J. Litchfield, Southbridge, Mass.

Cram.—*John of Hampton Falls, N. H.*, by John G. Cram, 105 Charles St., Boston, Mass.

Cronkhite.—*Henry of Litchfield, Mich.*, by Mrs. W. L. Proctor, 14 Caroline St., Ogdensburg, N. Y.

Croxall.—*Richard of Maryland*, by Mrs. Morris L. Croxall, 1346 Princeton St., N. W., Washington, D. C.

Cudworth.—*James of England*, by Wilford J. Litchfield, Southbridge, Mass.

CUSHING.—*Matthew of Hingham, Mass.*, by Henry Kirke Cushing, 786 Prospect St., Cleveland, Ohio; and James S. Cushing, 68 St. Matthew St., Montreal, Canada.

DAM.—*John of Dover, N. H.*, by Albert H. Lamson, Elkins, N. H.

DAMON.—*John of Scituate, Mass.*, by Wilford J. Litchfield, Southbridge, Mass.

DARLING.—*Dennis of Mendon, Mass.*, by Carlos P. Darling, Lawrenceville, Tioga Co., Pa.

DAVIS.—*Dolor of Barnstable, Mass.*, by Henry Herbert Smythe, Falmouth, Mass.

DAWSON.—*Robert of Connecticut*, by Mary Stevens Ghastin, 2297 North Hermitage Ave., Chicago, Ill.

DAY.—*Anthony of Gloucester, Mass.*, by Fred N. Day, Auburndale, Mass.

DAY.—*Robert of Hartford. Conn.*, by Wilson M. Day, 268 Huron St., Cleveland, Ohio; and Carlos P. Darling, Lawrenceville, Tioga Co., Pa.

DEAN.—*All lines*, by William Abbatt, 281 Fourth Ave., N. Y.

DEARBORN.—*Godfrey of Hampton, N. H.*, by Charles L. Dearborn, Muskegon, Mich.

DEMILL, OR DEMILT.—*Anthony of New York City*, by Wm. A. Eardeley, 466 State St., Brooklyn, N. Y.

DENTON.—*Of Yorkshire, England*, by Eugene F. McPike, 1 Park Row Room 606, Chicago, Ill.

DEWEY.—*All families of Westfield, Mass.*, by Louis M. Dewey, 279 Elm St., Westfield, Mass.

DEXTER.—*Thomas of Boston, Mass.*, by William A. Warden, Worcester, Mass.; and Robert L. Dexter, E. Mattapoisett, Mass.

DILLAWAY.—*All lines, before 1800*, by Henry Ernest Woods, 18 Somerset St., Boston, Mass.

DIMMOCK.—*Thomas of Barnstable, Mass.*, by George Dimmock, Springfield, Mass.; and Henry Herbert Smythe, Falmouth, Mass.

DOANE.—*John of Eastham, Mass.*, by Alfred A. Doane, 131 I St., So. Boston, Mass.

DOTY.—*Edward of Plymouth, Mass.*, by Carlos P. Darling, Lawrenceville, Tioga Co., Pa.

DOW.—*Henry of Hampton, N. H.*, by Herbert W. Dow, 136 Congress St., Boston, Mass.

DOWNE.—*Downes of America*, by H. Watson Downe, 55 Liberty St., N. Y. City.

DOWNES.—*Thomas of Dover, N. H.*, by William E. D. Downes, 71 Pearl St., Boston, Mass.

DRAKE.—*John of Windsor, Conn.*, by Louis Stoughton Drake, Auburndale, Mass.

DUMONT.—*Wallerand of Kingston, N. Y.*, by Eugene F. McPike, 1 Park Row, Room 606, Chiacgo, Ill.

DUNGAN.—*Thomas of Cold Spring, Bucks Co., Pa.*, by Warren S. Dungan, Chariton, Iowa.

DUNGAN.—*William of London, England*, by Howard O. Folker, Room 515, Reading Terminal, Philadelphia, Pa.

DUNHAM.—*Dea. John of Plymouth, Mass.*, by Prof. Isaac W. Dunham, 347 Summit Ave., Schenectady, N. Y.

DUNN.—*Hugh of Piscataway, N. J.*, by Oliver B. Leonard, 915 Madison Ave., Plainfield, N. J.

DUNNING.—*Andrew of Brunswick, Maine*, by Rev. Everett S. Stackpole, Bradford, Mass.

DURANT.—*George of Middletown, Conn., and John of Cambridge, Mass.*, by Rev. William Durant, Saratoga Springs, N. Y.

DURFEE.—*Thomas of Portsmouth, R. I.*, by Wm. F. Reed, 915 F St., N. E., Washington, D. C.

DURHAM.—*John of Perryville, Ky.*, by Joseph Pinckney Durham, 1131 West 30th St., Indianapolis, Ind.

DUTTON.—*John*, by William Tracy Eustis, 19 Pearl St., Boston, Mass.

DYER.—*William of Dorchester, Mass.*, by Mrs. Edward McClure Peters, 11 West 8th St., N. Y. City.

DYER.—*William of Truro, Mass.*, by Isaac W. Dyer, 36 Exchange St., Portland, Maine.

EAMES (see AMES).—*Robert of Boxford and Andover, Mass.*, by S. P. Sharples, 26 Broad St., Boston, Mass.

EAMES.—*Thomas of Dedham, Robert of Woburn, and Robert of Boxford, Mass.*, by Lucia Eames Blount, The Oaks, Georgetown Heights, Washington, D. C.

EARLL.—*Daniel of Marcellus (now Skaneateles), Onondaga Co. N. Y.*, by Edward A. Claypool, 309 Bush Temple, Chicago, Ill.

EASTMAN.—*All lines*, by Guy Scoby Rix, Concord, N. H.

EATON.—*All lines*, by Rev. A. W. H. Eaton, 20 East Fiftieth St., N. Y. City.

EDDY.—*Nathan of Pittsfield, Vt.*, by Byron Barnes Horton, Sheffield, Pa.

EGGLESTON.—*Bagot of Windsor, Conn.*, by W. E. Hagans, Elmhurst, Ill.

ELIOT.—*John of Roxbury, Mass.*, by Miss Mary C. Eliot, Clinton, Conn.

ELLIOT.—*Ebenezer of Newton, Mass.*, by John Elliot Bowman, 79 Elm St., Quincy, Mass.

ELLIS.—*John of Dedham, Mass.*, by Walter Fred Ellis, 1025 Fidelity Bldg., Buffalo, N. Y.

EMERSON.—*Michael of Haverhill, Mass.*, by Charles Burleigh, M.D., Malden, Mass.

EUSTIS.—*William*, by William Tracy Eustis, 19 Pearl St., Boston, Mass.

FAIRCHILD.—*Thomas of Stratford, Conn.*, by G. W. Fairchild, Oneonta, N. Y.

FANCHER.—*William of Harlem, Delaware Co., Ohio*, by James R. Clark, Maunie, Ill.

FANCHER, FANSHER, FANSHIER.—*All lines in America*, by Winfield Scott Potter, 305 North Front St., Columbus, Ohio.

FARRINGTON.—*Edmund of Lynn, Mass.*, by B. A. Leonard, De Pere, Wis.

FELLOWS.—*William of Ipswich, Mass.*, by G. M. Fellows, 208 West River St., Hyde Park, Mass.

FERNALD (see FIRNALD).—*Dr. Renald of Portsmouth, N. H.*, by Prof. Henry Torsey Fernald, Amherst, Mass.; and Henry W. Fernald, M. O. Division, Post Office, Boston, Mass.

FERRIS.—*Samuel of Groton, Mass.*, by Dr. Wm. Austin Macy, Kings Park, Long Island, N. Y.

FERRY.—*Charles of Springfield, Mass.*, by Aaron Ferry Randall, 350 Tremont Bldg., Boston, Mass.

FETTER.—*Jacob of Carlisle, Pa.*, by Harry Shelmire Hopper, 400 Chestnut St., Philadelphia, Pa.

FINNEMORE.—*John of Wicklow, Ireland*, by W. P. W. Phillimore, 124 Chancery Lane, London, England.

FIRNALD (see FERNALD).—*Jonathan Poor of Farmington, N. H.*, by Charles Augustus Fernald, 1483 Washington St., Boston, Mass.

FISH.—*Nathan*, by Henry Herbert Smythe, Falmouth, Mass.
FISHER.—*Samuel of Londonderry, N. H.*, by William P. Fisher, Andover, Mass.
FITZ-ALAN.—*Walter of Scotland*, by Geo. Washington Stuart, Box 364, Ayer, Mass.
FLANDERS.—*All lines*, by Fred W. Lamb, 452 Merrimack St., Manchester, N. H.
FLOWER.—*Tamrock of Hartford, Conn.*, by Mrs. M. A. Smith, 688 N. Park Ave., Chicago, Ill.
FOGG.—*Samuel of Hampton, N. H.*, by Mrs. Adna James Fogg, 601 Tremont Bldg., Boston, Mass.
FOLWELL.—*Nathan of Mansfield township, Burlington Co., N. J.*, by Roe Reisinger, Franklin, Penn.
FORD.—*Andrew of Hingham, Mass.*, by Miss Caroline Ford Lowery, 1604 South Grand Ave., St. Louis, Mo.
FOSKETT.—*All lines*, by Fred W. Lamb, 452 Merrimack St.. Manchester, N. H.
FOUNTAIN.—*Aaron of Conn., and Anthony of Staten Island, N. Y.*, by Wm. A. Eardeley, 466 State St., Brooklyn, N. Y.
FRENCH.—*Joseph of Adams Basin, Monroe Co., N. Y.*, by Mrs. Florence Danforth Stamp, Adams Basin, N. Y.
FRENCH.—*William of Billerica, Mass.*, by Miss Elizabeth French, 108 West 45th St., N. Y. City; and J. M. French, M.D., Milford, Mass.
FULLER.—*Robert of Salem and Rehoboth, Mass.*, by Newton Fuller, 16 Jay St., New London, Conn.
FULLER.—*Edward of Plymouth, Mass., Dr. Samuel, and Capt. Matthew*, by Homer W. Brainard, 88 Kenyon St., Hartford, Conn.
FULLER.—*Lt. Thomas of Dedham, Mass.*, by Francis H. Fuller, 18 Somerset St., Boston, Mass.
FULLERTON.—*John of Boston, Mass.*, by Dr. Murray Edward Poole, Ithaca, N. Y.
FURBUSH, or FURBISH.—*William of Kittery, Me.*, by F. B. Furbish, 25 Church St., Cambridge, Mass.
GAINES.—*Henry, Thomas, and Samuel of Lynn, Mass.*, by N. S. Hopkins, Williamsville, N. Y.
GALLUP.—*John of Boston, Mass., and New London, Conn.*, by Mary Stevens Ghastin, 2297 North Hermitage Ave., Chicago, Ill.
GARDNER.—*John of Newark, N. J.*, by Frank Gardner, 119 South St., Sunbury, Pa.
GATES.—*Stephen*, by Guy Scoby Rix, Concord, N. H.
GAYLORD.—*Isaac Thomas of Stowe, Ohio*, by T. O. Bailey, Cleveland, Ohio.
GERRITSON.—*Wolphert of Albany, N. Y.*, by Marcus N. Horton, 88 Essex Ave., Bloomfield, N. J.
GIBSON.—*John of Virginia*, by Collins B. Gibson, Box 244, Chicago, Ill.
GIFFORD.—*William of Sandwich, Mass.*, by Harry E. Gifford, 30 N. Water St., New Bedford, Mass.; and Henry Herbert Smythe, Falmouth, Mass.
GOODALE, or GOODELLE.—*Robert of Salem, Mass.*, by Lucy Hall Greenlaw, Sudbury, Mass.; and Rev. Isaac Goodell, 53 Stage St., Haverhill, Mass.
GOODSPEED.—*Roger of Barnstable, Mass.*, by Weston A. Goodspeed, Box 1122, Madison, Wis.
GOODWILL.—*Thomas*, by William Tracy Eustis, 19 Pearl St., Boston, Mass.

GOOKIN.—*Arnold of Co. Kent, England*, by Frederick William Gookin, 20 Walton Place, Chicago, Ill.
GORE.—*John of Roxbury, Mass.*, by Theodore W. Gore, Auburndale, Mass.
GOULD.—*Thomas of Salem, Mass.*, by Guy Scoby Rix, Concord, N. H.
GOWDY.—*All lines*, by Clarence E. Peirce, Box 981, Springfield, Mass.
GOWING.—*Robert of Lynnfield, Mass.*, by Robert H. Gowing, Wilmington, Mass.
GRAVES.—*Samuel of Lynn, Mass., Thomas of Charlestown, Mass., John of Concord, Mass., George of Hartford, Conn., Thomas of James City Co., Va., William of Dover, N. H.*, by John C. Graves, Lancaster, N. Y.
GREENLAW.—*All lines*, by William Prescott Greenlaw, 18 Somerset St., Boston, Mass.
GRIDLEY.—*Thomas of Hartford, Conn.*, by Eleanor Gridley, Orland, Ill.
GRIGGS.—*Thomas of Roxbury, Mass.*, by John W. Saxe, 16 State St., Boston, Mass.
GROSVENOR.—*John of Roxbury, Mass.*, by Mrs. H. M. Crissey, 1425 Massachusetts Ave., Washington, D. C.
GUENON, GENUNG, etc.—*Jean of Flushing, L. I.*, by Mrs. Josephine Genung Nichols, Snyder Hill, Ithaca, N. Y.
GUEST.—*Henry of New Brunswick, N. J.*, by Eugene F. McPike, 1 Park Row, Chicago, Ill.

[To be continued.]

PROCEEDINGS OF THE NEW ENGLAND HISTORIC GENEALOGICAL SOCIETY.

By GEO. A. GORDON, A.M., Recording Secretary.

Boston, Massachusetts, 4 October, 1905. The New England Historic Genealogical Society held a stated meeting this afternoon at half-past two o'clock, in Marshall P. Wilder hall, 18 Somerset street, the President, Hon. James Phinney Baxter, in the chair.

Charles Cowley, LL.D., of Lowell, being introduced, read a paper on *Boston in the Civil War, 1860-65, from a Naval View-Point*, which exhibited extensive research and the presentation of historical events not hitherto subjects of remark. It was a careful narration of deep interest to the audience, and was received with applause. After the reading, it was voted that Mr. Cowley be thanked for his effort, and a copy be requested for the archives of the Society.

The executive officers, severally, presented reports, which were received, read, accepted, and ordered on file.

Five new resident members and one corresponding member were elected.

The deaths of the late Treasurer, Benjamin Barstow Torrey, and Hon. James Madison Barker, LL.D., were announced, and committees appointed to prepare minutes expressive of the respect of the Society for their memory.

The Treasurer was empowered to release a mortgage on certain Kansas property, and to receive the legacy left to the Society by the late Robert Charles Winthrop, Jr., A.M., of Boston.

The meeting then dissolved.

1 November. A stated meeting was held to-day at the usual time and place, with the President in the chair. Under suspension of the rules, it was voted to proceed immediately to the election of a Nominating Committee, and tellers were appointed and the polls opened.

The operation of the rules being resumed, the chair introduced William Carver Bates, of Newton, who delivered, *ex tempore*, an address upon *Personal Experiences in Confederate Prisons, 1861-2*, to the acceptance of an interested audience. A vote of thanks was tendered the speaker.

On motion, it was

Voted, That the New England Historic Genealogical Society desires to express its approval of the work heretofore accomplished by the Boston Cemetery Department in publishing illustrated histories of certain of the more ancient burying-grounds of Boston; and, also, desires to express the hope that the Department will continue its work, until the histories of all such burying-places shall have been published.

The polls were closed, the vote canvassed and report made, which was read, accepted, and ordered on file. The chair then proclaimed the election of William Sumner Appleton of Boston, William Carver Bates of Newton, George Madison Bodge of West Roxbury, David Henry Brown of Medford, and Albert Alonzo Folsom of Brookline, as the Nominating Committee for 1905.

The executive reports were then made, and ordered on file.

William Carver Bates, of the committee to submit a minute *in memoriam* Benjamin Barstow Torrey, of Hanover, deceased, presented the following tribute, which was received, read, accepted, and ordered on file and to be spread upon the record of this meeting, viz:

Whereas, Death has removed from us one who was for many years a firm friend, an active member, and a trusted officer of this Society,

Therefore, We, the members of the New England Historic Genealogical Society, do hereby place upon record our deep sense of loss by the death of our associate, Benjamin Barstow Torrey, and our thankful remembrance and sincere appreciation of his work while with us.

Born of sturdy New England stock, he inherited those qualities of mind and heart which such an ancestry often transmits to its descendants. Beginning an active life at an early age, he remained a lifetime in the service of a great corporation and for nearly forty years was its trusted and faithful treasurer, serving it with ability and discretion, adding during ten years of that service the duties of the treasurership of a kindred corporation. Elected treasurer of this Society in 1871, succeeding the late William Blanchard Towne, he brought to its lesser duties those traits of integrity and honesty of purpose which characterized his life in broader fields; and for thirty-three years, a longer service than has been borne by any other treasurer of the Society, he was an efficient adviser and conservator in financial matters. As a member of the Council, his genial temper, good-fellowship, and sound judgment gave him the respect and friendship of his associates.

John Noble, LL.D., of Boston, of the committee to submit a minute *in memoriam* James Madison Barker, of Pittsfield, deceased, presented the following tribute, which was received, read, accepted, and ordered on file and to be spread upon the record of this meeting, viz:

James Madison Barker died in Boston the third day of October, 1905.

The New England Historic Genealogical Society places on record its sense of the great loss it has sustained in the death of a most honored and valued member. It records its recognition of a public career distinguished and remarkable in many fields of service and action.

He has been a legislator of broad and liberal views, of absolute independence, and of wisdom and foresight. He was a man of affairs, of sound judgment, sagacity and business capacity, proved in the many offices of trust and honor held by him through his life. A loyal son of Williams College, he was for many years a member of its Board of Trustees.

He was most widely known, perhaps, through his judicial service,—for nine years on the Bench of the Superior Court, under the appointment of Governor Long, in 1882, and on the Bench of the Supreme Judicial Court, under the appointment of Governor Russell, from June 18th, 1891, till the time of his death. He had, in a high degree, the essential qualities of a judge,—wide and accurate knowledge of existing law, legal learning and a grip of legal principles,—the legal instinct, acute perception, unusual power of analysis, the faculty of sifting and weighing evidence, the sure grasp of the controlling elements of a case, painstaking industry, scrupulous concientiousness, patience, dignified courtesy, and the aim to do exact justice always and everywhere.

As a citizen he was public spirited, alive to the highest duties of citizenship, and ready to do his full share therein. He was a man of fine culture and intellectual endowment, of great charm of manner and bearing, a lover of outdoor life with a keen enjoyment of all its manly sports, genial and cordial, a most attractive and welcome companion. He was a loyal friend, full of broad and tender sympathies, of generous kindness, hearty feeling, always faithful and true. He was a man in all the relations of life, of absolute integrity, of the highest sense of honor, and of stainless character.

Twenty new members were elected.

The proposed amendments to the By-laws, as reported by a committee at the special meeting in May, were given consideration and passage, viz:

That article 1, chapter II, of the By-Laws, be amended so that line numbered seven in the present edition shall read:—A majority of votes shall elect, but ten affirmative votes shall be required.

That article 1, chapter III, of the By-Laws, be amended so that the fourteenth line of the present edition shall read:—Ten members shall constitute a quorum for the election of members, and twenty members for all other purposes.

No further business being presented, the meeting dissolved.

NOTES AND QUERIES.

NOTES.

ODELL.—William Odell, the founder of an American family of that name, is traced as early as 1639 at Concord, Mass., where his children James (died 1641) and Rebecca were born. He may have been the brother of Ursula Wodell (also written Odle), who married Christopher Woolly (Wollie) at Concord in 1646.

William Odell died at Fairfield, Conn., in 1676; his will proved there June 6th of that year mentions, among others, his sons William and John Odell and daughter Rebecca Moorehouse, and disposes of lands in Concord and Fairfield.

William Odell's English ancestry seems likely to be ascertained from the following interesting clue:

Cranfield, Bedfordshire, England, is a small parish about eight miles from the village of Odell in the same county. The Cranfield Church Register records nearly seventy entries of Odell baptisms, marriages and burials, between the years 1602 and 1625, the name being variously written Wodell, Odell, Odle, Woddell, Woddle, etc. (See REGISTER, vol. 45, pages 7-8.) Among these entries are the following:—

1602, Feb. 24, William, son of William Wodell of Warleyend, baptized.

1615, July 22, William Odle of Worley, buried.

Perhaps this is the record of the baptism of William Odell who came to New England, and of the burial of his father.

The name "Warleyend" is doubtless that of a hamlet about one mile from Cranfield, which appears on an old map of Bedfordshire as "Wallerd or Wall End."

In Cranfield Parish there was, in 1632, a district, or possibly an estate, known as "Virginia." Now it is a very significant and suggestive fact, as disclosed by the local New England records, that at Concord, Mass., the original road, cut through the woods by the first settlers, has been called since 1650 "the Virginia Road," and the district through which it runs, "Virginy." It is also a fact that, at Concord, the plain just at the end of Virginia was described as "Cranefield" in the Town Records as early as 1648, and has so continued to be described almost to the present day. It would certainly seem that these names, "Virginia" and "Cranefield," were given by the early settlers of Concord in memory of their English home.

It should also be borne in mind that the first minister of Concord, the Rev. Peter Bulkeley, who came to New England in 1635, was from Odell Parish, Bedfordshire, where he had been rector for many years.

What has been related herein seems to furnish a good foundation for further research. RUFUS KING.

Yonkers, New York.

WASHINGTON.—The following extract from a letter of the Rev. R. T. Love, M.A., Rector of Purleigh, Maldon, co. Essex, England, to the Editor, will be of interest in connection with Mr. Waters's gleanings concerning the Washington family. The "printed circulars" refer to a plan for restoring the tower of Purleigh Church, an appeal in behalf of which will be found elsewhere in this issue.

"I enclose some printed circulars showing the object which I have in view—viz., a memorial to the connection between George Washington and Purleigh, as the last link with the old country. The American flag will be hung out every year on his birthday when the tower is repaired.

We have found the entry of Lawrence Washington's burial at Maldon. In the Dr. Plume's Library at that place, which is situated on the site of the old church of St. Peter's, may be seen a certified copy of the Parish Registers. The entry is as follows—amongst the burials:

'Mr Lawrence Washington 21 January 1653.'

Now this date fits in with Mr. Waters's theory, which necessitates the death of the father before 1655, when John Washington was of age and proved a will.

In a letter to 'The Times,' immediately before our Mansion House meeting, it was said that there was no proof of the marriage of the rector of Purleigh. But as I find that he resigned his fellowship at Brasenose 1632–3, about the same time as that in which he became rector of Purleigh, there appears a very strong *primâ facie* evidence of his marriage. A man does not resign £2-300 a year, the value of a fellowship, when he has no private means, except on compulsion. Mr. Lawrence Washington had little or no private means (his debt at Oxford is in evidence), and the only compulsion which could be applied to him to compel his resignation would be a marriage. Fellows did not (until the late new regulation) resign their fellowships on becoming beneficed clergymen, unless the benefice was a college living. Fellowships were held on life tenure, whether the fellows did work for it or not. But when they married, they lost their fellowships. It is stated that Lawrence Washington lost his fellowship 1632–3, therefore he married. He then received at about the same time the living of Purleigh on presentation of Mrs. Jane Horsmanden, widow; not a college living.

These two items—his burial at Maldon, and the fact that his marriage only would necessitate his resignation of his fellowship—I have not seen noted."

ROBY.—In the Public Library at Wayland, Mass., in a Journal of Dr. Ebenezer Roby during a visit to England and Holland in 1726, is the following genealogical record from a Roby family Bible which is briefly mentioned by Savage (vol. 3, page 548).

Dr. Roby was born in Boston, Mass., 20 Sept., 1701, graduated at Harvard College in 1719, settled in Sudbury, Mass., in 1725, and died in Sudbury, 4 Sept., 1772.

Castle Dunnington is in the East Riding of Yorkshire, England.

"A Memorandum of the Defcent of Father Roby's Family from ye Year 1586—as it was taken out of Uncle Thomas Roby's Bible—at Castle Duningtou, viz.

Mary Coxon Daughter of John Coxon of Caftle Dunington was born ye 20th of April 1586—wo was the Owner of the Bible.

Thomas Roby Marryed Mary Coxon September 29th 1606, had Ifsue viz.

Robert Roby born ye 11 July 1607. had Ifsue Thos: & Frances.

Mary Roby Born ye 4th May 1610 Maryed to Mr I. Burroughs.

Thom: Roby born 27 Sept 1611. had Ifsue Thos: Wm. & Mary.

John Roby born 12 May 1613 Ifsue Henry & 3 Daughters. One Maryed Mr Sherwin, ye other, Walker.

Henry Roby born 12 Febr 1618. wo went & lived in NEngd.

Edward Roby born 16 Sept 1620. had a Liberal Education & died a Bachelir

Saml Roby born 12 Febr 1628 went to New England.

Befides the sd Mary Coxon, had by ye Sd Thos Roby 8 other Children, dying very Young—

Thoms Roby our Grandfather was born Sept. 27th 1611. and Maryed the 26 of Auguft To Hellin Cherebough had Ifsue viz—

Mary Roby born the 3d July 1641. Maryed to Wm Riddiard of Bakewel, Derbyfs.

Thoms. Roby born 22d Septembr: 1645—was Maryed ye 8 Octobr 1676—To Ann Abbott Daughter of Luke Abbott of Hemington had Ifsue viz.

Thom^s^. Roby Born Octob: 31. 1677. Ifsue 2 Sons & 4 Daughters
Willm Roby Born July 26, 1680 Ifsue a Daughter it Died Jany 18. 1681.
Another Son born & Died March 11, 1683.
Ann Roby born Decem: 1^t^ 1685. Maryed to ye Revd Mr Wm Walton ye Diffenting Minifter of Donington. Ifsue 3 Sons & 5 Daughters Living.
William Roby my honour^d^. Father—born 26 April 1648—Went into NEngland Maryed Eliz^a^. Greenough Daughter of William & Elizabeth Greenough. Ifsue 15 Children. 7 of whom are Living. viz 4 Sons & 3 Daughters."

ALICE L. WESTGATE.

THAYER.—The following inscription from a gravestone in the Hancock Cemetery at Quincy, Mass., seems to have been omitted by Mr. William S. Pattee in his "History of Old Braintree and Quincy," 1878:

HERE LYES Y^e^ BODY | OF RICHARD THAYER senior | AGED 71 YEARS | DEC^d^ AUGUST Y^e^ | 27 1695.

(Footstone) R T

EDW. H. WHORF.

Boston, Mass.

[This is the Richard,[2] mentioned in my communication to the REGISTER (*ante*, vol. 37, page 84) in 1883, after visiting Thornbury, Gloucestershire, England, who appears in the registers of St. Mary's Church in that town as "Richard Tayer, baptized 10 February 1624[5]."

His father, Richard[1] Tayer (Thayer), who came to New England in 1641 with eight children—Richard, Sarah, Jael, Deborah, Zachariah, Hester, Nathaniel, and Cornelius—and settled at Braintree, Mass., was baptized at Thornbury, 5 April, 1601, and married there, 5 April, 1624, Dorothy Mortimore, who was buried at Thornbury, 17 January, 1640[1], and was the mother of his children above named.

There has been much confusion as to the dates of death of the various Richard Thayers. Richard[1] the emigrant was dead before 20th 2d mo. 1668, as shown in a deed (Suffolk Co. Deeds, V, 446) of his son Richard,[2] who died 27 August, 1695, and whose gravestone record Mr. Whorf has copied.

Richard[3] (Richard,[2] Richard[1]) died 4 December, 1705 (Braintree records); and his wife Rebecca (Micall) died 28 January, 1732, aged 73 years 8 days (gravestone).

Richard[4] Thayer (Richard,[3] Richard,[2] Richard[1]) died in 1774 (will probated 27 May, 1774, Suffolk Co.).

Richard,[4] son of Cornelius[3] and Abigail (Hayden), died 11 September, 1729, in his 33d year (gravestone).

Abstracts from the church registers of Thornbury, Gloucestershire, relating to the Tayer (Thayer) family, to be communicated by Mr. Faxon and Mr. Whorf, will appear soon in the REGISTER. EDITOR.]

BLACHLEY (*ante*, vol. 58, page 357).—The date of the deed of Thomas Blachley to William Maltby was 16 April, 1673, *not* 1653. William Maltby was born about 1645. (See "Maltby-Morehouse Family," page 7.) D. L. M.

New Haven, Conn.

A CORRECTION.—In the REGISTER, vol. 28, page 282, in tracing John Chamberlain the Roxbury church sexton of 1659, there mentioned, I find that line fifteen, commencing with: "It had a bell in 1658," etc., refers to the Rev. John Eliot's church in Roxbury. The First Church at Newton was not organized until 1664. The quotations in this paragraph are published in Ellis's History of Roxbury (1848), pages 23–24, and were taken originally from the town records of Roxbury, and without doubt refer to the First Church of Roxbury.

Weymouth, Mass. GEO. W. CHAMBERLAIN.

THE DEANE FAMILY (*ante*, vol. 3, page 386).—The will of Isaac[2] Dean (*John*[1]), of Taunton, names sons Nathaniel and Jonathan, and daughters Alice King, Abigail Terrey, Hannah Hodges, Mehetabel Dean, Abiah Dean, and Deborah Dean (Bristol Co. Probate, vol. 2, p. 281); and in a deed, dated 1726, of "Hannah Dean Widow Relict of Isaac Dean late of Taunton" and the "heirs," the heirs were John King and Alice King his wife of Taunton, Thomas Terrey and Abigail Terrey his wife of Freetown, Nathaniel Hodges and Hannah

Hodges his wife, William Stone and Mehitable Stone his wife of Norton, Benjamin Hodges and Abiah Hodges his wife, and Deborah Dean of Taunton (Bristol Co. Deeds, vol. 21, p. 175). * * *

SANFORD.—The following data is copied from the family Bible of Mr. Ellwood T. Sanford and the Dartmouth Records:

George Sanford born 22 2nd mo. 1736 } married 5 13. 1762
Rachel Gifford born 25 10th mo. 1744 }

Issue:

Gideon born 16 6. 1763; deceased 19 10. 1787 aged 24. 4. 2
Peleg born 10. 1. 1766; deceased 9 6 mo 1804 aged 38. 5
Alice born 21- 3 1771
Caleb born 25. 12. 1780; deceased March 26. 1834 aged 54. 3
Alice Ricketson died 26 2nd mo. 1826 aged 54. 11 & 5 days
Charles F. Ricketson died 1847 aged 36

George Sanford son of William Sanford Jr. & Rebeckah born 1735-6.

62 Buckingham St., Cambridge, Mass. GRACE WILLIAMSON EDES.

STIMPSON-FROTHINGHAM.—The article on the Stimpson family, *ante*, vol. 59, p. 248, errs in giving the date Dec. 25, 1776, as the date on the gravestone at Woburn of the death of Thomas Frothingham of Charlestown. The inscription reads: Jan. 1, 1776. (*Woburn Epitaphs*, p. 48.) Wyman's *Charlestown*, p. 392, says of Thomas Frothingham: "d. Dec. 25, 1775 (g. s. at Woburn has 1776)"; but the lack of sufficient words to complete the sense is a common fault of the style of literary composition adopted by Wyman in his monumental work. The latter part of the sentence would have been correct had it read: "(g. s. at Woburn has *Jan. 1*, 1776)."

On the other hand, the extract from Wyman's letter of Oct. 18, 1873, printed as a note to the epitaph of Thomas Frothingham, *Woburn Epitaphs*, p. 48, is full of errors when compared with Wyman's *Charlestown*, pp. 391, 392.

Woburn, Mass. WILLIAM R. CUTTER.

HERALDRY IN NEW ENGLAND.—The following extracts from a letter of Joseph L. Chester to William H. Whitmore, dated London, Mch. 19, 1864, seem worth preserving:

"Of course I do not mean to say that no early New England families were entitled to bear arms, for we all know better, but I do mean to assert that the proportion was very small. I rather take pride in my position that the greatest majority of the early settlers were of the hardy yeomanry of England, rather than from a socially higher class." * * * * "The use of arms is the very weakest of all evidence. I find them now on the old tombstones where it is certain that the individual buried had not the slightest claim to them. The very tombstones themselves are questionable evidence." EDITOR.

MUSSEY.—In my investigations of this family—also spelled Mussall, Mussell, Mudgett, Mussy, Muzzey, Muzzye—I have failed to discover any records earlier than those of the brothers Abraham and John who took the oath of allegiance, 26 March 1634, to pass to New England in the *John and Mary*. Of Abraham nothing further is known. John settled at Ipswich, Mass., in 1634, as did a Robert, who perhaps was a brother, and both had grants of land that year. Robert was made freeman in 1654. There was a Thomas at Cape Porpoise, Me., in 1663.

John, who was born about 1610, moved to Salisbury, Mass., in 1640, married Lydia —— of Cape Porpoise, who was living in 1690, and was the progenitor of the Portland, Me., branch of the family.

Robert, who married Bridget Bradstreet, also went to Salisbury, thence to Pulling Point and Malden, Mass. He bought land in Cambridge, that part adjoining Lexington, Mass., and was the progenitor of the Lexington branch of the family. A type-written list of his descendants, collated by me, is deposited with the Lexington Historical Society. WM. TRACY EUSTIS.

Brookline, Mass.

QUERIES.

SANDERS, TAYLOR.—On page 381 of vol. 5 of Middletown, Conn., Land Records is entered a document, of which the following is an abstract:

"To all Christon peple: know ye that I that haue passed by the name: of Willam Sandrs now in South-hamton am Taken to be Joseph Tayler formerly of South-hamton and haue declard that I am Joseph Tayler. and Chalend she that Now is the Wife of Samuel Biglow. to be my former Wife. and the estate that said Bigelow. Lieus on to be mine;"

He then quit claims to Bigelow all interest in the property for £10 consideration.

"In Witnees: and sett to my hand and sell this thord day of June in south hamton in year of our Lord 1730—

Ephraim: White	Willam *his* Sanders	
Ephraim Hildreth	O	[*seal*]
Dauid Roose	Josep *mark* taler	

June: 10th 1730—

Ephraim Hildreth & Dauid Roose did apear before Me one of his Maiesties Justices of the peace. and did make oath that the Witin instrument was the scubscribers fre and volantary act and Deed—

Test Daniel Sayre Just—"

"a True Record of the origenal Deed July: 6: 1731

Test. Joseph Rockwell Registr"

On the Town Records of Southampton, L. I., are entered the births, from February, 1722-3, to January, 1733-4, of five children of Samuel Bigelow: Abigail, Timothy, Mary, Isaac, and Samuel.

In April, 1723, Samuel Bigelow, ship carpenter of Southampton, L. I., bought land in that part of Middletown, Conn., now the town of Chatham.

In July, 1735, he made further purchases, and in September, 1736, had become a resident of Middletown. He made his will Oct. 14, 1748, which was probated eleven months later. In it he mentions his wife Mehetable, his five children, and "Elizabeth Spencer my Wifes Daughter."

The Middletown records show the marriage of John Spencer and Elizabeth Taylor, November 4, 1741. She died January, 1807, aged 90.

When and where was she born, and is there anything further known regarding her father, Joseph Taylor alias William Sanders?

Middletown, Conn. FRANK FARNSWORTH STARR.

HUNTER.—Correspondence is solicited with descendants of the following:

William Hunter (son of Robert and Sarah), born in Colrain, Mass., 1743; married Mary Anderson, at New Braintree, Mass., 1775; died in Brookfield, Mass., 1803 or '4.

Andrew Hunter (son of Robert and Sarah), born 1759; married first, Dorothy Howe, in 1782; married second, Mrs. Hannah Kelley; died in Oakham, Mass., 1835.

Sarah Hunter (daughter of Robert and Sarah), married Joseph Johnson, at New Braintree, Mass., 1768.

Robert Hunter, Jr., lived in New Braintree, Mass., between 1771 and 1782, and believed to have removed to Windham Co., Vt., where he was living in 1794.

Amos Hunter (son of William and Mary), born in New Braintree, Mass., 1781; married Hannah Lincoln of Oakham, Mass., 1810; died in Oakham, 1849.

Ira Hunter (son of William and Mary), born in Brookfield, Mass., 1790.

Eli Hunter (son of William and Mary).

Luther Hunter (son of Andrew and Dorothy), born in North Brookfield, Mass., 1789; married Betsey Lincoln of Oakham, Mass., 1813; died in Oakham, 1847.

Lucy Hunter, who married Dr. Cheeny Potter, May, 1806, both of Brookfield.

Sarah Hunter of New Braintree, Mass., who married John Potter 2d, of Brookfield, Jan., 1808.

And the following Hunters (children of Amos and Hannah), all born in Oakham, Mass.: Daniel T., born 1811; Levi L., born 1813; Ira, born 1814; Maryan, born 1816; Amos H., born 1818; Louise L., born 1820; George E., born 1823; Martha L., born 1826. GEORGE HUNTER.

Elgin, Ill.

ADAMS-ALEXANDER.—Capt. Stephen Adams, born 1792, son of William Adams of Henniker, N. H., married Abi, born 1791, daughter of Jonas Alexander of Henniker. Their first child, *William*, was born in 1810. When and where did their marriage take place? * * *

ADAMS.—Who were the parents of Abigail Adams, probably of Boston, who married, May 12, 1775, Enoch James of Boston and Hingham, and died Apr. 3, 1783? She was a sister of Dorcas Adams, who married Benjamin Silsbee of Salem, and who, dying young, left two children to be brought up by their uncle Enoch James. It is said that Abigail Adams was twice married before her marriage to Enoch James, first to —— Darracut, and second to —— Hart. Abigail Adams was born about 1755.

EATON.—Who were the parents of Anna Eaton who married John Butler of Connecticut, probably soon after the Revolution?

CORLIS.—Who were the parents of George Corlis of Providence, born Dec. 25, 1717, who married Mrs. Waitstill (Rhodes) Brown, and died June 16, 1790? He was a sea captain, and said to have been from Cape Cod.

51 Haller Building, Seattle, Wash. WALTER B. BEALS.

COOK.—What was the ancestry of Josiah Cook, who with wife Hannah joined the church in Middle Haddam, Ct., Oct. 4, 1741, having children *Elizabeth*, *Josiah*, *Elijah*, and *Joshua* baptized at the same time, and whose children, born subsequently, were *Moses*, *Mercy*, *Hannah*, *Rhoda*, and *Richard*, the latter born Mch. 17, 1753? F. J. COOKE.

225½ West Kennedy St., Syracuse, N. Y.

GILBERT.—Ancestry wanted of Moses Gilbert, who died in Brandon, Vt., in 1803, aged 81. Also, name and ancestry of his wife. Was she Mehitabel Bliss?

Bethiah, wife of Abraham Gilbert (son of above Moses), died Nov. 25, 1830. Further information is desired concerning her.

Univ. of Chicago Library, Chicago, Ill. CLARENCE ALMON TORREY.

STREET.—Emery's "Ministry of Taunton, Mass.," vol. 1, page 157, says that Rev. Nicholas Street, the early minister there, married a sister of Elizabeth Pole, the foundress of the place. Waters's "Gleanings," vol. 2, pp. 925-7, gives the wills of Elizabeth Pole's father and grandfather, and notes the names of her sisters and their husbands, but the name Street does not appear. Can any one *prove* Emery's statement? MURRAY E. POOLE.

Ithaca, N. Y.

REPLIES.

NELSON (*ante*, vol. 59, page 329).—Oyster River, a parish of Dover [N. H.], was incorporated as Durham in 1732. It had been made a parish in 1651; separated in 1675; incorporated in 1716. It had suffered severely during the Indian wars, the enemy frequently committing depredations within its limits." (McClintock's "History of New Hampshire," Boston, 1888, page 176.)

Full notices of "Oyster River" and "Oyster River Garrisons" will be found in Thompson's "Landmarks in Ancient Dover, N. H.," Durham, N. H., 1892, pages 168-189, including mention of Capt. John Woodman and his garrison, pages 179-180.

In "William Furber's Account. Ferriage," in "New Hampshire State Papers," Manchester, 1889, Vol. XVII., page 668, an entry has been found of ferriage "in June: 95: by the governor orders Mr. Nathenell ares and mathew Nellsonn with too men more and horses passing over." This ferriage in June, 1695—from another entry in the Account, "for passing of foot soldiers to oyester Rever to keep garisonn at Sundrey times, Eighty three"—was doubtless at Oyster River.

"Math Nelson" in June, 1678, was a resident of Portsmouth, N. H., and in 1693 seats were assigned to "Mathew Nelson" and to "Mathew Nelson's wife" in the Meeting House, Portsmouth. (Brewster's "Rambles about Portsmouth," First Series, Portsmouth, N. H., 1859, pages 60 and 64-65.)

Portsmouth, N. H. J. F.

Capt. John Woodman, of Oyster River, Dover (now Durham), N. H., will be found on page 366 of "Old Families of Salisbury and Amesbury," with corrections and additions on page 822. DAVID W. HOYT.
Providence, R. I.

HISTORICAL INTELLIGENCE.

PURLEIGH CHURCH.—An appeal is made to Americans for the restoration of the fine tower and the hanging of the peal of bells of this Church, at an estimated cost of £600 ($3000), to commemorate the connection with George Washington, President of the United States, whose ancestor Rev. Lawrence Washington was Rector of Purleigh, 1632–1643. Donations of any amount will be thankfully received, and may be sent to the Rector, Rev. R. T. Love, Purleigh Rectory, Maldon, co. Essex, England, or to Gen. James Grant Wilson, Buckingham Hotel, New York City.

SHERBURNE GENEALOGY.—The genealogy of the Sherburne family, prepared by the late William Sherburne and Edward Raymond Sherburne, the early generations of which, in condensed form, were contributed to the REGISTER (vols. 58 and 59), will be published during the next year. For information concerning it, address Frank S. Sherburne, 363 Marlborough St., Boston, Mass.

THE following copy of a circular issued by the State of New Hampshire will be of interest:

THE STATE OF NEW HAMPSHIRE, DEPARTMENT OF VITAL STATISTICS.

To Perfect the Records of Births, Marriages, and Deaths.

INSTRUCTIONS:—

Purpose of the Law.—The action of the last legislature emphasizes the fact that it is the policy of the state to secure, for the purpose of safety, record and ready reference, every record, or part of record, or scrap of personal history, connected with the births, marriages and deaths that have taken place in this state. Nearly one million such records are now on file in the Department of Vital Statistics, alphabetically arranged and grouped by family names, so that an individual record may be found in a moment.

It is intended to add to this group all the records in the possession of the towns and cities of the state not hitherto reported, as provided for in chapter 21, Laws of 1905.

Occasional losses of town records by fire and other causes, and the greater convenience of having a central office for all such records, always available to any individual in the state, upon application, without expense, and the fact that such records are becoming more valuable each year, and are sought for legal, personal, genealogical, historical and other purposes, makes it a matter of great importance that the provisions of this law be most carefully and conscientiously carried out.

Returns Made.—In 1849 the legislature enacted a law requiring births, marriages and deaths, to be returned annually by town clerks to the secretary of state. The first returns under this law were made in March, 1851. Some towns complied with the provisions of the law, others did not, and it is apparent that no attempt was made to enforce it by state authorities. It therefore follows that for a period of years, or for certain individual years, many towns made no report. All such will be required to complete the records under the law of last session.

Old Town Records.—We have examined some of the old town records, and have also received reports concerning them from several town clerks, all of which shows that in order to ascertain all the records of births, marriages and deaths in the possession of the towns, it will be necessary for the clerks to examine, page by page, these earlier books, as frequently the record of a family, or of a marriage or a birth, was inserted in the town records wherever convenient, not infrequently interspersed with other town matters, sometimes entered on the margin of a leaf, or on the fly-leaf, etc., so that a most careful search will be necessary to find all these entries. Many of them are very incomplete, marriages giving only the name of the bride and the groom, and the date of marriage, and a birth record, not infrequently giving only the name of the father; but no matter how meagre and fragmentary the records may be, each should be copied, and will constitute an individual record under the law.

How the Work will be Done.—In order to assist in the work of collecting these records, the registrar of vital statistics will request the returns to be made for stated periods, the first dating from the proprietor's records or the incorporation of the town down to a certain date, which will be stated. The second call for records will be from the latter date to a subsequent one, and so on until the work is completed. Town clerks will, therefore, be requested to take up the work in chronological order, as stated.

Each individual record must be made on a separate card (yellow); must give whatever data are found in their proper places; each must be signed by the town clerk, and be dated. The records may be transmitted to the Department of Vital Statistics at any time, preferable as often as once a month. A blank card (a few of which will be furnished with the record cards) must be filled, giving the number, each, of births, marriages, and deaths so returned, and the years covered in the search. When received at the Department of Vital Statistics, a receipt, which will be the town clerk's voucher for his fees, will be forwarded by mail. It is necessary that the transmittal blank be properly filled, in order that a statement of the work may be incorporated in the receipt.

Compensation.—The law provides that the town clerk shall receive five cents for each record returned in accordance with the law. This fee is not to be regarded as a part of his annual salary, nor to be accounted for in any way to the town other than by the presentation of the receipt from the Department of Vital Statistics, showing that the work has been done in accordance with the provisions of the Public Statutes.

No act of the town requiring the clerk to turn all fees into its treasury can apply in this case. The compensation is for a specific work required by the state, and no act can deprive the town clerk of that fee.

It is possible that the sum allowed will scarcely pay for the time required to make a careful search of the earlier town records, but later in this work the records of certain years will be called for which most towns now have entered upon special books, so that they can be readily copied, without research, and will prove remunerative, so that, taken as a whole, the town clerks will be reasonably well paid for their services.

Special Notice.—Black ink must be used in all cases. No hand stamps will be allowed. Each name must be written so plainly that every letter can be made out. The cards must be kept neat and clean. Any question on the card that cannot be answered should be left blank. The cards must not be folded. The cards should not be numbered. Transmit the records to the Department of Vital Statistics in long envelopes, by mail or express, prepaid. Additional blanks will be furnished upon application.

If there is anything not perfectly clear, or is not fully understood, the registrar of vital statistics will be glad to explain or to give further information at any time. We trust that everyone who has to do with this work will have a conscientious regard for exactness and accuracy, and may realize fully its imdortance to the state.

Concord, N. H., July, 1905. (Signed) IRVING A. WATSON, *Registrar.*

Note.—We have found that in some instances the certificates of births, marriages and deaths returned to the town clerk by the officiating clergymen and physicians were not recorded on the books, but put away in packages or into pigeon holes. All of these must be copied and returned. A return must be made of every record, no matter how it may have been kept, for the years called for by the registrar of vital statistics.

GENEALOGIES IN PREPARATION.—Persons of the several names are advised to furnish the compilers of these genealogies with records of their own families and other information which they think may be useful. We would suggest that all facts of interest illustrating family history or character be communicated, especially service under the U. S. Government, the holding of other offices, graduation from college or professional schools, occupation, with places and dates of birth, marriage, residence, and death. When there are more than one Christian name, they should all be given in full if possible. No initials should be used when the full name is known.

Bishop.—W. W. Cone, Brandsville, Mo., and George A. Root, Topeka, Kas., would be glad to receive information relating to the Bishop families in America.

Cass.—Alfred Cass, 271 West Rittenhouse Street, Germantown, Phila., Penn., is compiling a general history of the Cass family, and would be glad to correspond with members of that family or any persons who have knowledge of the ancestors of John Cass of Hampton, N. H., who died in 1675.

Smith.—Carroll F. Smith, 192 Lancaster St., Albany, N. Y., has in course of preparation a historical sketch and genealogical record of the descendants of Henry Smith and his children, *John, Henry, Daniel, Judith,* and *Elizabeth,* who came in the "Diligent" from co. Norfolk, England, to Hingham, Mass., in 1638, whence Henry Smith and his sons Henry and Daniel and daughter Elizabeth removed to Rehoboth about 1643. He desires to enter into correspondence with representatives of this family.

BOOK NOTICES.*

[The editor requests persons sending books for notice to state, for the information of readers, the price of each book, with the amount to be added for postage when sent by mail.]

Eliab Alden, of Middleborough, Massachusetts, and Cairo, New York. His Alden Ancestors and Descendants. Compiled by Charles Henry Alden, M.D., United States Army, Retired. Boston. Printed for Private Circulation. 1905. Large 8vo. pp. 55. Ill.

Eliab was of the family of John the Pilgrim. The compiler says that, so far as he is aware, no one of Eliab's descendants has been omitted. Persons and places are indexed.

The Allen Memorial. First Series. Descendants of Edward Allen of Nantucket, Mass. 1690–1905. By Orrin Peer Allen, Palmer, Mass. Palmer, Mass.: Press of C. B. Fiske & Co. 1905. 8vo. pp. 123. Ill. Price $2.50. Apply to Author.

This genealogy, which is arranged on the Register plan, contains all the descendants of Edward Allen excepting a few families whose records it has been impossible to discover. The appendix comprises the ancestry of the wives of the Allen ancestors of the author, their names being Coleman, Gaskel, Skiff, Coffin, Cady, and Doolittle. Good indexes are added.

Genealogical Chart of Balch Family of New England. Showing. Male Lines of Descent from the First Colonist, John Balch, to the Grandparents of the Present Generations. Copyright, 1905, by Samuel W. Balch, 67 Wall St., New York. 3 ft. 6 in. by 1 ft. 9 in.

History and Genealogy of the Descendants of Clement Corbin of Muddy River (Brookline), Mass., and Woodstock, Conn. With Notices of Other Lines of Corbins. Compiled by Rev. Harvey M. Lawson, Ph.B., B.D. Hartford Press: The Case, Lockwood & Brainard Co. 1905. Large 8vo. pp. 378. Ill. Price, in half Russia, $5.00; full cloth, $4.00.

The branches of the Corbin family included in this genealogy, besides the posterity of Clement Corbin, are those in western Connecticut, Dutchess Co., N. Y., and Vermont. Military services, from King Philip's War to the War of the Rebellion, are carefully recorded. Both as a genealogy and as a collection of biographies the work gives evidence of the pains bestowed upon it. The book is well printed, and is bound in cloth and Russia. There are sixty-five full-page portraits, besides other pictures. Following an excellent index are blank leaves for insertion of records.

* All of the unsigned reviews are written by Mr. Frederick Willard Parke of Boston.

New England Cox Families. By Rev. JOHN H. COX, of West Harwich, Mass. No. 17, 1905. Large 8vo. pp. 135–142. Price 25 cts.

Tables of Descendants of William Cumming, of Frederick County, Maryland. Compiled and arranged by MONTGOMERY CUMMING, Washington, D. C., July 1st, 1905. Chart. 3 ft. 10 in. by 2 ft. 6 in.

William Cumming was born near Inverness about 1725, married Sarah Coppage, became a large landed proprietor in Frederick Co., and died in March, 1793.

Davis Ancestral Chart. [By JOSEPH GARDNER BARTLETT.] 3 ft. 1 in. by 2 ft. 6 in.

This blue print gives the ancestors and children of William Davis, Jr., of Roxbury and Boston, who died 27 April, 1865, and of his wife, Maria Davis, who died 29 April, 1870.

History of the Fanning Family. A Genealogical Record to 1900 of the Descendants of Edmund Fanning the Emigrant Ancestor in America, who settled in Connecticut in 1653. To which is prefixed a General Account of the Fanning Family in Europe from Norman times, 1197, to the Cromwellian Confiscations, 1652-3. By WALTER FREDERIC BROOKS. Illustrated with Plates and Maps. In Two Volumes. Worcester, Massachusetts. Privately printed for the Compiler. 1905. Royal 8vo. pp. xvi+872. Price $20.00. Subscriptions to be sent to the Author, 54 Queen St., Worcester, Mass.

These very beautiful volumes are the product of fifteen years of labor both in this country and abroad. An account of the family in Ireland from the twelfth to the middle of the seventeenth century is given, as well as a record of ten generations of the descendants of Edmund Fanning in this country, which includes the descendants of Capt. James Fanning who settled in Long Island about 1715. Lists of those who performed military service from the Colonial to the Civil War will be found especially helpful. Mr. Franklin P. Rice, so well known for his historical work in Worcester County, has supervised the books typographically, and in addition to the pleasure thus afforded there are more than fifty illustrations in steel plate, photogravure, engravings in color, with maps and plans. The volumes are bound in half moroco with uncut edges and gilt top and printed on paper made for this work. Three full indexes are given.

Memorials of the Family of Forbes of Forbesfield. With Notes on Connected Morgans, Duncans and Fergusons. By ALEXANDER FORBES. Aberdeen: The King's Printers. 1905. 4to. pp. 134. Ill.

The body of this work consists of records of the Forbes of Forbes, Pitsligo, Newe, New Balgonen, and Forbesfield, with nearly fifty pages of "Forbes Appendices." The extensive index is general. The appearance of the book, which is in pamphlet form, is fine.

Major Alpin's Ancestors and Descendants. [By P. J. ANDERSON.] Aberdeen. Privately printed. 1904. 4to. pp. 32. Ill.

The "Major Alpin" of this sketch was Alpin Grant, whose ancestry is traced to the Grants of Glenmoriston, Scotland. Among his descendants the names of Mackay, Fraser, and Cameron are prominent. The pamphlet is beautifully printed and illustrated. No index.

Genealogy of the Greely-Greeley Family. By GEORGE HIRAM GREELEY. Boston, Mass. 1905. 8vo. pp. 911. Ill.

This genealogy comprises solely the descendants of Andrew Greele of Salisbury, Mass. It is not to be regarded as a history of the family, as biographical notices are too infrequent among the fourteen thousand descendants here recorded. As a genealogy it is apparently as exhaustive as works of this nature can be made. There are sixteen illustrations, nearly all portraits. It is well indexed.

Samuel Griffin of New Castle County on Delaware, Planter; and His Descendants to the Seventh Generation. Compiled and published by THOMAS HALE STREETS, M.D., U. S. N. Philadelphia, Pa. 1905. 8vo. pp. 235.

This well-printed book may be called a family history, so abundant are the biographical sketches. No attempt, however, is made to trace the history in Welsh records. The volume is carefully indexed. On the cover is the title, "Some Allied Families of Kent County, Delaware. Number Two."

The Pedigree of William Griffith, John Griffith and Griffith Griffiths (sons of Griffith John, of the Parish of Llanddewi Brefi, in the County of Cardigan, South Wales, Great Britain), who removed to the County of Chester, Pennsylvania, in the early part of the xviiith Century. Compiled in South Wales, Great Britain, by THOMAS ALLEN GLENN. One Hundred Copies privately printed. Phila. 1905. 4to. pp. ix+85.

The concluding paragraph of the preface of this genealogy is so remarkable that we copy it, as best showing the character of the work: "The compiler, having been practically unlimited by his principal in the matter of expenditure, can conscientiously state that no record likely to cast even a side light upon the subject has rested unexamined, and, finally, the following pedigree has been compiled from Family Archives, existing Official Records as cited or set forth at large, and from the ancient Welsh Authorities, some in one time, some in another, so that no man hereafter may either augment it or lessen it, or form a new pedigree or lose the old." It is only to the Welsh portion of the pedigree that this applies; the author does not consider himself responsible for the Pennsylvania section, as that has been supplied by members of the family. There are several facsimilies, and paper and type are excellent. There is no index.

A Record of the Descendants of Simon Henry (1766–1854), and Rhoda Parsons (1774–1847), His Wife. With Appendices containing some Account of their Ancestry and of Collateral Lines. Being a Contribution towards a Comprehensive Genealogy of the Descendants of Sergt. John Henry, Freeman of Topsfield, Mass., 1690. By FREDERICK AUGUSTUS HENRY, A.M., LL.B. Cleveland: Press of J. B. Savage. 1905. Large 8vo. pp. 65. Ill. Price $3.00 net, postage and packing 15 cts. extra. Apply to Printer or Author, Cleveland, O.

Of this excellently printed and finely illustrated volume it is only necessary to say that it amply fulfils the statement of the title-page, and has a thorough index of persons.

The Early Hildreths of New England. By ARTHUR HILDRETH. Read before the Reunion of the Hildreth Family, at Chelmsford, June 16, 1894. Privately printed. Copies can be obtained of the Author, Pierce Building, Copley Square, Boston. [Boston, n. d.] 16mo. pp. 60.

This little book relates to Richard Hildreth and his children. He was the ancestor of the New England Hildreths, and a character worthy of this animated sketch. There is no index.

Hills Family Genealogical and Historical Association. Eleventh Annual Report of the Directors. [Boston. 1905.] 8vo. pp. 13.

Captain Edward Johnson, of Woburn, Massachusetts, and Some of his Descendants. By EDWARD FRANCIS JOHNSON. Boston: Press of David Clapp & Son. 1905. Large 8vo. pp. 53.

This interleaved volume contains genealogical records only, extended biographical sketches having been excluded as not comporting with the design of the publication. The compiler vouches that all the statements he has admitted are accurate. There is a fine index. It should be mentioned that the greater part of the first twenty-nine pages has appeared in the REGISTER, Jan., April, and July, 1905.

The Lines Family. By DONALD LINES JACOBUS, of New Haven, Conn. [Reprinted from The Connecticut Magazine, April, 1905. New Haven. 1905.] Large 8vo. pp. 15.

The New Haven family of Lines is descended from Henry and Ralph Lines, supposed to be brothers.

William Luddington of Malden, Mass., and East Haven, Conn., and his Descendants. By JAMES SHEPARD. Boston: Press of David Clapp & Son. 1904. Large 8vo. pp. 13.

This is a reprint from the REGISTER, for Jan., 1904.

The Historical Journal of the More Family. Nos. 11, 12. June, Aug., 1905. Seattle, Washington. 4to. pp. 153-191. Ill.

Morse Genealogy, comprising the Descendants of Samuel, Anthony, William, and Joseph Morse, and John Moss. Being a Revision of the Memorial of the Morses, published by Rev. Abner Morse in 1850. Compiled by J. Howard Morse and Miss Emily W. Leavitt, under the Auspices of the Morse Society. Section Two. New York. 1905. 8vo. Variously paged.

This section begins with Ephraim[5] Morse, No. 370, and ends with Chester[6] Moss, No. 1087.

The Record of my Ancestry. By Charles L. Newhall. Addenda et Corrigenda. [n. p., 1905.] 8vo. pp. 16.

Palmer Groups. John Melvin of Charlestown and Concord, Mass., and his Descendants. Gathered and arranged for Mr. Lowell Mason Palmer of New York. By Miss Emily Wilder Leavitt. Private printed. Boston: Press of David Clapp & Son. 1901-1905. 4to. pp. x+450+xl.

In 1901 there appeared a volume by Miss Leavitt entitled "Groups of Palmer Families from Walter Palmer of Charlestown and Rehoboth, Mass., Stonington, Conn." This is reprinted here, and occupies two hundred and eighteen pages. Then follows "The Melvin Line," traced through five generations, succeeded by the "Spencer Line," "Rhode Island Ancestry," "Colonial Propositii," "Colonial Records," and forty-two pages of index. Two charts are inserted, viz., "Melville of Melville," and "Melville of Raith." Very noticeable is the abundance of biography, scarcely a page of mere genealogy occurring throughout the volume, while the "Rhode Island Ancestry" is wholly a series of biographical sketches. Nothing better could be desired than the style of print and paper, and the binding is attractive.

Dedication of Bowlders and Tablets to John Roundy and James Candage, a Founder, and an Early Settler of Bluehill, Maine, with Memorial Addresses by R. G. F. Candage, Esq., of Brookline, Mass., at Blue Hill Neck, Aug. 22, 1905. Ellsworth, Me.: Hancock Co. Publishing Company, Printers. 1905. 8vo. pp. 21. Ill.

Not a little genealogical information is contained in these addresses, the second of which, it is expressly stated, is based "on the town records, tradition and personal recollection."

Savery and Severy Genealogy (Savory and Savary). A Supplement to the Genealogical and Biographical Record, published in 1893, comprising Families omitted in that Work, and other Notes, Additions and Corrections; being a Continuation of the Notes, Additions, and Corrections in the Original Work from page xx. By the Author, A. W. Savary, A.M. Boston: The Fort Hill Press, Samuel Usher, 176-184 High St. 1905. Large 8vo. pp. 58. Ill. Price $1.50, with 12 cts. for postage and wrapper. Original Work with Supplement bound up with it, 324+xx pp. and 25 illustrations, $5.00, with 25 cts. for postage, etc.

Twelve years of research were required to produce the results embodied in this volume, which are, briefly stated, additional particulars respecting the name in Wiltshire, England, corrections of all ascertained mistakes in the original work, the connection with their proper lines of heretofore unattached families, newly found "Mayflower" pedigrees, and facts concerning Quakers of the name. The four illustrations are portraits. The book has two indexes.

Shannon Genealogy. Genealogical Record and Memorials of One Branch of the Shannon Family in America. Compiled by George E. Hodgdon. Rochester, N. Y. 1905. Square 4to. pp. xxxi+578. Ill.

The Shannons whose records are comprised in this volume are descendants of Nathaniel Shannon who came from the North of Ireland to Boston in 1687. In the Introduction is to be found the lineage, for sixteen generations, of the founder of the family, while in the "Genealogy" there are eight generations from the "Emigrant Ancestor." There are thirteen appendices consisting of correspondence, wills, petitions, affidavits, genealogies, and other valuable material. The illustrations are numerous and fine, besides which there are many facsimiles of autographs, private papers and public documents, together with a dozen tabular charts. The biographies are frequent, and many of them of extraordinary length. The print is excellent, the margins wide, and the binding substantial. There are two tables of index.

The English Ancestors of the Shippen Family, and Edward Shippen of Philadelphia. By THOMAS WILLING BALCH. Reprinted from the Pennsylvania Magazine of History and Biography, Oct. 1904. Philadelphia. 1904. Large 8vo. pp. 20. Ill.

Edward Shippen was a descendant of William Shippen of Methley, Yorkshire, Eng., and first settled in Boston, acquiring great wealth there before removing, in consequence of persecution for Quakerism, to the Quaker Province, where he won distinction in public life.

Thomas Steel, of Boston, and Some of His Descendants. 1664–1905. Also including the Family and American Ancestry of Samuel and Olive (Pierce) Steele, Pioneers of Koshkonong, Wis., 1842. Also the Families of Laura J. and Louisa L. (Pierce) Arkins, of Denver, Colorado. Prepared and Published by GEORGE W. STEELE. Times-Mirror Printing and Binding House, Los Angeles, Cal. 1905. 12mo. pp. xx+54. Ill.

This genealogy is confined mainly to the ancestry of the author, collateral lines being disregarded. Though covering so few pages, the fine print gives a great deal of matter in little space. The book is well made and indexed.

Genealogical Chart showing a part of the American Ancestry of Adelaide Bereman Walton. Prepared with loving care by her Father [CHARLES STRONG WALTON]. Los Angeles, Cal. 1905. 2 ft. 4 in. by 1 ft. 9½ in.

Genealogy of the Westervelt Family. Compiled by the late WALTER TALLMAN WESTERVELT. Revised and edited by WHARTON DICKINSON. New York: Press of Tobias A. Wright. 1905. Large 8vo. pp. vii+175. Ill. Price $5.00. Address T. A. Wright, 150 Bleeker St., New York.

The editor of Mr. Westervelt's work says it is done "in such a thorough and careful manner that the Editor has not deemed it necessary to alter the same in any material way or manner." A short sketch of the family in Holland precedes the American records. The book is splendid in appearance, and has a complete index.

Genealogy of the Descendants of John White, of Wenham and Lancaster, Mass., 1638–1905. In Three Volumes. By ALMIRA LARKIN WHITE of Haverhill, Mass. Vol. III. Haverhill, Mass.: Press of Nichols, "The Printer." 1905. 8vo. pp. 755. Ill. Price $5.00; after Jan. 1, 1906, $7.00.

The second volume of this work, published in 1900, is in a sense continued by the present volume, since both consist of branches of the family from the fifth generation until to-day. The book is printed on good paper, is well bound in cloth, finely illustrated, and completely indexed.

Some of the Ancestors and Children of Nathaniel Wilson, Esq., who was born Oct. 10, 1808, at Pelham, N. H., and died March 15, 1864, at Lawrence, Mass. Compiled by HENRY WINTHROP HARDON, A.M., LL.B. [60 Wall St., N. Y. City. 1905.] Chart. 2 ft. 1½ in. by 1 ft. 6½ in.

The Woods–McAfee Memorial, containing an Account of John Woods and James McAfee of Ireland, and their Descendants in America. Copiously illustrated with Maps drawn expressly for this Work, and embellished with one hundred and fifty handsomely engraved Portraits, Scenes, etc. By Rev. NEANDER M. WOODS, D.D., LL.D. With an Introduction by Hon. REUBEN T. DURRETT, A.M., LL.D., of Louisville, Ky. Louisville, Ky.: Courier-Journal Job Printing Co. 1905. Square 4to. pp. xiii+503. Price, full cloth, $5.00; half Morocco, gilt, $7.00; full Morocco, gilt, $10.00. Address Courier-Journal, etc.

The title-page further states that in this volume, "besides considerable new matter bearing on Virginia and Kentucky history, will be found mention of the families of Adams, Alexander, Armstrong, Behre, Bennett, Birkhead, Boone. Borden, Bowyer, Bruce, Buchanan, Butler, Caperton, Campbell, Clark, Coatse, Crawford, Curry, Daingerfield, Daviess, Dedman, Duncan, Dunne, Durrett,

Forsyth, Foster, Gachet, Gooch, Goodloe, Goodwin, Guthrie, Hale, Harris, Henderson, Johnston, Lapsley, McFarlane, Macgowan, Magoffin, McCoun, McDowell, McKamey, Phillips, Reid, Rickenbaugh, Rogers, Royster, Shelby, Sampson, Speed, Suddarth, Taylor, Todd, Thompson, Varner, Wade, Walker, Wallace, White, Williamson, Wood, Wylie, Young, and five hundred others. . . Also some hitherto unpublished documents which constitute a valuable contribution to the pioneer history of Virginia and Kentucky."

Herbert Cornelius Andrews. 1883–1905. Genealogist and Heraldist. [Lombard, Ill. 1905.] Portrait.

A biographical sketch, funeral addresses, correspondence, and verse constitute the memorial of one who, though young, was an authority on genealogy and heraldry, and, as a member of this Society and several other similar organizations, was recognized as one of great ability in the work of his choice.

Philip Augustus Chase: A Memorial Sketch of the First President of the Lynn Historical Society. By C. J. H. Woodbury. Reprinted from the Register of the Society. 1904. Large 8vo. pp. 14. Portrait.

Mr. Chase was a shoe manufacturer who, after acquiring wealth, devoted himself in various ways to the welfare of his native town.

In Memory of Elisha Slade Converse. Published by the City of Malden, Commonwealth of Massachusetts. Large 8vo. pp. 30. Ill.

This sumptuous pamphlet contains addresses made at the "Converse Memorial" held in honor of Mayor Converse, in Malden, Dec. 14, 1904, among the speakers on which occasion were Judge William Schofield, Rev. Richard Neagle, and Hon. John D. Long.

Gen. Charles W. Darling, M.A., Corresponding Secretary of the Oneida Hist. Soc. Born Oct. 11, 1830. Died June 22, 1905. Broadside. [Utica. 1905.] Portrait.

Major-General Michael Farly. Ipswich, Mass. 1720–1789. [Ipswich. 1905.] 8vo. pp. 4.

This sketch consists chiefly of extracts from Felt's History of Ipswich.

George Trumbull Hartshorn. 1860–1905. n. p.; n. d. 8vo. pp. 2.

Mr. Hartshorn was a chemist by profession, but his tastes were various, leading him to join several organizations, among them this Society.

Francis Edward Howard. n. d.; n. p. Small 8vo. pp. 81. Ill.

The Hon. Francis E. Howard was born and died in West Bridgewater, Mass., and was its most prominent citizen. This memorial contains, besides the "Funeral Service," "Memorial Addresses," "Personal Tributes," "Tributes of the Press," "Letters" and "Resolutions."

Captain Myles Standish. By Tudor Jenks. New York: The Century Co. 1905. 12mo. pp. viii+250. Ill.

A life of Captain Standish is necessarily little else than the history of the Pilgrims from the time of their landing at Plymouth to the date of his death, in 1656. Of the career of the Captain previous to his association with the Pilgrims we have the scantiest information. This book furnishes quite a history of the Pilgrim colony, preceded by exceedingly fine chapters on the "England of the Pilgrims," "The Separatists," and "The Standish Family." The characterization of Standish seems a correct one, and it is written in a very clear style.

Clara Louise Stewart. A Tribute. Printed for Arthur Collins Stewart, Boston, Mass. n. d. 12mo. pp. 31. Portrait.

Mrs. Stewart was born in Providence, R. I., in 1834, and died in Boston, April 1, 1903. She married, for her second husband, James Stewart, M.D., of Brooklyn, N. Y.

Catálogo Biográfico de la Casa de Thayer de Braintree. Por Luis Thayer Ojeda (Es Propiedad). Santiago de Chile. 1904. 4to. pp. 73.

This is a list of those of the "House of Thayer of Braintree" who have in any manner distinguished themselves.

In Memoriam. Lawrence Weldon. [Washington. 1905.] 4to. pp. 48.

The contents of this memorial consist of the "Proceedings of a Meeting of the Members of the Bar of the Court of Claims, to take action upon the death of Judge Lawrence Weldon." Judge Weldon was for twenty-one years judge of the Court of Claims, and was first connected with the operations of Federal justice in the time of Lincoln.

Records of the Sheriff Court of Aberdeenshire. Edited by DAVID LITTLEJOHN, LL.D., Advocate in Aberdeen, Sheriff Clerk of Aberdeenshire. Volume 1. Records prior to 1600. Aberdeen: Printed for the University. 1904. 4to. pp. xlvi+476.

This work consists of two parts, the first being "Records prior to 1600," the second, "Officials prior to 1600." The first part contains five volumes of "Diet Books" and one of "The Decree Books." The editorial treatment, with respect to each book, provides an introduction, a table of contents, and illustrative examples. In the "Table of Contents" of the entire work the "Illustrative Examples" are indexed. The "Officials" section is not a mere list of names, but a series of biographical sketches, though in mere outline. The verdict expressed in the "General Introduction" on the six books of part first is that the items of value to the legal antiquarian and genealogist will be found infrequent.

A Brief Account of the English Reformed Church, Begijhof, off Kalverstraat 130–132, Amsterdam. [Amsterdam.] n. d. 12mo. pp. 22. Ill. Map.

This church was founded about the year 1400, and to it is admitted anyone who understands English, of whatever nation he may be, provided his creed and morals are not in disagreement with the requirements for membership.

Old Bridgewater, Mass., a Classic Town whose Early Learned Ministers were Moulders of New England Character. An Address delivered by Rev. GEORGE A. JACKSON, M.A., before the Old Bridgewater Historical Society, June 25, 1904. Published by Edward Alden. Arthur H. Willis, Printer. 1905. 8vo. pp. 8. Price 10 cts.

Though chiefly commemorative of religious activities, this address has not neglected other interests.

The History of Concord, Massachusetts. Volume I. Colonial Concord. By ALFRED SERENO HUDSON. The Erudite Press. Concord, Massachusetts. 1904. 8vo. pp. 496+xiii. Ill. Portraits. Map.

The unique feature of this history is an entertaining Narrative which comprises Part I., and portrays minutely the every-day life of the early settler of Concord,—his natural surroundings and the obstacles he had to overcome in order to make his home, his relations with the Indians, religious, civil, and social life, superstitions, manners and dress. The author has employed both fiction and fact in order to produce this detailed pen-picture of colonial days.

Part II. gives chronologically the annals of the town from 1635 to 1692, and furnishes brief biographical sketches of the original grantees. Many old or famous houses now standing are described and located, and photographs of most of them, with portraits of noted Concord people, are among the fine illustrations which add to the pleasure derived from this well-printed, handsome volume. A good index is supplied. A. L. W.

Old Dartmouth Historical Sketches. No. 10. Historical Associations in North Dartmouth. Historical Glimpses of Dartmouth Schools. Pilgrimage of the Old South Historical Society to Old Dartmouth. [New Bedford. 1905.] 4to. pp. 20.

The Schools and Teachers of Dedham, Massachusetts, 1644-1904. By CARLOS SLAFTER. Privately printed. Dedham Transcript Press. 1905. Large 8vo. pp. 330.

The educational history of the town "which was the first to establish and support a public free school by *direct taxation*" is here abundantly and accurately detailed, the index of teachers who are noticed comprising a dozen pages. These notices are, in almost every case, biographical sketches which, in some instances, cover an entire page,—very thorough treatment, considering that the volume records the services of teachers who labored during a period of two hundred and sixty years. The various subjects connected with the main theme of the book are carefully indexed, and well show the interesting nature of the work. The volume is printed on heavy paper, and substantially bound in cloth.

Souvenir of Farmington, New Hampshire. Presented with the Compliments of the Farmington Old Home Week Association, Aug. 20, 1904. Farmington News Print. [1904.] Oblong 32mo. pp. 30. Ill.

This historical and descriptive account of Farmington is accompanied by numerous and fine illustrations.

An Historical Address delivered at Groton, Massachusetts, July 12, 1905, by request of the Citizens, on the Celebration of the Two Hundred and Fiftieth Anniversary of the Settlement of the Town. By SAMUEL ABBOTT GREEN. Groton: 1905. 8vo. pp. 52.

The influence of charters, governors, and changing policies, through two and a half centuries, upon the origins and bounds of a frontier town are here traced with remarkable clearness. Dr. Green shows his abiding affection for Groton, his deep insight into New England character, his knowledge along many lines, and his intercourse with men. He describes a visit to the English Groton, and adds notes on other towns of the name, on Indian words, and on subjects of local interest. The address will be read with pleasure for its accuracy of historical detail, its breadth of view, and its touches of happy philosophy. C. K. B.

Year Book. Parish of St. Paul's, Halifax, Nova Scotia. Easter, 1905. Holloway Bros., Printers. 12mo. pp. 116. Ill.

Ipswich in the Massachusetts Bay Colony. Part I. Historical. A history of the town from 1633 to 1700, containing the letters of Major Samuel Appleton, lists of soldiers in the Indian Wars, records and depositions of the Usurpation Period, and facsimiles of ancient documents, bearing many autographs of the early settlers. Part II. Houses and Lands. An account of the original grants of house lots and the successive owners of lands and houses, to the present time, illustrated with diagrams, ancient maps, and photographs of many ancient houses. With Seven Appendices. By THOMAS FRANKLIN WATERS, President of the Ipswich Historical Society. The Ipswich Historical Society, Ipswich, Mass. 1905. Large 8vo. pp. 586. Ill. Portraits. Maps. Facsimiles. Apply to the Ipswich Historical Society, Ipswich, Mass. Price $5.00. Postage 35 cents.

More than one kind of specialist, as well as the general student of history, will find here material of unusual interest and utility. Every aspect of the colonial development of the town has been carefully and scientifically investigated, and the results are presented in a well-made and well-printed book, with exceptionally beautiful illustrations. Specifications for building some of the old houses here photographed give us an insight into colonial architecture seldom obtained, and the witchcraft papers, early court records, military rolls and private letters are all valuable, but even more noticeable than these are the abstracts of land titles, extending from the original grantee to the present time. The appendices furnish a list of the first settlers, early inventories, letters of Rev. Nathaniel Ward, Giles Firmin, Samuel Symonds, Sarah Goodhue, and the narrative of Rev. John Wise. The analytical index is excellent. A. L. W.

Vital Statistics of the Town of Keene, New Hampshire, compiled from the Town Records, First Church and Family Records, the Original Fisher Record and the Newspapers. By FRANK H. WHITCOMB, City Clerk. Authorized by vote of the City Councils, June 1, 1905. Keene, N. H. Sentinel Printing Co. 1905. 8vo. pp. 268.

The marriage records in this volume extend from 1753 to 1854. The birth records are those contained in the first two record books of the town, together with about a thousand which have been copied from family records. The death records are brought down to April, 1881. The announcement says that "this publication is the first of a series of printed records of vital statistics of the town of Keene. It is expected that others will be issued in order to make all the records of a similar character available for public use to the year 1888, when the city began to print them in the annual reports."

Lexington Epitaphs. A Copy of Epitaphs in the Old Burying-Grounds of Lexington, Massachusetts. By FRANCIS H. BROWN, M.D. The Lexington Historical Society. 1905. Square 8vo. pp. 169. Plans.

The seven hundred and sixteen epitaphs here printed are from the Old Burying-ground, in the rear of the Unitarian Church, and from the Robbins Cemetery, in the East Village, and are exact transcripts. The addition of notes both of a genealogical and biographical character greatly increase the value of the work. Unstinted praise is due the compiler for thus preserving such interesting and valuable records.

Report of the Celebration of the Centennial of the Incorporation of the Town of Marlborough [*Conn.*], *Aug. 23d and 25th, 1903.* Compiled and published by MARY HALL. Hartford Press: The Case, Lockwood & Brainard Co. 1904. 8vo. pp. 96. Ill. Maps.

This centennial was marked by the delivery of the usual historical sermon and addresses, containing important portions of the annals of Marlborough, rendered serviceable by an index of the report.

History of the Maumee River Basin, from the Earliest Account to Its Organization into Counties. By CHARLES ELIHU SLOCUM, M.D., Ph.D., LL.D. Illustrated. Published by the Author, Defiance, Ohio. [1905.] 4to. pp. viii+638+xx. Map.

This is a work of the most thorough character, beginning with the geology of the region of which it treats, and its prehistoric inhabitants, and then proceeding to narrate the first explorations, the various wars of which the Basin has been the theatre, including that of 1812, the subjects of the concluding chapters being treaties with the Indians and missionary activities among them, the present drainage system, the first American settlers, the organization of counties, the development of communication, public lands, schools and libraries. While agreeing with the author that the actions of the aborigines should be related in the spirit of the historian and not of the sentimentalist, we doubt if everyone would describe their treatment by the government as "the ever magnanimous dealings with them of the United States."

Ancient Middlesex. With brief Biographical Sketches of the Men who have served the County officially since its Settlement. By LEVI S. GOULD. Somerville Journal Print. 1905. Large 8vo. pp. 336. Ill.

The contents of this finely printed and illustrated volume are described by the editor as a "collection of portraits and biographical sketches of faithful officials, considered worthy of preservation among the public archives and municipal libraries of the County." As to the number of portraits and facsimiles of signatures, the index of them covers nearly six pages. There are, in addition, copies of the seals of more than fifty towns. The portraits, with the exception of those in the supplement, are full-page illustrations.

Decoration Day, Peacham, Vt. May 30, 1905. Exercises at the dedication of Markers, Sons of the American Revolution, at the graves of the eleven Revolutionary soldiers in the Cemetery and old Graveyard. By JANE ELIZABETH COWLES. Peacham, Vt. [1905.] 16mo. pp. 12.

This booklet contains sketches of the life and service of each of the soldiers whose graves were marked.

The Old Families of Salisbury and Amesbury, Mass., with some Related Families of adjoining towns and of York County, Maine. By DAVID W. HOYT. Part eleven (part six of volume II), Providence, R. I. 1905. Large 8vo. pp. 781-852.

This is the concluding volume of this series, and the families recorded in it are Morrill, Morse, Mudgett, Monday, Mussey, Nichols, Page, Partridge, Peasley, Perkins, Philbrick, Pierce, Pike, Pressey, Purington, Quinby, Ring, Rolfe, Rowell, Rowlandson, Sammon, Sargent, Severance, Shepard, Smith, Somes, Stanwood, Stanyan, Stevens, Stockman, Stowers, True, Trussell, Tucker, Tuxbury, Wait, Warner, Webster, Weed, Wells, Wheeler, Wheelwright, Whitridge, Whittie , Williams, Winsley, Woodin, Woodman, Worcester, Worthen, Younglove. r

Shropshire Parish Register Society. Hereford. Vol. V. Part 2. Greete. Bedstone. Vol. X. Part 1. Claverly (Part 1). July, 1905. [London.] 2 vols.

8vo. Variously paged.

The Greete and Bedstone records extend from 1663 to 1899; those of Claverly from 1568 to 1685.

Shropshire Parish Register Society. July, 1905. Diocese of Lichfield. Vol. V, Part 2. Ruyton-in-the-Eleven-Towns. Leebotwood. Longnor. [London. 1905.] 8vo. Variously paged.

The Ruyton entries extend from 1719 to 1812; those of Longnor from 1586 to 1812; those of Leebotwood from 1548 to 1812.

The Ancient Crosses of Stortford. By J. L. GLASSCOCK. Bishop's Stortford Printed by A. Boardman & Son. 1905. 4to. pp. 32. Ill. Maps.

The author says that his design in writing this pamphlet is "To prove the existence of these ancient crosses by references from old documents; to endeavor to identify the sites they formerly occupied; and to suggest reasons for the names they bore.". After this method, six crosses are herein treated of.

[*No. 3.*] *Weymouth Historical Society. Wessagusset and Weymouth, an Historical Address by* CHARLES FRANCIS ADAMS, JR., *Delivered at Weymouth, July 4, 1874, on the Occasion of the Celebration of the Two Hundred and Fiftieth Anniversary of the permanent Settlement of the Town. Weymouth in its First Twenty Years, a Paper read before the Society by* GILBERT NASH, *November 1, 1882. Weymouth Thirty Years Later, a Paper read by* CHARLES FRANCIS ADAMS, *before the Weymouth Historical Society, September 23, 1904.* Published by the Weymouth Historical Society. 8vo. pp. 164.

This interesting and suggestive volume contains much to arrest attention. In his first address, Mr. Adams gave the history of Weymouth, but with no attempt to connect local events with other events elsewhere. Mr. Adams now recognizes that this was an error, and in his second address, prompted partly thereto by Mr. Nash, he shows that the real significance of the early years of Weymouth was the contest between Episcopacy and Puritanism, with the ultimate triumph of the latter. His thrust at Longfellow, and his vigorous protest against closing our eyes to the evils of the olden days and against the undue prominence given to wars, will meet with a sympathizing response from those whose aim in studying history is to attain the truth. A. M.

State of Connecticut. Public Document No. 41. Report of the Temporary Examiner of Public Records. 1904. Printed by order of the Legislature. Hartford Press: The Case, Lockwood & Brainard Co. 1904. Large 8vo. pp. 131. Ill.

This report shows that particular efforts have been made in forming a careful list of the Town and Probate records throughout the State, and is accompanied by recommendations regarding their preservation. A list of the ancient Court records, compiled under the supervision of the State Librarian and the Secretary of State, is also included in the report. Besides these, the report contains a list of Probate Districts, by the Librarian of the Conn. Hist. Society. The entire document is a labor of great importance, whose results will be inestimable.

Early Legislative Turmoils in New Jersey. By WILLIAM NELSON. April, 1905. The American Magazine of History. With Notes and Queries. New York. Large 8vo. pp. 221–231.

Mr. Nelson's paper helps to prove his assertion that they are deluded who suppose that human nature, and especially the nature of the politician, is less noble now than in the days of our patriotic forefathers.

Curious Features of some of the Early Notes or Bills used as a Circulating Medium in Massachusetts. By ANDREW MCFARLAND DAVIS. Reprinted from the Publications of the Colonial Society of Massachusetts. Vol. X. Cambridge: John Wilson and Son: University Press. 1905. Large 8vo. pp. 20.

In the conclusion of this paper Mr. Davis says, "The development of the topic under consideration has not involved new investigation or original research, but the collation of these notes will facilitate the study of their peculiarities."

Emergent Treasury-Supply in Massachusetts in Early Days. By ANDREW McFARLAND DAVIS. Reprinted from Proceedings of the American Antiquarian Society, April 26, 1905. Worcester, Mass.: The Hamilton Press. 1905. 4to. pp. 34.

In this paper Mr. Davis has been enabled, he says, "to round out the story of the participation of Massachusetts in attempts to supply a denominational currency based solely upon governmental credit."

The Limitation of Prices in Massachusetts. 1776–1779. By ANDREW McFARLAND DAVIS. Reprinted from the Publications of the Colonial Society of Massachusetts. Vol. X. Cambridge: John Wilson and Son: University Press. 1905. Large 8vo. pp. 20.

This paper was suggested by a schedule of prices in Hingham in 1779, and the period to which Mr. Davis's article relates was one of great disturbance caused by the inflation of the currency.

Journal of the One Hundred and Twentieth Annual Meeting of the Convention of the Diocese of Massachusetts, May 24, A.D. 1905. With Appendices. Boston: The Diocesan House. 1905. 8vo. pp. 282.

Joyce Junior. By ALBERT MATTHEWS. Reprinted from the Publications of the Colonial Society of Massachusetts. Vol. VIII. Cambridge: John Wilson and Son. University Press. 1905. Large 8vo. pp. 19.

As a frontispiece to this pamphlet there is a copy of a handbill which was posted in Boston, Jan. 17, 1774. It is signed "Joyce, jun. Chairman of the Committee for Tarring and Feathering." The meaning of this name Mr. Matthews is not able to explain.

Massachusetts Soldiers and Sailors of the Revolutionary War. A Compilation from the Archives prepared and published by the Secretary of the Commonwealth, in accordance with Chapter 100, Resolves of 1891. Vol. XIII. REA–SEY. Boston: Wright & Potter Printing Co., State Printers, 18 Post Office Square. 1905. 4to. pp. 1025.

Minutes of the Ninety-Sixth Annual Meeting of the General Association of the Congregational Churches of New Hampshire, held at Franklin, May 22, 23, 24, 1905. One Hundred and Fourth Report of the New Hampshire Home Missionary Society. Vol. VIII. No. 5. Nashua, N. H.: Telegraph Publishing Co., Printers. 1905. 8vo. pp. 452–570. Ill.

Public Papers of George Clinton, First Governor of New York. 1777–1795—1801–1804. Vols. VII., VIII. Published by the State of New York, compiled and arranged by HUGH HASTINGS, State Historian. Vol. VII. issued as Appendix "N," Third Annual Report of the State Historian. Albany: Oliver A. Quale, State Legislative Printer. 1904. 8vo. pp. lvi+633; xxxvii+467. Ill. Maps.

The North Carolina Booklet. Vol. V. No. 1. July, 1905. Published by the North Carolina Society of Daughters of the Revolution. [Raleigh, N. C. 1905.] 8vo. pp. 71. Ill.

The contents of this number of the "Booklet" are: "The Genesis of Wake County," "St. Paul's Church, Edenton, N. C.," "Life of William Hooper, Signer of the Declaration of Independence," and a supplement, to this last, on the Hooper family.

Blockade of Quebec in 1775–1776 by the American Revolutionists (Les Bastonnais). Published by the Literary and Historical Society of Quebec, and edited by FRED. C. WÜRTELE, Librarian. Quebec: The Daily Telegraph Job Printing House. 1905. 8vo. pp. xiv+307. Ill.

This is called the "Seventh Series of Historical Documents, 1905." It comprises "Historic Tablets at Quebec," "Ainslie's Journal," "Journal lent by D. James Bain," "Orderly Book," "List of Officers of Royal Highland Emigrants," "Roster of French Canadian Militia." The Ainslie Journal is by Thomas Ainslie, who at the time of the Blockade was Collector of Customs at the Port of Quebec. The other Journal was bought in London, and is called "Journal of the most remarkable occurrences in Quebec, since Arnold appear'd before the Town on the 14th November 1775."

List and Station of the Commissioned and Warrant Officers of the Navy of the United States and of the Marine Corps, on the Active List, and Officers on the Retired List employed on Active Duty. July 1, 1905. Washington: Government Printing Office. 1905. 8vo. pp. 161.

Official Records of the Union and Confederate Navies in the War of the Rebellion. Published under the direction of the Hon. PAUL MORTON, Secretary of the Navy, by Mr. CHARLES W. STEWART, Superintendent Library and Naval War Records. By authority of an Act of Congress approved July 31, 1894. Series 1—Vol. 19. West Gulf Blockading Squadron from July 15, 1862, to March 14, 1863. Washington: Government Printing Office. 1905. 8vo. pp. xvi+958. Ill.

Whalley and Goffe in New England. 1660–1680. An Enquiry into the Origin of the Angel of Hadley Legend. By GEORGE SHELDON. Reprinted from the Introduction to the New Edition of Judd's History of Hadley by H. R. Hunting & Co., Springfield, Mass. 1905. 8vo. pp. xxxiv. Portraits.

Doubtless there are many who will be glad to possess this reprint of Mr. Sheldon's "Enquiry," in which, as he says, he "has given a final quietus to the angel story being accepted as history."

Address of James P. Baxter, Mayor of Portland, Maine, at the Meeting of the American Institute of Instruction, July 10, 1905. [Portland. 1905.] Large 8vo. pp. 8.

Andover Theological Seminary. Alumni Letter. Andover, Mass., June 20, 1905. Large 8vo. pp. 16.

This "Letter" is a report of the year's work at the Seminary

Constitution and By-Laws and Membership California Society of the Sons of the American Revolution. 1905–1906. [San Francisco. 1905.] 32mo. pp. 31.

The Canadian Club of Harvard University. Cambridge, Massachusetts, U. S. A. 1905. 8vo. pp. 41.

This club consists chiefly of University students from Canada, and contains a list of such members as have attended the University during the last century.

Proceedings and Transactions of the Royal Society of Canada. Second Series. Volume X. Meeting of June, 1904. For sale by James Hope & Son, Ottawa; The Copp-Clark Co. (Limited), Toronto; Bernard Quaritch, London, Eng. 1905. Large 8vo. Variously paged. Ill. Maps.

The portions of the "Transactions" which treat of subjects of a historical and biographical nature are the first two sections, in which are found such papers as "L'honorable Joseph Royal—Sa vie—Ses œuvres," "Le Haut Canada avant 1615," "A Monograph of the Origins of Settlements in the Province of New Brunswick," and "Thomas Pownall—His Part in the Conquest of Canada."

Friday Afternoon Club. Farmington, New Hampshire. 1905–1906. [Farmington, N. H. 1905.] 32mo. pp. 8.

This booklet contains a "Calendar," members, constitution and by-laws, and officers of a ladies' club.

Proceedings of the Lexington Historical Society, and Papers relating to the History of the Town presented at some of its Meetings. Vol. III. Lexington, Mass.: Published by the Lexington Hist. Soc. 1905. 8vo. pp. 183+xxvi. Portrait.

The papers here published are "Hon. Thomas Hancock," "Dr. Stillman Spaulding," "Cambridge Farms," "Charles Follen," "Lexington Branch Railroad," "Lexington Centennial," "Third Meeting House," "Epitaphs in Burying-Grounds," "Concord Turnpike," "Early Days of High School," "The Monroe Tavern," "Clockmaking in Lexington," and "Saving Hancock-Clarke House." The portrait is one of Rev. Carlton A. Staples.

The Register of the Lynn Historical Society, Lynn, Mass., for the year 1903. Lynn, Mass.: Frank S. Whitten, Printer. 1905. 8vo. pp. 82. Ill.

Besides the usual contents of publications of this nature, this Register contains a section of "Necrologies," the sketches being accompanied by portraits.

Register of the Officers and Members of the Society of Colonial Wars in the State of Maine. Also History, Roster and Record of Colonel Jedidiah Preble's Regiment, Campaign of 1758, together with Capt. Samuel Cobb's Journal. Portland: Marks Printing House. 1905. Large 8vo. pp. 180. Ill.

Register of the Massachusetts Society of Colonial Dames of America. 1893–1905. Boston: Printed for the Society. 1905. Large 8vo. pp. 428. Ill.

By systematic and orderly arrangement of the names of the members and of the ancestors, by good print and good paper, the ladies in charge have not only secured individual credit in the production of this volume, but have issued a register which will serve as a model and enhance the regulation of the society. The concise, crisp citation of ancestors' service exhibits a wide acquaintance with colonial and provincial New England history, and will constitute this handy volume an authority in its peculiar field. GEO. A. GORDON.

Grand Chapter. Vol. XI. Part IV. The Eightieth Annual Convocation, held at Portland, May 2 and 3, 1905. Stephen Berry, Printer, 37 Plum St., Portland. [1905.] Large 8vo. pp. 299–438+iv.

Grand Council of Maine. Vol. V. Part X. 1905. The Fifty-first Annual Assembly. Held at Portland, May 3, 1905. Stephen Berry, Printer, 37 Plum St., Portland. 8vo. pp. 785–873+vi. Portrait.

The "Grand Council" of the title is the "Grand Council of Royal and Select Masters" of the Masonic fraternity.

Grand Lodge of Maine. Vol. XX. Part II. The Eighty-sixth Annual Communication, held at Portland, May 2, 3 and 4, 1905. Stephen Berry, Printer, 37 Plum St., Portland. [1905.] Large 8vo. pp. 199–334+vi.

Proceedings of the Most Worshipful Grand Lodge of Ancient Free and Accepted Masons of the Commonwealth of Massachusetts, in union with the Most Ancient and Honorable Grand Lodges in Europe and America, according to the Old Constitutions. Quarterly Communications, March 8, June 14, 1905. Special Communications, March 14, June 6, 10, 1905. Boston: The Rockwell and Churchill Press. 1905. Two volumes. 8vo. pp. 114.

The Proceedings and Transactions of the Nova Scotian Institute of Science, Halifax, Nova Scotia. Vol. XI. Part I. Session of 1902–1903. With 18 Plates. Halifax: Printed for the Institute by the McAlpine Publishing Co., Ltd. Date of Publication: 27th March, 1905. Price to Non-Members: One half-dollar. 8vo. pp. xv+162+iii.

Year Book No. 10 of the Oneida Historical Society, at Utica, N. Y., 1905. Munson-Williams Memorial. [Utica. 1905.] 8vo. pp. xxiv+168. Ill.

The papers contained in this number are: "The Genius of Anglo-Saxon Law and Institutions contrasted with the Latin Civilization of Imperialism," "The Mohawk Valley, a Channel of Civilization," "Colonization and Civil Government in the Tropics," "Recollections of the Oneida Bar," and "McKinley and the Spanish War."

Annual Proceedings. Pennsylvania Society of Sons of the Revolution. 1904–1905. Philadelphia. 1905. 4to. pp. 57. Ill.

Transactions of the Literary and Historical Society of Quebec. Sessions of 1903 to 1905. No. 25. Quebec: The Daily Telegraph Job Printing House. 1905. 8vo. pp. 75. Ill.

Besides various reports, and lists of officers and members, this number contains an article on "Education in Quebec in the 17th Century."

The John P. Branch Historical Papers of Randolph-Macon College. Published Annually by the Department of History. Vol. II. No. 1. June, 1905. Richmond: William Ellis Jones, Printer. 1905. 8vo. pp. 142. Price $1.00. Address Wm. E. Dodd, Editor, Ashland, Va.

The principal articles in this number are: "Spencer Roane," "Robert R. Livingstone," "Roane on the National Constitution," and "Roane Correspondence."

Proceedings of the Vermont Historical Society. 1903-1904. With Amended Constitution and List of Members. President's Address: The Recent Discovery and Recovery of the Original Records of the Early Vermont Conventions. Paper: "Commodore Thomas Macdonough," Hon. Charles H. Darling. Paper: "Soldiers of the Revolutionary War Buried in Vermont, and Anecdotes and Incidents Relating to Some of Them," Walter H. Crockett. With Lists of Revolutionary Soldiers Buried in Vermont. Burlington: Free Press Association. 1905. Large 8vo. pp. 168.

The contents have been indexed.

General Catalogue of the Officers and Graduates of Williams College. 1905. [1795-1905.] Williamstown, Mass. Published by the College. [T. R. Marvin & Son, Printers. Boston, Mass.] 1905. Large 8vo. pp. 231.

Proceedings of the Wiscasset Fire Society at its Four Hundred and Nineteenth Quarterly Meeting, July 20, 1905. Wiscasset, Maine: Reprinted from the Sheepscot Echo. 1905. 8vo. pp. 40. Ill.

The Grafton Chart Index. The Grafton Genealogical Notebook (Chart Index Form to accompany the Grafton Chart Index.) The Grafton Genealogical Notebook American Form. The Grafton Press, Genealogical Publishers, 70 Fifth Avenue, New York. Grafton Chart Index and Note Book, $1.25 net. Grafton American Form Note Book, 25 cents net.

This is a semi-circular chart providing space for recording ten generations by their names only. An index number for each name refers to a page of the Notebook, which consists of blank pages only, where data on each ancestor can be entered.

The American Form Notebook is convenient in size and is made up of six forms, each containing eight pages arranged to receive the data of a whole family. Among its most desirable features are noticed the perforated pages which can be detached when filled out and sent at once to the printer. Careful directions for use, with a reduced reproduction of four pages properly filled out, are furnished for the benefit of the amateur genealogist. A. L. W.

DEATHS.

Gustavus Adolphus Hinckley, a benefactor of this Society, was born in Barnstable, Mass., Aug. 15, 1822, and died at his home in that village, a few rods from his birthplace, on the 7th of August, 1905, in his eighty-third year. While Barnstable was always his home, his early manhood was spent elsewhere. Leaving his father's house at the age of eighteen, for Boston, he was in a store on Long Wharf for a few years, and then thoroughly learned the trade of a machinist, becoming well skilled in the various branches of that business, and was sent to different parts of this country and to Cuba, putting up engines and giving instruction in mechanics. He later went to Lake Superior, and was employed as Superintendent of the Pewabic Copper Mines, and after the discovery of oil in Pennsylvania, he became the manager of an oil-farm there for several years.

Returning to Barnstable in 1872, he was in 1874 urged to become the Treasurer of the Barnstable Savings Bank, then one of the largest banks in southeastern Massachusetts. In 1883 he retired from public service, but remained a tireless worker up to the year of his death.

Mr. Hinckley's tastes were scholarly and literary, and the "midnight oil" was freely burned. He was always greatly interested in historical and genealogical matters pertaining to the Old Colony. He was a lineal descendant of Gov. Thomas Hinckley, Rev. John Lothrop the first settled minister of Barnstable, Rev. John Robinson of Leyden, John Howland and others of the Mayflower, the old families of Gorham, Easterbrook, Davis, and others.

He took a great interest in his native town, and it is said that his "Rebellion Record," prepared at the expense of much time and labor and presented to the town of Barnstable, is one of the most complete in the Commonwealth.

Mr. Hinckley was very painstaking and accurate. He had copies made for himself of all the early records of the town of Barnstable, the early volumes of the County Probate Records, and the early Church records, and had the same carefully compared and fully indexed. He also personally visited all the burying grounds and cemeteries in all the different villages of the town, and had a complete record of the names and dates on all the tombstones and monuments, as well as pictorial representations of many of the headstones, engraved by himself. He was well known and appreciated by people dwelling in nearly every State in the Union, to whom he gladly and freely gave of his information concerning their ancestry, and was always ready to be interviewed by any one interested in the Old Colony and its early settlers. A well known genealogist writes of him: "Since the days of Amos Otis no man has done so much to preserve the records, monuments and history of his native town as he has done. But little of his work has been published, but it has all been preserved, and will be of great value to those interested in the early history of the town. He wrote the history of each man who represented Barnstable in the Civil War; he was an authority upon the history of the early settlers, and gave freely to all inquirers copies of his notes. Mr. Hinckley was a true country gentleman. He loved the history of Barnstable. He once said, 'In passing the old milestones I feel like taking off my hat in honor of the first settlers who placed them there.'"

Mr. Hinckley was never married. He lived a plain unostentatious life, and by reason of his modest living and quiet, economical habits he was enabled from his moderate earnings and careful savings to provide perpetually for the children of others. His gifts or bequests of $15,000 to the Boston University to assist deserving students not wholly able to get such education as they desired; $6000 to the St. Luke's Hospital at New Bedford to provide a free bed for those of his native town, or county, who should be unable to provide for themselves such needed medical treatment; and a bequest of $5000 to the State Board of Education for the benefit of those partially unable to bear the expense of a Normal School training, evince his interest in social and educational matters, and in the welfare of those yet to come to inhabit that portion of our Commonwealth so loved by Mr. Hinckley; while his bequest to this Society of all his "records relating to public or genealogical matters, whether bound or unbound, including several volumes of memorial inscriptions in the cemeteries and burying grounds in the town of Barnstable," not only shows his interest in its welfare, but a desire to furnish, after his death, to those interested, the help and information he so willingly and generously bestowed during his life.

Mr. Hinckley was in religious belief and training a Unitarian, and his bequests to the Orthodox, Baptist, and Episcopal Societies in Barnstable, as well as to the Unitarian Society, serve sufficiently to show that he was broad-minded, earnest and sincere, and desirous of assisting, as his means would allow, those who were trying to better themselves and to make others better and happier. F. H. L.

Barnstable, Mass.

Charles William Manwaring, genealogist and member of the Connecticut Historical Society, passed away on Saturday, Aug. 19, 1905, in Hartford, Conn., where he had resided many years.

He was born in Waterford, New London County, Conn., May 9, 1829, and was a descendant of one of the oldest families in Connecticut, the Manwarings being among the earliest settlers of that State, and their genealogy being easily traceable for many generations before the settlement of the New World. In his young manhood he became a builder and contractor, but his love for books and research led him to take up a line of work which has resulted in his leaving behind him a monument more enduring than stone, and a work which will be more and more appreciated as future generations come and go.

Mr. Manwaring was about seventy years old when he conceived the idea of putting into a concise and durable form the contents of the original books of probate records of Connecticut, part of which were in the State Capitol and part in the Halls of Record at Hartford, and all of which, from excessive use and the lapse of time, are rapidly approaching a condition when access to them will be obtained with difficulty. Having conceived the idea, he immediately began the work of putting it into a practical form, and for the remaining years of his life labored incessantly and under great physical disability, and succeeded in bringing his compilation down to 1750, comprising the first fifteen of the original books, and which is now being issued in three octavo volumes, two of them having already been published, and the third about to be issued. To this work he has given the title, "A Digest of Early Probate Records of Connecticut," and while it is a work of great value to reference libraries, genealogiets, and all who are interested in tracing their ancestry, it is also a pioneer work in its line, pointing the way to what may be done in other parts of the State and in sister States in the way of putting their ancient and valuable records into a form that will forever insure against their loss or destruction. Only great patience, determination, courage, and an abiding faith in the merits of the work could have brought about its production, especially at such an advanced age, and Connecticut was fortunate in possessing among her citizens one who was equipped with such necessary qualifications, and the State has recognized his labors by purchasing copies of the work for official use.

It is a sad fact that on the day following the completion of his great compilation he succumbed to the fatal disease which at last took him away—a cancerous affection of the throat—thus showing with what great courage and suffering he must have pursued his labors on the latter part of his work. For nine months he patiently bore his affliction, until death released him, leaving a work that will preserve his name forever. GEO. E. WRIGHT.

Hartford, Conn.

PHILIP ADSIT FISHER, minister and genealogist, compiler of the Fisher Genealogy, died of tuberculosis, Feb. 26, 1905, at Highland, Cal., aged 35 years.

He was born at San Francisco, Cal., Nov. 11, 1869, the younger of the two sons of Sidney Augustus and Julia (Brigham) Fisher, was educated in the San Francisco Boys' High School and University of California, and graduated from the San Francisco Theological Seminary in 1898, taking charge of the Walnut Creek Presbyterian Church, Contra Costa County, immediately after graduation.

On June 6, 1890, he married Emma Florence Donner, and a daughter, Angie Florence Fisher, was born to them, June 8, 1891. In Sept., 1902, Mr. Fisher became pastor of the Presbyterian Church of Mill City, Oregon, where he remained until his health failed, two years later. Thinking that a change of climate might benefit him he journeyed to Southern California, where he lived but a brief month. Mr. Fisher was a man of studious habits. He loved nature and had traveled extensively. He was very ambitious in his work, in spite of the fact that he was laboring under great physical infirmities which would have discouraged a less arduous man.

Los Angeles, Cal. * * *

JAMES R. B. HATHAWAY, for many years an antiquarian of repute in the history and genealogy of North Carolina, died at Merry Hill, N. C., Sept. 22, 1904. He was the editor and publisher of the "North Carolina Historical and Genealogical Register," a magazine full of historical material. The number of the magazine upon which he was at work was completed by his pen, and this will close the issuance of a most valuable publication. This "Register" is a witness of the wealth of material yet to be studied by the students of North Carolina history and family life. Mr. Hathaway was known as the "Old Mortality of the Albemarle." His home was at Edington, of which place he was mayor for a long series of years.

(Rev.) ANSON TITUS.

Somerville, Mass.

HENRY LEBBEUS OAK, an eminent author and scholar, died at his home at Seigler Springs, California, May 20, 1905. He was born in Garland, Maine, May 13, 1845. He attended Bowdoin College, thence to Dartmouth College, where he graduated in 1865. In 1865 he became librarian and chief assistant of Hubart H. Bancroft, who published a series of volumes upon the Pacific Coast. In this capacity Mr. Oak served eighteen years, when ill health forced him to retire. It is conceded that Mr. Oak wrote the five volumes concerning "The Native Races of the Pacific Coast." In semi-retirement he became interested in the genealogy of the Oak, Oaks, and Oakes families, and left a manuscript history of the same, which, if not published, will be deposited in the Library of this Society. His father was the Hon. Lebbeus Oak, historian of Garland, Maine. The following is his paternal line of ancestors: Lebbeus,^{5} Benjamin,^{4} Nathaniel,^{3} John,^{2} Nathaniel^1 of Marlborough.

(Rev.) ANSON TITUS.

Somerville, Mass.

Benjamin B. Torrey.

NEW ENGLAND
HISTORICAL AND GENEALOGICAL
REGISTER.

APRIL, 1906.

BENJAMIN BARSTOW TORREY.

By William Carver Bates, Esq.

The subject of this sketch was treasurer of the New England Historic Genealogical Society from 1871 to 1904, when he resigned on account of failing health, serving the Society with surpassing faithfulness and accuracy. When he became treasurer, the assets of the Society were about $10,000, and the yearly income no more than $1,500; at the termination of his service, the assets had increased to above $200,000, outside of the invaluable library, and the annual income was about $10,000. It is no small matter to have accounted for the finances for such a period without criticism or error, and Mr. Torrey's success in this field of activity might well have satisfied his desire to serve others with faithfulness, but he was for most of this long period the treasurer of the Boston and Providence Railroad, and, in the later years, also of the Old Colony Railroad, which meant the charge of one million to two million dollars annual income, for much of the time. Mr. Torrey's long service as treasurer of the Society, and as *ex officio* member of the Council, endeared him to many fellow workers and others who met him often in the various activities of a busy and long extended period. An opportunity was given to some of these friends to express briefly their appreciatiation of Mr. Torrey's character, and these tributes follow, somewhat condensed to meet the exigency of a limited space, and will precede a more detailed mention of the genealogy and outward events in his life.

It is with a mournful pleasure that I recall my memories of the late treasurer of the Society, Mr. Torrey. My acquaintance with him dates back through the past quarter of a century, and I met him frequently during that period, and at one time almost daily, either in the business world or at 18 Somerset Street.

His genial disposition was always apparent, something unusual in this world where one is apt to be depressed by upsets in business or by ill health. This genial nature was with him to the last, and at more social functions than the meetings of the Society, during the past two years, though he enjoyed the occasions, I marked with pain his increasing infirmities.

His appreciation of the eccentricities of his fellow-men was keen, and there is no class in which these weaknesses appear more frequently than in genealogists and students of history. His remarks, however, were never inspired by malice.

His labors were always highly valued by his fellow members, and when dissension entered the ranks he continued his labors, looking only to the welfare of the Society, and his position was appreciated by all.

To the late faithful librarian, John Ward Dean, this country and even England is indebted for advancing the study of New England genealogy and history. The people of the States owe him still more in the advantages derived from a free access to the store house mainly gathered through his labor. In this life work, he was wisely and conscientiously assisted, in its financial affairs, by Mr. Torrey, a busy man, but one who gave his time, quietly and gratuitously, without any desire for fame.

I can also testify to his devotion to family ties, in the care of his invalid wife.

His lack of a large estate at his death was a surprise to many, but it was only another proof of his devotion to his kindred and his disinterested services to the Society. WALTER KENDALL WATKINS.

Mr. Torrey was a good friend of mine for many years. The acquaintance began when he with Mrs. Torrey passed a winter in Milton in order to be near Mrs. Samuel Adams—a sister of Mrs. Torrey's—a neighbor and friend of ours. He always impressed me as eminently faithful and loyal in every relation of life. His devotion to his invalid wife was very beautiful—he seemed to be a token of strength to all of his family and friends—giving most liberally of his means to those less fortunate than himself. He was sent for several years as a delegate to the Diocesan Convention from his parish Church of St. Andrew at Hanover. It is needless to say he was faithful to his duties and responsibilities—as in every other position of trust where he was placed. We all knew of his long and honorable connection with the Providence Railroad as treasurer—and of the esteem and regard of his fellow officers for him. His devotion and interest in the Society and lasting effort in its behalf extending over a period of forty years —we all remember with gratitude. His genial and pleasant greeting will be long missed by his many friends so long identified with him in the New England Historic Genealogical Society. His love for the old Torrey homestead, so long in the Torrey family, was very noticeable, and I shall never forget a most charming visit enjoyed there during Mrs. Torrey's lifetime. It affords me much pleasure to add my simple tribute to that of others who hold a more clever pen. CORNELIA TOWNSEND.

My acquaintance with the late Mr. Benjamin Barstow Torrey, long time Treasurer of the New England Historic Genealogical Society, was very slight. The impression left on my mind is that of a courteous official with whom it was a pleasure to have dealings, a genial, kindly gentleman, whose abiding cheerfulness, closely akin to "Jest and youthful Jollity," often finding expression in jocose remarks, made him ever a welcome presence in the Society's rooms. MARY H. GRAVES.

My relations with Mr. Torrey were more as a personal friend than as an officer of the Society, as he was a relative of mine and we had many interests in common. As an officer he was kindness and indulgence itself, as a man he was genial and sweet natured, with many acquaintances but few intimate friends—I think he cared for very few in that way. He was a good raconteur, and enjoyed himself greatly when in contact with bright minds and exchanging good stories, and he was a devoted husband and brother.
SUSAN C. KENNEDY.

My acquaintance with Mr. Torrey began before I knew him in official relations, in the New England Historic Genealogical Society. That he was a gentleman in the true sense of the word cannot be doubted, and I found him to be so in my early intercourse with him. Honest, we know he was. Kind hearted, no one will dispute. Although I was not so intimate with him as were some others in our Society, I knew him well enough to know that all good qualities were his, and the reverse, never.

The Society does well to honor his memory with more than a passing notice.
AARON SARGENT.

Our associate, Benjamin Barstow Torrey, was a business man of ability, occupying a position where he had ample opportunity to exercise his characteristic courtesy and patience. As treasurer of the Boston and Providence Railroad Company for many years, and later also of the Old Colony Railroad Company, thousands of people knew him as an agreeable gentleman who performed his duties, especially those connected with the transfer of shares of the capital stock, in an exceptionally considerate and obliging manner. Thoroughly understanding his business, he never departed from fundamental principles, but would waive petty technicalities and did all in his power to unravel the legal tangles that peculiar conditions had created. Apart from the really difficult problems that came to him for solution, there were a multitude of instances where helpless people, some of them ignorant, were greatly puzzled as to what to do, and all such found in Mr. Torrey a kind friend, who cordially gave much time to assisting them. In many such cases, presumably, there was but slight recognition of his kindness, but a great number did appreciate it, and he was one of the most popular corporation treasurers in Boston. It does not appear that any court ever questioned an act of his or the correctness of his conclusions, or that the railroads or any individual ever lost a cent in consequence of his disposition to facilitate the transfer of stock. By his business associates Mr. Torrey was highly esteemed, and there was never a higher official that the humbler employees liked better than they did Treasurer Torrey. Absolutely honest, he possessed abilities that his quiet unassuming ways could not conceal, and the record of his life is that of a competent official and a kind and good man. To me it is a pleasure to pay even this inadequate tribute to his memory.
GEO. KUHN CLARKE.

I am glad to have an opportunity of expressing my admiration of the character of our late Treasurer, Benjamin Barstow Torrey, who in his quiet and unobtrusive life had endeared himself to a large number of friends and associates.

My intimate acquaintance with him was formed in the latter part of his life, beginning when I was elected one of the Auditing Committee of the Society, and in that capacity I had an opportunity of learning how devoted he was to the Society: how carefully he guarded its interests, and how painstaking he was in carrying out his work as its treasurer. When the time came for him to relinquish his duties, owing to steadily increasing physical infirmities, it was almost like the parting from a beloved friend to give up his books and accounts, which he had so long and patiently cared for: like a mother separating herself from a child for whom to sacrifice herself had become a part of her life.

Without disparaging by contrast the work of his predecessors, or of his successors, it can be truly said that he was a model officer, whose duties never have been nor ever will be more creditably carried out than during his administration.

When such a friend is taken from us, it creates a void which cannot easily be filled. CHARLES S. PENHALLOW.

I beg to say that, strong as were the words of commendation uttered and the resolutions adopted at the close of Mr. Benjamin Barstow Torrey's long services as Treasurer of the New England Historic Genealogicul Society, it still seems to me that we nevertheless scarcely appreciate the immense value of his quiet, constant service. He always had the welfare of the Society at heart, and no one took more pride than he in the growth of our funds from well nigh nothing at the beginning, to approximately three hundred thousand dollars at the close of his term of office as treasurer.

He did not, and indeed could not, personally contribute largely to the funds of the Society, but as auditor of the treasurer's accounts I have observed that he always favored strictly safe investments, and that he gave freely a vast amount of valuable time in order that the Society's books might be properly kept.

The Society is certainly to be congratulated that, while still in the full vigor of manhood, he consented to sit for the excellent portrait which Capt. A. A. Folsom and others of his friends secured for the office of the Society,—a fitting recognition of his long and valuable service.

HOSEA STARR BALLOU.

I saw in the Herald the other day a notice of the death of Mr. B. B. Torrey, and as he had led a good life, reached an advanced age, sustained a good name, and gained the love of all his friends and the respect of all who knew him, why should we mourn his decease when his powers had failed?. FRANCIS H. FULLER.

On receipt of the tribute of recognition of Mr. Torrey as treasurer, the Society adopted this at the meeting, May 4, 1904, in recognition of his services:

The members of the New England Historic Genealogical Society unanimously place upon its records their testimonial of regret that its late treasurer, Benjamin Barstow Torrey, has felt compelled to relinquish the duties of that responsible office.

Elected a member of this Society, May 4th, 1864, its assistant treasurer on January 5th, 1870, and its Treasurer on January 4th, 1871; Mr. Torrey has for forty years been an highly esteemed Counsellor and, as the custodian of the Society's moneys and securities for thirty three years, a trusted and valued official.

The Society's fund, increasing from $9,713.81, in 1870, to the sum of $313,671.37, at the termination of his trust, shows the painstaking care and labor he has performed; a laborious service, that he has cheerfully and freely rendered and made us his debtor.

For his steadfast and unswerving fidelity to our society's best interests, for his splendid financial record and for his uniform courtesy and good fellowship, we heartily thank him, and cordially wish him that tranquil rest and freedom from care that a faithful service of so many years merits.

The following Minutes and Resolutions were adopted at the stated meeting of the Society, November 1, 1905:

The Society should place upon its records an acknowledgment of its deep indebtedness and gratitude to the late Benjamin Barstow Torrey, a life member since 1864, and for his long continued and pecuniarily unrequited service to the Society as Treasurer from 1871 to 1904, a period of thirty-three years' continuous service. When he came to the treasurership the assets of the Society were about $10,000; when he resigned on account of failing health in 1904, the property of the Society had increased outside of the invaluable library, to over $200,000. To conduct these large accounts with faithful and accurate fidelity for more than thirty years would seem to be an accomplishment to gratify the ambition of an ambitious man, but Treasurer Torrey modestly pursued his way apparently unaware of doing anything out of the usual, and all this time he was Treasurer of the Boston and Providence Railroad, whose earnings increased from $1,066,000 annually to $1,905,000 annually, and during the last ten years he was also Treasurer of the Old Colony Railroad. In each of these positions Mr. Torrey betrayed not only an expected fidelity, but his intercourse with associates and with the public was always urbane and courteous, often under the irritating pressure of ill health, and his friends testify to the constant cheer of his presence.

A number of friends associated for many years in various relations of life with Mr. Torrey, have sent to the Society tributes of respect and affection; these will be preserved in the archives as a memorial volume constituting, we believe, a memorial tender and true, endearing and dignified as well befits the character of a man so faithful and pure.

Whereas, Death has removed from us one who was for many years a firm friend, an active member, and a trusted officer of the Society,

Therefore, We, the members of the New England Historic Genealogical Society, do hereby place upon record our deep sense of loss by the death of our associate, Benjamin Barstow Torrey, and our thankful remembrance and sincere appreciation of his work while with us.

Born of sturdy New England stock, he inherited those qualities of mind and heart which such an ancestry often transmits to its descendants. Beginning an active life at an early age, he remained a lifetime in the service of a great corporation and for nearly forty years was its trusted and faithful treasurer, serving it with ability and discretion, adding during ten years of that service the duties of the treasurership of a kindred corporation. Elected treasurer of this Society in 1871, succeeding the late William Blanchard Towne, he brought to its lesser duties those traits of integrity and honesty of purpose which characterized his life in broader fields; and for thirty-three years, a longer service than has been borne by any other treasurer of the Society, he was an efficient adviser and conservator in financial matters. As a member of the Council, his genial temper, good-fellowship, and sound judgment gave him the respect and friendship of his associates.

Benjamin Barstow Torrey of Boston was a native of Pembroke, Plymouth County, Mass., born November 22, 1837, son of Capt. Haviland and Salome (Barstow) Torrey, a lineal descendant of Captain William Torrey of Weymouth (1640), and numbered among his emigrant ancestors several other early settlers of the Massachusetts Bay and Plymouth Colonies. The Torrey line is William,[1] William,[2] Haviland,[3] William,[4] William,[5] Haviland,[6] Benjamin Barstow[7]. Capt. Haviland[6] Torrey was born at Pembroke, October 29, 1791, and died August 26, 1865. His wife Salome, born at Hanover, July 24, 1801, died May 3, 1878, was a daughter of John Burden and Betsey (Eells) Barstow, of Hanover. Her father, John Burden[5] Barstow, was born in 1764, and was a descendant, in the fifth generation, of William[1] Barstow who came to New England in 1635, was at Dedham in 1636, a freeman at Scituate in 1649, and the first recorded settler in the locality now called Hanover, Mass. The line of descent was through his son William,[2] Jr., born at Scituate in 1652; Benjamin,[3] born in 1690, whose second wife was Sarah Burden; Thomas,[4] who married Sarah, daughter of John Studley; to John Burden[6] Barstow, above named, who was a ship builder, and who held the rank of Colonel in the State Militia. His homestead at Hanover was known as "Broad Oak Farm." Col. John B. Barstow died in Hanover at the advanced age of ninety years, having survived his wife Betsey (Eells) Barstow, who died in 1852, in her ninety-first year.

Capt. Haviland Torrey and his wife Salome had five children, two of whom, Benjamin Barstow and Herbert, reached maturity. Herbert died suddenly, at the South Terminal Station, Boston, on July 24, 1901.

Benjamin Barstow Torrey was educated at the Hanover Academy, 1851–1855, and at the University Grammar School at Providence, R. I., which he attended about one year. He taught in one of the district schools of Milton, a few terms, making his home with the Misses Bent, of one of the old families there. In 1875 he married Miss Abbie Bent, who died Sept. 9, 1897. He died Sept. 11, 1905.

Mr. Torrey entered the service of the Boston and Providence Railroad in 1858, in the freight department as receiving clerk; in 1860 he was transferred to the General Passenger Office; was made Treasurer's Clerk in 1861; and became Treasurer in 1867. He retired from this latter position in 1904, receiving a moderate pension. In 1893 he became Treasurer of the Old Colony Railroad, and resigned his three treasurerships in 1904, on account of failing health. Mr. Torrey had been Treasurer of the New England Historic Genealogical Society since 1871, and a life member since 1864. He was a member of the Society of Colonial Wars, since 1900.

Inheriting his grandfather's estate, "Broad Oak," he occupied it a number of years as a summer residence, and was a communicant of St. Andrew's (Episcopal) Church and a frequent delegate from Hanover Parish to Diocesan Conventions.

It is not usual for the biographer to enter the cloister walls of home to scan the family influences which sweeten and sanctify the family life, and in the case of Mr. Torrey these were so uniform and pure it is a pleasure to recall the romance of the beginning, when the young school teacher turned to the mature matron as his ideal of a life long companion, she with maturer judgment gently chiding his enthusiasm, and only acceding after many months' observation assured her his was no fleeting whim. The many succeeding years of happy married life were to all observers an example that happiness is an inward state of peace, independent of all arbitrary conditions. Age and failing powers caused no subsidence from the high tide of reverent affection upon which the youthful suitor embarked.

Mr. Torrey would not have taken a degree in the modern school of High Finance; it was enough for him to administer faithfully the trusts committed to his care. The modern trust, frequently very temporary so far as the public is concerned, did not accord with his instincts. He did not, perhaps, originate schemes of investment for the funds in his charge, but at each scrutiny of the auditors the interest was all there, and the trustees or directors passed no sleepless nights on his account, the widow or orphan awoke to no hopeless days from his lapses from honor. We cannot doubt he will elsewhere receive the highest award — "Thou hast been faithful, enter thou into the joy of thy Lord."

INSCRIPTIONS FROM THE LONG SOCIETY BURYING GROUND, PRESTON, CONN.

Communicated by George S. Porter, Esq., of Norwich, Conn.

Long Society (Congregational) derived its name from its location on the long, narrow strip of land east of the Thames and Shetucket rivers which formed the eastern boundary of the original town of Norwich (then nine miles square), and extended from the present village of Poquetanuck to that of Plainfield. The church was organized in 1726, under the pastoral care of the Rev. Jabez Wight. The first meeting-house of the society stood where to-day stands its successor, about three miles from the centre of the city of Norwich. The church yard, from which many of the older gravestones have disappeared, lies immediately in the rear and on both sides of the meeting-house. When Norwich was divided, in 1786, Long society become a part of Preston.

Marget died Sept. 6, 1780, aged 11 days.
Mary died Oct. 5, 1782, aged 4 years and 7 months.
Children of Calvin and Marget Barstow.

Abel, son of Abel and Esther Benjamin, died Aug. 9, 1787, in his 22d year.

Mrs. Anna, wife of Elijah Benjamin, died June 5, 1794, in her 21st year.

Also their still-born child died April 31, 1794.

Deborah, wife of Elijah Benjamin, died Dec. 28, 1804, in her 29th year.

Eunice, wife of John Benjamin, born in the vicinity of Boston, Mass., 1729; died August 15, 1772, aged 43 years.

Elizabeth, wife of Elijah Brewster, died May 12, 1776, in her 45th year.

Priscilla Cook died Feb. 10, 1730–31, in her 15th year.

Sally, daughter of Amos and Alletty Corning of New York, died Dec. 15, 1794, aged 7 years.

Josiah Corning died Feb. 29, 1760, in his 51st year.

Jane, relict of Josiah Corning, died March 21, 1803, in her 88th year.

Nehemiah Corning died Oct. 7, 1797, in his 81st year.

Freelove, relict of Nehemiah Corning, died Nov. 8, 1809, aged 86 years.

Lydia P., wife of Jedidiah Corning, died Nov. 29, 1836, aged 41 years.

Hiram Burtis Corning, son of Jed^{h} and Lydia Corning, died Jan. 10, 1818, aged 1 year and 7 months.

Elisha Corning died May 28, 1805, aged 61 years.

Cyrus Corning died June 16, 1827, aged 59 years,

Hannah, wife of Elias Corning, died July 13, 1817, aged 30 years.

Russell Dennis died Jan. 20, 1840, aged 86 years.

Zipporah, wife of Russell Dennis, died Nov. 27, 1824, aged 69 years.

Zipporah, wife of James. Geer, died March 24, 1739, aged 18 years, 7 months and 24 days.

Mrs. Mary Giddings died April 29, 1733, aged 21 years.

Capt. Nathaniel Giddings died Feb. 6, [broken] in his 66th year.

Barshebe, wife of Levi Giddings, died Sept. 7, 1813, in her 36th year.

Solomon Giddings, Esq., died June 14, 1727, in his 73d year.

Andrew, son of Solomon and Sarah Giddings, was lost at sea Sept. 1804, in his 21st year.

Sarah, wife of Solomon Giddings, died July 6, 1784, in her 32d year.

Woodbury, son of Solomon and Sarah Giddings, died at Havana, Aug. 19, 1799, in his 24th year.

Ruth, relict of Solomon Giddings, died Dec. 15, 1836, aged 74 years.

John, son of Solomon and Ruth Giddings, died April 15, 1845, in his 50th year.

Anna, wife of Minor Grant, died July 24, 1820, aged 32 years.

Justin P. Grant, son of Minor and Anna Grant, died Jan. 9, 1824, aged 4 years.

Miss Anna Grant, daughter of Minor and Anna Grant, died Sept. 26, 1832, aged 24 years.

Elias B. Grant, son of Minor and Ann Grant, died Jan. 18, 1837, aged 23 years.
Denison L. Grant died Sept. 10, 1845, aged 32 years.
Peter Greene, Esq., died April 3, 1834, aged 82 years.
Sarah, wife of Peter Greene, died Jan. 7, 1834, aged 78 years.
Ebenezer Greene, son of Peter and Sarah Greene, died Aug. 17, 1808, aged 28 years.
Lucy, wife of Benjamin Fitch, died Aug. 20, 1796, in her 29th year.
Benajah Fitch died Jan. 25, 1805, in his 84th year.
Sarah, wife of Benajah Fitch, died Feb. 18, 1819, in her 93d year.
Rufus Fitch died Oct. 19, 1816, aged 51 years.
Zipporah, wife of Rufus Fitch, died June 7, 1821, aged 19.
Lyman Fitch died April 10, 1819, aged 34 years.
Washington, son of Russell and Julia A. Fitch, died July 3, 1823, aged one year and three months.
William G., son of Russell and Julia Fitch, died May 29, 1833, aged 11 months.
Deacon Benjamin Fitch died Oct. 10, 1727, in his 37th year.
Fanny, wife of Capt. George P. Harkness, died May 9, 1838, aged 32 years.
William L. Harkness, son of George P. and Fanny Harkness, died March 8, 1837, aged 6 months.
Paul Hervey died Aug. 13, 1778, in his 30th year.
Ruth, wife of Nathan Herrick, died Dec. 21, 1815, aged 60 years. [Her first husband was Paul Hervey; two stones bear this inscription. See Herrick.]
John Hervey, son of Paul and Ruth Hervey, died Sept. 30, 1787, in his 8th year.
Capt. Philip Harvey died Nov. 15, 1815, in his 72d year.
Elizabeth, relict of Capt. Philip Harvey, died March 20, 1826, aged 77 years.
Rhoda Hervey died March 6, 1776, aged 4 years and 4 months.
Philip Hervey died July 5, 1775, aged 1 year and 3 months.
Philip died at Demarara, Oct. 15, 1795, aged 20 years.
Children of Philip and Elizabeth Hervey.
Betsey, wife of Col. Paul Harvey, died Sept. 11, 1823, aged 34 years. [This stone stands in the Greene family row.]
Ramsford Harvey, son of Joseph and Betsey Harvey, died Aug. 6, 1833, aged 1 year.
Joseph H. Harvey, son of Henry and Elvira Harvey, died Feb. 14, 1845, aged 3 months and 15 days.
Roger Haskel died May 20, 1759, in his 69th year.
Mary Haskel died March 29, 1752, in her 52d year.
Roger Haskell died Aug. 14, 1791, in his 55th year.
John Haskell died Jan. 14, 1762, aged 23 years, 10 months and 12 days.
Chloe, wife of Benjamin Haskel, died May 20, 1769, in her 25th year.
Sarah Haskel, daughter of Roger and Anna Haskel, died Oct. 2, 1778, in her 6th year.
Gideon Haskel died June 16, 1798, in his 72d year.
Ruth, wife of Nathan Herrick, died Dec. 21, 1815, aged 60. [Her first husband was Paul Hervey, *q. v.*]
Benjamin Hillard died May 5, 1801, in his 49th year.

Sabra, wife of Benjamin Hillard, died April 5, 1808, in her 47th year.

Capt. Moses Hillard died Sept. 30, 1837, aged 57 years.

Sally, wife of Moses Hillard, and daughter of the late Capt. William Pride, died Sept. 26, 1823, aged 43 years. [See Pride.]

Sarah Hillard, wife of T. C. Stewart and daughter of Moses and Sally Hillard, died at Pass Cavello, Texas, May 10, 1852, aged 34 years. [See Stewart.]

Martha, wife of Capt. Moses Hillard, died Sept. 29, 1850, aged 60 years.

Capt. Chester Hillard died at Havana, Oct. 27, 1817, aged 31 years.

Benjamin F. Hillard was lost at sea near the coast of Spain, July 28, 1820, aged 19 years.

George W. Hillard died in the island of Medeira, March 3, 1830, aged 33 years. Also his wife Sarah C. Hillard died at the same place, Nov. 18, 1829, aged 29 years.

Col. Russell Hinckley died April 13, 1845, aged 41 years.

Sophia, wife of Col. Russell Hinckley, died May 3, 1837, aged 37 years.

Russell Hiram Hinckley died July 3, 1629, aged 1 year and 7 months.

Frederick J. Hinckley died June 19, 1831, aged 3 days.

Russell W. Hinckley was drowned in the River Thames Sept. 2, 1835, aged 6 years.

Frances S. Hinckley died Jan. 14, 1839, aged 7 years.

Children of Russell and Sophia Hinckley.

Samuel Holden died July 12, 1826, aged 61 years.

Ruth, relict of Samuel Holden, died Aug. 2, 1839, aged 74 years.

Rebekah, daughter of Samuel and Ruth Holden, died Sept. 22, 1806, in her 11th year.

Jacob Newton died Sept. 16, 1843, aged 95 years.

Lydia, widow of Jacob Newton, died Sept. 24, 1852, aged 96 years.

Benjamin Olin died July 31, 1848, aged 80 years.

Sally, wife of Benjamin Olin, died July 5, 1841, aged 68 years.

Mr. Jesse Palmer died Aug. 10, 1807, aged 65 years.

Mrs. Abigail, relect of Jesse Palmer, died June 14, 1825, aged 63 years.

Capt. William Pride died Jan. 9, 1811, aged 71 years.

Abigail, relict of Capt. William Pride, died July 3, 1835, aged 90 years.

Sally, wife of Moses Hillard and daughter of the late Capt. William Pride, died Sept. 26, 1823, aged 43 years. [See Hillard.]

Capt. Robert Pride died Aug. 10, 1819, aged 51 years.

Capt. James Richards died Feb. 19, 1778, aged 36 years. Also James Richards, Jr., died in Demerara, July 8, 1801, aged 23 years.

Deacon Joseph Roth died May 10, 1774, aged 55 years.

Sarah, wife of Deacon Joseph Roth, died [broken].

Samuel Roath died Dec. 28, 1804, in his 83d year.

Martha, relict of Samuel Roath, died March 26, 1818, in her 88th year.

Charlotte, wife of Zebulon R. Robbins, died Aug. 26, 1830, aged 24 years.

Infant daughter of Zebulon R. and Charlotte Robbins, died July 18, 1830, aged 1½ months.

[A tomb bears this inscription:] Capt. John Smith. 1780.

Samuel Stebbins died Nov. 6, 1838, aged 56 years.

Sarah Hillard, wife of T. C. Stewart and daughter of Moses and Sally Hillard, died at Pass Cavallo, Texas, May 10, 1852, aged 34 years. [See Hillard].

Ezekiel Story died Aug. 20, 1752, in his 52d year.

Jabez Story died June 10, 1817, aged 84 years.
Hannah, wife of Jabez Story, died Jan. 27, 1807, in her 73d year.
James S. Story died Nov. 8, 1778, in his 16th year.
Lucy Story died March 21, 1774, in her 16th year.
Mary Story died June 26, 1782, in her 22d year.
Children of Jabez and Hannah Story.
Jonathan Truman died Oct. 28, 1833, aged 70 years.
Mary, wife of Jonathan Truman, died Oct. 16, 1843, aged 78 years.
Capt. William H. Truman, son of Jonathan and Mary Truman, died at sea, on the coast of Africa, May 21, 1835, aged 27 years.
Rev. Jabez Wight, late Pastor of the Church of Christ in the 2d Society of Preston, who, in the 52d year of his ministry and the 82d of his age, on the 15th day of Sept. 1785, entered into the joy of his Lord.
Ruth, consort of Rev. Jabez Wright, died March 16, 1766, aged 63 years.
Capt. Jabez Wight died Aug. 9, 1787, aged 59 years.
Sarah, relict of Capt. Jabez Wight, died Oct. 3, 1788, aged 60 years.
Capt. John Williams died Jan. 11, 1741, aged 61 years, 10 months and 22 days.
Mary, wife of Capt. John Williams, died March 9, 1745, in her 67th year.
William Williams, son of Joseph and Eunice Williams, died Nov. 17, 1750, in his 2d year.
Hannah, wife of Joseph Williams, died Sept. 28, 1744, in her 22d year.
John Williams, son of Joseph and Hannah Williams, died March 27, 1745, in his 2d year.
Joseph Williams died March 10, 1768, in his 38th year.
Simeon Williams died Oct. 19, 1792, aged 18 years.
Betsey Williams died Dec. 13, 1792, aged 26 years.
Children of Simeon and Anna Williams.
Moses Williams died April 8, 1803, aged 80 years.

THE BELCHER FAMILIES IN NEW ENGLAND.

By Joseph Gardner Bartlett, Esq.

The name Belcher is of great antiquity in England, being found as early as 1176, when Ralph Belcher was witness to a deed. (Historical Collections of Staffordshire, Vol. 1, page 291.) The name is uncommon, however, and is found mostly in the county of Warwick and the surrounding counties of Stafford, Worcester, Oxford, Wilts, and Northampton. One line of the family was seated at Guilsborough in Northamptonshire for several generations, and was lineally descended from Hugh Belcher of Needwood, co. Stafford, who was living in the reign of Edward IV., about 1470. This branch of the family held landed estates, and bore for arms "*Paly of six or and gules, a chief vair*"; and their pedigree was entered in the Visitation of Northamptonshire in 1619, and also in the Visitation of Warwickshire of the same year. The will of Gregory Belcher, yeoman, of Berkeswell, co. Warwick, dated Mar. 20, 1620, mentions wife Joane; son Thomas Belcher; sons-in-law John Bonney and William Cook; daughters Elizabeth Cook, Isabel Bonney, and Alice Pemberton. (Putnam's Historical Magazine, vol. 4, page 183.) It seems likely that Thomas Belcher, son of Gregory of this will, was the Thomas Belcher who lived in the hamlet of Wardend, parish of Aston, co. Warwick, where he had three children recorded: John, bapt. Aug. 24, 1604; Gregory, bapt. Mar. 30, 1606; and Margery, bapt. July 9, 1615. Aston is about nine miles north-west of Berkeswell. As Gregory[1] Belcher, one of the emigrants to New England, in a deposition made in June, 1665, stated he was then about sixty years of age, it seems probable that he was identical with the Gregory Belcher, son of Thomas, who was born in Aston in 1606, who would be in his sixtieth year at the time of the deposition, and of whom no further mention appears in the Aston registers, although his brother and sister were married there. How these Belchers of Berkeswell and Aston were related to the armorial Belchers of Guilsborough has not been ascertained; but doubtless they were of the same original stock.

There were five persons named Belcher who settled in New England before 1650, and from two of them are descended practically all of the name in the United States. These five emigrants, in the order of their arrival in New England, were:

I. Mr. Edward[1] Belcher, born about 1595, came to New England in 1630 with Governor Winthrop, and was one of the founders of Boston. He was the fourth son of William Belcher of Guilsborough, Northamptonshire, England, and of positive armorial descent, but his male descendants became extinct with his grandson.

II. Jeremy,[1] or Jeremiah, Belcher, born about 1613, came to New England in the spring of 1635 and settled in Ipswich, where he died in March, 1692-3. He had eleven children, and his descendants are very numerous. Nothing is known of his ancestry, but he was probably in some degree related to the other emigrants of the name.

III. Gregory[1] Belcher, born about 1606, came to New England about 1637 and settled in Braintree, where he died Nov. 25, 1674. He had seven children, and many descendants live in the United States. He was perhaps the Gregory Belcher, son of Thomas, who was baptized in Aston, co. Warwick, England, Mar. 30, 1606, as suggested above.

IV. Andrew[1] Belcher, born about 1615, son of Thomas Belcher of London, and grandson of Robert Belcher, weaver, of Kingswood, Wiltshire, England. He first appears in New England in 1639, and settled in Cambridge. Although there was but one male who married in each generation of his descendants, this family attained great distinction. His son Andrew[2] Belcher was a Royal Councillor, and the greatest merchant of his day in New England; his grandson Jonathan[3] Belcher was Royal Governor of Massachusetts and also of New Jersey; his great-grandson Jonathan[4] Belcher was Chief Justice and Lieut. Governor of Nova Scotia; and his great-great-grandson Andrew[5] Belcher was a Royal Councillor of Nova Scotia, whose children settled in England, of whom a son, Sir Edward[6] Belcher, K.C.B., was a distinguished naval officer, attaining the rank of Rear Admiral in the British navy. A few descendants remain in England, but the name is extinct in the United States.

The descendants of Andrew[1] Belcher have always used the arms of the Belchers of Guilsborough, although their descent from that branch has not to the writer's knowledge been proven. For a full account of the descendants of Andrew[1] Belcher, see REGISTER, *ante*, vol. 27, pages 239–245.

V. THOMAS[1] BELCHER, stated to have been in the family of Nicholas[1] Frost of Kittery, as early as 1640, and to have died in 1652. ("Old Eliot, Me," vol. 1, pages 87 and 176.) The writer has no further knowledge of this individual, who probably died unmarried. It is a curious coincidence that, about 1693, John[3] Belcher* of Boston (Josiah[2], Gregory[1]) deserted his family there and went to Kittery, where he entered the service of Charles[2] Frost, son of Nicholas,[1] and remained in his employ and in that of his son and grandson for nearly forty years, until his death in 1730, leaving his property to his last employer, Charles[4] Frost.

EDWARD BELCHER OF BOSTON.

1. MR. EDWARD BELCHER, gent., fourth son of William and Christian (Dabridgecourt) Belcher of Guilsborough, Northamptonshire, England, was born about 1595, and came to New England in the fleet with Gov. Winthrop in 1630, and became one of the founders of Boston. His pedigree is recorded in the Visitations of Warwickshire and Northamptonshire in 1619. Although a member of an armorial family of the landed gentry of England, Edward[1] Belcher took a very inconspicuous part in the settlement of Boston, his descendants soon were reduced to very humble circumstances, and the family became extinct in the male line with the death of his grandsons. He was an original member of the First Church in Boston, and carried on the business of a pipestave culler. His houselot was located on the north side of the present Boylston street, between Washington and Tremont streets, and he also had a garden on the opposite side of Boylston street. In his will he calls himself "Edward Belcher, gent., of Boston, late of Guilsborough, Northamptonshire, England." As the witnesses to the will were doubtful whether or not he was of sound mind, the will was not allowed, and his son was appointed administrator of his estate, on Mar. 17, 1672–3. (Suffolk Co. Probate.) The name of his first wife, whom he married in England, has not been discovered. He married second, in Boston, about 1650, Christian, sister of William Talmage and widow of William Wornan, Wormwood, or Wornal. She was admitted to the First Church on Apr. 4, 1646, being then wife of Wormwood, by whom she had two daughters: Mary, born about 1635, who married her step-brother Edward[2] Belcher, Jr.; and Anne, born about 1638, who married, in 1658, Samuel Flack of Boston. (Suffolk Co. Deeds, vol. 21, page 647.)

Child of Edward[1] Belcher, by first wife:

2. i. EDWARD,[2] b. about 1627.

2. EDWARD[2] BELCHER (*Edward*[1]), born in England, about 1627, came in childhood to Boston, where he became a shipwright. On Apr. 30, 1670, he and his wife were deeded, by his father, Edward[1] Belcher, one-half of the latter's real estate. (Suffolk Co. Deeds, vol. 7, page 199.) In 1693, Edward[2] Belcher conveyed this estate to his sons-in-law Mark Pilkington and Edward Kettow, although these deeds were not recorded until Mar. 12, 1713, about which

* The suggestion in "Old Eliot," vol. 1, page 87, that this John Belcher was grandson of Thomas[1] above mentioned, is certainly erroneous. Perhaps Thomas[1] Belcher of Kittery was a brother of Gregory[1] of Braintree, and so grand-uncle of John[3] of Kittery.

time it is presumed Edward[2] Belcher died. (Suffolk Co. Deeds, vol. 16, page 176, and vol. 28, page 24.)

He married first, Jan. 8, 1655–6, his step-sister Mary,[2] born about 1635, daughter of William and Christian (Talmage) Wormwood of Boston, who died Mar. 21, 1693; and married second, June 24, 1708, when about eighty years of age, Abigail, daughter of Roger and Ruth (Stackhouse) Haskins of Beverly, and widow of John Swarton. She married third, Nathaniel Clark of Beverly, and died about 1730, having had no children by any of her husbands.

Children by first wife:

i. SATISFACTION[3] (son), b. Feb. 23, 1656–7, bapt. in First Church, July 31, 1670; took the oath of allegiance, Apr. 21, 1679; no further record, and probably d. unmarried.

ii. MARY, b. Apr. 4, 1659; d. young.

iii. FAITH, b. May 15, 1663; m. (1) ——— Cross; m. (2) Nov. 18, 1691, Mark Pilkington, cordwainer, of Boston, by whom she had four daughters: *Mary*, b. July 27, 1692, m. Nov. 23, 1709, Richard Jenkins; *Sarah*, b. Jan. 3, 1694–5, m. Jan. 20, 1712–13, James Woller; *Mercy*, b. Oct. 4, 1697, after being published to Richard Ould and also to William Wells, m. Jan. 4, 1716–7, John Hall; and *Abigail*, b. Feb. 12, 1700–1, d. young. The only descendants that now exist of Edward[1] Belcher of Boston derive their descent through the daughters of Mark and Faith (Belcher) Pilkington.

iv. MERCY, b. Feb. 7, 1665–6; m. Dec. 4, 1691, Edward Kettow, seaman, of Boston, who d. about 1701; probably no issue.

v. MARTHA, b. Sept. 15, 1671; d. young.

GREGORY BELCHER OF BRAINTREE.

1. GREGORY[1] BELCHER, born about 1606, was in New England as early as 1637, and on Dec. 30, 1639, was granted a lot of 52 acres at Mount Wollaston (Braintree), for thirteen heads, paying three shillings per acre for the same. (Boston Town Records.) Here he settled, was admitted freeman on May 13, 1640, and was made selectman in 1646. He deposed in June, 1665, aged about 60 years. (Essex Co. Court Files.) By occupation he was a farmer. On July 14, 1664, he purchased of John Smith 9 acres of land in Milton, which he gave to his son Joseph Belcher for a marriage portion. (Suffolk Co. Deeds, vol. 4, page 204a.) On Jan. 6, 1657–8, he obtained a lease of the Salter farm in Braintree, from the estate of William Tyng of Boston; and on Jan. 15, 1666–7, Gregory Belcher and others bought the Salter farm for £1900, Belcher's interest being one-eighth. (Suffolk Co. Deeds, vol. 5, page 229.) On Mar. 26, 1670, Gregory Belcher and his son-in-law Alexander Marsh purchased the iron works, with 200 acres of land, in Braintree; and on May 18, 1671, the same parties bought 40 acres in Braintree plain of Henry Crane. (Suffolk Co. Deeds, vol. 7, page 172.)

He died Nov. 25, 1674. The inventory of his estate, showing a total of £629-5-0, was presented by his widow, Jan. 29, 1674–5. (Suffolk Co. Probate.) His wife Catherine survived him, and died in the spring of 1680. Her will, dated Sept. 3, 1679, proved July 20, 1680, gives to son Josiah a cow "if he molest not my son Moses in his present dwelling and possessions"; to son John a cow and a horse; to daughters Elizabeth Gilbert and Mary Marsh, and granddaughter Mary Marsh, some household effects; "to son Moses (who hath all his life carried himself so dutifully to myself and his father) the great bible and the whole house and land he now possesses which I declare his father gave him." Sons Moses Belcher and Alexander Marsh executors.

On July 9, 1680, Josiah Belcher of Boston entered a caveat against the probate of any will said to be made by his late mother, Catherine Belcher of Braintree, widow, deceased, until he be present. (Suffolk Co. Probate.) It does not appear, however, that any contest was made over the estate.

Children:

i. ELIZABETH,[2] m. Thomas Gilbert, who was in Braintree in 1646. (Mass. Colonial Records, vol. iii, page 67.) Evidently he was the "goodman Gilbert" mentioned in Suffolk Co. Deeds, vol. 5, page 527, who owned land in Braintree in 1668, adjoining land of Thomas Gatlive, whose widow, Prudence, was a witness to the will of widow Catherine[1] Belcher.
2. ii. JOSIAH, b. about 1631.
3. iii. JOHN, b. about 1633.
4. iv. MOSES, b. about 1635.
5. v. SAMUEL, b. Aug. 24, 1637.
vi. MARY, b. July 8, 1639; m. Dec. 19, 1655, Alexander Marsh of Braintree.
6. vii. JOSEPH, b. Dec. 25, 1641.

2. JOSIAH[2] BELCHER (*Gregory*[1]), born in 1631, was a wheelwright, and settled in Boston, where he acquired an estate on the southeasterly corner of what is now Essex street and Harrison avenue, measuring 126 feet on Essex street, and running back 285 feet to the water. After the death of his widow, a partition was made of this estate among his surviving children, on Sept. 20, 1693, which is described and recorded in Suffolk Co. Deeds, vol. 19, page 158. Further deeds in relation to this property show that all his sons, except John and Benjamin, died without issue, and apparently unmarried, and that the daughter Dorothy died without issue soon after her marriage. (Suffolk Co. Deeds, vol. 40, page 225; vol. 41, page 210; vol. 46, page 90; and vol. 41, page 212.)

He was one of the founders of the third, or Old South, Church, and died Apr. 3, 1683, aged 52, being buried in the Granary burying ground, where his gravestone still remains. His will, made the day of his decease, names wife Ranis, sons John, Jonathan, Joseph, Edward, Nathan and Benjamin, and daughters Elizabeth, Rebecca, Anna, Dorothy, Abigail, and Ruth. (Suffolk Co. Probate.) He married, Mar. 3, 1654-5, Ranis,[2] born June 4, 1638, daughter of Elder Edward[1] and Elizabeth Rainsford of Boston. She died Oct, 2, 1691.

Children:

i. JOSIAH,[3] b. Dec. 23, 1655; served in Capt. James Oliver's Co. in the Narraganset campaign in King Philip's War, and took part in the Great Swamp Fight, Dec. 19, 1675. He died unmarried, and was evidently the Josiah Belcher who was drowned at Weymouth in the autumn of 1682, as mentioned in Judge Sewall's diary (vol. 2, page 19*).
ii. JOHN, b. Oct. 9, 1657; d. in infancy.
7. iii. JOHN, b. Dec. 23, 1659.
iv. JONATHAN, b. Sept. 1, 1661; was a goldsmith in Boston, and sold his interest in the paternal estate to his brother Edward, Nov. 22, 1693. (Suffolk Co. Deeds, vol. 16, page 220, and vol. 40, page 225.) He died soon after, unmarried.
v. ELIZABETH, b. July 10, 1663; m. John Paine of Swansey, Mass. (Suffolk Co. Deeds, vol. 35, page 248.)

vi. Joseph, b. Oct. 4, 1665; was a shipwright; d. unmarried, between 1700 and 1708. (Suffolk Co. Deeds, vol. 40, page 225, and vol. 41, page 210.)
vii. Rebecca, b. Dec. 31, 1667; m. in Lynn, Nov. 30, 1687, Joseph Fuller, shipwright, who settled in Boston. (Suffolk Co. Deeds, vol. 40, page 225.)
viii. Edward, b. Jan. 19, 1669-70; d. unmarried before May 14, 1700. (Suffolk Co. Deeds, vol. 40, page 225.)
ix. Anna, b. Feb. 13, 1671-2; m. (int. rec. Jan. 26, 1696-7) Joseph Johnson, cooper, of Boston.
x. Dorothy, b. Oct. 28, 1673; m. Feb. 19, 1693-4, Edmund Gross of Boston; she d. soon, without issue.
xi. Abigail, b. Mar. 10, 1674-5; living unmarried in Boston, June 8, 1717. (Suffolk Co. Deeds.)
xii. Nathan, b. 1677; d. July 3, 1699, unmarried.
xiii. Ruth, b. Dec. 21, 1678; m. Dec. 28, 1703, Benjamin Tolman. (Boston marriage records incorrectly call her Ruth Fletcher. For proof, see Suffolk Co. Deeds, vol. 41, page 212.)
8. xiv. Benjamin, b. Mar. 20, 1680-1.

3. John[2] Belcher (*Gregory*[1]), born about 1633, was a husbandman, and resided in Braintree. During King Philip's War he performed several months' service in the spring and summer of 1676 in the garrisons at Northampton, Milton and Medfield. He died intestate in 1693, leaving a very small estate, his son Josiah[3] Belcher being appointed administrator, Nov. 16, 1693. The inventory of the estate, valued at only £27-7-0, mentions "a poore house and ten acres of land, a piece of salt marsh, a little poore household goods, and an old spitt." (Suffolk Co. Probate.) He married, about 1655, Sarah ———, who survived him.

Children:

i. Sarah,[3] b. June 27, 1656; m. Nov. 13, 1677, Samuel Irons of Braintree.
ii. John, b. Jan. 1, d. Feb. 9, 1658-9.
9. iii. Joseph, b. Feb. 23, 1660-1.
iv. John, b. Mar. 10, d. Mar. 11, 1662.
v. Hannah, b. Apr. 6, 1664.
vi. Mary, b. Dec. 26, 1666.
10. vii. Josiah, b. June 26, 1669.
viii. Ruth, b. about 1672; d. June 23, 1675.

4. Moses[2] Belcher (*Gregory*[1]), born about 1635, was a husbandman, and resided in Braintree, inheriting his father's homestead. He is called "Corporal" Belcher on the records. He died July 5, 1691, and in his will, dated three days before, he mentions his wife; daughter Mary Bass; other daughters to have portions equal to that given to Mary; son Moses (then under age) to have the whole homestead; brother Alexander Marsh and cousin Joseph Belcher overseers; wife sole executor. (Suffolk Co. Probate.)

He married, May 23, 1666, Mary Nash, probably a daughter of James and Alice Nash of Weymouth, Mass., as Moses Belcher was a witness on a deed made by them, May 22, 1666, the day before his marriage. (Suffolk Co Deeds, vol. 5, page 82.)

On Dec. 30, 1707, Mary Belcher, widow, and Anna Belcher, spinster, Moses Belcher, Joseph Bass, Ichabod Allen and Elizabeth his wife, Jabez Athern and Katherine his wife, and Joseph Brackett and Mehitable his wife, being all the children of Moses and Mary Belcher, conveyed land of said Moses deceased. (Suffolk Deeds, vol. 36, page 70.)

Children:

i. MARY,[3] b. Sept. 8, 1668; m. June 5, 1688, Joseph Bass of Braintree.
ii. SARAH, b. Mar. 2, 1670–1; d. young.
iii. MERCY, b. Mar. 2, 1671–2; d. young.
11. iv. A SON [MOSES], b. 1674.
v. MEHITABLE, b. Sept. 12, 1676; m. Dec. 25, 1701, Joseph Bracket of Braintree.
vi. ELIZABETH, b. Apr. 25, 1679; m. Dec. 25, 1701, Ichabod Allen of Martha's Vineyard.
vii. CATHERINE, b. Nov. 23, 1681; d. Aug. 13, 1682.
viii. ANNA, b. May 21, 1684; m. Oct. 10, 1717, Nathaniel Wardell of Boston.
ix. CATHERINE, b. July 5, 1686; m. Nov. 30, 1705, Jabez Athearn of Martha's Vineyard; d. Apr. 3, 1752.

5. SAMUEL[2] BELCHER (*Gregory*[1]), born Aug. 24, 1637, resided in Braintree, where he died June 17, 1679. On May 6, 1680, administration on his estate was granted "to Roger Billing, Alexander March, and Moses Belcher – his father-in-law and two of his brothers." (Suffolk Co. Probate.) The inventory was £576–17–6. On Mar. 4, 1696, Thomas French and Elizabeth his wife conveyed to their brother Gregory Belcher their interest in the estate of their father Samuel Belcher. (Suffolk Co. Deeds, vol. 41, page 249.) On the same day, John Sanders of Westerly and Silence his wife conveyed their interest in the estate of their father Samuel Belcher. (Suffolk Co. Deeds, vol. 41, page 250.) On Sept. 21, 1693, Moses Belcher of Dorchester conveyed his interest in the estate of his father, Samuel Belcher, to his brother Gregory (Suffolk Co. Deeds, vol. 41, page 252). On Aug. 8, 1727, William Wattle and Abigail his wife, of Lebanon, Conn., conveyed to their brother Samuel Belcher their interest in the estate of their late mother Niles, deceased, in the estate of her former husband Samuel Belcher. (Suffolk Co. Deeds, vol. 41, page 253.) Samuel[2] Belcher married, Dec. 15, 1663, Mary, daughter of Roger Billings of Dorchester, Mass. She married second, Apr. 20, 1680, Samuel Niles of Braintree.

Children:

12. i. GREGORY,[3] b. Feb. 28, 1664-5.
13. ii. SAMUEL, b. Sept. 21, 1666.
iii. WILLIAM, b. May 3, 1668; served in Capt. John Withington's Co. in the expedition against Quebec in 1690; was a blacksmith; d. unmarried, in 1701; his brother Gregory appointed administrator. (Suffolk Co. Probate.)
iv. MARY, b. Oct. 16, 1670; m. Dec. 16, 1696, Capt. Nathaniel Vose of Milton, who d. Oct. 10, 1753; d. June 22, 1758.
14. v. MOSES, b. Aug. 4, 1672.
vi. ABIGAIL, b. Oct. 24, 1674; m. Apr. 28, 1697, William Waddel of Stonington, and later of Lebanon, Conn.
vii. ELIZABETH, b. June 22, 1677; m. Thomas French of Braintree.
viii. SILENCE, b. June 24, 1679; m. John Sanders of Westerly, R. I.

6. JOSEPH[2] BELCHER (*Gregory*[1]), born Dec. 25, 1641, on his marriage was given by his father 9 acres of land in Milton, where he settled (Suffolk Co. Deeds, vol. iv., page 204). His wife Rebecca was sole heiress to large tracts of land in Dorchester and Milton, from the estate of her father; but evidently incompatibility made their domestic life unhappy, causing a temporary separation and a

summons before the General Court. By the efforts of friends, however, a reconciliation was effected. (Dedham Historical Register, vol. 12, page 41.) On the breaking out of King Philip's War, Joseph Belcher served as quartermaster in the cavalry troop of Capt. Thomas Prentice in the first expedition against King Philip at Mt. Hope, and in a skirmish with the Indians at Swansey, on June 28, 1675, he distinguished himself by great bravery, being badly wounded in the knee, and having his horse shot under him. He died about 1678, the inventory of his estate, amounting to £472–4–9, being presented on Feb. 7, 1678–9. (Suffolk Co. Probate, vol. 12, page 318.) He married, in 1664, Rebecca,[2] baptized July 7, 1650, daughter of John[1] and Ann Gill of Dorchester.

Children:

i. ANNE,[3] b. in 1665; m. in 1682, Rowland Storey of Boston.
ii. JOHN, b. Apr. 2, 1667; d. Feb. 2, 1681–2.
15. iii. JOSEPH, b. May 14, 1669.
iv. REBECCA, b. Nov. 12, 1671; m. June 25, 1690, Samuel Miller of Rehoboth, later of Milton.
v. PATIENCE, b. Dec. 5, 1674.
vi. MARY, bapt. Nov. 12, 1676; m. Sept. 23, 1696, Benjamin Fenno of Milton.
vii. GILL, b. Sept. 22, 1678; was a sea captain in Boston, where he married, Sept. 21, 1702, Mary Howard. On Oct. 26, 1702, he gave power of attorney to his wife to dispose of his property, and on Sept. 3, 1703, she mortgaged his property in Boston. (Suffolk Co. Deeds, vol. 21, page 376.) On Feb. 6, 1705–6, Samuel Sewall sent a letter to Rev. Joseph Lord in Dorchester, South Carolina, by Capt. Gill Belcher. (6 Mass. Hist. Society Coll., vol. I, page 324.) No further trace of Gill Belcher has been found in New England; and he may have settled in South Carolina or been lost at sea. One Mary Belcher, possibly his widow, m. in Boston, June 7, 1716, John Flagg. In 1765, a Gill Belcher of Hebron, Conn., perhaps a grandson of Capt. Gill,[3] bought land in Great Barrington, Mass.

7. JOHN[3] BELCHER (*Josiah*,[2] *Gregory*[1]), born in Boston, Dec. 23, 1659, was baptized in the First Church, April 3, 1664, and admitted to the Old South Church, Apr. 30, 1680. By occupation he was a ship carpenter. In 1690 he was in the military service and stationed at Kittery, Me., and was dismissed and sent home on Nov. 9 of that year. (Me. Hist. Coll. Series 2, vol. 5, page 160.) He resided in Boston until about 1693, when he went to Kittery, Me., and entered the employ of the Frost family, who were extensive shipbuilders, where he continued until his death in 1730. His will, dated Feb. 17, 1729–30, calls himself "John Belcher, joiner, of Kittery, eldest son of Josiah Belcher of Boston," and states he has lived with the Frosts for near about forty years and none of his relatives have assisted him, and therefore he leaves all his property to Charles Frost. (York Wills, vol. 4, page 130; also Suffolk Co. Deeds, vol. 46, page 90.) Presumably it was this John[3] Belcher who married Theodora ———, in 1688, and had two children baptized in the Old South Church in Boston. He evidently deserted his family when he went to Maine in 1693, as his wife Theodora remained in Boston and married second, Dec. 9, 1698, Simon Lee, married third, Nov. 20, 1700, William Darnton, and married fourth, Sept. 13, 1709, Francis Pomeroy.

Children of John[3] and Theodora:

16. i. JOHN,[4] b. Dec. 11, 1689; bapt. in Old South Church, May 31, 1691.
ii. MARY, bapt. in Old South Church, Dec. 11, 1693; m. Oct. 7, 1712, John Milton of Boston, and had a son *John*,[5] b. in 1713, and a dau. *Theodora*, b. in 1715.

8. BENJAMIN[3] BELCHER (*Josiah*,[2] *Gregory*[1]), born in Boston, Mar. 20, 1680–1, was a shipwright, and about 1703 settled in Newport, R. I. (Suffolk Co. Deeds, vol. 41, page 210.) He was admitted freeman of R. I., May 6, 1707, and died about 1719. The information herein given of his descendants needs further verification. He married first, Phebe ——, who died after 1711; and married second, about 1715, Sarah, born Aug. 13, 1690, daughter of Arnold and Sarah Collins of Newport. She married second, about 1720, Josiah Bliss of Middletown, R. I.

Children by first wife:

17. i. BENJAMIN,[4] b. Nov. 7, 1704.
ii. PHEBE, b. June 11, 1708.
18. iii. EDWARD, b. Aug. 24, 1711.

Children by second wife:

19. iv. ARNOLD, b. about 1715.
v. SARAH (perhaps), bapt. May 17, 1717.

9. JOSEPH[3] BELCHER (*John*,[2] *Gregory*[1]) was born Feb. 23, 1660–1, and after his birth record, appears no further in any town, church, deed, or probate record that has been found by the writer. Nevertheless, it appears he had a family, as in the diary of John Marshall of Braintree is the following entry: "Joseph Belcher's child died Mar. 8, 1700–1." On Mar. 20, 1726, Joseph Belcher and his son, from Braintree, were warned from Boston. (Boston Record Com. Report, No. 13, page 154.)

It seems likely that he was father of the following Belchers who cannot otherwise be placed:

i. MERCY, m. in Boston, Nov. 11, 1709, Benjamin Johns.
ii. HANNAH, m. in Boston, May 25, 1713, Anthony Ennis.
ii. ELIZABETH, m. in Boston, Jan. 4, 1715-16, Alexander Fullerton. Possibly, however, she was dau. of Josiah[3] Belcher.
iv. MARY Belcher, m. in Boston, June 7, 1716, John Flagg (then in middle life), as his second wife. But possibly she was the widow of Gill[3] Belcher as previously suggested.
v. A SON, perhaps the Joseph Belcher, seaman, on ship "King George" in 1758, referred to under Josiah[3] Belcher.

10. JOSIAH[3] BELCHER (*John*,[2] *Gregory*[1]), born in Braintree, June 26, 1669, was a cordwainer, and lived in Braintree until Jan., 1713–14, when he went to Watertown, from whence he was warned two months afterwards. Later we find him in Boston, being warned from there before July 29, 1723. He then lived at Marblehead for a short time, but returned soon to Boston, he and his wife and two sons being warned in Boston on May 22, 1725. He remained, nevertheless, and on Feb. 25, 1726, bought of Thomas Bill (presumably his son-in-law) a portion of the dwelling house of the latter in Blackhorse lane, which he and his wife Margaret sold back to Thomas Bill, on Jan. 5, 1729–30. (Suffolk Co. Deeds, vol. 40,

page 266, and vol. 44, page 47.) This deal was probably for the purpose of securing a residence for Josiah and Margaret Belcher with their daughter Ruth Bill in Boston, free from the molestations of the authorities. In 1734, Josiah Belcher was refused a liquor license. No further record appears of him. He married Margaret, born May 11, 1670, daughter of Jonathan and Elizabeth (Ladd) Hayden of Braintree.

Children:

20. i. JOHN,[4] b. Aug. 28, 1694.
 ii. ELIZABETH, b. May 25, 1697; perhaps m. Jan. 4, 1715-16, Alexander Fullerton of Boston.
 iii. MARGARET, b. Apr. 8, 1699.
 iv. RUTH (probably), b. about 1702; m. June 6, 1723, Thomas Bill, shipwright, of Boston.
 v. A SON, name undiscovered.
 vi. JOSEPH, b. Nov. 1, 1709. Perhaps the Joseph Belcher of Braintree who served as seaman on the ship "King George," from Mar. 15 to Oct. 21, 1758; no further record.

11. MOSES[3] BELCHER (*Moses,*[2] *Gregory*[1]), born in Braintree in 1674, inherited the farm occupied by his father and grandfather, and resided in Braintree until his death, about 1745. He was called "Sr." on the records, to distinguish him from his cousin Moses[4] Belcher (born in 1692, son of Samuel[3]). Moses Belcher, Sr., held numerous minor town offices, such as fence viewer, constable, hogreive, and surveyor of highways, between the years 1712 and 1733. His name occurs in several land transactions, but no probate records of his estate appear. He married first, May 20, 1715, Anne, born about 1696, daughter of Samuel and Anne (Clay) Sarson of Martha's Vineyard, who died Jan. 28, 1721-2, having had three children; and married second, Jan. 3, 1726-7, Alice, born June 9, 1698, daughter of Dr. John and Sarah (Newton) Wilson of Braintree, and great-granddaughter of Rev. John Wilson, first pastor of the First Church in Boston. She died without issue, in 1754.

Children by first wife:

21. i. MOSES,[4] b. Mar. 8, 1715-16.
 ii. ANNE, b. May 19, 1718; probably m. Aug. 11, 1748, as his second wife, Maj. Joseph Crosby of Braintree.
 iii. MARY, b. Dec. 11, 1720; d. Aug. 18, 1725.

12. DEA. GREGORY[3] BELCHER (*Samuel,*[2] *Gregory*[1]), born in Braintree, Feb. 28, 1664-5, always resided there, where he held many minor town offices, and was deacon in the church for many years. Besides carrying on farming, he also followed the occupation of shipwright and carpenter. He was killed in an accident, by a plough, July 4, 1727. He married, Mar. 25, 1689-90, Elizabeth, born in 1669, daughter of John and Rebecca (Farnsworth) Ruggles of Braintree, who died Nov. 22, 1748.

Children:

22. i. GREGORY,[4] b. June 19, 1691.
 ii. ELIZABETH, b. Oct. 31, d. Dec. 30, 1693.
 iii. REBECCA, b. Nov. 30, 1694; m. (1) Sept. 14, 1720, Henry Carley, who d. at sea, Sept. 24, 1721, while on a return voyage from Ireland to New England; m. (2) July 1, 1727, Dr. Jacob Ealmanthorp of Braintree. (Suffolk Co. Deeds, vol. 41, p. 253.)

iv. ELIZABETH, b. Jan. 30, 1696-7; m. Feb. 12, 1724-5, David Bass of Braintree.
23. v. SAMUEL, b. Aug, 19, 1699.
vi. RUTH, b. Apr. 6, 1702; m. Oct. 10, 1728, Joseph Eddy of Bristol.
24. vii. JOSEPH, b. Aug. 19, 1704.
viii. CATHERINE, b. Dec. 24, 1706; m. (1) Nov. 30, 1732, William Clough of Boston; m. (2) Dec. 5, 1734, Rev. Elisha Eaton, Harvard College 1729, minister at Randolph, Mass.
ix. BENJAMIN, b. May 17, d. June 5, 1709.
x. ABIGAIL, b. May 24, 1711; m. Aug. 2, 1733, James Brackett of Braintree.

13. SAMUEL[3] BELCHER (*Samuel,[2] Gregory[1]*), born Sept. 21, 1666, was a farmer and resided in Braintree, where he held various minor town offices, and died Dec. 19, 1714. He married, in 1688, Comfort, born in 1666, daughter of John and Jael (Thayer) Harbour of Braintree and Mendon. (Suffolk Co. Deeds, vol. 17, page 216.) She married second, Jan. 10, 1722-3 (or Aug. 13, 1723), Stephen Crane of Braintree, and died in Milton, Dec. 21, 1745. Her will, dated 1744, mentions sons Moses and Nathaniel Belcher; daughter Mary Wales deceased; daughter Deborah Holten; and daughter Zipporah Curtis.

Children:

i. SAMUEL,[4] bapt. Mar. 3, 1688-9; d. in infancy.
ii. SAMUEL, bapt. Apr. 5, 1691; d. June 4, 1692.
25. iii. MOSES, b. Dec. 16, 1692.
iv. DEBORAH, b. Feb. 11, 1694-5; m. July 20, 1721, Nathaniel Houghton of Milton. (The Braintree records erroneously give his marriage to Mary Belcher.)
v. MARY, b. June, 1697; m. Jan. 13, 1718-19, Thomas Wales of Braintree.
vi. WILLIAM, b. July 14, d. Aug. 3, 1699.
vii. NATHANIEL, b. July 25, 1700.
viii. SARAH, b. Jan. 14, 1702-3; d. Jan. 14, 1716-17.
ix. ZIPPORAH, b. Aug. 27, 1704; m. Jan. 7, 1723-4, John Curtis of Braintree.
x. ANNE, b. July 19, d. Aug. 3, 1706.

14. DEA. MOSES[3] BELCHER (*Samuel,[2] Gregory[1]*), born Aug. 14, 1672, purchased a farm in Milton, where he resided until 1720, when he removed to Preston, Conn., where he died May 4, 1728. He and his wife were admitted to the Milton Church, Jan. 19, 1695-6, and dismissed to the second Preston church, Nov. 13, 1720, where he was elected one of the first deacons. In 1721, he represented Preston in the Connecticut General Assembly. On Sept. 12, 1729, Hannah Belcher, widow, William Belcher, Elijah Belcher, Stephen Tucker and Hannah his wife, all of Preston, Conn., and Ebenezer Clapp and Abigail his wife, of Stoughton, conveyed their interest in the land grant of George Lyon. (Suffolk Co. Deeds, vol. 49, page 171.)

He married, Dec. 19, 1694, Hannah, born Nov. 14, 1673, daughter of George and Hannah (Tolman) Lyon of Milton, who died Aug. 20, 1745, in Preston.

Children:

i. HANNAH,[4] b. Sept. 29, 1695; m. Aug. 30, 1716, Stephen Tucker of Milton, later of Preston, Conn.
ii. ABIGAIL, b. Sept. 18, 1697; m. Feb. 4, 1719-20, Ebenezer Clapp of Milton, later of Stoughton.

iii. MOSES, b. May 5, 1699; d. Oct. 13, 1722.
27. iv. WILLIAM, b. Dec. 20, 1701.
28. v. ELIJAH, b. Dec. 13, 1703.
vi. ELISHA, b. Nov. 12, 1706; d. July 20, 1729.
vii. MARY, b. Dec. 7, 1709; m. Nov. 20, 1729, Moses Tyler of Preston, Conn.
viii. EBENEZER, b. Feb. 23, 1713-14; d. Apr. 26, 1714.
ix. ELIZABETH, b. July 21, 1715; d. Feb. 9, 1718.
x. MEHITABLE, b. Nov. 4, 1718; m. Oct. 1, 1741, Timothy Lester of Preston, Conn.

15. REV. JOSEPH[3] BELCHER (*Joseph,*[2] *Gregory*[1]), born May 14, 1669, in youth inherited a considerable estate for those times, which enabled him to obtain a liberal education at Harvard College, where he was graduated in 1690. He then studied for the ministry, and began to preach in Dedham, in the spring of 1692, which resulted in a permanent call, and he was ordained and settled there on Nov. 29, 1693. He remained pastor there for nearly 30 years, until the autumn of 1721, when he was incapacitated by a paralytic shock, and was removed to the house of his son-in-law Rev. Thomas Walter, in Roxbury, to be under the care of his brother-in-law Dr. Philip Tompson, where he died Apr. 27, 1723. His portrait in oil hangs in the First Church in Dedham.

He married, Mar. 8, 1693-4, Abigail, born Nov. 25, 1670, daughter of Benjamin and Susanna (Kirkland) Tompson, whose father was a graduate of Harvard College, and for many years taught school and practiced medicine in Roxbury and Braintree, and also was noted as a poet and philosopher. She survived her husband.

Children:

i. ABIGAIL,[4] b. Aug. 23, 1695; m. Apr. 14, 1720, Perez Bradford, Harvard College 1717, who taught school in Dedham, Milton, and Attleborough.
ii. REBECCA, b. Mar. 14, 1696-7; m. Dec. 25, 1718, Rev. Thomas Walter of Roxbury, Harvard College 1713.
iii. JOSEPH, b. Oct. 16, 1699; Harvard College 1717; taught school in Dedham and Milton; d. about 1739; m. Dec. 24, 1731, Elizabeth, b. July 3, 1703, dau. of Nathaniel and Elizabeth (Breck) Butt of Dorchester, who had no children. She m. (2) Dec. 25, 1740, Capt. William Hunt of Braintree. (Suffolk Co. Deeds, vol. 65, page 228.)
iv. MARY, b. July 23, 1701; d. Jan. 11, 1702-3.
v. SAMUEL, b. Mar. 23, 1703-4; was a saddler, learning the trade with his uncle Benjamin Tompson of Roxbury; lived in Dedham and later in Milton, but about 1730 settled in Windsor, Conn., where he afterwards resided; d. Oct. 10, 1756, in an expedition against Crown Point, being a member of Capt. Benjamin Allen's Co.; m. Aug. 17, 1732, Mabel, b. Aug. 19, 1708, dau. of Capt. Thomas and Abigail (Edwards) Stoughton of Windsor, Conn. He had no children, according to Hinman's "Early Puritans of Conn.," page 177, which states that the will of Samuel left his estate to his wife Mabel and nephew Belcher Richards; but perhaps he was father of the Gill Belcher of Hebron, Conn., who bought land in Great Barrington, Mass., in 1765 (see 6, vii.).
vi. MARY, b. 1706; m. Aug. 10, 1726, Dr. Joseph Richards of Dedham, Mass., Harvard College 1721.
v. GILL, b. Oct. 11, 1711; lived in Milton and Swansey, and later in Dedham, where he d. May 16, 1752, apparently unmarried.

[To be continued.]

ESDRAS READE.

By Charles French Read, Esq., of Boston.

Among the great company of English people who joined in the Puritan movement which settled at the Massachusetts Bay early in the seventeenth century, the name of Esdras Reade finds a place, and it seems proper to publish this brief biography of him, that coming generations of his descendants may study the life of their first American ancestor of the name.

The earliest mention of Esdras Reade, which I have as yet found, is in the Records of the Town of Boston, under date of December 24, 1638. The entry reads that "Esdras Reade, a Taylor, is this day allowed to bee an Inhabitant and to have a great lot at Muddy River for 4 heads." Muddy River was then a part of Boston, and in 1705 became the present town of Brookline. But evidently conditions in Muddy River were not satisfactory to Esdras Reade, owing possibly to the fact that the hamlet was four miles from Boston, for we find that after a stay of a few weeks he removed to Salem, Mass., the records of that town telling us, under date of February 25, 1639, that "Esdras Reade is receaved to be an inhattant at the towne of Salem."

He received grants of land from the town, joined, with his wife Alice, the First Church of Salem, and was made a freeman of the Massachusetts Bay Colony, June 2, 1641. While a resident of Salem, his two children, Obadiah and Bethiah, the only ones he had, were baptized in the First Church, the record being "1640 31 3 Two children of Esdras Reade."

It is evident that the migratory habits of our ancestors of the seventeenth century fastened themselves upon the subject of this sketch, for in 1644, Esdras Reade with other members of the Salem church, including the pastor, Rev. John Fiske, founded the town of Wenham, Mass., which was called, before its incorporation, Enon, meaning much water.

While a resident of Wenham, he was a leading citizen of the town. Having, with his wife, become a member of the First Church of Wenham, when it was organized October 8, 1644, he was elected the first deacon, and he also represented the town in the General Court in the years 1648 and 1651.

A few years later brought another change of residence, for in 1655 he was one of the founders of the town of Chelmsford, Mass. A recital of the proceedings which led to the settlement of the new town may be interesting.

To quote from a history of Middlesex County:

In September, 1654, propositions were made to Rev. John Fiske and his church in Wenham to remove to Chelmsford, Mass., and the account of the proceedings which resulted in their removal there is preserved in the handwriting of Mr. Fiske. It is written in the quaint diction of the time, and reads as follows: "A day was set of meeting at Chelmsford. Upon the said day set divers of ye brethren accompanied ye pastor over unto Chelmsford where ye committee and divers others were present. A view was taken of ye place. The brethren present satisfied themselves about their accommodations, and proposals were then made to ye pastor for his accommodation and yearly maintenance, as to be tendered unto him by consent of ye whole of inhabitants and in the name of ye committee."

Soon after their return to Wenham, the larger part of the church, with their pastor, decided to accept Chelmsford's proposals. But at this time the proceedings were discontinued. We now return to Mr. Fiske's account. "Thus the matter lay dormant as 'twere all winter, until ye first month '55 at which time Brother Reade coming over, enformed us in such wise here at Wenham, as thereupon ye paster and ye said engaged brethren demurred upon ye proceedings, and some that had sold here at Wenham redeemed their accommodations again into their possession and a letter was suitably sent by Brother Reade to acquaint ye Chelmsford committee how things stood, and advised to stead themselves elsewhere."

The matter was not abandoned. Several letters passed between the parties. In June, 1655, a committee went with letters for Chelmsford, "with full power to then and there to treat and finalls to determine the business between both parties. The matter way referred to counsel. This case thus determined on either side, preparations were made for ye removal of ye church. Accordingly about ye 13th of ye 9th month '55 there were met at Chelmsford, ye pastor with ye engaged brethren of Wenham, seven in all, to whom such of the brethren of Woburne and Concord churches late at Wenham presented themselves and testimony given, were by a unanimous vote received in fellowship."

At the first town meeting in Chelmsford, held November 22, 1655, Esdras Reade was elected one of a "committee to officiate in ordering the publick affaires."

Three years later found him again on the move, for in 1658 he came to live in Boston a second time; and two years later, in 1660, the records of Chelmsford tell us that "John Webb is admitted to purchase all the rights and privileges granted by the town of Chelmsford to Esdras Reade." He joined with his wife, possibly a second one, the Second Church of Boston, August 4, 1661.

Nine years later he was living in Woburn, Mass., for in the deed of a sale of land which he made in 1670, he calls himself "Esdras Reade, Taylor of Woburn." But by the following year he had become a resident of Boston for the third time, as is shown in another deed, and he apparently lived there continuously until his death in 1680.

It is probable that his home was situated at the intersection of the thoroughfares which we call to-day Salem and Prince Streets. He sold this estate, January 12, 1674, to Samuel Brackenbury, physician, for the sum of £132, and the deed of sale gives the location as "at the intersection of a street that leads from the Second Meeting House in Boston towards Century Haven and a lane that leads from the said street towards Winnissimmet Ferry Place."

Esdras Reade, and here I quote the inscription on the gravestone of another ancestor, "after he had served his generation, by the will of God, fell on sleep" in Boston, July 27, 1680, at the advanced age of eighty-five years. He lies buried in Copp's Hill Burying Ground, Boston, and over his grave is to be seen to-day the double gravestone of himself and his second wife Sarah. It is inscribed in part: "Here lyeth buried | ye boddy of | Esdras Reade aged | 85 Years Died | July ye 27 | 1680."

He died intestate, and his small estate was administered by his son, Obadiah Read. The inventory of his property shows that he was, until his death, engaged in making a living by his trade, and he was possessed of a complement of tailor's tools.

And so we take leave of Esdras Read, taylor. When he came to the now great city of Boston, in 1638, it was a hamlet of about thirty families.

During his life, the Colonies of Massachusetts Bay and Plymouth were united in one, and seventy towns were incorporated by the General Court. He saw the persecution of the Quakers, and the havoc caused by King Philip's War. The closing years of his life were passed amid the political disturbances which resulted, four years after his death, in the annulment of the Charter of Massachusetts Bay by King Charles the Second.

INSCRIPTIONS FROM OLD CEMETERIES IN CONNECTICUT.

Communicated by Louis Marinus Dewey, Esq., of Westfield, Mass.

Glastonbury.

Josiah Benton died 9 Nov., 1783, in 78th year.
Joseph Fox died 24 May, 1733, in 38th year.
Hannah wife of Richard Goodrich died 23 Sept., 1721, aged 30 years.
Naomi Hale died 17 May, 1735, in 79th year.
Thomas Hale died 17 Jan., 1712, aged about 44 years.
Thomas Hale died 23 Dec., 1723, in 70th year.
Thomas Hale died 4 July, 1750, in 66th year.
Joseph Hill died 8 Nov., 1713, in 64th year. [On a table monument.]
John Hollister died 13 Dec., 1741, in 73d year.

Elizabeth daughter of John and Abi Hollister died 19 Feb., 1736, in 22d year.

Dorothy wife of Thomas Hollister died 5 Oct., 1741, in 64th year.

Thomas Hollister died 12 Oct., 1741, in 70th year.

Abraham Kilborn died 20 April, 1770, in 79th year.

Joseph Kilborn died 11 July, 1790, in 68th year.

Mary his wife died 14 Aug., 1806, in 84th year.

Eleazar Kimberly, late Secretary, the first male born in New Haven, died 3 Feb., 1709, aged 70. [Table monument.]

Thomas Kimberly. [No date.]

Experience wife of Thomas Loveland died 20 Dec., 1772, in 52d year.

John Loveland died 28 May, 1751, in 40th year.

Mrs. Mary Loveland died 28 March, 1789, in 74th year.

John Loveland died 15 Dec., 1794, in 31st year.

Elizabeth his wife died 3 May, 1846, aged 91.

Captain Abner Moseley died 11 Feb., 1766, in 66th year.

Capt. Joseph Maudsly, born 21 Dec., 1670, died 15 Aug., 1719.

Mrs. Abigail Merick, once the amiable consort of Capt. Joseph Moseley of this place, but late relict of Mr. James Merick of Springfield, died 18 April, 1773, in 93d year.

Capt. Isaac Mosely died 11 July, 1773, in 61st year.

Ruth his relict died 5 Sept., 1787, in 71st year.

Lucretia wife of Dr. Isaac Mosely died 3 Oct., 1770, in 28th year.

Wm. Mosely. [Monument.]

Ebenezer Plummer died 29 Nov., 1817, in 91st year.

Elizabeth his wife died 18 Feb., 1806, aged 73.

Gershom Smith died 28 Aug., 1747, in 68th year.

Capt. Richard Smith, Sr., died 4 July, 1716, about 63 years old.

Mary wife of Richard Smith, Sr., died 7 May, 1704, aged about 86 years.

Richard Smith died ——— 1774, aged 68.

Rev. Timothy Stevens died 14 April, 1726, in 61st year.

Deacon Benjamin Tallcott died 12 Nov., 1727, in 54th year.

John Webster died 1 Oct., 1781, in 34th year.

[Others of the Benton, Brown, House, Hubbard, Kinne, Lockwood, Risley or Wrisley, Sellew, Talcott, and Wells families appear.]

East Glastonbury.

Charles Andrews died 3 June, 1790, in 80th year.

Mary relict of Charles Andrews died 21 March, 1820, aged 72.

Elizabeth wife of Charles Andrews died 6 Aug., 1805, in 90th year.

Samuel Brooks died 2 Aug., 1810, in 43d year.

Isaac Chalker, pastor of the church at Eastbury, died 28 May, 1765, in 58th year, and 21st year of his ministry.

George Covell died 4 May, 1850, aged 68 years.

Clarissa his wife died 2 Nov., 1817, aged 28.

James Covell died — Sept., 1776, in 63d year.

Capt. Samuel Covell died 7 May, 1822, aged 77.

Mrs. Anna his consort died 8 July, 1816, in 66th year.

Samuel son of Samuel and Anna Covell died 27 Oct., 1793, in 22d year, at Point Peter.

Pitkin Eells died 25 Dec., 1816, aged 66.

Mary his wife died 1 Feb., 1815, aged 57.

Lieut. Gera Goodale died 8 May, 1813, aged 38.

Ruth wife of Capt. Joseph Goodale died 29 Jan., 1817, aged 68.
Joseph Goodale died 11 Oct., 1793, in 75th year.
Mrs. Betty wife of Moses Goodale died 7 Feb., 1794, in 21st year.
Clerenda daughter of Capt. Asa and Mrs. Goslee died 28 Aug., 1808, aged 3 years.
Mrs. Elizabeth wife of Joseph Hill died 8 April, o. s., 1754, aged about 81 years. [A table monument.]
Prudence Holcomb, former consort of David Hubbard Esq., and late of Judah Holcomb Esq., died 29 Nov., 1783, in 83d year.
Appleton Holmes. [No date.]
Annar wife of Theoder Hollister died 12 Nov., 1816, in 70th year.
Charles Hollister died 2 Feb., 1753, in 52d year.
Deacon Elisha Hollister died 14 Nov., 1800, in 78th year.
Mrs. Experience his wife died 7 July, 1765, in 38th year.
Hannah wife of Plen Hollister died 14 May, 1811, aged 62.
Moley wife of Plen Hollister died 19 March, 1786, in 47th year.
Deacon Gideon Hollister died 15 Feb., 1785, in 86th year.
Thomas Hollister died 17 Sept., 1784, in 76th year.
Daniel House. [No date.]
David Hubbard died 30 Sept., 1776, in 25th year.
David Hubbard died 15 Oct., 1760, in 63d year.
John Kimberly Esq. died 26 April, 1773, in 54th year.
Mary his wife died 30 June, 1812, aged 88.
Bezaleel Latimer died 12 Dec., 1811, in 64th year.
Levi Loveland. [No date.]
Sarah wife of Jonathan Shirtliff died 26 June, 1813, in 48th year.
Deborah wife of Elijah Sparks died 16 May, 1824, aged 33.
Benjamin Strickland died 7 June, 1806, in 76th year.
Enoch Strickland died 11 Jan., 1758, in 58th year.
Phebe Strickland wife of John Strickland died 10 June, 1750, in 46th year.
Mary wife of Lieut. Stephen Strickland died 26 Aug., 1784, in 60th year.
Lieut. Stephen Strickland died 2 May, 1803, aged 84.
Rhoda his consort died 31 Dec., 1822, aged 62.
Stephen Strickland Jr. died 6 Feb., 1802, aged 45.
Chloe Treat wife of Jonah Treat died 21 Nov., 1789, in 22d year.
Peleg Welden died 26 Oct., 1817, aged 77.
John Wickham died 2 July, 1804, aged 52.
Asa Williams died 19 April, 1790, in 26th year.
Eunice wife of Daniel Wright, died 29 May, 1768, in 64th year.
Samuel Wrisley died 6 Feb., 1756, in 77th year.
Thomas Wrisley died 1 Jan., 1813, in 88th year.

[Others of the Brewer, Delin, Hills, Nye, and Wier families appear.]

At Buckingham P. O. cemetery appear:
Alfred Benton died 17 May, 1865, aged 75.
Lorenda his wife died 23 Nov., 1863, aged 69.

[Also members of the Goodale, Goslee, Hale, House, Howe, Loveland, Strickland, and Weir families appear.]

In District No. 14 Glastonbury appears:
Nathaniel Tryon died 15 Dec., 1835, aged 70.
Mary his wife died 24 March, 1866, aged 85.

FRANCIS WEST OF DUXBURY, MASS., AND SOME OF HIS DESCENDANTS.

By EDWARD E. CORNWALL, M.D., of Brooklyn, N. Y.

1. "FRANCIS WEST, a house carpenter by trade, being a single man, invited by a Mr. Thomas of Marshfield, Massachusetts, left the town of Salisbury in England and came to N. England, and settled in Duxbury, Mass., and married Margrey Reeves, by whom he had five children, viz., Samuel, Thomas, Peter, Mary and Ruth." So wrote Judge Zebulon West (1707–1770), a great-grandson of the emigrant, who probably learned these facts from his father, also named Francis (1669–1731), who lived with the emigrant in Duxbury until he grew up.

Francis West married Margaret Reeves, in Duxbury, Feb. 27, 1639, and died in that town, Jan. 2, 1692, aged 86. He is spoken of as a carpenter in the Duxbury records, and the Plymouth Colony records show that he made a pair of stocks for the town of Duxbury in 1640. In 1640 and 1642 he was a member of the Grand Jury; in 1642 he bought a house and land in Duxbury (Millbrook); and in 1643 he was on the list of those able to bear arms. He was admitted freeman in Plymouth Colony in 1656. In 1658 he was surveyor of highways in Duxbury; constable in 1661; and in 1662, '69, '74, '78, '80 and '81 was a member of the "Grand Enquest." During the last years of his life his son Peter took care of him, and his estate, which amounted to only £16: 15: 00, was given to Peter by the Probate Court.

Children,* probably born in Duxbury:

2. i. SAMUEL,[2] b. 1643.
3. ii. DR. THOMAS, b. 1646.
4. iii. PETER.
   iv. MARY.
   v. RUTH, b. 1651; d. Dec. 31, 1741, aged 90; m. Nathaniel Skiff.

2. SAMUEL[2] WEST (*Francis*[1]), born in 1643, died May 8, 1689, aged 46, married, Sept. 26, 1668, Tryphosa, daughter of George and Sarah (Tracy) Partridge of Duxbury, Mass., who died Nov. 1, 1701. He lived in Duxbury, where he was constable in 1674.

Children, born in Duxbury:

5. i. FRANCIS,[3] b. Nov. 13, 1669.
   ii. JUEN, b. Sept. 8, 1671; d. young.
6. iii. SAMUEL, b. Dec. 23, 1672.
   iv. PELATIAH, b. Mar. 8, 1674; d. Dec. 7, 1756; m. July 12, 1722, Elizabeth Chandler. Lived in Duxbury, where he was selectman several years.
7. v. HON. EBENEZER, b. July 22, 1676.
8. vi. JOHN, b. Mar. 6, 1679.
   vii. ABIGAIL, b. Sept. 26, 1682; m. in 1714, Nathaniel Cole.
   viii. BATHSHEBA. Mentioned in the Zebulon West manuscript.

* Besides the five children mentioned in the Zebulon West Manuscript, two others, Pelatiah and Richard, have been ascribed to Francis West, though it would seem without good reason.

3. Dr. Thomas[2] West* (*Francis*[1]), born in 1646, died Sept. 6, 1706, aged 60, married Elizabeth ———, who died Feb. 16, 1728, aged 75. He was in Plymouth in 1667 and 1671, and after 1673 resided in Martha's Vineyard. He was a practicing physician, and perhaps also a lawyer, for he was called "The King's Attorney" in 1681, and "Their Majesties' Attorney" in 1690. He joined the Sabbatarian Baptist Church in Newport in 1692, from which he was dismissed in 1702. His will, dated Jan. 15, 1697/8, mentions his six sons, but not his daughters, who, however, are mentioned in a division of his real estate in 1722. His will also mentions "my brother Nathaniel Skiff."

Children, born in Martha's Vineyard

i. Abner,[3] b. June 9, 1683; d. 1756; m. Nov. 17, 1707, Jean, dau. of Thomas and Elizabeth (Bunker) Look, and widow of John Cottle. He was a carpenter in Martha's Vineyard. Among his children was *Rev. Thomas*,[4] who was father of Rev. Samuel,[5] D.D., b. 1738, of Boston, and Hon. Benjamin,[5] b. 1746, of Charlestown, N. H.
ii. Thomas, d. 1728, in R. I., from injuries received in a shipwreck; m. Jan. 29, 1713, Mary, dau. of Stephen and Deborah (Skiff) Presbury. He was an "innholder," "mariner," and "pilot" in Martha's Vineyard. Eight children.
iii. Peter, was excommunicated by the Newport Sabbatarian Baptist Church, in 1709, because he had "forsaken the Lord's Holy Sabbath and become very vain in his words and actions." He was a "planter" in Littletown, Albemarle Co., N. C., in 1715.
iv. William, mentioned in his father's will.
v. Dr. Sackfield, m. (1) Apr. 7, 1715, Mary Howes; m. (2) Ruth Jenkins; was a physician in Yarmouth and Barnstable, Mass. Among his children was *Rev. Samuel*,[4] D.D., b. 1730, of New Bedford, Mass.
vi. Judah, m. Sept. 28, 1718, Bethia Keen of Pembroke, Mass.; lived in Plymouth, Mass. Thirteen children.
vii. Abigail, m. 1722, Joshua Weeks.
viii. Elizabeth, m. (1) before 1708, John Millard of Newport; m. (2) Mar. 25, 1718, Jonathan Sabin of Newport.
ix. Ruth, m. Edward Cartwright of Martha's Vineyard.
x. Mary, m. 1717, John Cottle of Martha's Vineyard.

4. Peter[2] West (*Francis*[1]), died Feb. 20, 1720/1, married Patience ———, who died May 8, 1725, in Plympton, Mass. He lived in Duxbury, Mass., and inherited his father's estate.

Children, born in Duxbury:

i. Mary,[3] b. Oct. 3, 1675; d. young.
ii. Margaret, b. Mar. 12, 1678; m. Jonathan Bryant of Plympton.
iii. Esther, b. Sept. 20, 1680.
iv. Ann, b. Feb. 16, 1682; m. May 7, 1705, Elisha Curtis.
v. William, b. May 4, 1683; m. 1709, Abiah Sprague of Hingham, Mass.
vi. Mary, b. Dec. 7, 1685.
vii. Benjamin, b. July 7, 1688.
viii. Elisha, b. Mar. 2, 1693; m. (1) Dec. 10, 1718, Mary Bearse; m. (2) Martha ———. He lived in Kingston and Pembroke, Mass.
ix. Samuel, b. Apr. 4, 1697.

* For the account here given of Dr. Thomas West and his children I am indebted to the courtesy of Dr. Charles E. Banks, U. S. N., who has furnished it to me from the manuscript of his forthcoming History of Martha's Vineyard.

5. FRANCIS[3] WEST (*Samuel,*[2] *Francis*[1]), born Nov. 13, 1669, died in 1731, married, Dec. 20, 1696, Mercy, daughter of Captain Joseph and Mary (Avery) Minor of Stonington, Conn. He joined the church in Stonington, by letter from the church in Preston, Conn., Nov. 1, 1702. About 1720 he removed with the first settlers to Tolland, Conn., and was the first deacon in the church there, and also selectman.

Children, born in Preston and Stonington:

i. MERCY,[4] b. Oct. 30, 1697; m. Feb. 14, 1716–7, Nathaniel Wales of Windham, Conn.
9. ii. SAMUEL, b. 1699.
10. iii. JOSEPH, bapt. Nov. 30, 1701.
11. iv. AMASA, bapt. Mar. 27, 1704.
12. v. HON. ZEBULON, bapt. Mar. 16, 1707.
13. vi. CHRISTOPHER, bapt. June 19, 1709.
14. vii. PELATIAH, bapt. Sept. 30, 1711.

6. SAMUEL[3] WEST (*Samuel,*[2] *Francis*[1]), born Dec. 23, 1672, probably died about 1763, married, June 30, 1709, Martha, daughter of John and Mercy (Pabodie) Simmons, and widow of Ebenezer Delano of Duxbury, Mass. Her grandmother, Elizabeth (Alden) Pabodie, was daughter of John and Priscilla (Mullins) Alden. He lived in Duxbury, and, after 1723, in Lebanon, Conn. He was one of the organizers, in 1730, of the Goshen Church in Lebanon.

Children, born in Duxbury:

15. i. AMOS,[4] b. May 29, 1710.
16. ii. NATHAN, b. Aug. 18, 1711.
iii. SARAH, b. Nov. 8, 1712.
17. iv. MOSES, b. Mar. 4, 1716.

7. HON. EBENEZER[3] WEST (*Samuel,*[2] *Francis*[1]), born July 23, 1676, died Oct. 31, 1758, married, Jan. 14, 1713, Susannah, daughter of Nathaniel Wales of Windham, Conn., who died Oct. 14, 1723. He was an early settler of Lebanon, Conn., where he was constable in 1713, and was one of the organizers of the Goshen Church in Lebanon, in 1730, and its first deacon. He was a Representative in the Legislature for 46 sessions, Selectman, Justice of the Peace, and Judge of the County Court. His epitaph says he was "a person eminent for the strong powers of his mind, the honesty and integrity of his heart, and ye seriousness of his virtue. He long and faithfully served ye church of Christ in the office of a deacon, and his country in the character of a justice and a judge, and discharged duties of every relation with uprightness."

Children, born in Lebanon:

i. SARAH,[4] b. Jan. 25, 1714; living in 1746, unmarried.
18. ii. HON. JOSHUA, b. July 30, 1715.
iii. BATHSHEBA, b. Mar. 8, 1717; d. young.
iv. SUSANNAH, b. Jan. 17, 1719; m. ——— Delano.
v. EBENEZER, b. Apr. 11, 1721; d. young.
vi. JONATHAN [twin], b. Oct. 2, 1723; d. young.
vii. DAVID [twin], b. Oct. 2, 1723; d. young.

8. JOHN[3] WEST (*Samuel,*[2] *Francis*[1]), born March 6, 1679, died Nov. 17, 1641, married Deborah ———, who married second, John Lane of Killingworth, Conn. He settled in Lebanon, Conn., before 1714,

and was one of the organizers of the Goshen Church in Lebanon, in 1730.

Children, born in Lebanon:

i. JERUSHA,[4] b. Dec. 17, 1708; d. young.
ii. HANNAH, b. July 13, 1710; m. Feb. 14, 1739-40, Israel Everett of Windham.
19. iii. NATHAN, b. Nov. 10, 1712.
20. iv. JOHN, b. Mar. 12, 1715.
v. PRISCILLA, b. July 17, 1717; d. 1730.
vi. DOROTHY, b. Sept. 10, 1719; d. 1730.
21. vii. SOLOMON, b. Mar. 15, 1723.
22. viii. CALEB, b. July 3, 1726.

9. SAMUEL[4] WEST (*Francis,*[3] *Samuel,*[2] *Francis*[1]), born in 1699, died Feb. 3, 1779, married first, Nov. 4, 1724, Sarah, daughter of Jonathan Delano, who died Nov., 1752; and married second, Nov. 26, 1754, Abigail, daughter of Ichabod Lathrop. He lived in Tolland, Conn.

Children, born in Tolland:

i. PRUDENCE,[5] b. Sept. 5, 1726; m. Jan. 17, 1744, Joseph Lathrop.
ii. SARAH, b. Mar. 21, 1729; m. ——— Redington.
iii. SAMUEL, b. Mar. 30, 1732; m. Mar. 25, 1755, Sarah, dau. of Ichabod Lathrop, who d. May 7, 1784, in Pittsfield, Mass.; lived in Tolland. Children, born in Tolland: 1. *Sarah.*[6] 2. *Tryphena.* 3. *Ichabod*, served in the Revolution. 4. *Stephen*, served in the Revolution. 5. *Frederick.* 6. *Grace.* 7. *Prudence.*
iv. ABIGAIL, b. July 22, 1735; d. young.
v. ABNER, b. May 1, 1737; d. 1830; m. July 3, 1760, Mary, dau. of Joseph Hatch; lived in Tolland, Conn., and Lee and Richmond, Mass.; served in the expedition for the relief of Fort William Henry in the French and Indian War, 1757; served in the Revolution. Children, born in Tolland: 1. *Abigail.*[6] 2. *William*, served in the Revolution. 3. *Abner.* 4. *Mary*, m. Abraham Hand. 5. *Submit*, m. Samuel Southwick. 6. *Susannah*, m. Pardon Pierce. 7. *Eley*, m. Curtis Stoddard. 8. *Sarah*, m. Daniel Chamberlain. 9. *Pamelia*, m. Curtis Stoddard. 10. *Betsey*, m. Francis Chevevoy.
vi. JOANNA, b. Dec. 2, 1739; m. ——— Smith.
vii. ELISHA, b. Sept. 14, 1742; m. May 23, 1771, Olive Brewster of Sharon, Conn. Lived in Stockbridge and Lee, Mass. Children, born in Lee: 1. *Mary.*[6] 2. *Prudence.* 3. *Ann.* 4. *John Brewster.* Perhaps others.
viii. ANNA, b. Sept. 16, 1745; d. young.
ix. ANNA, b. Sept. 12, 1756.
x. RUTH, b. Dec. 24, 1759.

10. JOSEPH[4] WEST (*Francis,*[3] *Samuel,*[2] *Francis*[1]), baptized Nov. 30, 1701, died Jan. 27, 1764, aged 64, married, May 19, 1725, Joanna, daughter of Jonathan Delano. He lived in Tolland, Conn., and was selectman and deacon.

Children, born in Tolland:

i. MARY,[5] b. Apr. 21, 1726; m. Adoniram Grant.
ii. JOSEPH, b. Nov. 2, 1728; m. (1) Dorcas Redington; m. (2) Mar. 10, 1752, Lois Strong. Children, born in Tolland: 1. *Joseph,*[6] d. young. 2. *Sarah.* 3. *Charles*, d. young. 4. *Jonathan*, d. young. 5. *Dorcas*, d. young. 6. *Eunice*, d. young. 7. *Joseph.* 8. *Salome.* 9. *Hannah.* 10. *Zadock.* 11. *Joel*, m. Abina Chapman.
iii. JOANNA (or Jane), b. Aug. 21, 1732; m. (1) Dec. 26, 1751, Samuel Huntington; m. (2) William Stanley.

iv. RUFUS, b. Nov. 2, 1735; d. Aug. 12, 1814; m. Nov. 22, 1764, Sarah Nye; lived in Tolland; served in the expedition for the relief of Fort William Henry in the French and Indian War, 1757. Children, born in Tolland: 1. *Grace*,[6] m. John Barnard. 2. *Ephraim*, b. Sept. 3, 1767; d. Nov. 2, 1860; m. Ruth Cobb; Representative. 3. *Joel*, d. young.
v. DEBORAH, b. Jan. 30, 1738; m. Joshua Morgan.
vi. BATHSHEBA, b. July 9, 1741; d. Sept. 1, 1774; m. Dec. 5, 1765, Jonathan Hatch.
vii. ANDREW, m. Mehitable Palmer; lived in Tolland, Conn., and Stockbridge, Mass.; served in the Revolution. Children: 1. *Palmer*.[6] 2. *Jabez*. 3. *Orville*. 4. *Jane*. 5. *Hannah*. 6. *Abigail*.
viii. EPHRAIM, b. Dec. 5, 1747; d. Sept. 16, 1760.
ix. CAPT. JABEZ, b. Jan. 30, 1751; d. Nov. 24, 1817; m. May 22, 1788, Roxanna, dau. of Samuel Chapman of Tolland, who was b. Nov. 4, 1763; lived in Tolland; served in the Revolution. Children: 1. *Aaron*.[6] 2. *Dr. Eber*, of Otis, Mass. 3. *Roxanna*.

11. AMASA[4] WEST (*Francis*,[3] *Samuel*,[2] *Francis*[1]), baptized March 27, 1704, married first, Amy, daughter of Joseph Hatch; and married second, Sept. 20, 1757, Bathsheba Gibbs of Sandwich, Mass. He lived in Tolland, Mass.

Children, born in Tolland:

i. FRANCIS,[5] b. Nov. 1, 1731; d. June 22, 1769; m. Sept. 17, 1751, Abigail Strong of Coventry, Conn.; lived in Tolland, Conn. Children, born in Tolland: 1. *Beulah*,[6] d. young. 2. *Abigail*, d. young. 3. *Dorcas*, m. Amaziah Grover of Windham. 4. *Amasa*, d. young. 5. *Sarah*. 6. *Joanna*. 7. *Francis*. 8. *Irena*, d. young.
ii. OLIVER, b. Oct. 2, 1733; d. Apr. 23, 1816; m. June 20, 1757, Thankful Nye, who d. Mar. 13, 1806, aged 69; lived in Tolland, Conn., and Lee, Mass. Children: 1. *Ebenezer*,[6] m. Mehitable Nye. 2. *Anna*, d. young. 3. *Amy*, m. Seth Nye. 4. *Caleb*. 5. *Amasa*. 6. *Joshua*, m. Mary Newell. 7. *Anna*, m. Heman Bradley. 8. *Sarah*. 9. *Oliver*.
iii. PHEBE, b. Sept. 2, 1735.
iv. LUCIA, b. Aug. 9, 1738.
v. REBECKAH, b. Nov. 25, 1740; d. Dec. 10, 1774.
vi. AMY, b. Dec. 8, 1741; d. Aug. 8, 1756.
vii. MERCY, b. Sept. 16, 1744.
viii. MEHITABLE, b. Feb. 7, 1747; d. Mar. 24, 1755.
ix. AMASA, b. May 1, 1749.
x. SUSAN, b. Mar. 8, 1754; d. Mar. 25, 1755.
xi. LEVI, b. Apr. 27, 1760; d. Dec. 23, 1808; m. 1783, Bathsheba Rider, who d. Apr. 30, 1805; lived in Tolland and Lee; served in the Revolution. Children, born in Lee: 1. *Nabby*.[6] 2. *Nathaniel*. 3. *Patty*, d. young. 4. *Amasa*. 5. *Patty*. 6. *Mercy*, d. young. 7. *Ann*. 8. *Mercy*.

12. HON. ZEBULON[4] WEST (*Francis*,[3] *Samuel*,[2] *Francis*[1]), baptized Nov. 16, 1707, died Dec. 4, 1770, aged 64, married first, Oct. 7, 1731, Mary, daughter of Jonathan Delano, who died July 26, 1743; and married second, Feb. 12, 1744, Widow Sarah (Avery) Sluman of Groton, Conn. He lived in Tolland, Conn.; was the first Representative from Tolland in the Legislature, and represented the town at every session but one until his death, 53 sessions in all; Speaker of the Legislature for 10 sessions; member of the Governor's Council; town clerk; selectman; Judge of Probate; Justice of the Peace, and of the Quorum; Judge of the Hartford County Court; captain of militia. He held most of these offices at the same

time, and for long periods. He was author of a manuscript genealogy of the West Family.

Children, born in Tolland:

i. MARY,[5] b. Sept. 17, 1732; m. Ephraim Grant.

ii. REV. DR. STEPHEN, b. Nov. 2, 1735; d. May 13, 1819; m. (1) Elizabeth Williams, who d. Sept. 15, 1804; m. (2) Elinor Davis, who d. Mar. 14, 1827; graduated at Yale, 1756; received degree of D.D. from Dartmouth; preached in Stockbridge, Mass., 1759 to 1818; author of "Essay on the Atonement" and "Essay on Moral Agency," both widely celebrated in their day, and of numerous pamphlets, his fame as a theologian attracting many students whom he prepared for the ministry; vice-president of the first board of trustees of Williams College.

iii. ANN, b. Mar. 19, 1738; d. Jan. 8, 1775.

iv. THANKFUL, b. July 14, 1740; d. Dec. 15, 1754.

v. ELIJAH, b. Apr. 6, 1743; d. young.

vi. SARAH, b. Jan. 27, 1745; d. Aug. 19, 1750.

vii. PRUDENCE, b. Feb. 16, 1747; d. Aug. 16, 1748.

viii. NATHANIEL, b. Sept. 5, 1748; d. Feb. 2, 1815; m. Nov. 2, 1771, Lucretia Woodbridge of Hartford; lived in Tolland, Conn., and Stockbridge, Mass. Town clerk of Tolland. Graduated at Yale, 1768; served in the Revolution as Lieutenant. Children, born in Tolland: 1. *Nancy*,[6] m. ——— Chase. 2. *Fidelia*, m. Josiah Jones. 3. *Ashbel*, m. Delight Rudd. 4. *Desire*, m. Jabez Dudley. 5. *Russell*, d. young. 6. *Anna Woodbridge*, m. Horace Chase.

ix. DR. JEREMIAH, b. July 20, 1753; m. (1) Feb. 8, 1781, Amelia Ely, who was b. Dec. 26, 1750, and d. Apr. 28, 1786; m. (2) 1787, Martha, dau. of Dr. Thomas Williams of Deerfield, Mass.; lived in Tolland; was a physician; graduated at Yale, 1777; served five years in the Revolution as surgeon; an early member of the Society of the Cincinnati; justice of the peace; and representative. Children, born in Tolland: 1. *Laura*,[6] m. Capt. Joseph Abbott. 2. *Fanny*, m. Cyrus Williams. 3. *Amelia*, m. Col. Prentice Williams. 4. *Francis*, m. Fanny Chapman. 5. *Cynthia*, m. John Sergeant. 6. *Julia*, d. young. 7. *Edmund*. 8. *Lois*, m. (1) ——— Post; m. (2) Rev. ——— Nichols.

x. DESIRE, b. Aug. 18, 1755; d. Jan. 20, 1778; m. June 6, 1774, Benoni Shepherd.

xi. SARAH, b. May 27, 1758; d. young.

13. CHRISTOPHER[4] WEST (*Francis*,[3] *Samuel*,[2] *Francis*[1]), baptized Jan. 9, 1709, married, Oct. 25, 1732, Amy, daughter of Jonathan Delano. He lived in Tolland and Coventry, Conn.

Children, born in Tolland and Coventry:

i. PRISCILLA,[5] b. Aug. 26, 1733.

ii. PRINCE, m. Hannah ———; lived in Lee, Mass.; town clerk in 1777. Children, born in Lee: 1. *Bathsheba*.[6] 2. *Hannah*. 3. *John*. 4. *Sylvanus*, m. Wealthea Tracy. 5. *Christopher*. 6. *Heman*. 7. *Amy*. 8. *Philo*. 9. *Ezekiel*. 10. *Prince*, m. Lura Tracy.

iii. FRANCIS, b. Oct. 30, 1735; d. young.

iv. JONATHAN, b. Dec. 30, 1737; d. Sept. 17, 1795; m. Elizabeth ———; lived in Lee, Mass.: served in the Revolution. Children, born in Lee: 1. *Miner*.[6] 2. *David*, d. young. 3. *Lydia*, d. young. 4. *David*. 5. *Jared*. 6. *Betsey*. 7. *Laura*. 8. *Jonathan*. 9. *Thomas*. 10. *Lydia*, d. young. 11. *Lois*. 12. *Lydia*. 13. *Alvan*. 14. *Susannah*.

v. JERUSHA, b. Apr. 27, 1740.

vi. MINER, b. Jan. 9, 1743.

vii. LOIS, b. Apr. 5, 1745.

viii. LYDIA, b. Nov. 24, 1747.

ix. MARY, b. May 25, 1750.

x. SARAH, mentioned in the Zebulon West Ms.

14. PELATIAH[4] WEST (*Francis,*[3] *Samuel,*[2] *Francis*[1]), baptized Sept. 30, 1711, died July 11, 1778, married, Dec. 5, 1734, Elizabeth Lathrop, who died May 7, 1800, aged 88. He lived in Tolland, Conn., and Lee, Mass.

Children, born in Tolland:

i. ELIZABETH,[5] b. Sept. 17, 1735.
ii. SUSANNAH, b. Mar. 28, 1737; m. Oct. 9, 1757, Oziah Strong of Coventry, Conn.
iii. ELEAZUR, b. Nov. 9, 1738; m. Dec. 6, 1761, Olive Redington; lived in Tolland and Lee. Children: 1. *Charles.*[6] 2. *Thankful.* 3. *Olive.* Perhaps others.
iv. HANNAH, b. Mar. 28, 1740.
v. ZERVIAH, b. Aug. 2, 1743.
vi. EUNICE, b. Apr. 30, 1745.
vii. ELIJAH, b. Mar. 7, 1747: m. Marah ——; lived in Lee. Children, born in Lee: 1. *Jeduthan,*[6] m. Phebe Wilcox. 2. *Orange.* 3. *Erastus.* 4. *Deborah.* 5. *Pamelia,* d. young. 6. *Ashbel.* 7. *Wareham.* 8. *Sabara.* 9. *Alphæus.* 10. *Edna.*
viii. DANIEL, b. July 22, 1759; m. Elizabeth Tracy; lived in Lee and Lenox, Mass. Children, born in Lee and Lenox: 1. *Elizabeth,* d. young. 2. *Zerviah.* 3. *Thomas Tracy.* 4. *Daniel.* 5. *Lucy.* 6. *Sally.* 7. *Ira.* 8. *Elizabeth.* 9. *Orson.* 10. *Pelatiah.* 11. *Alvah.* 12. *Eunice.*
ix. PRUDENCE, b. June 1, 1751.
x. MARY, b. Jan. 28, 1753.

15. AMOS[4] WEST (*Samuel,*[3] *Samuel,*[2] *Francis*[1]), born May 29, 1710, married, July 21, 1738, Sarah Cutten of Watertown. He lived in Lebanon, Conn., Goshen parish.

Children, born in Lebanon:

i. BATHSHEBA,[5] b. May 1, 1739; d. young.
ii. ABIGAIL, b. July 9, 1741.
iii. BATHSHEBA, b. July 23, 1743; d. young.
iv. SARAH, b. Aug. 28, 1745; d. young.
v. ABIAH, b. Mar. 15, 1748; d. young.
vi. REUBEN, b. June 6, 1750.
vii. SIMEON, b. May 21, 1751.
viii. LEVI, b. May 20, 1754; served in the Revolution.
ix. JUDAH, b. Apr. 4, 1757; served in the Revolution.
x. AMOS, bapt. July 24, 1759; served in the Revolution.

16. NATHAN[4] WEST (*Samuel,*[3] *Samuel,*[2] *Francis*[1]), born Aug. 18, 1711, married, July 20, 1741, Jerusha, daughter of Gershom and Mary (Buel) Hinckley of Lebanon, Conn. He lived in the parish of Goshen in Lebanon.

Children, born in Lebanon:

i. JERUSHA,[6] b. Oct. 21, 1741; m. 1767, Eldad Hunt of Lebanon.
23. ii. Capt. SAMUEL, b. Aug. 23, 1743.
iii. NATHAN, b. May 26, 1746; d. young.
iv. MARY, b. June 7, 1747.
v. NATHAN, b. June 8, 1749.
vi. LUCY, b. May 16, 1751.
vii. WALTER, b. May 12, 1753.
viii. CHARLES, b. Apr. 22, 1755; d. young.
ix. CHARLES, b. July 4, 1756; d. Aug. 20, 1778; served in the Revolution, and was killed in battle.
x. SETH, b. June 2, 1758.
xi. CALVIN, b. June 11, 1761.
xii. GEORGE, b. May 13, 1762.

17. MOSES[4] WEST (*Samuel,*[3] *Samuel,*[2] *Francis*[1]), born Mar. 4, 1716, married, Aug. 18, 1751, Jemima Eaton of Tolland, Conn. He lived in Tolland.

Children:

i. DURA,[5] b. Jan. 23, 1752.
ii. LUNA, b. Jan. 9, 1754; m. Mar. 4, 1773, Jobin Bozworth of Lebanon.
iii. ALVAH, d. 1815; m. Susannah ——; lived in Stafford, Conn.; served in the Revolution. Children: 1. *Luna,*[6] m. Samuel Cushman. 2. *Amelia.* 3. *Asa Davis.* 4. *Susan.* 5. *Clarissa,* m. Zachariah Hale. 6. *Willis.* 7. *Horatio.* 8. *Orrin.*
iv. ANNA, mentioned in the Zebulon West Ms.

18. HON. JOSHUA[4] WEST (*Hon. Ebenezer,*[3] *Samuel,*[2] *Francis*[1]), born July 30, 1715, died Nov. 9, 1783, married first, Apr. 16, 1741, Sarah Wattles, who died Jan. 20, 1743/4, aged 20; and married second, June 24, 1745, Elizabeth, daughter of Ebenezer and Mary (Veach) Williams of Lebanon, Conn., who died May 16, 1791. He lived in Lebanon, Goshen parish; graduated at Yale, 1738; was representative in the Legislature, 27 sessions; judge of the County Court; Captain of militia; deacon; and served as Captain in the French and Indian War. In 1776, he was appointed by the Connecticut Legislature one of the nine members of the Revolutionary Committee of Safety of the Colony. His tombstone says: "His natural and amiable disposition, together with a liberal education, rendered him much beloved and extensively useful."

Children, born in Lebanon:

i. SUSANNAH,[5] b. Apr. 28, 1742; m. Dec. 2, 1762, David Mason of Norwich.
ii. JOSHUA, b. Dec. 12, 1743; d. Apr. 8, 1745.
iii. SARAH, b. Feb. 15, 1746–7; m. Mar. 25, 1773, William Buel of Lebanon.
iv. Lieut. EBENEZER, b. Sept. 17, 1748; d. Nov. 26, 1822; served in the Revolution as Lieut.; was taken prisoner on Long Island, Dec. 10, 1777, and exchanged Dec. 8, 1780; after he was taken prisoner, his horse found its way back to Lebanon alone.
v. MARY, b. Jan. 11, 1750; d. Sept. 13, 1753.
vi. JOSHUA, b. Dec. 20, 1751; d. May 22, 1839; m. (1) Nov. 5, 1773, Hannah Williams, who d. Mar. 26, 1781; m. (2) Mar. 19, 1789, Elizabeth Raymond, who d. 1843, aged 93; lived in Montville, Conn. Children: 1. *Olive,*[6] d. young. 2. *John,* d. young. 3. Capt. *Enos,* m. Nancy Latham.
vii. MARY, b. Jan. 2, 1754; m. Dec. 21, 1775, Eliphalet Metcalf.
viii. ELIZABETH, b. Jan. 22, 1756; d. Jan. 9, 1759.
ix. JONATHAN, b. Mar. 3, 1758; d. Mar. 19, 1759.
x. JONATHAN, b. May 31, 1761; m. (1) May 26, 1785, Parthena Clarke; m. (2) Nov. 14, 1798, Emma Newcomb; lived in Lebanon. Children: 1. *Elizabeth,* m. Samuel Newcomb. 2. *Samuel,* m. Nancy Griffin. 3. *Joshua,* m. Sarah Coggshall. 4. *Jonathan,* m. Sarah Griffin. 5. *Parthena,* m. Oliver Chatfield. 6. *Mary,* m. David T. Wood. 7. *David P.,* m. Sally Ladd.
xi. DAVID, b. July 11, 1763; m. Mercy, dau. of Capt. Gideon Clark; lived in Lebanon. Children: 1. *Harriet,*[5] d. young. 2. *David,* d. young. 3. *Mary,* d. young. 4. *Charles Ebenezer,* m. Lucy Clark. 5. *Jabez,* m. Fanny Balch.
xii. ELIJAH, b. Aug. 20, 1765, m. and removed to Pennsylvania.
xiii. ISAAC, b. Oct. 11, 1771; d. June 16, 1836; m. and went west, but after his wife and children were drowned while crossing Lake Erie, he returned to Lebanon.

19. NATHAN[4] WEST (*John,*[3] *Samuel,*[2] *Francis*[1]), born Nov. 10, 1712, died 1801, married Dec. 7, 1738, Mary, daughter of Gershom and Mary

(Buel) Hinckley of Lebanon, Conn. He lived in Bozrah, Conn.
Children, born in Bozrah:

i. DEBORAH,[5] b. Aug. 6, 1740.
ii. Capt. ELIAS, b. July 5, 1744; d. Feb. 9, 1835; m. Oct. 31, 1765, Mary Lathrop of Norwich, Conn.; lived in Bozrah; representative many times; served in the Revolution as lieut. Children: 1. *Jedidiah*,[6] m. Mary Backus of Hebron, Conn; lived in Manchester, Vt. 2. *Elias*, m. Mary Armstrong; lived in Montrose, Pa. 3. *Asahel*, m. (1) Sarah Wightman of Bozrah; m. (2) Sarah Hinman of Galway, N. Y.; lived in Galway. 4. *Zerviah*, m. Gurdon Gifford of Norwich. 5. *Pamelia*, m. Jabez West Throop of Bozrah. 6. *Hannah*, m. Edward Fuller of Montrose. 7. *Mary*, m. Samuel Fish of Litchfield, N. Y.
iii. NATHAN, b. Sept. 7, 1746; m. June 12, 1770, Sarah Chapman of Bozrah.
iv. CHILD, d. Sept. 13, 1748.
v. Lieut. JABEZ, b. Nov. 19, 1749; d. May 1, 1814; m. Jan. 3, 1773, Abigail Throop of Bozrah, who d. Oct. 29, 1825, aged 76; lived in Lebanon, Goshen parish; served in the Revolution as lieut.
vi. DANIEL, b. Nov. 20, 1751; served in the Revolution.
vii. GERSHOM, b. May 3, 1754; m. wid. Priscilla (Hinckley) Hyde, dau. of Jared and Anna (Hyde) Hinckley of Lebanon; lived in Troy, N. Y. Children: 1. *Jared*.[6] 2. *Christopher*. 3. *Calista*. 4. *Deborah*.

20. JOHN[4] WEST (*John*,[3] *Samuel*,[2] *Francis*[1]), born Mar. 12, 1715, died Jan. 31, 1766, married, June 16, 1738, Rebecca, daughter of John and Margaret (Post) Abel of Lebanon, Conn. He lived in Lebanon, Tolland, and Windham, Conn.

Children, born in Lebanon and Tolland:

i. JOHN,[5] b. Aug. 8, 1739; d. Nov. 23, 1810; m. Apr. 26, 1764, Phebe, dau. of Jonathan Strickland of Glastonbury, Conn.; lived in Windham and Glastonbury, Conn., and, after 1776, in Claremont, N. H. Children: 1. *Phebe*,[6] d. young. 2. *Lucretia*. 3. *Phebe*. 4. *John*. 5. *Anne*. 6. *Rufus*. 7. *David*. 8. *Aaron*, m. Elizabeth Leslie.
ii. DAN, b. Dec. 31, 1741: d. May, 1795; m. June 13, 1771, Mercy Cook; lived in Hadley, Mass. Children, born in Hadley: 1. *Dan*,[6] d. young. 2. *Thomas*, d. young. 3. *Dan*, d. young. 4. *Thomas*, b. Jan. 27, 1778; d. Jan. 16, 1865; m. Huldah Parsons. 5. *Ruby*. 6. *Polly*, d. young. 7. *Rebecca*. 8. *Polly*. 9. *Mary*. 10. *Roswell*, d. young. 11. *Hannah*, m. Chester Gray. 12. *Jerusha*, d. 1886, aged 91.
iii. DAVID, b. Feb. 4, 1744; m. Bethia Randall; lived in Vernon, Conn., and Middlefield, Mass.; served in the Revolution. Children: 1. *Horace*.[6] 2. *Percy*. 3. *Randall*.
iv. RUFUS, b. May 16, 1745; d. Aug. 19, 1747.
v. ABEL, b. May 11, 1747; d. Jan. 12, 1836; m. Hannah Chapman; lived in Lebanon and Bolton, Conn., and Washington, Mass.; impoverished himself purchasing supplies for the Revolutionary army. Children: 1. *John Chapman*,[6] d. young. 2. *Hannah*, m. Justus Chamberlain. 3. *Abel*, b. Nov. 26, 1780; d. 1871; m. Matilda Thompson. 4. *Rhoda*, m. Charles Cooley. 5. *Almira*, m. William Nichols. 6. *Elizabeth*, m. Alva Ames. 7. *Laura*, m. Asa Cone.
vi. HANNAH, b. Sept. 11, 1749; prob. d. young.
vii. DOROTHY, b. Oct. 1, 1751; d. young.
viii. REBECKAH, b. Apr. 7, 1755; d. young.
ix. OLIVE, mentioned in the Zebulon West Ms.

21. SOLOMON[4] WEST (*John*,[3] *Samuel*,[2] *Francis*[1]), born Mar. 15, 1723, died Aug. 9, 1810, married, Oct. 10, 1743, Abigail Strong of Leb-

anon, Conn., who died Aug. 12, 1807. He lived in the North district of Tolland, Conn., and was commissioned ensign of militia in 1762.

Children, born in Tolland:

i. SOLOMON,[6] b. Aug. 23, 1744: d. June 8, 1822; m. (1) Mar. 20, 1770, Prudence Lathrop; m. (2) Feb. 29, 1776, Catherine Carpenter; lived in Tolland. Children, born in Tolland: 1. *Solomon,*[6] d. young. 2. *Jesse.* 3. *Prudence,* m. Roswell Hatch. 4. *Sylvia,* m. Walter Badcock. 5. *Ruby.* 6. *Ebenezer.*
ii. RUBY, b. Aug. 1747; d. Oct. 5, 1781; m. Aug. 5, 1779, William Gurley.
iii. ABIGAIL, b. Dec. 19, 1748.
iv. LYDIA, b. Mar. 5, 1752; d. Oct. 28, 1772.
v. ESTHER, b. Mar. 17, 1754.
vi. CHLOE, b. Apr. 14, 1756.
vii. STEPHEN, b. Aug. 19, 1759.
viii. JERUSHA, b. June 6, 1763.

22. CALEB[4] WEST (*John,*[3] *Samuel,*[2] *Francis*[1]), born July 13, 1726, married, Aug. 12, 1747, Hannah Tuttle of Lebanon, Conn. He lived in Lebanon and Tolland, Conn.

Children, born in Lebanon and Tolland:

i. LOIS,[5] bapt. Apr. 10, 1748.
ii. HANNAH, b. Aug. 8, 1749.
iii. CALEB, b. Jan. 12, 1751; m. ———. Children: 1. *Darius.*[6] 2. *Aaron.* 3. *Hannah.* 4. *Pamelia.*
iv. IRA, b. June 26, 1752; m. Mar. 29, 1792, Sarah, dau. of Col. Samuel Chapman; lived in Tolland; served in the Revolution.
v. JONATHAN, b. June 20, 1754; probably d. young.
vi. ROGER, b. July 1, 1755.
vii. IRENE, d. Nov., 1763.
viii. SUSANNAH, d. young.
ix. PRISCILLA, b. Nov. 25, 1763.
x. KITTY, b. Mar. 20, 1768.
xi. PRUDENCE, mentioned in the Zebulon West Ms.

23. CAPT. SAMUEL[5] WEST (*Nathan,*[4] *Samuel,*[3] *Samuel,*[2] *Francis*[1]), born Aug. 23, 1743, died Jan. 10, 1835, married first, Sept. 12, 1765, Sarah, daughter of William and Sarah (Lyman) Hunt of Lebanon, Conn., who was born March 14, 1743, and died Aug. 12, 1816; and married second, Sarah Porter, who died Nov. 8, 1851, aged 84. He lived in the parish of Goshen in Lebanon, Conn., until about 1778, when he moved into that part of Lebanon which afterwards became the town of Columbia. He served in the Revolution as sergeant and was a Revolutionary pensioner; and was Representative.

Children, born in Lebanon:

i. Rev. JOEL, b. Mar. 12, 1766.
ii. SARAH, b. June 11, 1768; m. ——— Pease of Smyrna, N. Y.
iii. PARTHENA, b. May 15, 1770; m. Jared Bennett of Smyrna, N. Y.
iv. VILATIA, b. May 2, 1772; m. Gilbert Lincoln.
v. SUBMIT, b. Dec. 26, 1773; m. Benjamin House.
vi. Col. SAMUEL, b. Feb. 11, 1776.
vii. CHARLES, b. Nov. 10, 1777; d. Dec. 2, 1777.
viii. JERUSHA, b. Dec. 5, 1778; d. Nov. 21, 1781.
ix. LYDIA, b. May 1, 1782; d. 1866.
x. CHARLES, b. Mar. 11, 1784.
xi. SOPHIA, b. Apr. 13, 1786; m. Chester Lyman of Columbia.
xii. BETSEY, b. June 21, 1789; m. (1) ——— Hale; m. (2) ——— Hitchcock of Bayonne, N. J.

FAIRBANKS MARRIAGES IN THE PARISH OF HALIFAX, WEST RIDING OF YORKSHIRE, ENGLAND.

From 1538 to 1624.

Communicated by Rev. HIRAM FRANCIS FAIRBANKS, of Milwaukee, Wis.

INASMUCH as several early American emigrants came from the above named parish, this list may prove interesting.

The Fairbank, or Fairbanks, family was probably in this parish as early as 450 years ago. The earliest will, that of Richard of Heptonstall, in 1517, says his father lived, and he was born, in Kendall of Westmoreland. John Fairbank of Sowerby in 1517 was probably a brother of Richard, and Edmund Fairbank of Heptonstall was very likely his uncle. Edmund, who made his will in 1533, was probably born about 1460 or earlier. He seems to have been a man of considerable local importance. Two of his sons, Sir William and Sir George, were priests, and he had helped found a chapel. He seems to have had a chaplain, Sir John Grenwood; and to have possessed considerable land and money. He willed two "Macers," doubtless the symbol of some authority.

MARRIAGES.

Richard Saltonstall to Margaret widow of Hy. Fayrbanke, 24 Jan. 1539—40.
John Fayrebank to Eliz. Waterhous, 22 Oct. 1543.
Anth'y Fairbanke to Agnes Saybyll, 8 July 1544.
Robert Fourness to Sybell Fairebanke, 1 June 1545.
Wm Appillerd to Alice Fairbanke, 12 Sept. 1546.
Omfray Fairbanke to Johanna Heliwell, 31 Jan. 1546-7.
Edmund Fairbanke to Margt Denton, 20 June 1547.
Rd. Flemynge to Chrystabel Fairbanke, 6 July 1550.
Omfrey Fairebanke to Elsabeth Battes, 2 Sept. 1560.
William Fairebanke to Isabella Horton, 28 July 1562.
John Fairbank to Jane Banyster, 28 Jan. 1565-6.
John Northend to Magt Fairebank, 12 July 1566.
Humfrey Fairbanke to Sybell Wilson, 8 May 1570.
James Gawkroger to Jenet Fayrbank, 2 Dec. 1571.
Geo. Harryson to Agnes Fayrbank, 14 Oct. 1573.
Edw. Brodleys to Margt Fayrbank, 3 Feb. 1573.
Geo. Fayrbank to Jenet Brodly, 15 Feb. 1573-4.
John Fayrbank to Anne Stocke, 24 May 1574.
Matthew Brodley to Jane Fayrbank, 25 July 1575.
John Fayrbank to Margaret Symnes, 2 April 1578.
Hugh Fayrbank to Jane Mychell, 2 April 1578.
Rob. Hargreaves to Isabell Fayrbanke, 16 June 1578.
John Wylye to Eliz. Fairbanke, 13 June 1580.
Rob. Hargate to Eliz. Fayrbanke, 19 June 1580.
Mychaell King to Alice Fayrbanke, 7 Nov. 1580.
Richard Saltonstall to Marye Fayrbanke, 15 Jan. 1580-1.
Wm Wade to Susan Fairbanke, 7 Feb. 1590.

Sam'l Fayrbanke to Ellen Thorpe, 27 Sept. 1592.
Robert Fayrbanke to Ann Baxter of Birkine, 4 Aug. 1592.
Umfray Fairbanke to Grace Fairbanke, 27 Aug. 1593.
John Fairbanke to Isabell Stancliffe, 6 Aug. 1593.
Robert Fairbanke to Mary Barstow, 2 July 1593.
Richard Whittaker to Sibbil Fairbanke, 22 April 1594.
Thomas Pickels to Mary Fayrbanke, 3 May 1596.
Robert Holmes to Mary Fayrbanke, 10 May 1596.
(Churchwarden 1596, George Fayrbanke of Sowerby.)
Thomas Fayrbanke to Mary Mawde, 2 May 1598.
Robert Bevrleye to Alice Fayrbanke, 19 Feb. 1599.
John Bancroft (Hipp.) to Mary Fayrbanke, 20 Nov. 1599.
George Jackson (Hip.) to Susan Fayrbanke, 5 Feb. 1599.
(Churchwarden 1601, John Fayrebanke.)
Isaac Broadly (Hipp.) to Grace Fayrbanke, 11 July 1602.
Richard Wilson (Hipp.) to Anne Fayrbanke, 30 Jan. 1603.
Leonard Fayrbank to Agnes Ru[ ]sde, 22 April 1604.
Richard Fairbanke (Hal.) to Margt Pollard, 15 June 1607.
George Fairbanke to Ester Denton (Sowerby), 18 June 1607.
Samul Fairbank (Warley) to Edith Boulton, 14 Jan'y 1607.
John Fayrbanke (Hal.) to Mary Broadley, 16 Nov. 1609.
Richard Fayrbanke (Hal.) to Martha Haldsworth, 28 May 1610.
Abraham Bates to Susan Fayrbanke, 10 June 1611.
Hugh Fayrbank (Hal.) to Margt Brocksope, 11 Dec. 1611.
(Churchwarden 1612, George Fayrbanke of Sowerby.)
Abraham Boulton to Susan Fayrbanke (Hipp.) 12 April 1613.
Wm Wrigglesworth to Sibil Fayrbank (Hal.), 2 May 1613.
Mich'l Fayrbanke to Anne Dodson (Hal.), 20 June 1613.
Isaac Crowther to Grace Fayrbank (Skir.), 28 Aug. 1614.
George Fairbanke to Sarah Hargraves, 31 Aug. 1614.
George Fairbanke to Joice Denton (North), 25 May 1615.
John Bothamley to Ruth Fayrbank (Hal.) 22 May 1616.
Mich'l Fairbanke to Mary Sisar (Hal.), 1 July 1616.
Mich'l Fairbanke to Sarah Denton, 27 Oct. 1616.
Jonathan Fayrbanke to Grace Smith (Warley), 20 May 1617.

(This is the marriage of Jonathan Fayrbanke who came to New England in 1633, and settled at Dedham in 1636. All his children were baptized in the great parish church of Halifax, most of them having been born in Warley, which adjoins Sowerby, although Mary and George were born in Shelf, which is to the northeast of Halifax. All these townships are in the parish of Halifax. George Fayrbanke of Sowerby, who was churchwarden in 1612, and who died in 1620, was evidently a near relative of this Jonathan, for all his children had the same names as those of the emigrant. His son Jonathan graduated from Brazenose College, Oxford, and became Protestant Vicar of Bingley, Yorkshire, where he remained until more than eighty years of age.)

Robert Farebank to Eliz. Lambert (Hal.), 27 Dec. 1617.
Samuel Fayrbanke to Jenet Hodd (Hipp.), 23 Jan. 1618.
Francis Catlaw to Margaret Fayrbanke (Hal.), 21 Apr. 1618.
Leonard Fairbank to Susan Crowther (Hal.), 13 July 1618.
(Churchwarden 1616–1619, Simon Fairbanke of Hipperholme.)
Humphrey Fairbank to Susan Denton (Sowerby), 29 Ap. 1619.
John Hughe to Susan Fairbanke (Hip.), 3 June 1619.

John Fairbanke to Eliz. Blackburne (Hal.), 23 Sept. 1619.
Robert Fairbanke to Isabel Bamforth (Hip.), 28 June 1620.
Robert Field to Ruth Fairebank of Hipperholme, 23 Nov. 1624.

ATKINS FAMILY BIBLE RECORDS.

Communicated by STANLEY W. SMITH, Esq., of Boston.

THE following records appear in the old family Bible of William Atkins, now in the possession of his great-granddaughter Mrs. Mercy Atkins Hammond of Chatham, Mass.

Births.

William Atkins born August 30, 1748.
Lydia Atkins born Nov. 10, 1755.

Married.

William Atkins and Lydia Nickerson were married [the date not recorded].

Deaths.

William Atkins died Feb. 16, 1807 in the 59th year of his age.
Lydia Atkins died [date not given], in the 96th year of her age. 1850 [in pencil].

Births.

Joshua Atkins born May 15, 1777.
Susannah Atkins born May 17, 1780.
Tabitha Atkins born May 4, 1783.
Thomas Atkins born July 12, 1785.
John Atkins born June 14, 1787.
William Atkins born Sept. 4, 1791.
Prince Atkins, born May 17, 1794.
Lydia Atkins born Oct 28, 1799.

Marriages.

Joshua Atkins and Mehitable Eldridge were married March 22, 1799.
Susanna Atkins and Barney Taylor were married July 17, 1799.
Tabatha Atkins and ——— Pierce of Wellfleet were married Nov. 24, 1808.
Thomas Atkins and Tabatha Eldredge were married May 17, 1807.
John Atkins [never married].
William Atkins and Priscilla Baker were married April 20, 1813.
Prince Atkins [has no record of marriage or death].
Lydia Atkins [never married].

Deaths.

Joshua Atkins died May 30, 1845 aged 67 years.
Thomas Atkins died Aug 12, 1817 in the 33rd year of his age.
John Atkins died at Sea Oct. 3, 1810 in the 24th year of his age.
William Atkins died at Sea Aug. 26, 1815 in the 24th year of his age.
Lydia Atkins died July 14, 1878 aged 78 years.

THE BRISTOL BRANCH OF THE FINNEY FAMILY.

By FRANKLIN C. CLARK, M.D., of Providence, R. I.

[Concluded from page 73.]

16. THOMAS[4] FINNEY (*Jeremiah,*[3] *Jemiah,*[2] *John*[1]), born Nov. 16, 1737, in Bristol, R. I., married, June 5, 1760, Elizabeth Clark of Plymouth, Mass., who was born in 1742, and died Mch. 3, 1795. He died Jan. 5, 1791, at Plymouth. Both are interred on Burial Hill.

Children:

i. ELIZABETH CLARK,[5] b. Aug. 22, d. Dec. 16, 1761.
ii. CLARK, b. Nov. 6, 1762; d. Jan. 17, 1763.
iii. MOLLY, b. Dec. 5, 1763.
iv. JOSIAH MORTON, b. Nov. 10, 1765.
v. RUTH, b. Apr. 7, 1768.
vi. THOMAS (?).

17. WILLIAM[4] FINNEY (*Joshua,*[3] *Joshua,*[2] *John*[1]), born May 10, 1715, in Swansea, Mass., married first, Nov. 8, 1738, Elizabeth Clark of Swansea, Mass., who died in Oct., 1742; and married second, Nov. 2, 1747, Mrs. Abigail Black. He purchased land in Lebanon, Conn., in 1764, where he died in the early part of 1781.

Children:

i. WILLIAM,[5] b. Dec. 9, 1739.
ii. ELIZABETH, b. May 25, 1742.
iii. IRENE, b. Mch, 27, 1749.
iv. JOSEPH, b. June 4, 1751.

18. JOHN[4] FINNEY (*Joshua,*[3] *Joshua,*[2] *John*[1]), born June 2, 1721, in Swansea, Mass., married first, Aug. 25, 1743, Rachel Woodward of Lebanon, Conn., who died June 5, 1765; and married second, Oct. 17, 1765, Sarah Thomas. He resided in Lebanon and Warren, Conn., and died in 1788.

Children:

i. JOEL,[5] b. Sept. 1, 1744.
ii, RACHEL, b. 1745; m. ——— Barnum.
iii. LYDIA, b. Aug. 28, 1746; m. Amaziah Phillips of Southington, Conn., who d. before 1788.
iv. ELEAZAR, b. 1754.
v. RUFUS, b. May 18, 1760; m. Hannah Finney. (See No. 20, v.)
vi. JOHN, d. Jan. 12, 1762.
vii. DEIADEMA, bapt. July, 1767.

19. OLIVER[4] FINNEY (*Joshua,*[3] *Joshua,*[2] *John*[1]), born Nov. 11, 1728, in Swansea, Mass., married Aug. 9, 1749, Elizabeth Dunham. He removed to Lebanon, Conn., with his father; later resided in Warren, Conn.; and bought land in Kent, Conn.

Child:

i. ELIZABETH,[5] b. Sept. 10, 1750.

20. JOHN[4] FINNEY (*John,*[3] *Joshua,*[2] *John*[1]), born Oct. 14, 1718, in Swansea, Mass., married, June 14, 1744, Hannah Washburn. He removed to Lebanon, Conn., with his father, in 1728 or '9. He also resided in Kent and Warren, Conn.

Children:

i. TIMOTHY,[5] b. Aug. 28, 1746.
ii. MARTIN, b. June 20, 1751.
iii. ELIHU, b. July 14, 1755.
iv. JOHN, b. July 19, 1757.
v. HANNAH, b. Mch. 10, 1761, in Kent; m. May 20, 1779, her cousin Rufus, son of John Finney of Lebanon, Conn. (See No. 18, v.)

21. NATHANIEL[4] FINNEY (*John*,[3] *Joshua*,[2] *John*[1]), born Jan. 3, 1720–1, in Swansea, Mass., married Sept. 3, 1740, Hannah Wood of Swansea, Mass., who was born in 1718, and died Dec. 26, 1756, in Providence, R. I. He removed first to Providence, where he was made freeman in 1757; and in 1760, in company with others, he went to Nova Scotia, and settled in Sackville.

Children:

i. CALEB,[5]
ii, etc. Others.

22. DAVID[4] FINNEY (*John*,[3] *Joshua*,[2] *John*[1]), born Aug. 24, 1732, in Swansea, Mass., married, Feb. 26, 1759, Abigail Clark of Kent, Conn. He sold his property in Lebanon in 1760, and removed to Dutchess Co., N. Y.

Child:

i. ISAAC,[5] b. Oct. 3, 1759.

23. JABEZ[4] FINNEY (*John*,[3] *Joshua*,[2] *John*[1]), born Nov. 21, 1737, in Swansea, Mass., married, Nov. 8, 1764, Elizabeth ———. He resided in East Greenwich, R. I., where his father had purchased land as early as 1717. He was a soldier in the Revolution, in 1778.

Children:

31. i. GEORGE.[5]
ii. HANNAH, m. Feb. 29, 1784, John, son of Caleb Weeden of East Greenwich, R. I.

24. JOSIAH[4] FINNEY (*Joshua*,[3] *Josiah*,[2] *John*[1]), born Feb. 24, 1727–8, in Swansea, Mass., married Sarah, born Dec. 21, 1732, died June 16, 1777, daughter of Thomas and Sarah (Gilbert) Carter of Litchfield Co., Conn. He was one of the earliest settlers of Litchfield Co. He died Aug. 27, 1773.

Children:

i. JOSIAH,[5] about 1756.
ii. SYLVESTER, b. Mch. 15, 1759.
iii. SARAH, b. June 6, 1761; m. Judah Eldred.
iv. LUCINDA, b. Jan. 28, 1763.
v. ZENAS, b. Dec. 8, 1764; d. before Sept. 16, 1777.
vi. LEVINA, b. Oct. 28, 1766.
vii. CYRUS, b. Oct. 6, 1771.

25. DAVID[4] FINNEY (*Josiah*,[3] *Joshua*,[2] *John*[1]), born June 21, 1734, in Swansea, Mass., married first, Mch. 7, 1754, Jemima Warner, who died Nov. 14, 1770; and married second, May 6, 1775, widow Margaret Fuller. He removed with his family to Conn., and resided in Lebanon, where he owned land at the time of his second marriage.

Children by first wife:

i. ELEAZAR,[5] b. Jan. 20, 1755.
ii. ELIZABETH, b. Apr. 1, 1757.
iii. URIAH, b. Mch. 17, 1761; served in the Revolution, 1778-1780.
iv. JEMIMA, b. Aug. 15, 1763.
v. BENJAMIN, b. Aug. 9, 1771.

26. JONATHAN[4] FINNEY (*Josiah,*[3] *Joshua,*[2] *John*[1]), born June 1, 1736, in Swansea, Mass., married, Aug. 12, 1757, Phebe Phelps. He removed to Warren, Conn., where his father deeded him a farm of 112 acres on his marriage. He died Mch. 29, 1773.

Children:

i. JONATHAN,[5] b. Nov. 8, 1758.
ii. BETHUEL, b. June 11, 1760; removed to Lenox, Mass., in 1789.
iii. PHEBE, b. Feb. 22, 1762.
iv. RHODA, b. July 22, 1763.
v. ZINA, or ZERVIA, b. Jan. 14, 1765; removed to Hebron, Conn., in 1786.
vi. ASENATH, b. Jan. 28, 1767.
vii. BERIAH, b. Nov. 14, 1768; removed to Lenox, Mass., in 1789.
viii. LYDIA, b. June 28, 1770; d. June 19, 1771.
ix. ABRAHAM, b. Apr. 20, 1772; removed to Lee, Mass.

27. DANIEL[5] PHINNEY (*Elisha,*[4] *Jonathan,*[3] *Jonathan,*[2] *John*[1]), born Sept. 14, 1768, in Warren, R. I., married first, June, 14, 1798, Elizabeth, born Apr. 6, 1780, died Nov. 23, 1822, daughter of Thomas Kinnicutt and Mary (———) Coomer of Bristol, R. I.; and married second, Eliza, born May 22, 1792, died Apr. 30, 1891, in Providence, R. I., daughter of Stephen and Sarah Cranston of Bristol, and widow of George Cole of Warren. He was a farmer, residing in Warren, and died June 25, 1857. He had no children by his second wife.

Children:

i. EMMA,[6] b. Apr. 13, 1800; m. Aug. 23, 1818, Thomas Easterbrooks, b. Dec. 17, 1797, d. July 31, 1868, son of Ichabod and Rhoby (Cole) Cole of Warren; d. Nov. 25, 1860, in Warren. Children: *Sally, Benjamin, Betsey Phinney, Adeline, Nathan Phinney,* and *Burrill Bosworth.*
ii. ELIZA KINNICUTT, b. May 15, 1802; m. Sept. 15, 1823, her cousin Capt. William, b. May 16, 1800, son of Capt. Willam and Rebecca (Phinney) Champlin of Warren; d. May 22, 1831. (See 13, vii.) Children: *William, John Bowman,* and *Alexander Hodges.*
iii. THOMAS KINNICUTT COOMER, b. Mch. 21, 1804.
iv. HANNAH, b. June 20, 1806; m. Feb. 24, 1831, Capt. Ambrose, b. in 1803, d. May 21, 1883, son of Daniel and Hope Barnaby; buried in Warren, June 19, 1834. He m. (2) Hannah G. Vinnecum. Children: *Ambrose,* and *Margaret Mason.*
v. REBECCA PECK, b. Dec. 3, 1808; m. Nov. 17, 1836, Robert, b. June 3, 1803, d. Mch. 3, 1852, son of Bernard and Lydia (Ingraham) Miller; d. Nov. 1, 1851. Child: *George Robert.*
vi. NATHAN, b. Apr. 17, 1812; d. Jan. 27, 1843; unmarried.
vii. ELISHA PECK, b. Sept. 29, 1814.
viii. NANCY, b. Aug. 29, 1817; m. (1) Mch. 29, 1838, John Mason Bosworth of Dartmouth, Mass., who was b. in 1812, and buried Aug. 10, 1839; m. (2) her first husband's brother Alvin Bosworth; d. May 19, 1857. Child by first husband: *Daniel Phinney.* Children by second husband: *John, William,* and *Joseph.*

28. BENJAMIN[5] PHINNEY (*Elisha,*[4] *Jonathan,*[3] *Jonathan,*[2] *John*[1]), born Oct. 8, 1771, in Swansea, Mass., married Aug. 31, 1794, Betsey, born

Dec. 29, 1776, died Feb. 15, 1757, daughter of Mrs. Tabitha (Trafton) Vorce of Warren, R. I. He was a farmer, residing for a time in Swansea, and afterwards in Warren. About 1796 he removed with his family to Montpelier, Vt. He served as sergeant in the War in 1812, in Captain Timothy Hubbard's Co., of the "Plattsburg Volunteers" (1814). Later he was commander of an independent military company. He died Dec. 21, 1831, at Montpelier, Vt.

Children:

i. LYDIA PECK,[6] b. Apr. 8, 1795; m. Jan. 12, 1823, Josiah, b. Feb. 6, 1796, d. Aug. 10, 1870, son of Thomas and Abigail Parker of Oxford, Mass.; d. Feb. 12, 1883. Children: *Leander M.*, *Merville Josiah*, *Sabrina*, and *Leroy*.
ii. HANNAH, b. Oct. 8, 1797; m. March 2, 1818, Nathan, b. Mch. 6, 1798, d. Aug. 30, 1873, son of Solomon and Nancy (Taggard) Dodge of East Montpelier, Vt.; d. Aug. 23, 1851. He m. (2) his wife's sister Calista. Children: *Polly*, *Luther Collamore*, *Henry Lee*, *Jonathan W.*, *Omri Alonzo*, *Nathan Prentice*, and *Caira Caroline*.
iii. JOHN, b. Aug. 10, 1799.
iv. ELISHA, b. Aug. 1, 1801.
v. ELIZA, b. July 23, 1803; d. June 28, 1813.
vi. NATHAN, b. Mch. 9, 1806.
vii. DEXTER, b. Jan. 25, 1808; drowned, Apr. 17, 1811.
viii. TRUMAN, b. Mch. 26, 1810; d. Jan. 15, 1855; unmarried.
ix. CALISTA, b. June 9, 1812; m. May 25, 1854, her brother-in-law, Nathan Dodge (see Hannah, above); d. Oct. 20, 1872. Child: *Ella Calista*.
x. AMANDA, b. Aug. 11, 1814; d. Aug. 25, 1848; unmarried.
xi. WARREN, b. Sept. 6, 1816.
xii. CAROLINE, b. Apr. 17, 1819; m. Jan. 25, 1844, Thomas Crane, b. Feb. 4, 1819, son of Silas and Betsey (Greenough) Barrows of Montpelier, Vt.; d. Feb. 3, 1895. Children: *Laura Isabella*, *Abbie Lizzie*, *Ellen Caroline*, *Nellie Phinney*, *Lucy Caira*, and *Emily*.
xiii. CHARLES HENRY, b. Jan. 12, 1822; d. Jan. 4, 1843, at St. Jago, Cape Verde Islands.

29. LORING[5] FINNEY (*Jeremiah*,[4] *Jeremiah*,[3] *Jeremiah*,[2] *John*[1]). born June 18, 1760, in Bristol, R. I., married, Oct. 12, 1785 or '6, Experience, born May 4, 1764, in Plymouth, Mass., died Dec. 11, 1835, in Bristol, daughter of Samuel and Elizabeth (Atwood) Pearse and widow of Gideon Hersey. He was a shipmaster, served in the Revolution, at the Battle of Rhode Island, and resided in Bristol, where he died, Mch. 8, 1827.

Children:

i. THOMAS,[6] b. Mch. 23, 1787; d. Sept. 12, 1819, in North Carolina.
ii. MARY PEARSE, b. May 19, 1790; d. Mch. 13(?), 1866; m. Dec. 31, 1813, Capt. Josiah, b. May 7, 1784, d. Mch. 14, 1864, son of Capt. William and Molley (Finney, see 14, iv.) Coggeshall. Children: *Henry*, *Loring Finney*, *Martha*, *William*, and *George*.
iii. LEVI LORING, b. Dec. 28, 1791; lost at sea, June 26, 1815; unmarried.
iv. ELIZA ATWOOD, b. May 5, 1794; m. (1) Apr. 17, 1836, Samuel, b. Apr. 19, 1789, d. Mch. 29, 1849, son of Capt. Curtis and Rachel (Tew) Ladieu of Barrington, R. I.; m. (2) Dec. 5, 1850, John, b. 1778, d. Aug. 15, 1859, son of John Gregory of Seekonk, Mass.; m. (3) Isaiah Simmons, who was b. 1799, and d. June 19, 1877; d. without issue, June 22, 1884.
v. GEORGE, b. Jan. 4, 1797; d. in 1821, in North Carolina.

30. John[6] Finney (*Jeremiah,*[4] *Jeremiah,*[3] *Jeremiah,*[2] *John*[1]), born in 1772, in Bristol, R. I., married, July 8, 1798, Avis, born Feb. 24, 1780, daughter of James and Ruth (Arnold) Bowen of Warren, R. I. He removed from Warren, probably to Conn.

Child:

i. Avis.[6]

31. George[5] Finney (*Jabez,*[4] *John,*[3] *Joshua,*[2] *John*[1]), born in Warwick, R. I., married, May 4, 1792, Henrietta, born June 1, 1772, daughter of Caleb and Susanna (Pierce) Mathews of East Greenwich, R. I. He resided for a time in East Greenwich, but soon removed.

Children:

i. Betsey Ann,[6] b. Apr. 19, 1793.
ii. George, b. Apr. 11, 1795.

EDGARTOWN, MASS., CHURCH RECORD.

Communicated by Miss Mittie Belcher Fairbanks, of Boston.

The following entry in the records of the old Congregational Church at Edgartown, Mass., seems worthy of preservation in print.

"Records of the Church of Christ in Edgartown Mass. (M. V.) (Organized 1641) From 1717 to the Reorganization in 1827. [With some additional Records.]

[Previous History]

Finding no Record of the Church previous to the year 1717 I thought expedient here to infert the Account the Revrd Experience Mayhew gives vs of the firft Settlement of the Church He tells us that the same Year that is the first year the first Inhabitants came to this Island a Church was gathered (which was in 1641) & that the Revr[d] Mr. Thomas Mayhew was ordained Paftor of it. he was lost in a Voiage to England in the year 1657 He speaks of the Lofs of M[r] Mayhew so great to the whole Ifland both Natives & Englifh. It was many years before there was another Minifter settled in the Place. The Rev[d] M[r] Jonathan Dunham being the next. I find no account in what year that took Place the Rev[d] Samuel Wiswall was ordained as a Colleague with Mr Dunham in 1713, he died in 1746. The Rev[d] John Newman was ordained in 1747 he was difmifsed in 1758. The Rev[d] Samuel Kingsbury was ordained 1761, he died in 1778. The Rev[d] Joseph Thaxter was ordained 1780 Nov. 8th. I find on the old Records of the town that in Feb 1664 the Town invited Mr. John Colton to preach with them & to give him Forty Pounds a year I find that the 24 of May 1665 He accepted the Invitation there is no Record of his ordination or of the Time he continued among them. I believe it is a Fact that Governor Mayhew labored among the Indians & white people after the Death of his Son till a short Time before his Death Governor Mayhew died 1681 In the

[I find by the Chh Records of Plimouth that M[r] Dunham came from Plimouth in 1694 & was ordained Pastor of the Chh here]

94 Year of his age a short Biography of his Life informs us that after the Death of his son He preached to the white People & to the Indians & that at 70 years of age he travelled 20 miles thro' the Woods which might be from Edgartown to Gay Head to preach to the Indians & as there was no English House to lodge in He lodged in their Wigwams as mate. He continued his Labours till a short Time before his Death & retained his Reason & memory to the laſt what missionaries with all their pecuniary Rewards ever performed so much for the Glory of God & the Good of the natives as Governor Mayhew & his son did without Fee or Reward Great is their Reward in Heaven [Jos. THAXTER.]"

PASSENGER LISTS TO AMERICA.

Communicated by GERALD FOTHERGILL, Esq., of New Wandsworth, London, England.

[Continued from page 28.]

A List of Passengers who intend going to New York in the Ship *Cornelia* of Portland, sworn at Londonderry, 15 Apl., 1803.

Andrew Little	age	35	labourer	James Tracy	age	30	farmer
Jane "	"	26	spinster	Rose Tracy	"	32	spinster
John "	"	12	labourer	Margaret Tracy	"	2	a child
Margaret "	"	9	spinster	James McCarron	"	29	farmer
William "	"	6	a child	Jane McCarron	"	29	spinster
Eliza "	"	4	"	John McCarron	"	5	labourer
Jane "	"	2	"	Fanny "	"	3	a child
Hugh McAvery	"	24	farmer	John McQuoid	"	20	labourer
Jane McAvery	"	30	spinster	Robert Leonard	"	22	"
Jane McAvery	"	1	a child	Jane "	"	20	spinster
Simon Neilson	"	25	labourer	John Kelly	"	24	labourer
Mary "	"	25	spinster	Eliz Bruce	"	26	spinster
ArchibaldArmstrong	"	18	farmer	Robert Harper	"	30	farmer
James Neilson	"	3	a child	Jane Harper	"	24	spinster
Catherine Rodgers	"	30	spinster	Charles Harper	"	35	farmer
Wm Brown	"	20	labourer	John Forster	"	24	labourer
James McCann	"	25	"	Jane Little	"	21	spinster
David Henderson	"	20	"	James Harper	"	7	labourer
Cons Dougherty	"	20	"	Anthony O Donnell	"	19	"
Thos McDonogh	"	50	farmer	Manus Brown	"	19	"
Catherine "	"	50	spinster	Edwd Brown	"	20	"
" "	"	50	"	Patrick Collin	"	22	"
James "	"	15	farmer	John Gallougher	"	22	"
Hugh McDonogh	"	13	"	Chas Dougherty	"	23	"
Richard "	"	11	"	Rebecca Beatty	"	21	spinster
Thomas "	"	2	a child	James Muldoon	"	24	labourer
Hugh Donnelly	"	32	labourer	James King	"	25	farmer
Mary "	"	28	spinster	John Lenox	"	30	"
Hugh Kennen	"	51	labourer	William Coldhoune	"	30	labourer
Catherine Donnelly	"	4	a child	Patrick Caldwell	"	25	"
Hugh Kennen	"	3	"	Jane "	"	20	spinster

Thomas McKennen	age 3	a child	Mary McIver	age 17	spinster
John Beatty	" 28	farmer	Judith "	" 19	"
Isabella Beatty	" 22	spinster	Shane "	" 25	farmer
Stephen "	" 2	a child			

A List of Passengers who intend going to New York on the Ship *American*, 340 Tons burthen, Alexander Thompson Master, sworn at Londonderry, 9 Apl., 1803.

David Kerr	aged 28 of	Donegal	farmer
Hannah Kerr	" 25	"	spinster
Robert Virtue	" 22	"	farmer
Ann Virtue	" 25	"	spinster
Alexander Thompson	" 21	Fermanagh	farmer
L Jenkin	"	"	labourer
Andw Brander	"	"	"
L Miller		"	"
James McCafferty	"		
John Ward	"		
Robert Fitzpatrick	"		"
Robert Stinson	"	"	"
William Taylor	"	Sligo	"
Elinor "	"	"	spinster
Mary "		"	"
John Longhead	"	Donegal	labourer
R Longhead	"	"	spinster
Robt Longhead	"	"	labourer
John Longhead	"	"	"
John Whiteside		"	"
Ann "		"	spinster
Arthur Johnston	"	"	farmer
Mary "	"	"	spinster
Thomas Longhead	"	"	labourer
Thomas "	" 28	"	"
James McCrea	" 20	Ballantra	"
John "	" 25	"	"
Barbara Spence	" 24	"	spinster
Catherine "	" 23	"	"
John Coulter	" 23	Petigo	labourer
Dennis Carr	" 22	"	"
Catherine Carr	" 21	"	spinster
James Tremble	" 26	Donegal	farmer
Patk McGeragh	" 22	"	"
Alex McKee	" 27	"	"
Fanny McKee	" 26	"	spinster
Patrick McMullen	" 29	"	labourer
Hugh Devarney	" 26	Monaghan	"
Bryan Devine	" 28	"	"
Ann "	" 25	"	spinster
Mary McGinn	" 22	Cavan	"
Thos McGinn	" 27	"	labourer
James Murphy	" 27	"	"
Thomas Murphy	" 23	"	"

Thomas M^c^Surgan	aged 26	Cavan	labourer
Mary "	" 23	"	spinster
Mark O'Neill	" 25	Drunguin	labourer
Jane "	" 23	"	spinster
Henry "	" 17	"	labourer

A List of Persons who intend going to Philadelphia in the Ship *Mohawk* of and for Philadelphia, burthen 500 tons, John Barry Master, sworn at Londonderry, 23 Apl., 1803.

Neal Callaghan	aged 19	Ardmalin	labourer
Darby Dougherty	" 25	"	"
John Thompson	" 35	"	"
Charles Hethrington	" 40	Dungannon	
Christ[y] Hethrington	" 36	"	
Sus[na] "	" 40	"	
Jos[h] "	" 14	"	
Eliza "	" 16		
George "	" 10	"	
James Walker	" 32	Enniskillen	house servant
Ann Walker	" 30	"	
Ralph "	" 36	"	labourer
Anne "	" 32	"	
Alex[r] Wood	" 26	Lisnaska	"
Mary "	" 20	"	
W[m] Alexander	" 32	Donagheady	"
Jane "	" 30	"	
James "	" 11	"	
Martha "	" 10	"	
William Bacon	" 28	Taughbone	
Elizabeth "	" 27	"	
William "	" 12	"	
John M[c]Grenan	" 18	"	house servant
Pat M[c]Gafferty	" 19	"	labourer
Tho Donan	" 23	"	"
Anne Martin	" 20	Enneskillen	
Thomas Drum	" 36	"	
Nath[l] Drum	" 34	"	
Francis Smyth	" 29	"	
William Drum	" 20	"	
Mary Drum	" 16	"	
Pat Lunny	" 20	"	
John Bates	" 21	Donamanagh	"
James Murray	" 20	"	"
Rich[d] Jones	" 24	Strabane	house servant
Barry M[c]Ana	" 24	"	labourer
William Glin	" 25	Letterkenny	"
Owen M[c]Dade	" 28	Carne	"
Robert Hopkins	" 21	Bolea	
Robert Graham	" 20	"	
Abraham Philips	" 35	Urney	"
Robert M[c]Crea	" 30	Strabane	house servant
Pat Diven	" 28	"	"

Henry Forrester	aged 24	Clonis	labourer
Saml Faggart	“ 30	“	“
Marg^{t} “	“ 28	“	
Elizth Niely	“ 21	Newton	stewart
John McCoy	“ 20	Clougher	labourer
John Hastings	“ 21	Stewartstown	“
John Simpson	“ 25	“	“
George Walker	“ 20	“	
Samuel Thompson	“ 28	Dungannon	“
Anna “	“ 30	“	
And^{w} “	“ 25	“	
James	“ 6	”	
Sarah	“ 22		
James Campbell	“ 28	..	
Mary “	“ 20		
Pat^{k} Brodley	“ 19	Londonderry	house servant
Alex^{r} “	“ 28	Newtonstewart	labourer
Arch^{d} Anderson	“ 19	Armagh	“
James Tait	“ 36	“	“
James McGonegall	“ 25	Buncrana	“
Ferrol McAward	“ 21	“	“
Pat^{k} McDonnell	“ 20	“	“
Denis Lynchakin	“ 20		“
Neal Dougherty	“ 20		“
William Kelly	“ 23	“	
John Carton	“ 35	Claggen	
David McConaghy	“ 10	Ballyarton	
Robert McQuistin	“ 26	Dungiven	

List of Persons who have engaged their Passage on board the ship *Ardent*, Burthen 350 tons, Richard Williams Master, bound for Baltimore, sworn at Londonderry, 23 Apl., 1803.

Thomas Ramsey	aged 28	N^{r} Muff	co. Donegal	farmer
Hugh Elliott	“ 40	Rancel	“	“
M^{rs} “	“ 54	“	“	
James “	“ 20	“		
Hugh “	“ 14			
Jean Elliott	“ 18	“		
James Richey	“ 58	Donan	“	
M^{rs} “	“ 52	“	”	
W^{m} “	“ 18	“		
Cath	“ 16	“		
Ann	“ 14	..		
John “	“ 20	..		
And^{w} “	“ 12	“		
Ellen “	“ 10	“		
And^{w} McKee	“ 38	“		
M^{r}s “	“ 34			
Eliza Richey	“ 9			
Nancy McKee	“ 16	‘		
Pat “	“ 14	‘		
Eliz Finlay	“ 57	‘		

John Finlay	aged 22	Donan	Donegal	farmer
James "	" 17	"	"	"
Pat Cunigan	" 60	Killaughter		drover
James Manilus	" 26	Kilcar		"
Hugh Clark	" 30	Donan		farmer
Mrs Clark, Senr	" 28	"		
James "	" 17	"		"
W^{m} "	" 26	"	"	
M^{rs} " Junr	" 22	"	"	
Alex^{r}	" 8			
Mrs Richey	" 38	"		
George Richey	" 9	"		
Charles "	" 44	"		
And^{w} McCullough	" 40	"		
M^{rs} M^{c} "	" 34	"		
And^{w} "	" 16	"		
Jean "	" 14	"		
George "	" 12	"		
Alex^{r} "	" 10	"		
John Montgomery	" 24	Killybegs	"	gentleman
John Jones	" 20	"	"	"
Wm Graham	" 22	Tyrough	"	farmer
Francis "	" 22	"		"
James Cunningham	" 17	Glenery		
John Crawford	" 28	Ballybofey		
John Erwin	" 56	"	"	
George Crawford	" 32	Doren	"	
Ann Boyle	" 14	Mt Charles	"	
David Graham	" 48	Dergbridge	co. Tyrone	"
Sarah "	" 41	"	"	

[To be continued.]

LIEUTENANT GOVERNOR WILLIAM JONES, OF NEW HAVEN JURISDICTION, AND HIS DESCENDANTS.

Compiled by Hon. Ralph D. Smyth, and communicated by Dr. Bernard C. Steiner.

1. Lieut. Gov. William[1] Jones, emigrant to New Haven, styles himself, in a deed dated March 3, 1689/90, "sometime of Martins in the fields, Westminster, Esquire, now of New Haven in the County of New Haven in New England, Planter." He may have been a son of Col. John Jones the Regicide, executed Oct. 16, 1660, who married, as a second or third wife, Jane, the widow of Roger Whetstone and sister of Oliver Cromwell the Protector.

William[1] Jones is said to have been born in 1624, at London, where he was an attorney. He arrived at Boston, July 27, 1660, in the same ship with Whaley and Goffe, and brought his sons William and Nathaniel with him, born by a first wife. He married second, at London, Hannah, born in London in 1633, daughter of Gov. Theophilus Eaton of New Haven, July 7, 1659. By a deed of indenture, dated Mar. 20, 1658/9, Theophilus

Eaton of Dublin in Ireland, Esquire, son and heir to Theophilus Eaton, Governor, late of New Haven in New England, of one part, and Hannah Eaton of London, spinster, daughter of Theophilus Eaton, and Thomas Yale of New Haven in New England, Gentleman, of the other part, conveyed the estate of Gov. Eaton.

An agreement made by some of his heirs is on the New Haven County records. Among them are Andrew Morrison, in right of his wife Sarah, and John Morgan, in right of his wife Elizabeth. These women are spoken of as children of the whole blood of William Jones, Esq. "Jones's Bridge" in Guilford took its name from him. Lieut. Gov. Jones died Oct. 17, 1706, and Mrs. Hannah (Eaton) Jones died May 4, 1707.

Children:

2. i. WILLIAM,[2] lived at Guilford; d. May 23, 1700.
   ii. CALEB, d. unmarried, in 1677.
3. iii. NATHANIEL, d. Aug. 21, 1691.
   iv. HANNAH, b. in 1659 in England; m. (1) Oct. 2, 1689, Patrick Falconer of Newark, N. J., who died Jan. 27, 1692; and m. (2) in 1710, James Clark of Stratford.
   v. THEOPHILUS, b. in New Haven, Oct. 2, d. Oct. 5, 1661.
   vi. SARAH, b. in New Haven, Aug. 16, 1662; m. Oct. 21, 1687, Andrew Morrison.
   vii. ELIZABETH, b. in New Haven, Aug. 28, 1664; m. John Morgan of Groton. Did she marry ——— Williams?
   viii. SAMUEL, b. in New Haven, June 20, d. Dec. 16, 1666.
4. ix. JOHN, b. in New Haven, Oct. 6, 1667; A.B., Harvard College 1690; d. Jan. 28, 1718–19.
   x. DIODATE, b. in New Haven, Mar. 15, 1669; d. Apr. 5, 1670.
5. xi. ISAAC, b. in New Haven, June 20, 1671.
   xii. ABIGAIL, b. in New Haven, Nov. 10, d. Nov. 15, 1673.
   xiii. REBECCA, b. in New Haven, Nov. 10, d. Nov. 15, 1673.
   xiv. SUSANNAH, b. in New Haven, Aug. 18, 1675; d. in 1705; m. Apr., 1700, Nathaniel, son of Phinehas Wilson. He was a scapegrace, for account of whom see Savage's Gen. Dict., vols. 2, p. 568, and 4, p. 587, also 4 Conn. Col. Rec., 354.

2. WILLIAM[2] JONES (*William*[1]) was of Guilford, where he was listed in 1690 at £22.5.0, and had a quarter acre home lot and a cow. His inventory Mar. 19, 1701, was £141. He married, in 1687/88, Abigail, daughter of John Morse of Dedham or Boston. She died Sept. 23, 1737.

Child:

6. i. CALEB,[3] b. in 1688; d. May 24, 1754.

3. NATHANIEL[2] JONES (*William*[1]), of New Haven, married, Oct. 7, 1684, Abigail, daughter of David Atwater. His inventory was £308.8.6.

Children:

   i. HANNAH,[3] b. May 6, 1687.
7. ii. THEOPHILUS, b. Mar. 18, 1690.
   iii. ABIGAIL, b. Mar. 26, 1692, posthumous.

4. JOHN[2] JONES (*William*[1]) lived in New Haven. He married first, Hannah ———; and married second, Mindwell ———. About 1709, he preached a year and a half at Greenwich. He was drowned by breaking through the ice in New Haven harbor. His inventory was £242.12.9.

Children:

8. i. THEOPHILUS EATON,[3] b. Mar. 20, 1706.
   ii. HANNAH, b. Jan. 15, 1708; d. Feb. 16, 1709.

iii. HANNAH, b. July 28, 1710; d. Mar., 1730.
iv. JOHN, b. Feb. 7, 1712.
v. MINDWELL, b. Sept. 14, 1715.
vi. ABIGAIL, b. Jan. 25, 1718.

5. ISAAC[2] JONES (*William*[1]), of New Haven, married first, Nov. 21, 1692, Deborah Clark of Stratford, who died May 28, 1733; and married second, Oct. 1, 1735, Mrs. Abigail Chatterton, who died Sept., 1757.

Children, all by first wife:

9. i. SAMUEL,[3] b. Sept. 26, 1693; d. Aug., 1773.
10. ii. WILLIAM, b. July 20, 1694.
11. iii. TIMOTHY, b. Oct. 30, 1696.
iv. MARY, b. Oct. 6, 1698.
v. DEBORAH, b. Sept. 25, 1700.
vi. ISAAC, b. Dec. 23, 1702.
vii. HANNAH, b. Feb. 15, 1704; d. Jan. 3, 1709.
viii. JACOB, b. Mar. 20, 1706–07; living in Ridgefield in 1743.
12. ix. JAMES, b. May 16, 1709.
x. EBENEZER, b. Feb. 25, 1712; d. Sept. 23, 1713.

6. CALEB[3] JONES (*William Jr.*,[2] *William*[1]), of Guilford, died May 24, 1754. He married first, July 5, 1723, Mary, daughter of John Bishop, who died Jan. 23, 1724/25; and married second, Jan. 19, 1726, Elizabeth Lucas, who died Oct. 22, 1782. His list in 1716 was £49.16.0, and his faculty (carpenter trade and making wheels) was rated at £2.

Child by first wife:

i. MARY,[4] b. Oct. 26, 1724; m. Jan. 26, 1768, Nathaniel Foote of Bramford, and had four children, all daughters, who were unmarried. He d. Feb. 6, 1785.

Children by second wife:

ii. AARON, b. Oct. 4, 1727; d. Nov. 30, 1803; lived in Milford; m. Nov. 7, 1771, Anna, dau. of John Forsdick, who was b. Jan. 23, 1736, and d. Oct. 30, 1808; no children.
iii. SIBYL, b. Jan. 13, 1728; m. Sept. 11, 1756, Samuel Hoadley of Bramford, who d. June 6, 1804.
iv. TRYPHENA, b. Nov. 2, 1730; m. Joseph Roberts.
v. HANNAH, b. Jan. 3, 1735; d. Feb. 1, 1740.
vi. WILLIAM, b. Aug. 20, 1737; d. Nov. 24, 1739.

7. THEOPHILUS[3] JONES (*Nathaniel*,[2] *William*[1]) was a joiner, and lived in Wallingford. He married first, Dec. 26, 1711, Hannah Mix, who died Nov. 26, 1754; and married second, Sept. 22, 1755, Sarah Moss.

Children, all by first wife:

i. CALEB, b. Nov. 4, 1712; m. Mary, dau. of Zachariah Hard. Children: 1. *Anna*,[5] b. Aug. 19, 1742. 2. *Zachariah Hard*, b. Sept. 3, 1744. 3. *Hannah*, b. Jan. 8, 1746. 4. *Caleb*, b. Sept. 3, 1748. 5. *Samuel*, b. May 15, 1754.
ii. LYDIA, b. Nov. 4, 1714; m. Feb. 4, 1735, Joseph Moss.
iii. NATHANIEL,[4] b. Mar. 30, 1717; lived in Wallingford; m. June 8, 1743, Sarah Merriman, and had: 1. *Abigail*,[5] b. Sept. 26, 1744. 2. *Daniel*, b. Oct. 17, 1748. 3. *Sarah*, b. Aug. 16, 1750. 4. *Eunice*, b. Jan. 27, 1752. 5. *Benjamin*, b. Feb. 5, 1757. 6. *Amos*, b. Aug. 3, 1758. 7. *Reuben*, b. Oct. 11, 1759. 8. *Hannah*, b. Feb. 24, 1761.
iv. HANNAH, b. Oct. 4, 1720; m. Aug. 5, 1740, Jehiel Merriman.
v. THEOPHILUS, b. Nov. 1, 1723; d. Oct. 8, 1815; lived in Wallingford; m. May 24, 1757, Anna Street, who d. Aug. 10, 1811, aged 76.

Children: 1. *Sarah*,[5] b. Mar. 30, 1758. 2. *Nicholas*, b. Nov. 25, 1760; d. Aug. 25, 1848. 3. *Anna*, b. 1772; d. Oct. 1, 1776.

vi. ABIGAIL, b. Dec. 28, 1726; m. Mar. 16, 1747, Benjamin Dutton.

vii. NICHOLAS, b. Dec. 17, 1729; d. Apr. 24, 1760; m. (1) Mary ——; m. (2) Eunice ——. Children by first wife: 1. *Charles*,[5] b. May 19, 1752. 2. *Patience*, b. Mar. 27, 1754. Children by second wife: 3. *Mary*, b. Apr. 30, 1756; d. May 6, 1760. 4. *Eunice*, b. Feb. 26, 1758; d. Mar. 31, 1758. 5. *Mary*, b. Feb. 26, 1760.

viii. DANIEL, b. Oct. 28, 1731; d. May 1, 1737.

8. THEOPHILUS EATON[3] JONES (*John*,[2] *William*[1]) lived in Norwalk, and married, Oct. 17, 1728, Sarah, daughter of Paul Cornel.

Children:

i. HEZEKIAH,[4] b. Oct. 22, 1729; d. young.
ii. ABIGAIL, d. Sept. 14, 1737.
iii. HANNAH, b. Feb. 29, 1735-6.
iv. HEZEKIAH, b. Jan. 28, 1737-8.

9. SAMUEL[3] JONES (*Isaac*,[2] *William*[1]) lived in Wallingford. He married first, Sarah ——, who died Nov. 9, 1760; and married second, April 12, 1762, Esther Pratt.

Children, all by first wife:

i. MARY,[4] b. Dec. 5, 1720.
ii. WILLIAM, b. May 31, 1722.
iii. DIODATE, b. Mar. 5, 1724.
iv. HESTER, b. Mar. 9, 1727.
v. EATON, b. Aug. 26, 1730.
vi. DANIEL, b. Mar. 18, 1745-6.
vii. JOHN, b. May 24, 1747.

10. WILLIAM[3] JONES (*Isaac*,[2] *William*[1]) lived in Marblehead, Mass. He married Isabella (? Burrington), and died Oct. 17, 1730. She married second, July 22, 1735, John Jaggar.

Children:

i. BURRINGTON,[4] b. Apr. 16, 1721.
ii. WILLIAM, b. Sept. 5, 1723.
iii. BASIL, b. Apr. 29, 1725. He chose his grandfather, Isaac Jones, as his guardian, Apr. 26, 1739-40.
iv. DEBORAH, b. Oct. 29, 1727.

11. TIMOTHY[3] JONES (*Isaac*,[2] *William*[1]) lived at New Haven. His will was dated Aug. 20, 1781. He married first, Nov. 16, 1726, Jane Harris of Middletown: and married second, Anna ——.

Children:

i. ELIZABETH,[4] b. Nov. 29, 1729; m. —— Roberts.
ii. DEBORAH, b. Sept. 4, 1730; m. Isaac Gridley, and had a son *Isaac*, who graduated at Yale, 1773.
iii. ISAAC, b. Dec. 3, 1731; A. B. Yale, 1757; d. in 1812; lived in New Haven; m. (1) June 5, 1768, Elizabeth Trowbridge, who d. Apr. 4, 1769; m. (2) Sibyl ——. Child by first wife: 1. *William Trowbridge*,[5] b. Feb. 25, 1769. Children by second wife: 2. *Isaac*, Yale, 1792. 3. *Mary*. 4. *William*. 5. *Henry*. Yale, 1796. 6. *Timothy*, Yale, 1804. 7. *Algenon Sydney*, Yale, 1807. 8. *Frances*. 9. *Harriet*.
iv. SUSANNAH, b. Aug. 10, 1733; m. Aug. 28, 1755, John Hotchkiss of New Haven, A. B. Yale, 1748, who d. July 5, 1779.
v. HARRIS, b. Sept. 9, 1734.
vi. TIMOTHY, b. Oct. 1, 1737; A. B. Yale, 1757; d. May 14, 1800; lived in New Haven; m. (1) June 20, 1765, Mary Trowbridge; m. (2) Mrs. Rebecca (Hart) Lynde, dau. of Rev. William Hart, who d. Oct. 26, 1819. 1. A *son*,[5] b. Apr. 5, 1767; d. young. 2. *Elizabeth*,

m. Joseph Lynde. 3. *William Rosewell*, b. a deaf mute; never married; lived with his sister Elizabeth.

vii. JANE, b. Oct. 31, 1740.

viii. MARY, b. Dec. 12, 1743; m. Oct. 31, 1764, John Lothrop, who d. 1789; lived at New Haven.

ix. WILLIAM, b. Jan. 26, 1745–46; A. B. Yale, 1762; d. in 1783; lived in New Haven; m. ——, and had one dau., *Anna*,[5] who m. Solomon Huntington of Windham.

RICHARD SCOTT AND HIS WIFE CATHARINE MARBURY, AND SOME OF THEIR DESCENDANTS.

By STEPHEN F. PECKHAM, Esq., of New York City.

RICHARD[2] SCOTT was the son of Edward[1] and Sarah (Carter) Scott, and was born at Glemsford, Suffolk, England, in 1607. Edward Scott was of the Scotts of Scott's Hall in Kent,* who traced their lineage through John Baliol to the early Kings of Scotland. Richard Scott's wife was Catharine,† daughter of Rev. Francis Marbury and his wife Bridget Dryden, daughter of John Dryden, Esq., and his wife Elizabeth, daughter of Sir John Cope. Col. Joseph L. Chester says (*ante*, vol. xx., p. 367) "It will be seen therefore that Ann Marbury Hutchinson, by both parents, descended from gentle and heraldic families of England." Of course the same could be said of her sister Catharine, and of her husband.

Richard Scott and his wife probably came to New England with the Hutchinson party on the *Griffin* in 1634. Winthrop writes, "Nov. 24, 1634, one Scott and Eliot of Ipswich, was lost in their way homewards and wandered up and down six days and eat nothing. At length they were found by an Indian, being almost senseless for want of rest." But if this refers to Richard Scott, he might have come in Winthrop's party.

Richard Scott was admitted a member of the Boston Church, Aug. 28, 1634. He next appears of record at the trial of his sister-in-law Ann Hutchinson, March 22, 1638, when he said, "I desire to propound this one scruple, wch keepes me that I cannot so freely in my spirit give way to excommunication whither it was not better to give her a little time to consider of the things that is . . . . vised against her, because she is not yet convinced of her Lye and so things is with her in Distraction, and she cannot recollect her thoughts."

He next appears in Providence. What was then included in the "Providence Plantations" is now embraced in the towns of Woonsocket west of the river, North Smithfield, Smithfield, Lincoln, North Providence, Johnston, Providence and Cranston. Before 1700, the settlements centered in

* In the REGISTER, vol. xxxi., p. 345, will be found a review of "Memorials of the family of Scott of Scott's Hall in the County of Kent," by James Renat Scott, London, 1876.

† In the REGISTER, vol. xx., page 355, in an article on the Hutchinson Family, there is much relating to Ann Marbury Hutchinson, and incidentally to her sister Catharine Marbury Scott. In vol. xxi., p. 283, is an account of the Marbury Family with the will of the Rev. Francis Marbury. In vol. xxii., p. 13, is the pedigree of Richard Scott, the article containing much that later researches have proved to be erroneous and reaching conclusions wholly erroneous. In vol. xxiii., p. 121, is an article on the antiquity of the name of Scott. In vol. li., p. 254, will be found the will of George Scott of London, England, a brother of Richard Scott, which furnishes absolute proof of the ancestry of Richard Scott.

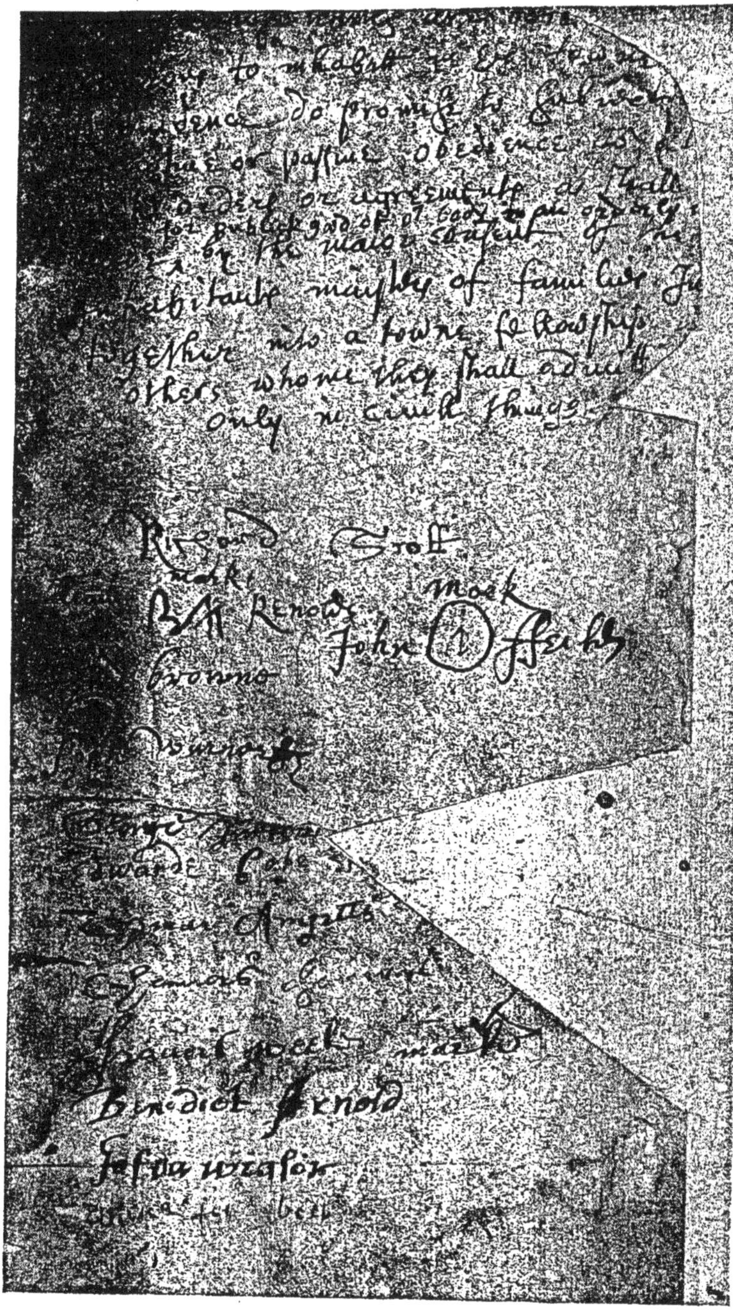

to inhabitt ye
do promise to subiect
or passive obedience
orders or agreements as shall
for publick good of ye body in an orderly
by the major consent of the
inhabitants masters of families
together into a towne fellowship
others whome they shall admitt
only in civill things

Richard Scott
marke
Reynolds
marke
John Field
browne
Benedict Arnold

PHOTO. OF THE PROVIDENCE, R. I., COMPACT.
(SLIGHTLY REDUCED.)

what is now the city of Providence, with farms extending north up the valley of the Blackstone river, west of Pawtucket and Lonsdale. Cumberland was then a part of the Massachusetts town of Rehoboth.

There is no record evidence of the time when Richard Scott first appeared at Providence. Familiar as I have been from childhood with the Blackstone valley, and after a careful study of the subject for many years, I have reached the conclusion that a mistake has been made in identifying Providence with Moshasuck. I believe that the latter settlement, while within the original limits of Providence, as first laid out, was about a mile west of Lonsdale, and a short distance west of Scott's Pond, where Richard Scott, Thomas Arnold, Thomas Harris, Christopher Smith, and others who became Quakers, made a settlement, which was begun before Roger Williams planted at the spring, the water of which still flows into a trough on Canal Street in the city of Providence. At Moshasuck, Richard Scott owned a very large tract of land, some of which remained in his descendants for 200 years, which included what is now Saylesville and Lonsdale and the land between them and around Scott's Pond. It became the Quaker settlement, as distinguished from the Baptist settlement at the head of Narragansett Bay.

The first document to which Richard Scott affixed his signature was the so-called Providence Compact,* which is pasted on to the first page of the earliest book of Records of the city of Providence. It is stated that when these records were copied in 1800, there was opposite the page on which the famous compact is inscribed an entry hearing date August 20, 1637. This date has been assumed to be the date on which the compact was signed. Until I obtained a photograph of this instrument, I supposed it was drawn up by Roger Williams and signed by the then citizens of Providence, but it is in the handwriting of Richard Scott, who was the first to sign it. He also signed for William Reynolds and John Field, who made their marks. Then, using the same ink, Chad Browne, John Warner and George Riccard signed. Then, using another ink that has faded, Edward Cope, Thomas Angell, Thomas Harris, Francis Weekes, Benedict Arnold, Joshua Winsor, and William Wickenden signed. Here are thirteen names, but not the names of the thirteen proprietors of the town of Providence, nor one of them.

It appears to me as almost certain that William Arnold and others had located at Pautuxet, and Richard Scott and others had located at Moshasuck, before Roger Williams and others crossed over from Seckonk, in June, 1636, began building near where St. John's church now stands in Providence, and named the settlement Providence. It is equally certain that Roger Williams secured from the Indians a deed that covered, or was afterwards made to cover, the land on which William Arnold and Richard Scott had located, thus sowing the seed for the perpetual feuds that existed betweeu Roger Williams and his "louing ffriends and Neighbors." In 1637, Richard Scott went to Boston and married Catharine Marbury. Returning to his home in Providence in March, 1638, he drew up and signed the celebrated compact, expecting that Roger Williams and his fellow sufferers, fleeing from the persecution of the triumphant Boston party, would all sign it, and thus found a commonwealth absolutely divested of the theocratic principle. In this he was mistaken. William Arnold, and his party, were joined by Stukeley Westcott, Thomas Olney, Francis Weston, and Richard Waterman, who had been banished from Salem, and they forced or persuaded Roger Williams, October 6, 1638, to deed to them an

* A slightly reduced facsimile from a photograph accompanies this article.

undivided interest in the town of Providence. In this, Richard Scott and his friends who signed the compact had no share. Finally, those who signed the compact and those who were grantees under the deed from Roger Williams, with others who had arrived meantime, joined in an arrangement by which they became "Purchasers of Providence." Under this agreement, the neck between Providence harbor and the Blackstone river was divided into town lots and distributed to 54 purchasers, of which Richard Scott was one. His lot was next north of Roger Williams, and extended up over the hill north of Bowen Street.

The conclusion therefore is inevitable, that whatever credit belongs to the author of this celebrated instrument belongs to Richard Scott alone, and that Roger Williams not only had nothing to do with it, but refused to sign it. It reads as follows:

> "We whofe names are hereunder defirous to inhabitt in ye towne of prouidence do promife to fubiect ourselves in actiue or paffiue obedience to all fuch orders or agreements as fhall be made for publick good of o^r body in an orderly way by the maior confent of the prefent Inhabitants maifters of families Incorporated together into a towne fellowfhip and others whom they fhall admitt into them
>
> only in ciuill things."

January 16, 1638, Winthrop notes, "At Providence things grow still worse; for a sister of Mrs. Hutchinson, the wife of one Scott, being infected with Anabaptistry, and going last year to live in Providence, Mr. Williams was taken (or rather emboldened) by her to make open professson thereof, and accordingly was rebaptized by one Holyman, a poor man late of Salem." There is no other evidence that Catharine Scott had, or wished to have, any influence upon Roger Williams. They never agreed, and upon two occasions Roger Williams had her, with other wives of his neighbors, arrested, but he did not carry his suits to a conclusion before the Court.

On the 27th of 5th month 1640, Robert Coles, Chad Browne, William Harris, and John Warner, were chosen Arbitrators to draw up what is known as the "Combination," which is a sort of agreement for arbitration for the adjustment of differences between "louing ffriends and Neighbours." Two of these arbitrators signed the compact, and two were grantees under the deed from Roger Williams, and the agreement adjusted differences between the Pawtuxet men, the Providence men, and the Moshasuck men. The Combination was signed by 12 who signed the compact, by Roger Williams and 8 grantees under the deed, and 18 others. Richard Scott was one of the signers of the Combination, which contains the following clause, "we agree As formerly hath ben the liberties of the Town: so still to hold forth Libertye of Conscience."

From 1640 to 1650, the Scotts appear to have been quiet and prosperous citizens. They sold their town lot and moved out into the country, upon their lands at Moshasuck. Richard[2] Scott shared in all the allotments of land, and acquired a large estate. Patience Island, in the Bay, was deeded to him "aboute ye year 1651," by Roger Williams.

The children of Richard[2] and Catharine were:

1. JOHN,[3] d. 1677; m. Rebecca Browne.
2. MARY, m. Christopher Holder.
3. HANNAH, b. 1642; d. July 24, 1681; m. Walter Clarke.
4. PATIENCE, b. 1648; m. Henry Beere.
5. DELIVERANCE, d. Feb. 10, 1676; m. William Richardson.
6. RICHARD (?).

Some time in 1656, Christopher Holder, a Quaker, came over from England and visited Providence. It is a tradition that Richard[2] Scott, his wife and daughters, soon became converts to the new faith. There is nothing to indicate that John[3] Scott was ever of that faith. Although the evidence concerning the identity of John Scott's wife is by no means certain, I think there is very good reason for believing her to have been the daughter of John and Sarah Browne of Old Swansea, who were baptists, members of John Myles's church. It is known that there was a second son, and there is reason for believing his name was Richard.

The daughter Mary[3] and Christopher Holder formed an attachment, and when two years later he was arrested in Boston on the charge of being a Quaker, and sentenced to lose his ears, Catharine Scott and her daughter Patience, then 11 years old, went to Boston to comfort the young man in his trial. The story is thus told by George Bishop in his "New-England Judged, by the Spirit of the Lord": "And Katharine Scot, of the Town of Providence, in the Jurifdiction of Rhode-Ifland (a Mother of many Children, one that had lived with her Husband, of Unblameable Converfation, and a Grave, Sober, Ancient Woman, and of good Breeding, as to the Outward, as Men account) coming to fee the Execution of the faid Three, as aforefaid [Christopher Holder, John Copeland and John Rouse, all single young men, their ears cut off the 7th of 7th month 1658, by order of John Endicott, Gov.] whofe Ears you cut off, and faying upon their doing it privately,—That it was evident they were going to act the Works of Darknefs, or elfe they would have brought them forth Publickly, and have declared their Offence, that others may hear and fear.—Ye committed her to Prifon, and gave her Ten Cruel Stripes with a three-fold-corded-knotted-Whip, with that Cruelty in the Execution, as to others, on the second Day of the eighth Month, 1658. Tho' ye confeffed, when ye had her before you, that for ought ye knew, fhe had been of an Unblameable Converfation; and tho' fome of you knew her Father, and called him Mr. Marbery, and that fhe had been well-bred (as among Men) and had fo lived, and that fhe was the Mother of many Children; yet ye whipp'd her for all that, and moreover told her—That ye were likely to have a Law to Hang her, if She came thither again—To which fhe anfwered,—If God call us, Wo be to us, if we come not; and I question not, but he whom we love, will make us not to count our Lives dear unto our felves for the fake of his Name—To which your Governour, John Endicot, replied,—And we shall be as ready to take away your Lives, as ye fhall be to lay them down—How wicked the Expreffion let the Reader judge."

The whip used is thus described by Bishop. "The whip used for these cruel Executions is not of whip cord, as in England, but of dryed Guts, such as the Base of Viols, and with three knots at the end, which many times the Hangman lays on with both his hands, and must needs be of most violent Torture and exercise of the Body."

Afterwards the daughter Mary[3] visited her lover in prison, but the Boston people sent her back to Providence without a whipping, a remarkable exercise of mercy for them, although they kept her in prison a month. In the spring of 1660, Mary[3] Scott and her mother went back to England, and on Aug. 12 she was married there to Christopher Holder. In a letter dated Sept. 8 of that year, Roger Williams wrote to Governor John Winthrop of Conn., "Sir, my neighbor, Mrs. Scott, is come from England, and what the whip at Boston could not do, converse with friends in England, and their arguments have in a great measure drawn her from the Quakers and wholly from their meetings." Catharine Scott's death is recorded in the Records of Friends at Newport, which is absolute proof that she died in full standing among them.

Feb. 26, 1676, Richard[2] Scott confirmed a deed, made many years before, of Patience Island to Christopher Holder and his wife Mary. A copy of this deed will be found in the REGISTER, vol. xxii, page 13.

Richard[2] Scott's daughter Patience[3] married Henry Beere, who was master of a sloop running between Providence and Newport. His daughter Hannah[3] married Walter Clarke, son of Jeremiah and Frances (Latham) Clarke, who was one of the Quaker Governors of the Colony.

In 1666, Richard Scott was chosen from Providence a deputy to the Legislature.

In 1672, George Fox visited New England and preached in Newport, R. I., with great acceptance, which greatly disturbed Roger Williams. In 1676, Roger Williams published in Boston, a book entitled "George Fox digg'd out of his Burrowes," which for scurrilous abuse has few equals, and which, when considered as the production of an apostle of Liberty of Conscience, is one of the most extraordinary books ever printed. In 1678, George Fox published in London, "A New-England Fire-Brand Quenched, Being Something in Answer unto a Lying, Slanderous Book, Entitled George Fox Digged out of his Burrows, &c. Printed at Boston, in the Year 1676, of one Roger Williams of Providence in New-England." It seems that George Fox addressed letters to William Coddiugton and Richard Scott, two of the most eminent Quakers in Rhode Island, and whom he had probably met at Newport, and asked them what manner of man Roger Williams was. They both replied at length, George Fox inserting the replies in his book as an appendix, from which I copy as follows:

"Friends,

Concerning the Converfation and Carriage of this Man Roger Williams, I have been his Neighbour thefe 38. years: I have only been Abfent in the time of the Wars with the Indians, till this prefent—I walked with him in the Baptifts Way about 3 or 4 Months, but in that fhort time of his Standing I difcerned, that he muft have the Ordering of all their Affairs, or elfe there would be no Quiet Agreement amongft them. In which time he brake off from his Society, and declared at large the Ground and Reasons of it: That their Baptifm could not be right, becaufe It was not Adminiftred by an Apoftle. After that he fet up a Way of Seeking (with two or three of them, that had deffented with him) by way of Preaching and Praying; and there he continued a Year or two, till Two of the Three left him.

That which took moft with him, and was his Life, was, To get Honor amougft Men, efpecially amongft the Great Ones. For after his Society and he in a Church-Way were parted, he then went to New-England,* and there he got a Charter: and coming from Bofton to Providence, at Seaconk the Neighbours of Providence met him with fourteen Cannoes, and carryed him to Providence. And the Man being hemmed in in the middle of the Cannoes, was so Elevated and Tranfported out of himfelf, that I was condemned in my felf, that amongft the Reft I had been an Inftrument to fet him up in his Pride and Folly, And he that before could reprove my Wife, for asking her Two Sons, Why they did not pull of their Hats to him? And told her, She might as well bid them pull off their Shoos, as their Hats (Though afterward fhe took him in the fame Act, and turned

* He went to Old England. Is not the *New* a mistake?

his Reproof upon his own Head) And he, that could not put off his Cap at Prayer in his Worſhip, Can now put it off to every Man or Boy, that puls of his Hat to him. Though he profeſſed Liberty of Conſcience, and was ſo zealous for it at the firſt Coming home of the Charter, that nothing in Government muſt be Acted, till that was granted; yet he could be Forwardeſt in their Government to proſecute againſt thoſe, that could not Join with him in it. as witneſs his Preſenting of it to the Court at Newport.

And when this would not take Effect, afterwards when the Commiſſioners were Two of them at Providence, being in the Houſe of Thomas Olney, Senior of the ſame Town, Roger Williams propounded this Question to them:

We have a People here amongſt us, which will not Act in our Government with us; what Course ſhall we take with them?

Then George Cartwright, one of the Commiſſioners asked him, What manner of Persons they were? Do they Live quietly and peaceably amongſt you? This they could not deny; Then he made them this Anſwer:

If they can Govern themselves, they have no need of your Government. —At which they were ſilent.

This was told by a Woman of the ſame Houſe (where the Speech was ſpoken) to another Woman, whom the Complaint with the reſt was made againſt, who related it to me; but they are both Dead, and cannot bear Witneſs with me, to what was ſpoken there. * * * * *

One particular more I ſhall mention, which I find written in his Book (pag. 7.) concerning an Anſwer to John Throckmorton in this manner: To which (ſaith he) I will not Anſwer, as George Fox Answered Henry Wright's Paper with a ſcornful and ſhameful Silence,—I am a Witneſs for George Fox, that I Received his Anſwer to it, and delivered it into Henry Wright's own hands; [Yet R. W. has publiſht this Lie So that to his former Lie] he hath added another ſcornful and ſhameful Lie; And then concludes, That they were his Witneſſes, that he had long ſaid with David (and he humbly hoped) he ſhould make it good that he hates and abhors Lying.

Providence in
New-England

RICHARD SCOT."

Richard Scott seems, from the meagre records that have come down to us, to have been a quiet man, attending to his own affairs, and having little part in the squabbles that disturbed the "louing ffriends and neighbours," which so often claimed the attention of Roger Williams.

There is no record known of Richard Scott's death, but from collateral evidence he is supposed to have died quite suddenly in the latter part of 1680 or early in 1681, leaving his affairs in considerable confusion. Catharine Scott died at Newport, R. I., May 2, 1687.

In Bodge's "Soldiers in King Philip's War," the name of Richard Scott appears in such manner as to make quite certain the presence of two persons bearing that name. In those accounts, Richard Scott, cornet, and Richard Scott, private, were both paid for services, Aug. 24, 1676. The services extended from December, 1675, to Aug., 1676. From these accounts it also appears that John[3] Scott served from June, 1675, to Aug., 1676. Richard[3] Scott, the younger, who is mentioned, but not named, in his father's letter to George Fox, no doubt perished, unmarried, in that terrible struggle.

John[3] Scott, who survived King Philip's War, had married, about 1661, Rebecca Browne. He took the oath of allegiance May 30, 1667, and was a juryman April 27, 1668. He paid taxes of £1–0–0 in 1671. He was acquiring property and rapidly becoming a prosperous citizen when he was shot by an Indian, on his own doorstep, and mortally wounded, dying in a few days, about June 1, 1677. As both Richard and John Scott's names are not in "A List of the inhabitants who Tarried in Providence during Philip's War—1675," it appears probable that the entire Moshasuck quaker settlement went to Newport during that struggle, and that John Scott and his family returned too soon for safety.

The children of John[3] and Rebecca, all born in Providence, probably a Moshasuck, were:

1. SARAH,[4] b. Sept. 29, 1662.
2. JOHN, b. March 14, 1664: d. 1725; m. Elizabeth Wanton.
3. MARY, b. Feb. 1, 1666; d. 1734.
4. CATHARINE, b. May 20, 1668.
5. REBECCA, b. Dec. 20, 1668; d. young.
6. SILVANUS, b. Nov. 20, 1772; d. Jan. 13, 1712; m. Joanna Jenckes.

The son John[4] lived in Newport, with his grandmother and aunts, became a merchant and carpenter, and married Elizabeth, daughter of Edward and Elizabeth Wanton. This Wanton family furnished five colonial governors, and are known as the "Fighting Quakers."

The widow Rebecca remained in Providence, and took up the task of straightening out her late husband's affairs, a task to which was soon added the tangled affairs of her father-in-law, Richard Scott; and there she married, April 15, 1678, John Whipple, Jr., who was one of the prominent men in the Providence colony, and had held nearly every office in the gift of the town, from constable to town clerk and moderator of the Town Meeting. He became blind, and several years thereafter, Dec. 15, 1700 he died.

Jan. 7, 1701, the widow Rebecca Whipple presented a will to the Town Council for probate, and was appointed administrator of her husband's estate, but delayed the settlement for nearly a year, until she and John Whipple's daughters and their husbands, on the one part, forced a deed of partition with young John Whipple, on the other part.

The youngest child of John[3] and Rebecca Scott, who was about six years old when his father died, lived with his mother in John Whipple's house He became Major Silvanus[4] Scott, and early in life entered into the politics of the town, becoming nearly as prominent in his generation as his step-father had been before him. He married, about 1692, Joanna, daughter of Joseph and Esther (Ballard) Jenckes. His wife was a sister of the Governor Jenckes so noted in R. I. annals in the first half of the 18th century. I have not learned that either Silvanus[4] or Joanna[4] Scott were Quakers; but many of their descendants were, and still are, of that faith Their great-grandson Job Scott was, in the latter half of the 18th century, one of the most noted Friends' ministers then living.

The children of Sylvanus[4] and Joanna were:

1. JOHN,[5] b. Sept. 30, 1694; d. July —, 1782; m. Mary Wilkinson.
2. CATHARINE, b. March 31, 1696; m. Nov. 1718, Nathaniel Jenckes.
3. JOSEPH, b. August 15, 1697; m. Elizabeth Jenckes
4. REBECCA, b. February 11, 1699; m. 1718, John Wilkinson.
5. ESTHER, b. December 5, 1700; m. Dec. 14, 1721, Thomas Sayles.
6. SILVANUS, b. June 20, 1702; d. young.

7. JOANNA, b. December 11, 1703; m. May 10, 1724, David Jenckes.
8. CHARLES, b. August 23, 1705; m. Dec. 16, 1713, Freelove Olney.
9. SARAH, b. June 15, 1707; d. 1753; m. Oct. 9, 1726, Stephen Hopkins.
10. JEREMIAH, b. March 11, 1709; m. Rebecca Jenckes.
11. NATHANIEL, b. April 19, 1711; m. Mercy, daughter of Edward,[3] (Edward,[2] Christopher[1]) and Mary Mowry Smith.

The only records of the Scott family that appear on the Providence ecords are the birth dates of the children of John[3] and Rebecca. It is robable that all of the homes and the records at Moshasuck were burned ıring King Philip's War. The records at Providence barely escaped. he Friends' records at Newport and East Greenwich begin in 1676; ıose at Union Village, Woonsocket, in 1719.

ECORDS OF THE SECOND CHURCH OF SCITUATE, NOW THE FIRST UNITARIAN CHURCH OF NORWELL, MASS.

Communicated by WILFORD JACOB LITCHFIELD, M.S., of Southbridge, Mass.

[Continued from page 66.]

A Catalogue of the Members of the second Church of Christ in Scitu-.e, Nov[r]: 13. 1751.*

ɔseph Cufhing: y[e] Deacon. Sen[r]:
lifabeth Curtice, y[e] Widow
ephen Clap.
emperance his Wife.
bagail Collamore, y[e] Widow
lifabeth Prouty, y[e] Widow
lifabeth Turner, Widow
ırah Pinchion,—Widow
nn Stetfon, Wife to M[r] Gerfhom S[n].
iriam Curtice.
ary Cufhing, Wife to M[r] .mes Cufhing.
lifabeth Tolman, Wife to M[r] enjamin Tolman.
eorge King, &
eborah, his Wife.
lifabeth Brooks.
ıchariah Damon, &
ehetabel, his Wife.
.mes Briggs, &
nna, his Wife.
ary Brooks, Wife to M[r] Nath[l] B.
hn James, Sen[r] &
Samuel Stockbridge, Sen[r]: &
Lidia his Wife.
Ierufha Church, wife to M[r]: Nath. Iun[r]
Eunice Sylvefter, wife to M[r]: Elisha S.
Rachel Spooner, Widow.
Mary Barker, wife to M[r]: Iames B.
Mary Cufhing, wife to Hon[l]. Iohn C., Esq:
Margarett Collamore, wife to M[r]: John.
North Eells, &
Ruth, his Wife.
Mary Sylvefter, wife to M[r]: Zebulon S.
Temperance Fofter Wife to M[r]: Elifha.
Ruth Perry.
Anna Lenthal Damon Wife to M[r]: Zach.
Iofeph Copeland &
Elifabeth, his Wife.

* The following entries are from the third book of records called "The Church Book Jonathan Darbys—1752." He was pastor until 1754, and was succeeded by Rev. Da-l Barns, D.D.

Lidia, his Wife.
Timothy Symmes, &
Elifabeth, his Wife.
Benjamin Perry.
Rachel Turner.
Abigail Hobart.
Ifaac Otis &
Deborah, his Wife.
Defire Sylvefter.
Ifaac Buck
Ionna Ruggles, Wife to Mr
Iohn Ruggles.
Elfe Benfon, Wife to Mr
Jofeph Benfon.
Sarah Lambert, Wife to Mr
Iames Lambert.
Iofeph Jacob, ye Deacon.
Mercy Turner, Widow.
Benjamin Curtice &
Rebecca, his Wife.
Abigail Turner, Wife to Mr: Wm: T.
Iemima Damon, Widow.
Lidia Simmons.
Ionah Stetfon &
Mercy, his Wife.
Ruth Perry.
Rebecca Prouty, Widow.
William Barrel &
Abigail, his Wife.
Iofeph Cufhing, Junr: ye: Deacon
Margarett Turner.
Rachel Stetfon, Wife to Mr: Saml: S.
Nathan Pickles.
Richard Turner.
Benjamin Randal &
Sarah, his Wife.
Abigail Fofter, Wife of Mr: Jofh: F.
Lufanna Turner, wife to Mr: Hawkins T.
Iudah Dwelly, Widow.
Iofeph Dunham &
Iane, his Wife.
Iohn Iames, Iunr &
Prudence, his Wife.
Lidia Sylvefter, Wife to Mr: Ioseph S.
Mary Barker, wife to Mr: Barnabas, Sr:
Hannah Merit, wife to Mr: David M.
Hannah Bowker, wife to Mr: Iames B.
Iofeph Clap, &
Sarah, his wife.
Iofeph Damon &
Ioanna his Wife.
Iofeph Palmer &
Iane, his Wife.
Iemima Farrow, Wife to Mr: Thos F.
Sarah Barker, Wife to Mr: Barnabas, Junr:
Sarah Stockbridge, Wife to Mr: Samuel, Junr:
Mary Neal, Wife to Mr: John N.
William Sylvefter &
Mary his Wife.
Mary Buck, Wife to Isaac B., Junr:
Prifcilla Hatch Wife to Mr: Michael H.
Deborah Turner, Wife to Mr: Ifrael T.
Edmond Grofs &
Olive, his Wife.
Mary Brooks, Wife to Mr: Wm:
Hannah Stetfon, Wife to Mr: Mathew S.
Mary Torry, Wife to Mr: Caleb T.
Hannah Collamore, Wife to Mr: Thos:
Abigail Turner, Wife to Mr: Jona: T.
Iemima Prouty, Wife to Mr: Wm: P.
Ruth Randal, Widow.
Abigail Bowker, Wife to Mr: Lazarus B.
Ifaac Damon &
Lidia, his Wife.
Benjamin Stoddard &
Mary his Wife.
Patience Iordan, Widow.
Cuba, a Servant to Mr: Ifaac Turner.
Deborah Oakman, Wife to Mr: Saml: O.
Abiel Bryant, Wife to Mr: Iohn B.
Mary Bryant, Wife to Mr: Saml: B.
Iael Whitton.
Hannah Turner, Wife to Mr: Lemuel T.
Mary Northy, Wife to Mr: Iames N.
Sarah Ruggles.
Abigail Bryant, Wife to Mr: Benjamin B.
Mary Sampfon, Wife to Mr: Charles S.

The Names of those Admitted into full-Communion

1752

April. 5. Mary, y^e: Wife of Robert Damon.
May. 3. Iofhua Lincoln & Huldah his Wife.
June. 7. Gilbert Brooks.
Nov: 5. Iofeph Tolman & Mary his Wife.
Thomas Pinchion & Agatha his Wife.

1753.

June. 10. Oliver Winflows, difsmifion from y^e: 1^t. Ch^h: of Marfhfield, was read & he recieved.
Oct^o: 7. Hannah, y^e. Wife of M^r: W^m: Stetfon.
15. The Hon^l: Iohn Cufhing Efq^r: being in full Communion with y^e: eftablifhed Ch^h: & defiring y^e: ordinances of Chrifti-anity with us & y^e: Privilidges of this. Ch^h: his Request Was granted by a Unanimous Vote.
Nov^r: 4. M^{rs}: Mary Cufhing & M^r: W^m: Cufhing—the Children of Iudge Cufhing.
December y^e 4th. 1754 M^r. David Barns's Dismifsion from the Chh in Littleton was Read & He Received into the 2^d. Chh in Scituate.
Attest Joseph Cushing Junr. Clerk of S^d. Church During the Vacancy.
$Octb^r$ 5. 1755 John Ruggles, Jun.
$Dcemb^r$: 3: Elifabeth Wife to Mr Jofeph Toleman
Ianuary 1756: Nehemiah Porter and his Wife. Prince Rofe
March: 7. John Cufhing Jun & Deborah his Wife
April: 4: Abiel Turner and Elifabeth his Wife
Grace y^e Wife of Elifha Sylvefter
May 2: the wife of Deacon Cufhing & his Son Jofeph
Sam^{ll} Clap Jun and his wife Lucy
Ruth Torry D. to Capt Torry
June 6. 1756 Nehemiah Hatch & Wife
The Widdow Hannah Bowker Lucy Bryant & Hannah Sparhawke
July 4. Elifha Tolman and his wife
Gilbert Brooks and Prifcilla Perry.
$Novb^r$. 4 Elifabeth Curtice

The Names of those who are baptized.

1751

Nov: 17. Lucy, daughter to Cap: Iohn Iames j^r:
Melzar & Mary, Children of Charles Sampfon.—By Rev^d: M^r: Bourn.
Dec^m:. 1. Deborah, daughter to M^r: Gerfhom Randal. Prudence, D. to M^r: Jofeph Stetfon. Iohn Son to M^r: Iohn Bryant. (This Child Was baptized ye: Sabbath before Viz. Nov^r: 24. y^e: 1st: I baptized).
8. Mary, daughter to M^r: Elifha Fofter. by Rev^d: M^r: Bourn.

Friday. 20. all y^{e}: Children of M^{r}: Richard Turner in his houſe, he being Sick. Viz. Iemima, upon her deſire. Iohn, Vine, Ioſeph, Conſider, & Ruth. (6)

1752

Jan^{y}: 26. Sarah, daughter to Iob Neal.
Feb. 23. Iohn, Son to Barnabas Barker Iun^{r}:
25. being Tueſday, Conſider, son to Ion^{a}: Elms, in his house it being Sick.
March. 8. Benjamin, Son to Benj^{a}: Randal jun^{r}:
29. Elijah, son to Saml: Briant, &
Nathaniel, son to Nathl: Turner.
April. 5. William, son to Ioſeph Copeland,
Thomas, son to Thos: Farrar, &
Caleb, son to amos Damon.
12. Caleb, son to Ioſeph Wade–William son to Willm: Brooks, & William son to M^{r}: Willm: Merchant of Boſton.
26. Lebeus, son to Sambo, a free Negro.
May. 3. Ruth, daughter to Iſaac Stetſon.
May. 10. Mary, D. to Deacon Ioſeph Iacob, &
Mary, D. to Robert Damon.
June. 7. Hannah, D. to Cap. Caleb Torey, &
Ionathan, Son to Lazarus Buker, [Bowker] &
Mary, D. to Iſaac Buck.
21. Eliſha, son to Benj^{a}: Buker. Iacob son to Iames Gilkey. Mary, D. to [omitted] Burrel. Deborah, D. to y^{e}: Widow Ruth Turner.
Iuly. 5. Deborah, D. to Dea^{n}: Ioſ^{h}: Cuſhing Iun^{r}:
12. Ioſeph, Abigail, & Peleg, Children of m^{r}: Iſrael Smith. North, son to M^{r}: North Eells.
Aug. 30. Abiel D to M^{r}: Saml: Stockbridge Iun^{r}:
N. Stile begins Simeon Son to M^{r}: Danl: Damon.
Sept. 24. David, S. to Widow Mary Clap. & David Clap Iun^{r}: dec^{d}:
Stephen, S. to Saml: Clap & Lucy his Wife.
Oct^{o}: 10. Tueſday. Simeon, S. to Thos: & Agatha Pinchion at her Deſire.
22. Zipporah, D. to M^{r}: Barnabas Barker Senr:
Celia, D. to Iſrael Sylveſter, by M^{r}: Bourn.
Oct^{o}: 29. Thos: Pinchion Senr: Thos: Pinchion jun^{r}:
Mary & Iudeth, Children of Thos: Pinchion Senr:
Enoch, Son to Saml: Curtice.
Nov^{r}: 5. Anna, D. to M^{r}: Iohn Bowker.
Nov^{r}: 12. Perſis, D. to M^{r}: Ion^{a}: Turner.
19. Elizabeth Hooper, AEt [omitted]:
Dec^{r}: 3. Edward, Son to Iohn Cuſhing Iun^{r}.

1753

Jan^{y}: 14. Bethiah, D. to M^{r}: Abiel Turner.
Feb. 18. Lydia, D. to M^{r}: Ieſse Turner.
Abigail, D. to M^{r}: Iohn Briggs.
Eliſha, Son to M^{r}: Eliſha Silveſter.
Feb. 25. Stephen, Son to M^{r}: Zach^{h}: Damon Junr:

March 22. Huldah, D. to Mr. Iofhua Lincoln, apprehended near its end, Was baptized in their house.
April. 1. David, Son to Mr: William Prouty, & Iames, Son to Mr: Iames Briggs Iunr:
15. Eunice, D. to Nathl: Clap, Esqr:
May. 13. Abigail (Smith) D. to ye: Widow Rachel Spooner, & Elifabeth, D. to Mr: Ionah Stetfon Iunr:
27. Marlborough, Son to Mr: Wm: Silvefter.
Iune. 3. Luke, Son to Mr: Luke Silvefter.
10. Edward, Son to Capt: Peleg Bryant.
July. 15. Thomas, Son to Capt Iohn Iames Iunr:
Sarah, D. to Bazaleel Palmer, by Mr: Bourn.
16. Mark, son to Philis, Negro Servant of Deacon Iofeph Cufhing Iunr:
29. Freeborn, Son to Samll: Bow, a Negro Man, free.
Augt: 5. Mary, D. to Samll: Randal & Sarah his Wife, Who own'd ye: Covenant.
Deborah, D. to Iacob Silvefter. Who ownd: Covenant.
26. Ionathan, Son to Iona: & Lydia Tower.
Sept: 2. Damaris, D. to Nehemiah & Lettice Prouty.
23. Submit, D. to Thos: & Hanh: Collamore.
Molly, D. to Mr: Saml: & Mary Bryant.
30. David, Son to Mr: Robert & Mrs: Mary Damon.
Octo: 14. David, Son to Mr: Ifrael & Mrs: Deb: Turner.
• William, Son to Mr: Iames & Mrs: Deb: Barrel.
21. Anna, D. to Mr: Luke & Ionna Bowker—yy: ownd: Covenant.
28. Iofeph, Son to Mr: Oliver Winflow. By Mr: Bourn.
Simeon, Son to Mr: Thos: & Mrs: Agatha Pincheon.
Ebenezer, Son to Mr: Iof: & Mrs: Elif: Copeland.
Novr: 4. Iob, Son to Mr: Iob Neal.
18. Martha D. to Mr: Iof: & Mrs: Iane Palmer.
Decr: 2. Hannah, D. to Mr: Benja: & Mrs: Hanh: Randal.
9. Sarah, D. to Mr: Elifha & Mrs: Merm: Toleman. By Mr: Bourn.

1754.

Iany: 10. Molly, D. to Nathl: & Mary Mayo being sick, Was baptized at her defire & upon her account.
13. Ruth, Dr: to Mr: Elifha & Temperance Fofter.
20. Lidia D. to Mr: Nathl: Mayo. & Mary his wife upon her account.
Feb. 24. William, Son to Mr: Wm: Iones of Marfhfield, Who own'd ye: Covenant.
March. 30. Ionathan, Son to Mr: Lazarus Bowker & Abigail his Wife, being dangeroufly ill.
April. 2. Mr: Ifaac Prouty AEt: 65, on his Death Bed.
7. Mary, D. to Mr: Barnbas Barker Iunr:

The Revd. Mr. Dorby Departed this Life April ye 22d. 1754 In the 28th. Year of His Age and in ye 3d. Year of His Ministry.

At a Church Meeting of ye 2d. Church of Christ in Scituate on ye 7th. Day of May A.D. 1754 being the first Chh. Meeting after the Death of the Rev^{d}. M^{r}. Dorby S^{d}. Church Chose ye Rev^{d}. Mr Bourn Moderator of S^{d}. Meeting.

Also S^{d}. Church Chose Joseph Cushing Iun^{r}. Clerk of S^{d}. Chh. during the present Vacancy

Baptized. 1754

April. 28th. Rebecca Curtis Daughter to Elisha and Sarah Curtis By ye Revd Mr Gay

May. 5th. Elisabeth Stetson Daughter to Isaac Stetson, By ye Rev^{d}. M^{r}. Perkins.

May. 19th. Betty Stodder Daughter to Benj^{a} Stodder Iun^{r}. Martha Daughter to Thomas Farrow and Amos Dammon Son to Amos Dammon all by the Rev^{d}. M^{r}. Bourn.

May 26 Abigail Iacob Daughter to Dea^{n}. Ioseph Iacob by the Rev^{d}. M^{r}. Smith

June y^{e}. 2^{d}. Desire Silvester Daughter to Nehemiah Silvester, Lucy Smith Daughter to Jsrael Smith. Lucinda Clap Daughter to Samuel Clap Iu^{r} Jsrael & Ruth Lappum Children of Thomas Lappum and Asher Son to Philis Slave to Doc^{tr} Otis all by the Rev^{d}. M^{r}. Wales

September ye 29th. 1754 Mehitabel Cole Daughter to James Cole and Ezekiel Sprague Son to Ezekiel & Priscilla Sprague. all by the Rev^{d} M^{r}. Smith of Wey^{o}. [Weymouth]

October ye 20th. 1754 Caleb Cushing Son to Dea^{n}. Ioseph Cushing Iu^{r}. Samuel Stetson Son to George Stetson and Samuel Randall Son to Samuel Randall all by the Rev^{d} M^{r}. Nat^{h} Eells of Stonington.

October ye 27th. 1754. Ann Briggs Daughter to Iohn Briggs and Iohn Bowker Son to Iohn Bowker by the Rev^{d}. M^{r}. Edward Eells of Middletown.

David Barns [his autograph]

The names of those y^{t}. were Baptized Since I was Ordained. Decem^{br}. 4: 1754

Decr 15: David, Son of M^{r}. Iesse Turner Chriſtopher, Son to Mr Sam^{ll}. Curtice

1755

Feb. 8 Thomas Son to M^{r} E: Sylveſter

Feb: 16: Robert, Son to M^{r} I: Cuſhing
Lemuel Son to Mr Laz: Bowker

Feb 23 Martha Daughter to M^{r} A: Turner

March. 2 Rachel Daugh^{tr}. to Nath: Clap Esq

March. 23 Elisabeth Daugh^{r} to Gerſh: Randal

April 6: James: Son to Caleb Tory

1755

Apr: 24 Ruth: D: to North Eells

May 18 Ceſar in Private by Reaſon of Sickneſs Sev^{t} [Servant to] John Elms

May 18 Rhoda D: to M^{r}. Peleg Briant
Edward Son to Zec^{h}. Damon
Joſeph Son to Ezra Randal.

May 25 Gilbert Son to W^m^. Brooks
Bathſhebah D to Luke Bowker
June 1 Eliſabeth: D: to Amos Damon
Hannah: D: to W^m^. Damon
June 8 Zine: D: to Sam^ll^. Briant
Aug: 3: Benjamin Son to Joſh Lincoln
Celia: D: to Jsrael Sylveſter
Job Son to Nathl: turner.
Lucy D: to James Cuſhing
Aug: 23: Abiah D: to John Briant
N: B: Sarah D to Waterman Eells. this Day w: Eells & wife y^r^ confeſsion . . . . . . owned ye cov^t^ and had y^r^ Child Babtized Sarah D: Nath Church
Octh^r^: 5: 1755/
Rebeckah D: to Joſeph Copeland
Nathl. Son to Na^th^ Broks [Brooks]
Huldah D: to Bezelael Palmer
Rachel: D: w^m^. Brigs
Octb^r^ 26/ Lydia D: to Jonah Stetſon
Anna D: to Job Neal
Nov^br^ 16/ Jonathan Son to Nehe^m^ Prouty
Nov: 23/ Sarah: D; Benja: Randal Ju
Dec^br^ 7/ Eliſabeth Wife to Joſeph toleman
Charles Son to Israel Smith
Feb 1: 1756 Ruth D: to Jona^th^. turner
Abigail D: to Ezek: Sprague
Feb/ 8/ Joſeph Son to John Brigs
Feb 29/ Lydia D: to Deacon Cuſh [Cushing]:
Sarah D: to Sam^ll^ Randal
May 16/ W^m^. Haden & wife made confeſsion and owned ye Cov^t^. and with his Children 5 in Number w^r^ Baptized
May 16: Damſon D: to John Bowker
Hannah D: to Jom [? John or James] Nicolſon
May 23: Mercy D: to a negro of Dr Otis
May 30/ John Son to Michael Hatch
Marcy D: to Eliph: Nothe [Northy]
June 20: Nath: ſon to Nath Clap
Johanna D: thom^s^ Farrar
Jemimah D: to Amos Damon
Sarah Da: Benja. Collomore
Mary *Ditto*
Hannah *Ditto*
Benja Son to S^d^ Collomore.
June 30/ Thomas Son to J^n^ Nicols
Sept: 19/ Betty Jones: D: to John Jones
Barnabas Son to B.^ar^ Barker

1757

Jan 16 Deborah D to Jsrael Turner
Abigail D to Ezra Randal
March 20:1757 Nehemiah Son to Mr Nehemiah Porter
26: Nabby: D: to Lazarus Bowker Baptized in private by Reaſon of Sickneſs

April: 3:	[blank] to Jonah Stetſon Jun
10	Barker Son to J^{n}: Cuſhing Jun
17	Sarah D to Widdow [blank] Palmer
24	Sam^{ll}: Son to Eliſha Tolman
	Ezekiel son to Peter Collmore
24	John Son to Sam^{ll} Bryant:
24:	Orphan D. to ye Widdo Peterſon owned ye covenant & was Baptized
May 8 1757	Ezekiel Son of Isai. Stoddard
15	Eliſha Son to Lemuel Sylveſter
	Lucy: D: to Isaac Damon
22	Sarah D: to John Homes
29:	Elijah Son to Joſeph Clap S^{r} [?]
	Lydia D: to John Curtice
	Abigail D: to M^{r}: Stephen Lapham
	Priſce [Priscilla]: D to Jsaac Prouty.
	Before Baptiſm ye same Day ye S^{d} Prouty and wife owned ye Covenant
June 19 1757	Allice: D: to Deacon Cuſhing Jun
July 3	Lydia D to Nath Brooks Jun
10	Barſtow Son to Capt. W^{m}. Sylveſter
	Rhoda D: to Michael Hatch
: 17:	Rachel: D: to R^{d} David Barns and Rachel his wife
23:	Thomas, Sam^{ll}. Abel, Sons, to Simeon Naſh and Lydia his Daughter
31	Cynthia D: to Elijah Curtice
Aug 14:	Thomas Barker Son to M^{r}. James Brigs
21.	Joſeph Son D^{cn}. Joſeph Jacob
28:	Unice: D: to Isaac Stetſon
Sept: 1757	Oliver Son of Oliver winſlow
	Ceberry [Sebre] D: to John Brigs
	Allice: D: to Israel Smith
	Eliphalet Son to Eliph Nothe [Northy]
Octbr 2 1757	Martha D: to Peleg Bryant
9	Damaris D: to: Nehe^{m}: Prouty
	Ruth: D: to Cornelius Brigs
16	Molly: D to Benj^{a}: Randall.
nov: 6:	Mary: D: to Math: Stetſon
	Abigail D to [blank] Tore [Torrey]
	Mercy: D: to Antony Eames
	Hannah his wife His wife owned ye Cov: Bapt: on His account
	Gidion Son to Gidion Roſe Jun brot out by her alone and Baptized on Her account
20	Gerſhom Son to Mr Nehemiah Sylveſter
	Betty: D: to Benj^{a} Collmore Baptized on Her Account
Decb^{r} 4:	Ebenezer & Grace Totman owned ye Covenant and y^{r} children w^{h} [were] Baptized Thomas and Stephen
	Charles Son to John Bowker
	Jenny D: to Nath Mayhew Baptized on Her Account

[To be continued.]

GENEALOGIES IN PREPARATION.

(Continued from page 89.)

HAIGHT.—*Jonathan of Rye, N. Y.*, by L. N. and Mrs. J. G. Nichols, Snyder Hill, Ithaca, N. Y.

HALEY, or HALLEY.—*All lines*, by Eugene F. McPike, 1 Park Row, Room 606, Chicago, Ill.

HAMMETT.—*Edward of Martha's Vineyard (?)*, by Mrs. Mary L. Alden, Troy, N. Y.

HANDY.—*Samuel of England or Wales*, by William Byron Handy, 585 Tremont St., Boston, Mass.

HANSBROUGH.—*Peter of Culpeper Co., Va.*, by John W. Hernden, 919 Prince St., Alexandria, Va.

HARRIMAN.—*Leonard of Rowley, Mass.*, by F. G. Harriman, Box 237, Santa Monica, Cal.; and Fred W. Lamb, 452 Merrimack St., Manchester, N. H.

HARRISON.—*Burr of Chappawamsic, Va.*, by Lelia H. Handy, 1331 12th St., N. W., Washington, D. C.

HARRISON.—*Richard, Jr., of Newark, N. J.*, by W. E. Harrison, Fort Madison, Iowa.

HARRISON.—*Richard of New Haven, Conn.*, by Mrs. Frances H. Corbin, 54 Dwight St., New Haven, Conn.

HART.—*Josiah of Manchester, N. S.*, by Howard C. Myers, 74 Spring St., Brighton, Mass.

HARWOOD.—*Andrew*, by W. H. Harwood, M.D., Chasm Falls, N. Y.

HARWOOD.—*Nathaniel of Concord, Mass.*, by F. H. Harwood, 126 Main St., Evansville, Ind.

HASEY.—*Lt. William of Reading, Mass.*, by William Prescott Greenlaw, Sudbury, Mass.

HATCH.—*Thomas of Barnstable, Mass.*, by Henry Herbert Smythe, Falmouth, Mass.

HATHEWAY.—*John of Taunton, Mass.*, by B. F. Hatheway, Stamford, Conn.

HATHWAY.—*John of Taunton, Mass.*, by Thomas G. Hatheway, U. S. Assay Office, Seattle, Wash.

HATHWAY.—*Nicholas of Gloucestershire, Eng. (?)*, by Arthur B. Paine, 120 Pleasant St., Brookline, Mass.

HAWKES.—*Adam of Lynn, Mass.*, by Adam Augustus Hawkes, Wakefield, Mass.

HAWKES, or HAWKS.—*John of Lynn, Mass.*, by J. M. Hawks, 16 Newhall St., Lynn, Mass.

HAWKESWORTH, *Thomas of Salisbury, Mass., and Adam of Wilmot Township, Annapolis Co., N. S.*, by Mrs. Sarah D. Cropley, Marblehead, Mass.

HAWKINS.—*James, Sr., of Union Co., S. C.*, by Edward A. Claypool, Suite 309 Bush Temple, Chicago, Ill.

HAWKINS.—*Robert of Charlestown, Mass.*, by Israel G. Hawkins, Stony Brook, Suffolk Co., N. Y.

HAWLEY.—*Jehiel of Arlington, Vt.*, by F. Phelps Leach, East Fairfield, Vt.

HAYWARD.—*Samuel of Mendon, Mass.*, by Mrs. W. L. Proctor, 14 Caroline St., Ogdensburg, N. Y.
HEDGER.—*Joseph of Flushing, L. I.*, by L. N. and Mrs. J. G. Nichols, Snyder Hill, Ithaca, N. Y.
HEDGES.—*Joseph of Monocacy, Md.*, by Mrs. W. Samuel Goodwyn, Emporia, Va.
HENDERSON.—*Robert of Hendersonville, Pa.*, by Miss Helen E. Keep, 753 Jefferson Ave., Detroit, Mich.
HERNDON.—*William*, by John W. Herndon, 919 Prince Street, Alexandria, Va.
HEWET, or HUIT.—*Thomas of Hingham, Mass.*, by Prof. W. T. Hewett, Cornell University, Ithaca, N. Y.
HIGGINS.—*Richard of Piscataway, N. J.*, by Mrs. M. P. Higgins, 228 West St., Worcester, Mass.
HILL.—*John of Guilford, Conn., and Luke of Guilford, Conn.*, by Edwin A. Hill, Room 348 U. S. Patent Office, Washington, D. C.
HILLS.—*Joseph of Newbury, Mass.*, by Smith Adams, Milltown, Me.
HILLS.—*John of Ashford, Eng., Joseph of Newbury, Mass., and William of Hartford, Conn.*, by William S. Hills, 294 Newbury St., Boston, Mass.; and Thomas Hills, 157 K St., South Boston, Mass.
HOAG.—*John of Rockingham Co., N. H.*, by Charles A. Hoag, Lockport, N. Y.
HOBART.—*Edmund of Hingham, Mass.*, by William Nelson, Paterson, N. J.
HOBBIE, or HOBBY.—*John of Greenwich, Conn.*, by William A. Eardeley, 466 State St., Brooklyn, N. Y.
HODGDON.—*John of Scarboro, Me.*, by Charles A. Beane, 213 Commercial St., Portland, Me.
HODGES.—*James of New Haven, Conn.*, by Edwin A. Hill, Room 348 U. S. Patent Office, Washington, D. C.
HOLLY.—*John of Stamford, Conn.*, by William A. Eardeley, 466 State St., Brooklyn, N. Y.
HOLMAN.—*Solomon of Newbury, Mass.*, by David Emory Holman, M. D., Attleboro, Mass.
HOLMES.—*David of Dorchester, Mass., Francis of Stamford, Conn., and George of Roxbury, Mass*, by William A. Eardeley, 466 State St., Brooklyn, N. Y.
HOLMES.—*George of Roxbury, Mass.*, by George Arthur Gray, 51 Botolph St., Atlantic, Mass.
HOPKINS.—*John of Hartford, Conn.*, by Timothy Hopkins, Mills Bldg., San Francisco, Cal.
HOPPER.—*John of Deptford Township, N. J.*, by Harry Shelmire Hopper, 400 Chestnut St., Philadelphia, Pa.
HORTON.—*Thomas of Springfield, Mass.* (?), by Marcus N. Horton, 88 Essex Ave., Bloomfield, N. J.
HORTON.—*William of Colchester, N. Y.*, by Barnes Horton, Sheffield, Pa.
HOSKINS, or HODSKINS.—*William of Taunton, Mass.*, by J. C. C. Hoskins, Sioux City, Iowa.
HOUGHTON.—*John of Lancaster, Mass.*, by Dr. Arthur W. Clark, Lawrence, Kansas.
HOWARD.—*Of Norfolk, Eng.*, by W. W. Bolton, 120 Howard St., So. Easton, Mass.
HOWARD.—*Robert of Dorchester, Mass.*, by William B. Handy, 585 Tremont St., Boston, Mass.

HOWE.—*Abraham of Watertown and Marlborough, Mass., Abraham of Roxbury, Mass., Edward of Lynn, Mass., James of Roxbury and Ipswich, Mass., and John of Sudbury and Marlborough, Mass.*, by Hon. Daniel Wait Howe, Indianapolis, Ind.

HUDSON.—*Ann of Philadelphia, Penn.*, or *N. J.*, by Harry Shelmire Hopper, 400 Chestnut St., Philadelphia, Pa.

HUDSON.—*Henry of England*, by Eugene F. McPike, 1 Park Row, Room 606, Chicago, Ill.

HUGHES.—*John ap Hugh of Gwynedd, Pa.*, by Mrs. Walter Damon Mansfield, California Hotel, San Francisco, Cal.

HUNT.—*Thomas of Rye, N. Y.*, by Dr. William Austin Macy, Kings Park, Long Island, N. Y.

HURD.—*John of Dover, N. H.*, by John Hurd Lord, Box 215, Berwick, Me.

HURRELL.—*All families of the name*, by W. G. Richards, 59 Hill Park Cresent, Plymouth, Eng.

HUSSEY.—*Capt. Christopher of Hampton, N. H.*, by Charles W. Tibbetts, Dover, N. H.

HUSSEY.—*Richard of Dover, N. H.*, by Henry S. Webster, Gardiner, Me.; and R. B. Hussey, 48 Linden St., Reading, Mass.

HYDE.—*Jonathan of Newton, Mass.*, by Frank C. Hyde, 31 Milk St., Boston, Mass.

HYDE, or IDE.—*Nicholas of Rehoboth, Mass.*, by Elizabeth J. Wilmarth, 73 North Main St., Attleboro, Mass.; and Herbert C. Ide, New Britain, Conn.

INGALLS.—*Edmund of Lynn, Mass.*, by Charles Burleigh, M.D., Malden, Mass.

IVES.—*William of New Haven, Conn.*, by Arthur S. Ives, 33 Sidney Place, Brooklyn, N. Y.

JACKMAN.—*James of Salisbury, Mass.*, by Geo. W. Jackman, 2403 North Ave., Bridgeport, Conn.; and Parmenio Adams Jackman, 263 North 3d East, Logan, Utah.

JACKSON.—*Robert of Hempsted, L. I.*, by George Cleo Jackson, 79 Hamilton Ave., Akron, Ohio.

JANES, or JEAN.—*Joseph of the Island of Jersey (?)*, by Albert James Walker, 18 Mt. Vernon St., Salem, Mass.

JOHNSON.—*William of Charlestown, Mass.*, by Orrin P. Allen, Palmer, Mass.

JONES.—*Dept. Gov. William of New Haven, Conn.*, by Edwin A. Hill, Room 348 U. S. Patent Office, Washington, D. C.; and George H. Andruss, 2437 Warring St., Berkeley, Cal.

KEHRT, or CART.—*Jacob of Ilbesheim, Bavaria*, by Harry Shelmire Hopper, 400 Chestnut St., Philadelphia, Pa.

KEMPTON.—*Ephraim, Jr., of Plymouth, Mass.*, by Mrs. Josephine Kempton Sedgwick, Parnia, Mich.

KENNY, KENE, or KENEY.—*Henry of Salem, Mass.*, by Mrs. Frederic L. Osgood, 194 Washington St., Norwich, Conn.

KEYES.—*John of Worcester, Mass.*, by Miss Idelle Keyes, 1077 Boylston St., Boston, Mass.

KIMBALL.—*Richard of Ipswich, Mass.*, by S. P. Sharples, 26 Broad St., Boston, Mass.

KING.—*James of Suffield, Conn.*, by Cameron H. King, 920 Fulton St., San Francisco, Cal.

KINGSLEY.—*John of Rehoboth, Mass.*, by J. S. Kingsley, Tufts College, Mass.

KINNEAR.—*William of Londonderry, N. H.*, by Mrs. John B. White, 616 East 36th St., Kansas City, Mo.

KIRKBRIDE.—*Matthew of Burlington, N. J.*, by Dr. William Austin Macy, Kings Park, Long Island, N. Y.

KIRTLAND.—*Nathaniel of Saybrook, Conn.*, by Carlos P. Darling, Lawrenceville, Tioga Co., Pa.

KNIGHT.—*Dea. Richard of Newbury. Mass.*, by Smith Adams, Milltown, Me.

KNOWLTON.—*All lines*, by George Henry Knowlton, 328½ Hudson Ave., Albany, N. Y.

LAKE.—*All Lake emigrants to America*, by B. Lake Noyes, M.D., Stonington, Maine.

LAMB.—*Thomas of Roxbury, Mass.*, by Frank B. Lamb, Westfield, N. Y.

LAMSON.—*William of Ipswich, Mass.*, by Albert H. Lamson, Elkins, N. H.; and Dr. W. J. Lamson, 120 Summit Ave., Summit, N. J.

LANCASTER.—*Thomas of England*, by Harry Fred Lancaster, Columbia City, Ind.

LANE.—*Robert of Killingworth, Conn.*, by Geo. B. Lane, Nowesna Bank Bldg., Minneapolis, Minn.

LANG.—*John of Portsmouth. N. H., and Robert of Portsmouth, N. H.*, by Henry W. Hardon, 60 Wall St., New York City.

LANGDON.—*Edward, John of Long Island (?), John of Boston, Mass., Peter of Cecil Co., Md. (?), Philip of Boston, Mass., and Tobias of Portsmouth, N. H.*, by J. G. Langdon, 46 Pelham St., Newton Centre, Mass.

LANGDON.—*Noah of Farmington, Conn.*, by Miss Grace Langdon, McMinnville, Tenn.

LANGDON.—*Peter of West Virginia*, by Mrs. H. A. Carroll, Charles Town, Jefferson Co., W. Va.

LANGDON.—*Philip of Boston, Mass*, by Miss Annie Laws, 818 Dayton St., Cincinnati, Ohio.

LANGFORD.—*John of Northampton, Mass.*, by Mrs. Mary L. Alden, 245 Pawling Ave., Troy, N. Y.

LANGTON.—*George of Northampton, Mass.*, by Robert Getty Langdon, 35 Nassau St., N. Y.; and J. G. Langdon, 46 Pelham St., Newton Centre, Mass.

LAPHAM.—*John of Dartmouth, Mass.*, by S. F. Peckham, 280 Broadway, Room 104, New York City.

LAY.—*John of Saybrook, Conn.*, by Edwin A. Hill, Room 348 U. S. Patent Office, Washington, D. C.

LAZELL.—*John of Hingham, Mass.*, by Theodore S. Lazell, 5 Nassau St., New York, N. Y.

LEACH.—*Lawrence of Salem, Mass.*, by F. Phelps Leach, East Fairfield, Vt.

LEIGHTON.—*Thomas of Dover, N. H.*—by Mrs. J. L. Comman, c/o Col. Daniel Comman, U. S. A., War Dept., Washington, D. C.

LILLY.—*George of Reading, Mass.*, by Julius W. Lilly, 637 East 67th St., Chicago, Ill.

LINNELL.—*Robert of Barnstable, Mass.*, by Arthur Ellsworth Linnell, 86 Davis St., Wollaston, Mass.

LITCHFIELD.—*Lawrence of Scituate, Mass.*, by Wilford J. Litchfield, Southbridge, Mass.

LOOMIS.—*All lines*, by Elisha S. Loomis, Berea, Ohio.

LORING.—*Thomas of Hull, Mass.*, by John Arthur Loring, Springfield, Mass.; and George F. Loring, 76 Highland Ave., Somerville, Mass.

LOUNSBURY.—*Richard of Rye, N. Y.*, by William A. Eardeley, 466 State St., Brooklyn, N. Y.

LOVEJOY.—*John of Andover, Mass.*, by D. R. Lovejoy, Niagara Falls, N. Y.

LOVEWELL.—*John of Nashua, N. H.*, by C. H. Lovewell, M.A., 6058 Wentworth Ave.. Chicago, Ill.

LUCE.—*Henry of Tisbury, Mass.*, by Wilford J. Litchfield, Southbridge, Mass.

LUDDINGTON.—*William of East Haven, Conn.*, by Dr. Horace Ludington, 135 North 31st Ave., Omaha, Neb.

LUMMUS.—*Edward of Ipswich, Mass.*, by Chas. A. Lummus, 3 William St., Newton, Mass.; and Henry T. Lummus, c/o Lummus & Barney, Item Bldg., Lynn, Mass.

LYON.—*Daniel of Greenwich, Conn.*, by L. N. and Mrs. J. G. Nichols, Snyder Hill, Ithaca, N. Y.

LYON.—*Isaiah of South Woodstock, Conn.*, by Eugene F. McPike, 1 Park Row, Room 606, Chicago, Ill.

LYON.—*Jacob of Ashford, Mass.*, by Mrs. Joseph H. Johnson, 2005 2d Ave., South, Minneapolis, Minn.

LYON.—*Thomas of Fairfield and Greenwich, Conn.*, by Robert B. Miller, 41 Van Buren St., Brooklyn, N. Y.

MACOMBER.—*John of Taunton, Mass., and William of Marshfield, Mass.*, by Rev. Everett S. Stackpole, Bradford, Mass.

MACOR, or MAKER.—*James of Yarmouth, Mass.*, by William A. Eardeley, 466 State St., Brooklyn, N. Y.

MADDOCK, MADOCK, or MADOX.—*All families of the name*, by W. G. Richards, 59 Hill Park Crescent, Plymouth, Eng.

MAIN, or MAYNE, *Ezekiel of Stonington, Conn.*, by E. G. Main, 28 Maple Ave., Waterbury, Conn.; and Algernon A. Aspinwall, 1305 Riggs St., Washington, D C.

MALTBY.—*John and William of New Haven, Conn.*, by Dorothy Lord Maltby, 58 Grove St., New Haven, Conn.

MANWARING.—*Ranalphus of England*, by G. A. Manwaring, Bayonne City, N. J.

MARKHAM.—*Daniel of Middletown, Conn.*, by E. A. Markham, M.D., Box 95, Durham, Conn.

MARSHALL.—*Anthony of Walpole, Mass.*, by Mrs. Sarah D. Cropley, Marblehead, Mass.

MARTIN.—*John of Piscataway Township, N. Y.*, by Charles W. Tibbetts, 22 New York St., Dover, N. H.

MARTIN.—*Samuel of Philadelphia, Pa.*, by Richard A. Martin, 145 West 82 St., New York City.

MASON.—*Sampson of Rehoboth, Mass.*, by Francis W. Plant, Joliet, Ill.; Carlos Parsons Darling, Lawrenceville, Penn.; and Alverdo Hayward Mason, East Braintree, Mass.

McGAFFEY.—*Neil of Epsom, N. H.*, by Rev. Frank Gardner, 119 South 4th St., Sunbury, Penn.

McNALLY.—*Michael of Clinton, Maine*, by Charles A. Beane, 213 Commercial St., Portland, Me.

McPIKE.—*James of Newport, Ky.*, by Eugene F. McPike, 1 Park Row, Room 606, Chicago, Ill.

MERCIER.—*Jean of Canterbury, Eng.*, by M. Ray Sanborn, Yale University Library, New Haven, Conn.

MERRITT.—*Henry of Scituate, Mass.*, by Wilford J. Litchfield, Southbridge, Mass.
MESSENGER.—*Henry of Boston, Mass.*, by Winthrop Messenger, 283 Vinton St., Melrose Highlands, Mass.
METCALF.—*Michael of Dedham*, by John Wilder Fairbank, 25 Upton St., Boston, Mass.
MILLER.—*James of Rye, N. Y.*, by Robert B. Miller, 41 Van Buren St., Brooklyn, N. Y.
MILLER.—*Frank of Waldoboro', Me.*, by Frank B. Miller, Rockland, Me.
MILLER.—*John of Wethersfield and Stamford, Conn.*, by Robert B. Miller, 41 Van Buren St., Brooklyn, N. Y.
MILLER, or MILLEN.—*Capt. Joseph of West Springfield, Mass.*, by C. S. Williams, 16 Rivington St., New York City.
MILLS.—*Daniel of Hadley, N. Y.*, by John R. Gray, 423 Prospect Ave., Buffalo, N. Y.
MILLS.—*George of Jamaica, Long Island, N. Y.*, by William A. Eardeley, 466 State St., Brooklyn, N. Y.
MILLS.—*John of Staunton, Va.*, by Edward C. Mills, 10 Y. M. C. A. Bldg., Columbus, Ohio.
MILTON.—*Robert of Hull, Mass.* (?), by William B. Handy, 585 Tremont St., Boston, Mass.
MOFFAT.—*William of Killingly, Conn.*, by Mrs. Grace Moffett Lansing, Watertown, N. Y.
MORRIS.—*Capt. Richard of Morrisania, N. Y.*, by Murray Edward Poole, Ithaca, N. Y.
MORSE.—*Anthony, Samuel, Joseph, and William*, by Emily W. Leavitt, 7 Walnut St., Boston, Mass.
MOSS.—*John*, by Emily W. Leavitt, 7 Walnut St., Boston, Mass.
MUNSEY.—*William of Dover, N. H.*, by William L. Palmer, 22 Sacramento Place, Cambridge, Mass.
MURRAY.—*Jonathan of Guilford, Conn.*, by W. B. Murray, 505 North Elizabeth St., Peoria, Ill.
MURRAY.—*Noah of Murraysfield, Penn.*, by Mrs. Louise Welles Murray, Athens, Penn.
NASH.—*All lines*, by Elizabeth T. Nash, Madison, Conn.
NEEDHAM.—*Anthony of West Peabody, Mass.*, by Sarah Jane Clarkson Needham, West Peabody, Mass.
NEILL.—*Filius of Scotland*, by William Nelson, Paterson, N. J.
NEWELL.—*Thomas of Hartford, Conn.* (?), by Carlos P. Darling, Lawrenceville, Penn.
NEWTON.—*Richard of Marlborough, Mass.*, by Mrs. E. N. Leonard, De Pere, Wis.
NICHOLAS.—*Rice of Madison, N. J.*, by N. L. and Mrs. J. G. Nichols, Snyder Hill, Ithica, N. Y.
NOYES.—*Rev. James of Newbury, Mass.*, by Smith Adams, Milltown, Me.
NUTT.—*William of Chester, N. H.*, by Charles Nutt, 7 Munroe Ave., Worcester, Mass.
NYE.—*Benjamin of Sandwich, Mass.*, by Henry Herbert Smythe, Falmouth, Mass.
OBITS, OBITTS, or OPITZ.—*John Michael of Lowville, N. Y.*, by Lieut. C. E. Johnston, Revenue Cutter Office, Treasury Department, Washington, D. C.
OLDHAM.—*Joshua of Scituate, Mass.*, by Mrs. James W. Carey, 22 Magazine St., Cambridge, Mass.

OLMSTED, OLMSTEAD.—*Capt. Jabez of Ware, Mass., Capt. Nicholas of Hartford, Conn., and Capt. Richard of Norwalk, Conn.*, by Frederick S. Hammond, Oneida, N. Y.

ORDWAY.—*James of Newbury, Mass.*, by John C. Ordway, 113 North State St., Concord, N. H.

OSBORN(E).—*All lines*, by John M. Bancroft, Bloomfield, N. J.

PABODIE (see PEABODY).—*Elizabeth of Plymouth, Mass.*, by Mrs. Mary L. Alden, 245 Pawling Ave., Troy, N. Y.

PAINE.—*David of Ludlow, Mass.*, by Mrs. Clara Paine Ohler, 559 West Market St., Lima, Ohio.

PAINE.—*Thomas of Eastham, Mass.*, by Josiah Paine, Harwich, Mass.

PALMER.—*William of Hampton, Mass.*, by William L. Palmer, 22 Sacramento Place, Cambridge, Mass.

PARDEE.—*George of New Haven, Conn.*, by Carlos P. Darling, Lawrenceville, Pa.

PARDEE.—*John of Sharon, Conn.*, by Miss Lydia Patchen, Westfield, N. Y.

PARKE.—*Richard of Cambridge, Mass*, by Frank S. Parks, 2104 H St., N. W., Washington, D. C.

PARKE.—*Robert of Mystic, Conn.*, by Frank Sylvester Parks, 2104 H St., N. W., Washington, D. C.

PARKER.—*All families in America*, by A. G. Parker, 878 Prospect Ave., Buffalo, N. Y.

PARKER.—*Dea. Thomas of Reading, Mass.*, by P. Hildreth Parker, 412 Pleasant St., Dracut, Mass.

PARKS.—*Lt. Richard of Concord, Mass.*, by C. W. Parks, U. S. N., Navy Dept., Washington, D. C.

PARMELE.—*John of New Haven, Conn.*, by Dr. George L. Parmele, 65 Pratt St., Hartford, Conn.; and Miss Helen Parmelee, 832 Euclid Ave., Cleveland, Ohio.

PARSONS.—*Ct. Joseph of Springfield, Mass.*, by Carlos P. Darling, Lawrenceville, Pa.

PARTRIDGE.—*George of Duxbury, Mass.*, by Mrs. Edward C. Chatfield, 613 Fulton St., Minneapolis, Minn.

PATCHING.—*Joseph of Roxbury, Mass., and Fairfield, Conn.*, by Miss Lydia Patchen, Westfield, N. Y.

PATTEE.—*Peter of Haverhill, Mass.*, by William Tracy Eustis, 19 Pearl St., Boston, Mass.

PATTERSON.—*Andrew of Stratford, Conn.*, by George L. Burton, 87 Church St., New Haven, Conn.

PEABODY (see PABODIE).—*Lt. Francis of Topsfield, Mass.*, by Miss Grace Peabody, 7424 Normal Ave., Chicago, Ill.

PEAKES, or PEAKS.—*William of Scituate, Mass.*, by Wilford J. Litchfield, Southbridge, Mass.

PEASLEE.—*Joseph of Salisbury, Mass.*, by George F. Beede, Freemont, N. H.

PECKHAM.—*Benjamin of North Stonington, Conn.*, by Byron J. Peckham, 52 Mechanic St., Westerly, R. I.

PECKHAM.—*John of Newport, R. I.* (?), by Stephen F. Peckham, 280 Broadway, New York City.

PEIRCE.—*Caleb of Rochester, Mass.*, by John Elliot Bowman, 79 Elm St., Quincy, Mass.

PENDLETON.—*Brian of Winter Harbor, Me.* (?), by Everett Hall Pendleton, Taunton, Mass.

PERLEY.—*Allan of Ipswich, Mass.*, by M. V. B. Perley, 22 Cabot St., Salem, Mass.

PERRIN.—*Daniel of Staten Island, N. Y.*, by Howland D. Perrine, 141 Broadway, New York City.

PERRY.—*Ezra of Sandwich, Mass.*, by William A. Eardeley, 466 State St., Brooklyn, N. Y.

PETTINGELL.—*Richard of Newbury, Mass.*, by Smith Adams, Milltown, Me.

PHELPS.—*William of Windsor, Conn.*, by F. Phelps Leach, East Fairfield, Vt.

PHILLIPS.—*George of Watertown, Mass.*, by Pauline Willis, 3 Kensington Gate, London, Eng.

PIATT, or PYATT.—*John of the Island of St. Thomas*, by Benj. W. Strader, 426 East 4th St., Cincinnati, Ohio.

PIERCE.—*Daniel of Newbury, Mass.*, by Smith Adams, Milltown, Me.

PIKE.—*James of Newport, Ky.*, by Eugene F. McPike, 1 Park Row, Room 606, Chicago, Ill.

PILCHER.—*James of Dumfries, Va.*, by Maj. James Evelyn Pilcher, U. S. A., Carlisle, Pa.

PITCHER.—*Pitchers of Albany and Schoharie Counties, N. Y.*, by George Thurston Waterman, 119 Hamilton St., Albany, N. Y.

PLACE.—*John of Rochester, N. H.*, by Guy Scoby Rix, Concord, N. H.

PLUMER, or PLUMMER.—*Francis of Newbury, Mass.*, by Smith Adams, Milltown, Me.; and Rev. George M. Bodge, 11 Flora St., West Roxbury, Mass.

POMEROY.—*Eltweed of Northampton, Mass.*, by Carlos P. Darling, Lawrenceville, Penn.; and Mrs. Henry Thorp Bulkley, Southport, Conn.

POOL.—*Patrick of Virginia or North Carolina*, by Murray Edward Poole, Poole Block, Ithaca, N. Y.

POOLE.—*Edward of Weymouth, Mass., John of Reading, Mass., William of Dorchester, Mass., John of Gloucester, Mass., Samuel of Boston, Mass., Matthew of Martha's Vineyard, Mass., Daniel of Virginia, Robert of Jamestown, Va., Robert of Bermuda and Virginia, Peter of Bound Brook, N. J., and Henry of Elizabeth City, N. C.*, by Murray E. Poole, Poole Block, Ithaca, N. Y.

POOLE.—*John of Reading, Mass.*, by William Prescott Greenlaw, Sudbury, Mass.

POSTE.—*Jeremiah of Morris Co.. N. J.* (?), by L. N. and Mrs. J. G. Nichols, Snyder Hill, Ithaca, N. Y.

PRAY.—*Quinton of Braintree, Mass.*, by J. L. Pray, 217 Rockingham St., Toledo, Ohio.

PRESTON.—*Roger of Lynn, Mass.*, by Charles H. Preston, Hathorne, Essex Co., Mass.

PRINCE.—*Robert of Salem, Mass.*, by Edward Prince, Quincy, Ill.

PRINDLE, or PRINGLE.—*William of New Haven, Conn.*, by Miss Mary L. Hine, 142 Main St., West Haven, Conn.; Franklin C. Prindle, U. S. N., retired, Navy Dept., Washington, D. C.; and Ruth S. Prindle, Sharon, Conn.

PUFFER, or POFFER.—*George of Braintree, Mass.*, by Loring W. Puffer, 15 Green St., Brockton, Mass.

PURDY.—*Gabriel of Annapolis Co., N. S.*, by L. N. and Mrs. J. G. Nichols, Snyder Hill, Ithaca, N. Y.

PUTNAM.—*John of Salem, Mass.*, by Eben Putnam, 26 Broad St., Boston, Mass.

[To be continued.]

THOMAS TREADWELL OF IPSWICH, MASS., AND SOME OF HIS DESCENDANTS.

By William A. Robbins, LL.B., of Brooklyn, N. Y.

[Continued from page 55.]

15. Jabez[4] Treadwell (*Nathaniel,[3] Nathaniel,[2] Thomas[1]*), born in Ipswich, Mass., 9 Aug., 1713, died testate in Ipswich, 22 Dec., 1780 (the correct year, although his gravestone states 1781), married (intention published in Ipswich, 20 Nov., 1736) Lucy Haskell of Ipswich, who died in Ipswich, 21 Sept., 1789, aged 74 years.

The church records in Ipswich would lead one to believe that Jabez married four times, whereas he had but one wife. He was a cooper, and resided in Ipswich.

Children, baptized in Ipswich:

- i. William,[5] bapt. 12 Mch., 1737-8.
- 31\. ii. Jabez.
- iii. Lucy, bapt. 21 Dec., 1740; d. in Ipswich, 7 Nov., 1763.
- iv. Hannah, bapt. 19 Dec., 1742.
- v. Hannah, b. 3 Jan., 1743-4; d. 16 Feb., 1823; m. (int. published in Ipswich, 14 Nov., 1767) Aaron, bapt. in Ipswich, 2 Sept., 1744, d. testate, 10 May, 1801, son of Jeremiah and Joanna (Smith) Perkins. He was a cooper, and resided in Ipswich. Children: 1. *Hannah*. 2. *Lucy*. 3. *Sarah*. 4. *Aaron*. 5. *Daniel*. 6. *Joanna*. 7. *Jeremiah*. 8. *Jabez*. 9. *Daniel*.
- vi. Sarah, bapt. 2 Feb., 1745-6; d. probably 4 Feb., 1782; m. (int. published in Ipswich, 19 Nov., 1768) Michael, probably bapt. 6 Apr., 1746, d. 25 Nov., 1795, son of Peletiah and Jane (Farley) Kinsman of Ipswich. Did he m. (2) Mary Knowlton of Ipswich?
- 32\. vii. Samuel.
- 33\. viii. William.
- 34\. ix. Nathaniel.
- x. Martha, bapt. 9 May, 1756.
- xi. Elizabeth, bapt. 26 Mch., 1758.
- xii. Daniel, bapt. 3 June, 1759.

16. Samuel[4] Treadwell (*Samuel,[3] Nathaniel,[2] Thomas[1]*), born in Wells, Me., 28 May, 1720; died probably after 27 Apr., 1803, on a salt marsh where he had been at work, his body having been found beside a heap of hay; married (intention published in Wells, 15 Oct., 1744) Hannah, born probably in Wells, 22 Aug., 1727, daughter of James and Lydia Littlefield of Wells. He apparently divided his property among his children during his lifetime. He was a yeoman, served in the French and Indian War, and resided in Wells, Me.

Children, born in Wells, Me.:

- i. Hannah,[5] b. 27 Sept., 1745.
- 35\. ii. Nathaniel.
- 36\. iii. James.
- 37\. iv. Masters.
- 38\. v. Samuel.
- vi. Hammond, bapt. in Wells, 15 May, 1757; killed in battle near Ticonderoga, reported dead 27 June, 1777, having enlisted 14 Dec., 1776, for three years or during the war.
- vii. Lydia, bapt. in Wells, 16 Sept., 1759.
- viii. Mary, bapt. in Wells, 31 Aug., 1760. Did she m. in Wells, 29 Oct., 1789, Joseph, b. 1 May, 1763, d. 17 Apr., 1836, probably the

son of Benjamin and Lydia (Morrison) Kimball of Wells and York, Me. This Joseph Kimball resided in Wells and York. Children: 1. *Hannah.* 2. *Joseph.* 3. *Charles.*

ix. JONATHAN, bapt. 31 Aug., 1760; d. probably in the army, on or before 1 Jan., 1782. He enlisted in the Continental Army to serve three years or during the war, after previous service.

x. LYDIA, bapt. in Wells, 24 Apr., 1763.

39. xi. JACOB.

17. JOSEPH[4] TREADWELL (*Thomas,*[3] *Nathaniel,*[2] *Thomas*[1]), born in Ipswich, Mass., 3 Feb., 1716/7, died in the army at Menas Bay, on Bay of Chagnecto, Nova Scotia, about 1763, married (intention published in Ipswich, 10 Jan., 1746/7) Sarah, baptized in Rowley Parish, Mass., 15 Feb., 1727/8, daughter of David and Mary (Platts) Hammond of Ipswich. Sarah (Hammond) Treadwell married second, in Newburyport, Mass., 25 Dec., 1769, Walter Davis of Newburyport, Mass., where she resided at that time.

Joseph[4] Treadwell was a yeoman, and resided in Ipswich and Dracut, Mass.

Children, baptized in Ipswich:

40. i. JOSEPH.[5]

ii. ELIZABETH, bapt. 5 Mch., 1748-9; probably d. young.

iii. MARY, bapt. 5 Mch., 1748-9; probably m. in Newburyport, Mass., 30 Dec., 1769, George Tryal.

iv. SARAH, b. in Rowley, Mass., 1751; bapt. 7 July, 1751; d. in Millbury, Mass., 25 Feb., 1837; m. in Oxford, Mass., 25 July, 1776, David Stone (name changed from Gale) of Oxford, b. in Waltham, Mass., 6 Dec., 1750, d. testate 9 Dec., 1827. She resided in Sutton, Mass., at time of her marriage. He was a yeoman, and resided in Oxford, that part now North Oxford. Children: 1. *David.* 2. *Joseph.* 3. *Sarah* (mother of Clara Barton, famous through her work in the Red Cross Society). 4. *Anna.* 5. *Jeremiah.*

18. THOMAS[4] TREADWELL (*Thomas,*[3] *Nathaniel,*[2] *Thomas*[1]), born in Ipswich, Mass., 6 Aug., 1732, died intestate, probably in 1766, married in Ipswich, 19 Feb., 1752, Esther, baptized 23 Feb., 1728, died probably in Ipswich, 5 Oct., 1809, daughter of Nathaniel and Hannah (Fossee) Hovey. He was a sea captain, and resided in Ipswich. Was he the "joiner," 1754?

Children, baptized in Ipswich:

41. i. NATHANIEL.[5]

ii. HANNAH, bapt. 12 May. 1754. Did she m. 27 Mch., 1777, Stephen Wyatt, Jr., of Newburyport, Mass.?

iii. ESTHER, bapt. 14 Nov., 1756. Did she marry in Ipswich, 22 May, 1778, Robert Newman of Ipswich? Perhaps it was their child who d. in Ipswich, 20 July, 1790.

19. SAMUEL[5] TREADWELL (*Thomas,*[4] *Thomas,*[3] *Thomas,*[2] *Thomas*[1]), born in Ipswich, Mass., 9 Mch., 1738, living 29 May, 1778, married in Templeton, Mass., 18 June, 1766, Sarah Nickless. He was a yeoman and blacksmith, was in the Canadian expedition in 1760-1, and served in the Revolution, probably as armorer. He resided in Littleton and Templeton, Mass., Fitzwilliam and Swanzey, N. H.

Children:

i. LYDIA,[6] b. in Templeton, Mass., 27 Aug., 1768; d. 6 Aug., 1836; m. 29 Mch., 1789, Thomas, b. 10 Jan., 1766, d. intestate 8 July, 1839, son of Moses and Ruth (Hill) Learned. He resided in Templeton,

Mass. Children: 1. *Mary*. 2. *John*. 3. *Joel*. 4. *Lydia*. 5. *Samuel*. 6. *Ruth*. 7. *Lyman*. 8. *Sarah*. 9. *Joel*. 10. *Moses*.

ii. SARAH, bapt. 10 Nov., 1771.

20. THOMAS[5] TREADWELL (*Thomas*,[4] *Thomas*,[3] *Thomas*,[2] *Thomas*[1]), baptized in Ipswich, Mass., 20 Oct., 1745, died testate, in Littleton, Mass., 7 May, 1796, aged 50 years, married in Littleton, 14 May, 1767, Jane, born in Littleton, 6 Mch., 1742, died in (? Waterford, Me., 6 Mch.) 1839, daughter of William and Hannah Jewett of Littleton. He was a yeoman, served in the Revolution, and resided in Littleton. After his death, his widow moved with her family to Waterford, Me.

Children, born in Littleton:

i. HEPZIBAH,[6] b. 7 Feb., 1769; m. in Littleton, 25 Nov., 1790, Dea. Solomon, b. in Groton, Mass., 7 Feb., 1763, d. in Waterford, Me., Sept., 1841, son of J. and Susannah (Moore) Stone of Groton. He was a farmer, and resided in Groton, Mass., and Waterford, Me. Children: 1. *Solomon*. 2. *Thomas Treadwell*. 3. *Susan Moore*.

ii. HANNAH, b. 13 (or 18) Sept., 1770; d. in Groton, Mass., 5 Jan. 1800; m. (int. published in Littleton, 18 May, 1788) Samuel, b. in Littleton, Mass., 1767, probably the son of Matthias and Mary (Preston) Farnsworth. Did he m. (2) Miss Hannah Tuttle of Littleton? He resided in Littleton and Groton, Mass. Children: 1. *Asahel*. 2. *Mary*. 3. *Thomas Treadwell*. 4. *Hepzibah*.

iii. JOHN, b. 18 Mch., 1772.

iv. WILLIAM, b. 30 Dec., 1773.

v. HULDAH, b. Sept., 1775; d. young.

vi. HULDAH, b. 29 July, 1777; buried in Littleton, 7 Sept., 1787, "in her 12th year" (?).

vii. ESTHER, b. 30 May, 1778; d. probably in 1873; m. Samuel Sanders of Rowley, Mass., who resided in Westbrook or Woodford's Corners, Me. Children: 1. *Hannah*. 2. *Thomas*. 3. *Joshua*. 4. *Samuel*. 5. *Jane*.

viii. THOMAS, b. 18 Nov., 1780; d. in Littleton, 23 Sept., 1782.

ix. SALLY, b. 26 Aug., 1782; d. probably in Bridgton, Me.; m. after 17 Apr., 1797, Gen. John Perley, who resided in Bridgton. Children: 1. *Susan H.* 2. *A son*.

x. MOSES HOBSON, b. 29 July, 1784; d. probably in Waterford, Me., before 1842; m. Jane Hawes. He was a deacon in the church; captain in the war of 1812; and resided in Waterford (Plummer District), Me. Children: 1. *Jane*.[7] 2. *Thomas*. 3. *Mariah H.* 4. *Samuel*. 5. *Sarah Perley*. 6. *William H.*

21. JOHN[5] TREADWELL (*John*,[4] *John*,[3] *Thomas*,[2] *Thomas*[1]), born in Ipswich, Mass., 20 Sept., 1738, died testate in Salem, Mass., 5 Jan., 1811, married first, in Topsfield, Mass., 15 Sept., 1763, Mehitable, who died in Ipswich, 1 (or 2) July, 1786, daughter of Dr. Richard and Mehitable (Putnam) Dexter of Topsfield, Mass.; married second, in Salem, 17 July, 1787, Dorothy, baptized 26 May, 1751, died in Salem, May, 1802, aged 51 years, daughter of Jacob and Mary (Ropes) Ashton and widow of Jonathan Goodhue of Salem; and married third, 12 June, 1804, Hannah, baptized 6 Jan., 1754, died in Charlestown, Aug., 1816, aged 63 years, probably the daughter of John and Hannah (Winslow) Austin of Charlestown.

He graduated at Harvard College in 1758; was minister, school teacher, representative, state senator, and judge of the Court of Common Pleas. He resided in Lynn, Ipswich, and Salem, Mass.

Children:

i. A SON, b. in Lynn, Mass., 6 Oct., 1764; probably d. young.

ii. JOHN DEXTER, b. in Lynn, Mass., 29 May, 1768; d. testate, in Salem, Mass., 6 June, 1833; m. in Salem, 4 Mch., 1804, Dorothy (A.), b. in Salem, 23 Feb., 1777, d. testate, in Salem, 29 Jan., 1858, dau. of Jonathan and Dorothy (Ashton) Goodhue. He graduated at Harvard College in 1788, and was a physician, residing in Marblehead and Salem, Mass. Child: *John Goodhue.*[7]

iii. MEHITABLE,[6] b. in Lynn, Mass., 27 July, 1775; d. in Boston, Mass., 20 Aug., 1840; m. in Salem, Mass., 17 Dec. (? 28 Oct.), 1797, Rev. Charles, b. in Norwich, Conn., 21 June, 1772, d. in Boston, Mass., 5 June, 1872, son of Aaron and Abiah (Hyde) Cleveland of Norwich, Conn. He m. (2) Lucy S. (Francis) Dunnels of Boston. He resided in Charlestown, Mass. Children: 1. *John Treadwell.* 2. *Charles Dexter.* 3. *George Putnam.*

iv. WILLIAM (?), bapt. in North Church, Salem, Mass., Apr., 1788; d. before 29 Jan., 1811.

22. ELISHA[5] TREADWELL (*John,*[4] *John,*[3] *Thomas,*[2] *Thomas*[1]), born in Ipswich, Mass., 3 Feb., 1754, died intestate, in Ipswich, Mass., 19 Dec., 1792, married in Ipswich, 21 June, 1780, Lydia, born in Ipswich, 7 Nov., 1754, died in Ipswich, 21 June, 1833, daughter of John and Mehitable (Burley) Crocker of Ipswich. Lydia (Crocker) Treadwell married second, in Ipswich, 18 Dec., 1804, Col. Joseph Hodgkins. Elisha[5] Treadwell was a yeoman, served in the Revolution, and resided in Ipswich.

Children, born in Ipswich:

i. WILLIAM,[6] b. 9 Feb., 1782 (1781, on a coffin plate); d. intestate, in Salem, Mass., 22 Aug., 1844; m. (1) in Salem, 29 May, 1803, Elizabeth, d. 7 Nov., 1804, probably the dau. of Daniel and Hannah (Symonds) Bancroft of Salem; m. (2) in Salem, 13 Oct., 1805, Hannah (Bancroft) Parker of Salem, a widow, and sister of his first wife, who d. Salem, 25 May, 1833, aged 57 years; and m. (3) in Salem, 21 Jan., 1835, Elizabeth Hyde Mansfield, b. in Norwich, Conn., 25 Apr., 1788, d. intestate, 16 May, 1847. He was a housewright, trader, and merchant, residing in Salem. Children, the first by wife Elizabeth, the others by wife Hannah: 1. *Elizabeth Bancroft.*[7] 2. *Hannah.* 3. *John Crocker.* 4. *Mary Irenea.* 5. *Lydia Asenath.* 6. *Charles William.*

ii. MARY, b. 11 Feb., 1783; d. in Ipswich, 23 (or 25) June, 1804.

iii. JOHN, b. 14 Mch., 1785; d. intestate and unmarried, 23 June, 1810, wrecked on the ship "Margaret." He was designated "Jr." in 1810, was a mariner, and resided in Salem and Ipswich, Mass.

iv. LYDIA, b. 14 Sept., 1787; d. in Ipswich, 20 Feb., 1819; m. in Ipswich, 20 Dec., 1810, Samuel Wade of Ipswich. He was a housewright, and resided in Ipswich. Children: 1. *Lydia.* 2. *Mary Crocker.* 3. *Priscilla Treadwell.*

v. EPHRAIM, b. 24 Sept., 1789; d. testate, in New York City, 4 Jan., 1857; m. 23 Dec., 1821, Mrs. Rachel R. (Taylor) Blackwood, b. in Philadelphia, Penn., 29 Mch., 1795, d. in New York City, 28 June, 1879, dau. of John R. Taylor of Philadelphia. He was a merchant, later in the baking business (ship bread and cracker), and resided in Salem and Boston, Mass., New York City and Tarrytown, N. Y. Children: 1. *Rachel Maria.*[7] 2. *Ephraim.* 3. *William Edward.* 4. *Mary.* 5. *Ephraim.* 6. *Ephraim.* 7. *Emily Augusta.*

vi. CHARLES, b. 26 July, 1791; d. in a hospital in New York City, 19 Aug., 1867; m. in Philadelphia, Penn., 25 Aug., 1820, Martha Reiff, b. (? in Philadelphia) 3 Apr., 1799, d. in Plainfield, N. J. (? Scotch Plains), 28 May, 1868, dau. of John Reiff Taylor of Philadelphia. His name was changed to Francis Charles Treadwell, by Act of the Mass. Legislature, 17 June, 1817. He was at first a commission merchant, then in the baking business, and later became an attorney-at-law. He resided in Salem, Mass., Richmond, Va., New York City, Portland, Me., and Brooklyn, N. Y. His widow resided in Plainfield, N. J., at time of her death. Children: 1. *Lydia.*[7] 2. *Francis Charles.* 3. *Martha.* 4. *John Reiff.* 5. *William.* 6. *William.* 7. *Martha Reiff.*

23. WILLIAM EARL[5] TREADWELL (*Jacob,*[4] *Nathaniel,*[3] *Nathaniel,*[2] *Thomas*[1]), born about 1727, died intestate, probably in 1793, before 19 Aug., married in Portsmouth, N. H., 21 Nov., 1764, Mehitable, born in Portsmouth, in 1733, died in Rye, N. H., Jan., 1820, daughter of Jotham and Mehitable (Cutt) Odiorne. Did he marry first Zerviah Stanley, who died May, 1750, aged 22 years, the daughter of Hon. William Parker? He served in the Louisburg Expedition in 1745, was a merchant, and resided in Portsmouth, N. H.

Children:

i. ROBERT ODIORNE,[6] d. 22 Apr., 1804, aged 38 years; m. in Portsmouth, N. H, 5 Dec., 1789, Ann Stocker Pearse (his cousin) of Portsmouth, d. testate, Sept., 1844, aged 75 years, dau. of Peter and Mary (Odiorne) Pearse. He was a merchant and sea-captain, and resided in Portsmouth. Children: 1. *Daniel Hearl.* 2. *A child.* 3. *A child.*

ii. DANIEL (?).

iii. A SON (?).

iv. A SON (?).

24. NATHANIEL[5] TREADWELL (*Jacob,*[4] *Nathaniel,*[3] *Nathaniel,*[2] *Thomas*[1]), born between 6 Dec., 1730, and 22 May, 1750, died testate, between 19 Oct., 1809, and 17 Oct., 1811, married, before 3 Mch., 1791, Catherine, who was living 14 Feb., 1818, probably the daughter of Jonathan Stoodley. Did he marry in Portsmouth, N. H., 9 Jan., 1759, Comfort, daughter of James Stilson of Portsmouth? He was a tanner, was designated "Jr." 1771–1809, and resided in Portsmouth, N. H.

Children:

i. JAMES,[6] probably d. in Boston, Mass., in 1816. Did he m. in Portsmouth, N. H., 14 Apr., 1793, widow Hannah Penhallow of Portsmouth? It is believed that he was a mariner.

ii. NATHANIEL, living 19 Oct., 1809. Did he m. in Boston, Mass., 10 Aug., 1803, Mary Card?

iii. JACOB, b. in Portsmouth, N. H.; d. intestate, and buried 16 Aug., 1824, aged 45 years; m. (possibly his second marriage) Ann (or Nancy), who d. in Lowell, Mass., 2 Mch., 1862, aged 74 years, 7 mos., probably the dau. of Nathaniel Paul. He was a merchant, residing in Portsmouth. Children; 1. *Ann S.*[7] 2. *Nathaniel Paul.* 3. *Charles.* 4. *Catherine.*

iv. HANNAH, bapt. in South Parish Church, Portsmouth, N. H., 24 Jan., 1762; living, 19 Oct., 1809.

v. CATHERINE. Did she m. in Portsmouth, N. H., 2 Mch., 1811, George H. Tuckerman of Portsmouth?

vi. JOHN, bapt. in South Parish Church, Portsmouth, N. H., 21 Mch., 1765.

25. SAMUEL[5] TREADWELL (*Jacob,*[4] *Nathaniel,*[3] *Nathaniel,*[2] *Thomas*[1]), born in Portsmouth, N. H., 4 Oct., 1741, died in Peterborough, N. H., 13 Dec., 1819, married first, 10 Apr., 1764, Mary, born 31 Mch., 1741 (? 1745), died 4 Oct., 1771, daughter of Jonathan Stoodley; and married second, 1 May, 1777, Mary, born in Townsend, Mass., 6

Sept., 1746, died in Peterborough, N. H., 27 Aug., 1833, daughter of Thomas and Elizabeth Cunningham, and widow of James McKean of Peterborough. He served in the Revolution, was a boat builder and yeoman, and resided in Portsmouth, Brentwood, and Peterborough, N. H.

Children by first wife:

i. DANIEL,[6] b. in Portsmouth, N. H., 28 Jan., 1766. Did he die in Huntington, Vt., 20 Sept., 1840? He was a farmer, and resided in Peterborough in 1790.

ii. MARY, b. in Portsmouth, 20 Feb., 1768; living, unmarried, 4 Feb., 1791.

iii. SARAH, b. in Portsmouth, 20 Nov., 1770; living, unmarried, 24 Nov., 1791, in Newington, N. H.

Children by second wife:

iv. ELIZABETH, b. in Peterborough, N. H., 15 Feb., 1778; d. near Peterborough, 5 July, 1862; m. Feb., 1796, Abel Weston, d. 17 Feb., 1860, aged 90 years. He was a shoemaker, residing in Peterborough. Children: 1. *Samuel.* 2. *Levi.* 3. *Mary.* 4. *Helen.* 5. *Nancy.* 6. *Harriet.* 7. *Clarrissa.* 8. *Timothy.* 9. *Amos.* 10. *Cummings.* 11. *Elizabeth.* 12. *Martha L.*

v. WILLIAM EARL, b. in Peterborough, 8 Feb., 1780; d. in Peterborough, 11 July, 1847; m. 21 Jan., 1810, Elizabeth, b. in Amherst, N. H., 24 Apr., 1785; d. 1 Apr., 1863, dau. of John and Eliza (Wheeler, born Carter) Secomb of Amherst. He was styled yeoman in 1809, gentleman in 1810, and resided in Peterborough. Children: 1. *A daughter.*[7] 2. *John S.* 3. *William Samuel.*

vi. ANNA (NANCY), b. 24 Feb., 1782; m. in Peterborough, 20 Jan., 1808, Solomon Buss of Wilton, N. H. They moved to Maine.

vii. SUSANNA, b. in Peterborough, 3 May, 1784; d. in New Ipswich, N. H., 27 Nov., 1835; m. in Peterborough, 6 Oct., 1803, Ezra, b. in Temple, N. H., 19 Apr., 1771, d. testate, in New Ipswich, N. H., 15 June, 1834, son of William and Isabella (Harvey) Mansur of Dracut, Mass. He was a yeoman, and resided in Temple, Wilton, and New Ipswich, N. H. Children: 1. *Mary Hay.* 2. *Samuel Crombie.* 3. *Eliza Cunningham.* 4. *Helen Maria.* 5. *William Earl.* 6. *Susan.* 7. *Nancy.* 8. *James Munroe.* 9. *Horace.* 10. *George Bradley.* 11. *Sarah.* 12. *Abby.*

viii. FRANCES, b. 18 June, 1786; d. unmarried, in Peterborough, 7 Feb., 1849.

26. JACOB[5] TREADWELL (*Nathaniel,*[4] *Nathaniel,*[3] *Nathaniel,*[2] *Thomas*[1]), baptized in Ipswich, Mass., 27 Oct., 1734, died testate, in Ipswich, 9 (3, in Bible) Dec., 1814, aged 82 years (Ipswich Town Records, but Bible states 81 years), married first, 11 Feb., 1762, Martha, baptized in Ipswich, 14 June, 1741, died in Ipswich, 27 Oct., 1780, in her 40th year, daughter of Rev. Nathaniel and Mary (Dennison, born Leverett) Rogers; and married second, in Salem, Mass., 2 Oct., 1782, Eliza[beth], who died in Ipswich, 20 Aug., 1801, aged 46 years, daughter of John White of Salem. He was an innholder, and in 1810 was styled merchant. He resided in Ipswich, Mass.

Children by first wife, born in Ipswich:

i. HANNAH,[6] b. 12 Dec., 1762; d. 4 May, 1814; m. in Ipswich, 29 Oct., 1788, Col. Nathaniel (a widower), b. in Ipswich, 27 Feb., 1750, d. 26 Oct., 1826, son of Timothy and Ruth (Woodbury) Wade. He served in the Revolution.

ii. NATHANIEL, b. 5 June, 1765; d. intestate, in Ipswich, 22 Feb., 1804; m. (1) in Ipswich, 13 Nov., 1788, Priscilla, b. in Ipswich, 17 Feb., 1763, d. in Ipswich, 15 Apr., 1796, dau. of Col. Isaac and Elizabeth (Day) Dodge of Ipswich. He m. (2) in Ipswich, 23 Dec., 1798, Hannah Treadwell, who may have been a widow, and born

Lord. She was living 10 Dec., 1805. He was styled yeoman in 1790, merchant in 1797, and was designated "3rd" from 1788 until his death. He resided in Ipswich. Children, first three by wife Priscilla, fourth by wife Hannah: 1. *Nathaniel Day.*[7] 2. *Rogers.* 3. *Priscilla.* 4. *Lucy Appleton.*

iii. JACOB, b. 10 Apr., d. in Ipswich, 19 Apr., 1770.

iv. MARY, b. 14 Dec., 1771; d. either 10 Dec., 1795, or 12 Jan., 1810; m. in Ipswich, 4 Sept., 1793, Joseph Knight, probably a widower, of Hampton, N. H., who d. probably 20 Nov., 1778. Child: *Antoine.*

v. JACOB, b. 20 (?29) Mch., 1774; d. intestate, in Boston, Mass., 12 Jan., 1810, probably unmarried. He was a baker, and resided in Boston.

vi. LEVERETT, bapt. in Ipswich, 13 Sept., 1778.

Children by second wife, born in Ipswich:

vii. JOHN WHITE, b. 12 July, 1785; d. testate, in Salem, Mass., 4 Apr., 1857; m. (1) in Ipswich, 14 Mch., 1810, Susanna Kendall, b. in Ipswich, 2 July, 1787, d. in Salem, 3 Oct., 1818, dau. of Robert and Susanna (Kendall) Farley of Ipswich; and m. (2) in Ipswich, 18 Oct., 1819, Harriet Kendall Farley (sister of his first wife), b. in Ipswich, 30 Jan., 1791, d. in Salem, 29 Sept., 1852. He was a sea captain, then a merchant, and also a bank cashier. He resided in Salem, Mass. Children: 1. *Susan Farley.*[7] 2. *John White.* 3. *Elizabeth White.* 4. *A son.* 5. *Harriet Farley.* 6. *Lucy.* 7. *Caroline.* 8. *Joseph Grafton.* 9. *Martha Johonnet.* 10. *George Johonnet.* 11. *Thomas White.* 12. *Anne Heard.*

viii. LEVERETT, b. 17 Apr., 1787 (Bible record).

ix. CHARLES, b. 18 Mch., 1789; d. in Ipswich, 28 Feb., 1855; m. in Salem, Mass., 2 May, 1819, Lydia Ropes, b. in Salem, 17 June, 1796, d. in Salem, 9 Nov., 1842, dau. of Benjamin and Jane (Ropes) Shillaber of Salem. He was a sea captain, and resided in Ipswich and Salem, Mass. Children: 1. *Eliza White.*[7] 2. *Charles.* 3. *Joseph Lee.* 4. *John Fenno.*

x. LEVERETT, b. 3 Oct., 1790; d. testate, in New York City, 13 Sept., 1860; m. 25 June, 1816, Martha (of the Long Island family), b. in East Chester, N. Y., 2 Apr., 1795, d. in New York City, 3 Jan., 1863, dau. of Capt. John and Phebe (Pell) Treadwell of East Chester. He was a merchant, also an inventor, residing in New York City. Children: 1. *Joseph Skinner.*[7] 2. *Phebe Ann.* 3. *Martha Eliza.* 4. *Emeline Adelia.*

xi. ELIZA[BETH], b. 19 Sept., 1792; d. suddenly, in Ipswich, 29 (or 31) Jan., 1861; m. Daniel[6] Treadwell (Moses,[5] Nathaniel,[4] Nathaniel,[3] Nathaniel,[2] Thomas[1]).

xii. MARTHA, b. 3 Sept., 1794; d. suddenly, in Ipswich, 1 Dec., 1803.

27. AARON[5] TREADWELL (*Nathaniel,*[4] *Nathaniel,*[3] *Nathaniel,*[2] *Thomas*[1]), baptized in Ipswich, Mass., 4 Sept., 1743, died testate, in Ipswich, 4 Mch., 1825, married (intention published in Ipswich, 18 Apr., 1767) Elizabeth, baptized 17 Apr., 1748, died in Ipswich, 27 Apr., 1827, daughter of John and Lucy (Boardman) Appleton of Ipswich. He was a yeoman, residing in Ipswich.

Children, born in Ipswich:

i. NATHANIEL,[6] b. 18 Apr., 1769; d. intestate, in Ipswich, 11 Apr., 1835; m. (1) in Ipswich, 28 Aug., 1791, Thankful, bapt. in Ipswich, 11 Dec., 1768, d. in Ipswich, 14 July, 1834, dau. of William and Abigail (Smith) Dennis of Ipswich; and m. (2) (int. published in Ipswich, 18 Oct., 1834) Liefa Homans of Beverly, Mass., b. Beverly, 10 Feb., 1792, d. testate, in Beverly, 26 Jan., 1876. He was a cabinetmaker, and later an innholder, designated "4th" in 1791, "3rd" in 1806, and "Jr." in 1834. He resided in Beverly and Ipswich, Mass., and his widow resided in Beverly, where she probably kept a shoe store. He seems to have left no child.

ii. AARON, b. 21 June, 1771; d. in Ipswich, 18 Nov., 1850; m. (1) in Ipswich, 18 Dec., 1796, Elizabeth Kilburn of Ipswich, who d. in Ipswich, 15 June, 1811, aged 39 years; and m. (2) in Ipswich, 16 Nov., 1812, Polly, baptized in Ipswich, 3 Feb., 1782, d. intestate, in Ipswich, 9 Oct., 1853, aged 73 years, dau. of Ebenezer and Sarah Lord, and widow of William Rust, of Ipswich. He was a farmer, residing in Ipswich. Children: 1. *A child.*^{7} 2. *Lucy.* 3. *Elizabeth.* 4. *Micajah.*

iii. ELIZABETH, b. 4 (or 14) Aug., 1775; d. 26 July, 1848; m. 14 Oct., 1799, William, b. 15 Feb., 1773, d. 26 Feb., 1832, son of Richard and Elizabeth (Foster) Sutton of Danvers, Mass. He resided in Danvers, Mass. Child: *William.*

iv. HANNAH, d. Ipswich, 22 Mch., 1865, aged 85 years; m. in Ipswich, 29 Dec., 1819, Capt. Daniel Lord, Jr. (widower), who d. testate about 1844. He was a mariner, residing in Ipswich. Child: *Lucy Treadwell.*

28. MOSES^{5} TREADWELL (*Nathaniel,*^{4} *Nathaniel,*^{3} *Nathaniel,*^{2} *Thomas*^{1}), born in Ipswich, Mass., 20 Sept., 1746, died testate, in Ipswich, 24 Jan., 1823, married in Ipswich, 13 Apr., 1769, Susanna, born in Ipswich, 3 Nov., 1749, died testate, in Ipswich, 30 Nov., 1842, daughter of Jonathan and Elizabeth (Wade) Cogswell of Ipswich. He was a farmer, served in the Revolution, and resided in Ipswich.

Children, born in Ipswich:

i. NATHANIEL,^{6} b. 27 Mch., 1770; d. intestate, in Hartford, Conn., 8 Mch., 1794, probably unmarried. He resided in Hartford, Conn.

ii. WILLIAM, b. 21 Oct., 1771; d. testate, in Ipswich, Oct., 1812; m. in Ipswich, 15 Oct., 1797, Elizabeth, d. in Ipswich, 26 Sept., 1803, aged 35 years, dau. of Bathsheba (Edwards) Gray of Charlestown, Mass. He was a shoemaker, also a trader, residing in Ipswich. Probably no child.

iii. HANNAH, b. 13 Feb., 1774; d. testate in Ipswich, 27 Aug., 1864, unmarried.

iv. MOSES, b. 17 Nov., 1775; d. testate, in Ipswich, 5 Dec., 1833; m. (1) in Ipswich, 22 Jan., 1805, Mary, b. in Ipswich, probably 22 July, 1777, d. in Ipswich, 6 Aug., 1812, dau. of Capt. Ephraim and Susanna (Perkins) Kendall of Ipswich; and m. (2) 13 Sept., 1814, Lydia Bowes, b. (? Shirley, Mass.) 20 Dec., 1786, d. in Ipswich, 10 Oct., 1830, dau. of James and Sarah (? Dickinson) Parker of Shirley. He was a merchant, and captain, residing in Ipswich. Children, first six by first wife, others by second wife: 1. *Moses D.*^{7} 2. *Mary.* 3. *George William.* 4. *Moses.* 5. *Mary Kendall.* 6. *Susan[na] T.* 7. *Lydia Bowes Parker.* 8. *James Parker.* 9. *Sarah Ann.* 10. *Leonard Lincoln.* 11. *Lucy Elizabeth Rogers.*

v. JONATHAN COGSWELL, b. 10 Feb., 1778; d. in Ipswich, 30 Dec., 1794.

vi. SUSANNA, b. 1 Oct., 1779; living 10 Aug., 1842; m. (1) in Ipswich, 30 Apr., 1809, Capt. William Caldwell, of Portland, Me., who d. intestate between 18 Apr., 1810, and Oct., 1811; and m. (2) (int. published in Portland, Me., 13 Nov., 1814) Ebenezer Webster (a widower) of Portland, who d. intestate, in Providence, R. I., before 10 Aug., 1842. Her first husband was a sea-captain, and her second a hatter. Child by first husband: 1. ——— (?); by second husband: 2. *Mary Cogswell.*

vii. ABIGAIL (NABBY), b. 28 Apr., 1785; living 5 May, 1862; m. in Ipswich, 31 Jan., 1833, Capt. Bickford Pulsifer (probably a widower), d. in Ipswich, 22 Mch., 1862, aged 89 years 6 mos. He was a sea-captain, residing in Ipswich.

viii. DANIEL, bapt. in Ipswich, 27 Sept., 1789; d. intestate (? abroad), 15 June, 1825; m. in Ipswich, 6 Aug., 1815, Eliza^{6} Treadwell (Jacob,^{5} Nathaniel,^{4} Nathaniel,^{3} Nathaniel,^{2} Thomas^{1}). He was a sea-captain, residing in Ipswich. Children: 1. *Eliza White.*^{7} 2. *Susan Cogswell.* 3. *Eliza White.* 4. *Daniel.* 5. *Martha Mathilda.*

[To be concluded]

RECORDS OF THE CHURCH IN VERNON, CONN. 1762–1824.

Communicated by Miss MARY KINGSBURY TALCOTT, of Hartford, Conn.

From the manuscript copy owned by the Connecticut Society of Colonial Dames.

[Continued from page 81.]

A.D. 1794.

Feb. 19. Jonas Sparks to Olive Smith.
May 15. Phinehas Naſh to Dorcas Tucker.
Nov[br] 13. Alexander Keeny to Eſther Talcott.— 27. Nathaniel Fields to Clariſſa King.— 27. Simon King to Marget Fletcher.— 27. Samuel Anders to Tryphena Loomis.

A Dom[l] 1795.

Feb[r] 19. Abel Driggs to Rachel King.
Oct[r] 21. Joſeph Tucker to Anna Brunſon.— 29. Joſeph Simons to Cynthia Carpenter.
Nov[br] 12. Timothy Steadman to Mehitabel Root.

1796.

May 12. Elias Skinner, to Widow Vahun.
June 27. William Boys to Jeruſha Payne.
Oct[r] 6. Oliver Thrall to Doratha Tucker.— 13. Zenas Carpenter to Rachel Loomis.

Anno Dom[l] 1797.

Jan[y] 25. Eraſtus Brounſon to Patty Lamfeer.
May 4. Auguſtus Grant to Aſenath Fuller.—Item, Elijah Skinner Ju[r] to Mary Hunt.— 9. Alvin Baker to Ruth Chapman.
June 15. Samuel Lyman to Sarah Cady.
Sep[t] 3. Eleazer McCray to Eunice Ladd.— 7. Thomas Deniſon to Widow Deborah Corning.— 14. Joſhua Stimſon to Anna Simons, both of Tolland.
Nov[br] 2. John Fitch to Rozana Pinney.— 8. Alvin Talcott to Philomela Root.

Anno Dom[l] 1798.

March 8. Ichabod Perry to Jane Tucker.
Ap[l] 13. Solomon Chapman to Molly Skinner.
Aug[t] 29. Timothy Pearl to Sally Perry.
Sep[t] 27. Epaphras Roberts to Sarah Chapman.
Nov. 4. Doct[r] Scotaway Hinkley to Eunice Kellogg.— 29. John King to Polly Driggs.

1799.

Janu[y] 9. Joel Thrall to Miriam Fitch.
May 22. James Sage to Sarah Fowler.— 29. Eliſha Grant to Electa Fuller.
Aug[t] 25. Brintnal Pain to Sarah Skinner.
Sep[t] 18. Alpheus Anders to Lucinda Darte.

1800.

Ap[l] 24. Ezekiel Baker to Anna Talcott.— 24. Asahel Cady to Mabel Smith.
Oct[r] 2. Solomon How to Perſis Baker.

Anno Dom[i] 1801.

Jan[y] 15. Roullin Jocelin to Polly Cheſebrough.

Anno Domini 1802.

Jan[y] 17. Daniel Thrall to Suſanna Baker.
March 8. Heman Hyde to Charity Burge.— 25. Martin Biſsel to Betsey Darte.
Apriel 8. Eliſha Ladd Ju[r] to Roxy Skinner.
May 13. ——— Burnham to Lydia Tucker.
June 23. Eraſtus M[c]Kinney to widow Lydia Talcott.
Aug[t] 2. Aaron Crane to Lodice Payne.
Nov. 12. John Scranton to Sally Button.— 25. Othmiel Clark, to Merren Walker.

Anno Dom[i] 1803.

March 24. ——— Stiles to Charlotte Brunſon.
April 14. Ephraim Williams to Vina Smith.
June 9. Ezekiel Olcott Jr to Perſis Cheeſbrough.— 14. Joſeph Loomis to Jeruſha Talcott.
Aug[t] 16. Zebulon Bidwel to Harriot Fuller.
Oct[r] 12. Larry Morriſon to Patty Robarts.
Nov[br] 24. John Bingham to Rhoda King.

A Dom[i] 1804.

Feb. 23. Beriah Brunſon, to Betsey Ladd.
March 21. Eli Millard, to Elisabeth Pearl.
April 5. Hoſea Brunſon to Healen Peaſe.
May 1. Seldin McKinney to Myrinda King.
Decem[br] 13. Jeremiah Hull to Lois Loomis.— 25. Thomas Studley to Debory Cady.

Anno Dom[i] 1805.

Oct[r] 30. Juſtus McKinney, to Phila Fuller.
Nov[br] 17. Salmon Thompſon to Clariſſa Waldo.— 28. Charles Bingham to Chloe McKinney.
Decem[br] 12. Alpheus Chapman to Abigail Carpenter.

A Dom[i] 1806.

Feb. 14. Thomas Jones to Betsey Matilda Sinnet.
April 21. Auguſtus Ruſſel to Nancy Paine.
June 26. Eliphalet Hancock to Lucy Chapman.
Aug[t] 3. Ceaſer Colman to Lucinda Lord.
Oct[r] 15. Solomon Carpenter to Eliſabeth Walker.
Nov[br] 27. Ebenezer Root to Anne Grant.
Decem[br] 17. Daniel Daniels to Damaris Olcott.

ADom[i] 1807.

Feb[y] 4. Gimerſon Cheeſbrough to Lydia Rogers.— 17. Daniel Thrall to Eliſabeth Strickland.— 25. Zera Hull to Electa Loomis.

Apriel 6. Harvey Wills to Rhoda Chapman.
Sep^{t} 3. Amasa Belnap to Betsey Chapman.
Decem^{br} 24. Curtis Crane to Nancy Chapman.

Anno Dom^{l} 1808.

Feby 4. Allen Morriſon Walker, to Clariſſa Foſter.— 9. Alpheus Winter to Sally Roberts.
March 9. John Simons Ju^{r} to Lucia Cheeſbrough.
Octr 27. Elijah Chapman to Lydia Pearl.

ADom^{l} 1809.

Feby 1. Levi Dart Junr to Buler Fuller.— 27. Samuel Millard to Sally Talcott.
May 9. Samuel Pratt to Susanna King.

A Domini 1810.

Jany 21. Revd Allen McLean to Sarah Pratt.
Augt 2. Green Capron to Betsey Brunſon.
Nov^{br} 15. Leonard Jones, to Sarah Driggs.— 29. Moses Bourn to Esther Chapman.

Anno Domini 1811.

Jany 13. Jehial Fuller to Else Grant.
Sep^{t} 3. Heury Hull to Harriot Humphrey.

Anno Dom^{l} 1812.

Apriel 30. Aaron Perrin to Lois Lee.
Augt 19. Chester McKinney to Sophia Talcott.
Sepr 23. ——— Cottrel of Columbia to Nancy Buckland.
Octr 12. Anson Biſſel to Anna Dart.
Nov^{br} 4. Benjamin Talcott Ju^{r} to Fanny Smith.— 26. Ruſſel Cady to Betsey Chapman.

Anno Domini, 1813.

Jany 7. Daniel Fitch to Jerusha Loomis.
March 31. John Abbott to Acsah Cone.
Apriel 22. Salmon Loomis to Betsey Dart.

Anno Domini, 1814.

March 31. Minor White to Nancy Fitch.
May 22. James Bebee to Phebe Sweney, both of Colchester.
June 16. Amasa Daniels of Palmira, State of Pennſyl^{a} to Olivia Hammond of Vernon, State of Conn^{t}.
July 13. Joel King to Laura Hunt.
Nov^{br} 23. ——— Torry of Ashford to Ruth Sage.

AD 1815.

June 8. Alexander McLean Eſq^{r} to Elizabeth Kellogg, relict of Ebenezer Kellogg Eſq^{r}.
Octob^{r} 18. William Baker to Harmony Newton.— 26. William Fuller to Olive Davis.
Nov^{br} 6. Justus Talcott Junr to Lovinia Tryon.

Anno Domini 1816.

Jany 15. Col^{l} Francis McLean to Sarah Child.
Decem^{br} 31. Samuel Leonard to Cynthia Burdwyn.

1818. Married by William Ely.

April 7th Chester White to Philenda Roberts.
Sept. 9th Orrin Pelton (of Glastenbury) to Sarah Fuller.
Nov. 23d Amos Wakefield (of Andover) to Mary Cottrell.
Dec. 30th Adam Newton to Lucinda Loomis (of E. Windsor.)

AD 1819.

Feb. 11th John Walker to Widow Rebecca Fitch.
March 3d Flavel Hunt to Pamelia Cheesebrough.
Oct. 19th Harry Landfear (of Orford) to Sarah Talcott.
Nov. 18th Reuben Skinner Jun to Lydia S. Wheadon.
Dec. 30th Chauncey Fitch to Anna Loomis of E. Windsor.

AD 1820.

May 24th Eli Hammond Jun to Mary Anne Chapman.
Aug. 3d Clark Tucker to Zina King.

AD 1821.

April 4th John Hyde Nye of Tolland, to Almira Payne.
August 29. Alfred Roberts to Sarah Lee.

AD 1822.

Jany 1st George W. Griswold of E. Hartford to Betsey Talcott.
Cornelius Roberts to Jerusha Hunt.
Feb. 27th Gurdon Smith to Lydia Roberts.

The Persons under Written have owned the Covenant—March 27, 1763. Mehetabel Wright.—Oct. 30, Hesekh Wells, 1764. Mercy the Wife of Roger Strickland.— Octbr 21. Cynthia the Wife of Gideon Searl.—Elijah Loomis & his Wife recomendd by Revd Mr Perry of Windſor, Novbr 4 Oliver Hills.— 1765, Octr 20. Reuben Searl and his Wife.— May 11, 1766. Moſes Thrall and his Wife.— Augt 20. Joſeph Bliſh and his Wife recommended by Revd Benjn Dunning, Paſtor of the Chh in Malborough—March 15, 1767. Abigail the Wife of Saml Blackmer.— Octr 25. David Woodworth & his Wife.— July 17, 1768, the Wife of Nathan Darte.— Septr ye Wife of James Pendal.— Decembr Alexander Kinny & his Wife. — May 14, 1769, Ebenr Darte & his Wife.— Jany 21, 1770. Zadoc How & his Wife.—Abigail the Wife of Elijah Brunſon Recomdd.— Novbr 16, 1771, by Revd Ells Pastor of the Chh in East Glaſtenbury. Augt 14, 1774, Reuben Skinner & his Wife.— Decr 4. Jabes Emerſon Jur & his Wife.— Apl 6, 1775, Stephen King & his Wife.— Septr 10, Timothy Pain & his Wife.—David Dorcheſter Jun and his Wife Recommend by Revd Bliss of Elington Sept 11, 1775. April 5, 1776, David King and his Wife.—Novbr 3 Lemuel Chapman & his Wife. Feby 3, 1777, Benjamin Bliſh & his Wife—Recommended by Mr Colton.— Augt 10 The Wife of Willm Little.— Decembr 14. Jonathan Shirtlaft and Abigail his Wife, Recommended by Mr Norton of East Hampton in Chatham.— June 27, 1779, Sarah ye Wife of John Walker.

Anno Doml 1780.

January 30. Hezekiah Loomis and his Wife.
Feb. 6. Nathan Chapman and his Wife.— 13. Phinehas Jones.

Anno Doml 1782.

May 19. John Phelps & Wife.

June 2. Martha Brownson.— 30. Elifabeth Carpenter, July 7, Widow Johnfon.

A Dom[l] 1783.

April 20. Roxana Fitch.

1784.

March 20. Noah Carpenter & Wife, Recommend by M[r] Strong Cov[ty].
June 20. Sarah Pain.—Alexander Keney & his Wife Recommended by M[r] Williams of East Hartford.

1786.

June 23. Betty Skinner.
July 27. Paul Pitkin & his Wife.
Octob[r] 8. Lydia, the Wife of Leveritt Millard.
Novb[r] 5. Loudon Millard, and his Wife.

1787.

June 10. Elnathan Grant.
Aug[t] 4. George Hall & Wife, Recom[d] by M[r] Potwine of East Windfor.

1788.

May 27. Elijah Tucker Jun[r] & his Wife.
Oct[r] 26. Alexander Kinney Jun[r] & his Wife.
Nov[br] 2. Jacob Strong & his Wife.— 9. Jabez Brunfon & his Wife.

1789.

Oct. 11. Wareham Grant.

1789.

Novb. 26. Reuben Sage recommended by M[r] Bulkley of Middletown upper Houfes.

1789.

November 8. Hannah Driggs.

1790.

January 17. Ozias Humphry and his wife.
July 25. Luke Loomis and his Wife.
August 8. Talcott Flint & his Wife.— 20. Allen Bronfon & his Wife.— 22. Daniel Dorchefter & his Wife.
Sep[t] 26. The wife of Thaddeus Fitch.

1791.

June 19. William Hunt & his Wife.— 26. William Thrall & his Wife.
July 17. Charles Wells & his Wife.
Oct. 30. Lemuel King & his Wife.

1792.

Feb. 12. Henry Lawrance & his Wife.— 26. Mabel Smith.
June 9. D[r] Elijah F. Reed & his Wife.
July 15. Jane Tucker.

1793.

June 2. Ranfford Webfter & his wife.

1794.

Aug[t] 3. Converfe Fitch & his wife.
Octo[r] 26. Ebenezer Webfter & his wife.

1795.

June 28. Samuel Anders & his wife.
Agust 30. Benajah Pain & his wife.

1796.

April 3. John McCray & his wife.— 11. David Dorchefter Junr & his wife.
June 19. Jerufha Paine.
Decem^br 19. Oliver Thrall & his wife.

1797.

March 26. The wife of James Lyman Ju^r

1800.

Octr 12. Afbur Ifham & wife recommend by Mr Wills, Tolland.
Nov^br 16. Joel Thrall & his wife.

1801.

July 19. Francis McLean & his wife.

1802.

Warren McKinney & his wife.

1803.

Nov^br 27. Lemuel Abbot & his wife.

1806.

Jonathan Smith Tucker & his wife.

N. Bolton 1762.

Church Communicants.

Isaac Jones—Titus Alcott & Damaris his Wife—Elifabeth Allis—John Chapman, & Hannah his Wife—Isaac Brunfon and Abigail his Wife—Charles King & Sarah his Wife—David Allis, & Sarah his Wife—Seth King—Thomas Darte—Afabel Root & Mehetable his Wife, Thomas Chapman, & Mary his Wife—Sarah the Wife of Stephen Johns—Jabez Rogers—Elifabeth the Wife of John Darte—Abiatha Wife of Jared Knowlton—Solomon Loomis—Nathan Meffenger & Abigail his Wife—Caleb Talcott, Hezekiah King & Ann his Wife—Stephen Pain—Lydia the Wife of Stephen Pain Ju^r—Experience Lord & Ruth Lord—Dorcas Olcott—Eunice Marfhal, Sarah Blackmore.

The above Perfons were Members of the C^hh in ye 1 Society in Bolton, & Recommended by the Revd Thomas White, Paftor of S^d C^hh.

David Smith recommended by ye 5 C^hh in Windfor, Oct. 30, 1763, Elijah Tucker and his Wife Violet—Philip Smith. Recommend by ye Revd Joseph Perry Paftor of the 2 C^hh in Windfor—Feb 20 1763, Nathan Jones & Elifabeth his Wife—Augt 6, 1730, Jonathan Smith & Miriam his Wife—Gideon King—Roger Lomis & Prifcilla his Wife—David Dorchester & his Wife—Recommended by the C^hh at Somers—Benjamin Kilborn Recommended by ye Revd Eleazer Wheelock, Paftor of the 2 C^hh in Lebanon—Daniel Carpenter, and his Wife, recommend by ye Revd Nath^n Strong, Paftor of ye 2 C^hh in Coventry—Elijah King & Mary his Wife—John M^cray Recommended by Revd Danl Welch Pastor of ye 2 C^hh of Christ in Manffield—Seth Johnfon Recommended by Mr Wheelock Paftor of the 2 C^hh in Lebanon—Eliakim Hitchcock & Izada his Wife—Beriah Brunfon Recommended by Revd John Bliss Paftor of ye C^hh in Elington,

Windſor—Ezekiel Ladd & his Wife Recommended by ye Revd Nathn Williams of Toland—William Hunt & his Wife, and Solomon Hovey Recommended by Revd Eleazer Wheelock, Paſtor of the 2 Chh in Lebanon—Allen McLean Recommend by the Revd Eliphalet Williams, Paſtor of the Chh in E. Hartford.

Alexander McLean & his Wife—John Hodge & Hannah his Wife, Lucretia Johns, Febr 1765, Hannah the Wife of Revd Ebenr Kellogg—Mary Carly Recommended by Revd N. Webb of Uxbridge—Ann the Wife of Philip Smith Recommended by Revd N. Strong Paſtor of the 2 Chh in Coventry—Sarah Brown Recommend by the Chh in Elington—Bethiah Thatcher Recommend by Jacob Eliot—Paſtor of ye 3d Chh in Lebanon—Phebe the wife of James Fitch Recommended by Mr Strong of Coventry—Ann Hitchcock Recomd by Revd Ephm Little Paſtor of the 1 Chh in Colcheſter—The Wife of, Thomas Darte—Ann ye Wife of Danl Reed, Recommendd by Mr Lockwood of Andover—Miriam Grant—The Wife of Jaſon Millard—The Wife of Jonathan Bliſs—1770, Eliſabeth the Wife of Henry Baldwin Recommended by Mr Salter Apr 2, 1770. Octr 14, Edward Pain & his Wife—Octr 28 Saml Root—Joel Naſh Recommend by Mr Williams of Tolld, Decembr 30, Ichabod Carly—Gurden Fowler & Sarah his Wife Recomdd by Mr Williams of Lebanon—July ye 8, Charity ye Wife of Gideon King—March 1771—Martha Carrier—Oct 6, Silas King & his Wife—Decembr 2, Lemmi Thrall & his Wife—Sarah ye Wife of John Rogers Recommendd by Mr Boardman Paſtor of ye Chh in Middle Haddam, Lucy Ladd Recommended by Mr Williams of Tolland—Henry Bauldwin Recommended by ye Chh in Newent. Feb. 23, 1772, Jeruſha ye Wife of James Lyman—March 8 Elijah Brunſon—March 22 Elijah Skinner, and his Wife—Apriel 19, Aſahel Webſter & his Wife—July 12 Daniel Skiner & his Wife—item Ezial Lomis—July 19 Daniel Fowler & his Wife—July 26, Eunice the Wife of David Smith—Augt 19 Thomas Chapman Jur & his Wife—Rachel Wife of Ezra Lomis recommended by Revd George Colton Pastor of ye 1 Chh in Bolton—Decembr 12, 1773, Rachel ye Wife of Caleb Talcott. July 17, 1774, Sarah ye Wife of Jabez Emerſon— Augt 21. Joſhua Pearl and his Wife—May 14, 1775, the Wife of David West—June 4, Danl Ladd, Perſis the Wife of Daniel Ladd, Recommended by Mr Lockwood of Andover— June 11. Suſannah Wife of Reuben King. Augt 2 Abel West & his Wife—Septembr 17, Azubah ye Wife of Jeremiah Chapman. The Wife of Jonathn Chapman, Recommend by the Chh in Millington—Apl 3, 1775 Novbr 26. Mable Kellogg. — Decembr 10. Mary Smith— May 5, 1776. Eliakim Root and his Wife, also the Wife of Jedediah Leonard— 25. Ephraim Ladd & Lois his Wife, — June 9. The Wife of John Allis—Sylvanus Delano & his Wife recommended by Mr Williams of Tolland— 30. Hannah Ladd.—July 7, The Wife of Jeremiah Fuller— 14. Mary Wife of Gurdeon Fowler—Septembr 8 Widow Sarah Pain— Octr 13. The Wife of Dean Seth King—Januy 29, 1777, Eliſha Ladd & his Wife— March 9. Phinehas Chapman—May ye 4th Prudence Darte. June 7. Eliſabeth Pendal.

1780.

May 28. Abijah Johns & his Wife.

Augt 6. Aſenah Dorcheſter.—Joel Drake & his Wife Recomendd by Mr Perry.—Aſahel Phelps & his Wife Recommended by Mr Pomroy of Hebron.

[To be concluded.]

PROCEEDINGS OF THE NEW ENGLAND HISTORIC GENEALOGICAL SOCIETY.

By Geo. A. Gordon, A.M., Recording Secretary.

Boston, Massachusetts, 6 December, 1905. The New England Historic Genealogical Society held a stated meeting in Marshall P. Wilder hall, 18 Somerset street, at half-past two o'clock this afternoon, the President, Hon. James Phinney Baxter, Litt.D., in the chair.

After the reading and approval of the minutes of the November stated meeting, Hon. George Sheldon, of Deerfield, was introduced as the essayist for this day. He presented to the meeting his son, who read the paper entitled *The Conference at Deerfield, August 27–31, 1735, between Gov. Belcher and several tribes of Indians*, to relieve the author, his father, on account of the infirmities of advanced age. It was greatly enjoyed and, on motion, it was voted that thanks be tendered Mr. Sheldon for his paper, of large historical importance, with the hope that a copy will be prepared for the Society's archives.

The ordinary routine business followed, at which six new members were elected, and Messrs. Edmund Dana Barbour and George Sherburne Penhallow, A.B., appointed the auditing committee for 1905.

The meeting then dissolved.

3 January, 1906. In the absence of the President, a stated meeting was called to order by the Secretary, at half-past two o'clock this afternoon, at the usual place.

Charles Sidney Ensign, LL.B., was called to the chair.

Mr. Sidney Perley, of Salem, delivered an address on the *Study of Local History*, at which he enjoys the reputation of an expert. The thanks of the meeting were voted therefor.

The reports of the executive officers were duly made, read, accepted, and ordered on file.

Seventeen new resident members and one corresponding member were elected.

On motion, it was

Voted, That the principal of the Bond fund be fixed at twenty-five hundred (2500) dollars, and that all sums hereinafter received, from sales or otherwise, be credited to General Income.

The chair then declared the meeting dissolved.

10 January. The annual meeting of the Society was held, to-day, agreeable to article 1, Chapter III, of the By-laws. A full report of the proceedings may be found in the supplement to the present number of the Register.

7 February. The President being absent, in Europe, a stated meeting was called to order by the Secretary, this afternoon, at the usual place and time, at which Charles Sidney Ensign, LL.D., of Newton, was invited to serve as Chairman *pro tempore.* He accepted, and performed the duty.

Charles G. Chick, Esq., of Hyde Park, read a paper on *The Boston Port Bill (1774)*, to which the audience gave good attention and hearty applause. Mr. Chick was thanked, and invited to deposit a copy of his important paper in the archives of the Society.

Confirmation of the minutes of the January meetings, and the reports of the executive officers, were heard, as usual, and filed.

Eleven new members were elected.

A Committee was appointed to submit, at some future meeting, resolutions *in memoriam perpetuam* of Rev. George Moulton Adams, D.D., Historian of the Society.

P. Hildreth Parker, Esq., of Dracut, presented a copy of graveyard inscriptions in Pelham, N. H., for which thanks were returned.

Amendment to Article 1, Chapter III, of the By-laws was submitted, agreeable to article 1, Chapter XIII, of the By-laws, and a committee appointed to consider and report on the same.

7 March. The President being still absent, a stated meeting, at the usual time and place, was called to order by the Secretary, and Charles Sidney Ensign, LL.B., was called to the chair.

George Sumner Mann, Esq., of Brookline, read a paper of remarkable interest on *The Shays Rebellion, 1786–7*, which was very entertaining. The historical character of these events was interspersed with personal details and incidents, gathered in Petersham, Pelham, Athol, Worcester, and Springfield, the theatre of the demonstration. Much personal history of Shays and his principal supporters was given. The thanks of the Society were ardently voted, and request made for a copy of the paper for the Society's archives.

Twelve new members were elected.

The executive reports were presented, read, and filed.

The committee on the proposed amendment to the By-laws submitted a report, which was received, read, and filed. The proposed amendment was made the order of business at the stated meeting in April.

No further business being presented, the meeting dissolved.

NOTES AND QUERIES.

NOTES.

WASHINGTON.—The following is a further communication from Rev. R. T. Love, M.A., Rector of Purleigh, Maldon, co. Essex, England, whose interesting letter and an appeal for repairs upon whose church appeared *ante*, pages 91 and 97.

"The marriage of Lawrence Washington, Rector of Purleigh 1642-43, rests on much more substantial grounds than *primâ facie* evidence drawn from the resignation of his Fellowship, as mentioned in your issue of January—which Fellowship, I am informed by the Master of Brasenose College, was resigned 30 Nov. 1633. Not only are we now in a position to prove his marriage, which I am inclined to suggest took place the day of the resignation, but also the name of his wife, and his relationship as father of the first Washingtons who settled in Virginia.

First, his marriage is placed beyond doubt by the appearance of Mrs. Washington before Commissioners on Plundered Ministers at Chelmsford, in 1649, when a "fifth part of Purleigh" was "ordered to the plundered Rector's wife." (The word "plundered" (deprived) was first used in England 1642. Skeat's Etymological Dictionary, The Clarendon Press, Oxford.)

Secondly, the Rector of Purleigh's wife is proved to be Mrs. Amphillis Washington, whose children benefited under the will of Mr. Andrew Knowling of Tring, 1649-50. In addition to the circumstantial evidence collected by Mr. Waters, in his "Ancestry of Washington," reprinted from the REGISTER, proof positive may be found in *The Nation*, Dec. 22, 1892, and Sept. 21, 1899, based on the axiom that 'when one's brother has the same name as one's niece's father, these must be one and the same person.' Mrs. Mewce's brother was Lawrence Washington, Rector of Purleigh; and her niece's father was Lawrence Washington, husband of Amphillis Washington. Therefore, the Rector of Purleigh was the husband of Mrs. Amphillis Washington.

Thirdly, having identified the Rector of Purleigh as the husband of Mrs. Amphillis Washington, the next step is to prove that her children were the Virginian settlers. This proof is obtained by comparison between the wills of these emigrants on the one hand, and the names, on the other hand, of the children of Mrs. Amphillis Washington, as contained in the very important will of Mr. Andrew Knowling. By this comparison it is shown that the three settlers, John, Lawrence, and Martha, had two sisters, Elizabeth and Margaret; and these five names correspond with the names of Mrs. Amphillis Washington's children in the above mentioned will. Moreover, the use of the words 'eldest' and 'other,' in the American wills, when compared with the baptismal entries in England, establishes the order of birth to be the same in both cases. It is therefore absolutely certain that John, the eldest of these settlers, found in Virginia 1659, and whose will is authenticated by endorsement in the handwriting of Gen. George Washington, was the eldest son of Mrs. Amphillis Washington and of her husband, the Rector of Purleigh.

The details of this evidence have been put at length in a 'Summary of Evidence,' which the present Rector has drawn up from the writings on this subject; and which he proposes to put into print, should he find any encouragement on the part of Americans."

FEW persons of the present day are aware how general was piracy two centuries ago. The following extract from "The Boston News-Letter," August 21, 1721, shows that in early times pirate ships, carrying many guns and heavily manned, sailed the high seas and pursued their unlawful calling. The "Mary" was taken somewhere in the Sargasso Sea, off the coast of Africa.

SAMUEL A. GREEN.

"THESE are to Certifie all Persons concerned that on the 7th Day of May last, William Russel Master of the Ship Mary of Charlestown, in his Voyage from Madera to Surranam in the Lat. 22 Deg. and 27 N. and Long. 25 and 27 W. from London was taken by a Pirate Ship upwards of 50 Guns, Commanded by Capt, Roberts, about 300 Men, who robb'd him of part of his Cargo, and Forced away from him two of his Men, against his and their own consent, viz. Thomas Russel born in Lexintown near Charlestown and the other Thomas Winchol born in Portsmouth, New-Hampshire in New England."

BRAINTREE MARRIAGES.—In the article on page 43 of the last issue of the REGISTER, in the marriage under the date of "1760, Apr. 24," the name of the man was Caleb Bailey, not Bagley. (See Deane's *Scituate*, page 214.)

ELLA T. BATES.

EDGARTOWN DEATHS.—In the REGISTER, vol. 59, page 303, in the article entitled "Deaths at Edgartown," it is stated (page 307) that the Beulah Coffin who died Jan. 19, 1812, age 86, was the daughter of Enoch and Jane (Claghorn) (Whellen) Coffin. The contributor has made a mistake, as the Beulah, daughter of above, was born Oct. 10, 1748, married, Jan. 5, 1769, Jonathan Pease, and died Jan. 29, 1773. The Beulah who died Jan. 19, 1812, was the daughter of Enoch and Beulah (Eddy) Coffin.

C. H. C.

Philadelphia, Penn.

COTTON.—The daughters Joanna (born Mar. 5, 1690), Mary (born Apr. 10, 1692), and Elizabeth (born Sept. 2, 1694), given in the REGISTER, vol. 8, page 43, as the children of Rev. Caleb Cushing, were the children of his wife, Mrs. Elizabeth (Cotton) Alling, by her first husband, Rev. James Alling of Salisbury, Mass.

LAWRENCE B. CUSHING.

Newburyport, Mass.

PROCTOR.—Benjamin[3] Proctor (John[2], John[1]), born June 10, 1659, at Ipswich (see *ante*, vol. li., page 410), married Mary, daughter of William and Sarah (Smith) Buckley of Ipswich and Salem Village, widow of Sylvester Witheridge, and granddaughter of Thomas Smith of Ipswich, as shown by the following records:

Lynn.—Benjamin Proctor to Mary Buckley married Dec. 18, 1694. (Essex County Records.)

Benjamin Proctor and Mary Witheridge married Dec. 18, 1694. Children: *Mary*, born Oct. 12, 1695: *Priscilla*, born Dec. 11, 1699: *Sarah*, born Jan. 2, 1701-2. (Salem Town Records.)

Admitted to the First Church of Salem, June 5. 1709, Prudence Witheridge, dau' of Mary, w' of Benj' Proctor. (Records of First Church, Salem.)

Silvester Whitterage and Mary Buckley married Nov. 17, 1684. (Essex Co. Records.)

Children of Silvester Witheridge and Mary his wife: *Prudence*, born Oct. 8, 1686; *Silvester*, born March 17, 1688. (Salem Town Records.)

Administration on the estate of Benjamin Proctor of Salem granted to his widow Mary. June 27, 1717. (Essex Co. Probate, vol. 812, page 70.)

Mary Proctor of Salem, widow, formerly Mary Buckley, daughter of William Buckley formerly of Ipswich, but more lately of Salem, deceased, and Sarah his wife, who was one of the daughters of Mr. Thomas Smith of Ipswich, deceased, conveyed to John Higginson of Salem all interest in the estate of her grandfather Thomas Smith and of her father William Buckley, May 27, 1727. (Essex Co. Deeds, vol. 57, page 51.)

"Jan. 2, 1702. Old William Buckley dyed this evening. He was about 80 years old." (Diary of Rev. Joseph Green of Salem Village.)

Petition of William Buckley to the General Court, Sept. 13, 1710, "in ye name of our family." "My Honoured Mother Sarah Buckley and my sister Mary Witherige were both in prison from May until January following" [1692–1693].

Thorndike Proctor of Salem formerly purchased a certain farm in Salem known as the Downing Farm, and afterwards sold a part to his brother Benjamin Proctor, since deceased, and John Proctor, only son and heir of said Benjamin, May 14, 1726. (Essex Co. Deeds, vol. 53, page 40.)

Cambridge, Mass. VIRGINIA HALL.

BURRELL.—In the REGISTER, vol. 59, page 352, there is a mistake in the line of descent of Sergt. John Burrell, who was a great-grandson, not grandson, of John Burrell the emigrant. The line is as follows:

John[1] Burrell arrived in Weymouth, Mass., in 1639; married Rebekah ——, and had these three (if not more) children: *John*,[1] b. 1658, d. 1731; *Thomas*, b. 1659; *Ephraim*, b. 1664.

John[2] Burrell (John[1]) married, June 26, 1688, Mercy[3] Alden (Joseph,[2] John[1] of the "Mayflower"), and had: *Elizabeth*,[3] b. 1689; *Thomas*, b. 1692; *Capt. John*, b. 1694.

Capt. John[3] Burrell (John,[2] John[1]), who moved to Abington in 1741, married, Jan. 8, 1717, Mary[4] Humphrey (Joseph,[3] Thomas,[2] John[1]) of Hingham, and had: *Sergt. John*[4] b. Sept. 24, 1719; *Joseph*; *Abraham*, b. 1721; *Humphrie*, b. 1723, d. at Lake George, 1756; *Thomas*; *Mary*.

Sergt. John[4] Burrell (John,[3] John,[2] John[1]) married Ann[4] Vinton (Thomas,[3] John,[2] John[1]), and had: *Mary*, b. Feb. 22, 1741; *Ann*, b. Mar. 17, 1743; *Elizabeth*, b. Aug. 7, 1745; *Miriam*, b. Mar. 17, 1749; *John*, b. Oct. 5, 1752; *Bela*, b. May 20, 1756; *Nathaniel*, b. May 17, 1761; *Ziba*, b. Mar. 12, 1765.

Cambridge, Mass. WM. LINCOLN PALMER.

STIMPSON.—In the REGISTER, vol. 59, page 368, it is stated that [19] John[5] Stimpson (John,[4] John,[3] Andrew,[2] Andrew[1]) married Mary, daughter of Nathaniel and Mary (Kemball) Harrington, but this is an error, for in 1784 she was the wife of David Whitney, as shown in the will of Nathaniel Harrington, in Middlesex Co. Probate, file 7316. The oldest child of Daniel Whitney was named *Mary Kimball*.

John[5] Stimpson probably married Mary, daughter of Edward and Anna (Bullard) Harrington of Watertown, who, according to Bond, was born Aug. 23, 1752, for in the division of Edward Harrington's estate, in 1794, Middlesex Co. Probate, file 7280, one share was allotted to "the heirs of Mary Stimson, deceased." ARTHUR M. JONES.

Boston, Mass.

QUERIES.

A GENEALOGICAL PUZZLE.—Judge Sewall, in his Diary, vol. 1, p. 215, under date, May 30, 1688, says: "Mr. Joseph Eliot here, says the two days wherein he buried his Wife and Son, were the best that ever he had in the world." The editors, in a foot-note, facetiously add, "The kindest construction should be put upon this remark of the bereaved husband and father."

The context shows that Mr. Joseph Eliot was the Rev. Joseph Eliot, son of the "Apostle," who was the minister at Guilford, Conn. But there are confusing facts. He had two wives. The first, Sarah Brenton, died prior to 1685, leaving four daughters. The second wife, Mary Wyllys, died in 1729, thirty-five years after the death of her husband. There were two sons, born to this second marriage, who lived many years after the death of their father.

Could the wellnigh infallible Judge have made a mistake in attributing this remark to the son Joseph, instead of his father, the "Apostle," whose wife,

"Hanna Mumford," died March 22, 1687, and whose son Benjamin died Oct. 15, 1687? The words, "the two days wherein," stand in the way of this explanation, but words spoken, and written subsequently, may not be correctly reported. It would be interesting to have some expert straighten this matter.
48 W. 36th St., New York, N. Y. ELLSWORTH ELIOT.

ADDIS, BEEBE, HAWKE.—I should like the dates of birth, marriages, and death of Millicent, daughter of William Addis, or Addes, of Gloucester, Mass., 1642. She married first, William Southmaid, second, William Ash, and third, Thomas Beebe, by which last husband she had a daughter *Hannah*, who married, in New London, Conn., 16 Jan., 1688-9, John Hawke. Has anybody discovered the maiden name of Millicent's mother? And was John Hawke of *Mayflower* descent? (Miss) LUCY D. AKERLY.
550 Park Ave., New York City.

BOYCE.—Who were the parents of Ruth Boyce who married, Apr. 20, 1728, Nathaniel Jillson, Jr.? (Gillson-Jillson Genealogy, page 25.)
University of Chicago Library, Chicago, Ill. C. A. TORREY.

DAVIS.—Where can I find references to Peter Davis and his family, Quakers, who went from Boston to Rhode Island? Some of them were preachers of that faith.

STONE.—Aaron Strong, Jr., born Nov., 1768, married, 25 Jan., 1813, as his second wife, Polly, of Guilford, Conn., born 23 Dec., 1771, died May, 1830, without issue, daughter of Daniel and Sarah (King) Stone of South Hampton. Information is wanted as to the ancestry and rest of the family of Daniel Stone. A. H. STONE.
3931 S. Thomas Ave., Minneapolis, Minn.

FOSTER.—I am trying to indentify Abigail ——, who married, about 1692, Jonathan[3] Foster (Thomas,[2] Thomas[1]). Jonathan was born probably in Dunstable, Sept. 21, 1671, and died Jan. 5, 1755. He first appears in Billerica, and later was a resident of Stow and Chelmsford. Abigail is said to have died in Chelmsford, July 9, 1761. Some think she was a child of Arthur[2] Warren (Arthur[1]), who was born in 1639, married Abigail Rogers of Billerica, date unknown, and died Apr. 5, 1671. His widow died June 15, 1671.
523 Altman Building, Kansas City, Mo. (Dr.) WILLIAM DAVIS FOSTER.

MERRITT.—Who were the parents and wives of the following Merritts: Benjamin of Rye, N. Y., first wife Hannah, 1741; Benjamin of Newcastle Co., Del., born 1700; George of Stratfield, Conn., 1738; Edward, freeholder of New York, 1701; George of Perth Amboy, 1694; Henry of Scituate, Mass., 1628; Henry of Norfolk, Va., 1650; Isaac of Lebanon, 1741; James of Barkhampstead, Conn., 1770, wife Hannah; John of North Castle, N. Y., 1730; John of Block Island, 1702; Lovering of Kent Co., Md., 1700; Meyer of East Ward, New York, 1703; Nathaniel of Rowley, Mass., 1773; Nicholas of Lyndeboro, N. H., 1736; Pheleck of Hopkinton, R. I., 1774; Philip of Boston, born 1662, died 1741; Richard of Richmond Co., N. Y., 1701; Samuel of Scarborough, N. Y., born 1719; Samuel of Hopkintown, R. I., 1774; Thomas of Delaware, 1664-76; Thomas of Rye, N. Y., 1670-1722; Thomas of ship "Little Baltimore," 1693; William, mayor of New York, 1662, wife Margery; William of New York, 1730; William of Hartford, Conn., 1780, son William; William of North Carolina, 1790, son Berry. DOUGLAS MERRITT.
Rhinebeck, N. Y.

MALTBY.—In the REGISTER, vol. 59, page 255, it is stated that John[3] Kirkham (Samuel,[2] Thomas[1]) married Esther, daughter of David Maltby of Northford. This I believe to be an error, and that she was the daughter of Daniel Maltby, Jr., who married, in 1736, Mary Harrison. Daniel and Mary had a daughter Esther, born Aug. 30, 1739. Can anybody give me definite information on this point? (Miss) DOROTHY LORD MALTBY.
58 Grove St., New Haven, Conn.

OLMSTED, BROWN, SMITH.—Thankful Olmsted of Brookfield and Ware, Mass., born Feb. 15, 1712, married ——— Brown, and died before 1752, leaving children. Her sister Abigail Olmsted, born Mar. 24, 1731, married, before 1752, ——— Smith of Ware, Mass. They were daughters of Capt. Jabez Olmsted, and are mentioned in his will, dated Feb. 24, 1752. Further information about these families is desired. F. S. HAMMOND.
Oneida, N. Y.

TEMPLETON.—What was the ancestry of Polly Templeton, born Jan. 18, 1785 or '6, who married, about 1802, William Curtis, born Sept. 13, 1781 or '3, of Simsbury, Conn., son of Eliphalet, Jr., and Mary (Wilcox) Curtis? He died June 26, 1815, at Marcellus, N. Y., and she died July 11, 1835, at Oswego, N. Y.
530 So. Madison Ave., Pasadena, Cal. (Mrs.) L. E. STEELE.

POMEROY.—I desire information of the military commission of Gen. Seth Pomeroy which was among his effects when he died at Peekskill, N. Y., Feb. 19, 1777. MORRIS P. FERRIS.
33 Nassau St., New York City.

HISTORICAL INTELLIGENCE.

ENGLISH RESEARCH.—The Committee on English Research, of the New England Historic Genealogical Society, begs to call attention to the desirability of reviving investigation concerning the English ancestry of the pioneers of New England. From 1883 to 1899, former Committees secured funds by which valuable researches among the wills of the Prerogative Court of Canterbury in London were carried on by Henry F. Waters, Esq., the results of which were published in the REGISTER, giving clues which lead to determining the ancestry of many of the early settlers of New England; but since Mr. Waters's work was relinquished, comparatively little has been accomplished by the Society in that direction.

The Committee now solicits funds for continuing research in England, on the ancestry of the early New England colonists, the results to appear in the REGISTER, and it would be glad to receive suggestions and information on this subject.

Clues, not generally known, as to the origin of several early emigrants, have come into the Committee's hands, and the Secretary of the Committee will be glad to give information to anyone who may desire to make investigations.

CHARLES SHERBURNE PENHALLOW, *Chairman*,
FRANCIS APTHORP FOSTER,
JOSEPH GARDNER BARTLETT, *Secretary*,
} Committee on English Research.

WOOD GENEALOGY.—Clay W. Holmes, Elmira, N. Y., compiler of the genealogy of the Descendants of William Wood of Concord, Mass., 1638, published in 1900, 8vo, pp. 365, will be glad to present to any public library or historical society making a specialty of genealogical publications, which is not already supplied with the book, a complimentary copy if the transportation charges will be paid.

GENEALOGIES IN PREPARATION.—Persons of the several names are advised to furnish the compilers of these genealogies with records of their own families and other information which they think may be useful. We would suggest that all facts of interest illustrating family history or character be communicated, especially service under the U. S. Government, the holding of other offices, graduation from college or professional schools, occupation, with places and dates of birth, marriage, residence, and death. When there are more than one Christian name, they should all be given in full if possible. No initials should be used when the full name is known.

Lee.—Joseph L. Edmiston, 1129 W. 17th St., Los Angeles, Cal., is collecting material for a genealogical record of the descendants of Dea. Benjamin Lee of Manchester, Mass., who died in 1757, and desires correspondence with representatives of the various branches.

Pike.—A collection of notes from English archives, relating to the Pike family, is now being formed, with the assistance of an experienced and reliable record-searcher in London, England. The latter has already supplied several interesting notes on this subject. The material consists of unpublished data obtained from the Public Record Office, British Museum, etc. These original gleanings will be of considerable interest to many other families, and will probably be published. For particulars, address Eugene F. McPike, 1 Park Row, Chicago, Ill.

Talmage, or Talmadge.—Chas. M. Talmadge, Newport, Wash., would like to hear from anyone interested in the history or genealogy of this family, especially that branch in Connecticut.

Woodcock.—Jno. L. Woodcock, 1218 Washington Boulevard, Chicago, Ill., has in preparation a genealogy of the Woodcock family in America, and would be pleased to correspond with any persons interested.

BOOK NOTICES.*

[The editor requests persons sending books for notice to state, for the information of readers, the price of each book, with the amount to be added for postage when sent by mail.]

Data concerning the Families of Bancroft, Bradstreet, Browne, Dudley, Emerson, Gamble, Goodridge, Gould, Hartshorne, Hobson, Kemp, Kendall, Metcalf, Nichols, Parker, Poole, Sawtell, Wainwright, Woodman, etc., etc., in England and America, 1277 to 1906, A.D. Compiled from Official Sources by Thomas Gamble, Jr., Savannah, Ga. Printed for the Subscribers. [Savannah.] 1906. Square 4to. pp. viii+248. Ill. Price $5.00.

The compiler in his introduction says that "it has not been the endeavor to embrace a wide scope, but rather to prepare concise biographical and genealogical data, that, while it might be of some broader interest, would be more particularly valuable to a few who trace their ancestry to the fountain sources of American life mentioned herein." There are two genealogical charts, and at the end of the volume are blank leaves for additional records. The book is indexed, is bound in flexible covers, and has many illustrations.

Caleb Benton and Sarah Bishop. Their Ancestors and Their Descendants. By Charles E. Benton. Press of The A. V. Haight Co., Poughkeepsie, New York. 1906. 4to. pp. 92. Ill. Price $2.00 net. Apply to Publishers.

Caleb Benton was a descendant from Edward Benton who died at Guilford, Conn., in 1680, and Sarah Bishop is traced to John Bishop who died in the same place, in 1660. A division is made between the historical and genealogical materials of this work, which will be found of great convenience to those particularly interested in the latter, and there is a tabular pedigree at the end of the book. The book is printed on heavy paper, substantially bound, and provided with three indexes.

Band of Botsford. Act of Organization. Buffalo, Erie Co., N. Y., 101 Rodney Ave., Wed., Oct. 18, 1905. [Buffalo. 1905.] 12mo. pp. 8.

This "Band" consists of the descendants of Elizabeth and Henry Botsford, of Leicestershire, Eng., and Milford, Conn.

The Genealogy of the Cushing Family, an Account of the Ancestors and Descendants of Matthew Cushing, who came to America in 1638. By James S. Cushing. Montreal: The Perrault Printing Co. 1905. 12mo. pp. 598+lxx. Ill.

The first edition of this work was published in 1877 by Lemuel Cushing. The Matthew Cushing of the title-page came to Hingham, Mass., in 1638, and it is

* All of the unsigned reviews are written by Mr. Frederick Willard Parke of Boston.

said that all the Cushings in the United States and Canada are his descendants, with the exception of a few who came to America in the nineteenth century. Although much that is new respecting these descendants has been collected in this edition, it is not pretended that this is a complete genealogy. Nevertheless, a vast amount of information respecting the family is here presented, the arrangements of the records being on the REGISTER plan. Biographical notices are numerous, and to be expected in the history of a family which has "probably furnished more judges for our Probate, Municipal, and Supreme Courts than any other." The volume is fully indexed, its print is clear, and the binding cloth.

Derby Genealogy. Being a Record of the Descendants of Thomas Derby of Stow, Massachusetts. By VIOLA A. DERBY BROMLEY. The Grafton Press: Genealogical Publishers. New York. 1905. Large 8vo. pp. 141. Ill.

The system of page reference employed in this genealogy greatly facilitates the tracing of pedigrees. The "Owner's Lineage" at the end of the volume, comprising a couple of pages of genealogical blanks, is also a useful feature. The genealogy is brought down to the eighth generation, and is well indexed. The book is printed on heavy paper with wide margins, and the binding is substantial.

Gamble and Hobson Families, England and America, 1480 to 1905, A.D. [By THOMAS GAMBLE.] Chart. 30 in. by 19 in.

This is one of the genealogical charts contained in Mr. Gamble's "Data concerning the Families of Bancroft, Bradstreet, etc.," which is noticed in this issue.

Annals of the Hilton-McCurda Family. Concord, N. H.: Rumford Printing Co. 1905. 12mo. pp. 12.

The Hiltons of this pamphlet are descendants of William Hilton who came to Plymouth in 1621, and afterwards settled on the Piscataqua River, near Dover. One of these descendants, Anna Hilton, married John McCurda, of Bristol, Me.

The Lindsay Family Association of America. Second Annual Report. [Boston. 1905. 8vo. pp. 14.

Lyon Memorial. Massachusetts Families, including the Descendants of the Immigrants William Lyon. of Roxbury, Peter Lyon, of Dorchester, George Lyon, of Dorchester. With Introduction treating of the English Ancestry of the American Families. Editors: A. B. Lyon(s), M.D., of Detroit, Mich.; G. W. A. Lyon, M.D., of Philadelphia, Pa. Associate Editor: EUGENE F. MCPIKE, of Chicago, Ill. Detroit, Mich.: Press of William Graham Printing Co. 1905. 8vo. pp. 491. Ill. Price $5.00 net. Address Dr. A. B. Lyons, 72 Brainard St., Detroit, Mich.

Besides the immigrants mentioned on the title-page, this work contains a notice of Matthew Lyon who settled in Vermont, and who has been called "the American Pym." The investigations in England have not only confirmed what had already been asserted but have supplied new information respecting the Lyon origins. The American portion of the genealogy has for its principal object the sifting of the materials regarding the first generations, the definite separation of the historic from the traditional. The history of this family necessarily contains biographies of importance, as so many of the name have acquired distinction. The book is well indexed, is printed on unbleached paper, and bound in cloth. The illustrations are chiefly portraits.

Estate of Daniel Rogers, Merchant. n. p.; n. d. Folio. pp. 7.

Daniel Rogers was born in Kittery, Me., in 1734, and died in Gloucester, Mass., in 1800. This document gives his descendants, among whom was distributed a sum awarded for a "French Spoliation Claim."

Schuremans of New Jersey. Supplement, January, 1906. Copyright, 1906, by RICHARD WYNKOOP. *Additions and Corrections.* n. p. [1906.] 8vo. pp. 23. Ill. Price, 25 cts.

Shepardson. A Family Story. By FRANCIS W. SHEPARDSON, Ph.D., [Chicago.] n. p.; n. d. 8vo. pp. 6.

This pamphlet gives descendants of Daniel Shepardson of Charlestown, Mass., earlier of Salem.

Annals of the Sinnott, Rogers, Coffin, Corlies, Reeves, Bodine and Allied Families. By MARY ELIZABETH SINNOTT. Edited by JOSIAH GRANVILLE LEACH, LL.B. Printed for private circulation by J. B. Lippincott Company, Philadelphia. MDCCCCV. 4to. pp. 254. Ill. Charts. Facsimiles.

For centuries the Sinnotts have held a prominent position in County Wexford, Ireland, and various branches of the family are shown on charts, in addition to the immediate line which came to America in 1854.

The Annals of the Allied Families are a scholarly compilation of reliable data on the early lines of the Rogers, Coffin, Hammond, Winslow, Reeves, Jess, Lippincott, Bodine, Corlies, Wing, West and Mayhew families. Preceding each of these accounts is a chart showing the connection with the Sinnott family. We notice the usual careful attention to detail which is characteristic of Mr. Leach's editorial work. The illustrations are of unusual beauty, and facsimiles of documents and signatures, with many portraits and coats-of arms, are scattered through the book, which is a fine specimen of the printer's art. There is an excellent index. A. L. W.

A Genealogy of the Southworths (Southards), Descendants of Constant Southworth. With a Sketch of the Family in England. By SAMUEL G. WEBBER, A.B., M.D. (Harvard). The Fort Hill Press, Samuel Usher, 175 to 184 High St., Boston, Mass. 1905. Large 8vo. pp. 487. Ill.

The record of the descendants of the sons of Constant Southworth—Edward, Nathaniel and William—occupies the body of this work; in the two appendices are found descendants of John Southard of Boothbay, Me., and of Isaac Southworth, of Sharon, Ct. The chapter on the Southworths in England, which is of considerable length, ascribes the origin of the family to Gilbert de Croft who, in consequence of a grant of land in Southworth, assumed that name. There are two extensive indexes. Paper, print and illustrations are excellent. An error occurs in the list of contents, the first chapter having a wrong title assigned to it.

Andrew N. Adams. By ERASTUS HIBBARD PHELPS, Esq., of Fair Haven, Vt. n. p. [1906.] Large 8vo. pp. 4.

This is a reprint from the REGISTER for January, 1906.

The Diary of William Bentley, D.D., Pastor of the East Church, Salem, Massachusetts. Volume 1. April, 1784—December, 1792. Salem, Mass.: The Essex Institute. 1905. 8vo. pp. xlii+456. Ill. Price $3.50 postpaid. Address: The Essex Institute, Salem, Mass.

Dr. Bentley was born in Boston in 1759, and was pastor of the East Church in Salem from 1783 to 1819, the year of his death. He was remarkable as a student and linguist, and displayed an original and independent mind. The diary of such a person must necessarily be of exceeding interest as a portrayal of the social, political, and religious aspects of the community in which he lived, and time which it represents, from the close of the Revolution to 1819. An introduction to the diary consists of a "Biographical Sketch," an "Address on Dr. Bentley," "Bibliography," and an "Account of the East Meeting-House." The footnotes are principally those of Mr. Edward Stanley Waters, a former resident of the East Parish.

Lucius Manlius Boltwood. By Hon. GEORGE SHELDON. Boston: Press of David Clapp & Son. 1905. Large 8vo. pp. 15. Portrait.

This is a reprint from the REGISTER for October, 1905.

Memorial of Mary Francis, Born, November 6, 1803, Died, December 14, 1884, and William Boardman, Born, February 25, 1805, Died November 3, 1887. By WILLIAM F. J. BOARDMAN. Hartford, Conn. Printed for Private Distribution. n. d. Large 8vo. pp. 54. Ill.

Mr. Boardman was one of the most influential business men of Hartford, and his wife was a woman exceptionally beneficent. Besides the biographical sketches, this volume contains an account of the Boardman Memorial Chapel erected by Mr. Boardman in memory of his wife.

Memoir of Col. Henry Lee. With Selections from His Writings and Speeches. Prepared by JOHN T. MORSE, Jr. Boston: Little, Brown & Company. 1905. 8vo. pp. viii+441. Ill.

The index of this fine volume is sufficient to show that it is a work of great interest, not only as to what relates to Mr. Lee, but also as to the many whose obituaries by him are included in the "Selections from his Writings." His own life is amply treated under the heads of "Youth," "Matters Theatrical" (referring to his passion for the amateur drama), "Civil War," "Public Affairs," "Harvard University," "Traits," "Library Labors," "Religion." Besides twenty-five obituaries of persons of eminence, the "Selections" contain "Personal Reminiscences of Gov. Andrew," "Broad Street Riot," "The Shaw Memorial," and other articles. The book is fascinating reading, and is a splendid tribute to the man. Paper, type, illustrations, and binding are of the best.

In Memoriam. Stephen Salisbury. [Worcester, Mass. 1905.] 8vo. pp. 4.

This "appreciation" of the munificent patron of the Art Museum, Worcester, was presented at a special meeting of the directors of the Museum, Nov. 16, 1905.

Memoir of James Swift Rogers. By ALMON DANFORTH HODGES, Jr. Boston: Press of David Clapp & Son. 1906. Large 8vo. pp. 7. Portrait.

This is a reprint from the REGISTER for January, 1906.

Tryphena Ely White's Journal. Being a Record, written one hundred years ago, of the Daily Life of a Young Lady of Puritan Heritage. 1805–1905. Published by her only remaining granddaughter, FANNY KELLOGG. [1904. Grafton Press. New York City.] 12mo. pp. 46. Ill.

In the introduction it is stated that Tryphena Ely White "received her birth" in West Springfield, Mass., March 25, 1784. It was in the town of Camillus, N. Y., however, that the journal was written, Miss White's father having settled there late in life. In 1813 she married Frederik Kellogg, and died in 1816. The journal, which is of exceeding simplicity, relates to the most commonplace incidents of everyday life. A few other brief documents are included in the volume.

Half Century at the Bay. 1636—1686; Heredity and Early Environment of John Williams, "The Redeemed Captive." By GEORGE SHELDON. W. B. Clarke Co., 26 and 28 Tremont St., Boston. 1905. 12mo. pp. 149+10.

This deeply interesting volume portrays life in Roxbury, Mass., and its neighborhood under Puritan domination with truth and vividness. The biography of Williams up to the time he settled in Deerfield is the slender thread which winds in and out among baptisms, funerals, executions, fasts, wars, lectures, sports, collegiate activities, and a multitude of other things. The style of the book is unpretentious and clear, and the opinions expressed seem to be void of prejudice.

Mental and Moral Heredity in Royalty. A Statistical Study in History and Psychology. By FREDERICK ADAMS WOODS, M.D. With one hundred and four portraits. New York: Henry Holt & Co. 1906. 8vo. viii.+312. Price $3.00 net, postage extra.

This book is designed primarily to prove the predominating influence of heredity in the formation of traits of character. Records relating to royal families, as contained in dictionaries, histories, and court memoirs, are here brought together, averaged, and arranged according to scientific formulæ. Tables and charts show the proportionate influence which each ancestor exerts on descendants, according to his remoteness. The origin and descent of exceptional ability, insanity, extraordinary perversities, degenerations, or even altruistic traits, are shown on various charts and discussed at length. Genealogists interested in royal families will find many pedigrees, compiled completely (including all maternal branches), not to be found in any other book. ***

A History of the United States and Its People. From their earliest records to the present time. By ELROY MCKENDREE AVERY. In Fifteen Volumes. Volume II. Cleveland. The Burrows Brothers Company. MCMV. 4to. pp. xxxvi. +458. Ill. Maps. Facsimiles.

An unusual opportunity is here afforded to study the unity of our colonial history, and contrast its diversified development from Massachusetts to Virginia, during the formative period from 1600 to 1660. New Netherlands and New France are also included, and maps, contemporaneous and otherwise, are lavishly used, as well as innumerable illustrations, to give a clear-cut, accurate and readable account of the United States during those years. The manner of placing dates and leading topics in the broad margins is admirable, and the biographical appendix will be found useful in making further investigations. The frontispiece of this volume is a portrait of John Winthrop, in color, and the other numerous portraits and illustrations are made from copper etchings. Owing to the increase of material, the work is extended to fifteen volumes, instead of twelve, without additional cost to the original subscribers. A. L. W.

Vital Records of Dalton, Massachusetts, to the Year 1850. Published by the New England Historic Genealogical Society, at the charge of the Eddy Town-Record Fund. Boston, Mass. 1906. 8vo. Cloth. pp. 82.

Systematic History Fund. Vital Records of Douglas, Massachusetts, to the end of the year 1849. Worcester, Mass.: Published by Franklin P. Rice, Trustee of the Fund. 1906. 8vo. Cloth. pp. 192.

Vital Records of Edgartown, Massachusetts, to the Year 1850. Published by the New England Historic Genealogical Society, at the charge of the Eddy Town-Record Fund. Boston, Mass. 1906. 8vo. Cloth. pp. 276.

Vital Records of Lynn, Massachusetts, to the end of the Year 1849. Volume I.—Births. Published by The Essex Institute. Salem, Mass. 1905. 8vo. Cloth. pp. 429.

Vital Records of Norton, Massachusetts, to the Year 1850. Published by the New England Historic Genealogical Society, at the charge of the Eddy Town-Record Fund. 1906. 8vo. Cloth. pp. 405.

Systematic History Fund. Vital Records of Royalston, Massachusetts, to the end of the Year 1849. Worcester, Mass.: Published by Franklin P. Rice, Trustee of the Fund. 1906. 8vo. pp. 196.

Vital Records of Wenham, Massachusetts, to the end of the Year 1849. Published by The Essex Institute. Salem, Mass. 1904. 8vo. Cloth. pp. 227.

Taylor's Connecticut Legislative History and Souvenir. Vol. V. 1905-1906. Portraits and Sketches of State Officers, Senators, Representatives, Commissioners, etc. Group Cuts of Committees. List of Committees. Putnam, Conn. William Harrison Taylor. 1905. Large 8vo. pp. 300.

To the description of the volume given by the title-page it is only necessary to add that every page, with but few exceptions, contains a portrait and biographical sketch, or a group.

Registry Department of the City of Boston. Records relating to the Early History of Boston. (Formerly called Record Commissioners' Reports.) Vol. 34. The Town of Roxbury, its Memorable Persons and Places, its History and Antiquities, with numerous Illustrations of its Old Landmarks and Noted Personages. By FRANCIS S. DRAKE. Boston: Municipal Printing Office. 1905. Large 8vo. pp. vi+475. Map.

A note states that this volume "is reprinted from the original plates purchased from the estate of the late Francis S. Drake." The work was published by the author in 1878, and was reviewed in the REGISTER for January, 1879.

The Bostonian Society Publications. Vols. 1, 2. Boston: Old State House. 1905. 2 vols. Large 8vo. pp. 84; 142. Ill. Map.

These volumes contain seven articles. The longest one, "Jean Lefebvre de Cheverus," is deeply appreciative of its subject. The paper on "Abel Bowen," printer and engraver, will be enjoyed by the antiquarian, and it is accompanied by a number of the copper-plates and wood-cuts engraved by him. The volumes are extremely handsome, printed on excellent paper, and thoroughly indexed.

Brookline. The Chronicle Souvenir of the Bicentennial. C. A. W. Spencer, Publisher. The Riverdale Press, Brookline, Mass. 1905. Square 4to. pp. 64. Ill.

Alfred D. Chandler's article, "Brookline," which fills half of the volume, gives the reasons why Brookline is "supreme as a municipality, the most notable example of successful autonomy—self-government—in the world's history." This is followed by W. K. Watkins's "Naming of Brookline," and other papers, the book concluding with an account of the Bicentennial. The illustrations are numerous and very fine, including sixty portraits, accompanied by biographical notes.

Old Dartmouth Historical Sketches. No. 12. Being the proceedings of the Winter Meeting of the Old Dartmouth Historical Society, held at the Rooms of the Society, Dec. 8, 1905, and containing the following paper: *Friends Here and Hereaway* Continued, MARY JANE HOWLAND TABER. [New Bedford. 1905.] 4to. pp. 17.

An Historical Sketch of the Town of Deer Isle, Maine. With Notices of Its Settlers and Early Inhabitants. By GEORGE L. HOSMER. The Fort Hill Press, Samuel Usher; 176 to 184 High St., Boston, Mass. [1905.] 8vo. pp. 289. Portrait. Map.

Mr. Hosmer in his Introduction says that the sources of his compilation are oral. While the work as a whole is excellent, the third chapter, which occupies the greater part of the book, is of the most general interest on account of the genealogical information it contains. The volume is indexed, and is well printed and bound. The map shows the location of the first settlers.

A Dorchester Religious Society of Young Men. By ALBERT MATTHEWS. Boston: David Clapp & Son. 1905. Large 8vo. pp. 13.

This reprint from the REGISTER for January, 1906, refers to Dorchester, Mass.

Two Hundredth Anniversary of the Birth of Benjamin Franklin. 1706-1906. Franklin, Massachusetts. [Franklin, 1906.] 12mo. pp. 24. Ill.

Addresses delivered at Groton, Massachusetts, July 12, 1905, by request of the Citizens, on the Celebration of the Two Hundred and Fiftieth Anniversary of its Settlement. Groton. 1905. Large 8vo. pp. 100.

Among the addresses in this publication is one by Dr. Samuel Abbott Green, that was issued separately and noticed in the REGISTER for January of this year. The other addresses of length are by Gen. William A. Bancroft, Hon. Chester W. Clark, and Hon. Charles S. Hamlin.

Hyde Park Historical Record. Vol. V—1905. WILLIAM A. MOWRY, Editor. Published by the Hyde Park Historical Society, Hyde Park, Mass. [1905.] 8vo. pp. 72. Ill.

The principal articles in this volume are "Sketch of the Life of James Read," "The Damon Family of Dedham," "The Greenwood School," and "Proceedings of the Society since 1892 (continued)."

Perfecting of Valuation Lists of Kittery, Maine, 1760. By NATHAN GOULD. n. d.; n. p. Large 8vo. pp. 18.

History of Newburyport, Mass., 1764-1905. By JOHN J. CURRIER. With Maps and Illustrations. Newburyport, Mass. Published by the Author. 1906. Large 8vo. pp. 766.

In the first five chapters the events constituting the history of the town are related in order. Then follows an account of the various activities of the community—ecclesiastical, educational, literary and military—together with notices of enterprises not comprised under these heads. In the historical narrations, particular attention has been paid to the part played by the merchants of Newburyport in supplying clothing and military stores to the patriot army in the Revolution, and in fitting out privateers. As to the later history of the town, space did not permit an adequate treatment, on which account biographical sketches have been omitted. The appendix contains lists of collectors of the port, representatives, town and city clerks, and treasurers. The index occupies more than seventy pages. The quality of the paper used does not comport with the general excellence of the work.

The New York Historical Society. 1804–1904. By ROBERT HENDRE KELBY, Librarian of the Society. New York. Published for the Society. 1905. Large 8vo. pp. 160. Ill.

The history of the Society—which, with the exception of the appendix, fills this volume—consists mainly of materials collected for a paper read by Mr. Kelby "as a retrospect of the century which had elapsed since the foundation of the Society." The appendix, besides the lists usually found in such volumes, also contains a list of the Society's publications.

Neighbors of North Wyke. Part II. In South Tawton (continued). Part III. In South Tawton (continued). Part IV. North and South Tawton in the Pipe Rolls. Part V. Ash and South Zeal in South Tawton. By ETHEL LEGA-WEEKES. Reprinted from the Transactions of the Devonshire Association for the Advancement of Science, Literature, and Art. 1902.—xxxiv. pp. 578–647; 1903.—xxxv. pp. 497–538; 1904.—xxxvi. pp. 415–444; 1905.—xxxvii. pp. 325–374. 4 vols. 8vo. pp. 71; 42; 30; 325–374. Ill.

The first part of this series was noticed in the REGISTER for April, 1902. In the introduction to that publication, the compiler says that her object is "to repeople, with Wykes and their successors, some of the old houses . . . that awakened in her especial interest," adding that she "had not the heart to throw overboard such bits of information concerning *other* inhabitants as happened to be caught in its meshes." It is evident that the same aim has been followed in the parts of the work which have since appeared, the Wykes by no means receiving exclusive attention.

History of the Town of Lanesborough, Mass. 1741–1905. Part I. By CHARLES J. PALMER. n.p.; n.d. 8vo. pp. 168. Ill. Price $1.00 postpaid. For sale by William Lincoln Palmer, 66 Cornhill, Boston.

The main contents of this volume consist of appendixes to a "Historical Address delivered at Old Home Week Celebration, July 27, 1902," which is preceded by an "Account of Origin of Present Name of Town." The appendixes contain sketches of the Lanesborough, Howard, Mowbray, and Bigod families, "Extracts from Old Newspapers and Records relating to Early History," "Vital Statistics," "Revolutionary Soldiers," "Miscellaneous Stories," "Inscriptions in the Various Cemeteries," and other papers of similar importance.

The Penhallow Panels. [Boston. 1905.] 8vo. pp. 3. Ill.

These panels, now in the Victoria and Albert Museum, South Kensington, London, were erected by John Penhallow in the reign of Charles II., in Clifford's Inn, which is the oldest Inn in Chancery.

The Depredation at Pemaquid in August, 1689, and Events that led up to it. By VICTOR HUGO PALTSITS. Read before the Maine Historical Society, Jan. 18, 1900. Portland, Maine: Press of Lefavor-Tower Co. 1905. Large 8vo. pp. 15.

Shropshire Parish Register Society. Dec., 1905. Diocese of St. Asaph. Vol. IV. Part II. Contents: Oswestry. pp. 161–256. *Indexes. Contents: Greete, Bedstone, Chirbury, Ruyton-in-the-XI-Towns, Leebotwood, Longnor.* Variously paged. [London.] 1905. 2 vols. 8vo.

Historic Record of St. Paul's Episcopal Church, Stockbridge, Mass. A Sermon preached on the Twenty-first Anniversary of the Consecration of the Church, by ARTHUR LAWRENCE, Rector of the Parish. Nov. 12, 1905. Pittsfield, Mass.: Press of Sun Printing Co. 1905. 8vo. pp. 15.

Reminiscences of Wilmington and Smithville—Southport, N. C. 1848–1900. By Dr. Walter Gilman Curtis. Pph. 8vo. pp. 62.

A commendable chronicle of public events, social customs, and political changes in the Cape Fear region of North Carolina, covering the periods before and during the civil war, the reconstruction era, and recent improvements. The author has been a practising physician in Brunswick county, N. C., for the last fifty years. He was born in New Hampshire, and graduated at Dartmouth college. This labor of mingled love and duty will increase in value as time moves onward. *

Inaugural Address of Hon. John T. Duggan, Mayor of Worcester, Mass. Jan. 1, 1906. Worcester, Mass.: The Blanchard Press. 1906. 8vo. pp. 17.

Gravestone Records in the Ancient Cemetery and the Woodside Cemetery, Yarmouth, Mass. From literal Copies of the Inscriptions made at the expense of Thomas W. Thacher and Stanley W. Smith. Compiled by George Ernest Bowman. Published by the Mass. Soc. of Mayflower Descendants at the charge of the Cape Cod Town Record Fund. Boston, Mass. 1906. Large 8vo. pp. 45.

These inscriptions, which are arranged alphabetically, similar to the plan of the Massachusetts Vital Records publications, will be found of great value and easy reference to the genealogist. *

Economies of the Iroquois. A Dissertation presented to the Faculty of Bryn Mawr College for the Degree of Doctor of Philosophy. By Sara Henry Stites. 1904. Press of the New Era Printing Co., Lancaster, Pa. 1905. 8vo. pp. 159.

Minutes of the General Conference of the Congregational Churches in Maine; Seventy-Ninth Anniversary. Maine Missionary Society, Ninety-Eighth Anniversary. Held with the Church at Gardiner, Sept. 26, 27, 28, 1905. Vol. III, No. 1, New Series. Portland: Press of Southworth Printing Co. 1905. 8vo. pp. 244. Portrait.

The True Mecklenburg "Declaration of Independence." By A. S. Salley, Jr. A. S. Salley, Jr., Columbia, S. C. 1905. Square 4to. pp. 18. Ill. Price $1.00.

This "Declaration of Independence" is one that is "alleged to have been passed by a convention of Mecklenburg County, North Carolina, May 20, 1775."

Quakerism and Politics. Essays. By Isaac Sharpless, LL.D. President of Haverford College. Phila.: Ferris & Leach, 29 South Seventh St. 1905. 12mo. pp. 220.

The purpose for which this book was written has been admirably accomplished. Its design is to show that the beneficent results of Quaker policy were the inevitable consequences of the application of uncompromising moral principle in the transactions of government. From the first chapter, "A government of Idealists," to the last, "The Basis of Quaker Morality," this truth is vividly illustrated. In the two concluding chapters, the distinctly Quaker sentiments of the author are most plainly, and by no means offensively, obvious. The whole work, which chiefly relates to the early history of Pennsylvania, shows unmistakably that it is the production of a Friend.

The Case for an United States Historical Commission. A Letter to Members of the Fifty-ninth Congress and Others, with Previous Correspondence, and a Bibliography of Historical Documents issued by European Governments. [By Lothrop Withington. London.] 1905. 32mo. pp. 48.

Mr. Withington's advocacy of the establishment of a Historical Commission for the United States is vigorously expressed. Three Senate bills are inserted after the correspondence on the subject between Mr. Withington and President Roosevelt, Hon. Henry Cabot Lodge and others. The bibliography occupies fifteen pages.

The Journal of the American-Irish Historical Society. By Thomas Hamilton Murray, Secretary-General. Volume V. Boston, Mass., Published by the Society. 1905. Large 8vo. pp. 212. Portrait.

Besides showing the work done by the Society during the year, this volume contains valuable historical articles, among which are "Goody Glover," "Capt. Daniel Neill," "The New Hampshire Kellys," "Master John Sullivan of Somersworth and Berwick, and his Family," "Martin Murphy, Sr., an Irish Pioneer of California," and an extensive array of "Historical Notes of Interest."

Constitution, By-Laws and Hand Book of the Texas Society of the Sons of the American Revolution. 1905. [Galveston. 1906.] 32mo. pp. 22.

Society of Colonial Wars in the State of California. 1906. Decennial Register. Proceedings at the Eleventh General Court, Dec. 25, 1905. [Los Angeles. 1906.] 4to. pp. 15. Ill.

Publications of the Ipswich Historical Society. XIV. The Simple Cobler of Aggawam, by Rev. Nathaniel Ward. A Reprint of the 4th Edition, published in 1647, with Fac-Similes of Title Page and Preface, and Head-Lines, and the Exact Text, and an Essay, Nathaniel Ward and the Simple Cobler, by THOMAS FRANKLIN WATERS, *President of the Ipswich Historical Society. Proceedings at the Annual Meeting, Dec. 5, 1904.* Salem Press: The Salem Press Co., Salem, Mass. 1905. Large 8vo. pp. 132.

Annual Report of the Historical and Philosophical Society of Ohio. For the Year Ending Dec. 4, 1905. Cincinnati: The University Press. 1906. 8vo. pp. 23.

Thirty-fourth Annual Meeting, Second Mass. Infantry Ass'n, at Charles Russell Lowell Post 7, G. A. R. Headquarters, Boston, Mass. Sept. 18, 1905. [Boston. 1905.] 8vo. pp. 29.

Grand Commandery of Maine, 1905. Vol. VIII. Part IV. The Fifty-fourth Annual Conclave. Held at Portland, May 4, 1905. Stephen Berry, Printer, 37 Plum St., Portland. 8vo. Variously paged.

Proceedings of the Most Worshipful Grand Lodge of Ancient Free and Accepted Masons of the Commonwealth of Massachusetts, in union with the Most Ancient and Honorable Grand Lodges in Europe and America, according to the Old Constitutions. 1792-1815. Cambridge: Press of Caustic-Claflin Co. 1905. 8vo. pp. 685.

Proceedings of the Most Worshipful Grand Lodge of Ancient Free and Accepted Masons of the Commonwealth of Massachusetts, in union with the Most Ancient and Honorable Grand Lodges in Europe and America, according to the Old Constitutions. Quarterly Communication: Sept. 13, 1905. Special Communications: Sept. 28, Oct. 11, and Nov. 16, 1905. M. W. Baalis Sandford, Grand Master. R. W. Sereno D. Nickerson, Recording Grand Secretary. Ordered to be read in all the Lodges. Boston: The Rockwell & Churchill Press. 1905. 8vo. pp. 115-155.

Society of Mayflower Descendants in the Commonwealth of Massachusetts. Organized 28 March, 1896. Officers, Committees, Membership Roll. Publications. 1 Feb., 1906. Rooms 7, 8 and 9, Number 53 Mt. Vernon St., Boston, Mass. 8vo. pp. 25.

The First Record-Book of the Society of Mayflower Descendants in the State of Rhode Island and Providence Plantations. Providence: Standard Printing Co. 1904. 12mo. pp. 39.

Ninth Annual Report of the Peabody Historical Society. [Peabody. 1905.] 8vo. pp. 9.

Sketches of the Early History of Amherst College, prepared by President HEMAN HUMPHREY, D.D., at the Request of the Trustees. [Amherst. 1905.] 8vo. pp. 32.

A prefatory note says that this is "an undated manuscript of President Heman Humphrey, D.D. It has never before been printed but was frequently quoted from by Prof. W. S. Tyler in his 'History of Amherst College.' The original text appears here without change. The manuscript is the property of Amherst College Library. It is published and distributed by the kindness of Mr. Frank W. Stearns, of the class of 1878."

Annual Register United States Naval Academy, Annapolis, Md. Sixty-first Academic year, 1905–1906. Government Printing Office, Washington, D. C. 1905. Large 8vo. pp. 168.

A Pamphlet descriptive of Bowdoin College and the Medical School of Maine. Brunswick, Maine. Printed for the College. 1905. 8vo. pp. 22. Ill.

The interesting text of this pamphlet is embellished with numerous illustrations of the College buildings, etc.

Library of Harvard University. Bibliographical Contributions. Edited by William Coolidge Lane, Librarian. No. 56. Catalogue of English and American Chap-Books and Broadside Ballads in Harvard College Library. Printed at the expense of the Richard Manning Hodges Fund. Cambridge, Mass. Issued by the Library of Harvard University. 1905. Large 8vo. pp. xi+171.

A List of Winners of Academic Distinctions in Harvard College during the Past Year. Together with Lists of the Scholars of the First Group since 1902, and the Winners of the Bowdoin Prizes. Cambridge, Dec. 18, 1905. 8vo. pp. 60.

The Handbook of Princeton. By John Rogers Williams, General Editor of the Princeton Historical Association. With an Introduction by Woodrow Wilson, LL.D., President of Princeton University. The Grafton Press. 70 Fifth Avenue, New York City. [1905.] 8vo. pp. xvii+154. Ill.

Besides the introduction, the contents of this volume are the "History of the University," "Grounds and Buildings of the University," "Upperclass Clubs and the University Athletic Grounds," "The Town," "The Princeton Theological Seminary," and "The Lawrenceville School." There are more than sixty illustrations, all excellent, and the book is a beautiful specimen of the artistic work of the Grafton Press.

Heralds' College and Coats-of-Arms, Regarded from a Legal Aspect. Third Edition, revised. With a Postscript concerning Prescription, and an Appendix of Statutes and Cases. By W. P. W. Phillimore, M.A., B.C.L. London: Phillimore & Co., 124 Chancery Lane. 8vo. pp. 48. Price One Shilling net, postage extra.

In this interesting pamphlet, which every student of heraldry should read, Mr. Phillimore takes the side of the College of Arms against certain recent writers in *The Ancestor*, and others. In a "Note," he says: "It has been thought expedient in this third edition to deal fully with the subject of Prescription, of late so persistently put forward as a justification for the use of bogus Coats-of-Arms, and to add an Appendix of statutes and modern cases."

The Law and Practice of Change of Name. With Cases and Precedents. By W. P. W. Phillimore, M.A., B.C.L., Solicitor. London: Phillimore & Co., 124 Chancery Lane. 1905. Price One Shilling net, by post 1s 1d. 8vo. pp. 32.

The Family Chest. Hints for the Preservation, Arrangement, and Calendaring of Family Muniments. By W. P. W. Phillimore, M.A., B.C.L. Phillimore & Co., 124 Chancery Lane, London. 1905. Narrow 8vo. pp. 16. Price Sixpence net; by post, Sevenpence.

Reception and Entertainment of the Honourable Artillery Company of London, Two Hundred and Sixty-sixth Annual Record of the Ancient and Honorable Artillery Company of Massachusetts, 1903–1904, and Sermon of Rt. Rev. William Lawrence, Bishop of Massachusetts. Printed at the Norwood Press for the Ancient and Honorable Artillery Company of Massachusetts. n. d. 8vo. pp. viii×382. Ill.

The reception and entertainment described, while tendered principally at Boston, were also participated in by other cities in the United States, and by

Canada. The "Record" of the Massachusetts Company occupies the last hundred pages of the book. The illustrations are numerous, and the print and binding of superior quality.

The Word Palatine in America. By ALBERT MATTHEWS. Reprinted from the Publications of the Colonial Society of Massachusetts, Vol. VIII. Cambridge: John Wilson & Son. University Press. 1905. Large 8vo. pp. 24.

The origin of the different significations in which the word "Palatine" has been used in America is here carefully traced, the latter part of the paper relating to the "Palatine Light" and the wreck of a Palatine vessel at Block Island.

Library of Congress. List of Cartularies (principally French) recently added to the Library of Congress, with some Earlier Accessions. Compiled under the direction of APPLETON PRENTISS CLARK GRIFFIN, Chief Bibliographer. Washington: Government Printing Office. 1905. 4to. pp. 30.

Library of Congress. List of the Benjamin Franklin Papers in the Library of Congress. Compiled under the direction of WORTHINGTON CHAUNCEY FORD, Chief, Division of Manuscripts. Washington: Government Printing Office. 1905. 4to. pp. 322.

DEATHS.

WILLIAM PHINEAS UPHAM, who died in Newtonville, Nov. 23, 1905, was one of the best-known antiquarians in New England. He was the son of Rev. Charles W. Upham of Salem, author of the "History of the Salem Witchcraft," and his mother was a sister of Oliver Wendell Holmes. Mr. Upham was a graduate of Harvard College, class of 1856, and was a life member of the American Historical Association, and of the Massachusetts Historical Society. For many years he was engaged in restoring, classifying and indexing the manuscript records of Essex County and of Suffolk County, through which work, together with his own independent researches, he became an authority on the early history of these counties. He was the author of numerous pamphlets on antiquarian subjects, and at the time of his death had nearly completed, in collaboration with Mr. John Noble, clerk of the Supreme Court of Massachusetts, an edition of "Records of the Court of Assistants of Massachusetts Bay," never before published. His exhaustive knowledge of the systems of shorthand in use during the Colonial period enabled him to decipher manuscripts that must otherwise remained unintelligible, a notable achievement being his recent recovery of the phonetic alphabet employed by Jonathan Edwards. He invented a "rational" system of shorthand, which is extensively used in England. He was recently elected to membership in the Harvard Chapter of the Phi Beta Kappa Society, in recognition of his antiquarian scholarship. Mr. Upham was a member of the Essex bar. He leaves a widow and two daughters.—*Boston Transcript.*

ERRATA.

Vol. 59, page xiii, line 24, *for* Wharf, *read* Whorf.
Vol. 59, page 376, line 40, *for* 1847, *read* 1857.
Vol. 60, page 23, line 27, *for* 1805, *read* 1803.

THE

NEW ENGLAND

HISTORICAL AND GENEALOGICAL REGISTER.

SUPPLEMENT TO APRIL NUMBER, 1906.

PROCEEDINGS

OF THE

NEW ENGLAND HISTORIC GENEALOGICAL SOCIETY

AT THE

ANNUAL MEETING, 10 JANUARY, 1906,

WITH

MEMOIRS OF DECEASED MEMBERS, 1905.

BOSTON:
PUBLISHED BY THE SOCIETY.
MDCCCCVI.

BOSTON.
Press of David Clapp & Son.

CONTENTS.

OFFICERS OF THE SOCIETY

FOR THE YEAR 1906.

President.

JAMES PHINNEY BAXTER, A.M., Litt.D., . Portland, Maine.

Vice-Presidents.

CALEB BENJAMIN TILLINGHAST, A.M., Litt.D., Boston, Massachusetts.
WILLIAM DAVIS PATTERSON, ... Wiscasset, Maine.
JONATHAN EASTMAN PECKER, B.S., . . . Concord, New Hampshire.
HOYT HENRY WHEELER, LL.D., ... Brattleboro', Vermont.
GEORGE CORLIS NIGHTINGALE, ... Providence, Rhode Island.
JAMES JUNIUS GOODWIN, ... Hartford, Connecticut.

Recording Secretary.

GEORGE AUGUSTUS GORDON, A.M., . . . Somerville, Massachusetts.

Corresponding Secretary.

HENRY WINCHESTER CUNNINGHAM, A.B., Manchester, Massachusetts.

Treasurer.

NATHANIEL CUSHING NASH, A.M., . . . Cambridge, Massachusetts.

Librarian.

WILLIAM PRESCOTT GREENLAW, ... Sudbury, Massachusetts.

The Council.

Ex-Officiis.

JAMES PHINNEY BAXTER, A.M., Litt.D.
CALEB BENJAMIN TILLINGHAST, A.M., Litt.D.
GEORGE AUGUSTUS GORDON, A.M.
HENRY WINCHESTER CUNNINGHAM, A.B.
NATHANIEL CUSHING NASH, A.M.
WILLIAM PRESCOTT GREENLAW.

For 1906.

WILLIAM TAGGARD PIPER, A.M., Ph.D., . Cambridge, Massachusetts.
RUFUS GEORGE FREDERICK CANDAGE, . Brookline, Massachusetts.
WILLIAM RICHARD CUTTER, A.M., . . . Woburn, Massachusetts.

For 1906, 1907.

MARY ALICE KEACH . . . . Providence, Rhode Island.
CHARLES KNOWLES BOLTON, A.B., . . . Shirley, Massachusetts.
FREDERICK LEWIS GAY, A.B., ... Brookline, Massachusetts.

For 1906, 1907, 1908.

HELEN FRANCES KIMBALL, ... Brookline, Massachusetts.
FRANCIS APTHORP FOSTER, ... Falmouth, Massachusetts.
MYLES STANDISH, A.M., M.D., ... Boston, Massachusetts.

OFFICERS AND COMMITTEES

FOR THE YEAR 1906.

APPOINTED BY THE COUNCIL.

Historian.

WILLIAM RICHARD CUTTER, A.M. . . . . Woburn.

Editor of Publications.

HENRY ERNEST WOODS, A.M. . . . . Boston.

Committee on Finance.

JAMES PHINNEY BAXTER, A.M., Litt.D., *Chairman* . . Portland, Me.
HENRY WINCHESTER CUNNINGHAM, A.B. . . . . . . Manchester.
NATHANIEL CUSHING NASH, A.M. . . . . Cambridge.
FREDERICK LEWIS GAY, A.B. . . . . Brookline.
WILLIAM TAGGARD PIPER, A.M., Ph.D. . . . . . . Cambridge.

Committee on Real Estate.

JAMES PHINNEY BAXTER, A.M., Litt.D., *Chairman* . . Portland, Me.
NATHANIEL JOHNSON RUST . . . . Boston.
EDMUND DANA BARBOUR . . . . Sharon.
HENRY WINCHESTER CUNNINGHAM, A.B. . . . . . . Manchester.
THOMAS HILLS . . . . Boston.

Committee on the Library.

GEORGE BROWN KNAPP, A.M., *Chairman* . . . . . . Boston.
HELEN FRANCES KIMBALL . . . . Brookline.
MYLES STANDISH, A.M., M.D. . . . . Boston.
JOSEPH GARDNER BARTLETT . . . . Boston.
WILLIAM PRESCOTT GREENLAW, *ex-officio* . . . . . Sudbury.

Committee on Heraldry.

HENRY ERNEST WOODS, A.M., *Chairman* . . . . . . Boston.
FRANCIS APTHORP FOSTER . . . . Falmouth.
BOYLSTON ADAMS BEAL, A.B., LL.B. . . . . Nahant.

Committee on Publications.

CALEB BENJAMIN TILLINGHAST, A.M., Litt.D., *Chairman* Boston.
DON GLEASON HILL, A.M. . . . . Dedham.
CHARLES KNOWLES BOLTON, A.B. . . . . Shirley.
FRANCIS EVERETT BLAKE . . . . Boston.
EDMUND DANA BARBOUR . . . . Sharon.

Committee on Papers and Essays.

ALBERT ALONZO FOLSOM, *Chairman* . . . . Brookline.
DAVID HENRY BROWN, A.B. . . . . Medford.
WILLIAM CARVER BATES . . . . Newton.

Committee to Assist the Historian.

ANDREW FISKE, Ph.D., *Chairman*	Weston.
SILVANUS HAYWARD, D.D.	Southbridge.
ANSON TITUS	Somerville.
ERNEST LEWIS GAY, A.B.	Brookline.
EDWARD CHAUNCEY BOOTH, A.B., M.D.	Somerville.
ABRAM ENGLISH BROWN	Bedford.
ARTHUR WENDELL BURNHAM	Newton.

Committee on English Research.

CHARLES SHERBURNE PENHALLOW, A.B., *Chairman*	Boston.
FRANCIS APTHORP FOSTER	Falmouth.
JOSEPH GARDNER BARTLETT	Boston.

Committee on Epitaphs.

JOHN ALBREE, Jr., *Chairman*	Swampscott.
CHARLES SIDNEY ENSIGN, LL.B.	Newton.
JOHN BLISS BRAINERD, M.D.	Brookline.
NELLIE CHAMBERLIN PRAY	Boston.
RUFUS GEORGE FREDERICK CANDAGE	Brookline.
CHARLES FRENCH READ	Brookline.
GEORGE WALTER CHAMBERLAIN, B.S.	Weymouth.

Committee on Collection of Records.

JOHN BLISS BRAINERD, M.D., *Chairman*	Brookline.
ARTHUR GREENE LORING	Woburn.
ALBERT MATTHEWS, A.B.	Boston.
IDA LOUISE FARR MILLER	Wakefield.
ETHEL STANWOOD BOLTON, A.B.	Shirley.
STEPHEN PASCHALL SHARPLES, S.B.	Cambridge.
WILLIAM PRESCOTT GREENLAW	Sudbury.

Committee on Consolidated Index.

FRANCIS APTHORP FOSTER, *Chairman*	Falmouth.
WILLIAM PRESCOTT GREENLAW	Sudbury.
NATHANIEL CUSHING NASH, A.M.	Cambridge.

Committee on Sale of Publications.

CALEB BENJAMIN TILLINGHAST, A.M., Litt.D., *Chairman*	Boston.
HENRY ERNEST WOODS, A.M.	Boston.
HENRY WINCHESTER CUNNINGHAM, A.B.	Manchester.
GEORGE AUGUSTUS GORDON, A.M.	Somerville.
WILLIAM PRESCOTT GREENLAW	Sudbury.

Committee on Increase of Membership.

GEORGE SUMNER MANN, *Chairman*	Brookline.
CHARLES KNOWLES BOLTON, A.B.	Shirley.
ALBERT ALONZO FOLSOM	Brookline.
FRANK ERNEST WOODWARD	Malden.
HELEN FRANCES KIMBALL	Brookline.

ADDRESS OF THE PRESIDENT.

FELLOW MEMBERS OF THE NEW ENGLAND
HISTORIC GENEALOGICAL SOCIETY:

It has long been the custom for the president to make an annual address to the Society, though I have sometimes thought that perhaps it was a custom that might be more honored in the breach than the observance, inasmuch as it seems to be expected that the president shall review the proceedings of the year, which have already been fully set forth in the various reports. Last year the incongruity of presenting the same facts in three different forms suggested to the Society the propriety of printing the reports instead of reading them to those of the Society present, and this suggestion was adopted and the reports accordingly printed. As it is wholly unnecessary for me to repeat what is of necessity embodied in the reports, I shall only touch upon a few points in them to which I desire to call particular attention; and, first, the house we live in, which we all realize has been outgrown by the Society, and is wholly inadequate to its requirements. Not only are we crowded for space but we are exposed to danger from fire, and the loss of our library and collections would be irreparable. Fortunately, we have acquired sufficient land in the rear of our building to enable us to erect thereon a fire-proof structure for our library, and should our property not be taken for public use, we should, during the year, take some steps towards building. Our finances are in extremely good condition, and we have reason to be pleased that we have this year lived within our appropriations, a consummation devoutly to be wished hereafter. Our library too, shows a healthy growth, and the Librarian and Committee in charge are entitled to no small measure of credit for their able and intelligent conduct of its affairs.

The same may be said of the editor of the REGISTER and your Publication Committee; in fact, all of your active committees merit the regards of the Society.

Genealogy is now generally considered a legitimate subject of study. Fifty years ago this was far from the case, and those who gave themselves only in a moderate degree to this branch of history, were looked upon as at least erratic. Now, however, a man can hardly be regarded as educated who does not know something of his own family history, and something, too, of that of the larger characters of history, for education, once confined to the narrowest limits, has overleaped its bounds and now finds the widest fields of knowledge all too narrow for its exploration. Even the imagination, once the unquestioned prerogative of Art, has been made tributary to Science, and may now be as legitimately employed by an Agassiz and a Pierce, as by a Longfellow and a Holmes. At the same time, we are far from being an educated people in a real sense. Our system of popular education has produced imperfect fruit; indeed, much of the product of our colleges and universities is coarse and unsound. How many men who boast a diploma are devoid of that ethical sense which is the test of true culture. The other day a party of young men, higher classmen in one of our colleges, who had evidently been participants in a football game, entered a car upon which I was coming to Boston. Proceeding at once to monopolize the vacant places, they sprawled over the seats, placing their feet in many instances over the backs of those in front of them, and by loud talk, snatches of college songs, and horse play made themselves obnoxious to their fellow travellers. I wondered if an intelligent foreigner would not have supposed these fellows to have been descendants of one of our aboriginal tribes, rather than of respectable American families, and I wondered still farther what they would be likely to become when they entered upon the real business of life. Certainly, most of them could never become cultivated, well balanced christian gentlemen; rather would they, the spiritual side of their nature having in the process of their education been left fallow, become exploiters of selfish business-schemes, attaches of yellow journalism, and political bosses, to whom all games, if successful, are orthodox; in other words, apt devotees of commercialism, to use a popular and expressive term, which embodies all forms of greed for gain, and of which the consummate flower is graft. Yes, with all our boasted devotion to education, we are still far from being an educated people. We have learned enough to use slang more copiously and more graphically than it was ever used before by any people, and to exploit fads most convincingly to shallow thinkers; but having neglected moral and religious education in the schools, we are losing our morals and our faith. It seems to me that the most crying need of the time is education in morals, particularly that phase of morals relating to one's private and public duties. In these respects the moral sense seems to have become woefully blunted.

So strong has the spirit of commercialism become, that a man cannot perform a service to a fellow man, and especially to the public, without being suspected of being influenced by selfish motives; in fact, men as a rule wholly fail to recognize disinterestedness in any service, hence men of character very largely refuse to accept public office in which they might render valuable service, because they shrink from attracting to themselves the attention of illnatured critics, which would not only render them personally uncomfortable, but tend to lower them in the esteem of their fellows. Party papers, whose only function should be to instruct their readers in the principle of their party, showing by fair arguments their superiority over those of their opponents, are largely responsible for this; too many of them ignoring argument and indulging in inuendo and personal criticism bordering often upon libel. Nothing debauches public morals and lowers the character of public service more than this, and if the boycott is ever justifiable, it should be applied to papers which resort to such reprehensible methods.

I have intimated that commercialism has invaded every field of human activity, even people who were taught in older fashioned times to regard the ballot as a sacred thing to be used only in promoting the public welfare, have found out that it really possesses commercial value and employ it for private advantage. I have been astounded at this new phase of graft. Said an alderman in a good New England city to me, Mr. X has withdrawn his trade from me much so my loss, because I failed to get his street paved. This attracted my attention, and investigation disclosed the fact that men owning property upon some street frequently traded their votes in order to secure the nomination or election of men who would pledge themselves, as an offset, to make improvements to their pecuniary benefit. Citizens, whatever their private interests may be, who have no higher conception of the sanctity of the ballot than to prostitute it to private gain in any form, might as well join the despicable army of floaters and sell their votes to the highest bidder. It is strange that men cannot see that such practices must inevitably result in giving the direction of government to venal men to their own injury as well as to that of the public.

It is high time that the pupils in our public schools should be given the advantage of a course of instruction in good citizenship; in fact, I believe that such a course of instruction is necessary if we would make this country the abode of a free people. Evidences of the need of such instruction are constantly multiplying. Within a month, a candidate was visited on the eve of an election by a considerable number of boys from one of the best wards of the town. They had chosen a spokesman who informed the candidate that they wanted a valuable piece of ground which he owned, part of the lawn of a fine old estate, for a ground for football and other games, and they backed up their demand by informing him in the most significant manner that their fathers were all voters. Not contented with this, they called the next day upon a member of the city committee and requested him to use his influence with the candidate, who could have their fathers' votes if their request was granted. These boys had, of course, learned the commercial value of votes in their own homes, where education begins, and must begin if education in the schools is to achieve its best results.

It is certainly a hopeful sign to see that writers are taking up the subject of the duties of citizenship. Such works as "The Citizen and the Neighbor" and "The American Citizen," written by Rev. Charles F. Dole of Jamaica Plain, are invaluable, and can be made of great public service. If the contents of these little books could be made available to the youth of this country, the benefit to them would be incalculable, because it would put them on the highway to the knowledge that the man who holds a ballot has had bestowed upon him by the nation a sacred trust to be used solely, in accordance with his best light, for the public good. To use his ballot for personal profit renders a man unworthy of the franchise.

PROCEEDINGS.

THE Annual Meeting of the NEW ENGLAND HISTORIC GENEALOGICAL SOCIETY was held in Marshall P. Wilder hall of the Society's house, No. 18 Somerset Street, Boston, on the afternoon of Wednesday, 10 January, 1906, at 2.30 o'clock, the President, Hon. JAMES PHINNEY BAXTER, A.M., Litt.D., presiding.

The call for the meeting was read and the meeting declared open for business, agreeable to article 1, chapter III., of the by-laws.

The annual reports, as hereinafter printed, were presented, received, read, accepted, and ordered on file.

On motion, it was

Voted, To proceed to the election of officers for 1906, agreeable to article 1, chapter IV., of the by-laws.

That the polls be now opened and stand open until three o'clock this afternoon.

That three tellers be appointed by the Chair, who shall receive, sort and count the ballots and make report to this meeting.

The Chair appointed, as tellers: WILLIAM SUMNER APPLETON, of Boston, ERNEST LEWIS GAY, A.B., of Boston, and CHARLES FRENCH READ, of Brookline, who accepted the duty and conducted the election.

The limit of the poll having arrived, the Chair, after inquiry if all, who wished to, had voted, declared the polls closed. The President vacated the chair, calling Capt. ALBERT ALONZO FOLSOM, of Brookline, to preside as Chairman *pro tempore*. Capt. FOLSOM accepted and assumed the gavel.

The tellers made a report of the election, which was received, read, accepted, and ordered on file.

Proclamation was then made of the result of the election, as follows:

President.

JAMES PHINNEY BAXTER, A.M., Litt.D., of Portland, Me.

Vice-Presidents.

CALEB BENJAMIN TILLINGHAST, A.M., Litt.D., of Boston, Mass.
WILLIAM DAVIS PATTERSON, of Wiscasset, Me.
JONATHAN EASTMAN PECKER, B.S., of Concord, N. H.
HOYT HENRY WHEELER, LL.D., of Brattleboro', Vt.
GEORGE CORLIS NIGHTINGALE, of Providence, R. I.
JAMES JUNIUS GOODWIN, of Hartford, Conn.

Recording Secretary.

GEORGE AUGUSTUS GORDON, A.M., of Somerville, Mass.

Corresponding Secretary.

HENRY WINCHESTER CUNNINGHAM, A.B., of Manchester, Mass.

Treasurer.

NATHANIEL CUSHING NASH, A.M., of Cambridge, Mass.

Librarian.

WILLIAM PRESCOTT GREENLAW, of Sudbury, Mass.

Councillors for the term of two years, 1906, 1907.

CHARLES KNOWLES BOLTON, A.B., of Brookline, Mass.
FREDERICK LEWIS GAY, A.B., of Brookline, Mass.

Councillors for the term of three years, 1906, 1907, 1908.

HELEN FRANCES KIMBALL, of Brookline, Mass.
FRANCIS APTHORP FOSTER, of Falmouth, Mass.
MYLES STANDISH, A.M., M.D., of Boston, Mass.

The Hon. JAMES PHINNEY BAXTER, Litt.D., of Portland, Me., was then presented as the President elect, who accepted the position and delivered an inaugural address. (See page ix.)

On motion, it was

Voted, That the annual reports this day accepted; the inaugural address of the president; the biographical notices of deceased members; the charter and other acts of the General Court of Massachusetts, extending the rights and privileges of this Society; an estimate of the financial needs of the Society; with the proceedings of this meeting, be printed in pamphlet and mailed to the members (including the families of members deceased during the past year, donors and exchanging societies), the number to be determined by the Committee on Publication, including fifty copies for the use of the Council.

That the Council be charged with the execution of this order.

On motion, it was

Voted, That hereafter, the Executive Officers and the Council present their annual reports in print.

No other business being presented for consideration, on motion, it was

Voted, That this meeting do now dissolve.

So attests

GEO. A. GORDON,
Recording Secretary.

REPORT OF THE COUNCIL.

Prepared by ALBERT MATTHEWS, A.B.

THE subject of names is a large one, and has been treated frequently and extensively. Nevertheless, it will perhaps be possible, in brief space, to throw out some suggestions which may prove of value to the members of a society like this. Do not some of us, in our genealogical researches, feel that our labor is in a somewhat narrow field? The facts we accumulate about a certain person are doubtless of extreme interest to ourselves and to the descendants and family of that person, but are they so to others? Can we not broaden the field, and so make the labor more interesting at once to ourselves and to others?

Let us consider for a moment the matter of Christian names. There are instances of double names in the seventeenth century, and they were perhaps more common in the eighteenth century than is generally supposed. At that time, they were apparently more frequently given to girls than to boys. At the present day our English cousins are as heavily burdened in this respect as we are; but in England boys seem seldom to be named after distinguished persons. With us, on the contrary, this practice is most pronounced. Its origin is to be found in the political turmoil engendered by the Stamp Act. On October 16, 1766, a Boston boy "was Baptized by the Name of *Wilkes*, when it had *No.* 45, in Bows, pinn'd on its Breast." Within the next few years children in Boston were baptized by the names of William Pitt, Oliver Cromwell, Paschal Paoli, Catharine Macaulay, George Whitefield, Samuel Adams, George Washington, Charles Lee, Henry Knox, and Benjamin Franklin. It is hardly an exaggeration to say that, were other material lost, the history of our country might be reconstructed from Christian names. Thus from a source so seemingly unpromising as baptismal registers facts of interest can be drawn.

In investigating the origin and history of literary usages, it is surprising how often it becomes necessary to inquire minutely into the lives of persons. Wherever we find a term containing a proper name, there seems to be an ineradicable tendency in the human mind to explain the term by referring it to some person or thing of the same name. Thus,—to take but a few instances,—it has been alleged that *Brother Jonathan* is derived from Governor Jonathan Trumbull of Connecticut, *Uncle Sam* from Samuel Wilson of Troy, *Yankee* from Jonathan Hastings of Cambridge, *lynch law* from Charles Lynch of Virginia.

The Sons of Liberty have not received the attention they deserve. The name itself was coined by Colonel Isaac Barré in the debates on the Stamp Act in the House of Commons in 1765. They appear to have had a regular organization, and the warning notices issued by them were sent out in the names of "M. Y., Secretary," "O. C., Secretary," "P. P., Clerk," etc. Were these the initials of the members who held the positions? Again, what was the significance of "Joyce, Jr."—the name under which the chairman of the committee for tarring and feathering masqueraded? Once more, was the father of Samuel Adams actually, as he is said to have been, the founder of the Caulkers' Club, and did the Caulkers' Club give rise to a word which has played so important a part in the political history of our country—*caucus?* Those searching for genealogical facts relating to the prominent actors of the Stamp Act period may at any moment stumble on letters or documents which would solve these questions.

These remarks have been desultory and inadequate in the extreme, but perhaps enough has been said to show that genealogical researches and investigations into the origin of literary usages, besides satisfying a natural desire to ascertain the facts, often throw light on the manners, the customs, the political beliefs, and the history of our colonial or provincial or national periods.

The Report of the COMMITTEE ON FINANCE, by Hon. James Phinney Baxter, Litt.D., William Tracy Eustis, Esq., Nathaniel Johnson Rust, Esq., Henry Winchester Cunningham, A.B., William Taggard Piper, Ph.D., and Nathaniel Cushing Nash, A.M., the Committee:

The total expenditure from the unrestricted income of the Society, for the year ending 31 December, 1905, has been $9,158.48. The details of this expenditure are given in the report of the Treasurer.

Legacies have been received from Walter Titus Avery, amounting to $950.00, and from Robert Charles Winthrop, Junior, amounting to $3,000.00.

The Committee has authorized the purchase of four Chicago, Rock Island & Pacific, three Detroit, Grand Rapids & Western, three Central of New Jersey, three New York Central & Hudson River, three Missouri Pacific, and three Chicago, Burlington & Quincy Railroad bonds, each of one thousand dollars, as an investment of the principal on hand.

The Committee also reports that by practising the strictest economy—restricting the work in the Library merely to what was indispensable—the Society has lived within its income this year, and has used none of its invested funds to pay current expenses; but expenses have been so reduced, by cutting off many things that would improve the Library, that the Committee earnestly hopes the friends of the Society will come to its aid by generous gifts and bequests during the coming year.

The Report of the COMMITTEE ON REAL ESTATE, by Hon. James Phinney Baxter, Litt.D., Henry Winchester Cunningham, A.B., Thomas Hills, Esq., and Nathaniel Johnson Rust, Esq., the Committee:

The Committee, appointed early in the year, has examined the present House and the adjoining real estate owned by the Society, and considers that it has great possibilities, and can hardly be improved upon as a home for the Society. The Committee also looked at several sites and buildings in the neighborhood, but found prices high and buildings not adapted to the Society's purposes, and came to the conclusion that the present situation was as good a one as means permitted, particularly as it was important for genealogical work to be near the State House and the Court House. And as there seemed to be no immediate prospect of the present House being taken for public purposes, the Committee abandoned further search.

The Report of the COMMITTEE ON THE LIBRARY, by George Brown Knapp, A.M., Helen Frances Kimball, Myles Standish, M.D., Joseph Gardner Bartlett, Esq., and William Prescott Greenlaw, Esq., the Committee:

The danger of the total and irreparable loss by fire of the Library of our Society has oppressed the Committee on Library for several years. It was known to them that the construction of the Library building made it a very hazardous fire risk and that the building was structurally weak.

It was evident to the most casual observer that the original structure, a lightly built dwelling house, had been weakened by the removal of all the interior partitions except those surrounding the stairs, that the heavily loaded library floor was supported upon unprotected iron columns incapable of withstanding any great amount of heat. It was known that a weak floor had been laid above the old library floor in such a way as to leave an open space from wall to wall both ways between the floor and the ceiling below it. That the upper floor added weight without giving additional strength and left an open space which would allow fire to spread rapidly, weakening the light timbers, so that there would be a collapse of the building in a short time if fire once got under way in that space. The timbers of this floor were known to be neither large enough nor near enough together for a building used for public purposes, and that they had been very much weakened by cutting to accommodate gas pipes in the centre of the span.

It was also known that the old-fashioned construction created open spaces running vertically between the brick walls and the plaster on all sides behind the bookcases, and would be exceedingly difficult to reach in case of fire, so that enormous damage to the books by water and otherwise would result from even a slight fire. These spaces would, in all probability, also serve as flues to conduct fire into the dangerous places, namely, the space between the library floor and the ceiling below it, and the loft above the library ceiling.

The furnace room was low studded, so that it was evident that the ceiling was dangerously near the top of the furnace, and that in cold weather the room was frequently overheated.

It was remembered that when the building was enlarged, years ago, the rear wall of the original structure had been removed up to the level of the balcony in the library, leaving the weight of the roof and the remaining portion of the rear wall supported by brick piers over that portion of the library room. These facts, and a general sense of insecurity, induced the Library Committee to appoint a sub-committee to investigate the condition of the building. Mr. J. Gardner Bartlett for that sub-committee made the following report:

"The edifice was originally built over 100 years ago for a dwelling house, was altered for their use when bought by the Society about 35 years ago, and has since been enlarged and altered twice. In 1891 the bulging of the north wall rendered the building liable to collapse, and this wall was strengthened by piers and the building tied together with cross rods in the floors.

The whole construction of the building from cellar to roof is totally unsuited for the purpose of a Library or the deposit of valuable books or manuscripts. Investigations at various times have shown that dangerous conditions exist, like exposure of woodwork to heat and smoke flues, timbers so cut for piping as to reduce their strength by half, exposure of the building to explosion from escaping gas, etc. The whole construction of the building is too light for the purpose for which it is used, and is also of an inflammable character; the construction of the library floor and roof, especially, is of such a nature as in case of fire to afford a clean sweep for flames and a total loss of the contents of the building.

Nor is the safe at all a secure place for the valuable treasures of the Society, as the roof is not tight, and in case of a fire the contents of the safe would surely be damaged if not ruined by water; moreover, if the safe be made water-tight, as the limit of its capacity has been reached, further fire-proof space is necessary for new accessions.

Besides the risk from fire in the present building, the rapidly increasing accessions of the Society require larger quarters.

As the collections of the Society are not only of great money value, and historical importance, and besides the manuscripts, over 1,000 printed titles could not be replaced at any expense, we recommend that all such unreplaceable matter should be deposited at once in some safe place until the Society shall have a modern, thoroughly fire-proof building, the need of which is imperative."

The Committee accepted the report, and voted to approve and forward the recommendation in the last paragraph to the Council of the Society.

A sub-committee was then appointed to inquire into the expense of making the building less dangerous in case of fire. This sub-committee invited Messrs. Wheelwright & Haven, the well known architects, to make an examination of the building and an estimate as to the probable cost of such structural changes. These gentlemen reported as follows:

"BOSTON, 29 Nov. 1905.

MYLES STANDISH, M.D.,
N. E. Historic Genealogical Society.

Dear Sir:—In response to your request we submit the following report on the danger from fire in the Building of the N. E. Historic Genealogical Society and as to the possible and advisable precautions to be taken to lessen fire risk without complete reconstruction of the building, together with thr cost thereof.

The building is an old dwelling house which has been altered over from time to time as requirements made necessary.

The walls, with the exception of an addition on the rear, are of less thickness than are now required by the Boston Building Laws (see Note A) and that on the north side is badly cracked and bulged. The party wall is 12" thick and further it is perforated by the timbers of the adjoining building. This perforation may also be the case in the lower stories, but this we were not able to ascertain without removing bookcases and plastering.

The floors are not stiff enough to carry the heavy load of the books without considerable vibration on the second and third floors. The ceiling of the third story in the old part is badly out of level and is held up by a light truss of old pattern and very light wood ties from the rafters supporting the ceiling joists. The roof is composition for the addition and slate for the old part. All walls with the exception of parts of the Basement and First Story are plastered on wooden laths and furring.

Note A.—The building is 50 ft. high to the highest point of the roof, and for a building of this height the Boston Building Laws require the following thicknesses of walls.

	Building Law.	*As Existing.*		
		Front & Party Wall.	Side Wall.	Addition.
Basement	20"	12	16	16
1st	20"	12	16	16
2d	16"	12	12	16
3d	16"	12	12	16

1. Fire Risk from External Causes.

The perforation of the party wall at the level of the third story ceiling may be easily remedied by closing the draft space with brick or metal lath and plaster, but the bearing of the timbers 8″ into the wall is a more serious matter.

With this condition, if there were a severe fire in the adjoining building the party wall would probably be thrown by falling beams causing a section of the roof construction and all of the ceiling joists to fall upon the third floor which is already heavily loaded. If the floor joists of the third floor run 8″ into the north outside wall, as we have reason to suppose, this wall already very weak would undoubtedly fall between the buttresses. If this should occur the library building would be a total wreck, and even if this wall should not fall the building, even if it were not wholly destroyed, would probably be so damaged that it would be poor economy to reconstruct.

The slate of the old roof when exposed to fire from the outside would crack and fall, leaving the roof boarding unprotected.

2. Fire Risk from Internal Causes.

The ceiling of the boiler room is of the ordinary construction of wood laths on plaster applied to the bottom of the floor joists. The plaster of the ceiling has been knocked away in places, leaving the laths and space between the timbers exposed. Fire might be caused in this room by overheating in the furnaces or by leaking gas, and in the basement in general, might be caused by rats or by spontaneous combustion in oiled rags or waste. A fire started in the cellar would be likely to ignite the wood lathed ceilings, thence, by the air spaces between the floor beams to the side and party walls of the building it could spread to all stories and the roof. The large number of wall cases renders it difficult to gain access to the furring space in case of fire.

Another way for fire to spread is offered by the light shaft starting at a little below the level of the second floor and running through the roof. The sides of this shaft are of stud construction and the party wall is framed with wood and plastered on wood lathing. Fire originating in the basement could follow up the under side of the stairs from first to second stories directly into this light shaft as there are unprotected glass doors on the stair landing and above this there is a window in the third story.

Hot air pipes to the various floors run behind wood casings and in many places are surrounded by cases filled with books, making fire channels hard of access.

To render the building a less dangerous fire risk we would propose:

1. To strip the party wall in all stories, fill solid with mortar between the wood furrings and then metal lath and plaster, leaving no air space.

2. To remove all ceilings plastered on wood lath and replace with metal lath and plaster.

3. To fire stop with plaster at both sides of each floor to prevent the spread of fire behind the furrings. In the basement to cross stop between the joists at several points the whole length of the building, to prevent the spread of fire in a horizontal direction between the floor beams.

4. To strip the plastering from staircases, fire stop them in accordance with the requirements of the Building Laws and plaster on metal lathing.

5. To build new roof of steel and concrete, carrying the weight on the party wall side by four steel columns extending from the new roof level to the basement floor. These should be located against the party wall in the adjoining building owned by the Society. On the side opposite the party wall three steel columns will carry the weight of new roof to the tops of the present buttresses. This method will relieve the party wall from any roof load, except that coming on it from the adjoining building, and the wall opposite the party wall will receive no roof load above the level of the third floor at which point the wall is reinforced by the buttresses.

6. To protect the furnace pipes by some effective insulating material.

The electric light installation should be thoroughly inspected by competent experts and all possible precautions taken for its proper insulation.

We would suggest replacing the present wooden bookcases with metal cases. This is especially desirable in the vaults and storage spaces in the basement and first story.

With the building in its present condition a night watchman should be employed and his service checked by a watchman's clock.

The total cost of fire-protecting the structure and of building a new roof of incombustible material as herein advised would not be less than $15,000, not reckoning the cost of storage of the books, etc., of replacing the present wood cases with metal, or of inspecting and further insulating the electric light installation.

Yours truly,

WHEELWRIGHT & HAVEN."

The architects' figures, it will be noticed, do not cover the expense of the metal cases and shelves, nor the cost of handling and storing the books during the reconstruction of the building, which would easily double the expense, and we should still have a building with weak walls, wooden floor timbers, and lacking space for the future growth of the Library.

Even at the present time, every available inch of space is occupied, and we have more than 20,000 volumes and pamphlets in storage. Our most valuable papers would still be stored in the brick vault of the present building, which is a structure of doubtful security. It is a brick arch construction, supported by iron beams. These beams, being unprotected like the iron columns in the hall above, would collapse if heated, and the entire manuscript collection would be lost. The roof of the safe is now badly cracked and thin, and probably would not be strong enough to survive the fall of the party wall, if the building itself should be destroyed.

We have land in the rear of the present building on which a building approximately 65×70 ft. and 80 ft. high, built of brick, with steel and tile arch floor construction, equipped with steel stacks, could be erected for $125,000, even at the present high prices of material and labor. A building 65×70 ft. and 80 ft. high would have four times the capacity of the present building, and if planned aright, ought to be sufficient for the growth of the next fifty years.

The construction of such a building is earnestly recommended, and the Committee on the Library hopes that the Society will take such action in the immediate future.

The Report of the COMMITTEE ON PUBLICATIONS, by Caleb Benjamin Tillinghast, Litt.D., Chairman:

The activities of the Committee on Publications for the year 1905 embrace

(1). The quarterly publication of the REGISTER and the annual Proceedings of the Society, which are now comprised in one volume.

(2) The publication of Register *Soame*, 1620, of the wills recorded in the Prerogative Court of Canterbury.

(3) The publication of volume 6 of the Memorial Biographies and the partial preparation of volume 7.

(4) The publication of the Vital Records of the towns of Palmer and Medway, and the city of Newton. The records of Edgartown, Norton and Sturbridge will be published during the coming year, and those of a large number of other towns are in various stages of preparation.

The preparation and publication of all the volumes issued by the Society is carried on as rapidly as is consistent with careful editing and the best mechanical results.

The Report of the COMMITTEE ON PAPERS AND ESSAYS, by Albert Alonzo Folsom, Esq., Chairman:

4 January. Reading of Paper postponed on account of the inclemency of the weather.

1 February. Paper by Charles G. Chick, Esq., President of the Hyde Park Historical Society, on "Side-Lights upon Colonial Taxation in England and America, 1762–1774."

1 March. Paper by James Duncan Phillips, A.B., of Salem, on "Salem Commercial Enterprise."

5 April. Paper by Thomas William Silloway, A.M., of Boston, on "Rev. Joseph Morse, A.M., Minister at Weston, Mass., and first Minister at Canton, Mass."

3 May. Paper by Edgar Oakes Achorn, A.B., of Brookline, on "The German Settlement at Waldoboro', Maine."

4 October. Paper by Charles Cowley, LL.D., of Lowell, on "Boston in the Civil War, from the Naval View Point."

1 November. Paper by William Carver Bates, Esq., of Newton, on "Personal Experiences in Confederate Prisons, 1861–1862."

6 December. Paper by Hon. George Sheldon, of Deerfield, on "The Conference at Deerfield, August 27–31, 1735, between Gov. Belcher and several tribes of Indians."

The Report of the COMMITTEE TO ASSIST THE HISTORIAN, by William Richard Cutter, A.M., Chairman:

The Historian confesses that in seeking help from surviving friends of our deceased members he has neglected the help this Committee stood ready to furnish. Mr. Heywood of the Committee has died.

The sixth volume of the Memorial Biographies has been published during the year. The volume has been edited and printed under the direction of the Historian, and members of the Committee have assisted in the work when they have been called upon. The Historian is now at work on the material for the seventh volume.

The chairman has written a number of sketches for the Proceedings. Where the work has been only a condensation from a single article, no signature has been appended, and the same omission has been made in the case of sketches prepared from material formerly contributed by deceased members to the archives of the Society.

It is not easy at times to get the exact date of death of members living at a distance, and if persons residing in other states, than Massachusetts, would inform the Society of the dates of death of members belonging in their vicinity, which come to their knowledge, it would be a help.

Rev. Anson Titus is writing a sketch of President Elmer H. Capen.

This is all that the Committee is doing at the present time.

The Report of the COMMITTEE ON ENGLISH RESEARCH, by Charles Sherburne Penhallow, A.B., Chairman:

In behalf of the Committee on researches in England, I have to report that there have been no meetings during the year, there having been no funds to use in connection with that branch of the Society's work.

The Report of the COMMITTEE ON HERALDRY, prepared by Francis Apthorp Foster, Esq., Secretary of the Committee, and presented by Henry Ernest Woods, A.M., Chairman:

The Committee on Heraldry begs to report that during the past year it has had a much smaller number of inquiries than usual to answer.

Two books published in 1904 seem worthy of special mention:

Macdonald's "Scottish Armorial Seals," and Fox-Davies's "Art of Heraldry."

Of another character is Crozier's "General Armory: a Register of American Families entitled to Coat Armor." With the attitude of the Society towards the wholesale use and abuse of arms, it is impossible for your Committee to recommend this work.

The Report of the COMMITTEE ON EPITAPHS, by John Albree, Esq., Chairman:

The Committee on Epitaphs reports that during the year there have been added to the Library by donation copies of inscriptions from the following cemeteries:

1. Cedarville Cemetery, East Sandwich, Mass., from Levi Henry Elwell, M.A., Amherst, Mass.
2. North Cemetery, Salem Road, North Billerica, Mass., from Miss Martha Ann Dodge, Billerica, Mass.
3. First Presbyterian Churchyard, Schenectady, N. Y., from Nathan Van Patten, Schenectady, N. Y.
4. Old Burying Ground, North Andover, Mass., from Hollis Bailey, Cambridge, Mass.
5. Old South, Farm, Brush Hill, Plain, Central, West, and New South Burying Grounds, Sherborn, Mass., from John Bliss Brainerd, M.D., Brookline, Mass.
6. St. John's Church Graveyard, Providence, R. I., from Miss Mary Alice Keach, Providence, R. I.

And through the Committee on Vital Records:

7. Hinsdale, Mass., Cemetery Records, and
8. Partridgefield (now Peru), Mass., Inscriptions, both from James Hosmer, Hinsdale, Mass.

The preparation of these manuscripts has required a great amount of time, patience and careful work, and the Committee takes this occasion to express appreciative thanks to those who have contributed to the results.

It is to be noted with pleasure that the seven old grave-yards in Sherborn, Mass., have been copied in excellent form by Dr. Brainerd, who reports that he found a large number of inscriptions illegible, a condition that unfortunately is too often noted in old graveyards; and that again emphasizes the need of prompt action in preserving the data recorded in graveyards which have not yet been cared for.

The circular "Suggestions as to Copying Inscriptions," the preparation and printing of which was mentioned in the report for last year, has been found to be of decided assistance in the work, especially in securing greater accuracy and more uniformity in the manuscripts.

Co-operation in the work of copying, one instance of which was reported by this Committee in the last report, namely, the excellent results attained by the Daughters of the American Revolution at Cohasset, has been adopted by the local chapter of the Daughters of the American Revolution at Hingham, the adjoining town, and the final copy is being prepared. The Daughters of the American Revolution in Milford, N. H., have made substantial progress along the same line, and the final copy is being made there also. The Sons of the American Revolution at Springfield have made a beginning in that place. The Arlington Inscriptions, contributed by the Arlington Historical Society some years ago, is another instance of the successful working of the plan of co-operation. These instances are mentioned to call the attention of the patriotic orders and the local historical societies to a field that falls within the scope of their operation. Experience shows that a leader can soon gather around himself or herself enough helpers to allow the field work to be speedily completed.

Additions to the card catalogue of this Committee are being continually made, showing in what places the inscriptions have been copied and where the copies are to be found. If a copy has been made and deposited in safe-keeping, sooner or later the facts will be printed.

The work of the Committee seems to be peculiarly in accord with the motto on the seal of the Society, "In Memoriam Majorum," in that it seeks to fulfil and render certain of accomplishment the purposes the "great multitude" had in mind when they erected the humble slate memorials as "sacred to the memory of" those they loved.

The Report of the Committee on Collection of Records, by Arthur Greene Loring, Esq., Chairman:

This Committee has had several meetings during the year.

The members of the Committee, personally, have continually urged upon the proper officials the importance of printing their records, but so far as has come to their notice but little has been done in this line during the year.

The Report of the Committee on Consolidated Index, by Francis Apthorp Foster, Esq., Chairman:

The Committee on the Consolidated Index begs to report that a sufficient number of subscriptions at $5 per part have been received to cover the cost of publication.

The Committee's attempt to get a proper price on printing the Index caused a delay of some months, which was still further increased by the death of the chairman, Captain James Swift Rogers;

but it is now happy to report that the work is progressing rapidly. Three numbers have been issued this year, and, at the present rate of progress, six parts may be expected annually until the work is finished.

As 600 copies of the rarest volume of the REGISTER were printed, and as there are probably about 500 complete sets of the REGISTER in existence, holders of nearly complete as well as of complete sets should secure the Index before it is out of print. The fact that a complete set of the REGISTER lacking the Index will be less useful and probably less valuable than a set with the Index but lacking the rare volumes should not make it difficult to dispose of the remaining unsold sets before the work is completed.

The Committee believes that the Society should not profit pecuniarily by this undertaking, and proposes that the subscribers shall benefit by the $2,400 donated originally for the preparation of the Index. It further proposes, after reimbursing the Society for money advanced, to give to subscribers *pro rata* any balance on hand at the completion of the work.

REPORT OF THE LIBRARIAN.

PRESENTED BY WILLIAM PRESCOTT GREENLAW.

THE LIBRARIAN has attended to the duties of his office throughout the year, devoting from one to two hours per day more than is required of his assistants in forwarding the interests of the Society. He has usually been the first to enter the building in the morning and the last to leave it at night, exercising the most rigid vigilance over the heating and lighting apparatus as a safeguard against fire. In his endeavors to build up the Library and increase its usefulness, he has enjoyed to a remarkable degree the coöperation of the officers, members and employees of the Society. Below he submits a statement of the growth, progress and needs of the Library, to which is appended the required list of donors.

Accessions.

Again, as in 1904, the additions to the Society's collections in the Library and the Cabinet have been eminently appropriate. Two hundred and fifty-three genealogies have been acquired in 1905, which, with the six hundred and twenty-five secured in 1902, the three hundred and sixty-two in 1903, and the same number again in 1904, makes a total of over sixteen hundred genealogies added in four years. The accessions for the year number 829 volumes, 763 pamphlets, and 1098 miscellaneous articles. Of these, 217 volumes, 99 pamphlets, and 15 miscellaneous articles were purchased, 542 volumes, 639 pamphlets, and 1083 miscellaneous articles were given, and 70 volumes and 25 pamphlets were received in exchange. Adding to the last published estimate, the accessions received since, and deducting the duplicate municipal reports (40 volumes and 2560 pamphlets) disposed of in 1904, gives 32,498 volumes and 32,479 pamphlets as the approximate number in the Library, December 31, 1905.

Manuscripts.

The Society has been fortunate in securing genealogical manuscripts during the year. Among these worthy of special mention at this time are genealogies of various Rogers families compiled by the late Capt. James Swift Rogers of Boston, and presented by his widow; genealogies of several Cook families, and partial copies of local records in the vicinity of Pittsfield, Mass., gathered by the late Rollin H. Cooke of Pittsfield; an Adams genealogy compiled by the late Hon. Andrew N. Adams of Fair Haven, Vt., and presented by his widow; an Eldred genealogy given by Mrs. Marian Strong Baker of Washington, D. C.; a Pulsifer genealogy given by Mrs. Cornelia Lucretia Boardman Pulsifer of New Bedford; Ward, Plummer and Lang genealogies given by Mrs. Harriet Emeline Richardson of Aurora, Ill.; a collection of manuscripts from the library of the late Hon. Charles Henry Bell of Exeter, N. H., given by Mr. Hollis Russell Bailey of Cambridge; several volumes of English records gathered by the late Joseph Jackson Howard of Blackheath, Kent, Eng.; an original Diary, kept by Israel Litchfield, given by Miss Ella Farmer of Hingham, Mass.; an original list of marriages by Rev. John Webb, 1714–1749, and the second volume of the records of the New North Church of Boston, of which Mr. Webb was the first minister, given by Mary Lincoln Eliot of Boston; and a very large collection of copies of town, church, and probate records, epitaphs and deeds, relating to Barnstable, Mass., made by the late Gustavus A. Hinckley of Barnstable, and bequeathed by him to the Society.

Growth and Use of the Library.

The efforts put forth in recent years to increase the Library have been directed mainly toward the acquisition of genealogical publications and manuscripts, and properly so, for the Society has become widely known as the *Genealogical Society*, and the chief use of its Library, both by members and visitors, is for the purpose of making genealogical investigations. Probably less than five per cent of the books consulted are examined for all other purposes. The historical side, however, has not been wholly neglected, especially when opportunity occurred to secure desiderata at low or moderate prices; yet it has been thought wise to leave to the various state and local historical societies of New England the opportunity for each to excel in its own special field of activity. To gather and preserve for public use the records of the families who have lived within the confines of New England since its settlement is a task sufficiently large to engross the energy and to absorb the means of any one institution. And it is certainly more in accordance with modern ideas, for the Society to specialize in what to some, perhaps, may seem a narrow interpretation of its founders' purposes, accomplishing much in the more restricted field, than for it to divide its energy and means among a wider range of objects, failing to obtain more than a moderate degree of success in each. The remarkable growth of the Library along genealogical lines is to a large extent due to the general demand of visitors for genealogical information.

Danger from Fire.

The wooden buildings on the adjoining land recently purchased by the Society have been demolished this year, making a slight change for the better in external conditions. See the former reports of the Librarian. For expert opinions of the dangerous condition of the Society's Building, read the Report of the Committee on the Library.

Binding.

Finding it impossible to purchase duck of an uniform texture and color, in small quantities, for binding, the Librarian has had made to order a quantity of cloth sufficient for several years.

Economy and Service.

In response to a general demand "to take in sail" at the beginning of the year, it has been necessary to curtail expenses wherever possible. As a result, fewer books have been purchased, less binding has been done, and scarcely anything worth mentioning has been accomplished on the card catalogue. Miss Chapman and Miss Rayne of the Library staff have been assigned temporarily to the Consolidated Index, and jointly given charge of the editorial work on it. This transfer has materially lessened the pay roll of the library and has provided efficient editors for the Index, but it has also seriously interfered with the progress of the library work. Miss Stickney has been appointed by the Council as Assistant Librarian, and continues to attend to the routine work of the Library.

The Treasurer's report for the year indicates that the Society has lived within its income. The Librarian regrets the necessity of reporting that, in order to do this, it has been impossible to purchase desirable books frequently called for, to keep up the cataloguing and binding, and to give the best service in assisting members and visitors.

LIST OF DONORS TO THE LIBRARY.

Names.	Names:
Canada:	*States:*
Superintendent of Immigration.	Massachusetts.
United States:	*Cities:*
Secretary of the Navy.	Beverly.
Smithsonian Institution.	Boston.
	Cambridge.
Towns:	Chelsea.
Durham, Conn.	Hartford, Conn.
Framingham.*	Newton.
Lexington.	
Provincetown.	
Ware.	

Names.	Addresses.
Abbot Academy	Andover.
The American Antiquarian	Chicago, Ill.
American Antiquarian Society	Worcester.
American Catholic Historical Researches	Philadelphia, Pa.
American Catholic Historical Society	Philadelphia, Pa.
American Congregational Association	Boston.
American Exchange National Bank	New York, N. Y.
American Jewish Historical Society	New York, N. Y.
American Statistical Association	Boston.
Amherst College	Amherst.
Ancient Free and Accepted Masons	Boston.
Andover Alumni Association	
Andover Theological Seminary	Andover.
Boston City Hospital	Boston.
The Boston Five Cents Savings Bank	Boston.
Boston Floating Hospital	Boston.
Boston and Maine Railroad	Boston.
Boston Public Library	Boston.
Boston Transcript	Boston.
Boston University	Boston.
Bostonian Society	Boston.
Bowdoin College	Brunswick, Me.
The Brooks Company	Cleveland, O.
Buffalo Historical Society	Buffalo, N. Y.
Bunker Hill Monument Association	Boston.
The Burrows Brothers Company	Cleveland, O.
California Society of the Sons of the American Revolution	
The Canadian Club of Harvard University	Cambridge.
Cemetery Department of the City of Boston	Boston.
The Century Company	New York, N. Y.
Chicago Historical Society	Chicago, Ill.
Children's Hospital	Boston.
Ye Chipman Printery	Poland, Me.
City Registry Department	Boston.
Colby College	Waterville, Me.
The Colonial Society of Massachusetts	Boston.
Connecticut Historical Society	Hartford, Conn.
Connecticut State Library	Hartford, Conn.
Courier-Journal Job Printing Company	Louisville, Ky.
Dartmouth College	Hanover, N. H.
Drake University	Des Moines, Ia.
Essex Antiquarian	Salem.
Essex Institute	Salem.
Estate of Mrs. Anne Williams Cushman	Greenfield.
Estate of Charles E. French	Boston.
Estate of Gustavus A. Hinckley	Barnstable.

* All places are in Massachusetts unless otherwise specified.

Fairmount Park Art Association	Philadelphia, Pa.
Family of Mr. and Mrs. Matthew Gault Emery	
Franklin and Marshall College Alumni Association	Lancaster, Pa.
General Theological Library	Boston.
The Grafton Press	New York, N. Y.
Groton School	Groton.
The Gulf States Historical Magazine	Birmingham, Ala.
Harvard Law School	Cambridge.
Harvard University	Cambridge.
Hemenway Trustees	Boston.
Hills Family Genealogical and Historical Association	Boston.
Historical and Philosophical Society of Ohio	Cincinnati, O.
Historical Society of Delaware	Wilmington, Del.
The Historical Society of Pennsylvania	Philadelphia, Pa.
The Huguenot Society of South Carolina	Charleston, S. C.
H. R. Huntting & Company	Springfield.
Hyde Park Historical Society	Hyde Park.
Industrial Aid Society	Boston.
Kansas State Historical Society	Topeka, Kan.
Kentucky State Historical Society	Frankfort, Ky.
Lexington Historical Society	Lexington.
C. F. Libbie & Company	Boston.
Library of Congress	Washington, D. C.
J. B. Lippincott Company	Philadelphia, Pa.
Literary and Historical Society of Quebec	Quebec, Can.
Lynn Historical Society	Lynn.
Maine Genealogical Society	Portland, Me.
Maine State Library	Augusta, Me.
Maine Historical Society	Rutland, Me.
Maryland Historical Society	Baltimore, Md.
Massachusetts College of Pharmacy	Boston.
Massachusetts General Hospital	Boston.
Massachusetts Historical Society	Boston.
The Massachusetts Medical Society	Boston.
Massachusetts Society of the Colonial Dames of America	
Massachusetts Society of Mayflower Descendants	Boston.
Meadville Theological School	Meadville, Pa.
Missouri Historical Society	St. Louis, Mo.
The Morse Society	New York, N. Y.
Museum of Fine Arts	Boston.
The Nation	New York, N. Y.
National Society of the Daughters of the American Revolution	Washington, D. C.
New England Moral Reform Society	Boston.
New England Society of Cincinnati	Cincinnati, O.
New England Society in the City of New York	New York, N. Y.
New Hampshire Historical Society	Concord, N. H.
New Haven Colony Historical Society	New Haven, Conn.
New York Genealogical and Biographical Society	New York, N. Y.
New York Historical Society	New York, N. Y.
Northwestern University	Evanston, Ill.
Nova Scotia Historical Society	Halifax, N. S.
Nova Scotia Institute of Science	Halifax, N. S.
Oberlin College	Oberlin, O.
Ohio Society of New York	New York, N. Y.
Old Dartmouth Historical Society	New Bedford.
The "Old Northwest" Genealogical Society	Columbus, O.
Oneida Historical Society	Utica, N. Y.
Ontario Historical Society	Toronto, Can.
Pennsylvania Society of Sons of the Revolution	Philadelphia, Pa.
Phillips Exeter Academy	Exeter, N. H.
Princeton University	Princeton, N. J.
The Publishers' Weekly	New York, N. Y.
Quinabaug Historical Society	Southbridge.
Record Commissioner	Providence, R. I.
Registry Department	Boston.
The Research Publication Company	Boston.
Roxbury Latin School	Boston.
Royal Historical Society	London, Eng.
Royal Society of Canada	Ottawa, Can.
Second Massachusetts Infantry Association	Boston.
Sharon Historical Society	Sharon.
Shropshire Parish Register Society	Oswestry, Eng.
Societe Historique de Montreal	Montreal, Can.
Society of Antiquaries	London, Eng.
Society of Colonial Wars in the District of Columbia	Washington, D. C.
Society of Colonial Wars in the State of Maine	Portland, Me.
Society of Mayflower Descendants in the State of New York	New York, N. Y.
Society of Middletown Upper Houses	Cromwell, Conn.
Somersetshire Archæological and Natural History Society	Taunton, Eng.
South Carolina Historical Society	Charleston, S. C.
Southern Historical Society	Richmond, Va.
State Agricultural College	Fort Collins, Colo.

State Historian	Albany, N. Y.
State Historical and Natural History Society	Denver, Colo.
The State Historical Society of Iowa	Iowa City, Ia.
State Historical Society of North Dakota	Bismarck, N. D
State Historical Society of Wisconsin	Madison, Wis.
Surrey Archæological Society	Guildford, Eng.
Syracuse University	Syracuse, N. Y.
The Texas State Historical Association	Austin, Tex.
Topsfield Historical Society	Topsfield.
Towle Manufacturing Company	Newburyport.
Trinity College	Hartford, Conn.
Tufts College	Tufts College.
United States Court of Claims	Washington, D. C.
United States Naval Academy	Annapolis, Md.
University of California	Berkeley, Cal.
University Club	New York, N. Y.
University of Colorado	Boulder, Colo.
University of North Carolina	Chapel Hill, N. C.
University of Texas	Austin, Tex.
University of Vermont	Burlington, Vt.
Vermont Historical Society	Montpelier, Vt.
Virginia Historical Society	Richmond, Va.
Wendell Brothers	Minneapolis, Minn.
Whitcomb, Wead & Company	Boston.
William and Mary College	Williamsburg, Va.
Williams College	Williamstown.
Wiscasset Fire Society	Wiscasset, Me.
Worcester Society of Antiquity	Worcester.
Yale University	New Haven, Conn.

Members.

Charles Francis Adams, LL.D.	Lincoln.
James Bourne Ayer, A.M., M.D.	Boston.
Edmund Dana Barbour	Boston.
Joseph Gardner Bartlett	Boston.
William Carver Bates	Newton.
Hon. James Phinney Baxter, A.M., Litt.D.	Portland, Me.
Francis Everett Blake	Boston.
John Taggard Blodgett, A.M.	Providence, R. I.
William Francis Joseph Boardman	Hartford, Conn.
Charles Knowles Bolton, A.B.	Shirley.
Edward Augustus Bowen	Woodstock, Conn
Sumner Eli Bowman	West Somerville.
John Bliss Brainerd, M.D.	Brookline.
Lloyd Vernon Briggs, M.D.	Hanover.
Walter Frederic Brooks	Worcester.
David Henry Brown, A.B.	Medford.
Rufus George Frederick Candage	Brookline.
Rev. Charles Carroll Carpenter, A.M.	Andover.
George Walter Chamberlain, B.S.	Weymouth.
John Denison Champlin, A.M.	New York, N. Y.
Col. Albert Clarke, A.M.	Boston.
George Kuhn Clarke, LL.B.	Needham.
Deloraine Pendre Corey	Malden.
Frank Ethridge Cotton, A.B.	Woburn.
Henry Winchester Cunningham, A.B.	Manchester.
Horace Davis, LL.D.	San Francisco, Cal.
Horatio Davis	Boston.
Gen. John Watts de Peyster, LL.D.	Tivoli, N. Y.
Martha Ann Dodge	Billerica.
Rev. Arthur Wentworth Hamilton Eaton, D.C.L.	New York, N. Y.
Mary Lincoln Eliot	Boston.
William Tracy Eustis	Brookline.
Mrs. Hattie Sturtevant Everit	Framingham.
John Wilder Fairbank	Boston.
Mittie Belcher Fairbanks	Farmington, Me.
Charles Allcott Flagg, M.A.	Washington, D. C.
Capt. Albert Alonzo Folsom	Brookline.
Thomas Gamble, Jr.	Savannah, Ga.
Alexander McLellan Goodspeed	New Bedford.
Charles Eliot Goodspeed	Boston.
George Augustus Gordon, A.M.	Somerville.
Mary Hannah Graves	Boston.
Hon. Samuel Abbott Green, M.D.; LL.D.	Boston.
Lucy Hall Greenlaw	Sudbury.
William Prescott Greenlaw	Sudbury.
Charles Henry Hart, LL.B.	Philadelphia, Pa.
Frederick Augustus Henry, LL.B.	Cleveland, O.
Lew Cass Hill	Boston.
Thomas Hills	Boston.
Frederick Hills Hitchcock, A.B.	New York, N. Y.

Almon Danforth Hodges, Jr., A.M.	Boston.
Clayton Wood Holmes, A.M.	Elmira, N. Y.
James Hosmer	Hinsdale.
Hon. Sir Walter Francis Hely-Hutchinson, G.C. M.G.	Cape Town, So. Africa.
Rev. George Anson Jackson, Ph.B.	Swampscott.
Robert Tracy Jackson, S.D.	Cambridge.
Edward Francis Johnson, LL.B.	Woburn.
Mary Alice Keach	Providence, R. I.
Idelle Keyes	Louisville, Ky.
Helen Frances Kimball	Brookline.
George Brown Knapp, A.M.	Newton.
James Henry Lea	South Freeport, Me.
Emily Wilder Leavitt	Boston.
Wilford Jacob Litchfield, M.S.	Southbridge.
Arthur Greene Loring	Woburn.
John Jacob Loud, A.M.	Weymouth.
Rev. Willard Francis Mallalieu, D.D., LL.D.	Newton.
John Miner Carey Marble	Los Angeles, Cal.
William Theophilus Rogers Marvin, A.M.	Brookline.
Albert Matthews, A.B.	Boston.
Samuel May, Jr.	Boston.
Samuel Merrill, LL.B.	Cambridge.
Rev. Charles Langdon Mitchell, A.M.	Winchester.
Tyler Seymour Morris	Chicago, Ill.
John Graham Moseley	Boston.
Joseph James Muskett	Stoke Newington, Eng.
William Nelson, A.M.	Paterson, N. J.
Charles Lyman Newhall	Southbridge.
Sereno Dwight Nickerson, LL.B.	Cambridge.
George Corlis Nightingale	Providence, R. I.
John Noble, LL D.	Boston.
Nathaniel Paine, A.M.	Worcester.
William Lincoln Palmer	Cambridge.
Pearl Hildreth Parker	Lowell.
Charles Sherburne Penhallow, A.B.	Boston.
William Phillimore Watts Phillimore, M.A., B.C.L.	London, Eng.
Mrs. Anna Maria Pickford	Lynn.
Eben Putnam	Wellesley Farms.
Mrs. Anna Margaret Riley	Claremont, N. H.
Hon. George Sheldon	Deerfield.
Rev. Thomas William Silloway, A.M.	Allston.
Rev. Carlos Slafter, A.M.	Rockford, Ill.
Rev. Edmund Farwell Slafter, D.D.	Boston.
Charles Elihu Slocum, LL.D.	Defiance, O.
Susan Augusta Smith	Dorchester.
Francis William Sprague	Brookline.
Alexander Starbuck	Waltham.
Henry Reed Stiles, A.M., M.D.	Hillview, N. Y.
Robert Thaxter Swan	Boston.
Mary Kingsbury Talcott	Hartford, Conn.
Rev. John Phelps Taylor, D.D.	Andover.
Walter Eliot Thwing	Roxbury.
Rev. Anson Titus	Somerville.
John Harvey Treat, A.M.	Lawrence.
Henry Edward Waite	Newton.
Joseph Burbeen Walker, A.M.	Concord, N. H.
John Collins Warren, M.D., LL.D.	Boston.
Charles Frederick White	Brookline.
Edward Henry Whorf	Boston.
Belvin Thomas Williston	Somerville.
Henry Ernest Woods, A.M.	Boston.

Not Members.

Mrs. Andrew N. Adams	Fair Haven, Vt.
Arthur Adams, B.A.	New Haven, Conn.
Charles Henry Alden, M.D.	Kendal Green.
Orrin Peer Allen	Palmer.
Azel Ames, M.D.	Wakefield.
Michael Anagnos, A M.	Boston.
Peter John Anderson, LL.B.	Aberdeen, Scotland.
Mr. and Mrs. Alfred Hinsdale Andrews	Lombard, Ill.
Henry Franklin Andrews	Exira, Ia.
Gustave Anjou, Ph.D.	Hasbrouck Heights, N. J.
James Newell Arnold	Providence, R. I.
Col. John Jacob Astor, B.S.	New York, N. Y.
Mrs. Margaret Lindsay Atkinson	Boston.
Mary Farwell Ayer	Boston.
Benjamin Aymar	New York, N. Y.
William Plumb Bacon, A.M.	New Britain, Conn.
Hollis Russell Bailey, A.M., LL.B.	Cambridge.
Edward Wild Baker, A.B.	Brookline.

Hon. Henry Moore Baker	Concord, N. H.
Mrs. Marion Strong Baker	Washington, D. C.
Francis Noyes Balch, A.M.	Jamaica Plain.
Thomas Willing Balch, LL.B	Philadelphia, Pa.
Frank Amasa Bates	South Braintree.
Stephen Berry	Portland, Me.
Paul Blatchford	Chicago, Ill.
James Knox Blish, M.A.	Kewanee, Ill.
Hon. Walter H. Blodget	Worcester.
Clarence Saunders Brigham, A.B.	Providence, R. I.
Mrs. Willard Irving Tyler Brigham	Littleton, N. H.
Benjamin Myer Brink	Kingston, N. Y.
Edward Judson Brockett	East Orange, N. J.
Francis Henry Brown, A.M., M.D.	Boston.
Mrs. Maria Annette Brush	Brooklyn, N. Y.
Percy Bryant, M.D.	Brooklyn, N. Y.
F. C. Burbank	Taunton.
Clarence Monroe Burton, B.S.	Detroit, Mich.
Mrs. Harriet Blackstone C. Butler	Dorchester.
Mrs. Florence E. Buzzell	Bangor, Me.
Augustine Caldwell	Ipswich.
Rev. Seth C. Cary	Boston.
James Read Chadwick, A.M., M.D.	Boston.
Francis M. Chandler	Cleveland, O.
Mrs. Alice B. Chase	Lynn.
Henry F. Church	Boston.
Harold Benjamin Clark, S.B.	New York, N. Y.
John Howe Clark, M.D.	Amherst, N. H.
Silas R. Coburn	Dracut.
Mary Louisa Trumbull Cogswell	Worcester.
Holdridge Ozro Collins, LL.B.	Los Angeles, Cal.
Maj.-Gen. Cyrus Ballou Comstock	New York, N. Y.
George Edward Congdon	Sac City, Ia.
Hon. William Ashmead Courtney	Newry, S. C.
Jane Elizabeth Cowles	Peacham, Vt.
J. Meadows Cowper, F.S.A.	Canterbury, Eng.
Rev. John Hosmer Cox	West Harwich.
J. Percy Crayon	Dover, N. J.
Irwin Chandler Cromack	Dorchester.
John F. Cronan	Boston.
F. H. Crossman	Berlin.
Francis Boardman Crowninshield, A.M.	Boston.
Montgomery Cumming	Washington, D. C.
Harvey Lear Currier	Manchester, N. H.
William S. Curtis	Colchester, Conn.
Samuel Newton Cutler, A.B.	Somerville.
Andrew McFarland Davis, A.M.	Cambridge.
William G. Davis	East Mansfield.
Ralph Davol	Taunton.
Judson Keith Deming	Dubuque, Ia.
Clarence Holbrook Denny, LL.B.	Boston.
Prof. Samuel Carroll Derby, A.M.	Columbus, O.
Louis Marinus Dewey	Westfield.
Walter G. DeWitt	New York, N. Y.
William E. Dodd, Ph.D.	Ashland, Va.
Richard Henry Winslow Dwight	Boston.
Mrs. Grace Williamson Edes	Cambridge.
Robert Holmes Edleston, F.S.A.	Darlington, Eng.
Rev. Lester H. Elliot	Waterbury, Vt.
W. C. Elliott	Reynoldsville, Pa.
Levi Henry Elwell, M.A.	Amherst.
Mrs. Wilimena Hannah (Eliot) Emerson	Detroit, Mich.
Ella Farmer	West Hingham.
Edgar Conway Felton, A.B.	Haverford, Pa.
Alexander Forbes	Aberdeen, Scotland.
Rev. Samuel Lankton Gerould, D.D.	Hollis, N. H.
Daniel Coit Gilman, LL.D.	North East Harbor, Me.
J. L. Glassock	Bishop's Stortford, Eng.
Lt.-Col. Thomas Allen Glenn	Tregaron, South Wales.
Alphonso Landon Goding	Elburn, Ill.
Nathan Goold	Portland, Me.
Lysson Gordon, A.B.	West Medford.
George S. Gould	Norwich, Conn.
Hon. Levi Swanton Gould	Melrose.
Henry Gray	London, Eng.
George Hiram Greeley	East Boston.
B. Frank Green	Newark, N. J.
Henry Winthrop Hardon, LL.B.	New York, N. Y.
Col. Sidney M. Hedges	Boston.
Arthur Hildreth	Boston.
Henry B. Hill	Boston.
Edward Hitchcock, LL.D.	Amherst.

Mrs. Orlando John Hodge	Cleveland, O.
Mrs. Frances Keturah Holton	Southwick.
Abel Hosmer	Oakland, Cal.
Edith Frances Howard	West Bridgewater.
David Webster Hoyt, A.M.	Providence, R. I.
Rev. Alfred Sereno Hudson	Ayer.
George W. Humphrey	Boston.
Jonas Sewall Hunt	Sudbury.
Fanny B. Hunter	Alexandria, Va.
David Russell Jack	St. John, N. B.
Donald Lines Jacobus	New Haven, Conn.
Charles William Jenks, A.B.	Bedford.
Cereno Percy Jones	Bath, Me.
Frederick John Kingsbury	Waterbury, Conn.
Rev. Harvey Merrill Lawson, Ph.B.	Putnam, Conn.
A. F. Lewis	Fryeburg, Me.
Charles C. Lord	Hopkinton, N. H.
Henry Morton Lovering	Taunton.
Fred Bates Lund, M.D.	Boston.
Robert Hall McCormick, LL.B.	Chicago, Ill.
Rev. Leander Cornelius Manchester, D.D.	Boston.
William Henry Manning	Ayer.
Charles William Manwaring	Hartford, Conn.
Mrs. Sophia (Smith) Martin	Hartford, Conn.
Walter K. Means	Milwaukee, Wis.
Capt. Joe Vincent Meigs	Boston.
Mrs. Ellen Stevens Melcher	New York, N. Y.
Rev. William Henry Meredith	Lynn.
Douglas Merritt	Rhinebeck, N. Y.
Thomas Middlemore	Melsetter House, Orkney.
Edward A. B. Mordaunt	London, Eng.
David Fellows More	Buffalo, N. Y.
Col. John P. Nicholson	Philadelphia, Pa.
Mrs. Edward Orton, Jr.	Columbus, O.
Alfred B. Page	Needham.
Moses Greeley Parker, M.D.	Lowell.
Langdon Brown Parsons	Rye, N. H.
Samuel F. Patterson	Concord, N. H.
Erastus Hibbard Phelps	Fair Haven, Vt.
George S. Porter	Norwich, Conn.
Mrs. Cornelia Lucretia Boardman Pulsifer	New Bedford.
George E. B. Putnam	Newton Centre.
Thomas C. Rand	Keene, N. H.
Sarah Elizabeth Read	Boston.
Col. Philip Reade	Washington, D. C.
Daniel H. Reed	Fitzwilliam, N. H.
Edward F. Reed	Everett.
Howard I. Reynolds	Philadelphia, Pa.
Hon. R. Goodwyn Rhett	Charleston, S. C.
Mrs. Harriet Emeline Richardson	Aurora, Ill.
Mrs. James Swift Rogers	Roxbury.
James Hardy Ropes, S. T. B.	Cambridge.
Elias Harlow Russell	Worcester.
Ely Morgan Talcott Ryder, Ph.B.	New Haven, Conn.
A. S. Salley, Jr.	Columbia, S. C.
Franklin Haven Sargent, A.B.	New York, N. Y.
Alfred William Savary, M.A.	Annapolis Royal, N. S.
W. Clark Schafer	Boston.
Mrs. Elizabeth Hubbell Schenck	Washington, D. C.
Philip Schuyler	Irvington-on-Hudson, N. Y.
Mrs. Mary Dow Scott	Newton.
Richard Cutts Shannon, LL.D.	Brockport, N. Y.
Mrs. Frederick C. Shattuck	Boston.
James Sheldon, Jr.	New York, N. Y.
James Shepard	New Britain, Conn.
John Kelley Simpson	Arlington Heights.
Rev. Charles N. Sinnett	Edmore, N. D.
Mary Elizabeth Sinnott	Philadelphia, Pa.
Caroline Smith	Newton Centre.
Frank Smith	Dover.
Arthur Willis Stanford, M.A.	Auburndale.
Rev. Charles Jason Staples, S. T. B.	Burlington, Vt.
Robert Edwards Carter Stearns, Ph.D.	Los Angeles, Cal.
George W. Steele	Pasadena, Cal.
Charles Ellis Stevens, LL.D.	Brooklyn, N. Y.
Arthur Collins Stewart	Jamaica Plain.
Henry Randolph Storrs, A.B.	Brookline.
Thomas Hale Streets, M.D., U.S.N.	Philadelphia, Pa.
Mrs. Elizabeth Orne Paine Sturgis	Worcester.
Martha Jane Tenney	Haverhill.
Rev. George A. Tewksbury	Concord.
George A. Thayer	Cincinnati, O.

Thomas Baldwin Ticknor, A.B.	Cambridge.
Frederic C. Torrey	Lakehurst, N. J.
Benjamin Franklin Trueblood, LL.D.	Boston.
John Atherton Tucker	Mattapan.
Rollin Usher Tyler, LL.B.	Haddam, Conn.
William Phineas Upham, A.B.	Boston.
Mrs. Alice B. Vail	Bangor, Me.
Nathan Van Patten	Schenectady, N. Y.
Mrs. Adelaide Cilley Waldron	Farmington, N. H.
Rev. Edwin S. Walker	Springfield, Ill.
Charles Strong Walton	Los Angeles, Cal.
Rev. Thomas Franklin Waters	Ipswich.
Samuel Gilbert Webber, M.D.	West Newton.
Charles T. Wells	Hartford, Conn.
Samuel Calvin Wells, A.M.	Philadelphia, Pa.
Mrs. Spier Whitaker	Raleigh, N. C.
Frank Herbert Whitcomb	Keene, N. H.
James Arthur Whitcomb	Boston.
Almira Larkin White	Haverhill.
Rev. Charles Harold Evelyn White, B.A., F.S.A.	Cambridge, Eng.
Mrs. Edwin Whitefield	Reading.
Frederick H. Whitin	New York, N. Y.
Charles Collyer Whittier	Roxbury.
Charles Henry Wight	New York, N. Y.
Charles S. Williams	New York, N. Y.
Henry Moreland Williams, LL.B.	Cambridge.
George Dikeman Wing	Kewanee, Wis.
William Arthur Wing	New Bedford.
Charles Jeptha Hill Woodbury	Lynn.
Francis Eben Woodruff, B.A.	Morristown, N. J.
Charles Woodruff Woolley	Buffalo, N. Y.
Tobias A. Wright	New York, N. Y.

REPORT OF THE CORRESPONDING SECRETARY.

PRESENTED BY HENRY WINCHESTER CUNNINGHAM, A.B.

BOSTON, December 30, 1905.

DURING the year 1905 the following persons have joined the Society:

William Fitzhale Abbot, A.B.	Worcester.
William Lothrop Allen, A.B.	Newton.
Edward Stevens Beach, A.B.	New York, N. Y.
Samuel Arthur Bent, A.M., LL.B.	Brookline.
Mrs. Sarah Delina Cropley	Boston.
William Horace Davis, M.D.	Boston.
Alfred Alder Doane	Boston.
Rev. William Phineas Fisher, A.B.	Andover.
Horace Tower Fogg	Norwell.
Mary Alice Frye	Wellesley.
Thomas Gamble, Jr.	Savannah, Ga.
Edmund Le Breton Gardiner, B.M.E.	Ridgewood, N. J.
Warren Fisher Gay, A.B., M.D.	Boston.
Theodore Woodman Gore	Newton.
Arthur Fairfield Gray	Watertown.
Francis Byron Greene	Boothbay Harbor, Me.
Rev. William Austin Hill, A.M.	Arlington.
Frederick Hills Hitchcock, A.B.	New York, N. Y.
Georgiana Elizabeth Holbrook	Sherborn.
Arthur Kinsman Hunt	Portland, Me.
Mrs. Elizabeth Bowers Jenny	Boston.
Nathaniel Thayer Kidder, B.A.S.	Milton.
Frank Bird Lamb	Westfield, N. Y.
Lambert Bigelow Lawrence	Northborough.
Henry Lefavour, B.A., Ph.D., LL.D.	Boston.
John Miner Carey Marble	Los Angeles, Cal.
George Ritchie Marvin, A.M.	Brookline.
Harriet Louise Matthews	Lynn.
Emory McClintock, A.M., Ph.D., LL.D.	Morristown, N. J.
Frank Palmer McIntyre	Boston.
Frank Remick Moore	Newton.
Elizabeth Todd Nash	Madison, Conn.
Mrs. Elisa White Osgood	Norwich, Conn.
Mrs. Annie Currier Pratt	Chelsea.
Henry Mellen Prentiss, A.M.	Bangor, Me.
Thomas Frazer Reddy, LL.B.	Boston.
Albert Edward Rhodes	Quincy.

Alexander Starbuck	Waltham.
James Arthur Stiles, A.B.	Gardner.
Reuben Samuel Swan	Brookline.
Charles Dana Thomas	Boston.
Edith May Tilley	Newport, R. I.
Dwight Tracy, M.D., D.D.S.	Norwich, Conn.
Mrs. Mary Duston Page Watson	Andover.
Mrs. Kate Haswell (Whitcomb) Wead . . .	Brookline.
Henry Adelbert Whitney	Bellingham.
John Barber White	Kansas City, Mo.

And the following who joined in December, but whose membership will date from January 1, 1906:

Edgar Oakes Achorn, A.B.	Newton.
Henry Austin Clark	New York, N. Y.
Jedidiah Dwelley	Hanover.
Thomas Bellows Peck, A.B.	Walpole, N. H.
William Joseph Rotch	Tisbury.
William Tudor, A.B.	Boston.

These Resident and Life Members joined the Society before 1860:

William Blake Trask, A.M.	August, 1851.
Alfred Poore	October, 1851.
Aaron Sargent	September, 1855.
Samuel Abbott Green, A.M., M.D., LL.D. . . .	June, 1858.
George Oliver Sears	October, 1859.

Rev. Edward Everett Hale, A.M., S.T.D., was elected a member in August, 1846, resigned in January, 1851, and was re-elected in June, 1891.

And these Corresponding Members joined before 1860:

Asa Warren Brown	May, 1852.
Edward Peacock, F.S.A.	January, 1858.
Charles Combault Moreau	October, 1858.
Seth Hastings Grant, A.M.	November, 1858.
Isaac John Greenwood, A.M.	April, 1859.
John Watts de Peyster, A.M., LL.D. . . .	June, 1859.
Henry Reed Stiles, A.M., M.D.	November, 1859.

REPORT OF THE TREASURER.

THE Treasurer submits herewith his annual report for the year ending December 31, 1905: —

The following is a detailed statement of all the investments of the Society, excepting the Real Estate: —

N. Y., N. H. & Hartford R. R. 5% Deb. due 1947	5	Bonds	$5,262.50
Butte Water Company 5% due 1921	5	"	4,000.00
Western Telephone & Telegraph Co. 5% due 1932 . . .	3	"	3,147.50
Northern Pacific & Great Northern R. R. 4% due 1921 . . .	5	"	2,243.75
Western Union Telegraph Co. 4½% due 1950 . . .	5	"	5,207.50
Flint & Pere Marquette R. R. 5% due 1939 . . .	5	"	5,756.25
Concord & Montreal R. R. 3½% due 1920 . . .	5	"	5,125.00
City of Providence 3% due 1930	1	"	1,194.01
American Telephone & Telegraph Co. Collateral Trust 4% due 1929	10	"	10,000.00
Fremont & Elkhorn R.R. 6% due 1933	3	"	3,000.00
Chicago Stock yards 4% due 1940	10	"	10,250.00
Chicago, Rock Island & Pacific R. R. 4% due 1934	4	"	3,890.00
Detroit, Grand Rapids & Western R.R. 4% due 1946 . . .	3	"	2,985.00
Central R. R. of New Jersey 4% due 1913	3	"	3,000.00
N. Y. Central & Hudson River M. C. 3½% due 1998	3	"	2,700.00
Missouri Pacific R. R. Collateral 5% due 1917	2	"	2,135.00
Chicago, Burlington & Quincy R. R. South Western Div. 4% due 1921	3	"	3,036.67
West End Street Railway . . .	50	Shares	4,256.25
Boston & Maine R. R. . . .	50	"	9,918.75
Old Colony R. R.	100	"	17,559.76
Cambridge Gas Light Co. . . .	15	"	3,011.15
Austin City Water Co.	25	"	500.00
Mortgage on Real Estate In Roxbury		"	1,000.00

Total Stocks, Bonds and Mortgages $109,179.09

General Income Account.

This account has been charged with the following items, viz.: —

Maintenance, House and Repairs	$ 691.89	
Heat and Light	419.38	
Taxes and Insurance	12.00	
Printing, Stationery, and Postage	1,028.16	
Miscellaneous Expenses	482.35	
Printing Register	2,023.09	
Books for Library, balance of account	84.24	
Salaries	4,417.37	
Total charges for the year to this account		$9,158.48

and has been credited with the following, viz.: —

Unrestricted Investment Income	$4,149.86	
Subscriptions to Register	1,319.22	
Miscellaneous Registers sold	526.46	
Admissions and Annual Dues	2,711,00	
Books sold	25.00	
Interest	414.52	
Waters Gleanings in England	70.50	
Donations, etc.	194.07	
Total credits for the year to this account	$9,410.63	
Excess of income over expenses	252.15	
		$9,158.48

Bonds Purchased in 1905.

$4,000 Chicago, Rock Island & Pacific 4% due 1934	$3,890.00	
$3.000 Detroit, Grand Rapids & Western 4% due 1946	2,985.00	
$3,000 Central R. R. of N. J. 4% due 1913	3,000.00	
$3,000 New York Central & H. R. R. R. 3½% due 1998	2,737.33	
$2,000 Missouri Pacific Collateral 5% due 1917	2,178.88	
$3,000 Chicago, Burlington & Quincy S. W. Division 4% due 1921	3,036.67	17,827.88

The total receipts of Cash for the year have been $30,070.79, derived from the following sources, viz.

Income Bond Investment	$2,800.00
Income Stock Investment	1,030.63
Income Mortgage Investment	99.30
Humphrey Mortgage paid off	600.00
William Sumner Appleton Fund	6.00
Walter Titus Avery Fund	950.00
Henry Bond Fund	16.00
Henry Bond Fund Income and Principal	1,843.18
Cushman Genealogical Fund	33.00
Cushman Genealogical Fund Income and Principal	193.10
Robert Henry Eddy Town Record Fund	500.00
William Blanchard Towne Memorial Fund	88.86
Robert Charles Winthrop, Jr. Fund	3,000.00
Life Membership Fund	692.00
General Income	94.07
Prerogative Court of Canterbury Wills, sales	459.49
Waters' Gleanings in England, sales	70.50
New-England Historical and Genealogical Register, Consolidated Index, subscriptions	4,075.60
Printing, Stationery and Postage	11.34
Miscellaneous Expense	7.33
Interest on Deposits	94.52
Books Sold	26.75
Books for Library, rebate	4.63
Donations for Binding	11.00
Admission Fees and Annual Dues	2,713.00
Subscriptions to N. E. H. G. Register	1,319.22
Miscellaneous Registers Sold	526.46
Proceeds of sale of Bushnell Street Houses, Ashmont, including Rents	5,214.29
Rents, Westmoreland Street Houses, Ashmont	391.69
" Houses on Somerset St. and Allston Place	3,198.83
Total Cash Receipts	$30,070.79

The total Cash disbursements for the year have been $39,435.16, paid out for the following purposes: —

Society's House, Care and Repairs . . .	$ 691.89	
Heating and Lighting	419.38	
Binding	336.77	
Salaries	4,417.37	
Printing, Stationery, and Postage . . .	1,039.50	
Miscellaneous Expenses (Telephone, Safety Vault, etc.)	489.68	
Printing New-England Historical and Genealogical Register	2,183.09	
Books Purchased	1,048.87	
Profit on Books Sold	1.75	
Consolidated Index, Publication Account .	3,993.66	
Admissions Fees (rebate)	2.00	
Taxes and Insurance	12.00	
Prerogative Court of Canterbury Wills, Publication account	700.39	
Towne Memorial Income, printing Volume VI of Memorial Biographies	1,139.25	
Purchase of Bonds (details on last page):	17,827.88	
Premium on purchase and sale of securities .	147.77	
Purchase of 2 shares Cambridge Gas Light Co.	413.75	
Real Estate, 2 Westmoreland Street, repairs, taxes, etc.	294.06	
Real Estate, 4 Westmoreland Street, repairs, taxes, etc.	151.91	
Real Estate, 69 Bushnell Street, repairs, taxes, etc.	222.06	
Real Estate, 73 Bushnell Street, repairs, taxes, etc.	141.01	
Real Estate, 3 Allston Place, repairs, taxes, etc.	399.04	
Real Estate, 5 Allston Place, repairs, taxes, etc.	906.93	
Real Estate, 7 Allston Place, repairs, taxes, etc.	368.64	
Real Estate, 16 Somerset Street, repairs, taxes, etc.	2,007.89	
Cataloguing	78.62	
		$39,435.16

Cash Resumé.

Cash on hand, January 1, 1905	$10,749.37	
Cash Receipts as above stated	30,070.79	
		$40,820.16
Cash Disbursements as above		39,435.16
Balance of Cash, December 31, 1905		$1,385.00

Balance Sheet, December 31, 1905.

	Resources.	Liabilities.
Society's Building	65,486.90	
Library, Fixtures and Furniture	$ 96,450.42	
Stocks, Bonds and Mortgages	109,179.09	
Real Estate Investment on Somerset Street and Allston Place	26,011.30	
Real Estate in Ashmont	14,942.95	
N. E. Hist. and Gen. Register Consolidated Index, Publication account	7,391.62	
Registers on hand	3,987.92	
Prerogative Court of Canterbury Wills, Publication account	1,560.08	
Cash	1,385.00	
Premium on purchase and sale of securities	712.95	
Uncollected Coupons and dividends	500.00	
Society's Building Fund		$62,804.21
Donors' Free Fund		1,305.00
Librarian Fund		12,763.13
Library Fund		90,929.85
Ebenezer Alden Fund		1,000.00
William Sumner Appleton Fund		6.00
Walter Titus Avery Fund		950.00
John Barstow Fund		1,200.00
Robert Charles Billings Fund		5,000.00
Robert Charles Billings Book Fund		5,000.00
Henry Bond Fund		2,459.83
John Merrill Bradbury Fund		2,500.00
Edward Ingersoll Browne Fund		1,000.00
Jonas Gilman Clark Fund		2,000.00
Thomas Crane Fund		1,000.00
Cushman Genealogical Fund		382.55
Pliny Earle Fund		1,000.00
Robert Henry Eddy Fund		56,787.00
Charles Louis Flint Fund		5,000.00
John Foster Fund		5,000.00
Moses Kimball Fund		5,000.00
William Latham Fund		1,000.00
Ira Ballou Peck Fund		1,000.00
Mary Warren Russell Fund		3,000.00
Samuel Elwell Sawyer Fund		4,000.00
Anne Elizabeth Sever Fund		5,000.00
George Plumer Smith Fund		10,000.00
Joseph Henry Stickney Fund		1,000.00
William Cleaves Todd Fund		11,000.00
William Blanchard Towne Memorial Fund		4,000.00
William Blanchard Towne Memorial Fund Income		1,520.07
Robert Charles Winthrop, Jr., Fund		3,000.00
Cyrus Woodman Fund		1,000.00
Life Membership Fund		18,639.74
J. Henry Lea, Balance of account		76.90
Binding, Accumulated Income		283.95
	$327,608.23	$327,608.23

Nathaniel C. Nash, *Treasurer*.

The undersigned hereby certify that they have examined the accounts of the Treasurer of the New-England Historic Genealogical Society for the year 1905, and find his books properly kept. The securities were examined and found to be in accordance with the books.

Boston, January 4, 1906.

Chas. S. Penhallow, } *Auditors.*
E. D. Barbour, }

REPORT OF THE TRUSTEES OF THE KIDDER FUND.

Boston, Dec. 30, 1905.

Balance on hand, December 31, 1904		$65.63
Dividend July 1, 1905		40.00
Interest on deposit		2.29
		$107.92
Paid Walford Bros., books	$50.70	50.70
Balance on hand		$57.22

W. Tracy Eustis,
Nathaniel J. Rust,
Elbridge H. Goss.
} *Trustees.*

REPORT OF THE HISTORIAN.

Presented by Rev. George Moulton Adams, D.D.*

NECROLOGY FOR 1905.

[*The dates in the first column indicate the years of election.*]

Corresponding Members.

1846. Lucius Manlius Boltwood, A.B., of Grand Rapids, Michigan, was born in Amherst, Massachusetts, June 8, 1825, and died in Grand Rapids, February 28.

1885. Charles William Darling, of Utica, New York, was born in New Haven, Connecticut, October 11, 1830, and died in Asbury Park, New Jersey, June 22.

1847. George Edward Day (Rev.) D.D., of New Haven, Connecticut, was born in Pittsfield, Massachusetts, March 19, 1815, and died in New Haven, July 2.

1883. Joseph Foster, M.A., of London, England, was born in Sunderland, England, March 9, 1844, and died in London, July 29.

1877. George William Marshall, LL.D., F.S.A., of London, England, was born in Warwickshire, England, in 1839, and died in Barnes, Surrey, England, September 12.

1847. James Davie Butler (Rev.) D.D., LL.D., of Madison, Wisconsin, was born in Rutland, Vermont, March 15, 1815, and died in Madison, Nov. 20.

Life Members.

1870. William Claflin, LL.D., of Newton, Massachusetts, was born in Milford, Massachusetts, March 6, 1818, and died in Newton, January 5.

1865. Otis Brigham Bullard, of Washington, District of Columbia, was born in Holliston, Massachusetts, August 18, 1815, and died in Washington, April 25.

1881. Joshua Montgomery Sears, A.B., of Boston, was born in Yarmouth, Massachusetts, Dec. 25, 1854, and died in Southborough, Massachusetts, June 2.

1886. Robert Charles Winthrop, Jr., A.M., of Boston, was born in Boston, December 7, 1834, and died there June 5.

1889. Leander Miller Haskins, of Rockport, Massachusetts, was born in Rockport, June 20, 1842, and died there August 1.

* Rev. Dr. Adams died 12 January, 1906.

1885. FREDERICK HASTINGS RINDGE, A.B., of Los Angeles, California, was born in Cambridge, Massachusetts, December 21, 1857, and died in Yreka, California, August 29.

1864. BENJAMIN BARSTOW TORREY, of Brookline, Massachusetts, was born in Pembroke, Massachusetts, November 22, 1837, and died in Brookline, September 11.

1889. STEPHEN SALISBURY, A.M., LL.B., of Worcester, Massachusetts, was born in Worcester, March 31, 1835, and died there November 16.

Resident Members.

1895. ANDREW NAPOLEON ADAMS (Rev.), A.B., of Fair Haven, Vermont, was born in Fair Haven, January 6, 1830, and died there March 13.

1904. ELMER HEWITT CAPEN (Rev.), D.D., LL.D., of Somerville, Massachusetts, was born in Stoughton, Massachusetts, April 5, 1838, and died in Somerville, March 22.

1899. JAMES SWIFT ROGERS, A.B., of Boston, was born in Danby, Vermont, March 28, 1840, and died in Boston, April 9.

1891. WILLIAM HENRY PULSIFER, of Newton, Massachusetts, was born in Boston, November 18, 1831, and died in Washington, District of Columbia, April 9.

1900. JAMES CLARK DAVIS, A.B., of Boston, was born in Greenfield, Massachusetts, January 19, 1838, and died in Boston, May 11.

1887. WILLIAM SWEETZER HEYWOOD (Rev.), of Dorchester, Massachusetts, was born in Westminster, Massachusetts, August 23, 1824, and died in Dorchester, May 27.

1904. HERBERT CORNELIUS ANDREWS, of Los Angeles, California, was born in Chicago, March 19, 1883, and died there, May 31.

1896. JACOB CHESTER CHAMBERLAIN, B.A., M.S., of New York City, was born in India, July 3, 1860, and died in New York, July 28.

1892. GEORGE TRUMBULL HARTSHORN, A.M., of Taunton, Massachusetts, was born in Worcester, Massachusetts, October 20, 1860, and died in Taunton, August 22.

1884. TIMOTHY THOMPSON SAWYER, Litt.D., of Charlestown, Massachusetts, was born in Charlestown, January 7, 1817, and died in Magnolia, Massachusetts, September 4.

1890. ELIJAH BRIGHAM PHILLIPS, of Brookline, Massachusetts, was born in Sutton, Massachusetts, August 20, 1819, and died in Brookline, September 13.

1901. JAMES MADISON BARKER, LL.D., of Pittsfield, Massachusetts, was born in Pittsfield, October 23, 1839, and died in Boston, October 3.

1897. GEORGE EDWARD ATHERTON, of Brookline, Massachusetts, was born in Charlestown, Massachusetts, May 2, 1845, and died in Brookline, October 31.

1899. MYRON SAMUEL DUDLEY (Rev.), A.M., of Newington, New Hampshire, was born in Peru, Vermont, February 20, 1837, and died in Newington, November 17.

1899. GEORGE ALLEN DARY was born in Taunton, Massachusetts, November 30, 1842, and died December 30.

Deaths that occurred in previous years, but not recorded until now.

1886. Hezekiah Spencer Sheldon, of West Suffield, Connecticut, a life member, was born in Suffield, June 23, 1820, and died August 29, 1903.

1875. L'Abbé Henri Raymond Casgrain, D.Litt., F.R.S.C., of Quebec, Canada, a corresponding member, was born at Rivière Ouelle, Canada, December 16, 1831, and died in Quebec, February 11, 1904.

1847. Amos Bugbee Carpenter, of West Waterford, Vermont, a corresponding member, was born in Waterford, May 25, 1818, and died there April 26, 1904.

1871. Walter Titus Avery, A.B., of East Moriches, New York, a corresponding member, was born in New York City, January 18, 1814, and died in East Moriches, June 10, 1904.

1902. Louis Pindle White, of Whatcom, Washington, a resident member, was born in Preston County, Virginia (now West Virginia), December 20, 1856, and died July 10, 1904.

1898. Ira Davenport, of Bath, New York, a life member, was born in Hornellsville, New York, June 28, 1841, and died in Bath, October 6, 1904.

MEMOIRS

OF THE

NEW ENGLAND HISTORIC GENEALOGICAL SOCIETY.

Arranged by Rev. GEORGE MOULTON ADAMS, D.D., Historian.*

THE following pages contain obituary notices of members who died during the year 1905, with the addition of six deceased in preceding years. The notices are arranged in the order in which the deaths occurred.

1903.

HEZEKIAH SPENCER SHELDON, of West Suffield, Connecticut, a life member since 1886, died August 29, 1903. He was a native of Suffield, and was born June 23, 1820. His father was Julius Curtis Sheldon, and his mother's maiden name was Mindwell Spencer. He was a descendant of Isaac Sheldon, of Dorchester, Windsor, and Northampton, through Jonathan,[2] Elijah,[3] Martin,[4] Julius C.[5]† Julius Curtis Sheldon was born in Suffield, where the family had lived for several generations, December 12, 1791, and died December 5, 1873. His mother was born in Suffield, April 22, 1797, and died August 23, 1885.

The subject of this sketch was married, November 1, 1843, to Almira C., daughter of Barlow Rose. They had no children. He died in Suffield, leaving only a brother, Martin J. Sheldon, of Suffield. In his letter of acceptance to the Society he says, "My education to the age of seventeen years, was in the common school; polished up with a few terms at the Connecticut Literary Institution of Suffield. Then I commenced a most instructive course in the study of human nature, by teaching district schools five winters, boarding 'round, and working on the homestead farm in the summers. The broad acres of that farm, through five successive generations, are still in the family name. Alas, only the sons of the Green Isle till its soil!

"I was a Suffield representative in the Connecticut legislature, for the years 1857 and 1881, and have held many local town

* After the death of Rev. Dr. Adams, William Richard Cutter, A.M., who was appointed Historian, completed the arrangement and editing of the Memoirs.

† Mr. Sheldon preserved the following facts regarding these ancestors:—Isaac, d. July 27, 1708; Jonathan, b. May 29, 1687, d. Suffield, April 10, 1769; Elijah, b. Northampton, Nov. 2, 1719, d. Suffield, June 1, 1785; Martin, b. Feb. 1, 1762, d. Sept. 4, 1848.

offices. I am vice-president (serving as president) of the First National Bank of Suffield. I am collecting, transcribing, and printing (privately) the 'Documentary History of Suffield in the Colony and Province of the Massachusetts Bay in New England, 1660–1749.' I have printed already, in pamphlet form, 195 pages, and I hope to complete it. I am the author of a pamphlet entitled 'Suffield and the Lexington Alarm in April, 1775,' 22 pp. I have written the article 'Suffield' for the 'Hartford County Memorial History.'" An examination of his documentary history of Suffield shows it to be a work of much merit. He adopted the documentary, in preference to the narrative form, because it was his belief that "no history can be so complete, or valuable, as the records themselves, accurately transcribed."

1904.

Henri Raymond Casgrain, D. Litt., F. R. S. C., was born December 16, 1831, at Rivière Ouelle, Province of Quebec, Canada, and died February 11, 1904, in the Convent of Les Religieuses du Bon-Pasteur, Quebec, where he had retired during the last thirty years of his life. His father was Hon. Charles Eusèbe Casgrain, his mother Elizabeth Anne Baby, daughter of Hon. James Baby, of Sandwich, Ontario.

Henri Raymond Casgrain was educated at Sainte Anne College, and made his entry in the world as a medical student at McGill University, Montreal. About a year afterwards, he left to enter the Seminary of Quebec, where he was admitted to holy orders. He devoted a few years to the ministry and was professor at Ste. Anne College, until he was obliged to take rest on account of his eyes, which were gradually losing sight as the result of his night studies.

Generally, during fifteen or sixteen consecutive years, he used to pass the winters in Europe, particularly in Paris, where he formed the acquaintance of divers literary and scientific men. There he collected a considerable number of historical documents, the greater part of which were printed in Quebec by the Provincial Government.

The principal works of l'Abbé Casgrain are: "Légendes Canadiennes," "Biographies Canadiennes," "Histoire de l'Hotel Dieu de Québec," "Un Pélérinage au Pays d'Evangéline," which was crowned by the Académic Française, and "Montcalm et Lévis," 2 vols.

The Abbé was a friend of Parkman. Their correspondence relating to the Acadians, in which he rectified some historical errors of his friend, brought forth the "Documents inédits sur le Canada et l'Amérique," in 1888. They are intended to be the counterpart and correction of Akin's collection of "Nova Scotia Archives," published in 1869. In view of writing the Pélérinage, the Abbé twice visited the principal places of the old Acadian settlements, and examined the Archives of Nova Scotia, at Halifax. Then he crossed to London for additional researches, more particularly in the British Museum. From thence he continued to Paris for the same object.

The Abbé Casgrain was a corresponding member of this Society, elected in 1875.

By Hon. PHILIPPE BABY CASGRAIN, K.C.

AMOS BUGBEE CARPENTER, of West Waterford, Vermont, a corresponding member, elected in 1847, was born in Waterford, May 25, 1818, and died in that town, April 26, 1904. He lived all his life on the home farm in West Waterford, and married, June 24, 1847, Cosbi B., daughter of Ezra and Hannah (Burleigh) Parker, of Littleton, New Hampshire, who was born June 24, 1828, and died March 25, 1904. He was appointed postmaster when the post office at West Waterford was first established, in 1855, and resigned the office in 1888, being succeeded by his wife, who was postmistress at the time of her death. He was elected in 1888 a representative in the legislature for two years. He was survived by five of a family of seven children.

His life extended back to the first generation of Waterford inhabitants, and almost to the beginning of the town's history. He was identified with nearly every one of its enterprises, had an excellent memory, and knew thoroughly its history and its people, and no one was better qualified to write its history. Instead, however, his time for twenty years was devoted to an effort to prepare a history of the Carpenter family, involving an extensive correspondence and travel into different parts of New England. This work was published by him in 1898, under the title "A Genealogical History of the Rehoboth Branch of the Carpenter Family in America." In the preparation of this work,—like other genealogists of his day,—he went from town to town in quest of every one of his name, making note of every record, tradition, item of information, land ownership, and probate record,—not forgetting the memorials of the dead in the different burial-places of the towns which he visited.

By S. F. CUTTING, and others.

WALTER TITUS AVERY, A.B., of East Moriches, New York, a life member since 1871, died on June 10, 1904. He was born in the city of New York, January 18, 1814, the only child of John Smith[6] Avery and his wife Amelia Titus. His parents were natives of Huntington, Long Island. John S. Avery, his father, was a successful merchant of New York City. His mother was a daughter of Israel and Temperance (Norton) Titus. His father was the son of John[6] and Ruth (Smith) Avery. John[6] Avery was graduated at Yale College in 1761; son of Rev. Ephraim,[4] who was graduated at Harvard College in 1731 (REGISTER, 9: 173); son of Rev. John,[3] Harvard College 1706; son of Robert[2]; son of Dr. William,[1] of Dedham.

Walter Titus Avery was graduated from Columbia College in 1832. He began in the profession of civil engineering on the location of the New York and Croton Aqueduct in 1836, and was civil engineer on the Hudson River Railroad, from 1847 to 1850. He then became a merchant, located in Stockton, California, from 1851 to 1856, and then in New York City, from 1856, and onwards till his retirement.

He was a benefactor of the Society, leaving to it a bequest of one thousand dollars.

Mr. Avery left to the Dedham Historical Society of Dedham, Mass., the sum of one thousand dollars, and quite a collection of books and genealogical manuscript of the Avery family. He also left to the Pocumtuck Valley Memorial Association of Deerfield, Mass., the sum of one thousand dollars. A friend writes: "Mr. Avery was greatly interested in the genealogy of the Avery family, and spent both time and money in quest of information relating to the early history of the family, not only in all parts of this country, but in England as well. In features and complexion he resembled his mother, though possessing strongly the Avery characteristics. In California he was engaged in selling supplies for the miners under the firm name of Avery and Hewlett. He returned to New York in 1856, and formed a partnership with an old friend as importers and commission merchants under the firm name of H. E. Blossom and Co. At Mr. Blossom's death in 1863, Mr. Avery continued the business with a former associate, the firm being Avery and Lockwood. Retiring from business in 1885, Mr. Avery passed most of his time in a quiet village on the Great South Bay, Long Island, dividing his time between his favorite pastimes of yachting, driving and reading. He was well known among his friends as a student of Shakespeare." He was unmarried.

LOUIS PINDLE WHITE was born in Preston County, Virginia (now West Virginia), December 20, 1856, the son of Thornton and Bersheba Ann (Davis) White. His father was a native of Maryland and his mother of Virginia. The names of his mother's parents were Thomas H. Davis and Mary Hawley. He was educated in the common school branches only, and previously to 1892, conducted a department store at Elk Garden and Terra Alta, both in West Virginia. He was cashier of the Terra Alta Bank, from 1892 to 1897, and afterwards president and manager of the Bank of Whatcom, at Whatcom, State of Washington. He also held the office of vice-president of the Washington State Bankers' Association, and president of the board of regents of the State Normal School in Whatcom, and belonged to the Knights Templar, Mystic Shrine, and Knights of Pythias. Of the last named organization he was a past chancellor.

He married, May 4, 1882, Mary Ellen, daughter of George Washington and Margaret Ann (Silbaugh) Burke. By this marriage there were eight children, born between 1883 and 1899, by name Clarence George Thornton, Jessie Pearl, Lewis Pinckney, Lilly, Harry Stanhope, William Bruce, Helen Frances Luella, and Margaret Virginia.

Of his ancestors, his grandfather William White married Charlotte Johnson, and his great-grandfather Henry White married Mary Felton. Thomas H. Davis, his mother's father, was a soldier of the war of 1812, and Capt. John Davis, his mother's grandfather, was a soldier in the Revolutionary War. His father Thornton White was born March 29, 1823, and his mother Bersheba Ann (Davis) White was born October 6, 1827.

Louis P. White died July 10, 1904. He was a resident member of this Society since 1902.

IRA DAVENPORT, of Bath, New York, a life member of this Society, to which he was elected in 1898, was born in Hornellsville, New York, June 28, 1841, and died in Bath, in that state, October 6, 1904. He was the son of Ira and Lydia (Cameron) Davenport, and a descendant of Thomas Davenport, who settled in Dorchester, Mass., in 1635.

Ira Davenport was educated at the Union school, Bath, N. Y., and at Russell's school, New Haven, Conn. He was state senator, 1878–82; state comptroller, 1882–84; the unsuccessful Republican candidate for governor of New York in 1885; and a representative from Bath in the forty-ninth and fiftieth Congresses, 1885–89. In the New York senate, he served both terms as chairman of the Committee on Commerce and Navigation. He was married to Katherine Lawrence Sharpe, on April 27, 1887. On his mother's side of the family he was a descendant of Ewen Cameron, of Inverness, Scotland, born 1730. Dugald Cameron, son of Ewen, and father of Lydia (Cameron) Davenport, was born in Inverness, in 1776, and became one of the first settlers of Bath, N. Y. Dugald Cameron died at Albany, while a member of the Legislature, March 30, 1828.

1905.

Rev. Elmer Hewett Capen, D.D., LL.D., was born in Stoughton, Massachusetts, April 5, 1838, the son of Samuel Capen and his wife Almira Paul. His paternal line of ancestry was Samuel,[7] Elisha,[6] Samuel,[5] Samuel,[4] Samuel,[3] Samuel,[2] Bernard[1] Capen. His maternal line of ancestry was Almira,[7] Samuel,[6] Samuel,[5] Samuel,[4] Samuel,[3] Samuel,[2] Richard[1] Paul. His remaining ancestral lines are in the Bailey, Payson, Gay, Withington, Fales, Fisher, Fenton, Shepherd, and Morse families.

Dr. Capen was fitted for College at Green Mountain Institute, Woodstock, Vermont, and entered Tufts College in 1856, graduating in 1860. At the first election after he was twenty-one years of age, he was elected to the Massachusetts House of Representatives, and bore an honorable part in the conduct of its business. He studied at Harvard Law School, and was admitted to the Bar in 1863. He soon, however, determined to enter the Christian ministry. He was ordained and installed as pastor over the Independent Christian Church at Gloucester, Massachusetts, October 5, 1865, where he remained nearly five years, and because of the ill-health of his wife, removed to St. Paul, Minnesota. But change of climate did not grant the needed restoration, and he returned to New England, becoming pastor in Providence, R. I. He came to the presidency of Tufts College, March 13, 1875, and presided over its interests until his decease, March 22, 1905.

His services for Tufts College can scarcely be estimated. Under his presidency the enrollment of students rose from eighty-three to one thousand, and the number of the faculty from fifteen to nearly two hundred. President Capen was an administrator. He had great concerns in his charge and executed them with skill and foresight. He was a person of commanding presence, and was recognized as a leader among the people. From 1889 to his death he was a member of the Massachusetts State Board of Education.

In the Christian pulpit, Dr. Capen was in the foremost rank, and as an orator concerning academic subjects had few equals. While alert in promoting the freest spirit in scholastic affairs, and in the furtherance of Christian ideals, he was ever foremost in his adherence to the central principles of the Universalist Church. He was a student among students, and a man among men. The world is richer and better because of his service, and his memory is cherished not only by the student body and alumni of his College but by citizens and lovers of good government throughout our country.

President Capen married, January 3, 1866, Letitia Howard, daughter of Hon. Thomas Mussey, one time a resident of New London, Connecticut. She died September 5, 1872. He married, February 12, 1877, Mary Leavitt, daughter of Oliver Edwards,

Esq., of Brookline, Massachusetts, who survives him. Their three children are Samuel Paul Capen, professor of Modern Languages, Clark University, Worcester; Ruth Paul Capen, Tufts College 1902; and Rosamond Edwards Capen. President Capen became a resident member of this Society in February, 1904.

By Rev. Anson Titus.

William Henry Pulsifer, was born in Boston, November 18, 1831, the eighth in descent from Benedict Pulsifer, who settled at Ipswich, Massachusetts, in 1662, and who is the first of the name of Pulsifer known to have lived in America.

Mr. Pulsifer attended the Grammar and High Schools of the city of Boston. Upon leaving school, he engaged in mercantile business in Boston, and resided there, with occasional extended business visits to the West, until 1859, when he removed to St. Louis, Missouri, where he became engaged in the manufacture of white lead and other chemical products. He continued to reside in St. Louis until 1890, when he retired from active business and returned to the east, residing in the winter at Newton Centre, Massachusetts, and at Washington, District of Columbia, and passing the summer at his country place at Nonquitt, on Buzzard's Bay, Massachusetts.

During his residence in St. Louis, Mr. Pulisifer was prominent in many business and financial enterprises. He was for many years President of the St. Louis Lead and Oil Company, Treasurer of the American Central Insurance Company, a director of the National Bank of Commerce and of several other corporations. He was a fellow of the American Association for the Advancement of Science; a member of the St. Louis Academy of Science; of the Anthropological Society of Washington; of the National Geographic Society; of the American Folk Lore Society; of the American Forestry Association; of the New England Historic Genealogical Society, admitted in 1891; of the Society of the Sons of the American Revolution; and of the Bostonian Society. He was also a member of the Union Club in New York and of the Cosmos and Metropolitan Clubs in Washington.

Mr. Pulsifer died April 9, 1905, at the Highlands in Washington. He leaves a widow, and one daughter, Mrs. H. Duncan Wood of New York.

Otis Brigham Bullard. Like very many of the older families of New England, the Bullards emerge into our history in the fourth decade of the seventeenth century. Benjamin Bullard was one of the group of pioneers who ventured to settle west of Charles River, near where Medfield, Sherborn, and Millis (formerly East Medway) corner together; and doubtless he and his growing family shared with the Fairbanks, Lelands, Morses, Daniels, and others, the protection of their good stone garrison-house on the shore of Bogistow Pond, when King Philip's war party attempted its destruction by means of the cartload of burning flax.

Isaac and three generations of Samuels succeeded Benjamin in the ancestry of him whose career we now call to mind. Of these, Samuel Bullard, Esq., of Holliston (1742–1816) was a noted surveyor and almanac-maker. Capt. Samuel Bullard (born 1777) inherited the homestead of four generations of Bullards of Holliston, a daughter town of old Sherborn, which Benjamin Bullard helped to found. At this homestead Otis Brigham Bullard was born, August 18, 1815, when Madison was president of the United States, when the sterner aspects of Puritanism still prevailed in old New England homes, when still "a man was famous according as he had lifted up axes upon the thick trees."

The boy had a mind receptive toward the educational opportunities that came to him. Enough of the grandfather's blood ran in his veins to make him interested in mathematics and surveying, and under Matthew Metcalf he assisted as engineer on the old Boston and Worcester railroad in 1839. He had flattering opportunities to make some application of mathematics his life-work, but somehow he early felt himself drawn away from family traditions and so-called practical affairs into the pursuit of music as a profession. Availing himself of such training in this direction as circumstances then allowed, he devoted his best energies during the most active years of his long life to the elevation of public taste through this chosen fine-art. As choir-master and as teacher of singing classes of boys and girls in his native town and elsewhere, he left a distinct mark upon his time, and very many bear testimony to his usefulness. He was greatly aided in this work by his self-effacing, devoted wife, Abigail Cutler, whom he married January 11, 1843, and with whom he lived in most helpful relations for more than sixty-one years.

As a successful public school teacher in his young manhood, later as a member of the school board for many years, as town treasurer, as loyal and efficient member of his home church to his life's end, as neighbor, citizen, and friend, many of his best qualities were brought into exercise. He was one of the first to support the Free-soil party. He was always in warmest sympathy with the cause of public righteousness. Having once adopted an opinion or allied himself with a cause, he, with innate persistency, held to it faithfully at all hazards. His mathematical instincts and training made him accurate in observation and statement of facts, and just because of this quality he was a valuable source of information concerning the past.

In 1869 he left Holliston for permanent residence in Washington, District of Columbia, where for twenty years or more he was proprietor of the Washington Conservatory of Music. His death there, from a street accident, April 25, 1905, may have come to him somewhat as a relief in the loneliness of old age, without children or near relatives. Yet a long life, spent, as his was, in close contact with the men and events of his time, gathers up a fund of knowledge and experience which the world loses with regret.

He was a life member of this Society, admitted in 1865.

By Prof. U. WALDO CUTLER.

JAMES CLARKE DAVIS, born in Greenfield, Massachusetts, January 19, 1838, died at his home in Jamaica Plain, May 11, 1905. His father, George T. Davis, was born in 1810, graduated at Harvard in 1829, lived in Greenfield from 1833 to 1865, and died in Portland in 1877. He was an excellent lawyer, a noted wit, a singularly agreeable converser, a most hospitable entertainer, a genial, lovable man. He was a son of Wendell Davis of Sandwich, and grandson of Thomas Davis of Plymouth. His mother, Harriet T. Davis, was a daughter of Nathaniel P. Russell of Boston, and was described by James Freeman Clarke, for whom James Clarke Davis was named, as having a brilliant intellect, easy flashing wit, self-possessed graceful demeanor—all the qualities which charm society. She died in 1862.

Mr. Davis attended school at the Deerfield and Phillips Exeter Academies, graduated at Harvard in 1858, belonged to five college societies, studied law in his father's offiee and at the Harvard Law School, was admitted to the bar in 1861, entered his father's firm, and in 1862 removed to Boston where he practised until his death. For several years he was clerk to the attorney general, and afterwards was assistant attorney general. He prepared for the city of Boston a "Digest of Massachusetts Decisions of Municipal Interest," which was published by the city in 1866. He belonged to the Union and St. Botolph Clubs, and was secretary of the former for four years, and one of its trustees. He was secretary and a trustee of the Adams Nervine Asylum, one of the council of the Boston Bar Association, and one of the class committee and also secretary of his college class. For several years he was one of the school committee of Boston. He was a resident member of this Society, elected in 1900.

On June 3, 1873, he was married to Alice W. Paine of Worcester, daughter of Charles Paine. They had two daughters. They lived on Mt. Vernon Place in Boston till 1883, and afterwards in Jamaica Plain, where they maintained a delightful home, made sad in 1902 by the death of the elder daughter. Mrs. Davis and the younger daughter survive. His only brother, Wendell, and his only sister, Ellen, died several years ago, both unmarried.

Mr. Davis had little taste for court practice and gradually withdrew from it, and at last devoted himself almost exclusively to the care of trust funds and the management and settlement of estates. He was often appointed receiver of insolvent companies, and in all such cases did his work to the great satisfaction of the court. In his experience there was no such thing as swerving from the strictest ideas of right. Those who knew him well reposed implicit confidence in his integrity, fidelity and accuracy.

In politics Mr. Davis was a Republican; and in religious faith a Unitarian. He attended the church of Rev. Dr. James De Normandie of Roxbury, with whom he had a warm friendship.

By Hon. CHARLES ALLEN, LL.D.

WILLIAM SWEETZER HEYWOOD was born in Westminster, Massachusetts, August 23, 1824, the son of John and Betsey (Edgell) Heywood. His ancestors in the direct line were John,[1] who was settled in Concord in 1656, John,[2] Phineas,[3] Timothy,[4] John.[5] On his mother's side he was descended from William[1] Edgell of Woburn, through William,[2] William,[3] and Betsey.[4] Reared on his father's farm in the southerly part of Westminster, he was educated in the common schools of his native town, and at Leicester Academy, also at Clinton Liberal Institute, Clinton, Oneida County, New York. It has been said of him that he was "endowed by nature with a superior mental and moral constitution."

His father attended the Universalist Church at Westminster, and under the direction of Rev. Varnum Lincoln of that church, and later of Rev. Adin Ballou at Hopedale, Mr. Heywood prepared for the christian ministry and was ordained May 25, 1849. He early became interested in the great moral reforms of temperance, anti-slavery, woman's rights, and the cause of peace. In 1848 he took up his residence with the Hopedale Community, an attempt at "practical christian socialism." At Hopedale he preached as an independent practical christian, and was also associate editor of the *Practical Christian*, published by the Hopedale Community, meantime serving the Community as its president, until it virtually failed in 1856.

On May 11, 1851, Mr. Heywood married Abigail Sayles, daughter of Rev. Adin and Abigail (Sayles) Ballou. With her he established in 1856 the Hopedale Home School, which continued successfully for seven years. In 1864 he left Hopedale, and entering into fellowship with the Unitarian denomination, he was settled as pastor of Unitarian societies in Scituate, Hudson, Holyoke, the Parmenter St. Chapel in Boston, and at Sterling. Everywhere he was a devoted teacher and pastor, and always charmed by his "simple, guileless goodness."

In 1888 his native town of Westminster voted an appropriation for a history of the town, and he was selected as the town's historian. The history is a work of great merit, a volume of nearly a thousand pages, published in 1893. More recently he edited and published some of the writings of his father-in-law, Rev. Adin Ballou. Mr. Heywood was elected a resident member of this Society in 1887. He made frequent use of its library, and was actively interested in its affairs, particularly as a member of the committee on graveyard inscriptions.

An invalid for more than two years, Mr. Heywood died at his home in Dorchester, Massachusetts, May 24, 1905. Besides his widow he left an only child, Lucy Florence, born July 28, 1861, the wife of John Holden, Esq., of New York, and two young grandchildren. Those who were privileged to know William Sweetzer Heywood have remarked the singular beauty of his domestic life, his entire genuineness, and his spiritual helpfulness.

By Hosea Starr Ballou.

Herbert Cornelius Andrews, son of Alfred Hinsdale and Ella Cornelia (Matson) Andrews, was born in Chicago, Illinois, March 19, 1883. He was descended from John Andrews (often spelt Andrus) and Mary, his wife, who were among the earliest settlers of Farmington, Connecticut, John Andrews being admitted to the church there on May 9, 1658; made freeman May 20, 1658; and his name appearing among the 84 proprietors in 1672.

From these ancestors his line of descent was as follows: John[1] Andrews and Mary ——— ; Daniel[2] Andrews and Eunice ——— ; Daniel[3] Andrews and Mabel Goffe; Hezekiah[4] Andrews and Anna Stedman; Ezekiel[5] Andrews and Roxana Hinsdale; Alfred[6] Andrews and Mary Lee Shipman; Alfred Hinsdale[7] Andrews and Ella Cornelia Matson; Herbert Cornelius[8] Andrews.

As a child he was far from robust, and during his later years there were always physical limitations. He was absorbed in his studies, including music, and every study possessed for him an intense interest. He graduated from the High School at Oak Park, Illinois, in 1899, with high honors, and later attended the University of Chicago, and Colorado College, Colorado Springs. At school and college, in addition to the regular studies, he mastered stenography and typewriting; took a course in advertising, and salesmanship; and for a time studied designing. While at Colorado College he studied harmony, and showed marked ability in musical composition.

After a year at Colorado College, he became so broken in health that he was obliged to give up all further thought of school and devote himself to an outdoor life. He spent a year alone in Flagstaff,

Arizona. He next went to Pasadena, California, where after a few months his health had so much improved that he became anxious for definite occupation, and accepted an engagement with the Los Angeles agents of the A. H. Andrews Co. of Chicago, of which his father is President. After spending a year in business, he refused the offer of a fine position in San Francisco, as the opportunity had now come to him to devote his entire time to genealogical research, a work absolutely congenial to him and to which he had for several years devoted all time not otherwise engaged. That he came naturally by his great love for genealogical research is plainly seen when we consider that he was the grandson of Alfred Andrews of New Britain, Connecticut, who spent so many years in work of this kind, and whose labors bore fruit in the "Andrews Memorial," "Hart Genealogy," and "Genealogy and Ecclesiastical History—First Church, New Britain."

He established a studio at Los Angeles, and devoted himself exclusively to genealogical work, becoming in a very short time the recognized authority in genealogy and heraldry on the Pacific Coast. The work which he accomplished in the few years in which he was engaged in genealogical matters was surprisingly large. He compiled many family histories—making a specialty of this line of work, in the execution of which he was enabled to show his superior artistic taste, in addition to partially compiling and entirely editing the Hinsdale Genealogy (the manuscript of which is completed and the publication expected at an early date), and he had also compiled the Matson Genealogy, which is now ready to go into the hands of the printer, as well as completed a manuscript of 1,000 pages on "Early Connecticut Families," besides having devoted much time and attention to the foreign ancestry of many of the early families in this country. For some months before and at the time of his last illness, he was principally engaged on the history of a branch of the Rindge family, and he kept at the dearly beloved manuscript days after he should have laid it down, so eagerly did he hold on to his life work.

In December, 1904, he was obliged to undergo an operation for appendicitis, but which upon examination proved to be sarcoma of a very aggravated type. He apparently recovered from the operation and was able to get to his studio and to attend to some work, but a relapse occurring, he was brought back to Chicago in April, and failing very rapidly, died, after much intense suffering, on May 31, 1905. His funeral took place at the home of his parents in Lombard, Illinois, and his remains were laid to rest in the cemetery at that place. The following tribute was paid to him by a relative: "What makes it so clear in regard to the future of this young man is that he seemed before he left us to have made adjustment to all the conditions passing or probable. He had the open mind and the forward look. That attitude discovers and reveals. It is not too much to say that he had native ability to enter upon any of the paths open to human effort. But better, he had the disposition to work along any or all of them as exigency might seem to require. A fine scholar, yet he made a valued hand in a lumber mill. He kept the guiding thread in any department of thought and action to which he was introduced. The last year of his life shows his Plato read and marked. His mind was opened once and forever to the treasures of literature. When he left us he was an authority in genealogy and heraldry, a remarkable result for a man so young. Some of us thought that this study would inevitably make of him an historian. We are sure that from his fine sensibility and keen perception, we should have had something that would rank high in truth and taste."

Although only twenty-two years of age at the time of his death, he has left a distinct mark, and this Society is a loser by his untimely decease. Realizing what he had already accomplished in his short life, one cannot but deplore the loss of what he undoubtedly would have done had he been allowed to live the allotted "three score years and ten."

He was a resident member of the New England Historic Genealogical Society, elected in 1904.

By Alfred Lyman Holman.

Joshua Montgomery Sears, A.B., whose death occurred at his farm in Southborough, Massachusetts, June 2, 1905, after a somewhat protracted illness, was born at Yarmouthport, Massachusetts, December 25, 1854. He was descended in direct line from Richard Sears, the Pilgrim, who came to this country in the "Leyden" in 1630.

His father, Joshua Sears, born at Yarmouthport, August 20, 1791, came to Boston and established himself in business, where from small beginnings he accumulated a large fortune. He married, in February, 1854, Phœbe, daughter of Deacon Robert Snow of Brewster, by whom he had only one child, the subject of this sketch. Mrs. Sears died January 1, 1855; and Mr. Sears two years later, February 7, 1857.

A good part of the early life of Joshua M. Sears was passed in the family of the late Alpheus Hardy, who was one of the trustees of his father's estate. He attended school at Andover, Massachusetts, going later to Stuttgardt and Berlin, and from there to Yale College, where he graduated in the class of 1877. While in Europe, he became the owner of the Freiligrath and Curtius Libraries, the former of which is now a part of the fine library in the

Boston house on Arlington Street; the latter he presented to Yale College.

He married, September 17, 1877, Sarah Carlisle, daughter of Charles F. Choate, then of Cambridge, Massachusetts, who, with two children, a son and daughter, survives him. In college, Mr. Sears was a member of the base-ball nine of his class, and all through life he showed an active interest in athletics. As a business man, he was connected with many important interests. He was for many years a director of the Second National Bank, the Massachusetts Hospital Life Insurance Company, and the Old Colony Railroad. He was treasurer for over twenty years of the Children's Hospital.

He was prominent in the yachting world, as one of the syndicate which built the defender "Puritan," and as the owner of many fine yachts. His latest purchase, the steam yacht "Sultana," was being fitted out for a summer cruise at the time of his death. He passed much of his time—as much as his business cares would permit—on his beautiful farm in Southborough, and devoted a great deal of thought and energy to its development. Of all his possessions, this was the nearest and dearest to him; and it was there he turned when his last and fatal illness came upon him.

Mr. Sears was a man of generous impulses, devoted to his friends, and always ready to help others, giving freely of his time and money. In college he assisted many of his class-mates; many struggling musicians have been the recipients of his bounty; and his charities to all have been without number—all done without ostentation or show of any kind, known to none outside the beneficiaries except those intimately connected with his business affairs.

He was a life member of this Society, elected in 1881.

By Charles Sherburne Penhallow, A.B.

Charles William Darling died June 22, 1905, in Asbury Park, New Jersey. He was born October 11, 1830, in New Haven, Connecticut, and was the son of Rev. Charles Chauncey Darling, a Presbyterian clergyman of New York City, by his wife Adeline E., daughter of William and Eliza Dana of Boston, Massachusetts, and granddaughter of Robert Davis, an officer of artillery in the war of the Revolution. His grandfather, Dr. Samuel Darling, a graduate of Yale, and a physician of New Haven, married Clarinda, daughter of Rev. Richard Ely of Saybrook, Connecticut. His great-grandfather, Judge Thomas Darling of New Haven, who married Abigail Noyes (granddaughter of Rev. James Pierpont of New Haven, one of the founders of Yale College), was the son of Samuel Darling, who was born in England in 1695, and came to New Haven in 1722' where he died in 1760.

Charles William Darling was educated in New York City, and graduated from New York University. After his graduation, he traveled in England and on the continent. Upon his return to the United States he connected himself with the National Guard of the State of New York, and when Edwin D. Morgan was elected Governor he became a member of his staff. In 1864 he was appointed aid-de-camp on the staff of Gen. Benjamin F. Butler, then in command of the Army of the James. The following year, when Reuben E. Fenton was elected Governor, he received an appointment on his staff as assistant paymaster general, and in 1867 he was appointed military engineer-in-chief of the State of New York, with the rank of brigadier-general.

Gen. Darling in 1869 again visited England, and was the recipient of many courtesies from the English authorities. He subsequently traveled extensively in Europe, Asia and Africa, and his absence abroad covered a period of about ten years. Upon his return, in 1879, he removed from New York City to Utica, New York, where he resided until his death. He was connected with many historical and scientific societies; was a member of the American Authors' Guild; associate member of the Victoria Institute of India; honorary member of the Egyptian Exploration Company, and secretary of the fund for the promotion of its work. For several years he was president of the Young Men's Christian Association. He was a corresponding member of this Society, elected in 1885.

Gen. Darling married, in 1857, Angeline E., daughter of Jacob A. Robertson of New York City. He left no immediate family.

From the *New York Genealogical and Biographical Record.*

REV. GEORGE EDWARD DAY, D.D., elder son of Gad and Roxanna (Rice) Day, was a descendant of Robert Day, who came from Ipswich, England, to Boston, Massachusetts, in the bark "Elizabeth" in April, 1634, and was one of the original proprietors of Hartford, Connecticut, having probably journeyed thither through the wilderness with Rev. Thomas Hooker in 1636. Through his mother he was descended from Thomas Yale, uncle of Elihu Yale, in whose honor Yale College received its name. He was born March 19, 1815, in Pittsfield, Massachusetts, but in 1822 removed with his parents to New Haven, Connecticut.

After graduation from Yale College in 1833, he taught two years in the Institution for the Deaf and Dumb in New York City. In the education of this class he was deeply interested, and in 1836, while a student in the Yale Seminary, wrote on the subject for the American Journal of Science. The results of his investigations, made by request during subsequent visits abroad, were published in a "Report on Institutions for the Deaf and Dumb in Europe, especially Germany," in 1845, and in one on similar institutions in Holland and Paris, in 1861. On completing his theological course in 1838, before entering the active ministry, he was Instructor in Sacred Literature in the Yale Divinity School for two years. He was ordained pastor of the Union (Congregational) Church in Marlborough, Massachusetts, December 2, 1840, continued there seven years, and then from January, 1848, to May, 1851, filled the pastorate of the Edwards Church, Northampton, Massachusetts.

Following ten years of pastoral work, he was for fifteen years Professor of Biblical Literature in Lane Theological Seminary at Cincinnati, Ohio. In 1863 he established *The Theological Eclectic*, which he edited through seven volumes, when it was merged with the *Bibliotheca Sacra.* While abroad in the summer of 1865 he purchased in Great Britain and on the continent large additions for the library of Lane Seminary. In April, 1866, he returned to New Haven as Professor of the Hebrew Language and Literature and Biblical Theology in the Yale Divinity School, and maintained his official connection with the school to the close of his long life. The value of his services in the erection of the present buildings was gratefully acknowledged by his associates, and his self-sacrificing devotion to his work, both in instruction and outside of the class-room, was manifest. In 1888 he became Dean of the Divinity School, and for three or four years thereafter shared the duties of his professorship with Professor Harper, afterwards President of Chicago University. Upon his retirement from the office of Dean in 1895, he was made Professor Emeritus.

Professor Day retained his enthusiasm for linguistic study, acquiring new languages even in his later years. He translated from the Dutch Van Oosterzee's "Biblical Theology of the New Testament" in 1871, and edited an American edition of Oehler's "Biblical Theology of the Old Testament" in 1883. By taste and experience he was well fitted for his share in the revision of the English version of the Bible, and served as secretary of the American Revision Committee, and a member of the Old Testament Company from its formation in 1871. He was thoroughly familiar with the history and present condition of the great missionary work of the church, and at his own expense collected and catalogued an exceedingly valuable missionary library, now numbering about seven thousand five hundred volumes. This he gave to the Yale Divinity School, and also provided funds for its maintenance and increase. He was active in efforts which resulted in the erection of a monument to Rev. John Robinson, the "Pilgrim" pastor in Leyden.

Professor Day died July 2, 1905, in his ninety-first year. Injuries resulting from a fall had confined him to his house for fifteen months previous. He married, in 1843, Amelia H., daughter of Henry and Mary Oaks. She died in 1875, and he afterward married Olivia Clarke Hotchkiss, who survives him. The latter was the daughter of Lewis and Hannah (Trowbridge) Hotchkiss. There were no children by either marriage.

Professor Day compiled "A Genealogical Register of the Descendants in the Male Line of Robert Day, of Hartford, Conn., who died in 1648," first edition, New Haven, 1840; second edition, 1848. He was a corresponding member of this Society from 1847, a member of the Royal Asiatic Society of Japan, and a corresponding member of the American Oriental Society from 1848.

By THOMAS ROSSITER BARNUM, A.B.

JACOB CHESTER CHAMBERLAIN, B.A., M.S., died in New York, July 28, 1905, aged forty-five. Descended in the seventh generation from William[1] Chamberlain of England, whose appearance of record in New England was in 1648, he was born in India, July 3, 1860, eldest son of Jacob[7] Chamberlain, M.D., D.D. (Jacob,[6] Isaac,[5] Isaac,[4] Jacob,[3] Jacob[2]), and Charlotte (Birge) Chamberlain, daughter of Chester Birge. He married at Albany, New York, June 12, 1895, Annie Mary Irwin, daughter of William P. Irwin. Mrs. Chamberlain and an only child, Anna Irwin, survive.

Having been graduated with honor from Rutgers College, New Brunswick, New Jersey, in 1882, he took a post-graduate course in chemistry, and thereafter devoted himself to electrical research and engineering. He was actively connected with several of the great electrical undertakings of the last twenty years in this country, and patented important electrical inventions. A pioneer and leader in the application of electric motive-power to boats, he was, at the time of his death, general manager of the Automatic Refrigerating Company. Holding the degree of Master of Science, he became one of the early members of the American Institute of Electrical Engineers. He was one of the governing board of the New York Engineers' Club, and an influential member of the Colonial Club, the Marine Field Club, and the Grolier Club. In the objects of the Grolier Club he was specially interested, and his collection of first editions of early American authors was already regarded as one of the best in the United States. To the enlarging and perfecting of that collection, he was constantly and enthusiastically devoted.

He was also an experienced, accomplished genealogist. One of the founders and most generous supporters of the Chamberlain Association of America, he gave to it much of its early inspiration in genealogical directions. At the time of his death he was engaged in genealogical researches whose scope far exceeded the Chamberlain ancestry in America. Yet his highest excellence was not in his notable electrical discoveries and achievements; nor in his marked business success; nor in his skilful, important work as bibliophile and genealogist. His highest worth was in his character and personal culture. He was faithful to the welfare of both his city and his country. In him gentleness was blended with strength, and amiableness with resolute integrity. Well born and well brought up, he appeared, even to those who knew him most intimately, to have no remotest inclination to any form of dishonor. Comely, courteous, joyous, with a genius for friendship, he was the light of his beautiful home, a centre of attraction among many acquaintances, and an example of perfect uprightness in wide business relations. He was, all in all, a Christian gentleman of rarely noble type.

He was a resident member of this Society, elected in 1896.

By Rev. LEANDER TROWBRIDGE CHAMBERLAIN, D.D.

JOSEPH FOSTER, M.A., the antiquary and genealogist, was born in Sunderland, England, March 9, 1844, the son of Joseph and Elizabeth (Taylor) Foster. He was a nephew of Birket Foster, the artist. Educated in private schools of North Shields, Sunderland, and Newcastle-on-Tyne, he inherited his genealogical faculty from his grandfather, Myles Birket Foster. After editing four volumes of Lancashire and Yorkshire pedigrees, he transcribed the admission registers of the four Inns of Court, a herculean task, extending over several years. The acquisition of the register of our oldest University, coupled with those of the Inns of Court, with which they dovetail, illustrating and annotating each other, materially strengthened Mr. Foster's position; but still, before he could hope to grapple effectually with so arduous a task as the annotation of the earlier "Alumni Oxoniensis," it was necessary that all the Bishops' certificates of institutions to livings (since the reformation), now deposited in the Public Record Office, should be laid under contribution, with the result that we have these 150,000 institutions, etc., alphabetically arranged as a clergy list, and have Mr. Foster's greatest work comprised in eight volumes.

His best known critical work was undoubtedly "Chaos," under which category he classed for the first time all known "soi-disant baronets." "Chaos" formed a minor portion of the "Peerage, Baronage and Knightage," compiled and edited by Mr. Foster in 1880–1884, for the pedigrees of which the records of the Heralds' College were unreservedly placed at his service. From the study of this prolific worker have also emanated such useful works as "Men at the Bar," "Scottish Members of Parliament, 1857–1882," "Gray's Inn Admission Register, 1521–1889," "Our Noble and Gentle Families of Royal Descent," and several minor family histories. Within recent years have been published "Some Feudal Coats of Arms," "Two Tudor Books of Arms," "Some Feudal Lords and their Seats," and "Banners, Standards, and Badges," the last three of which Mr. Foster edited for the De Walden Library.

Mr. Foster married, August 12, 1869, Catherine Clark, daughter of George Pocock. He was a corresponding member of this Society, elected in 1883. He died in London, July 29, 1905.

This sketch is chiefly from the London *Times*.

LEANDER MILLER HASKINS, of Rockport, Massachusetts, who died in that town, August 1, 1905, aged sixty-three, was a life member of this Society from 1889. He was a native of Rockport, born June 20, 1842, was fitted for college at Phillips Andover Academy, and was graduated at Dartmouth College in 1862. He then taught school in his native town, and afterwards employed himself in civil engineering. In 1863, during the Civil War, he was appointed clerk in the commissary department of the army, and was attached to the Nineteenth Army Corps. He became later a clerk in the Navy Department.

After the war, he engaged in the fish and commission business on Long Wharf, Boston, and in this business he was engaged at the time of his death. He was one of the pioneers in the fish isinglass business. He served as a representative in the legislature for one year. He was a director in the Faneuil Hall National Bank of Boston, and in the Rockport National Bank, and other corporations; and was a member of the Boston Art Club, and many other organizations. He was also interested in yachting. He was married, his wife dying some years before him, and he is survived by an adopted daughter, Louise Canfield, of Montclair, New Jersey.

By his will, Mr. Haskins named his adopted daughter as residuary legatee, and provided that there shall be established first a trust fund of $65,000, to continue fifteen years after the execution of the will. After enumerating how the income shall be distributed among relatives and friends, direction was given that the income of one thousand dollars be given to the First Congregational Church of Rockport for general purposes, and the income of another thousand to the public library in that place, for the purchase of books. From the trust fund the following religious organizations in Rockport will receive the amounts named: First Congregational Church, ten thousand dollars for a parsonage fund; Methodist, Baptist, Universalist, Episcopal, and Catholic churches, each three hundred dollars. The house and thirty acres of land in Rockport, and forty acres more in Rockport, are to be used for hospital and park purposes. After these provisions are carried out, ten thousand dollars is to be set apart, the income to be used to aid worthy indigent students of Rockport in taking courses in Dartmouth College or the Massachusetts Institute of Technology, the first named to be preferred.

GEORGE TRUMBULL HARTSHORN, A.M., was born in Worcester, Massachusetts, October 20, 1860, and the only child of George Franklin and Isabella Frink (Trumbull) Hartshorn.

He was fitted for college at Adams Academy, Quincy, and entered Harvard in 1878. After graduating from Harvard College in 1882, he pursued the study of chemistry, and, in 1883, took the degree of Master of Arts. He was for three years instructor of chemistry in Harvard College, working in association with Professor Charles Jackson. In 1886 he gave up his work at Harvard and went to Taunton, where for some years he went on with his chemical research work.

On November 17, 1891, he married Miss Alice Roberts of Cambridge, Massachusetts. They had one son, George Dean Hartshorn. The last few years of Mr. Hartshorn's life were devoted almost entirely to the study of musical composers and their works. Of an intensely musical nature, and gifted with a rare facility of playing easily any musical instrument, all branches of the study interested him, and he collected a fine library of old and rare musical books.

Mr. Hartshorn died August 22, 1905, at his home in Taunton, after an illness of several months. He was a resident member of this Society, elected in 1892.

By ALICE ROBERTS HARTSHORN.

FREDERICK HASTINGS RINDGE was born in Cambridge, Massachusetts, December 21, 1857, and died in Yreka, California, August 29, 1905. He was the son of Samuel Baker Rindge, a merchant of large estate, whose acts of private beneficence and public liberality have left a permanent impress upon Boston and Cambridge.

In early youth he attended the schools of Cambridge and Boston, receiving his final preparation for college from Dr. James Laurence Laughlin. During his vacations, and while a young lad, his mind was broadened by extensive travel under the direction of his father. In 1870 he went to California, and during 1871 and 1872 he visited most of the places of interest in Europe. Entering Harvard College, he was graduated in 1879. His whole life was an exemplification of the stern rule of probity and religious adherence to the principles which characterized his forefathers, softened by a gentle consideration for the opinions of those differing from him, and by charity for the frailties of the erring.

After the close of his college career, he was called to assume the grave responsibilities of his father's estate. Those responsibilities were borne in a manner surpassing the expectations of his most sanguine friends, as the record of the many official and private resolutions and testimonials from his native city, and his many benefactions, public improvements and religious endowments, in the land of his chosen home on the Pacific Coast, show.

He was prostrated in the last year of his college course by an illness, from which he suffered during the remainder of his life.

On May 27, 1887, he was married to Miss Rhoda May Knight, of Trenton, Michigan, the daughter of James and Rhoda Lathrop Knight, and from this marriage were born two sons and a daughter:—Samuel Knight, at Los Angeles, April 9, 1888; Frederick Hastings, Jr., at Redondo, September 5, 1890; and Rhoda Agatha, at Santa Monica, April 20, 1893.

Early in his California life, Mr. Rindge purchased the historic Rancho Topanga Malibu, a tract of many thousands of acres of most picturesque mountain, valley and canon. Here he erected a commodious residence, and in his charming book, "Happy Days in Southern California," he has given a graphic account of this mountain home and his happy life there with his family.

A few years since he changed his residence to Santa Monica, of which he was one of the most enterprising and progressive citizens.

The evils of intemperance had been impressed upon his heart from his youth, and he gave neither countenance nor excuse for the sale of intoxicating spirits. He devoted his best energies to abolish the traffic. A member and trustee of the Methodist Episcopal Church of Santa Monica, by his generosity the religious edifice was greatly enlarged, beautified, and furnished. Nor did his activities in the religious life cease with his removal to Los Angeles. He wrote for private distribution several books of meditations, and upon his election as President of the Young Men's Christian Association in Los Angeles he instituted measures which in their fruition will give to that organization a home whose equal does not exist upon the Pacific Coast. He once said: "I derive the greatest satisfaction in my life in Christian work."

In his private charities, and relief for the destitute, he took none into his entire confidence, and not until the great record shall be read will be known the story of all his good deeds.

His public benefactions have for the most part become known. In testimonial of the love for his native place, and the home of his ancestors, he erected and presented to the city of Cambridge its municipal building, a public library, and the Didactic Public Buildings, and he founded and supported for many years the Manual Training School for boys. In Salem, he founded and endowed the Children's Island Sanitarium.

In the management of his estate, with keen foresight and discriminating judgment he invested largely in California, principally in the central and southern sections, and with the improvements made thereon, these have greatly increased in value. As a relaxation from his many business obligations, he gave considerable attention to scientific research and the early history of America. He was a life member of the New England Historical and Genealogical Society, elected in 1885, and of the Archæological Institute of America. His collections in numismatics and in the aboriginal fine arts were of such value, that he was induced to place them in the loan exhibition of the Peabody Museum of Harvard College and the Boston Museum of Fine Arts; and in the hall, erected as an annex to his spacious mansion in Los Angeles, he gathered an exhibit of the Pacific Coast archæology, and memorials of the early history of California, which has no equal among private collections.

Upon the instititution of The Harvard Club of Southern California, he was unanimously elected its President; and in view of the expected visit to Los Angeles of Mr. Roosevelt, who was his friend and associate in college, he was elected for a second term.

Mr. Rindge was a descendant of Robert Kinsman, of England, who was born in 1629, and came to the Massachusetts Bay Colony, settling in Ipswich. His daughter Mary was married to Captain Daniel Rindge of Ipswich.

Mr. Rindge was also a descendant of Daniel Harrington, who was born and died in Lexington, Massachusetts, a participant in the fight of Lexington and Concord, and who gave patriotic service during the War of the Revolution, retiring with the rank of Captain. His young son, Levi Harrington, was drummer of his father's company, and participated in the siege of Boston and in subsequent campaigns. He was also descended from Samuel Baker, one of the Ipswich Company, which marched for the relief of Lexington on April 19, 1775.

By Holdridge Ozro Collins.

Timothy Thompson Sawyer, Litt.D., was born in Charlestown, Massachusetts, January 7, 1817, the son of William and Susanna (Thompson) Sawyer. His father was a descendant of Thomas Sawyer who settled in Lancaster, Massachusetts, in 1634. Mr. Sawyer's mother was the daughter of Timothy and Mary (Frothingham) Thompson of Charlestown, who were descendants of James Thompson and William Frothingham, both of whom were members of the company who came over with Governor Winthrop, to establish a colony, in 1630.

Mr. Sawyer's uncle was engaged in the hardware and ship chandlery business in Merchants' Row, and there when he was fourteen years old, Mr. Sawyer commenced his business career, and there he remained until the death of his uncle, June 27, 1837. He then engaged in the ship chandlery business on his own account, until a promising opportunity offered to join a new firm to engage in the shipment of ice. The style of the Ice Company was originally Gage, Hittinger and Company, afterwards Gage, Sawyer and Company. The business was interesting and successful, and Mr. Sawyer continued in it until 1860.

Mr. Sawyer was a director in the Bunker Hill Bank, from 1851 until his death, and was president from 1885 to 1890. In 1854 he was chosen one of the trustees of the Warren Institution for Savings, and was president of the Institution from 1880 till 1903, when he resigned on account of advanced age. After holding many minor offices in Charlestown, Mr. Sawyer was mayor of the city for three years, 1855–1857, and was in 1857 also a member of the House of Representatives of Massachusetts. In 1858 he was a member of the Senate. In 1872, after the resignation of Edward Lawrence, the first president of the Mystic Water Board, he was chosen Mr. Lawrence's successor, and held the position until Charlestown was annexed to Boston. Afterwards, when the Cochituate and Mystic Water Boards were merged and the new Boston Water Board commenced its duties, he was chosen chairman of that Board, and held the position for the three years succeeding.

Mr. Sawyer has shown some literary ability and has written many articles for the local papers. Some of these articles have been assembled in a book of over five hundred pages, entitled "Old Charlestown, Historical, Biographical, Reminiscent." The book is an interesting and graceful memorial of the many eminent citizens who have in times past lived under the shadow of Bunker Hill. But it is more than that. It is a complete illustration of the author's abounding loving kindness towards his fellow men.

Mr. Sawyer was one of the original organizers and one of the most efficient promoters of the Public Library of Charlestown, and gave to it liberally from his private funds. He was president of its board of managers from the time of its opening, January 1st, 1862, until it became a branch of the Boston Public Library, after the two cities were annexed in 1874. He was for many years chairman of the standing committee of the First Universalist Church in Charlestown. For more than forty years, he was one of the board of trustees of Tufts College. In 1903 the degree of Litt. D. was conferred upon him by the college.

Mr. Sawyer was a citizen of Charlestown until the fall of 1885, when he removed to Dartmouth Street in Boston. He died in Magnolia, Massachusetts, September 4, 1905. He was a most lovable gentleman, actuated through his long career by the highest and best motives only, rejoicing in and aiding the successes or sympathizing in and relieving the failures of others, dispensing affectionate good cheer to the world he met, and ever striving to make it a better and happier world for his having lived in it. He was a resident member of this Society, admitted in 1884.

By C. P. Sampson.

Elijah Brigham Phillips, (Ebenezer Morgan,[7] Dr. Ebenezer Humphrey,[6] Ensign Jonathan,[5] Joseph,[4] Theophilus,[3] Rev. George,[2] Christopher[1]), was born in West Sutton, Massachusetts, August 20, 1819, and died at his home in Brookline, September 13, 1905. His ancestry of the seventeenth century was wholly of the Puritan migration and within the Bay Colony. The three best known of that clergy were among his ancestors, George Phillips of Watertown, Richard Mather of Dorchester, and John Cotton of Boston.

Mr. Phillips's schooling was obtained in the Westborough village schools, supplemented by a year at Leicester Academy. He was, his life long, an insatiable reader. He commanded a style in his correspondence and reports, ready, clear and direct. He liked to recall that as a boy he had trundled flour on his barrow from the Concord store to the door of the Philosopher. When nineteen years old, he entered the employ of the Boston and Worcester Railroad Company at Boston, and thus began an exceptional career of fifty years in railroad service. These years coincided with the half century which witnessed the commencement and development of steam transportation, with all which that meant to the world. He played a not unimportant part in that development. He was in turn Boston freight agent of the Company, its general agent, and its master of transportation.

In 1852 he was called to Ohio, as superintendent of the Cleveland, Norwalk and Toledo Railroad, then building. Six years later he returned to Boston, as superintendent of the Boston and Worcester Railroad, where he remained seven years. He was elected in September, 1865, president of the Michigan Southern and Northern Indiana, which Company united with its neighbor, in 1869, to form the present Lake Shore and Michigan Southern, and he was the first president of the consolidated company. The following year he organized the Phillips and Colby Construction Company to build the Wisconsin Central. For several years he operated it in conjunction with the Milwaukee Northern.

In May, 1879, he was chosen president of the Eastern Railroad of Massachusetts. Shortly after, he was one of a commission of three to arbitrate between the State and the Fitchburg Railroad. The early part of 1883 he devoted to the management of the Toledo, Cincinnati and St. Louis Railroad; later in that year he was elected president of the Fitchburg Railroad. Four years of negotiations with the governor and his council representing the State ownership of the Hoosac Tunnel, and with the two corporations immediately to the west of it, resulted in the union of the four properties in one organization. He retired from railroad affairs in 1890, having completed a half century of strenuous railroad work, during which he had been foremost in introducing, as railroad science progressed, the many new methods and appliances which made for efficiency, economy and safety.

As the late Henry Pratt of the Michigan Central Railroad said of him, he was "a good disciplinarian; he set an example of fidelity; he hated shams; faithful to the interests committed to his care; straightforward; an example of commercial honesty." Bishop Charles Edward Cheney, of Chicago, speaks of:—"The Christian faith, the spotless integrity, the fidelity to conscience, the family affection, the never wavering loyalty to friends which marked the long life of Elijah Brigham Phillips."

He married, February 2, 1845, Maria Rebecca, daughter of Henry (born in 1784 in Walberton, co. Sussex, England) and Mehitable (Copeland) Ayling, of Boston. A devoted and happy union of forty-nine years was severed by the death of his wife, May 2, 1894. Their three children survive them.

Mr. Phillips became a resident member of this Society in 1890.

Hon. JAMES MADISON BARKER, LL.D., of Pittsfield, Massachusetts, Judge of the Supreme Court of the State, died suddenly in Boston, October 3, 1905. He was a resident member of the Society since 1901. He was born in Pittsfield, October 23, 1839, the son of John V. and Sarah (Apthorp) Barker.

He enjoyed the best educational advantages, preparing for college in the public schools of his native town, at Hinsdale Academy and at Williston Seminary. Entering Williams College in 1856, he was graduated with high rank in the class of 1860. He studied law, first in a law office at Bath, New York, and in 1862 and 1863 at Harvard Law School. In the latter year he was admitted to the Massachusetts bar, and at once formed a partnership with Major Charles N. Emerson of Pittsfield, a lawyer of note, who served with distinction through the Civil War. Two years later, Major Emerson was appointed to the internal revenue service, and Mr. Barker became associated with Thomas P. Pingree in the practice of the law, the partnership continuing until Judge Barker's elevation to the bench. This was in November, 1882, when a vacancy occurred on the Superior Court bench.

His wide knowledge of the law, keenness of comprehension, analytic quality of mind, and aptitude for clear incisive statement, contributed to his success as a judge, and the record shows that while on that bench his rulings were upheld in large measure upon appeal to the Supreme Court. His reputation for courtesy and firmness was equally in his favor, and when Judge William Allen died, in 1891, he was appointed to the vacant seat on the bench of the Supreme Judicial Court. Before his connection with the judicial branch of government removed him from active participation in politics, Mr. Barker was prominent in the councils of the Republican party. He was in the Massachusetts House of Representatives in 1872 and 1873, serving on the Committee on Railroads. In consequence of the great fire in Boston, which occurred on the 9th and 10th of November, 1872, the Legislature was convened in special session. It was during this extra session that the memorable resolution censuring Charles Sumner was adopted by a vote of 103 yeas and 66 nays. Mr. Barker was recorded in the negative.

Near the close of the session of 1874 a resolve authorizing the appointment of a commission to inquire into the expediency of revising and amending the laws of the State relating to the taxation and exemptions therefrom was passed, and Mr. Barker was appointed on the commission. In 1881 and 1882, Mr. Barker was a member of the State Commission to revise the Public Statutes. In June, 1880, Mr. Barker was a member of the delegation sent by Massachusetts to the Republican National Convention at Chicago. He was foremost among the opponents of a third term for General Grant. He also was a worker for the civil service reform plank that went into the platform of that year.

Mr. Barker married at Bath, New York, September 21, 1862, Helena, daughter of Levi Carter and Pamelia (Nelson) Whiting. Mrs. Barker died April 11, 1889. The Barker home has always been in Pittsfield. Justice Barker had seven children, and five survive him. His son John is a member of the bar. His daughter Mary was married to Harry G. Day, Esq., of New Haven. His other daughters were Alice, Olive, and Elizabeth.

George Edward Atherton, a resident member of this Society since 1897, died in Brookline, Massachusetts, October 31, 1905. He was born in Charlestown, Massachusetts, May 2, 1845. His father, Samuel Atherton, was a descendant of Maj.-Gen. Humphrey[1] Atherton who came to this country in 1635. The line to George Edward[8] was through Consider,[2] Humphrey,[3] John,[4] John,[5] Samuel,[6] Samuel.[7] His mother, Temperance Holbrook, was the daughter of Col. Joseph and Mary (Rich) Holbrook.

He was educated at Chauncy Hall School, Boston, and in the public schools of Dorchester, Massachusetts. He spent his early life in Dorchester, and started in his business life with his father in the leather business, from which he retired about 1894. He was married first, September 15, 1869, to Emma A. Coffin of Wakefield, Massachusetts, by whom he had two children, Edith and George Edward. His first wife was the daughter of Nathaniel R. Coffin, and her death occurred December 11, 1879. He was married second to Isabelle King Ray of Andover, Massachusetts, June 2, 1881. His second wife was the daughter of Frederick Ray.

By his second marriage he had three children, Ray, Ellen Parker, who died when an infant, and Emma. After his second marriage, he removed from Dorchester to Brookline.

Mr. Atherton was a member of the Union Club of Boston, and trustee of several estates.

Rev. Myron Samuel Dudley, A.M., a resident member of this Society since 1899, died November 17, 1905. At the time of his death he was acting pastor of the Congregational Church in Newington, New Hampshire. He was born in Peru, Vermont, February 20, 1837, was graduated with honor at Williams College in 1863, and from Union Theological Seminary in 1869, and also studied a year in Andover Theolgical Seminary. He was acting pastor at Otego, New York, 1869–'70; ordained September 28, 1871; acting pastor, Peacham, Vermont, 1871–'72; pastor, Cromwell, Connecticut, 1874–1885. Later he had pastorates in North Wilbraham, Massachusetts, 1886–'89, and Nantucket, 1889–'97.

He was a descendant of the Dudleys of Concord, Massachusetts, through Francis,[1] Samuel,[2] Samuel,[3] Stephen,[4] Gen. Peter,[5] and Gen. Stephen[6], his father. ("Dudley Family," page 599.) His parents were Stephen and Lydia (Davis) Dudley. He received his education first in the common schools, and later in academies in Londonderry, Vermont, and Manchester, Vermont. At first he had planned to become a civil engineer, and at one time he taught Latin and Greek in Burr and Burton Seminary, at Manchester, Vermont. In 1863, while teaching school in place of a brother, in Kentucky, he carried out his resolution to enter the army. Therefore he returned to Vermont, and enlisted in the Fifth Vermont Volunteers, then stationed in Virginia. From a private in this veteran regiment he rose through the grades of sergeant and first lieutenant to the position of captain. He was wounded in the Battle of the Wilderness, but shared, however, with his regiment in the victories of the Shenandoah Valley, and in the campaign about Petersburg. He was mustered out with his regiment in June, 1865.

He was married first to Martha M. Hale, August 20, 1873, who died July 20, 1876. By this marriage he had a daughter, who died young. He was married second to Sarah D. Todd, a daughter of Rev. John Todd, D.D., the well-known author. This wife died October 26, 1884; and he was married third to Mary Elizabeth Marrett, September 14, 1892, who survives him.

He published a "Historial Sermon at the re-dedication of the Congregational Church, Peacham, Vt., 1874"; a "History of Cromwell, Conn.," 1881; "Funeral Sermon of Ira Hutchinson, M.D.," Cromwell, 1881; a sketch of Cromwell, in the History of

Middlesex County, Connecticut, 1884. He had also written a history of his college class: "Class of Sixty-Three, Williams College. By the Class Historian, 1903." And there were other publications. His history of Cromwell, Connecticut, his studies in the early history of Nantucket, and his memoir of Edward Griffin Porter, president of this Society, were all marked by his characteristic thoroughness. He was a man of great public spirit, and interested especially in civil service reform, and in forestry and village improvement.

After joining this Society, Mr. Dudley became a very active member, and was appointed on the committee on the library. One of his earliest duties was the preparation of a memoir of its president for the REGISTER, which was afterwards published separately. The article on the "Churches and Pastors of Nantucket, Mass., from the First Settlement to the Present Time," in the REGISTER, January, 1902, was enlarged and published separately, as was also his article entitled "Historical Sketch of Newington, New Hampshire," July, 1904.

REV. JAMES DAVIE BUTLER, D.D., LL.D., of Madison, Wisconsin, a corresponding member of this Society since 1847, died November 20, 1905, at the age of ninety-one.

He was born March 15, 1815, in Rutland, Vermont. In his letter of acceptance, dated from Norwich University, March 20, 1847, and still preserved, he mentions a manuscript volume giving a history of his family, and the fact that he was a member of the New York Historical Society; and that he presented to the New England Historic Genealogical Society the first pamphlet published by the Vermont Historical Society. His family, he said, originated in Massachusetts.

From a notice published in 1888, the following facts are gleaned.

His father settled in Rutland, Vermont, in 1787, but was born in Boston, where his lineage is traced from 1637.

Mr. Butler was graduated at Middlebury College in 1836, with high honor. After a year in Yale theological seminary, he returned to Middlebury and served five years as a tutor. He finished his course in Andover theological seminary, and was immediately elected Abbot resident. During the second year of his residence he accepted an invitation from Prof. Edwards A. Park to accompany him to Europe. Their passage (in 1842) lasted forty-seven days. After a stormy return passage he reached America near the close of 1843. He was advised to prepare European lectures, and did so, and one or another of these descriptions he was invited to deliver more than three hundred times in, or near, New England. After supplying the Congregational church in Burlington, Vermont, for half a year, he became a professor in Norwich (Military) University, now the Military College of Vermont, of which, at one time, he was acting president. He resigned his position there in 1847. He was pastor of churches in Wells River, Vt., South Danvers (now Peabody), Mass., and in Cincinnati, O., followed by professorships of Greek in Wabash College, Crawfordville, Indiana, and in the State University of Wisconsin, at Madison.

In 1867 he again went abroad, extending his travels to the Orient, and to other European countries which he had not before visited.

In 1869, he penetrated into the Yosemite, and crossed to the Sandwich Islands in a sailing bark, and reached the volcano Kilauea.

He visited Europe a third and fourth time, in 1878 and 1884. He passed down into Colorado, Mexico, and Cuba. In 1883, he entered Portland, Oregon, by the first train on the Northern Pacific, and then went on through the Puget Sound to British Columbia. In 1890, then in his seventy-sixth year, he undertook a tour around the globe. It was accomplished in seventeen months, and he went alone.

He was elected to the American Antiquarian Society in Worcester at a date that ranks his name as one of the earliest members on its roll.

His writings were widely circulated. One of the most notable, from the literary standpoint, was his paper on words used once for all in Shakespeare. His lecture on "Commonplace Books" was called for more than a hundred times.

He was married, in 1847, to Anna, daughter of Joshua Bates, President of Middlebury College, by whom he had four children.

George Allen Dary died at his home in Roxbury, Massachusetts, on December 30, 1905. He was born in Taunton, Massachusetts, November 30, 1842. His father was George Leonard Dary, the son of Allen Dary, a farmer of Rehoboth, and a soldier of the war of 1812. Allen's father was John Dary, a private in the Revolutionary War, and John was the son of Lewis Dary, the first of the family name in this country.

George Allen Dary took great interest in genealogical study, and published the Dary Genealogy in 1903. He was a member of the Society of Mayflower Descendants, the Sons of Colonial Wars, and Sons of the Revolution. His father dying when the son was only six years old, and the mother when the son was only thirteen, he was placed under the care of a guardian in Taunton until the year 1855, when, coming to Boston, he entered the law office of Samuel E. Sewall, and was admitted to the Suffolk Bar in 1872. He was later a partner in the firm of Sewall and Angell, and then of Sewall and Dary. He held many trusts, which he administered with most scrupulous care. He was regarded as a most expert and reliable conveyancer. He was a founder and a member of the Abstract Club, the Massachusetts Title Insurance Company, and the Conveyancers Title Insurance Company. In 1901 he was chosen Government expert to report all the titles for the Nahant fortifications. He examined the title of the various purchases of President Cleveland at Gray Gables.

Among other things he was extremely fond of music. For many years he was on the music committee of the First Religious Society of Roxbury. He attended the Symphony Orchestra concerts from the first, and was a contributing member of the Philharmonic Society and the Orpheus Musical Association.

His greatest rest and pleasure was in out-of-door life. He was fond of the deep woods and of fishing with the fly. Fifteen years in succession he passed his summer vacations camping in the woods of Maine and New Brunswick.

He shunned prominence as much as others seek it. He had no desire to be known by many, but valued highly the friendship and loyalty of a few. He was absolutely honest, and never had any money which he did not earn by hard work. He was a most industrious man; worked hard and fast at his desk, and frequently until late in the evening; was worried if every account was not paid and up to date, and every probate account allowed. At his death, —unforeseen by him,— he left all his papers, accounts, and affairs, in as perfect condition as if he had known the hour of it months in advance.

He was a resident member of the Society, elected in 1899.

By William Hoag, Esq.

1904.

[The following sketch of Hon. Ira Davenport, arranged for by the late Rev. Dr. Adams, was not found until after the sketch on page liii was printed.]

Ira Davenport. His grandfather, Noah Davenport, was a soldier in the Revolutionary War, and his maternal grandfather, Dugald Cameron, was a prominent citizen of Steuben County, New York, in its early development, having come from Scotland in the latter part of the 18th century. Ira Davenport, the father of the subject of this sketch, when a young man, removed from Columbia County, New York, to Steuben County, where he established his home and married Lydia, the daughter of the above-mentioned Dugald Cameron. The late Ira Davenport was the youngest child of this marriage.

His father's death, in 1868, threw upon him the responsibility of the management of important interests in various States, but he found time to devote himself to all measures which he believed would make for the material and intellectual welfare of the people of his county. He was largely instrumental in securing for the town of Bath the New York State Soldiers' and Sailors' Home. He endowed liberally the Davenport Home for Female Orphan Children at Bath, an institution founded by his father, and he left to the village of Bath the library which bears his name, with a fund to properly maintain it. In politics he was a member of the Republican party.

In 1877 he entered public life. In that year he was elected to the State Senate, and in 1879 was re-elected to the same office. During the four years he served as a Senator in the New York Legislature he made such an impression upon his party and the people of the State that in 1881 he was nominated and elected comptroller, in which office he demonstrated his sterling business methods and sagacity. In 1884 he was elected a representative in Congress, and the following year his party honored him by naming him as its candidate for Governor of the State; but the Democratic party carried the election and he was defeated. In 1886 he was re-elected to Congress, and at the end of his second term he retired to private life. In 1887 he married Katharine, only daughter of General George H. Sharpe of Kingston, New York.

Mr. Davenport was a wide reader, a man fond of and versed in the humanities, of a nature broadly tolerant, keen of insight and humor, a lover and judge of painting. Public honors were never sought by him; they came to him unsolicited, and evidenced the esteem in which he was held by his county, his district, and his State.

By Severyn B. Sharpe, Esq.

Memoirs of the following named members of the Society may be found as indicated: —

Hon. Lucius Manlius Boltwood, in the Register of October, 1905; James Swift Rogers, A.B., and Hon. Andrew Napoleon Adams, in the Register of January, 1906; and Benjamin Barstow Torrey, in the Register of April, 1906.

It is expected that a memoir of Robert Charles Winthrop, Jr., A.M., will appear in the Register of July, 1906, and one of Hon. Stephen Salisbury, A.M., and George William Marshall, LL.D., in the Register of October, 1906.

INDEX OF MEMOIRS.

FINANCIAL NEEDS OF THE SOCIETY.

The attention of all persons interested in historical and genealogical research is called to the following estimate of the financial needs of the Society:

For a new five-story fire-proof Library building in rear of Society's House, with a hall to seat 300 persons, stack room for 250,000 books, and a reading room to accommodate 80 readers (tentative plans can now be seen at the Society's rooms, and suggestions are invited)	$60,000	
Library fixtures, furniture, etc.	30,000	
Land, 5,000 square feet, purchased, but not yet paid for	30,000	$120,000
For addition to permanent fund, for purchase and binding of books, and increased expenses of a new building (calling for $3,000 additional income per annum)		75,000
For copying records of births, marriages and deaths from court files, church records, clergymen's and undertakers' private records, graveyard inscriptions, and family bibles		10,000
For preparing and printing a catalogue of the 60,000 books and pamphlets belonging to the Society		8,000
For Alphabetical Abstracts or Digest of personal items in the Boston News-Letter and other New England newspapers, from 1704 to 1815, estimated to be equal to 8000 printed pages		6,000
For Genealogical research in England, a permanent fund		15,000
For printing Abstracts of Wills from the Prerogative Court of Canterbury, England		10,000
For estimated loss in printing Vital Records to 1850 of Massachusetts towns		5,000

The Treasurer, NATHANIEL C. NASH, 18 Somerset St., Boston, and all other officers of the Society, will be glad to advise persons intending to give or bequeath money to the Society.

CHARTER.

An Act to Incorporate the New-England Historic Genealogical Society.

Be it enacted by the Senate and House of Representatives, in General Court assembled, and by the authority of the same, as follows:

SECT. 1.—Charles Ewer, J. Wingate Thornton, Joseph Willard, their associates and successors, are hereby made a corporation, by the name of the New-England Historic Genealogical Society, for the purpose of collecting, preserving, and occasionally publishing, genealogical and historical matter, relating to early New England families, and for the establishment and maintenance of a cabinet; and for these purposes, shall have all the powers and privileges, and be subject to all the duties, requirements and liabilities, set fourth in the forty-fourth chapter of the Revised Statutes.

SECT. 2.—The said corporation may hold and possess real and personal estate, to an amount not exceeding twenty thousand dollars.

Acts and Resolves, 1845, chapter 152.

An Act to Enable the New-England Historic Genealogical Society to Hold an Additional Amount of Property.

[This Act enables the Society to hold real and personal estate not exceeding one hundred thousand dollars, in addition to the amount authorized in 1845.]

Acts and Resolves, 1868, chapter 100.

An Act to Enable the New-England Historic Genealogical Society to Hold Additional Real and Personal Property.

[This Act enables the Society to hold real and personal estate not exceeding two hundred thousand dollars, in addition to the amount authorized in 1845.]

Acts and Resolves, 1888, chapter 227.

The following is from the *Revised Laws of 1902, Corporation Acts, chapter 125, section 8:*

Any corporation organized under general or special laws for any of the purposes mentioned in section two [educational, charitable, antiquarian, historical, literary, scientific, etc.] . . . may hold real and personal estate to an amount not exceeding one million five hundred thousand dollars.

An Act to Enable Women to Become Members of the New-England Historic Genealogical Society.

Be it enacted, etc., as follows:

The New-England Historic Genealogical Society, a corporation organized under the laws of this Commonwealth, may admit women to membership, subject to such restrictions as the By-Laws of said corporation may from time to time impose.

Acts and Resolves, 1897, chapter 275.

Robert C. Winthrop, Jr.

Engraved for The Colonial Society ...
from the original ...

NEW ENGLAND HISTORICAL AND GENEALOGICAL REGISTER.

JULY, 1906.

ROBERT CHARLES WINTHROP, JR., A.M.

By HENRY HERBERT EDES, Esq.

ROBERT CHARLES WINTHROP, the younger of that name, was born in his father's house, No. 7 Tremont Place, Boston, on the 7th of December, 1834, the elder son of Robert Charles and Eliza Cabot (Blanchard) Winthrop. Descended from forebears who for many generations had occupied a distinguished place in society and in all branches of the public service, he never forgot the admonition of Young that—

> "They that on glorious ancestors enlarge
> Produce their debt, instead of their discharge."

Neither should his biographer fail to remember that "no man is wholly accounted for, or known as well as he can be, who is studied apart from the genealogical tree on which he grew."

The line of Mr. Winthrop's descent from ADAM[1] WINTHROP, of Lavenham, in the county of Suffolk, England, who was living in 1498, was through ADAM[2] (1498–1562), of Groton Manor, Suffolk, Master of the Clothworkers Company of London; ADAM[3] (1548–1623), of Groton Manor, a lawyer and county magistrate; JOHN[4] (1587–1649), of Groton Manor, afterward Governor of the Colony of the Massachusetts Bay, and the founder of Boston in New England; JOHN, Jr.[5] (1605–1676), of Groton Manor, afterward of Ipswich, Massachusetts, and New London, Connecticut, Fellow of the Royal Society of London, and Governor of the Colony of Connecticut; WAIT STILL[6] (1642–1717), of Boston, Commissioner of the United Colonies of New England, Major-General of the Colony, and Executive Councillor and Chief-Justice of the Province of the Massachusetts Bay; JOHN[7] (1681–1747), of Boston, afterward of New London, Connecticut, a graduate of Harvard College in the Class of 1700, Fellow of the Royal Society, and the plaintiff in the *cause célèbre* of Winthrop *v.* Lechmere, which was an appeal to the Privy Council from the decision of the Connecticut Courts involving the English law of primogeniture; JOHN STILL[8] (1720–1776), of Boston, afterward of New London, Connecticut, a graduate of Yale College in the Class of 1737; THOMAS LINDALL,[9] LL.D. (1760–1841), of New London and later of Boston, a graduate of Harvard in the Class of 1780, and an Overseer of the College (1828–1841), member of the American Philosophical Society, Treasurer of the American Academy of Arts and Sciences, President of the Massachusetts Historical Society and of the American Antiquarian Society, Fellow of the Royal Society of Northern Antiquaries and of other learned bodies in Europe, and from 1826 till 1833 Lieutenant-Governor of Massachusetts; and ROBERT CHARLES,[10] LL.D. (1809–1894), of Boston, a graduate of Harvard in the Class of 1828, President of the Alumni Association, and an Overseer of the College (1852–1856), in the Corporation of which he had twice refused a seat, member of the American Philosophical Society, American Academy of Arts and Sciences, Society of Antiquaries of London, and other learned societies abroad, President of the Massachusetts Historical Society, Speaker of the Massachusetts House of Representatives and of the Thirtieth Congress, and a Senator of the United States from Massachusetts, succeeding Daniel Webster.

Mr. Winthrop's mother was born in Boston on the 27th of May, 1809. She was the daughter of Francis Blanchard, Esq., of Wenham, Massachusetts, and later of Boston, a graduate of Harvard in the remarkable Class of 1802, who studied law with Judge Charles Jackson and became his law partner before his appointment to the Bench of the Supreme Judicial Court in 1813, the year in which Mr. Blanchard died on the 26th of June. On the 29th of August, 1808, he had married his second cousin, Mary Ann Cabot, daughter of Francis and Ann (Clarke) Cabot and widow of Nathaniel Cabot Lee of Salem, who died on the 25th of July, 1809, soon after the birth of her daughter, who, in November, 1814, was taken into the family of her father's uncle, Samuel Pickering Gardner, where she remained until her marriage to Robert Charles Winthrop on the 12th of March, 1832. She died on the 14th of June, 1842, leaving three children, of whom the eldest is the subject of this notice.

More might be said of those distinguished ancestors of Mr. Winthrop who bore the names of Dudley, Bowdoin, and Temple, to name no others, but enough has already been told to show the environment in which he was born and bred and to account for his inheritance of abilities of a high order.

Owing to the early death of his mother and the absence of his father in Washington in the public service, much of Mr. Winthrop's boyhood was spent with his kinsfolk in Salem and elsewhere. One of his cousins recently recalled the picture of young Winthrop lying upon the floor of his uncle's library devouring Scott's novels and other of the best English literature of that day, utterly oblivious of all that was passing around him.

Mr. Winthrop received his early education in the private school of Mr. John Adam Weisse,* in Roxbury, in whose establishment he was a boarding pupil from 1840 to 1847, when he went abroad with his father. Of this, their first, visit to Europe, the son thus speaks in his Memoir of his father:

"He had friends and relatives both in England and France, and he took with him flattering letters of introduction from Mr. Webster and Mr. Everett, which made his first experience of London society an exceptionally agreeable one. In a fragment of autobiography privately printed by him not long before his death and now to be found in many public libraries, he gave some account of his intercourse with European celebrities at different periods, and it need only be mentioned here that among the persons of distinction of whom he was privileged to see a good deal in 1847 were the Duke of Wellington, Sir Robert Peel, the poet Rogers, the historians Thiers, Mignet, Milman, Thirlwall and Hallam, Archbishop Whately, Bishops Wilberforce and Blomfield, Lord Landsdowne (then President of the Council), Lords Aberdeen and Stanley (both afterward prime ministers), Prince Louis Napoleon (then in exile in London), and King Louis Philippe, who twice received Mr. Winthrop informally at Neuilly" (page 64).

Returning home in the autumn of 1847 from an experience which cannot have failed to make a lasting impression upon his youthful mind, young Winthrop, then well advanced in his studies, entered the Boston Public Latin School, where his father and grandfather had been prepared for college, as well as seven other members of his family, Professor John Winthrop, of the Class of 1721, who graduated at Harvard College in 1732, having been the first. In 1848 he left the School, where the course was then five years, and entered Phillips Academy, Andover, where he remained till 1850, when he entered Harvard, from which he graduated in 1854.

Of Mr. Winthrop's college life, the following extracts from letters of a few of his classmates and contemporaries not classmates will furnish an interesting glimpse:

I.

For more than two years we were at the same club table at Mrs. Guthrie's in Church Street, and we were in the Hasty Pudding and Porcellian Clubs together. . . . Winthrop's rooms were at Mrs. Guthrie's, and Payson Perrin Ellis, who had rooms in the same house, Charles Thorndike, Theodore Lyman and I were quite intimate with him. His other friends

*A sketch of Mr. Weisse is in Appleton's Cyclopædia of American Biography (1889), vi., 423. His school in Roxbury was on the northwesterly side of Hawthorne Street, on an estate subsequently owned by Roland Worthington. John Chandler Bancroft (H. C. 1854) and the Rev. Dr. Alfred Porter Putnam (B. U. 1848) were also pupils of Mr. Weisse between 1840 and 1847. Nicholas Weisse, Sr., of Roxbury was his brother. Mr. Weisse married, 27 June, 1841, Jane Lee, daughter of William Hunt, of Watertown, Mass., and his wife Jane, daughter of George and Mary (Faneuil) Bethune, of Boston. Mrs. Weisse compiled: Records, Genealogical Charts, and Traditions of the Families of Bethune and Faneuil, New York, 1866; Records and Traditions of the Families of Hunt and Weisse, New York, 1866; and A History of the Bethune Family, Together with a Sketch of the Faneuil Family, New York, 1884.

See also W. L. G. Hunt's Genealogy of the Name and Family of Hunt, Boston, 1863, p. 322; Bond's Genealogies and History of Watertown, pp. 174, 304.

at that time, who continued to appreciate him while they lived, were John Quincy Adams, Theodore Chase, George B. Chase, Langdon Erving, William Frick, Jr., John C. Bancroft, William S. Haseltine, James Savage, Charles Russell Lowell, William Thorndike, and S. Parkman Blake; and Charles Francis Adams, Dr. Hall Curtis, George Putnam, Robert H. Renshaw, Dr. B. Joy Jeffries, and Horace H. Furness are among the living who cared for him.

Winthrop was popular with his class; his abilities were recognized and he was made Class Orator. He had plenty of brains, but was more disposed to use them in reading than in studying what did not interest him. .... With more work [he] could have been celebrated as a lawyer or politician in the best sense, but he preferred to read, work in his library or travel and lead the life of a cultivated gentleman. He was fond of detail, accurate and methodical, and would have made a good business man had he been obliged to turn his attention in that direction. He was indolent about exercise. With a large frame he might, as his classmate Dr. Windship, the well known strong man, told him, have become an athlete, though the fashion did not then point in that direction for fame.... He was most loyal to his old friends and took a good deal of pains to see them.

II.

In college he made no mark as a student, although always a reader, and endowed with an extraordinary memory for what he read. Here, as in after life, his bookish interests were mainly in history, especially American history. He was, however, indifferent to the way in which history, and indeed most other things, were then taught at Harvard; and when called up at recitation he was apt to say nothing or to say "not prepared." Once, however, the story goes, after a long series of these "not prepareds" he was called up for examination in the presence of the Visiting Committee, and at once gave a fluent talk upon the point in question for almost five minutes, and until told he need go no further.

His main distinction in the Class lay in his inherited faculty as a presiding officer. He was at the head of the two great clubs, the Porcellian and the Hasty Pudding,* and was usually selected to preside at any Class election or meeting. He belonged to neither of the Greek letter societies, and in their contests in the Hasty Pudding Club he, as President, sometimes maintained the balance of power in a salutary, if, perhaps, somewhat despotic, way.

III.

In college Winthrop lived rather apart. He appeared to wholly neglect his studies, and except by a small circle of intimates he was very little known. In the last two years of his college course, however, he acquired a reputation as an admirable presiding officer and amateur actor in the Hasty Pudding Club, and he was always selected, as a matter of course, to preside at all festivities of the Class, both before and after graduation. He was outside of the bitter hostilities of the Class factions and was chosen Class Orator by a compromise as one whom neither faction objected to.... On our twenty-fifth anniversary [24 June, 1879] he gave [at Young's] a dinner to the Class at which he presided with the same felicity and charm which had characterized him in college days.

* Mr. Winthrop was also a member of the Institute of 1770.

IV.

He was certainly a man of cultivation and literary distinction. . . . I remember thinking his oration witty, able, and worthy of his reputation.

V.

He was popular with his Class but not with the Faculty. . . . Katharine Winthrop whom he defended was my ancestor, and he sent me his "Defence" of her. The spirit is the same he had in college days *versus* the Faculty.

VI.

His Oration was rather more jocular and sarcastic, but at the same time more interesting, than such performances are generally apt to be. On the evening, I think it must have been, of Class Day, there was a supper in Mr. Winthrop's room, the memory of which long lasted in college; it has perhaps not yet entirely faded away.

VII.

It was his utter lack of ambition which caused his failure to take any rank, but all his classmates knew the power and force that was in him, if he could but be induced to put them forth. . . . Although he had no college rank, which is never an ultimate criterion, so deeply had his talents and ability impressed themselves upon his classmates that he was elected, almost without opposition, their Class Orator.

It was through no direct fault of his own that his degree was taken away from him. His offense in the eyes of the Faculty was that he had provided means for an entertainment on the evening of Class Day a little too lavish for the occasion. . . . The supper was given in one of the rooms of Holworthy, on the ground floor, and its distinguishing feature was that it was open to all the world and not restricted to any Class. The Faculty, I believe, looked upon it as an act of bravado on Winthrop's part. No thought of this, I am sure, entered Winthrop's mind. It was merely done in the exuberance of his gratitude to his classmates for having elected him their Orator,—an election which, it was said, keenly gratified his father.

The withholding of Mr. Winthrop's first degree was only temporary, and it was conferred at the next Commencement, in 1855. He received his Master's degree in 1858.

After Mr. Winthrop's death, one of his classmates prepared for the College Class Book a brief sketch from which the following extracts are taken:

Robert C. Winthrop, Jr., would have been more at place in Cambridge after the College became a liberal University.

Placed so that he was free to follow the bent of his mind and the interests surrounding his position, he developed his critical acumen and became a very interested and interesting member of the genealogical and historical societies of his State and City.

Those of his Class who knew him well and saw him often, could not but have been surprised in later years, at the recital of his pleasant Cambridge reminiscences, called up by talk of the past.

If he and the Faculty never exactly agreed, he and his classmates always did, as shown by the prominence they accorded him so readily. The former seemed never quite to understand him, the latter did more loyally.

After graduation, Mr. Winthrop spent a year in the Harvard Law School under Professors Joel Parker and Theophilus Parsons, and then entered the law office of Mr. Leverett Saltonstall. He was admitted to the Suffolk Bar in 1857, but never practised.

On the 15th of October, 1857, Mr. Winthrop was married, in Boston, to Frances Pickering Adams, youngest daughter of Mr. Benjamin Adams, and immediately sailed for Europe. Till Mrs. Winthrop's death, their time was passed in travelling, the winters being divided between the south of France, Malta, and Italy, while the summers were devoted to Paris, England, and Germany. Mrs. Winthrop died, childless, in Rome on the 23d of April, 1860, at the age of twenty-four. Early in the following summer Mr. Winthrop returned to America, and from that time till 1866 he made frequent short trips to Europe, generally confining his travels to France and England. In the autumn of 1866 he again went abroad, remaining two years, during which time, in addition to long stays in Paris, he visited Spain, Portugal, Russia, and Italy. Besides travel and sightseeing, Mr. Winthrop found time while in Europe for the study of languages and to familiarize himself with European politics of which his knowledge was thorough.

One of his contemporaries writes that—

With the history of modern Europe, especially on its family and genealogical side, he was as familiar as with that of America. The Almanach de Gotha he had at his fingers' end, almost at his tongue's end, and he was apt to reply to any question, "You will find that in the Almanach."

Mr. Winthrop was a good French scholar, and his command of Spanish and Italian was sufficient for all purposes of travel and sightseeing. A connoisseur in art, he knew little of music although he enjoyed the Opera. As a young man and in early middle life he was an inveterate theatre-goer; later, however, he cared only for really fine acting; but whenever there was a good French company in Boston he rarely missed a single performance.

On the 1st of June, 1869, Mr. Winthrop was married, in Boston, to Elizabeth Mason, eldest daughter of Robert Means Mason and granddaughter of the Hon. Jeremiah Mason, the greatest lawyer of New England in his day, who was also a Senator of the United States from New Hampshire. In the following July, Mr. and Mrs. Winthrop went to Europe, where they remained till September, 1871, travelling in Great Britain, France, Italy, and Germany. In the autumn of 1872 they established themselves at No. 37½ Beacon Street, Boston, where they passed their winters till 1884, when they removed to No. 10 Walnut Street. Their summers were passed in various places till 1896, when they occupied the house at Manchester-by-the-Sea which they began to build in 1894.

On returning to Boston, Mr. Winthrop found abundant leisure to pursue his literary and historical studies, and during the next few years he was welcomed to fellowship in some of the leading Clubs and Societies. He had been a member of the Somerset Club since his graduation from Harvard, and now he also found enjoyment in the meetings of the Wednesday Evening Club, organized in Boston as early as 1777, and of the Essex County Club, to which he belonged from its formation. He was also a member of the Bostonian Society.

Mr. Winthrop's connection with this Society dates from the 7th of April, 1886. On its reorganization, in 1889, he was elected a member of the Council for three years, and rendered efficient service. From 1891 till 1902 he served on the Committee on English Research, and he was also a working member of other important committees. When the Consolidated Index of the first fifty volumes of the New England Historical and Genealogical Register was undertaken, he made a generous contribution toward its cost.

It was to the work of the Massachusetts Historical Society, however, that for nearly a quarter of a century Mr. Winthrop devoted his best energies. His connection with that venerable organization is best described in the following words of its President, Mr. Charles Francis Adams:

Mr. Winthrop was chosen a Resident Member May 8, 1879, and during the presidency of his father. . . . For over twenty of the twenty-six years of his connection with the Society, Mr. Winthrop was one of the most active, interested, and influential of its members. More recently, owing to a marked tendency to seclusion,—due, as he claimed, to bodily infirmities and especially to a growing imperfection of hearing,—he had ceased to attend our meetings, the last at which he was present, and in which he took characteristic part, having been that of February, 1901.

His first committee service was in 1880, in connection with the Winthrop Papers, in the preparation and publication of which he took a natural and hereditary pride. The finances of the Society were at that time in a far from flourishing state, and it was Mr. Winthrop who quietly came forward and met the cost, some $1200, of printing the volume (Part IV.) published after he had been made a member of the committee. Subsequently, in 1889, 1892, and 1897, he served on the similar committees for the publication of Parts V. and VI. of the Winthrop Papers and of the volume of Bowdoin and Temple Papers. Between 1886 and 1898 his service on other committees was almost continuous and never merely nominal. He was essentially a working member. . . .

Passing to his communications and share in our proceedings, besides two lesser memoirs, that on R. M. Mason and that on David Sears, he prepared the more elaborate biography of the elder Robert C. Winthrop. This last, let me say in passing, was not only a most creditable piece of literary work, done with much judgment and good taste, but it stands in lasting evidence of that abiding and admiring respect for his father which was in him so marked a characteristic. Besides the above, the list of Mr. Winthrop's miscellaneous formal contributions . . . . is too long for detailed enumeration; suffice it to say, it includes many of the most valuable as well as entertaining papers read at our meetings between 1880 and 1900. During those years no one was listened to with more instruction, certainly no one at times did so much to enliven a series of meetings not characterized, as a rule, by sallies of humor or aggressiveness of speech. Nor was his participation confined to formal papers; and the older members of the Society will bear me out in the statement that, when Mr. Winthrop took the floor, whatever degree of listlessness might before have been apparent at once disappeared from our gatherings. All was alertness and attention.

An accomplished host as well as a generous giver, to him we owe that most valuable double autograph of Governors Bradford and Winthrop which ornaments our entrance chamber, one of the most precious of the Society's possessions; and on two occasions at least, the special meeting after the death of Charles Deane and the Annual Meeting of April, 1898, he entertained the Society at his home.

Altogether, I may confidently assert that through a score of years no member of our organization was more constant in attendance, more fruitful in matter, more entertaining as well as instructive in his contributions, more generous in gift and more lavish in hospitality than was that friend and associate of fifty years whose death I to-day announce.*

While Mr. Winthrop's services to the Massachusetts Historical Society, as author and editor, were various and valuable, his great work was his Memoir of his father. This substantial volume of more than three hundred and fifty pages is remarkable for many things besides those mentioned by Mr. Adams: it is just and discriminating; notable for what it omits, both of persons and events; frank to a degree unusual in family biographies; and, when we remember Mr. Winthrop's filial attitude, and that certain political events ended the elder Winthrop's public career, for which he had most unusual qualifications, the reader marvels at the calm self-restraint, the perfect candor and the absence of passion and resentment which characterizes the portrayal of this period of his father's public life. Reverence and affection, the truest sympathy in his father's domestic joys and sorrows, and determination to vindicate his character from the unjust aspersions and misjudgments of political enemies and thoughtless contemporaries are everywhere apparent. One of Mr. Winthrop's early friends writes:

His after life was quiet and domestic. He kept up his historical studies, but wrote much less than his friends had hoped for. His Life of Robert C. Winthrop is, however, everywhere recognized as a model of biographical writing, perfectly impartial, never allowing his filial relation to interfere with a clear statement of all phases of his father's character and career.

A Classmate adds this estimate of the volume:

I think Robert Winthrop's Memoir of his father gives an impression of his own character and abilities. . . . I have long considered it equal to the very best biographies extant,—indeed, I cannot name another that I consider as good,—and it is quite as much a monument to the writer as to the subject. The Defence of Katharine Winthrop I have not seen. . . . Except the exquisite biography of which I have already spoken, he did nothing to my knowledge which disclosed his remarkable gifts.

* 2 Proceedings of the Massachusetts Historical Society, xix. 301, 302.

There was, however, another literary production of Mr. Winthrop, already mentioned, which, although in an entirely different vein from the Memoir of his father, is nevertheless entitled to prominent mention in any biographical notice of its author. One of our younger scholars has pronounced it "the brightest historical gem we have produced." On the cover of this pamphlet is printed—"A Few Words in Defence of an Elderly Lady," while the more formal title-page runs, "A Difference of Opinion concerning the reasons why Katharine Winthrop* refused to marry Chief Justice Sewall." In an Address on the Life and Character of Chief Justice Sewall, delivered in the Old South Meeting House, in October, 1884, Dr. George E. Ellis had styled Madam Winthrop a "worldly minded woman" and had intimated "that she first encouraged an old man to make her an offer of marriage and then refused him from mercenary motives." A few months later, when the Address had been printed and distributed, these passages fell under Mr. Winthrop's notice, aroused his indignation, and called forth his "Defence" of the lady. This paper was read at a meeting of one of the Societies with which he was in fellowship, in February, 1885. Declaring that "sufferance is not the badge of *all* my tribe," and that "the angelic attribute of Patience has ever been imperfectly developed in my composition," Mr. Winthrop proceeded to deal with his subject in a manner peculiarly his own. As a piece of literature it is brilliant, discovering a sagacious insight into character, a masterly power of statement and of analysis, dry humor, keen wit, an equally keen sense of the ludicrous, generous appreciation of the worth and rights of others, pungent phrases expressive of his indignation at the injustice done to Madam Winthrop, and therewithal a rollicking good-humor which disarms at once the criticism of unprejudiced and disinterested readers. The Publishing Committee of the Society, however, in the exercise of the discretion conferred upon it by the By-Laws, did "not think fit" to include it in the printed Proceedings of the Society. As might have been foreseen, Mr. Winthrop promptly had his "Defence" printed and distributed to his friends and public institutions. The pamphlet is divided into two Chapters. Chapter I., "Wherein the Champion of an Elderly Lady recites her Wrongs," is introduced by the exclamation of Angus—

> "*And darest thou then*
> *To beard the lion in his den,*
> *The Douglas in his hall?*"

Chapter II., "Wherein an Elderly Lady's Champion unfolds a

* Katharine Winthrop, born 26 September, 1664, was a daughter of Thomas Brattle, the richest merchant of his day in New England, and widow of John Eyre of Boston at the time of her marriage to Chief-Justice Wait Still Winthrop, 13 November, 1707. She died 2 August, 1725 (Boston Record Commissioners' Reports, ix. 91, xxviii. 17; Sewall's Diary, iii. 363; Paige, History of Cambridge, p. 499).

Penitential Tale," begins with a passage from the lamentations of King David—

"All they that see me . . . . they shoot out the lip, they shake the head."

The second chapter is, in a way, autobiographical and sheds light upon Mr. Winthrop's college career and his relations to the Faculty, of which mention has been already made. It also reveals his unwillingness to conceal any shortcomings of his own, knowledge of which may be necessary to a proper understanding of his personal relation to events he is describing,—a delicious frankness, indeed, which it behooves his biographer not to forget. A portion of this chapter, which comprises Mr. Winthrop's Remarks at the April meeting of the same Society, follows:

The explanation I am about to make is, as I said before, a short one; but in order to make it, I am obliged to go back to a period when some of the younger members of this Society were in their cradles, to a time—two and thirty years ago—when, as a member of the Junior Class of Harvard College, and in compliance with an official summons, I waited upon the President of the University, the lamented Dr. James Walker, to hear from his venerable lips the announcement that the College Faculty, by a unanimous vote, had awarded to me what was then known as a "Public Admonition" for an offence which, after this lapse of time, I blush to describe, and which consisted in the consumption and distribution of peanuts in the College Chapel during a Dudleian Lecture. I could not in conscience deny the charge; and I was aware that any attempt to do so would be futile, as I had not long before been credibly assured that no less competent an authority than a well-known Professor of Political Economy had personally identified a heap of shells under my seat. I ventured, however, to insinuate some slight palliation of the enormity of which I had been guilty, by pointing out that no inconsiderable portion of that Dudleian Lecture had been devoted to undermining certain religious tenets which I had from childhood been taught to reverence. Dr. Walker rejoined, in accents of unmistakable severity, although, as it seemed to me, there played across his expressive features the shadow—the momentary shadow—of a smile: "Mr. Winthrop, your conduct in this, as in some other matters, has been marked by an incorrigible want of decorum."

Well-nigh a third of a century has passed away since I was privileged to enjoy, on that and at least one other somewhat similar occasion, a few minutes of close personal intercourse with so remarkable a man; and, viewed in the light of subsequent experiences, those memorable words of his which I have just quoted seem now to me to have been instinct with a sort of prophetic pathos. Again and again have I been made the subject of such misconceptions. Endowed by nature with the keenest appreciation of whatever is grave and solemn and respectable in this world; animated as I have long been, by an eager desire to concentrate these qualities in an eminent degree in my own person,—I yet seem, somehow or other, only to have succeeded in encountering, from time to time, a perverse disposition to attribute to me an ill-judged levity wholly foreign to my temperament. It has even been broadly hinted to me that in a communication which I felt it my duty to make to this Society at its February meeting, I was considered in some influential quarters to have transcended the very climax of previous indiscretion. And so I stand up here this afternoon, figuratively attired in sackcloth, bowing a gray head in what is intended to be a penitential attitude, indicative of contrition; and as I look around me, while I seem to discern here and there on some expressive features the shadow—the momentary shadow—of a smile, yet in my heart of hearts I realize that if some venerable lips saw fit to speak, they would only, I fear, re-echo the language of James Walker two and thirty years ago, and impute to me "an incorrigible absence of decorum."

To those gentlemen who may not have been present at the February meeting, I will briefly explain, that I hurried here that afternoon, bursting, I may say, with what I thought a righteous indignation,—fired, as it were, by a pious zeal to vindicate the memory of an aged lady, who would, had she been able, have risen here herself before us, from her grave just below that window, the great-great-grandmother of the retiring President of this Society, whose character had been, as I conceived, somewhat cruelly bespattered in a recent pamphlet from the authoritive pen of our revered Senior Vice-President, soon, as I magnanimously hope, to be hailed by us by an even more august title.

After the meeting was over, it occurred to me to put to one of our leading members, with whom I was in casual conversation, this crucial question: "How much," I inquired, "of what I said this afternoon would you advise me to send in for publication?" His countenance fell,—he looked at me somewhat askance,—and, taking refuge in periphrastic ambiguity, he replied: "They are likely to be very short of space in the forthcoming volume. Several memoirs have unexpectedly come in, and the Doctor is said to have prepared one more than forty pages long." Well, I confess, such is the egregious vanity often resulting from literary composition, that for an instant I felt like exclaiming, "How hard—how hard—that this little ewe lamb of mine—this widow's mite of a communication, so to speak —must be sacrificed because some one has unexpectedly prepared a memoir more than forty pages long!" But in a twinkling my better nature asserted its supremacy, and I said to myself, "Age before merit,—I will go home and shear that little ewe lamb!" And I went home, and I clipped away a little here and I expurgated a little there, making a not inconsiderable reduction; and the next day, with a light heart and an easy conscience, I dispatched what was left to our admirable Recording Secretary, Professor Young. Bitter, bitter deception! About a week after, I got a letter from him, couched in most courteous language,—he could pen no other,—delicately but frankly intimating to me that my little ewe lamb was a source of no small embarrassment to the Publishing Committee. One eminent member of the Society (whom he did not name) was substantially of the opinion that so misbegotten a beast had no proper place in our sheepfold. Another eminent member (whom he equally did not name) considered that, if admitted at all, the process of shearing should be continued even to the bone. A third contented himself with the general suggestion that my method of treating such subjects was hardly in accordance with the dignified traditions of this body. I took all these criticisms in good part. I realized that the gentlemen who made them could have no possible bias, that they were actuated only by a sense of duty or by a desire to promote what they believed to be the best interests of this Society. I deferred to their better judgment. I drew the sacrificial knife. I said, "I have been willing in moderation to shear, but I cannot vivisect this animal; I prefer to cut its throat." In other words, I withdrew the communication; substituting for it that half-page of innocuous manuscript which you will find printed in the volume of Proceedings this day laid upon the table.*

And here, so far as this Society is concerned, I drop the subject; merely adding that, while I freely consented to make this little sacrifice, while I was even ready to humble myself as I have done here to-day, yet I could not find it in my heart to abandon one who, as I firmly believe, has rested her defence upon my shoulders. I reflected that the pamphlet, the accuracy of passages in which I called in question, has not merely been distributed among the personal friends of its distinguished author, but that it has unquestionably found a place—a place of permanent record—on the shelves of numerous public libraries in New England and elsewhere; and I thought it only fair, only right, that the future student of provincial domestic history should be enabled to discover in some obscure and dusty corner of the same shelves another little pamphlet, issued solely upon my own responsibility, disengaging wholly the dignity of this Society, and which will embody the substance of my remarks upon this subject, accompanied, not impossibly, by some slight annotation. I shall be happy to send a copy of this little pamphlet to any member of the Society who may feel the smallest interest in the matter, and in the mean time I should be really grateful if any one of them—Mr. Charles Francis Adams, Jr.,† of course, necessarily excepted—would supply me with an appropriate classical quotation for my titlepage. Those I have hitherto thought of do not quite satisfy me, and I have been obliged thus far to content myself with the following sentence, or rather half-sentence, which I take from an inspired source: "And David put his hand in his bag, and drew thence a stone, and *slang* it!"

NOTE.—An obliging person has pointed out to me, what I supposed I had made sufficiently evident, that I have not the blood of the lady of whom I have constituted myself the champion. He seems to think that because I am descended from her step-son, I must necessarily be indifferent to her good name. I can only reply that such has not been my own experience of the state of mind resulting from such family connections.

I regret to add (and I only mention it because I am afraid Dr. E. may, if I do not) that this step-son, after his father's death, became an imprudent person in money matters. Katharine Winthrop was put to great annoyance by his delay in refunding a considerable sum she had allowed him the use of; and though she eventually got back her principal, I doubt if she ever saw a penny of her interest. I venture to hope that she may regard my activity in her behalf in the light of a tardy reimbursement; and if I am fortunate enough to obtain from her any distinct manifestation on this subject, I shall communicate it to the Society for Psychical Research. R. C. W., Jr.

Mr. Winthrop led, from preference, a retired life, and although a loyal American he took no active part in politics and held no public office. He was, however, constantly employed in important historical and biographical work, of which his Memoir of his father and his Defence of Katharine Winthrop are the best fruit. He especially liked biography, and was an incessant reader. While he shunned publicity and ostentation, he was most kind and obliging, especially to strangers and historical students and scholars

* Proceedings, 1884–1885, p. 379.

† This reference to Mr. Adams was doubtless prompted by his Oration, entitled "A College Fetich,"—a term by which he characterized the traditional study of Greek,—delivered in June, 1883, before the Harvard Chapter of Φ.B.K.

who wrote or called upon him for information concerning persons or events that possibly are mentioned in his unrivalled collection of family papers. He was also thoughtfully kind-hearted, as is seen in the gift, after his father's death, of all his father's spectacles to one of the leading oculists of Boston, to be given to his poor patients. Like his father, Mr. Winthrop was himself very near-sighted, and in consequence often passed his most intimate friends on the street without bow or recognition of any kind,—a fact that caused him to be regarded as snobbish by persons who knew him but slightly,—an amusing misapprehension, since he was one of the most democratic of men, appreciating individuality of character in whatever walk of life he found it. One of Mr. Winthrop's friends writes:

> He always had a very strong family feeling, and every Sunday night during my mother's life nothing would prevent his paying her a regular Sunday evening visit.
>
> He certainly had remarkable talents. . . . . He was a man who loved accuracy and hated nebulosity. What some people, I think, regarded as hardness on his part was a desire to prevent the possibility of future mistakes.

He also hated injustice and loved fair play.

In his beautiful home in Walnut Street, adorned by a great and matchless collection of portraits of his ancestors and kinsfolk of many generations, and of his own and his father's friends among famous men, Mr. Winthrop died, in consequence of a surgical operation, in the evening of Monday, the 5th of June, 1905, in his seventy-first year. The funeral was held on the following Friday, in St. John's Memorial Chapel in Cambridge, built nearly thirty years before by Mrs. Winthrop's father. During the service on that beautiful summer afternoon, as the setting sun streamed through the painted windows as if in benediction upon the scene, the opening lines of one of Longfellow's sonnets involuntarily came to mind:

> "I stand beneath the tree whose branches shade
> Thy western window, Chapel of St. John!
> And hear its leaves repeat their benison
> On him whose hands thy stones memorial laid."

Mr. Winthrop was survived by his widow, a son, Robert Mason Winthrop, a graduate of Harvard in the Class of 1895 and now Secretary of Legation at Madrid, and two daughters, Clara Bowdoin Winthrop and Margaret Tyndal Winthrop, the name of the younger being a pleasant reminder, after the lapse of nearly three centuries, of the saintly woman who for nearly thirty years shared the joys and sorrows of Governor John Winthrop the elder. In his will he describes himself as "Robert Charles Winthrop, the younger of that name," having always retained the "Junior" after the death of his father. His public bequests of more than thirty thousand dollars were to the Massachusetts Historical Society, the New England Historic Genealogical Society, The Colonial Society of Massachusetts, the Bostonian Society, the Boston Episcopal Charitable Society, Bowdoin College, and Phillips Academy, Andover, the income of the last two bequests "to be used for the encouragement of the study of Greek and Latin authors." Mr. Winthrop's modesty is recognized in his two bequests to the Historical Society, both of which are to be added to existing Funds already named for those who gave them.

EXTRACTS FROM THE JOURNAL OF CONSTANTINE HARDY, IN THE CROWN POINT EXPEDITION OF 1759.

Communicated by CHARLES A. FLAGG, Esq., of Washington, D. C.

THE writer of this diary was born in Westborough, Mass., 6 Mar., 1736-7. Enlisting in Apr., 1759, his company evidently formed a part of the 2d battalion of Col. Ruggles's Worcester County regiment.

Hardy passed the remainder of his days in Westborough, and died there 16 Mar., 1777. By his marriage with Jemima Brigham of Shrewsbury (intention recorded 15 Jan., 1763), he had two sons and five daughters. The elder son, Constantine, removed to Upton, and later to Shelburne, Mass. The latter's great-granddaughter, Miss Elizabeth Hardy, of Shelburne, is the present owner of the diary. This consisted originally of a book of twenty-two leaves, but only twelve and part of another of the leaves are now remaining.

April the 2 1759. I inlested in to his maiestys Seruice to Serue my King and Cuntry Under Capten Sephen Maynard*

May the 10. 1759. I Past muster at Worcester Before Capt. Whelock and then the Next time we Past muster at Springfield Before a helander† officer and the Next Day we was ordered to march and we marched as fur as the Sig of the Black horse and then we halted and then we was ordered to march from there to go ouer the Riuer and we Stad for our billingtin we stod till Corl Rugls‡ Came out and then we marched ouer the Riuer and Lay in an old house one Night and all the Next Day till about Sundown and then orders Came for us to march ouer to westfield and from theire wee went to Glascho§ and the Next Day we went throw the greenwoods and then from thir we went to Sheffield their we Staid til monday and then went to go to Canter hook‖ and Lay in the woods one Night and the Next Day we went in to Canter Hook and tarried their one Night and the Next Day we arriued Safe to Green bush and tarried their one Night and the

* Undoubtedly Capt. Stephen Maynard, a prominent man of Westborough.

† Highlander, or Scotch.

‡ Timothy Ruggles of Hardwick, colonel and brigadier general in this war, and later a prominent tory in Revolutionary days.

§ Blandford, which had earlier borne the name of Glasgow.

‖ Kinderhook.

Next day we went in to Albany and we went Up onto the Hil aboue the Sitty and their we Lay about a fort net or three weeks.

Staats Van Sanstoord opposit to the Kings Coot of Arms Eight huts Lef hear Albony June: the: 1 Ano Domine 1759

June the 18. 1759. Coneticut Jerzy Blews* and the Royal Scotch From Ford Edward to go to the Lake.

June the 20. we Sot out to go to the Lak and at Night wee ariued Safe at the Lake their was Six or seuen thousand got to the Lake that Night.

June the 24. mr for Bushes† text was in Mathew the 5 Chapter and the Forty forth Verse.

June ye 28. all the Batallion Went out to Shooting Plattoons and We Shot three Rounds a Piece and then Brock off

July the 2. the French and Endions Came upon a Party of Jarzy Blews that was apealing Bark and kild and Took Eleuen they Came in open Sight of the Camp their Rallied out Maier Rogers‡ with a Number of the Rangers and they Pursued after them and they Came in Sight of them Jest as they got in to their Battoes and So they got away.

July ye 2. [Duplicating the last entry] there Came fourteen Batooes from tantrabogus Parte of the Way to the Lakes to the Camps and then there Came about Twenty Indians vpon a party of the Jerzy Blews of Eighteen men and killed and Scalped and Took thirteen out of Eighteen and they Came Within one Hundred and fifty Rod of the Camps in open Sight of us all and we Dont know that We killed any one of them But the Raingers folowed hard after them and they had got into their Batooes and had got off about twenty Rods from the Land and So got away

July the 9. 1759. The Reu. Mr. Forbush Preached a Sermon From the first of Samuel the Seuetentnth Chapter and the Forty fifth Verse.

July the 12: 1759. Mier Rogers Went out with about Five hundred men with him and a Cannon or two he went Down the Lake as Far as the first Narrows and He Came uppon a Party of french and Endions they met and they had a Small Scurmey and they Cild one Serient and wounded one man more but we dont know as we Cilled any of them but it Looks Very Likely that they Cilled Some of them for we Shot one of their battoes in two and Droue them and took a Small Brest work and Burnt it up and then Came of and Left them and he got in the Same Night.

July the 13: 1759. There was a man Shot to Deth for Desertion amongst the regulars.

July the: 14: 1759. the first Battallion Came up to the Lake and Joyned the Second Battallion and their was a Ridgment or a Part of a Ridgment of Coneticots and Some Jerzey Blews.

July the 15: 1759. The Rev. mr. Forbush Preached a Sermon from Jeremiah the Forty Eight Chapter and the tenth Veirce.

July the 17. their was a french flag of truce Came in here and what they Came in for I know not.

The Eighteenth Day. their was a Number of men went out to Shoot of their guns and their was Very hot fighering for Some Considerable time

July the 21. the army all im barct to Set out for tiantorogo and we got with in three or four miles of the Landing Place and then Lay upon our ores all Night and a teedious Night we had and in the morning the Rangers and Conl: Willems Ridgment and the Second Battallion of

* The New Jersey troops were commonly designated Jersey blues.

† Rev. Eli Forbes of North Brookfield, chaplain of Ruggles's regiment.

‡ Maj. Robert Rogers, the commander of the celebrated Rangers.

Bregidear Rugles Ridgment all Landed upon the East Side of the Lake and we marched Round upon the mountains and came In by the mils and then the Second Battalion marched up By the East side of the Lake against their brest work and Built a Brest woork annd then Cap: Maynard with about Fifty men went upon the Rocks upon a Point of Land wheir Lake george and the South Bay Emtyed in to Lake Cham Plain and their they built another Smal Brest woork wheir they Cept a guard of twenty fiue men

Augst the 5 1759. The Second Batalion of Brigedar Rugilses Ridgment Set out for Crown Point and about half way between Sundown and Dark we all a Riued Safe at Crown Point and then we had to on Lod our Battoes and then we marched upon the grass wheir the gras was fit to mough and Canpt Down that Night Some of us Pitched our tents and Some of them Neuer Stood to Pitch their Tents But Lay Right Down upon the grass till morning

August the 6: 1759. We was ordered to pitch our tents in order

Crownpoint Avgust the 10 1759. Recevd a Letter from home Dated July the 25 Anadomine 1759

Crownpoint August ye 26: 1759. the Reverend mr. forbush went over to Col. Whitings Ridgments to Preach for all our men was gon out of the Camps and he had None to Preach to he Dident Preach to None of ourn onely what went to that Ridgment and that want mayny only a few Sick ones that want able to go upon feteague

Crownpoint September 23. the Reu Mr ——— Preached a Sermon from Mathew the fifth Chapter and the Eight Verse

---

GEORGE BETHUNE OF CRAIGFURDIE, SCOTLAND, AND BOSTON, MASS.

By Charles P. Noyes, Esq., of St. Paul, Minn.

George Bethune, son of William and grandson of Robert and Marion (Inglis) Bethune of Craigfurdie, Scotland, arrived in Boston about 1710. The approximate year of his arrival is obtained from Sewall's Diary, where, under date of Mar. 11, 1710–1, we find this note: "Thomas Lee, and George Bethune fin'd for Constables."

It has been stated that George Bethune came to Boston about 1724, established himself as a banker there, and married a Miss Carey; but after a most thorough search in Boston for the ancestry of Miss Carey, I became satisfied that this was an error, and my later discovery of the following records proves it to be so.

In the Boston Book of Marriage Intentions we find George Bethune was published June 10, 1713, to Mary Waters of Marblehead, while in the Marblehead town record of Marriages appears this record: "George Bethune of Boston and Mrs. Mary Waters Je 3 1713." Another record gives the date as June 30. Mary Waters, born Feb. 25, 1691–2, baptized at Marblehead Apr. 24, 1692, was the eldest daughter of William and Elizabeth (Latimer) Waters of Marblehead, Mass.

Further confirmation of the marriage was found in the following: George Bethune of Boston deeded property, Sept. 10, 1722, to Nathaniel Norden, Mary Waters's uncle, to settle the estate which Nathaniel Norden held in his own right, and which, on his decease, was to go to Latimer

Waters (Mary's brother) and his heirs; and in default of such heirs it was to go to the next of kin of Latimer's deceased mother, Elizabeth (Latimer) Waters. (Essex Co. Deeds, Vol. 41, p. 209.) Sept. 14, 1722, Nathaniel Norden of Marblehead, "for love of his kinswoman Mary wife of George Bethune," deeded to her a certain house "now in possession of Benjamin Stacy called The Three Codds Tavern." (Essex Co. Deeds, Vol. 41, p. 210.) In a deed of settlement in 1722, Nathaniel Norden gave to Latimer Waters, Mary Petherick, spinster, of Marblehead, George Bethune of Boston and Mary his wife, two dwellings which were part of the estate of Christopher Latimer, set off to Nathaniel Norden in lieu of debt. (Essex Co. Deeds, Vol. 44, p. 88.) In the final distribution of Christopher Latimer's estate, Jan. 6, 1726, the division was between Latimer Waters of Marblehead and George and Mary Bethune of Boston—"One half to Latimer Waters and the other half to Mary Bethune, children of William and Elizabeth Waters, said Elizabeth being a daughter of Christopher Latimer." (Essex Deeds, Vol. 53, p. 180.) There appears to have been no other George Bethune of Boston at that time, so the above seems to establish beyond question the fact that his wife was Mary Waters.

George Bethune was undoubtedly engaged to some extent in shipping trade, as, Dec. 18, 1727, he bought of Daniel Law "the sloop Mayflower all ready for a voyage to Honduras." He was one of the members of the Scots Charitable Society of Boston, and in 1732 was Justice of the Peace. The date of his death is not known, but it was probably in 1735, as an inventory of his estate was taken Feb. 20, 1735-6, in Boston.

The children of George and Mary (Waters) Bethune were:

i. JANE, b. June 15, 1714; m. (1) Feb. 1, 1737-8, Dr. (or Capt.) Moses, son of Samuel and Mercy (Hinckley) Prince, who d. July 6, 1745, at Antigua, W. I.; and m. (2) Sept., 1761, as his third wife, Hon. Peter, son of Col. John and Elizabeth (Coffin) Gilman. She died at Newburyport, Mass., Mar. 9, 1795.

ii. NATHANIEL, b. July 25, 1715; m. probably Hannah (or Abigail), daughter of Job and Sarah (Palmer) Lewis. He was Justice of the Peace in 1760; and d. in Boston. His will was dated Feb. 1, and probated Mar. 15, 1771.

iii. MARY, b. Apr. 27, 1717; d. young.

iv. ELIZA (or ELIZABETH), b. June 1, 1718; m. in 1758 (intention published Oct. 26), Ezekiel Lewis. She probably d. before 1771, as her brother Nathaniel in his will mentions only her husband, "Brother Ezekiel Lewis."

v. GEORGE, b. in 1719; d. the same year.

vi. GEORGE, b. Dec. 7, 1720; m. in 1754 (intention published July 15, 1751), Mary, daughter of Benjamin Faneuil, and niece of Peter Faneuil, of Boston. He was Justice of the Peace in 1774; and d. in Cambridge, in 1785.

vii. SUSANNA, b. Dec. 11, 1722; m. Benjamin Pemberton.

viii. HENRY, b. Aug. 18, 1724.

ix. SARAH, b. June 27, 1728; m. in 1760 (intention published June 30), Rev. Sylvanus Conant of Middleborough, Mass.

x. MARY, b. Oct. 7, 1730.

Mary Waters, wife of George Bethune, was daughter of William Waters (d. 1704); and granddaughter of William Waters (d. 1684), of Marblehead, and his wife Hannah (Peach) Bradstreet, the daughter of John Peach (d. 1694) of Marblehead.

Her mother, Elizabeth Latimer (d. 1699), was daughter of Christopher Latimer (d. 1690), of Marblehead, and his wife Mary (d. 1681), daughter of William Pitts (d. after 1679), of Marblehead and Boston, Mass.

PASSENGER LISTS TO AMERICA.

Communicated by GERALD FOTHERGILL, Esq., of New Wandsworth, London, England.

[Continued from page 164.]

List of Passengers who intend to proceed on board the American Ship *Jefferson* to New York from Sligo, James Adams, Master, sworn at Sligo, 16 Apl., 1803.

Peter Gonagle	Labourer	Pat Nelis	Labourer
James Clenten	"	Edmd Gilfeader	"
Edm[d] Leyonard	"	Thomas Reily	"
Pat. Waterson		James M[c]Key	
John M[c]Gan	"	James Curry	
Thos Wymbs	Dealer	Dan[l] Gilmartin	
Mich[l] Wymbs	"	Thos Farrel	
Pat Hangdon	Labourer	John Higgins	
John Harken	"	William Kalens	
Fran[s] Kelly	"		

The following duplicate of the foregoing, sworn 28 Apl., 1803, by James Adams, the Master, gives fuller information.

Peter Nangle	aged 40 of	Sligo		Labourer
James Clenton	26	Clurbagh	Sligo	"
Edm[d] Leynerk	20	"	"	"
Pat Waterson	55	"	"	"
John M[c]Gan	32	Carns	Sligo	"
Thos Wymbs	36	"	"	Dealer
Mich[l] "	30	"	"	"
Pat Haregdon	41	Moneygold	"	Labourer
John Harken	26	Grange	"	"
Fra[s] Kelly	29	Bunduff	"	"
Pat Nelis	27	Creery	"	"
Edm[d] Gilfeader	23	M[t] Temple	"	"
Tho[s] Reilly	29	" "	"	"
Ja[s] M[c]Key	36	Sligo		
Ja[s] Curry	28	"		
Dan[l] Gilmartin	29	"		
Tho[s] Farrell	23	Clurbagh	Sligo	"
Jno Higgins	37	"	"	"
W[m] Kalens	42	"	"	

A List of Passengers who intend going to Baltimore in the Ship *Serpent* of Baltimore, Arch[d] McCockell, Master, sworn at Londonderry, 30 Apl., 1803.

Joseph	Neilson	26	Farmer	Strabane
Margt	"	24	———	"
Jane	"	14	spinster	"
Elizabeth	"	12	"	"
John	"	10	———	"
James	"	10	———	"

Sam[l] McCarthy	25	Labourer	Omagh
Dav[d] Falls	25	"	"
Sam[l] Turner	30	"	Strabane
Jn[o] Neilson	27	"	"
Pat Mounigle	28	"	Rosquill
Neal McPeak	30	"	"
Mich[l] McCann	40	Farmer	"
Phelix McCann	35	"	
Pat[k] "	28	"	
Peter "	18	"	
Nelly "	37	——	"
Susan "	40	——	"
Hannah "	16	spinster	"
Mary "	14	"	
James McBride	25	Farmer	"
Catherine "	24	——	"
Peter Corbitt	25	Farmer	Rathmullen
Isabella "	23	——	"
John Mundell	40	Farmer	Gortgarn
Margaret Mundell	39	——	"
Samuel "	46	Farmer	"
W[m] Jn[o] "	25	"	
Isabella "	37	——	"
Isabella "	20	spinster	"
Jane "	16	"	"
Mary "	14	"	"
Eliz[h] "	12	"	"
Margt Craig	36	——	"
Geo Laird	25	Farmer	"
Sam[l] "	22	"	"
Mary "	24	——	"
Rach[l] "	25	spinster	"
Peter Kenedy	27	Farmer	"
Margaret "	25	——	"
Emelia "	6	——	"
James Reed	40	Farmer	Maghera
Agnes Reed	37	——	"
Sally "	15	spinster	"
Mary McCool	45	——	"
James McCool	24	Farmer	"
Jn "	20	"	"
Nelly Ross	35	——	"
James Rolls	18	Labourer	"

Passengers List of the Ship *Strafford* for Philadelphia, sworn at Londonderry, 14 May, 1803.

John	McGan	aged 34	Farmer of	Coagh
Elizabeth	"	30	Spinster	"
Sarah	"	2	——	"
Elinor	"	infant	——	"
W[m]	Walker	30	Farmer	"
Mary Anne	"	20	Spinster	"
Eliz	"	18	"	"

Wm Mitchel	20	Farmer	Cumber
Thos Coningham	18	"	Ballymony
Alexr Stewart	20	Labourer	Ketreights
John Moore	19	"	Loughgin
James Hamilton	23	"	"
Wm Smily	23	"	Ketreights
Edw Clarke	40	Farmer	Enniskillen
John Milley	45	"	"
Wm Loughridge	30	"	Cookstown
Mg "	24	———	"
Jane "	7	———	"
James "	5	———	
Eliza "	2	———	"
Nancy Harkin	30	Seamstress	Birdstown
Nelly "	4	———	"
Wm "	6	———	"
John Chamber	20	Farmer	County Tyrone
Wm Gray	24	"	" "
James Ralston	45	"	" "
Mary Ralston	40	———	" "
James Ralston	15	———	" "
Mary "	12	———	" "
Davd "	9	———	" "
Josh "	5	———	" "
Anne "	2	———	" "
Anne "	34	Seamstress	" "
Robt	19	Labourer	" "
Davd	15	"	
John	11	———	" "
Jane	8	———	" "
Anne "	5	———	" "
Josh	2	———	" "
John "	40	Farmer	" "
Sarah "	40	Seamstress	" "
Davd	9	———	" "
Andw	7	———	" "
Wm	3	———	" "
James "	5	———	" "
Elinor Shean	60	———	County Down
Mary Anderson	24	———	" "
Mary "	2	———	" "
John Wilson	22	Farmer	———
Wm Carr	20	"	———
James Moore	19		Ballykelly

A List of Passengers to go on board the Ship *Patty*, sworn at Newry, 5 May, 1803.

Wm Griffis	34	Labourer	Down
Andrew Hurs	30	"	"
John Kenedy	41	"	"
Saml McBride	28	"	Tyrone
John Gibson	50	Farmer	"

Patk Lynch	27	Laborer	Tyrone
David Hunter	28	"	"
Edward "	34	"	"
George "	14		"
Alexr Armstrong	29	"	Armargh
Mary Harvey	45	Spinster	"
Eliza "	23	"	"
Robt "	48	Farmer	"
Biddy Brown	38	Spinster	Down
Henry Williams	28	Gentleman	Armagh
Saml Patton	32	Laborer	Down
Joseph "	36	"	"
George Tilforde	28	"	"
John Blair	29	"	
John McDale	36		
Walter Potts	25		
William Roncy	19	"	
James Eakin	46	Farmer	"
Samuel "	50	"	
James Fitspatrick	37	"	
Mary "	32	Spinster	"
Edward Maugher	26	Laborer	Queens County
John Fleming	24	"	" "
Thomas Dick	32	Farmer	Down
James Nelson	28	"	"
John Armstrong	29	"	"

[To be continued.]

THE BELCHER FAMILIES IN NEW ENGLAND.

By Joseph Gardner Bartlett, Esq.

[Continued from page 136.]

16. John[4] Belcher (*John,[3] Josiah,[2] Gregory[1]*), born in Boston, Dec. 11, 1689, was a mariner and lived in Boston, where he died, Oct. 3, 1713, just one month after his marriage. He was buried in the Granary burying ground, where his gravestone still remains. He married, Sept. 3, 1713, Sarah,[8] born Oct. 11, 1695, daughter of Dea. Samuel[2] and Ruth (Rawlins) Marshall of Boston, who married second, Nov. 17, 1715, Capt. John Bonner, Jr., mariner, of Boston, and died about 1761. (Suffolk Co. Probate, vol. 60, page 80.)
Child:

i. John,[5] b. in Boston, June 2, 1714; was a mariner and lived in Boston, where he m., June 12, 1735, Anne Jones, and had two children.

17. Capt. Benjamin[4] Belcher (*Benjamin,[3] Josiah,[2] Gregory[1]*), born in Newport, R. I., Nov. 7, 1704, resided in his native town, where he was a shipwright and sea captain. He married, Dec. 24, 1724, Abigail Arnold, who died in Newport, Dec. 7, 1773, aged 67·

She was probably the Abigail Arnold, born Mar. 28, 1706, daughter of Josiah and Mary (Sanford) Arnold of Jamestown, R. I. Their children were baptized in Trinity Church, Newport.

Children:

i. BENJAMIN,[5] bapt. Jan. 16, 1725-6.
ii. JOSIAH, bapt. Aug. 20, 1727; d. young.
iii. PHEBE, bapt. Nov. 10, 1728; probably m. Aug. 8, 1755, Henry Perkins.
iv. ABIGAIL, bapt. May 3, 1730; d. young.
v. ABIGAIL, bapt. July 7, 1732; perhaps m. Aug. 13, 1758, Owen Belcher.
vi. MARY, bapt. Sept. 29, 1734.
vii. ARNOLD, bapt. Sept. 30, 1736.
viii. JOSIAH, bapt. Aug. 9, 1737.
ix. COMFORT, bapt. Aug. 21, 1739.

18. CAPT. EDWARD[4] BELCHER (*Benjamin,[3] Josiah,[2] Gregory*[1]), born in Newport, R. I., Aug. 24, 1711, was a shipwright and mariner, and was admitted freeman of R. I. on May 6, 1735. He married first, Dec. 5, 1734, Catherine Arnold, who was probably the Catherine Arnold born Feb. 7, 1713, daughter of Josiah and Mary (Sanford) Arnold of Jamestown, R. I.; and married second, June 22, 1747, Lydia Howland.

Probable children by first wife:

i. ARNOLD,[5] b. about 1735; of Jamestown, R. I.; m. Feb. 18, 1758, Catharine Austin.
ii. OWEN, b. about 1737; m. Aug. 13, 1758, Abigail Belcher.
iii. CATHARINE.
iv. ELIZABETH.

Child by second wife:

v. BENJAMIN, bapt. Aug. 12, 1751.

19. ARNOLD[4] BELCHER (*Benjamin,[3] Josiah,[2] Gregory*[1]), born about 1715, lived at Westerly, R. I. He married Elizabeth, born Jan. 10, 1719, daughter of Christopher and Elizabeth (Dennison) Champlin of Westerly. The record of this family does not appear, but the following children were probably theirs.

Children:

i. SILVESTER,[5] m. July 2, 1761, Olive Babcock.
ii. ELIZABETH, m. Nov. 11, 1764, Job Stanton.

20. JOHN[4] BELCHER (*Josiah,[3] John,[2] Gregory*[1]), born Aug. 28, 1694, lived in Braintree until after his marriage, and then in Boston, where he died about 1720. He apparently owned no real estate, and there is no reference to him in probate records. He married, Aug. 16, 1717, Sarah Cook of Brookline, who married second, in Boston, Feb. 7, 1722–3, John White.

Children:

i. REBECCA,[5] b. Oct. 29, 1718; m. Oct. 18, 1739, Philip Newton of Boston. She was bapt. as an adult, and admitted to the New South Church on Feb. 17, 1739–40.
ii. SARAH (?), b. about 1720. There was a Sarah Belcher bapt. and admitted to the New South Church on the same day as Rebecca (Belcher) Newton, and it is probable that they were sisters. Sarah Belcher's m. int. was pub. to Samuel Barns, July 31, 1740.

21. Moses[4] Belcher (*Moses,*[3] *Moses,*[2] *Gregory*[1]), born Mar. 8, 1715-16, lived in Braintree. On Apr. 20, 1736, his father was appointed guardian for him and his sister Anne, for property left them by their grandfather Samuel Sarson. (Suffolk Co. Probate.) On Oct. 7, 1740, Moses Belcher, Jr., yeoman, and Anne Belcher, spinster, both of Braintree, sold to Nathaniel Wardwell of Boston (husband of their aunt Anna Belcher) their interest in an estate in Boston formerly belonging to their grandfather Samuel Sarson deceased. (Suffolk Co. Deeds, Vol. 59, page 271.) On the records he is called Moses, Jr., and Moses *tertius*, to distinguish him from his father and from his cousin Maj. and Dea. Moses[4] Belcher. He married Eunice, born Apr. 4, 1716, daughter of Experience and Remember (Bourne) Mayhew of Chilmark, Martha's Vineyard.

Children:

- i. Eunice,[5] b. Dec. 25, 1736.
- ii. Lucy, b. Mar. 2, 1738-9.
- iii. Capt. Sarson, b. June 21, 1741; settled in Boston, where he carried on the business of hatter; joined the Ancient and Honorable Artillery Co. in 1765; during the Revolution he was Capt. of the 8th Co. of Boston Militia in Col. Hatch's regt.; m. Mar. 24, 1763, Fenton (or Fanny), dau. of John and Elizabeth Hill, who was b. Mar. 7, 1742-3, and d. Aug. 25, 1793; d. Dec. 24, 1794. They had issue.
- iv. Mary, b. May 24, 1744; d. Sept. 23, 1748.
- v. Mayhew, b. Mar. 12, 1746; located in Bridgewater, and there d. unmarried, in 1778; served in the Revolution, a few days on the Lexington alarm in 1775, later in an expedition to Rhode Island, in Dec., 1776.
- vi. Anne, b. about 1747; m. in Bridgewater, Apr. 21, 1774, John Keith of Hardwick.

22. Gregory[4] Belcher (*Dea. Gregory,*[3] *Samuel,*[2] *Gregory*[1]), born June 19, 1691, was a carpenter and lived in Braintree, where he died, Jan. 20, 1727-8, in his 37th year. His will, dated Jan. 17, 1727-8, names wife Abigail and daughter Abigail. He married, Aug. 6, 1719, Abigail Brackett, who died a few months after her husband.

Child:

- i. Abigail,[5] b. July 16, 1720; m. Nov. 6, 1740, Samuel Nightingale; removed to Pomfret, Conn. (Suffolk Co. Deeds, vol. 64, p. 173.)

23. Sergt. Samuel[4] Belcher (*Dea. Gregory,*[3] *Samuel,*[2] *Gregory*[1]), born in Braintree, Aug. 19, 1699, was a husbandman, and resided in Braintree until his death, June 21, 1738, administration being given to his widow Sarah. Between 1728 and 1738 he held several minor town offices, usually surveyor of shingles and clapboards, and in 1736 became sergeant of one of the military companies. He married, Jan. 13, 1725-6, Sarah, born Oct. 19, 1705, daughter of Jonathan and Sarah (Ruggles) Hayward, who married second, Sept. 7, 1742, Dea. Thomas Wales.

Children:

- i. Samuel,[5] b. Nov. 7, 1726; d. Jan. 25, 1726-7.
- ii. Sarah, b. Dec. 1, 1729; m. Dec. 4, 1744, Atherton Wales; d. 1816.
- iii. Elizabeth, b. Nov. 22, 1733; m. Moses Wales.
- iv. Susanna, b. Apr. 19, 1736; m. (int. pub. Jan. 24, 1756) Col. Jonathan Bass, who d. May 12, 1790, aged 57 yrs.

v. SAMUEL, b. Nov. 21, 1738; lived in Randolph; m. (int. pub. July 3, 1758), Sarah, b. Sept. 7, 1731, dau. of Joseph and Hannah (Allen) Wales, who d. June 6, 1806; d. June 6, 1795. Six children.

24. REV. JOSEPH[4] BELCHER (*Dea. Gregory,[3] Samuel,[2] Gregory[1]*), born Aug. 19, 1704, graduated from Harvard College in 1723, and studied for the ministry. After preaching at Walpole, Mass., and other places, he received a call to Easton, Mass., where he was settled and ordained, Oct. 6, 1731. He was a man of peculiar temperament, and was subject to periodical attacks of partial insanity, which resulted in serious difficulties in his church, and in his dismission on Apr. 16, 1744. Financial embarrassments finally induced him, shortly after the death of his wife, to desert his children and flee from his creditors. He was for a while at Wiscasset, Me., but on Dec. 3, 1757, acknowledged a deed at Taunton, Mass. (Suffolk Co. Deeds, vol. 94, page 67.) His further history is unknown to the writer, but the catalogue of Harvard College states that he died in 1773.

He married, in 1732, Deborah, born Mar. 8, 1710–11, daughter of Rev. Samuel and Hannah (Pope) Hunt of Dartmouth, who died Mar. 21, 1753.

Children:

i. HANNAH,[5] b. Jan. 23, 1732–3; m. in Bridgewater, Dec. 14, 1769, as his second wife, Capt. Moses Curtis of Braintree.

ii. REBECCA, b. Apr. 1, 1735; m. in Bridgewater, Jan. 5, 1764, Jesse Edson.

iii. "DR." JOSEPH, b. Apr. 1, 1735; served in Capt. Simeon Carey's Co. in two Crown Point expeditions, in 1758 and 1759; settled, about 1762, in Stoughton, where he carried on a farm and also posed as a physician, his specialty being a quack eye lotion; m. Mar. 2, 1762, Abial Hollis, who d. Feb. 14, 1838, aged 94; d. Apr. 20, 1803. Eight children.

iv. BENJAMIN, b. about 1737 (?). A Benjamin Belcher appears on the roll of Capt. Simeon Cary's Co. in 1758, on a Crown Point expedition. This individual cannot be placed unless he was a son of Rev. Joseph.[4]

v. GREGORY, b. Jan. 26, 1738–9; lived in Easton; m. (1) Deborah ———, by whom he had one child; m. (2) June 29, 1775, Elizabeth Pratt, by whom he had three children.

vi. DEBORAH, b. Mar. 31, 1741; m. in Bridgewater, Dec. 3, 1761, Seth Dunbar.

vii. SAMUEL, b. Feb. 4, 1742–3; d. Jan. 29, 1755.

viii. ELEAZER, b. Sept. 1, 1745; went to Stoughton, and settled in that part which in 1778 became Foxborough; served in the Revolution; m. (int. pub. Nov. 10, 1766) Elizabeth,[6] b. Sept. 10, 1745, dau. of Timothy[5] and Elizabeth (Partridge) Morse of Stoughton, who d. in Apr., 1838; d. Dec. 24, 1818. Nine children.

ix. WILLIAM, b. Jan. 29, 1748; is said to have been killed or captured near New York, in Sept., 1776, in the Revolution. (History of Easton, page 100.)

x. JONATHAN, b. in Feb., 1753; lived in Stoughton and Needham during the Revolution, and rendered protracted service in the army; later settled and d. in his native town of Easton; m. Jan. 4, 1778, Abigail, b. in 1751, dau. of Daniel and Hannah (Rose) Corthrell of Bridgewater. They had issue.

25. MAJ. and DEA. MOSES[4] BELCHER (*Samuel,[3] Samuel,[2] Gregory[1]*), born in Braintree, Dec. 16, 1692, passed his life in his native town, where he became an influential man and the most prominent of the Bel-

chers descended from Gregory. Up to 1735 he is called "Jr." on the records, to distinguish him from his elder cousin Moses[3] (born in 1674, son of Moses[2]), and after that year (when Moses,[4] son of Moses,[3] became of age and a town voter) he is designated either as "Mr." or "Deacon," or by his military title. As early as 1726 he began to hold minor town offices, and for over 30 years he was continuously prominent in the affairs of the town; selectman from 1737 to 1742, and in 1746; sergeant 1737–1742; lieutenant 1742–1748; captain 1748–1751; and major from 1751 to 1759. During the French and Indian war, from 1756 to 1759, he rendered service as a muster and training officer, but on account of his age probably did not take the field. On May 29, 1747, he was elected deacon of the first church, holding the office for thirty years, until his death. The exact time of his decease is not recorded, but he was living as late as 1775. The probate files show no record of his estate.

He married first, in Boston, May 20, 1715, Mary Williams; and married second, May 23, 1765, Abigail, born Oct. 11, 1704, daughter of Benjamin and Hannah Beale, and widow of Benjamin Baxter of Braintree.

Children by first wife:

i. SAMUEL,[5] b. Sept. 19, 1719, in Braintree; settled in Boston about 1752, where he engaged in the trucking business; and d. in Feb., 1762. His residence was at the corner of Bury Street and Sister's Lane (now Channing Street and Leather Square), and his name appears on the alarm list for Ward 12, Boston, dated Dec. 7, 1754. Children by wife Abigail: 1. *Samuel,*[6] b. Oct. 24, 1743; settled in Boston, where he m., Apr. 9, 1765, Deborah Thompson. Children: i. Samuel Thompson,[7] b. Apr. 18, 1767; m. Jan. 12, 1792, Sally, b. Apr. 28, 1775, dau. of Lewis and Sarah (Tuckerman) Tucker; settled in Foxborough, Mass., where he d. Jan. 22, 1846, and she d. May 15, 1842, leaving children. ii. Deborah, b. Aug. 11, 1768; m. June 20, 1790, Edward Reynolds, merchant, of Boston, and had Dr. Edward, H. C. 1811, a distinguished oculist in Boston. iii. Mary Thompson, bapt. Feb. 7, 1773. iv. Jenny Thompson, bapt. in Weston, Sept. 24, 1775. 2. *A child,* b. and d. May, 1745 (?). 3. *A child,* b. and d. July 17, 1747. 4. *Mary,* bapt. Apr. 30, 1749; probably the one who m. in Boston, Aug. 15, 1767, Edward Stow, Jr. 5. *Abigail,* bapt. Nov. 3, 1751; m. in Boston, May 21, 1772, Benjamin Callender. 6. *William,* bapt. in New South church, Boston, Feb. 17, 1754; was a tailor; settled in Northfield, Mass., where he d. Mar. 14, 1827; m. June 8, 1775, Huldah, bapt. July 3, 1757, dau. of Alexander and Lydia (Chamberlain) Norton of Northfield. Thirteen children. 7. *Richard,* bapt. June 13, 1756; probably the Richard, of Boston, who enlisted June 10, 1775, as matross in Maj. Thomas Pierce's Co.; not further traced.

ii. MARY, b. Mar. 10, 1721–2; further history unknown.

iii. MOSES, b. Apr. 27, 1724.

iv. ELIJAH, b. Oct. 21, 1729; resided in Braintree, where he d. June 1, 1800; served for two days, in June, 1776, in a Co. commanded by Capt. Edmund Billings, assembled to drive the British ships from Boston, also in a regt. of guards at Roxbury, from Mar. 25 to Apr. 7, 1778; m. (1) Oct. 4, 1753, Mary, b. Apr. 21, 1736, dau. of John and Mary (Horton) Glover of Dorchester, who d. Nov. 2, 1754, leaving one child; m. (2) (int. pub. Sept. 15, 1758) Mary, b. Jan. 24, 1732, dau. of William and Deliverance (Woodward) Pierce of Milton, who d. Mar. 22, 1819. Five children.

v. WILLIAM, bapt. June 24, 1733; was a merchant of Boston, of the firm of Richard Cranch & Co., candle manufacturers.

26. LIEUT. NATHANIEL[4] BELCHER (*Samuel,[3] Samuel,[2] Gregory[1]*), born in Braintree, July 25, 1700, resided there and held various minor town offices from 1729 to 1759, in which latter year he was chosen selectman. From 1749 to 1756 he was ensign, and after 1756 lieutenaut of one of the Braintree military companies. In his old age he went to reside with his son Joseph in Randolph, where he died in the winter of 1780, aged 80 years.

He married first, Nov. 18, 1731, Hannah, born Nov. 20, 1702, daughter of Thomas and Mary Holbrook of Braintree, who died Feb. 3, 1754–5; married second, Sarah ———, who died June 24, 1761, aged 61; and married third, June 1, 1768, Bethia Bass.

Children by first wife:

i. CAPT. NATHANIEL,[5] b. Sept. 19, 1732; resided in Braintree, where he was a prominent man during the Revolutionary period; served as sergeant and as lieutenant in the French and Indian War in the campaigns of 1759, 1760, and 1762; was captain in the Continental army in the Revolution; d. in 1786; m. Dec. 10, 1755, Lydia, b. Oct. 26, 1734, d. about 1787, dau. of Richard and Lydia Brackett. Ten children.

ii. JOSEPH, b. Aug. 5, 1734; lived in Braintree, and later in Randolph; served in the Revolution; d. Oct. 18, 1818, in his 85th year, and administration on his estate was given to his eldest son, John, in 1819 (Norfolk Co. Probate); m. Jan. 6, 1763, Susanna, b. June 16, 1736, d. Oct. 28, 1821, dau. of John and Mehitable (Willard) Baxter of Braintree. Nine children.

iii. HANNAH, b. Sept. 14, 1736; d. June 21, 1744.

iv. THOMAS (or THOMAS HOLBROOK), b. Oct. 20, 1739; lived in Braintree, and later in Randolph; served in the Crown Point expeditions of 1758, '59, '61, and '62, and later in the Revolution; m. (1) Nov. 3, 1764, Sarah Bracket, who d. about 1766, leaving one child; m. (2) (int. pub. Aug. 6, 1768) Mary, b. about 1742, dau. of Ebenezer and Deborah (White) Copeland of Braintree, who d. in 1810, having had six children; d. Feb. 28, 1824.

v. MARY, b. Oct. 8, 1741; d. June 6, 1744.

vi. EBENEZER, b. Dec. 2, 1744; served at Castle Island, from Dec. 1, 1762, to May 2, 1763; probably the Ebenezer who served in the Revolution from Scituate, and who m. there, Mar. 2, 1780, Ruth Peterson.

27. WILLIAM[4] BELCHER (*Moses,[3] Samuel,[2] Gregory[1]*), born in Milton, Mass., Dec. 20, 1701, was taken by his parents to Preston, Conn., where he afterwards resided, and died Feb. 7, 1731–2. His will, dated Sept. 6, 1731, mentions his wife, son William, mother Hannah, and brother Elijah.

He married Mehitable ———.

Child:

i. CAPT. WILLIAM,[5] b. Aug. 29, 1731; lived in Preston, where he d. June 27, 1801, in his 70th year; commanded a company in the Revolution; m. Apr. 23, 1752, Desire, b. Feb. 27, 1736, d. May 15, 1801, dau. of Daniel and Elizabeth (Gates) Morgan of Preston. Nine children.

28. DEA. ELIJAH[4] BELCHER (*Moses,[3] Samuel,[2] Gregory[1]*), born in Milton, Mass., Dec. 13, 1703, went to Preston, Conn., with his parents, in 1720, where he afterwards resided, and was deacon in the Preston (now Griswold) second church. In 1748 he was Representative to the Conn. General Assembly.

He married first, in Preston, Sept. 17, 1724, Abigail Kinney, who died Sept. 21, 1727; married second, in Milton, Aug. 21, 1729, Elizabeth, born Apr. 5, 1704, daughter of Edward and Elizabeth (Morey) Blake of Milton, who died Feb. 13, 1753; married third, in Preston, June 6, 1753, Mrs. Hannah Williams, who died Nov. 26, 1771; and married fourth, July 15, 1773, Mrs. Judith Morse of Preston.

Children by first wife:

i. MOSES,[6] b. Oct. 20, 1725; d. Jan. 11, 1732-3.
ii. ELIJAH, b. Sept. 18, 1727.

Children by second wife:

iii. ELIZABETH, b. May 8, 1730; m. Dec. 12, 1753, John Starkweather.
iv. MOSES, b. Mar. 11, 1734; lived in Preston, where he d. Apr. 15, 1782; m. Nov. 8, 1758, Esther Rudd of Windham, Conn. Ten children.
v. ABIGAIL, b. May 30, 1736; m. May 27, 1752, Joseph Johnson of Preston.

JEREMIAH BELCHER OF IPSWICH.

1. JEREMY, or JEREMIAH,[1] BELCHER came to New England in the ship "Susan and Ellen," in the spring of 1635. On the ship's list his age is stated to be 22 years, so he was born about 1613. (Hotten's "Original Lists," page 59.) He is said to have been born in Wiltshire, England, but the writer has found no evidence of this. He settled at Ipswich, Mass., where he became a proprietor, was admitted freeman Mar. 13, 1638-9, and acquired extensive lands by grant and by purchase. In the records he is usually styled "merchant," but sometimes he appears as "sergeant." On May 28, 1659, he was granted 300 acres, by the General Court, to be located outside the settled plantations, but he did not take up this grant, which was revived in favor of his son Jeremiah[2] over sixty years later, Nov. 17, 1722. (Province Laws, vol. x, page 220.) On May 15, 1661, he deeded lands in Haverhill to his sons Jeremiah[2] and John.[2] (Pope's "Pioneers of Massachusetts.") He deposed on Mar. 21, 1671-2, then aged 59 years. (Essex Co. Court Files.) On July 1, 1721, John Gould of Charlestown, Walter Russell of Cambridge, Daniel Gould of Charlestown, and Moses Burnham and Thomas Andrews of Ipswich, heirs to Jeremiah Belcher of Ipswich, deceased, released to Samuel Adams all claims to a farm in Ipswich formerly owned by said Jeremiah Belcher, and they also defended the grantee from the heirs of Richard Belcher and from the heirs of David Belcher, sons of said Jeremiah, and from the heirs of John Andrews who married one of the daughters of said Jeremiah Belcher. (Essex Co. Deeds, vol. 40, page 9.)

Jeremiah[1] Belcher died in Ipswich, in Mar., 1692-3, aged about 80 years, the eldest son, Rev. Samuel,[2] being appointed administrator of the estate, Mar. 31 of that year.

The name of his first wife, whom he married about 1637, does not appear, but it should be noted, however, that a Mary Clifford, aged 25 years, emigrated to New England in the same ship with him in 1635, her name standing next to his on the passenger list, and that Edward[3] Belcher, grandson of Jeremiah,[1] had a son *Clifford*.[4]

Jeremiah[1] married second, in 1652, Mary Lockwood, with whom he made a marriage contract Sept. 30, 1652, conveying lands to trustees for her benefit for life. She survived him, and died in Oct., 1700.

Children by first wife:

2\. i. SAMUEL,[2] b. in 1639.
3\. ii. JEREMIAH, b. in June, 1641.
iii. JOHN, b. about 1643; was deeded land in Haverhill by his father, on May 15, 1661 (Pope's "Pioneers of Massachusetts," page 43); not further traced; probably d. when a young man, unmarried.
iv. MARY (first), b. about 1645; m. June 23, 1662, Joseph[2] Russell of Cambridge, and had eleven children, among whom *Walter*,[3] the oldest surviving son, signed the deed of 1721, previously mentioned. On Nov. 27, 1686, Jeremiah[1] Belcher of Ipswich conveyed to his two sons, Jeremiah Belcher of Rumney Marsh, and Joseph Russell of Cambridge, part of a tract of land he bought of an Indian in 1651. (Original deed in possession of Warren[7] Belcher, Esq., of Winthrop, Mass.)

Children by second wife:

v. ABIGAIL, b. about 1653; m. in 1670, John[2] Gould of Charlestown End (Stoneham), and had seven children, of whom the eldest son, *John*,[3] signed the deed of 1721.
vi. DORCAS, b. in 1656; m. Daniel[2] Gould of Charlestown End (Stoneham); her eldest son, *Daniel*,[3] signed the deed of 1721.
vii. JUDITH, b. Aug. 19, 1658; m. John[2] Andrews of Ipswich. (Essex Deeds, vol. 40, page 9.)
viii. MARY (second), b. July 12, 1660; m. Feb. 9, 1681–2, Thomas[2] Andrews of Ipswich, brother of John[2] who married her sister Judith; her son *Thomas*[3] signed the deed of 1721.
4\. ix. DAVID, b. in 1662.
5\. x. RICHARD, b. Sept. 10, 1665.
xi. ANN, b. probably about 1668; m. Moses Burnham of Ipswich, who signed the deed of 1721.

2\. REV. SAMUEL[2] BELCHER (*Jeremiah*[1]), born in 1639, graduated from Harvard College in 1659, and studied for the ministry, and was preaching at Kittery, Me., as early as 1663. (Sibley's "Harvard Graduates," vol. II, page 42.) About 1665 he went to the Isles of Shoals, where he was preaching as late as 1686 (York Deeds, vol. IV, page 64), but finally ill health obliged him to leave that place about 1692. Before 1695 he was preaching in the West church at Newbury, where he was ordained and settled Nov. 10, 1698. About 1711, the infirmities of age compelled him to retire from the ministry, and he removed to his native town, Ipswich, where he died Mar. 10, 1714–15. A contemporary minister, Rev. John Barnard, refers to him as "a good scholar, a judicious divine, a holy and humble man."

He married first, about 1668, Mary,[2] daughter of Rev. Thomas[1] Cobbett of Lynn and Ipswich, who died about 1679; and married second, Mercy,[3] born Feb., 1655–6, daughter of Rev. Michael[2] and Mary (Reyner) Wigglesworth of Malden, and widow of Rev. Samuel Brackenbury of Rowley. She survived her second husband, and died Nov. 14, 1728.

Children by first wife:

i. ELIZABETH,[3] b. about 1671; m. Apr. 5, 1697, John, son of George Taylor of Cape May County, N. J. On May 21, 1716, they signed a receipt for her inheritance in her father's estate, she being the only surviving child. (Essex Co. Probate.) Six children.
ii. SAMUEL, b. about 1674; mentioned in the will of his grandfather Cobbett; d. young.

3\. JEREMIAH[2] BELCHER (*Jeremiah*[1]), born in June, 1641, located about 1665 at Rumney Marsh (which embraced what is now Revere,

Chelsea, and East Boston, and was a part of Boston until 1739, when the town of Chelsea was incorporated). He first leased a farm of Gov. Bellingham (the original indenture, in the beautiful handwriting of the governor, being now in the possession of Warren[7] Belcher, Esq., of Winthrop, Mass.), and later purchased lands in what is now Lynn, Revere, and on Breed's Island (then called Hog Island). He appears to have been a prosperous farmer, as in 1702 he paid the highest tax in Rumney Marsh, on a farm worth £25 rent per year, two oxen, eight cows, two horses, one hog, and one hundred sheep. (Boston Record Commissioners' Report, vol. 10, page 143.) Late in life, he deeded lands to his sons Edward, Joseph, and Ebenezer, which they divided among themselves. (Suffolk Co. Deeds, vol. 28, page 136.)

He made a will, the original of which is in the possession of his descendant Warren[7] Belcher, Esq., of Winthrop, Mass., but the instrument was not offered for probate, and therefore never recorded in any registry, so it is herewith given in full, for preservation:

"The last Will and Testement of Jeremiah Belcher, Living in Boston, being at this present time through God's goodness in health, Revoking all other Wills.

1. I do commit my Soul into the hands of God who gave it, who I trust hath redeemed it, and purchased it with his precious Blood. And my body to decent Christian burial in hope of a blessed resurrection.

2. And as to my worldly goods I do give and bequethe forever to my three sons, Edward, Joseph, and Ebenezer Belcher, all that my Farm, lying and being within the bounds of Boston and Lin, as they have already divided it, as also the salt-marsh lying within Boston bounds.

3. I do give unto my Daughter, Sarah Dole, my house and land in Boston which I am now possessed of after my desese, that is to say she paying to me the just sume of £30 money as I shall have occasion to call for it, but if it so be I shall have no occassion to call for it, then my will is that after my desese the £30 be paid to my three sons, Edward, Joseph and Ebenezer to be equetly divided, that is to say, ten to each of them, within one year after my desease.

4. I do give to my son Edward my silver Tankard and two silver spoons. My will is that my Grandson Jeremiah the son of Edward Belcher, may have the silver Tankard, after his father's deseace.

5. I do give to my two sons Joseph and Ebenezer each of them a silver cup and two silver spoons. I also give to my daughter Dole two silver spoons.

6. What remains of my estate after my desease to be equetly divided amongst my children. Lastly, I do appoint my three sons already named, Executors of this my last Will and Testiment.

As Witness my hand and seal, Aug. 28, 1719.

In the presence of us
James Gooding JEREMIAH BELCHER."
Henry Emmes
Mark Day

Jeremiah[2] Belcher died Feb. 6, 1722–3, aged 81 years, 6 months, according to his gravestone, which is still standing in the old Revere cemetery.

He married, about 1667, Sarah,[2] daughter of Edward[1] and Elizabeth Weeden of Boston, who died Jan. 20, 1715–16. On Mar. 20, 1716–17, he entered his intention of marriage with Rebecca Nash of Boston, but it is doubtful if the marriage was consummated. She was the widow of John Nash, cooper, of Boston, who had died in 1712.

Children:

i. JEREMIAH,[3] b. Oct. 31, 1668; no further record; probably d. young.
6. ii. EDWARD, b. Feb. 14, 1669-70.
iii. SARAH, b. Feb. 23, 1671-2; m. Jan. 5, 1698-9, Abner Dole of Newbury.
iv. NATHANIEL, b. Oct. 27, 1673; no further record; probably d. young.
7. v. JOSEPH, bapt. June 6, 1675.
vi. REBECCA, b. Apr. 11, 1677; d. Apr. 21, 1699.
8. vii. EBENEZER, b. Feb. 21, 1678-9.

4. DAVID[2] BELCHER (*Jeremiah*[1]) was born in Ipswich, in 1662, and was living there Dec. 11, 1678, when he took the oath of allegiance. (Waters's "Ipswich in the Mass. Bay Colony," page 99.) In the deed of July 1, 1721, previously mentioned (Essex Co. Deeds, vol. 40, page 9), the grantors, who were some of the grandchildren of Jeremiah[1] Belcher, defended the grantee from the heirs of David[2] Belcher; so it may be inferred that the latter had descendants, although no further record or mention of him of any kind can be found. Possibly he perished in the Canadian expedition of 1690. He was probably father of the following.

Child:

9. i. JOSEPH,[3] b. about 1685.

5. RICHARD[2] BELCHER (*Jeremiah*[1]), born in Ipswich, Sept. 10, 1665, was a mason, settled and lived in Charlestown about 1708, where he died Sept. 14, 1720.

He married first, Mar. 20, 1688-9, Mary,[2] born June 2, 1664, daughter of Thomas[1] and Mary (Jordan) Simpson of Salisbury and Ipswich, who died about 1703; and married second, Oct. 11, 1705, Ruth,[3] born May 7, 1682, daughter of Joseph[2] and Ruth Knight of Woburn, who married second, John Harris.

Children by first wife:

i. JANE,[3] b. Mar. 26, 1689-90; m. Nathaniel Lawrence.
10. ii. DAVID, b. Dec. 19, 1691.
iii. RICHARD, b. Oct. 22, 1693; lived in Stoneham, where he d. early in 1758. His will, dated Jan. 20, 1758, filed Mar. 13 following, gave trifling bequests to sister Ruth Blacklock, and brothers Jeremiah, Jonathan, and Samuel Belcher, and the remainder of his estate to his friend James Wiley. He had a wife Mary, but probably no children.
11. iv. THOMAS, b. May 29, 1696.
12. v. SAMUEL, b. June 20, 1699.
13. vi. JEREMIAH, b. Sept. 13, 1701.

Children by second wife:

14. vii. JONATHAN, b. Jan. 29, 1706-7.
viii. JOSEPH, b. Sept. 20, 1708; was a mariner, and in 1768 "had been at sea for over thirty years"; probably never married.
ix. MARY, b. Aug. 13, 1712; m. Feb. 22, 1732-3, Joseph Tarbox of Lynn; moved to Biddeford, Me.
x. RUTH, b. in 1715; m. (1) in Boston, Oct. 21, 1732, James Tite; m. (2) Oct. 28, 1739, Robert Simpson; m. (3) Jan. 6, 1746-7, Christopher Blaycock, or Blacklock.
xi. DANIEL, b. 1718; d. in youth.

6. ENS. EDWARD[3] BELCHER (*Jeremiah*,[2] *Jeremiah*[1]), born Feb. 14, 1669, was a husbandman, and inherited a portion of his father's estate in Revere, which also extended into Lynn, where he held the

office of Ensign of the local company, and resided until 1720, when he sold his homestead to Thomas Cheever and moved to Milton, where he lived for a short time, but finally bought a large farm in that part of Stoughton which was later Stoughtonham (Sharon), where he died Mar. 16, 1744–5, aged 76 years 1 month 2 days, according to the record, which agrees with the record of his birth.

He married, about 1700, Mary ———, born about 1675, said by tradition to have been Mary Clifford, who died in Stoughton, Mar. 5, 1752, in her 78th year. The births of his children are recorded in Lynn.

Children:

i. SARAH,[4] b. Aug. 4, 1701; d. Nov. 3, 1702.
15. ii. JEREMIAH, b. Mar. 23, 1702–3.
16. iii. SAMUEL, b. Mar. 8, 1704–5.
17. iv. EDWARD, b. Jan. 16, 1706–7.
v. PRESERVED, b. June 14, 1708; d. young.
18. vi. CLIFFORD; b. Oct. 12, 1710.
vii. MARY, b. Nov. 22, 1713; m. July 9, 1729, Eleazer Hawes of Stoughton.
viii. MARTHA, b. 1716; d. Nov. 17, 1764; m. Sept. 13, 1739, Ebenezer Esty of Stoughton, who was b. Oct. 15, 1705, and d. Apr. 10, 1769.

7. ENS. JOSEPH[3] BELCHER (*Jeremiah,*[2] *Jeremiah*[1]), baptized June 6, 1675, was born in Rumney Marsh, where he passed his life, inheriting part of his father's lands. He also owned two estates on North street in Boston. He resided in that part of Rumney Marsh called Hog Island (now Breed's Island), and with his wife Hannah became a member of the Rev. Thomas Cheever's church, in 1716. He was prominent in the affairs of the precinct, holding the offices of constable and of ensign in the military company for many years. He died Nov. 15, 1739. His will, made the day before his decease, names wife Hannah, sons Joseph, Nathaniel, and Jonathan, and daughters Sarah and Hannah.

He married, Jan. 7, 1697–8, Hannah,[4] born about 1676, daughter of Lieut. Jonathan and Frances Bill of Boston and Pulling Point (Winthrop), who married second, July 29, 1742, Richard Hunnewell of Boston.

Children:

19. i. JOSEPH,[4] b. Oct. 25, 1698.
20. ii. NATHANIEL, b. Oct. 5, 1703.
iii. JAMES, b. Oct. 30, 1707; d. Dec. 1, 1723.
iv. HANNAH, b. Feb. 20, 1712–13; m. June 22, 1732, Samuel Cleveland of Charlestown.
21. v. JONATHAN, b. Feb. 27, 1717–18.
vi. SARAH, b. July 6, 1721; m. Dec. 9, 1740, John Floyd, Jr., of Chelsea.

8. EBENEZER[3] BELCHER (*Jeremiah,*[2] *Jeremiah*[1]), born Feb 21, 1678–9, lived in Rumney Marsh (Revere), and for some years in Lynn, until about 1714, when he removed to Boston, where he bought an estate in the southerly part of the town. (Suffolk Co. Deeds, vol. 28, page 137.) He was a mariner, and on July 24, 1734, was appointed sealer of cordwood. He died in 1735. His daughters Sarah, Mary, and Mercy inherited his estate. (Suffolk Co. Deeds, vol. 94, page 75, and vol. 131, page 23.)

He married, Nov. 23, 1708, Ruth, born Mar. 18, 1680–1, daughter of Joseph Hichings of Lynn, who died in Boston, Jan. 23, 1732–3, and is buried in the Granary burying ground.

Children:

i. Sarah,[4] b. Sept. 8, 1709; m. Apr. 22, 1736, Samuel Smith, mariner, of Boston.
ii. Mary, b. Sept. 4, 1711; m. (1) Nov. 30, 1736, Thomas Wyat of Boston; m. (2) Apr. 29, 1740, Moses Eayres of Boston.
iii. Mercy, b. Aug. 5, 1713; m. Sept. 16, 1754, Samuel Hichings of Marblehead.
iv. A child, b. 1715; d. young.
v. Ebenezer, b. June 30, d. Aug. 12, 1717.
vi. Ebenezer, b. June 1, 1719; d. Apr. 24, 1723.
vii. Ruth, b. Aug. 30, 1722; d. Aug. 16, 1724.

9. Joseph[3] Belcher (*perhaps David,[2] Jeremiah[1]*), born perhaps about 1685, lived in Chebacco parish, Ipswich. His house was burned in 1742, and a contribution was taken in the Chebacco Church for his assistance. He died Jan. 12, 1748–9; and his widow Ruth died June 29, 1757.

Child:

22. i. Joseph,[4] b. perhaps about 1708.

10. David[3] Belcher (*Richard,[2] Jeremiah[1]*), born Dec. 19, 1691, was a cordwainer, and lived in Ipswich, and Charlestown until about 1722, when he settled in Boston, where he had previously joined the Second Church on Mar. 14, 1714–15, and later his children were baptized there. The record of his death has not been found, and there are no probate records of his estate. He married, Aug. 20, 1724, Rely, born Apr. 4, 1699, daughter of John and Rely (Holmes) Simpson of Boston, and widow of Thomas Smith.

Children:

i. Mary,[4] b. Aug. 29, 1726; perhaps m. Dec. 27, 1743, Stephen Nazro of Boston.
ii. David, b. Aug. 1, 1728; probably identical with "David Belcher, aged 30, born in Boston, a tailor," who enlisted Mar. 27, 1762, in Capt. Jonathan Haight's Co., in Westchester Co., N. Y. (N.Y. Historical Society Collections, 1891, page 430.)
iii. Sarah, b. Nov. 30, 1731; probably m. Dec. 10, 1750, John Chilcott of Boston.
iv. Jonathan, b. Aug. 29, 1736; lived in Boston; served at Louisbourg in Capt. Edward Blake's Co., from Nov. 2, 1759, to Apr. 13, 1761; d. in Boston, probably unmarried, Apr. 26. 1764, and was buried in the Granary burying ground.

11. Thomas[3] Belcher (*Richard,[2] Jeremiah[1]*), born May 29, 1696, was a mariner, and settled in Boston, where he died in 1735, administration on his estate being given, Sept. 16 of that year, to Jonathan Farnum, and guardians appointed for his children. His sons died unmarried. He married, Apr. 21, 1720, Susanna,[2] born Jan. 24, 1700–1, daughter of Humphrey[1] and Susanna (Wakefield) Richards of Boston, who died before her husband.

Children:

i. Thomas,[4] b. Nov. 4, 1722; was a mariner, of Boston; d. unmarried, in 1750.
ii. John, b. June 29, 1725; living in Boston in 1745; d. soon after, unmarried.
iii. Susanna, b. Apr. 20, 1727; living, unmarried, in Boston, in 1755 (Suffolk Co. Deeds, Vol. 86, page 249); perhaps m. July 28, 1763, John Thompson.

iv. MARY, b. 1729; living unmarried in Boston in 1755 (Suffolk Co. Deeds, Vol. 86, page 249); perhaps m. in 1758, Henry Farley.
v. SAMUEL, b. July 4, 1731; d. young.

12. SAMUEL[3] BELCHER (*Richard,[2] Jeremiah[1]*), born in Ipswich, June 20, 1699, was taken to Charlestown by his parents, where he lived until after he became of age. He then located in Cambridge, where he resided until 1742, when he removed to Wrentham, where he died in 1773. By occupation he was a tailor and husbandman. His will, dated Sept. 28, 1773, names wife Sarah, daughters Mary, Abigail and Elizabeth, unmarried; daughter Martha Jewett; grandsons David and Jonathan Winchester; and sons John, Andrew, David, and Woodbridge; the homestead being given to the son John.

He married, Dec. 27, 1726, Sarah, born Sept. 26, 1706, daughter of Ichabod and Martha (Woodbury) Brown of Cambridge.

Children;

i. SAMUEL,[4] b. Dec. 5, 1727; no further record; probably d. unmarried.
ii. SARAH, b. Oct. 13, 1729; m. Dea. Elhanan Winchester.
iii. MARY, b. Mar. 21, 1731-2.
iv. MARTHA, b. Mar. 22, 1733-4; m. June 17, 1762, Jonathan Jewett of Rowley.
v. ABIGAIL, b. Dec. 16, 1735.
vi. ELIZABETH, b. Aug. 3, 1738.
23. vii. ANDREW, b. Sept. 10, 1740.
24. viii. JOHN, b. June 20, 1744.
25. ix. DAVID, b. Aug. 14, 1746.
26. x. WOODBRIDGE, b. Oct. 10, 1749.

13. JEREMIAH[3] BELCHER (*Richard,[2] Jeremiah[1]*), born Sept. 13, 1701, chose, when his father died, William Bryant of Reading for his guardian. When a young man, he lived in Woburn for a time, but later located in Stoneham. On Sept. 11, 1747, he was warned from Woburn. He later settled in Lunenburg, Mass., where he died about 1778, administration on his estate being given that year. (Worcester Co. Probate.) He was in the military service from May 20 to Aug. 15, 1724, in the Co. of Capt. Eleazer Tyng and of Capt. Josiah Willard, and also in Capt. William Canedy's Co. from Nov. 21, 1724, to May 14, 1725.

He married, Apr. 12, 1733, Arminal, born July 30, 1707, daughter of Eliah and Mary (Palmer) Tottingham of Woburn.

Children, born in Stoneham:

i. MARY,[4] b. June 12, 1734.
ii. SARAH, b. Oct. 20, 1735.
iii. JEREMIAH, b. about 1737 (?). A Jeremiah Belcher of Sheffield, Berkshire Co., was in the military service in 1761; and it was probably the same Jeremiah who enlisted in the Continental army, from Lanesborough, Berkshire Co., at the age of 45, in 1781. This soldier cannot be placed unless he was a son of Jeremiah.[3] No further positive information has been secured of him, but there are Belchers in that vicinity who are probably descended from him.

14. JONATHAN[3] BELCHER (*Richard,[2] Jeremiah[1]*), born Jan. 29, 1706-7, settled in Framingham when a young man. His name appears as a trumpeter in Capt. Josiah Brown's Co., from Sept. 23 to Oct. 27, 1747, and he served as corporal in Capt. Ebenezer Newell's Co.,

from Apr. 4 to Nov. 6, 1755, on a Crown Point expedition, also as corporal in Capt. John Nixon's Co., from Apr. 10 to May 25, 1758. He died in 1787. He married, about 1733, Hannah,[4] born in 1712, daughter of Joseph[3] and Mary (Read) Seaver of Roxbury, who died in 1796.

Children:

27. i. JONATHAN,[4] b. about 1734.
28. ii. DANIEL, b. June 14, 1736.
iii. HANNAH, b. Mar. 10, 1743; d. young.
iv. ANDREW, b. June 16, 1748; d. young.
29. v. EZRA, b. 1751.
30. vi. JOSEPH, bapt. July, 1755.
vii. SHUBAEL, d. young.

[To be concluded.]

THE CONFERENCE AT DEERFIELD, MASS., AUGUST 27–31, 1735, BETWEEN GOV. BELCHER AND SEVERAL TRIBES OF WESTERN INDIANS.

By Hon. GEORGE SHELDON, of Deerfield.

WHILE engaged in gathering material for the history of Deerfield, some thirty-five years ago, I heard from Miss Harriet Hitchcock a tradition, told her by Charles Hitchcock, her father, that a treaty had been made with the Indians at Deerfield a long time ago, aud that the meeting was held on the home-lot then owned by Jonathan Hoyt,* who was our common ancestor. This tradition was unsupported by any record which had come to my knowledge, and observation had taught me that local traditions with no records to back them were, as a rule, to be taken with a great many grains of salt. However, with this tradition had come down a single Indian word. This word had apparently been so often repeated, I reasoned, that it stuck, and may have become a by-word in the town. Therefore, there must be some foundation for the story of the Meeting. This word was "squawottock," meaning "more rum."

With this fantastic foundation for my faith, I set about an exhaustive search for traces of this convocation in the formidable mass of manuscript at the State House, and was at length rewarded by finding some bills of expenses attending a Conference with the Housatonics and other tribes at Deerfield, in August, 1735. But at this point I was confronted with a statement by our eminent historian, Gen. Epaphras Hoyt,† in his "Antiquarian Researches," that the Conference of 1735 was held at Fort Dummer. Further

* Born 1688, died 1779.
† Born 1765, died 1850.

search revealed the record of a similar Conference at Fort Dummer two years later, October, 1737. In the very first speech at this Conference, made by Ontosogo, the Indian orator of the Caghnawagas said to Gov. Belcher, "Brother of the Broadway, Two Years Past I was at Deerfield, the matter then delivered to us by you was, that the old Covenant of Peace and Unity between our brother of the Broadway and us might be continued." In replying to Ontosogo, the Commissioners allude to "the Covenent of friendship renewed two years ago at Deerfield between this Government and the Cagnawaga Tribe." This settled the question that the meeting in 1735 was at Deerfield. Gen. Hoyt had evidently seen the report of this meeting at Fort Dummer, and in quoting from it had substituted "Fort Dummer" for "Deerfield." Having no clue to a conference in his native town, and according to Miss Hitchcock held on his grandfather's own home-lot, Hoyt interpreted "Deerfield" as covering the whole frontier, as "Boston" often stood in Canada for the whole colony. This slip of Gen. Hoyt should not discredit his general accuracy.

The question of location being settled, I renewed my search with ardor, but unfortunately I confined my efforts to the records of Indian Conferences and the manuscript Archives, and brought but little more to light. From these slight traces, and knowledge of the procedure in like Conferences, was made up the account of the Treaty printed in the History of Deerfield. It is primarily to give a fuller and more correct account of the Conference at Deerfield, August, 1735, that this paper is prepared. At this point I quote from the History of Deerfield.

"As I have said, no record of this conference at Deerfield has been found, but we are indebted to Miss C. Alice Baker for two important papers relating to it, which she has lately discovered in the manuscript Archives at Quebec. One is a 'Letter from M. de Beauharnois to the Minister [in France], 1735 12th October.'" In this letter, written six weeks after the Conference, is enclosed the full text of a speech which Beauharnois says he had prepared and sent to Deerfield to be delivered by Ontosogo, the Caghnawaga Chief, as his own. Beauharnois writes, "My Lord, You will see by the words subjoined that I have had a journey to Deerfield made by trustworthy people, and the speech I have had made to them . . . . which astonished them not a little."

This speech is skilfully drawn to hide all trace of French origin, and made to appear as if it were a spontaneous outbreak of the Caghnawaga chieftain, enraged by the reports of an English settlement on lands which he claimed as his own. These two papers were printed in full in the History of Deerfield as authentic addition to my sketch of the Conference. The reason for calling attention to this incident will appear in the next stage of this narration.

Years later, Judge Francis M. Thompson, while hunting material for his History of Greenfield, in the Public Library at Boston, happened upon an official printed pamphlet containing the entire record of the Conference at Deerfield, August, 1735.* Here was a "find" indeed, and Judge Thompson was desirous of making a perfect copy for his history, but proper facilities were denied, and he was hampered in his efforts. Later, however, I was conceded the privilege needed for making a verbatim copy of this document.† Now, the record thus brought to light reveals a queer sequel. The proceedings of each day of the Conference, and the speeches of each day, are given minutely, and from first to last there is not a word, or a hint, of the speech or subject matter of the speech, which M. de Beauharnois says he prepared for Ontosogo, and which, when delivered by Ontosogo at Deerfield, "astonished them not a little." It may be here added that at the Conference at Fort Dummer, two years later, there was neither word nor hint of this incendiary speech by Ontosogo. Instead of waving the bloody axe and breathing threatenings and slaughter at Deerfield, as represented by Beauharnois, the Caghnawaga chief appears to be the most serene and happy man alive. In his farewell speech, August 29, he says, "I salute the Governor and all the Gentlemen here. I have been so handsomely treated since I have been with you that I have almost fancied myself in Heaven." Could Gov. Belcher and Ontosogo read the Canada version of this Conference, they would no doubt be "astonished not a little." How are these contradictions to be explained? How is the official Report of Gov. Belcher and the official letter of Gov. M. de Beauharnois to the Court of France to be reconciled?

One is reminded of a conumdrum founded upon what a boy declared to be an impossible relationship to certain people. The solution of the puzzle given was, "The little brat lied." Does not the solution in this case, at least, squint in the same direction? But who was the author of this old conundrum? Each must be his own judge. Could Gov. Belcher have suppressed such a speech after he had promised to send each tribe a printed copy of the proceedings? Indians never forget. Did Ontosogo keep the speech in his breast and report its delivery to Beauharnois with its astonishing effect on the English? Hardly, when 142 Indians present could bear testimony against him. Were the grievance, and the threatening speech, made up and sent to France, to show the King what a faithful and watchful governor he had as his representative in Canada? Did Beauharnois assume that his report would be forever buried in the Archives of France? He could not then have reckoned with Miss Baker a century and a half later.

* See Thompson's History of Greenfield, vol. 1, pages 141-162.

† It is the writer's intention to reprint this article, adding to it his copy of the document.

One more document should be preserved, and explained in this connection. Oct. 28, 1903, Rev. Ansón Titus published in the Boston Transcript a manuscript found in the Archives of the New England Historic Genealogical Society, which he called "A Diary of Surpassing Interest, for the first time published." This Diary was written by a gentleman who attended the Deerfield Conference in the train of Gov. Belcher; but it was devoted mainly to the incidents of travel by the way. So far as it goes, in reciting the action of the Conference, it bears out the text of Gov. Belcher's report with a single exception. The diarist says that one of the tribes present was "the tribe of Mohegans." Knowing the history of the Mohegans, it was a justifiable presumption which led me to question the statement of one of the actors in the Conference, as to the presence of this tribe. Thinking there might have been an error in the copyist or typesetter, I examined the original, and ascertained there was no error in the printed copy; "Mohegan" it was. But the doubt still remained, and a comparison of the diary with the Official Report revealed the fact that the diarist unwittingly or ignorantly used the name "Mohegan" to designate the Mohawks, who were actually present, associated with the Scattakooks and not otherwise named by him as a distinctive body. Where he writes "Mohawks" it applies to the French Mohawks, or Caghnawaga tribe.

It was the discovery of this error, and the untoward incident of the Beauharnois letter, which moved me to publish this paper, that the close student of Indian affairs of the period might not be misled by the writer of the diary, or by the historian of Deerfield, in their reports of the Conference in 1735.

There is another word that might be said touching this representative gathering, but by no means confined to it. It shows in general the parliamentary method of procedure in the public business meetings of the savage and the intruding white man. We see here the native savage imposing upon the representative of the highest civilization his own modes and forms of conducting public affairs. This emphasizes the fact that the impact of civilization upon savagery in this direction had been successfully resisted. These forms and ceremonies of the Indians handed down from a far-off age, from generation to generation, were so deeply rooted as to defy all inducements for conformity to the English methods. I have said elsewhere, from information obtained chiefly in conversation with Miss Alice Fletcher, an eminent authority on Indian affairs:—

"The red man is generally spoken of as the child of freedom; but no galley slave was more firmly bound to his oar, than was the North American Indian to the customs and traditions of his tribe. He had no will of his own. His costume, his habits, his conduct in war or peace, were all marked out for him by inexorable law. . . . Contact with civilization made not a whit of change in his mode of conducting public business, whether in the State House at Boston, or by the Council fire in the wilderness. At the Court of the 'Grande Monarche' Louis XIV., etiquette was not more strictly enforced than with the tribes, in their conferences and treaties with the whites. The latter were obliged to conform as best they could to the ceremonial forms of the savage. Governors and Embassadors gravely smoked the Pipe of Peace . . . ; lifted or buried the hatchet, brightened the Covenant chain, sent or received the wampum belts, and gave the inevitable present; for no promise was sacred and no treaty binding which was not ratified by an exchange of gifts."* With this strong attachment to their international civil forms, it would seem an utterly hopeless task to attempt a change in their religious rites relating to the unseen and controlling powers all about them. But the fact remains, account for it as you may, that the devoted English missionaries were partially successful in their attempts to "convert" the natives to Christianity; albeit it generally proved in the end a ruinous operation to the natives, as they took more readily to the vices than the virtues of their Christian neighbors. At this same Conference of which we write, a minister was ordained to go among the people of one of the tribes, to labor for their conversion. The history of the Housatonic Indians shows that this effort met with a considerable measure of success. They as a tribe accepted the new Deity, the new forms of worship, and many of the ways of civilization; thus they were held constant friends of the English in subsequent French and English wars.

The Diary quoted below had never before, so far as known, been published. In his introduction Mr. Titus said:—

"The following diary was kept by a member of the council of Governor Jonathan Belcher, on the tour to consult with the Indians in the western part of the Bay Province. It is not known by whom it was written."

This itinerary is condensed, but the entries bearing on the Conference are given in full.

DIARY.

"On Wednesday morning August 20th. 1735. about six o'clock His Excellency, attended by a number of Gentlemen, set out from Boston on a Journey to Deerfield, about 120 miles."

That day they reached Col. Chandler's at Worcester; August 21st, reached Col. Dwight's at Brookfield; the 22d, Col. Stoddard's at Northampton; the 25th, they went up to Deerfield.

"26th. Tuesday tarry'd at Deerfield.

27th. Wednesday at Deerfield. There was a Tent erected of about 100 Foot long, where the Govr. din'd with the rest of the

*July 10, 1735, John Wheelwright was allowed by the Council six hundred pounds, for the purchase of "a present to the Western Indians to be given them at the intended Interview at Deerfield."

Gentlemen, & where in the afternoon the Tribe of the Cagnaroagas (or French Mohawks)* was sent for, & after the usual Salutations & Conference they were dismist.

28th. Thursday at Deerfield. The same was done to the Hoasetonnocks, & to the Scattacooks & Mohegans [Mohawks] together, in the forenoon. In the afternoon the Mohawks [French Mohawks] were sent for again, & had a conference. It lasted about an hour & an half.

29th. Friday at Deerfield. The Housetonnocks were sent for, & had a conference: it lasted about an hour & an half (in the forenoon) Then the Mohawks [French Mohawks] were sent for, reciev'd their Presents after a short Conference, & din'd with the Governour & Gentlemen in the Tent, & after Dinner the Govr. took his Leave of them.

30th. Saturday at Deerfield. The Housetonnocks were sent for, & after some Conference reciev'd their Presents, & were dismist. Then the Scattacooks were sent for & in like manner reciev'd their Presents, the Mohegans [Mohawks] reciev'd theirs after Dinner without any further Conference. These three Tribes [Housatonics, Scattakooks, Caghnawagas] din'd with the Governour.

31st. Sabbath Day at Deerfield. In the forenoon, the Revd. Mr. [John] Sergeant was ordain'd to preach the Gospel to the Tribe of the Housetonnock Indians. The Revd. Mr. [Jonathan] Ashley of Deerfield began with Prayer, the Revd. Mr. [Nathaniel] Appleton of Cambridge preach'd from 2 Tim: 2: 21. 'If a man therefore purge himself from these he shall be a Vessell unto Honour, sanctified & meet for the Master's use, & prepared unto every good work.' The Revd. Mr. [William] Williams of Hatfield gave the charge, & the Revd. Mr [Stephen] Williams of Springfield the right hand of Fellowship. In the afternoon the Revd. Mr Williams of Springfield preach'd from 2: Is: 4: 'And he shall judge among the nations, & shall rebuke many peoples: and they shall beat their swords into ploughshares, & their Spears into Pruning Hooks.'"

Sept. 1, Monday, they rode up to Fort Dummer; Sept. 2, they rode through Northfield, Montague, Sunderland, and Hadley, to Kelloggs ferry, where the Governor and party crossed over to Northampton; Sept. 3, they went to Westfield, and thence to Springfield; Sept. 4, homeward bound, they reached Brookfield; Sept. 5, at Marlborough; and Sept. 6, arrived at Boston.

In the official report of the Conference by Gov. Belcher, there is a notable lack of the picturesque and embellished oratory which writers generally put into the mouths of Indian speakers. In fact, the language of Gov. Belcher is more figurative than that of the Indians.

*The Caghnawagas were an offshoot of the Mohawks. one of the Five Nations. They had been converted by Catholic missionaries and induced to remove and settle on the Sorel River in Canada. There they were a bulwark against invasion from the South. They were known as "French Mohawks."

RECORDS OF THE CHURCH IN VERNON, CONN.

1762-1824.

Communicated by Miss MARY KINGSBURY TALCOTT, of Hartford, Conn.

From the manuscript copy owned by the Connecticut Society of Colonial Dames.

[Concluded from page 205.]

1781.

Octr 6. The Wife of Dea^n Dorchefter.—The Wife of Squire Recm^d by Mr Persons.

1782.

Jany. Oliver King & his Wife.
Augt 4. Eunice Root. Sep^t 22. Wealthy Carpenter.
Sep^t 29. Samuel Rogers.—Jofiah Whitney.
Oct. 6. Nathaniel Rogers. 27. Charles Warner.—Elijah Loomis Junr.
Nov^br 3. Abigail Root. 10. Seth King and his Wife. 17. Leonard Rogers and his Wife.
Decem^br 1. Caleb Talcott Junr.
Decem^br 15. James Chapman.

Anno Dom^l 1783.

Jany 26. Amafa Loomis & his Wife.
Feb. 2. Rachel Hunt. 23. Elijah Loomis & his Wife.
March 16. Solomon Loomis Ju^r.
Apriel. Jofeph Seffions & Wife Recommended by ye 5th C^hh in Windham.

1784.

Augt 10. Jofeph Loomis & his Wife Lois.—Eunice the Wife of Daniel Carpenter recomend^d by Mr Willard.
Sep^t 12. Jerufha Wife of Ezek^l Richardfon, Recmd^d by Mr Strong.

1785.

June 5. Lucy, the Wife of Afahel Root, Recommend by Mr Strong Covty.
Augt 5. Henry Waldo & Hannah his Wife Recom^d by Mr Colton.
Sept. 19. Daniel Field & his Wife Recommended by Mr Colton.

1786.

March 12. Juftus Talcott & Sarah his Wife.
Apriel 16. Rufus Safford & Mary his Wife.
May. Elifabeth the Wife of Phinehas Chapman.
June 18. Jonathan Fowler & his Wife Sarah.
Augt 12. Benjn Talcott Junr & his Wife Recomended by Mr Colton.

1787.

June 17. Rachel the Wife of Elijah Loomis Junr.

1788.

John Olcott & Wife.
Nov^br 2. Oliver Hunt & his Wife.

1789.

May 3. Guftavus Kilborn & his Wife Elifabeth.
June 7. Ebenezer Kellogg Jun. & Abigail his Wife.
Nov. 8. Jofeph King.

1790.

March 7. Lucy the wife of Mofes Thrall.
May 30. Phinehas Talcott & his Wife.
July 11. Lucy, Wife of Thos Field recommend by Mr Colton.
Sep^t 12. Cornelius Roberts & his Wife. 26. Daniel Lord & his Wife.
Octr 3. The wife of James Chapman. 3. Sarah Torry.

1791 1791.

June 5. Seth Talcott & Wife recommended by Mr Elles of E. Bury.*
Augt 15. Samuel Talcott.
Sep^t 18. Rofwell Smith & his Wife.—Mabel the wife of Stephen Richardfon recommend by Mr Strong of Coventry.
Decem^b 4. Leverett Biffel and his Wife.

Anno Domini 1792.

June 9. Rachel the wife of Zadok How.
July 15. The Widow Simons.
Augt 26. Sarah, the wife of Samuel Talcott.
Sep^t 30. David Smith & Olive his Wife.
Nov^br 4. Reuben King.

A. Dom^l 1793.

Ap^l 7. Hezekiah Loomis & his Wife.
June 16. Rofwell Pain & his Wife.
Sep^t 29. Eli Hammond and his Wife.
Decem^br 15. Reuben Carpenter & Miriam his Wife.

ADomini 1794.

June 22. Roger Darte & his wife recommended by ye C^hh in Surry, N. Hamfhire.
Decem^br 7. Sarah, the wife of Capt Fuller, recom^d by Mr Persons, E. H.†

ADom^l 1795.

Marc^h 1. Eliakim Hitchcock Junr & his Wife.
Ap^l 19. The wife of Jofeph Hyde recommend by Mr Willar^d.
Augt 9. Samuel Field.

1796.

Jany 17. Thomas W. Kellogg & Mary his Wife.
June 19. Abel Driggs and Rachel his Wife.
July 17. Ebenezer Hunt and Mary his Wife.
Augt 28. Capt Jehiel Fuller.
Nov^br 20. The wife of John Olcott. 20. The wife of Caleb Talcott Junr. 27. Widow Mary Hyde, recommended by Mr Nott of Franklin.

1797.

Jany 29. John Darte.
Mar^h 19. Simon King & his Wife.

* East Glastenbury.
† Easthampton.

Ap[l] 2. Salmon King. 17. Sarah, the wife of Ebenezer Reed. 30. Ebenezer Reed.
June 11. Lois y[e] wife of Nath[l] Hurlburt.
Sept 3. Jacob Talcott & Anna his wife. 17. Achſah, wife of John Pearl, recommended by M[r] Alden of Willington.

Anno Dom[i] 1798.

Jan[y] 7. Daniel Talcott & his wife.
May 13. Alvin Talcott and his wife.
Aug 5. Doc[t] Eleazer Maccray & his wife.
Oc[t] 21. Alvan Baker & his wife.

Anno Dom[i] 1799.

Feb 17. Elijah Skinner Jun[r] & his wife.
Nov[br] 24. D[r] Hinckly & his wife.

Anno Domini 1800.

March 23. Clariſsa Ladd.—Sarah Pratt.
May 24. Lyman Hunt.—John Delano.
Aug[t] 10. Abigail Carpenter. 31. Elijah Tucker Ju[r] & his wife.
Oct[r] 6. Allen McLean.
Nov[br] 23. John Chapman.

Anno Dom[i] 1801.

March 29. Samuel Anders & his wife.
May 31. Elijah Hammond & Martha his wife recommend by M[r] Colton.
Aug[t] 2. Suſannah King. 16. Alpheus Anders & his wife.

Anno Dom[i] 1802.

Janu[y] 17. Hannah the 2[d] wife of Eben[r] Kellogg Jun[r].
May 9. Percy the wife of Joſeph Hyde Jun[r] recommended by M[r] Pond Paſtor of the 1st C[hh] in Aſhford.
June 6. Benjamin Kilbourn & his wife recommended by M[r] King Paſtor of y[e] 2 C[hh] in East Hartford.
Nov 7. Caleb Parſsons & his wife recommended by M[r] Hayes of South Hadley.

ADom[i] 1803.

April 3. Solomon Perrin & Anna his wife recommended by M[r] Gillet Paſtor of y[e] C[hh] in Gilead.
May 8. Eraſtus M[c]Kinney.
Sep[tr] 25. Hannah 2[d] wife of Benjamin Talcott Jun[r].
Oct[r] 2. Lucy wife of Hope Tucker, recommend by Salmon King, Paſtor of the C[hh] in Orford.
Nov[br] 6. Lois the wife of Nathan Chapman.
Decem 1. Will[m] Worthington & Wife, and their daughters Sarah & Celina, recommended by M[r] Forward of Belcherftown in Maſſachuſetts.

ADom[i] 1804.

March 30. Betsey 3[d] wife of Ebenezer Kellogg Jun[r], recommended by M[r] Judſon of Sheffield Maſſ[ts].
Aug[t] 5. Abraham Whedon & Lydia his wife recommended by M[r] Eells Paſtor of y[e] 2[d] C[hh] in Branford.
Oct[r] 7. Widow Rachel Brunſon.
Decem[br] 2. Nabbe the wife of John Chapman recommend by Rev[d] Mr. Colton of Bolton.

ADom[l] 1805.

Aug[t] 4. John Pain & his wife.
Oct[r] 20. Hope Tucker.

Anno Domini 1806.

June 29. Salley Roberts.—Clariſſa Coming.
Aug[t] 24. Ezekiel Baker & his wife. 31. Sarah the wife of Brint Pain.

A.D. 1807.

May 31. Francis King A.B.
July 12. Darius Hunt & his Wife.

Anno Dom[l] 1808.

May 8. Daniel Cone & Keziah his wife, recommended by the Rev[d] W[m] Lyman Pastor of the church in Millington.
June 26. Emely Bow.
Oct[r] 2. The wife of Daniel Fuller.
Nov[br] 20. Charles Lee.
Decem[br] 4. Alexander M[c]Lean & wife recommended by Rev[d] Salmon King of Orford. 25. Miriam Sheldon.

1809.

Jan[y] 8. John Bingham recommended by the Rev[d] Eph[m] Woodruff N. Coventry.
Apriel 9. Mary Corning.—Olive Hammond. 16. Joanna Johns.—Patty Talcott.
May 14. The wife of Francis M[c]Lean. 28. The wife John A. Hall.
June 4. Polly Woodard.
Oct[r] 22. Elijah Hammond Jun[r]. 29. Harriet Humphry.—Betsey Rogers.—Nancy Rogers.—Lydia Cady.
Nov[br] 5. Anna, the wife of Doct[r] Dart, recommended by y[e] Rev[d] W[m] B. Riply of Lebanon Goſhen.

Anno Dom[l] 1810.

Jan[y] 7. Sarah Thrall.—Zina King.
Feb[y] 25. Eunice Rogers.—Lydia Root.—Fanny Smith.—Electa Smith.

Anno Dom[l] 1811.

June 16. Widow Sibel Barstow, recommend[d] by the Church in Columbia.
Oct[r] . Susannah wife of Elijah King.
Nov 24. Josiah Fox, recommended by the C[hh] in Enfield of which Rev[d] N. Prudden is Pastor.

Anno Dom[l] 1812.

March 1. The wife of Jonathan S. Tucker.
May 10. Delano Abbot & his wife. [They only "owned the Covenant." —A. S. K.]
Nov[br] 22. Clark Tucker.

Anno Dom[l] 1813.

Apriel 18. Sally, the wife of Elam Tuttle, recommended by the Pastor & C[hh] in North Haven.
May 6. Ruth the wife of Reuben Skinner recommend by Rev[d] M[r] Ripley & C[hh] in Malborough.
Aug[t] 15. Anna, the wife of Elliot Palmer.
Oct[r] 3. Betsey Pran [Pain?].

Anno Dom^{i} 1814.

July 24. Ruth, wife of ——— Scott.
Augt 14. Martin Kellogg.—George Kellogg. 21. Ammariah Knox.—Nancy Talcott.—Zilpha Perkins.
Sept 25. Lydia Corning.
Decem^{br} 18. Hulda Millard.

Anno Dom^{i} 1815.

Jany 8. Anne, wife of Col^{l} L. P. Tinker.
March 5. Ruth Sage, widow of Reuben Sage.—Jemima Hills, widow.
April 23. Ephraim Tucker & his wife. 30. Lyman Ransom & his wife.—Sophrona Wheadon.—Meliscent Wheadon.—The widow Anna Carpenter, recommended by doct^{r} Nathan Williams, Pastor of ye C^{hh} in Tolland.
May 7. Joshua Pearl Junr & his wife.—Oliver Baker & his wife.—The widow Mary Warburton.—The widow of Stephen Johns.—Warren McKinney & his wife.—The wife of Lemuel Abott, (Lucretia).— 21. Rachel Carpenter.—Anna Talcott.—Milla Talcott.—Amanda Stedman.
June 11. The wife of Reuben Sage.—The wife of John R. Phelps.—The wife John Abbott.—The wife of Aaron Perrin.—Hannah Wells.—Calista Cone.
Augt 6. Cyntha, wife of Russel King.— wife of Russel Sage.—Henry Kellogg. 20. Sarah Talcott.—Clarissa McLean.

Anno Dom^{i} 1816.

Feb 25. Eunice Chapman.—Docia Wells.—Mary the wife of Ralph Eaton.
March 24. Flavel Talcott & his wife Eunice, who were recommended by ye Revd Mr Parmele of Bolton.
June 16. Miriam Root.
Sep^{t} 1. Lydia Millard.—Roxy King.

A.Domini 1817.

May 25. Eliza, wife of George Kellogg recommended by Revd E. Cook of Orford, E. H.

1818.

June 28th. Widow Mary Scarborough recommended by the church of Christ in Brooklyn by letter dated Jany 30th 1818.
July 5th. Eldad Barber and his wife.—Agustus Grant and his wife.—The wife of Wareham Grant.—Margery Drown.
Sept 6th. Joel Talcot & the wife of Francis McLean.
Nov 1st. Sylva the wife of George Holden.—Olive Abbot.—Gurdon Grant.—Electa Grant.

1819.

Jany 3rd. Asa Cone.—wife of Asa Cone.—Henry Dixon.—Sarah, the wife of Elijah Lee.—Anne, the wife of Curtis Crane.—Olive Smith.—Hannah P. Talcott.
March 7th. Wife of Harvey Cunningham,—Lucy Cunningham.—Martha Hammond.—Sarah Lee.—Lucy Lee.—Deborah Pearl.—Elizabeth Talcott.—Maria Kellogg.
July 4th. Erastus McCollum.—Baca Wife of John Walker.—Miriam Wife of Joel Thrall.—Hannah Talcott.—Elizabeth Warburton.—Mary Anne Chapman.—Eunice Hincley.—Elizabeth Hincley.—Mary Cunningham.

Sept 5th. Francis Grant.—Wife of Francis Grant.—Royal Talcott.—Sarah Carpenter.—Jerusha, Wife of John Lucas.—Betsey Talcott.—Julia Talcott.

Nov 7th. Mrs Lydia Hall (by letter from the church of Christ in Orford).

1820.

Jany 2rd. George Tryon.—Wife of George Tryon.—Josiah Hammond.—Benjamin Talcott Jun.—Seneca Gale.

May 7th. Sally, wife of Eliphalet C. Parker, by letter from the church of Christ in Montville.

July 3rd. Bathsheba Talcott.—Lucretia Hunt.

Sept. 3rd. Else Fuller (by letter from the Church of Christ in East Haddam).

Feby 25th. Harriet W. Ely (by letter from the church of Christ in Hartford).

Feb 13th. Deac Elisha Ladd, (by letter from the Church of Christ in North Wilbraham.)

Feb.25th. Nathaniel Hubbard Jun and Wife (by letter from the Church of Christ in Bolton.)

Aug 25th 1822. Eliza, wife of Allyn Kellogg Recommended by Revd A. B. Collins, Pastor of the Church in Andover.

25th. Wealthy Hayden Recommended by Revd Henry Lord Pastor of the Church in Williamsburgh Mas.

Sept 29th. Mary Johns.

Oct 27th. Martha, wife of Royal Talcott recommended by letter from Bolton.

1823 May 25th. Elisabeth Kellogg wife of Nathaniel O Kellogg Recommended by the Church of Christ in Stock,bridge; Mas, David D Field Pastor.

Oct. 26th. Thomas Wells and Wife Recommended by the Church of Christ in Tolland, Ansel Nash Pastor.

Nov 9. Sybel Tuttle the Wife of Miles Tuttle Recommended by the Church in North Haven.

1824 Jan 11. Betsey Talcott the Wife of Benjamin Talcott Recommended by the Revd Ansel Nash Pastor of the Church in Tolland.

Jan 11. Alithea Kellogg Wife of Henry Kellogg. Recommended by the Church of Christ in Bolton.

June 14th 1818. By vote of the church, Oliver Baker and his wife recommended to the church of Christ in Springfield.

Letter sent Oct. 1819.

Sept 27th. The wife of Russel King recommended by vote of the church to the fellowship of the churches wherever Providence may call her.

1819 Aug 1st. Rachel Lyman (formerly Rachel Carpenter) by vote of the church recommended to the church of Christ in Paris, N. York, society of Hanover.

1820 May 18th. George Tryon and wife recommended to the church of Christ in Gilead.

Aug 9th. Amaziah Knox recommended to the Church in the South Society in Hartford.

April 27th 1821. Sarah Landfear (formerly Sarah Talcott) by vote of the Church recommended to the Church of Christ in Orford.

The following persons have been Recommended from this Church since Mr Ely,s Dismission—Viz—

About, April 1st 1822. Abraham Whedon & Wife and Melicent Whedon, reced certificate of good standing in this church, upon which they were received into the church in N. Branford.

About June 1st 1823. Widow Ruth Skinner received a letter of Dismission, Recommended to the Church in Marlborough.

May 2d. The Church voted letters of Dismission—To Betsey the Wife of George W. Griswold to the Church in Manchester.

To Sally Wife of Eliphalet C. Parker to the Church in Montville.

To Elizabeth Wife of Silas Drake to the first Church in Hartford.

P. Talcott.

DEACON JOHN CHEDSEY, OR CHIDSEY, AND HIS DESCENDANTS.

Compiled by Hon. Ralph D. Smyth and communicated by Dr. Bernard C. Steiner.

1. Dea. John[1] Chidsey, of East Haven, Conn., was an early settler at New Haven, and took the oath of fealty in 1647. He married Elizabeth ———, and died Dec. 31, 1688. His wife died the same year.

Children:

i. Mary,[2] b. Sept. 22, 1650; d. Oct. 9, 1650.
ii. John, b. Oct. 21, 1651; d. 1693.
iii. Sarah, b. Oct. 21, 1653; m. Oct. 26, 1683, Samuel Alling.
2. iv. Joseph, b. Dec. 5, 1655; d. 1712.
v. Daniel, b. July 30, 1657; d. June 4, 1667.
vi. Mary, b. Nov. 24, 1659; m. Mch. 2, 1695, Jonathan Gilbert.
3. vii. Caleb, b. Nov. 20, 1661; d. Feb. 20, 1713.
viii. Hannah, b. Jan. 9, 1663.
4. ix. Ebenezer, b. Feb. 10, 1665; d. Sept. 26, 1726.
x. Elizabeth, b. Dec. 16, 1668; d. July 16, 1688.

2. Joseph[2] Chidsey (*John*[1]) married Sarah ———.

Children:

i. Hannah,[3] b. Jan. 28, 1696; m. Nov. 30, 1718, Levi Bradley.
ii. Joseph, b. Aug. 15, 1698; d. young.
iii. Sarah, b. May 13, 1700; d. Mch. 7, 1778; m. May 16, 1721, Ebenezer Lee of Guilford, who d. Sept. 24, 1751.
iv. Abigail, b. Apr. 28, 1702; m. Mch. 12, 1729, Daniel Hitchcock.
v. Rachel, b. Mch. 16, 1704.
vi. Dinah, b. May 14, 1707.
vii. Abel, b. Mch. 7, 1708-9; d. Mch. 24, 1709-10.
5. viii. Joseph, b. Aug. 8, 1710; d. May 19, 1790.

3. Caleb[2] Chidsey (*John*[1]) married first, May 10, 1688, Anne Thompson, who died Jan. 15, 1691-2, without issue; and married second, Jan. 6, 1693, Hannah Dickerman, who died Dec. 25, 1708.

Children by second wife:

i. DANIEL,[3] b. Mch. 25, 1695; d. Oct. 27, 1716.
6. ii. CALEB, b. May 9, 1697.
7. iii. ABRAHAM, b. Mch. 31, 1699.
iv. MARY, b. Oct. 13, 1701.

4. EBENEZER[2] CHIDSEY (*John*[1]) married Priscilla Russell, who died Jan. 1, 1728.

Children:

i. SARAH,[3] b. Dec. 8, 1689.
ii. JOHN, b. Nov. 6, 1691.
iii. ELIZABETH, b. Feb. 6, 1693.
iv. JOHN, b. Mch, 4, 1694–5.
v. SAMUEL, b. June 6, 1699; d. Oct. 8, 1726.
vi. EBENEZER, b. Dec. 6, 1701; killed by upsetting a cart, June 28, 1716.
vii. JAMES, b. Aug. 23, 1704.

5. JOSEPH[3] CHIDSEY (*Joseph*,[2] *John*[1]), of North Guilford, married, Oct. 22, 1735, Bathshua, daughter of Timothy Baldwin of North Guilford, who died Sept. 15, 1792, aged 76.

Children:

8. i. JOSEPH,[4] b. July 11, 1738.
ii. LOIS, b. July 3, 1741; m. July 2, 1760, John Bartlett of North Guilford, who d. Mch. 13, 1801; d. Feb. 15, 1820.
iii. SAMUEL, b. Dec. 4, 1743.
iv. ASENATH, b. July 15, 1746; m. Feb. 16, 1774, Selah Dudley.
v. SARAH, b. Aug. 24, 1748.
vi. MARY, b. Oct. 14, 1751; m. Jan. 27, 1779, Luther Dudley.
9. vii. NATHAN, b. Mch. 14, 1755; d. Nov. 3, 1832.

6. CALEB[3] CHIDSEY (*Caleb*,[2] *John*[1]) married widow Abigail Smith.

Children:

i. ISAAC,[4] b. Nov. 8, 1731.
ii. CALEB, b. Sept. 1, 1738.

7. ABRAHAM[3] CHIDSEY (*Caleb*,[2] *John*[1]) married first, Mabel ———, who died Mch. 8, 1734; and married second, Mary ———, who died Apr. 3, 1737.

Children by first wife:

i. DANIEL,[4] b. 1719; d. 1720.
ii. DANIEL, b. 1728; d. 1729.
iii. DANIEL, b. 1729; d. 1730.
iv. HANNAH, d. July 1, 1730.
v. ABRAHAM.

8. JOSEPH[4] CHIDSEY (*Joseph*,[3] *Joseph*,[2] *John*[1]) married Zerviah, daughter of Daniel Collins.

Children:

i. LOIS,[5] b. Sept. 7, 1761; d. Feb. 13, 1774.
ii. AUGUSTUS, b. Jan. 27, 1764.
iii. SAMUEL, b. Aug. 14, 1766.

9. NATHAN[4] CHIDSEY (*Joseph*,[3] *Joseph*,[2] *John*[1]), married first, Dec. 27, 1786, Rachel Benton, who died Nov. 25, 1820; and married second, Apr. 8, 1821, Mary Kimberley, who died Feb. 13, 1850.

Children by first wife:

i. JOSEPH,[5] b. July 5, 1787; m. Mch. 16, 1809, Molly Coe of Durham, and had: 1. *Helen*,[6] b. June 6, 1818; m. John Wadsworth of Washington, D. C. 2. *Maria Theresa.* 3. *Joseph.* 4. *Charles Philip*, b. June 6, 1817; m. Sarah C. Squire of Durham, who was b. Oct. 4, 1821, in Granville, Mass.; lived in New York. Children: Charles Adrian,[7] Marian Augusta, Sarah Squire, Frank Bates, Joseph, Herbert Chauncey, Nathan, Anna Catharine, ——— (a daughter), Nathan A., and Helen B.

ii. Abraham, b. Oct. 13, 1791; was very talented but wild, and went away about 1815.

GARDINER FAMILY BIBLE RECORDS.

Communicated by Ernest Lewis Gay, A.B., of Boston.

The following items are copied from a leaf of the family Bible which belonged to David Gardiner (David,[4] John,[3] David,[2] Lion[1]), of Gardiner's Island and New London, born 3 June, 1718, A.B. Yale 1736, died 17 Jan., 1776. This leaf is now in the possession of his great-great-granddaughter Miss Jane Richards Perkins of New London, Conn. The items form distinct additions to the data found in Curtiss C. Gardiner's "Lion Gardiner and his Descendants" (1890), page 118.

David Gardiner and Elizabeth Gardiner was married A.D. 1741, March 29.

Samuel Gardiner ye Son of David and Elizabeth Gardiner was born A.D. 1742/3 Febr. 4. Departed Life September (?) 14, 1775.

Elizabeth Gardiner ye Daughter of David and Eliz^{a}. Gardiner was born A.D. 1744 October 15. Departed Life Aug. 6, 1757.

Mary Gardiner ye Daughter of David and Elizabeth Gardiner was born A.D. 1746 May 12.

David Gardiner ye Son of David and Elizabeth Gardiner was born A.D. 1748/9 March 18.

Elizabeth Gardiner ye Daughter of David and Eliz^{a}. Gardiner was born A.D. 1750/1 Jan. 25.

Joseph Gardiner ye Son of David and Elizabeth Gardiner was born A.D. 1753 April 17.

Lucretia Gardiner ye Daughter of David & Elizabeth Gardiner was born A.D. 1755 Apr^{l}. 18.

Thomas Gardiner ye Son of David & Elizabeth Gardiner was born A.D. 1757 Nov. 5.

Elizabeth Gardiner the Wife of David Gardiner Departed this Life Octob^{r} 13, 1772 in the Fifty First year of Her Age.

David Gardiner Departed this Life Jany 17, 1776—In the Fifteth Eaight year of his age.

Samuel Gardiner Son to David and Elizabeth Gardiner departed this life June 14, 1775.

July 9, 1792, departed life at N. York, Thomas Gardiner Son of David & Eliz^{a}. Gardiner Aged 34—.

David Gardiner son of David & Elizabeth Gardiner Departed this life at Flusing Long Island Sept. 2, 1809 Aged 60.

RECORDS OF THE SECOND CHURCH OF SCITUATE, NOW THE FIRST UNITARIAN CHURCH OF NORWELL, MASS.

Communicated by WILFORD JACOB LITCHFIELD, M.S., of Southbridge, Mass.

[Continued from page 182.]

May 15. 1791*		Clarriſsa & Lucinda twins Daughters to Sam^{ll}: Damon and Wife.
May	22	Lydia Daughter to Simeon Daman & wife
June	5	Clarriſsa D. to abiel Turner Junr. & wife
		Galen Clapp Son to Capt John James & wife
		Rebeckah in Private D. to Thos. Lapham Junr & wife
July	3	George & Ruth, Son and D. to Thos. Lapham Jun and wife
		Deſire Eells D. to Calvin Daman and Wife
		Elias Son to James Barrell Junr. And Wife
Augst	7:	Quintus Carolus, Son of Charles Turner Eſq^{r}. & Wife
		Lucinda D: to Elijah Turner and wife
Augst	14	Tryphine D to Thos. Sylveſter Junr. & Wife
Augst.	21	Sylveſter Son to Charles Tolman & wife
Augst	27	Joseph Son To Roland Turner and wife
Sept	7:	Thomas Son to Thos. Waterman and Wife
Jany 9 1792		Luſstanos. Son to Bryant Stephenſon & wife
Feb	14	Mary Collier[?] D to Galen Daman & Wife in private
Feb^{y}	20	Zacheriah adult in ye other Pariſh very Sick. His other name Naſh.
May	27	Charles, Son to Noah Meritt in private
June	3	Eliſha Son to Eliſha Young & wife
		Benj^{a} Turner Son to Benj^{a} Lane & wife
May	13	Horace Son to Capt Enoch Collmomore [*sic*] and wife
June	10	Experence D to Sam^{ll}. Randall and Wife
June	17	Hannah D to Capt John James and wife
June	24	Hannah D to Nath^{ll} Waterman and wife
July	1	Thirzby D to Joſhua Bryant Junr. & wife
		Betſy D. to Mathew Tore [Torrey] & Wife
		Chloe D to Benj^{a} Bowker Junr. and wife
July	15	Thomas Son to tho^{s}. Ruggles & wife
July	22	Sam^{ll}. Son to Charls Turner Eſq^{r}. & Wife.
July	29	Mary D to Sam^{ll}. Curtis & wife
		Leafe D to Joſeph Cuſhing & wife
		Harris Son to Gerſhom Bowker in Private
Sept	9	Lucy & Ruth Daughters to Willm Barrell and wife
Augst.	19	Samuel Son to Charles Turner Eſq^{r}. and wife
Sept.	16	Lydia, Betſy, Hannah, D^{s}: William Joſiah Levitt Sons to William James & wife.
		Polly D: to s^{d}. James & wife Baptized in private

* This entry begins what is left of the church baptisms of Rev. David Barnes—contained in loosely-sewed sheets, without covers, preserved at the Norwell Bank. There appears to be a hiatus in these records from 1757 to this entry. Rev. Dr. Barnes retired from the ministry in 1809, and was succeeded by Rev. Samuel Deane. Besides the baptisms, there are marriages, church admissions, dismissals, etc.

Sept 16	Elijah Stowers Son to Elijah Curtice Junr & wife
	Lucy Cuſhing D. To Stephen Bowker & wife
Sept 23	Elijah Son to John Hatch and wife.
Sept 31 [*sic*]	Calvin Son to Calvin Daman & wife
	Artimiſsa: D to Jonathan Hatch Junr. and wife
Octobr: 7	James Son to Jeſse Wright & wife
	Juda Litchfield D. To Joſhua Daman & wife
	Polly D: to Thos. Lapham Junr. and wife
Octob. 14	Eleanor Wife of Robert Northy.
	Eleanor D: & James Son to Robert Northy and Wife
Novb 3	Joſeph Son to Samll. Simmons & Wife
Novb 4	Mary Turner D. to Joſeph Tolman Junr & Wife
Decbr	Thankfull Wife to Samll. Simons Adult
	Peleg & Samll. Sons to Samll. Simons and wife
Jany 13 1793	Luther son to Luther Barrell and Wife
Feb 24	Benja. Hearſsy son to Braddock Jacobs and wife
May 5	Marcus Son to Samll. Tolman & wife
	John Son to Elijah Bowker and wife
June 2	Elijah Son to William Brooks Junr & wife
Augt 4.	Clarriſsa D: to Joſeph Jacobs and Wife
Augt: 18.	Lucy D. to Benja Lane and Wife
Sept 8.	Anna D. to Eliſha Briggs and wife
Sept 22	Bettſy D: to Israel Turner & wife
Octobr 6	Gorham Son to Joſeph Benſon & wife
Octobr. 13	Betſey D. to Nathll. Cuſhing & wife
Novbr. 24	Lucy D. to Joſeph Cuſhing and wife
Decmr. 7	Abigail D to Gerſhom Bowker and wife in private
Feby 3 1794	Eliſha Son to David Clapp & wife in private
april 13.	Lucy D. to Nathll Chittenden & Wife
	Nancy D to Lemuel Jacobs & wife
May 22	Horrace Son to John James and wife
June 8	Hannah Tolmon D. to Charles Turner Eſqr. & Wife
	Eſther D to Charles Cole & wife
June 29	Alpheus Son to Micah Stetſon & wife
Augst. 24	Eſther D to Charles Cole and wife
Augſt. 31	Eldward [or Edward] son to Nathll. Cuſhing Junr. and wife
Sept 14.	Benjamin son to Roland Turner and wife
	Johannah D. to Eliſha Young and wife
	Turner son to Jonath. Hatch Junr: and wife
Sept 28	Samll. Stanly Son to Samll. Bowker Negro and wife
	Harriot, Stanly Dr to Prince Freeman Negro & wife
Octobr 5	Nabby D: to Stephen Bowker and wife
	Samll. Litchfield Son to Simion Daman & wife
	Betſey. D to Thos. Ruggles and wife
Novbr 2.	Fanny D to David Clapp and wife
	Elijah Son to David Clapp and wife
	Tryphoſy D to Thos. Sylveſter & wife
Decmbr. 7	Eliza. Bailey. Son to Elijah Turner Eſqr. and wife
May 10 1795	Ruth Tillden D: to Calvin Daman & Wife
June 7	Son to Pickles Cuſhing Junr. and wife
	Joſeph Copeland son to Samll. Tolman & wife
June 14	Sarah Jacobs Daughter to Eliſha Briggs & wife
July 26	Loring Cuſhing son to Micah Lapham & wife

Augst	9:	Nabby Leavet D. to Luther Barrell & wife
Augst.	23	Affee[?] D: to Co^{ll}. Willm. Turner & wife
		Fanny D. to Benj^{a} Lane and wife
Sept	27	Theadore son to Charles Turner Eſq^{r}. and wife
Octob^{r}.	4	John son to John Foſter Junr. & Wife
		Lydea D. to Braddock Jacobs and wife
Octo^{br}	18	Betſy. D to Gerſhom Ewell and wife
Octo^{br}.	25.	Charles. son to David Clapp and wife
Nov^{br}	1	Seth Stoddard Junr. and wife Owned the Covenant He was Baptized with two of y^{r}. Children Named Benjamin and Temperance
Nov^{br}.	8	Lucinda an adult D to Sylvanus Daman.
April 4	1796	Demick Bowker son to Galen Daman & wife in private
May	1	Joſiah son to Charles Briggs and wife
May	8	Joſhua Dauis son of Harris Turner and wife
May	20	Charles son to Stephen Totman & wife
May	29	Thomas son to Sam^{ll}: Simmons and wife
July	5.	Nabby an adult Wife to Ezra Dingley of Duxbury
Augst.	14	Lydia D. to Elijah Curtice & wife.
Augst.	14	Cloe Stowers D. to John Turner & wife
Augst.	21	Anna D. to Simeon Daman & wife
Augst.	28	Abiah Joice D to Thos Lapham Junr and wife
		Harriot D to Nath^{ll}. Chittenden & wife
Sept	4	Hannah an adult wife to Elijah Briggs
		James Buffinton son to Elijah Briggs & wife
		Eliſabeth Daughter to Elijah Briggs & wife
Sept	6.	Baptized the Children of Conſider Merritt & wife in private they being Sick of ye Canker Raſh—Polly: D. Joce[?] D: Benjamin Son. Roxa[?] D: Conſider son Joſeph son Priſsa D
Octo^{br}.	23.	Delight D to Elijah Bowker and wife
Nov^{br}.	13	Lydia Ford. D: to Micah Stetſon & wife
	20	Molly Dau^{tr}. to William James & wife
May 21	1797	Mary Rand. D: to Charles Turner Eſq^{r}. & wife
July.	9.	Hannah Chandler Daug^{h} to Cha[n]dler Cole and Wife
		Anſon son to Jonth Hatch Junr. & wife
Octo^{br}:	8:	Ruth Turner D to Thos. Cuſhing & wife
		Ruth Thomas D to Picles Cuſhing & wife
Octo^{br}.	29	Lazerus Bowker, Son to Galen Daman & wife
		Bethyah Woodard: D to Willm Gallop[?] Junr & wife
		Stephen. Son to Joſeph Cuſhing & wife.
Nov^{br}.	2	Debbe Cuſhing D. to John Naſh & Wife in private
Nov^{br}.	5.	Samuel Oakman son to Thos. Ruggles & wife
Nov^{br}.	12.	William son to Charles Lapham & Wife
		Lucy D: to Nath^{ll} Winſlow Junr. & wife
Nov^{br}.	19	Sarah Turner D. to Benj^{a} Turner Lane & wife
Jany 11	1798.	Nathan Son to William Brooks and wife in private
April.	28.	Turner. Son to Sam^{ll}. Tolman and wife in private
May	19:	Sarah D to Eben^{r}: Copeland & wife
July	1.	Noah Son to Joſhua Bryant and wife
		Deborah Richmond: D to Perez Jacobs and wife
July	8	Sam^{ll}. Weſt son to Nath^{ll}. Cuſhing and wife
		Gracy D to James Torry & wife

July	22	Lucy Daughter to John James and wife
Augst	5	James Newton Son to James Sparrell and wife
Augst.	5.	Hannah Waterman. D to Joſhua Jacobs Junr. and wife
Sept	30	Fanny D to Luther Barrel and wife
Octobr.	7	Juda Hatch D to Harris Turner & wife
June 16	1799	Lucy Sylveſter D to John Ewell and wife
		Mary D to Elijah Curtice & wife
June	30	James Son to Thomas Southward & wife
July	7	Eliſha son to Micah Stetson and wife
Sept	1	Joanna & Hannah Daughters to Braddock Jacobs & wife
		Sarah Stockbridge D to Perez Turner & wife
Sept	29	Joanna Turner. D to Capt Benja Lane and wife
Octobr.	6:	Francis Son Coll. Charles Turner and wife
		Charles son to Charles Cole and wife
		Abiel son to Roland Turner and wife
		Mary D to Nathll Winſlow Junr. & wife
		Charlotte D to Charles Lapham & wife.
Octobr.	13	James So[n] to John Foſter Junr & wife
Octobr	20	John son to John Naſh and wife
		Hannah Stowel D to Eliſha Briggs and wife
		Sally D to Robert Northy and wife
Novbr.	3	Howard son to Galen Daman and wife

[To be continued.]

GENEALOGIES IN PREPARATION.

(Continued from page 190.)

QUIMBY.—*John of Stanstead Co., P. Q., Canada*, by Rev. Frank Gardner, 119 South 4th St., Sunbury, Pa.

QUINBY.—*Robert of Amesbury, Mass.*, by Henry Cole Quinby, Union League Club, New York City.

QUINTARD.—*Isaac of Stamford, Conn.*, by William A. Eardeley, 466 State St., Brooklyn, N. Y.

RANDALL.—*Matthew of Hopkinton, R. I., and Stephen of Westerly, R. I.*, by Aaron Ferry Randall, 350 Tremont Bldg., Boston, Mass.

RANDALL.—*Matthew of Philadelphia, Pa.*, by Miss Elizabeth Deland, Haverford, Pa.

RANDALL.—*Robert of Weymouth, Mass.*, by Rev. W. L. Chaffin, North Easton, Mass.

RANDALL.—*William of Scituate, Mass.*, by George Leander Randall, Marion, Mass.

RANNEY.—*Thomas of Cromwell, Conn.*, by Charles Collard Adams, Cromwell, Conn.

RANSOM.—*Matthew of Saybrook, Conn., and Robert of Plymouth, Mass.*, by John E. Ransom, 26 West Avenue, Buffalo, N. Y.

RAYNOR.—*Thurston of Hempstead, L. I., N. Y.*, by Murray Edward Poole, Poole Block, Ithaca, N. Y.

RENAUD, ROYNO, or RYNO.—*John of Elizabeth, N. J.*, by Dr. Wakeman Ryno, Benton Harbor, Mich.

REYNOLDS.—*John and Jonathan of Greenwich, Conn.*, by Spencer P. Mead, 139 West 43d St., New York City.

RICE.—*Dea. Edmund of Marlborough, Mass.*, by George L. Burton, 87 Church St., New Haven, Conn.

RICHARDS.—*All lines*, by W. G. Richards, 59 Hill Park Crescent, Plymouth, England.

RICKER.—*George of Dover, N. H.*, by Percy L. Ricker, 227 T St., N. E., Washington, D. C.

RICKETSON.—*William of Dartmouth, Mass., and William of Portsmouth, R. I.*, by Mrs. Henry H. Edes, 62 Buckingham St., Cambridge, Mass.

RIDER.—*William of Sherborn, Mass.*, by Henry F. Ryther, Newport, Vt.

RIX.—*Thomas of Salem, Mass.*, by Guy Scoby Rix, Concord, N. H.

ROBERTS.—*Thomas of Dover, N. H.*, by Oliver H. Roberts, 67 Oakland St., Melrose, Mass.

ROBESON.—*Hon. Andrew of Pa.*, by Mrs. Joseph P. Osborne, 287 Ridge St., Newark, N. J.

ROBINSON.—*Isaac of Falmouth, Mass.*, by Henry Herbert Smythe, Falmouth, Mass.

ROCKET, or ROCKWOOD.—*Richard of England*, by Elmer E. Rockwood, Box 163, Attleborough Falls, Mass.

ROE, or ROWE.—*John of East Jefferson, L. I., N. Y.*, by Alfred Seelye Roe, 5 Dix St., Worcester, Mass.

ROGERS.—*Luke of Watertown, Mass.*, by Mrs. Ethel Brigham Leatherbee, 274 Waverley Oaks Road, Waltham, Mass.

ROOT.—*John of Farmington, Conn.*, by Mrs. Harriet C. Fielding, 30 Winans St., East Orange, N. J.

RYERSON.—*Martin of Brooklyn, N. Y.*, by Albert Winslow Ryerson, 60 Canfield Ave. E., Detroit, Mich.

RYNO.—(See Renaud.)

SABIN.—*William of Rehoboth, Mass.*, by Rev. Anson Titus, 10 Raymond Ave., Somerville, Mass.

ST. BARBE.—*Wyatt of England*, by William Tracy Eustis, 19 Pearl St., Boston, Mass.

ST. HILL.—*All lines*, by W. G. Richards, 59 Hill Park Crescent, Plymouth, England.

SALISBURY.—*Thomas of Northumberland Co., Va.*, by Rev. Joseph Brown Turner, 62 State St., Dover, Del.

SANDES, SANDS, or SANDYS.—*James of Block Island, R. I.*, by James Thomas Sands, Roe Bldg., St. Louis, Mo.

SATTERLEE.—*Nicholas of Westerly, R. I.*, by John C. Satterlee, 172 Washington St., Chicago, Ill.

SAWTELL.—*Richard of Watertown, Mass.*, by Nelson S. Hopkins, Williamsville, N. Y.

SAYLES.—*John of England*, by Henry A. Sayles, Box 31, Chepachet, R. I.

SAXE.—*John of Highgate, Vt.*, by John W. Saxe, 16 State St., Boston, Mass.

SAXTON.—*George of Westfield, Mass.*, by Harold Newell Saxton, Custom House, New York City.

SCOFIELD.—*Daniel of Stamford, Conn.*, by Wm. A. Eardeley, 466 State St., Brooklyn, N. Y.

SCOTT.—*Richard of Providence, R. I.*, by Stephen F. Peckham, 150 Halsey St., Brooklyn, N. Y.

SEARLE, or SERLE.—*All lines*, by W. G. Richards, 59 Hill Park Crescent, Plymouth, England.

SEYMOUR.—*Richard of Norwalk, Conn.*, by Miss Mary K. Talcott, 135 Sigourney St., Hartford, Conn.; and Edward Seymour Beckwith, Elkhorn, Wis.

SHACKFORD.—*William of Newington, N. H.*, by Mrs. Mary B. Morse, 24 Park St., Haverhill, Mass.; Samuel Shackford, Winnetka, Ill.; and S. B. Shackford, 151 Central Ave, Dover, N. H.

SHEAR.—*Johannes of Fishkill, N. Y.* (?), by George Thurston Waterman, 119 Hamilton St., Albany, N. Y.

SHEDD.—*Daniel of Billerica, Mass.*, by Frank E. Shedd, 93 Federal St., Boston, Mass.

SHIVERICK.—*Rev. Samuel of Falmouth, Mass.*, by Henry Herbert Smythe, Falmouth, Mass.

SHURTLEFF.—*William of Marshfield, Mass.*, by Benjamin Shurtleff, Jr., 85 Cushman St., Revere, Mass.

SILVER.—*Thomas of Newbury, Mass.*, by H. A. Silver, 45 Palmer St., Roxbury, Mass.

SISSON.—*Richard of Dartmouth, Mass.*, by Arthur A. Wood, Slocum, R. I.

SKINNER.—*Thomas of Marlborough, Mass.*, by Fred Skinner Wood, Foxborough, Mass.

SLOCUM, SLOCUMB, or SLOCOMB.—*Volume II.*, by Dr. Charles E. Slocum, Defiance, Ohio.

SMALL.—*Francis of Truro, Mass.*, by Rev. U. W. Small, West Leeds, Me.; and Mrs. Edward McClure Peters, 501 West 113th St., New York City.

SMITH.—*Ebenezer, Jr., of Woolwich, Me.*, by Walter H. Sturtevant, Richmond, Me.

SMITH.—*Henry of Hingham, Mass.*, by Carroll F. Smith, 192 Lancaster St., Albany, N. Y.

SMITH.—*Ralph of Eastham, Mass.*, by L. Bertrand Smith, 48 McDonough St., Brooklyn, N. Y.

SMITH.—*Richard of Smithtown, L. I., N. Y.*, by Mrs. Edward C. Hawks, 165 Summer St., Buffalo, N. Y.

SMITH.—*Lieut. Samuel of Hadley, Mass.*, by George L. Burton, 87 Church St., New Haven, Conn.; and Rev. William Durant, Saratoga Springs, N. Y.

SNEDEKER.—*Jan of Flatbush, Kings Co., N. Y.*, by Isaac S. Waters, 1233 Fulton St., Brooklyn, N. Y.

SNOW.—*Nicholas of Eastham, Mass.*, by F. W. Snow, 972 Massachusetts Ave., Cambridge, Mass.; and Mrs. Charles L. Alden, 245 Pawling Ave., Troy, N. Y.

SNOW.—*William of Bridgewater, Mass.*, by Mrs. Charles L. Alden, 245 Pawling Ave., Troy, N. Y.

SOUTHWICK.—*Lawrence of Salem, Mass.*, by John Herbert Barker, 53 Park St., Somerville, Mass.

SPEAR.—*George of Braintree, Mass.*, by William Spear, North Pembroke, Mass.

SPELMAN.—*Richard of Middletown, Conn.*, by Mrs. Thomas J. Barbour, 169 Hicks St., Brooklyn, N. Y.

SPENCER.—*Gerard of Haddam, Conn.*, by Dr. Horatio N. Spencer, 2725 Washington Ave., St. Louis, Mo.

SPICER.—*Peter of Groton, Conn.*, by Susan S. Meech, Groton, Conn.

SPINK.—*Robert of Narragansett or Portsmouth, R. I.*, by Kate Louise McMillan, 155 East North St., Wooster, Ohio.

SPINNEY.—*Thomas of Kittery, Me.*, by Eugene N. Spinney, Shelburne Falls, Mass.

STAMP.—*William of Lincolnshire, Eng.*, by Mrs. Florence Danforth Stamp, Adams Basin, Monroe Co., N. Y.

STANSBURY, or STANBOROUGH.—*All Massachusetts, Long Island and Maryland lines*, by Mrs. Walter Damon Mansfield, San Francisco, Cal.

STANTON.—*George of New York City*, by Dr. William Austin Macy, Kings Park, Long Island, N. Y.

STARK.—*Aaron of New London, Conn.* (?), by James R. Clark, Maunie, Ill.

STEPHEN.—*Nicholas of Taunton, Mass.*, by Mary Stevens Ghastin, 2297 N. Hermitage Ave., Chicago, Ill.

STEVENS.—*Cyprian of London, Eng.*, by E. H. Stevens, 25 Banks St., West Somerville, Mass.

STEVENS.—*Henry of Boston, Mass.*, by William A. Robbins, 178 Garfield Place, Brooklyn, N. Y.

STEWARD, STEWART, STUART, or STEUART.—*Duncan of Rowley, Mass.*, by Mrs. Willard B. Steward, Box 195, Skowhegan, Me.; Joseph A. Stuart, Palo Alto, Cal.; and George S. Stewart, 15 Irving St., Melrose, Mass.

STEWART.—*William of Mercer, Pa., and Lieut. William of Indian Run, Pa.*, by Miss Helen E. Keep, 753 Jefferson Ave., Detroit, Mich.

STOCKBERGER.—*All lines*, by W. W. Stockberger, U. S. Dept. of Agriculture, Bureau of Plant Industry, Washington, D. C.

STOKES.—*Capt. Jonathan of Branford, Conn.*, by Edwin A. Hill, U. S. Patent Office, Washington, D. C.

STONE.—*Simon of Watertown, Mass.*, by Frederic C. Stone, Hyde Park, Mass.

STOUGHTON.—*All lines*, by Rev. L. H. Stoughton, Saco, Me.

STOW.—*John of Roxbury, Mass.*, by A. S. Wiester, P. O. Box 104, Berkeley, Cal.

STREETER.—*Stephen of Charlestown, Mass.*, by Carlos P. Darling, Lawrenceville, Pa.

STURDEVANT.—*William of Norwalk, Conn.* (?), by Walter H. Sturtevant, Richmond, Me.

STURTEVANT.—*Samuel of Plymouth, Mass.*, by Walter H. Sturtevant, Richmond, Me.

SWAN.—*John of Cambridge, Mass.*, by Reuben S. Swan, 91 Babcock St., Brookline, Mass.

SWEET.—*John (Isaac) of Providence, R. I.*, by J. S. Sweet, 607 Cherry St., Santa Barbara, Cal.

SWEETING.—*Lewis and Henry of Rehoboth, Mass.*, by Mrs. Charles L. Alden, 245 Pawling Ave., Troy, N. Y.

SWETLAND.—*William*, by Rev. Frank Gardner, 119 South 4th St., Sunbury, Pa.

SWETT.—*John of Newbury, Mass.*, by Rev. Everett S. Stackpole, Bradford, Mass.

TALMAGE, or TALMADGE.—*All lines*, by Charles M. Talmadge, Newport, Wash.

TAYLOR.—*John of Co. Suffolk, Eng.*, by William Othniel Taylor, Box 1505, Orange, Mass.

TAYLOR.—*William of Peekskill, N. Y., or vicinity*, by John Elliot Bowman, 79 Elm St., Quincy, Mass.

THACHER.—*Anthony of Yarmouth, Mass.*, by John R. Totten, 44 West 54th St., New York City.

THACHER.—*Peter of Salisbury, Eng.*, by John R. Totten, 44 West 54th St., New York City.

THOMAS.—*Capt. John of Braintree, Mass.*, by Frank W. Thomas, 56 4th St., Troy, N. Y.

THURLOW.—*Richard of Newbury, Mass.*, by Miss Georgianna Thurlow, 204 Water St., Newburyport, Mass.

THURSTON.—*Job of Rehoboth or Hingham, Mass.* (?), by George Thurston Waterman, 119 Hamilton St., Albany, N. Y.

TIBBETTS.—*Henry of Dover, N. H.*, by C. W. Tibbetts, 22 New York St., Dover, N. H.

TILDEN.—*Nathaniel of Scituate, Mass.*, by John W. Linzee, Jr., 96 Charles St., Boston, Mass.

TILTON.—*Samuel of Chilmark, Mass.*, by Mrs. Martha J. Cottle, Box 42, West Tisbury, Mass.; and N. P. Tilton, West Tisbury, Mass.

TILTON.—*William of Lynn, Mass.*, by John P. Tilton, Salem, Mass.; Frank W. Hine, 7 Norris Block, Grand Rapids, Mich.; and George Washington Stuart, 54 Washington St., Ayer, Mass.

TINCOMBE, or TINGCOMBE.—*All lines*, by W. G. Richards, 59 Hill Park Crescent, Plymouth, England.

TINKER.—*John of Hartford, Conn.*, by Rev. William Durant, Saratoga Springs, N. Y.

TITCOMB.—*Moses of Newbury, Mass.*, by William Tracy Eustis, 19 Pearl St., Boston, Mass.

TITUS.—*Robert of Rehoboth, Mass.*, by Rev. Anson Titus, 10 Raymond Ave., Somerville, Mass.

TOMPKINS.—*John of Concord, Mass.*, by Mrs. Harriet C. Fielding, 30 Winans St., East Orange, N. J.

TORSEY.—*Dr. Gideon of Gilmanton, N. H.* (?), by H. T. Fernald, Amherst, Mass.

TRACY.—*Nicholas of Wexford, Eng.*, by William Tracy Eustis, 19 Pearl St., Boston, Mass.

TRAFFORD.—*All lines*, by W, G. Richards, 59 Hill Park Crescent, Plymouth, England.

TREADWELL.—*Thomas of Ipswich, Mass.*, by William A. Robbins, 178 Garfield Place, Brooklyn, N. Y.

TREDWELL.—*Edward of Huntington, Co. Suffolk, Eng.*, by William A. Robbins, 178 Garfield Place, Brooklyn, N. Y.

TREGO.—*Peter of Chester Co., Pa.*, by Dr. A. Trego Shertzer, 25 W. Preston St., Baltimore, Md.

TRUE.—*Henry*, by Miss Annie A. Clarke, 639 Congress St., Portland, Me.

TWITCHELL.—*Joseph of Dorchester, Mass.* (?), by H. K. Twitchell, 153 South Oxford St., Brooklyn, N. Y.

TYRRELL.—*William of Weymouth, Mass.*, by Mrs. Charles L. Alden, 245 Pawling Ave., Troy, N. Y.

UDALL.—*Dr. Lionel of Stonington, Conn.*, by G. Louis Arner, Jefferson, Ohio.

VAN BOERUM.—*William Jacob of Flatbush, L. I., N. Y.*, by J. E. Bookstaver, 6 Lockwood St., Binghamton, N. Y.

VAN DEUSEN.—*Abraham of New Amsderdam, N. Y.*, by Albert H. Van Deusen, 2207 M St., N. W., Washington, D. C.

VAN HORN.—*Christian of Wilmington, Del.*, by C. S. Williams, 16 Rivington St., New York City.

VAN HORNE.—*Jan Cornelius of New York City*, by C. S. Williams, 16 Rivington St., New York City.

VOSE.—*Robert of Milton, Mass.*, by Miss Ellen F. Vose, Mattapan, Mass.
WADDINGTON.—*All lines of Yorkshire, Eng.*, by Eugene F. McPike, 1 Park Row, Room 606, Chicago, Ill.
WADE.—*John of Lyme, Conn.*, by Rev. William Durant, Saratoga Springs, N. Y.
WALES.—*Ebenezer of Dorchester and Milton, Mass., Union and Hebron, Conn.*, by Lyndon P. Smith, 27 Charter Oak Place, Hartford, Conn.
WALKER.—*Richard of Lynn, Mass.*, by Everett Worthington Foster, Maltby Building, Washington, D. C.
WALTER.—*All lines*, by W. G. Richards, 59 Hill Park Crescent, Plymouth, England.
WARDWELL.—*Col. Samuel of Bristol, R. I.*, by Stephen F. Peckham, 150 Halsey St., Brooklyn, N. Y.
WARNE.—*Thomas of Perth Amboy, N. J.*, by George W. Labaw, R. F. D. Route 1, Paterson, N. J.
WATERBURY.—*John of Stamford, Conn.*, by William F. Waterbury, 125 Grove St., Stamford, Conn.
WATERHOUSE.—*Nathan of Leyden, Mass.*, by A. J. Waters, c/o Citizens Nat'l Bank, Los Angeles, Cal.
WATERMAN.—*Richard of Providence, R. I.*, by William H. Waterman, New Bedford, Mass.
WATERMAN.—*Robert of Marshfield, Mass.*, by George Thurston Waterman, 119 Hamilton St., Albany, N. Y.
WATERS.—*Anthony of Jamaica, Queens Co., N. Y.*, by Isaac S. Waters, 1233 Fulton St., Brooklyn, N. Y.
WEBB.—*William of Perch River, N. Y.*, by James B. Webb, 117 Clinton Ave., Oak Park, Ill.
WEBSTER.—*All New England lines except descendants of Gov. John*, by Stephen P. Sharples, 26 Broad St., Boston, Mass.
WEED.—*John and Jonas of Stamford, Conn.*, by Edward F. Weed, Rowayton, Conn.
WEEKS.—*Joseph*, by Mrs. J. W. Cary, 22 Magazine St., Cambridge, Mass.
WELD.—*Edmund of Sudbury, Eng.*, by J. Edward Weld, New York City.
WEST.—*All lines*, by George H. West, Ordway, Col.
WEYBURN.—*All lines*, by S. Lyon Weyburn, 464 Fayerweather Hall, Yale College, New Haven, Conn.; and L. A. Weyburn, Rockford, Ill.
WHEAT.—*Moses of Concord, Mass.*, by Silas A. Wheat, 987 Sterling Place, Brooklyn, N. Y.
WHEELER.—*John of Newbury, Mass.*, by Clarence E. Pierce, Box 981, Springfield, Mass.
WHELDEN, or WHELDON.—*Gabriel of Malden, Mass.*, by John M. Bancroft, Bloomfield, N. J.
WHITAKER.—*William of Pownall, Mass.* (?), by Mrs. James W. Cary, 22 Magazine St., Cambridge, Mass.
WHITE.—*Edward of Cranbrook, Co. Kent, Eng.*, by Frank M. White, North Attleborough, Mass.
WHITE.—*Elder John of Dorchester and Hadley, Mass., and Hartford, Conn.*, by Lyndon P. Smith, 27 Charter Oak Place, Hartford, Conn.
WHITE.—*Matthew of Albany, N. Y.*, by Rev. William Durant, Saratoga Springs, N. Y.
WHITIMORE.—*Francis of Cambridge, Mass.*, by Mrs. William T. H. Purdy, 1411 Hill Road, Reading, Pa.
WHITNEY.—*John of Watertown, Mass.*, by Rev. Charles G. Fogg, Staffordville, Conn.

WHITTIER.—*John Greenleaf of Haverhill, Mass., and Thomas of Haverhill, Mass.*, by Charles C. Whittier, 374 Blue Hill Ave., Boston, Mass.

WILLET.—*Thomas of Co. Leicester, Eng.*, by J. E. Bookstaver, 6 Lockwood St., Binghamton, N. Y.

WILLIAMS.—*Emmanuel of Taunton or Freetown, Mass.; Oliver of Sunderland, Mass., and Samuel of Groton, Conn.*, by John Oliver Williams, 171 West 75th St., New York City.

WILLIAMS.—*John of Haverhill, Mass.*, by Miss Cornelia Barton Williams, Cor. Ontario and N. State Sts., Chicago, Ill.

WILLIAMS.—*Robert of Roxbury, Mass.*, by E. H. Williams, Jr., Andover, Mass.; and Lyndon P. Smith, 27 Charter Oak Place, Hartford, Conn.

WILLIAMSON.—*Timothy of Marshfield, Mass.*, by Mrs. Henry H. Edes, 62 Buckingham St., Cambridge, Mass.

WILLIS.—*Benjamin of Haverhill, Mass.*, by Miss Pauline Willis, 3 Kensington Gate, London, England.

WILLISTON.—*John of Milton or Boston, Mass.*, by B. T. Williston, 3 Monmouth St., Somerville, Mass.

WILLITS.—*Richard of New York*, by Le Roy Willits, Seaton, Ill.

WILLMOT.—*Thomas of Rehoboth, Mass.*, by Elizabeth J. Wilmarth, 73 North Main St., Attleborough, Mass.

WINCHELL.—*Robert of Windsor, Conn.*, by A. H. Winchell, 113 State St., Minneapolis, Minn.

WISWALL.—*Thomas of Newton, Mass.*, by Rev. Anson Titus, 10 Raymond Ave., Somerville, Mass.

WITHERELL.—*William of Scituate, Mass.*, by Mrs. James W. Cary, 22 Magazine St., Cambridge, Mass.

WOOD.—*Isaiah of Ipswich, Mass.*, by Edwin A. Hill, U. S. Patent Office, Washington, D. C.

WOOD.—*John of Groton, Conn.*, by Frank B. Lamb, Westfield, N. Y.

WOODCOCK.—*All lines*, by John L. Woodcock, 1218 Washington Boulevard, Chicago, Ill.

WOODFORD.—*Thomas of Northampton, Mass.*, by Carlos P. Darling, Lawrenceville, Pa.

WOODRUFF.—*Matthew of Farmington, Conn.* (?), by Carlos P. Darling, Lawrenceville, Pa.

WOODWARD.—*Robert of Scituate, Mass.*, by Frank E. Woodward, 93 Rockland Ave., Malden, Mass.

WOODWORTH.—*Walter of Scituate, Mass.*, by Newell B. Woodworth, 718 James St., Syracuse, N. Y.

WOOLSON.—*Thomas of Sudbury, Mass.*, by Le Roy L. Woolson, Hopkinton, Mass.

WORTHINGTON.—*John of Maryland*, by Mrs. Laura A. Madden, 2880 Broadway, New York City.

WORTHINGTON.—*Nicholas of Hatfield, Mass.*, by William Tracy Eustis, 19 Pearl St., Boston, Mass.

WRIGHT.—*Peter of Virginia*, by Dr. William Austin Macy, Kings Park, Long Island, N. Y.

WRIGHT.—*Samuel of Northampton, Mass.*, by Rodney P. Wright, 47 Granite St., Cambridge, Mass.

WRIGHT.—*Simeon of Croton, Ohio*, by G. Eastman Wright, Granville, Ohio.

WRIGHT.—*Stephen of Freeport, Ill.*, by Mrs. James W. Cary, 22 Magazine St., Cambridge, Mass.

WYETH.—*Nicholas of Cambridge, Mass.*, by John Herbert Barker, 53 Park St., Somerville, Mass.
WYMAN.—*John of Woburn, Mass.*, by Walter Channing Wyman, Union League Club, Chicago, Ill.
YATES.—*William of Greenwood, Me.*, by Edgar Yates, 28 Sherman St., Everett, Mass.

[To be concluded.]

TAYER (THAYER) FAMILY ENTRIES IN THE PARISH REGISTER OF THORNBURY, GLOUCESTERSHIRE, ENGLAND.

Communicated by WALTER FAXON, Esq., and EDWARD HENRY WHORF, Esq.
With Introduction and Notes by HENRY ERNEST WOODS, A.M.

THE parish of Thornbury is in the western part of Gloucestershire, the town being a short distance from the river Severn. It is eleven miles north from Bristol, from which port it is probable that Thomas and Richard Tayer sailed for New England.* The Thornbury parish register is from 1538, with breaks from 1645 to 1650 and from 1679 to 1684.

Thomas Tayer was in Boston, Mass., before 24 Feb. 1639-40, when land was granted to him at Mount Wollaston (Braintree, Mass.) for "9 heads" in his family,† these consisting of himself and wife Margery, his sons Thomas, Ferdinando and Shadrach, perhaps two daughters, Sarah‡ and Hannah,§ born soon after his arrival in New England, and possibly two servants.

Richard Tayer, a widower, presumably a younger brother of Thomas, came to New England in 1641 with eight children,‖ and settled at Braintree, Mass., afterwards removing to Boston. His children are identified as Richard, Sarah, Jael, Deborah, Zachariah, Hester, Nathaniel and Cornelius.¶

It is likely that the Nathaniel Thayer who was in Taunton before 1668,** and the Benjamin Tayer who died in Newport, R. I., in 1716,†† were related to Thomas and Richard.

The root of the family name, from "taw": to dress skins,‡‡ is made clear in the earlier spelling of the name at Thornbury. The letter "h" was added soon after the emigrants came to New Eng-

* REGISTER, vol. 37, page 84, and vol. 58, page 225 and note.
† Boston Record Commissioners' Report, No. 2, page 50.
‡ Sarah Thayer and Jonathan Hayward were married 6 May, 1663, in Braintree.
§ Hannah Thayer and Samuel Hayden were married 28 Oct., 1664, in Braintree.
‖ 4 Massachusetts Historical Society's Collections, vol. 5, page 105, and Pattee's History of Old Braintree and Quincy, Mass., page 48.
¶ REGISTER, vol. 60, page 93.
** Emery's History of Taunton, Mass., page 110, and The Harvey Book, page 37.
†† Austin's Genealogical Dictionary of Rhode Island, page 197.
‡‡ REGISTER, vol. 37, page 84.

land; but in the line of the family descended from Ferdinando[2] (Thomas[1]) of Mendon, Mass., that letter was silent—as in Thomas and Thompson—until early in the last century. No coat-of-arms appears on any tablet or monument of the family at the parish church (St. Mary) at Thornbury, and the fact that Edward Tayer of Oldbury-on-Severn, in the parish of Thornbury, was disclaimed by the heralds at their Visitation of Gloucestershire in 1623, for using arms without proof of authority, would show that the family was not armorial. The name is now extinct in Thornbury.

A family spelling the name *Theyer* and *Thayer*, and having the same root from "taw,"* has long been at Brockworth in Gloucestershire,† a parish 25 miles north-east of Thornbury; and there was an armorial family of *Tawyer* at Raunds in Northamptonshire,‡ about 80 miles north-east of Brockworth and 105 miles from Thornbury; and also an armorial family of *Thayer* at Great Baddow and later at Thaydon Garnon in county Essex,§ afterwards of London‖; but no connection between these families has been established, so far as known.

In an account¶ of "Able and Sufficient Men in Body fit for His Majesty's Service in the Wars, within the County of Gloucester, . . in the Month of August, 1608," which is given in three classes, (1) those about 20 years of age, (2) those about 40 years of age, and (3) those between 50 and 60 years of age, there appear in Thornbury: Edward, John, Nicholas, and Richard *Tayer*, all of the second class, and William Martimer, of the first class; in Stinchcomb, 8 miles north-east from Thornbury: John *Thayer* (gent.), of the second class; and in Brockworth and its vicinity: John *Theyer*, of the first class, Richard, Roger, Thomas, Walter, and William *Theyer*, of the second class, Gabriel, Giles, John, and Thomas *Thayer*, of the first class, and William *Thayer* of the second class.

In Shakespeare's "A Midsummer Night's Dream" there is a stage direction in the First Folio: "[*Enter*] Tawyer with a trumpet." This refers to a William Tawier, or Tawyer, a subordinate in the employ of John Hemminge who was one of the members of the Globe Theatre Company and one of the editors of the First Folio. William Tawier was buried in St. Saviour's Church, Southwark, in June, 1625.**

---

* Wood's City of Oxford (Oxford Historical Society, xv), vol. 1, page 476, note 5.
† Notes and Queries, 6th Series, vol. 12, page 31, and Wood's Athenæ Oxonienses, 1813, vol. 3, page 996.
‡ Metcalfe's Visitations of Northamptonshire, page 49.
§ Howard's Bysshe's Visitation of Essex, page 92.
‖ Visitation of London (Harleian Society, xvii), vol. 2, page 280.
¶ Smith's Men and Armour for Gloucestershire in 1608 (London, 1902).
** Midsummer Night's Dream, Furness's Variorum Edition, act v, scene i, line 134 and note, and Halliwell-Phillipps's Outlines of the Life of Shakespeare, 7th ed., vol. 2, page 260, note 22.

Baptisms.

4 Jan. 1557–8. Johes Tayer. Godfathers: Johanes Williams, Johanes Tyther. Godmother: Elizabeth Cooke.

15 Oct. 1558. Johanes Tayer, son and heir to Thomas Tayer. Godfathers: William Merick, Henricus Lydat. Godmother: Jone Rede.

7 Nov. 1559. Thomas Tayer. Godfathers: Thomas Moore, Johanes Barton. Godmother: Elizabeth Whitfield.

25 Apr. 1560. Thomas Jamis. Godfather: Thomas Tayer. Godmother: Margareta Tayer.

13 Oct. 1560. Margareta Tawier. Godfather: Willhelmus Mawle. Godmothers: Margareta Busher, Agneta Tayer.

6 May 1561. Johanes Tawier. Godfathers: Johanes Roocs, Richardus Baker. Godmother: Margaretta Wallis.

1 Sept. 1561. Cuthberta Tawier. Godfather: Thomas Pullen. Godmothers: Susan Birton, Johana Selmon.

2 Aug. 1562. Richardus Tawier. Godfathers: Richardus Cheyre, Walter Howks. Godmother: Elizabeth Picher.

21 Sept. 1563. Johanes Jamis. Godmother: Maria Tawier.

8 Feb. 1563[–4]. Thomas Tawier. Godfathers: Thomas Search, Thomas Moore. Godmother: Margerate Floyde.

28 Feb. 1563[–4]. Johannes Tawier. Godfathers: Johannes Moore, Humfridus Whitfield. Godmother: Elenora Barton.

1 Nov. 1564. Wilihelmus Tawier. Godfathers: William Bruton, Johannes Jonis. Godmother: Joyce Griffings.

6 May 1565. Richard Tawier. Godfathers: Richardus Wilcox, Merricus ———. Godmother: Marie Tawier.

16 Dec. 1565. Alicia Tawier. Godfather: Richard Griffing. Godmothers: Alicia D[ ]rnt, Elizabeth Howell.

20 Dec. 1567. Secillia Tawier. Godfather: Richard Wilcox. Godmothers: Secilia White, Catherine Ripe.

23 Sept. 1568. Luci Tawier. Godfather: Johanes Driver. Godmothers: Luci Baker, Catherina Rippe.

12 Feb. 1569–70. Thomas Tawyer. Godfathers: Thomas Stevens, Richard Wilkokes. Godmother: Isabella Fowler.

13 Aug. 1570. Anna Tawier. Godfather: Thomas Marten. Godmothers: Agneta Ady, Alice Laurence.

23 Mar. 1572[–3]. William Tawyer. Godfathers: Robert Eslineton, Johanes Jonis. Godmother: Johana Bartone.

25 Jan. 1573[–4]. Nicholas Tawier. Godfathers: Nicholas Adams, Thomas Holdbrooke. Godmother: Johana Tocker.

26 Oct. 1577. Edward Tawier. (Christened.)

25 Apr. 1579. Ursula Tawier. (Christened.)

6 Jan. 1581[–2]. Anthony Tawier. (Christened.)

24 June 1586. Catherine Tawier. Godfather: Thomas Tawier. Godmothers: Catherine [ ]ippe, Susannah Jones.

23 Oct. 1587. Alice Tawyer. Godfather: Thomas Jones. Godmother: Alice Joanes.

23 Dec. 1589. Margaret Tawier. Godfather: Thomas Gibbs. Godmothers: Margaret Griffin, Mary Werryat.

7 Mar. 1589–90. Francis Tawier. Godfathers: John Tawier, William Williams. Godmother: Ussly Tawier.

22 Oct. 1590. Jane Tayer. Godfather: Richard Pullen. Godmothers: Jane Tyler, Jone Gibbs.
10 Nov. 1590. Ann Tawier. Godfather: Richard Pullen. Godmothers: Sicely Jones, Margaret Griffins.
4 Dec. 1591. Elinor Tawier. Godfather: John Comely. Godmothers: Elnor Carle, Jone Tawier.
26 Dec. 1591. John Tawier. Godfathers: John Lyilyn, James Lawrence. Godmother: Ann Watson.
6 Jan. 1592[-3]. Joane Tawier. Godfather: Thomas Holdbrooke. Godmothers: Joane Barton, Margery Dimery.
17 Apr. 1593. John Tayer. Godfathers: John Tayer, Richard Dimery. Godmother: Als Tayer.
21 Jan. 1594[-5]. Thomas Tayer. Godfathers: Thomas Tayer, Thomas Shurman. Godmother: Edy Midlton.
7 Feb. 1594[-5]. Edward Tayer. Godfathers: Edward Knight, John Jones. Godmother: Mary Tratman.
1 Mar. 1595[-6]. Mary Tayer. Godfather: Thomas Holdbrook. Godmothers: Als Hilpe, Agnes Jones.
16 Aug. 1596. Thomas Tayer.* Godfathers: Thomas Gibbs, William Dimery.
18 Aug. 1597. Judith Tayer. Godfather: Edmond Pytcher. Godmothers: Judith Stones, An Tayer.
1 Mar. 1597-8. Ferdinand Tawyer. Godfathers: Thomas Porkwood (gent.), John Carle. Godmother: Ann Thurston.
13 Aug. 1598. John Tayer. Godfathers: John Tayer, Nicholas Baker. Godmother: Jone Wither.
13 Jan. 1598-9. Catherine Pitcher. Godfather: John Tayer.
1 Jan. 1599[1600]. Wilfry Tayer. Godfathers: Wilfry Waker, Robert Smith. Godmother: Joice Griffing.
1 May 1600. Sicely Tayer. Godfather: Thomas Pytcher. Godmothers: Als Hilpe, Mary Tratman.
5 Apr. 1601. Richard Tayer.† Godfathers: Richard Dimery, Nicholas Tayer. Godmother: Elizabeth Griffing.
7 Oct. 1602. Alice Tilladam. Godmother: Alice Tayer.
21 Aug. 1603. Thomas Tayre. Godfathers: Thomas Tayer, Richard Wytheed.
24 Feb. 1603[-4]. Catherine Tayer. Godfather: Thomas Dimery. Godmothers: Catherine Russell, Grlian[?] Smith.
5 May 1605. William Tayer. Godfathers: William Coke, John Walker. Godmother: Jone Taire.
10 June 1606. Margaret Tayre. Godfather: John West. Godmothers: Jane Walker, Joice Griffing.
14 July 1606. Elizabeth Tayre. Godfather: Nicholas Purnell. Godmother: Sisly Wicksteed.
15 Mar. 1607[-8]. Agnes Taire the daughter of Richard Taire. Godfather: Nicholas Barly. Godmothers: Agnis Grainge, Jone Walker.
15 Jan. 1609[-10]. Thomas Tawyer son of Edward Tawyer. Godfathers: Thomas Tawyer, James Eddis. Godmother: Elizabeth Wilcox.

* It was probably he who married, 13 Apr. 1618, Margerie Wheeller, and later emigrated to New England with his family.

† It was probably he who married, 5 Apr. 1624, Dorothy Mortimore, and, after her death, emigrated to New England with his children.

29 Apr. 1610. John Taire. Godfather: John Clarke. Godmother: [erased] Taire.

23 June 1611. Anna Tayer. Godfather: William Gwatkins. Godmothers: Anne Breadston, Joyse Haris.

26 Dec. 1611. John Tayer. Godfathers: John Whitfield, John Steevens. Godmother: Jobane Patche.

13 Nov. 1614. John Tawyer. Godfathers: James Eddys, Richard Wicksteed. Godmother: Agnes Ganner.

13 Oct. 1616. Frederick Badmanton. Godfathers: Thomas Tayer, Francis Tayer.

15 Feb. 1617. Cordelia Badmenton. Godfather: Ferdinando Tayer. Godmothers: Agnes Tayer, Sisley Tayer.

4 July 1619. Frances Davys. Godfather: Edward Tayer. Godmother: Anne Tayer.

18 Nov. 1619. Ursula Tayer. Godfather: Gyles Wheeler. Godmothers: Ursula Tayer, Secilly Davys.

28 Jan. 1620–1. John Davys. Godfather: John Tayer.

20 May 1621. Welfrey Tayer. Godfathers: Welfrey Tayer, John Bayne [or Boyce]. Godmother: Katherin Hurd.

19 Aug. 1621. Bartholomew Tayer. Godfathers: John Curtys, gent., Thomas Parker. Godmother: Alys Eddys.

15 Sept. 1622. Thomas Tayer.* Godfathers: Thomas Budden, Richard Tayer. Godmother: Joyce Harris.

10 Feb. 1624[–5]. Richard Tayer.† Godfathers: Richard Tayer, Wm. Mortimore. Godmother: Bridgett Seagar.

18 Apr. 1625. Ferdinando Tayer.‡ Godfathers: Ferdinando Tayer, William Tayer. Godmother: Margarett King.

8 Sept. 1626. Jonathan Tayer. Godfathers: John Callaway, Thomas Tayer. Godmother: Dorothy Tayer.

8 Oct. 1626. Ursula Tayer. Godfather: Nicholas Tayer. Godmothers: Ursula Tayer, Elizabeth Jones.

29 June 1627. Marie Tawyer. Godfather: Richard Callaway. Godmothers: Agnes Tayer, Katheryne Bruidwor.

10 May 1628. Elizabeth Tayer. Godfather: William Jones. Godmothers: Joyce Harrys, Margaret Byrde.

15 Jan. 1628[–9]. Jonathan Tayer. Godfathers: Richard Tayer, John Dynty. Godmother: Alice L[ ]ker.

9 May 1629. Shadrach Tayer.§ Godfathers: John Alpas, John Pendock. Godmother: Katherin Tayer.

4 Feb. 1629–30. Deborah Tayer. Godfather: John Purlyn. Godmothers: Katheren Dymery, Sarah Thurston.

17 Apr. 1630. Elizabeth Tayer. Godfather: George Speck. Godmothers: Isabel Mershe, Agnes Tayer.

* Son of Thomas and Margerie (Wheeller), who came to New England with his parents, settled in Braintree, Mass., married, about 1646, Anne ——, and died in Braintree, 9 Aug. 1692, "aged neer seventy."

† Son of Richard and Dorothy (Mortimore), who came to New England with his father, settled in Braintree, Mass., where he married, 24 Dec. 1651, Dorothy Pray, and died there 27 Aug. 1695, "aged 71."

‡ Son of Thomas and Margerie (Wheeller), who came to New England with his parents, married in Braintree, Mass., 14 Jan. 1652–3, Huldah Hayward, and later settled in Mendon, Mass., where he died 28 Mar. 1713.

§ Son of Thomas and Margerie (Wheeller), who came to New England with his parents, settled in Braintree, Mass., where he married (1), 1 Jan. 1654–5, Mary Barrett, and (2), about 1661, Deliverance Priest, and died in Braintree, 19 Oct. 1678.

24 June 1630. Mary Tayer. Godfather: William Tayer. Godmothers: Katheryn Tayer, Ellizabeth Moore.

14 Aug. 1631. John Tayer. Godfathers: John Dawniee, John Dymerie. Godmother: Katheryne Teakle.

2 Feb. 1631[-2]. Thomas Tayer. Godfathers: ——— Mershe, Francis Tayer. Godmother: Agnes Tayer.

9 Feb. 1631[-2]. Sara Tayer.* Godfather: Thomas Tayer. Godmothers: Agnes Jones, Katheryne Dawney.

16 Sept. 1632. Marie Tayer. Godfather: Francis Mountayne. Godmothers: Ann Stadurd, Katheryne Dymerie.

2 June 1633. Jaell Tayer.† Godfather: Rychard Dymmerie. Godmothers: Katheryne Dawney, Agnes Tayer.

12 Nov. 1633. Ann Tayer. Godfather: Richard Peaseley. Godmothers: An Tayer, Elizabeth Mershe.

27 Mar. 1633-4. Deborah Tayer.‡ Godfathers: William Jones, John Busher. Godmother: Elizabeth Wenkl.

6 Mar. 1634[-5]. Zacaria Tayer.§ Godfathers: John Ford, William Banton. Godmother: Agnes White.

12 Apr. 1635. Elizabeth Tayer. Godfather: William Callaway. Godmothers: Elizabeth Dymerie, Jaine Callaway.

26 Nov. 1635. Charles Tayer. Godfathers: Thomas Smithe, Thomas Pach. Godmother: Eliz. Peaseley.

24 Nov. 1636. Hester Tayer.‖ Godfather: John Dymery. Godmothers: Alice Parker, Marie Tayer.

16 Nov. 1637. Edee Tayer. Godfather: George Baker. Godmothers: Anne Tayer, Ann Hornes.

27 Dec. 1637. Jonathan Tayer. Godfathers: Rich. Tayer, John Dymery. Godmother: Marie Kelloway.

11 Apr. 1639. Nathaniel Tayer.¶ Godfathers: Thomas Dymrie, Edward Dymrie. Godmother: Abigail Purlene.

10 May 1640. Nathaniel Tayer. Godfathers: Thomas Dymerie, William Hancock. Godmother: Elizabeth Purlen.

31 May 1640. Judith Tayer. Godfather: John Tayer. Godmothers: Elizabeth Peslie, Jane Whitfield.

10 Dec. 1640. Cornelius Tayer.** Godfathers: Robert Thurston, Giles Wheler. Godmother: Alice Hopkins *als* Seaborn.

22 Apr. 1644. Gabriel Tayer. Godfathers: William Callaway, John Briggs. Godmother: Marie Callaway.

* Daughter of Richard and Dorothy (Mortimore), who came to New England with her father, and married in Boston, Mass., 20 July 1651, Samuel Davis.

† Daughter of Richard and Dorothy (Mortimore), who came to New England with her father, married in Braintree, Mass., 17 Mar. 1654, John Harbour, Jr., and died there 10 Mar. 1701.

‡ Daughter of Richard and Dorothy (Mortimore), who came to New England with her father, married in Braintree, Mass., 11 Apr. 1653, Thomas Faxon, Jr., and died there 31 May 1662.

§ Son of Richard and Dorothy (Mortimore), who came to New England with his father, and settled in Braintree, Mass., where he died, unmarried, 29 July 1693.

‖ Daughter of Richard and Dorothy (Mortimore), who came to New England with her father, and in 1695 was the wife of Joseph Gray, probably of Taunton, Mass.

¶ Son of Richard and Dorothy (Mortimore), who came to New England with his father, settled in Boston, Mass., married, about 1670, Deborah Townsend, and died in 1693.

** Son of Richard and Dorothy (Mortimore), who came to New England with his father, and settled in Weymouth, Mass., where he died in 1663.

The following names appear, either as godfather or godmother, in other baptismal entries.

Agnes (Annis) Tayer, 1600, 10, 14, 17, 22, 27, 30, 41; Alice Tawier, 1566; Alice Tawyer, 1601; Alice (Als, Allice) Tayer, 1567, 95, 99, 1602, 22, 24, 26, 28, 30, 35; Ann Tayre, 1606; An Taire, 1608; An (Anne, Ann) Tawyer, 1608, 13, 15; An (Anne) Tayer, 1620, 23, 33, 36; Cicely (Sissily) Tayer, 1592, 1617; Edward Tayer, 1597, 1600, 20, 22; Edward Taire, 1608; Edward Tawyer, 1612, 15; Elinor Tawyer, 1612; Ellyn (Elen) Taire, 1607, 10; Ellyne Tayer, 1611; Ellyne Tawyer, 1612; Frances Tawyer, 1613; Frances Tayer, 1618; Francis Tayer, 1619, 20, 26, 31; Ferdinand (Ferdinando) Tayer, 1618, 33, 34; Ferdinando Tawyer, 1638; Jone (Joane) Tayer, 1595, 1603, 5, 11; Joane Tawyer, 1601, 28; Jone Tay[r], 1604; Joane (Jone) Tayre, 1604, 6; Jone Taire, 1605; Johanes Tawier, 1565, 67, 68, 69; Johan Tayer, 1623, 25, 29; John Tawyer, 1585, 1603, 15; John Tayer, 1591, 96, 99, 1605, 16, 21, 24, 34, 36, 37, 39, 42; John Tawier, 1590, 93; John Tayar, 1592; John Taire, 1597; John Tayre, 1605; Judith (Judeth) Tayer, 1617, 18, 19; Katheryne (Catherine, Katheren, Katherine, Katheryn) Tayer, 1613, 15, 17, 21, 25, 27, 28, 30, 37; Lucie Tayer, 1636; Lewcey Tawyer, 1638; Margareta (Margaret) Tawier, 1563, 74; Margareta (Margarett, Margaret) Tayer, 1564, 83, 1625, 30, 32; Margaret Tawyer, 1586; Maria Tayer, 1557, 59; Maria Tawier, 1560, 61, 63; Mary Taire, 1608; Nicholas Tayer, 1596, 1613, 21, 22, 32; Nicholas Taire, 1608; Richard Tayer, 1613, 18, 19, 21, 24, 38; Susanna Tayer, 1626; Symon Taire, 1641; Thomas Tayer, 1557, 58, 59, 62, 99, 1621; Thomas Tawier, 1560, 62, 67, 83; Thomas Tawyer, 1596, 1608, 14; Usly Tayer, 1599.

Marriages.

15 Nov. 1553. Thomas Jamys to Jone Taw[i]er.
19 Feb. 1560[-1]. Thomas Holdbrooke to Constans Tawier.
3 Aug. 1589. John Tawyer to Joan Lawrence.
30 Apr. 1597. Thomas Tillad to Alice Tawyer.
3 May 1597. Thomas Tilladame to Alice Tawyer.
15 Oct. 1599. Nicholas Tayer to Jone Stones.
4 Nov. 1599. William Pytch[r] to Ussly Tayer.
24 Nov. 1614. Thomas Badmanton to Ellnor Tayer, at Gloucester.
13 Apr. 1618. Thomas Tayer* to Margerie Wheeller.†
11 June 1618. James Davisse to Sysley Tayer, at Gloucester.
22 Nov. 1619. Christopher Grymer to Mabell Tayer.
29 Apr. 1622. John Tayer to Alce Vyzard, at Bristol.
5 Apr. 1624. Richard Tayer‡ to Dorothy Mortimore.§
19 Jan. 1625[-6]. William Tayer to Mary Kellaway.
27 Jan. 1630[-1]. William Barton to Agnes Tayer.
4 July 1631. John Dawnce to Katheryne Tayer.
29 June 1640. Richard Tayer to Jane Solles.

*Came to New England with his family, and settled at Mount Wollaston (afterwards Braintree), Mass., where he died 2 June, 1665.

† Died at Braintree, Mass., 11 Feb., 1672-3.

‡ Came to New England with eight children, and settled first in Braintree, Mass., afterwards removing to Boston, Mass., where he married, soon after 15 July 1646, Jane, widow of John Parker of Boston (formerly of Marlborough, Eng.), and died before 20 Apr. 1663.

§ Died in Thornbury, 17 Jan. 1640[-1].

Burials.

21 Aug. 1558. Jobes Tawier.
11 Feb. 1561[-2]. Johes Tawier.
11 Feb. 1561[-2]. Willihelmus Tawier.
19 Mar. 1561[-2]. Constans Tawier.
13 Jan. 1565[-6]. Willihelm Tawier.
6 Mar. 1565[-6]. Thomas Tawier.
5 May 1571. Agneta Tawier.
20 Nov. 1572. Wilihelmus Tawier.
17 Mar. 1573[-4]. Thomas Tayer.
4 May 1576. Johana Tawier.
4 July 1579. Secilia Tawier.
12 Oct. 1584. John Tawier.
11 Sept. 1586. Catherine Tayer.
13 Dec. 1586. Alice Tawier.
16 Aug. 1587. Anthony Tayer.
8 Nov. 1590. Jane Tayer.
10 Nov. 1590. An Tawier.
10 Nov. 1590. Ann Tawier daughter of above born, and buried at the same time as her mother.
5 Feb. 1592[-3]. Jone Tayer.
26 Apr. 1593. Margaret Tayer.
14 Feb. 1594[-5]. Thomas Tayer.
1 Jan. 1600-1. John Tayer died, buried 4th day.
18 June 1603. Margaret Tayer.
15 Mar. 1606-7. John Taire, son of Richard Tayre.
11 Feb. 1609[-10]. Thomas Taire, son of Edward Taire.
12 Oct. 1610. John Taire, son of Richard Taire.
20 Apr. 1611. Mrs. Mary Cooke (whose Sister [*sic*] in law was Thomas Tawyer who died in Anno 1593).
15 Nov. 1612. Alice Tawyer.
13 Dec. 1619. Ursula Tayer.
10 July 1621. Wilfrey Tayer.
12 June 1622. Welfrey Tayer.
25 Feb. 1622[-3]. Bartholomew Tayer.
3 Mar. 1622[-3]. Thomas Tayer.
3 Oct. 1626. Jonathan Tayer.
2 May 1627. Ursula Tayer.
24 Sept. 1627. Marie Tayer.
5 Nov. 1627. Edward Tayer.
3 Dec. 1627. Thomas Tayer had a child buried not baptised.
20 Feb. 1627[-8]. John Tayer.
25 Jan. 1628[-9]. Jonathan Tayer.
16 Mar. 1630[-1]. Deborah Tayer.
18 Aug. 1631. John Tayer.
23 May 1632. Francis Tayer.
— Dec. 1632. Thomas Tayer had a child buried not baptised.
18 May 1634. Ursula Tayer.
17 Jan. 1640[-1]. Dorothie Tayer.*
19 Jan. 1642[-3]. Ferdinando Tayer.
9 Feb. 1642[-3]. Lucie Tayer.
16 Feb. 1642[-3]. Jonathan Tayer.
16 Mar. 1642[-3]. Anne Tayer.

* Wife of Richard who emigrated to New England in 1641.

ABSTRACTS OF WILLS RELATING TO THE TAYER (THAYER) FAMILY OF THORNBURY, GLOUCESTERSHIRE, ENGLAND.

Communicated by HENRY ERNEST WOODS, A.M.

WILL of JOHN TAYER of Thornbury, co. Gloucester, yeoman. Dated 31 December 1600; proved March 1600 [-1]. To be buried at Thornbury. To 3 daughters Alice, Agnes and Evelyn (?) Tayer a messuage and tenement in Thornbury. To son John a gold ring. To wife Jone Tayer all goods and she Executrix. To mother Mary Cooke. To brother Thomas 3s 4d. To Mr. Manning, minister of Thornbury, 10s. Overseer: John Hilse, Senior, and appoints to be joined with him as overseers John Hilse, Junior, and brother Thomas Tayer, and to them 20d for their pains. Witnesses: John Manning, Thomas Tayer, John Hylse and Jo: Hylse. Memorandum (after sealing will): To daughters Alice and Agnes Tayer £8, being £4 to each of them. (*Consistory of Gloucester.*)

Will of THOMAS TAWYER of Thornbury, gent. Dated 13 February 1622; proved 20 May 1623. To the Parish Church of Thornbury 6s 8d. To Poor people of Thornbury and Kington 40s. Desires that Mr. Sprinte, Minister at Thornbury, should preach 4 Sermons on such texts of Holy Scripture as he should appoint before his decease and at such times as he should mention, one at funeral and the other at intervals of a month, and to be paid 6s 8d for his trouble. To son Ferdinando and his heirs house, land and appurtenances at Thornbury, and failing issue, to son Francis and his heirs, and failing issue, to daughter Elinor Smith and her heirs. To son Francis £40 and a signet ring. To son Ferdinando £70 and a gold ring. To daughter Elinor Smith 12d. To Frederick Badminton, son of daughter Elinor, £20. To Hanna Smith and Elinor* Smith, daughters of said Elinor Smith, £10 apiece. If wife should marry again, then to son Francis £50, to Frederick Badminton £20, and to Hanna and Hester* Smith £10. Due on Bond from Thomas Smith £100, this amount to be for the use of Frederick Badminton. To each of children various silver articles. All residue of goods to present wife Ann, who is to have use of all silver plate till her death or second marriage, and she to be Executrix, if she refuse, then sons Ferdinando and Francis to be Executors. Overseers: William Rider, Richard Atwells, John Parker and John Champneys, gent., and sons Francis and Ferdinando Tawyer. Witnesses: John Baker, John Champneys, Francis Tawyer and Ferdinando Tawyer. (*Consistory of Gloucester.*)

Will of KATHERINE TAYER of Kington in the parish of Thornbury, co. Gloucester. Dated 21 January 1656; proved 26 June 1658, by the executor named. To my daughter Anne Barton, my best stuff gown, and one holland sheet which I bought of my father James Ellys, and £20; she and her now husband giving a receipt in law to my executor. To my grandchildren John Tayer the younger, Thomas Tayer and Sara Tayer, £10 apiece. To my 4 grandchildren, viz. the 4 daughters of my son John Tayer, £5 apiece. To my 2 grandchildren Sarah Tayer and Mary Tayer,

*The testator mentions Hanna and *Elinor* Smith the two daughters of Elinor Smith, but afterwards, in several places, he refers to Hanna and *Hester* Smith the two daughters of Elinor Smith. Probably the word Elinor, first used, was an error.

all my gloves, purses and silk girdles. 20s to be laid out by my executor in smocks and aprons for my cousin Elizabeth Jaine. To my cousin Edward Parker 10s. To my cousin William Parker, if he shall be living at my death, and come in person to receive it, 10s. To everyone of the sons and daughters of John Baker of Thornbury, gentleman, my kinsman, 12d. To Alice Eedes, wife of Henry Eedes, my market petticoat. To my godson Samuel Eedes 10s. To my late servant Marie White, now called Marie Syer, 40s. To my servant Martha Gawney 10s. Residuary legatee and Executor: my son John Tayer. Overseers: John Baker aforesaid and Thomas Baker his eldest son. Witnesses: Jo: Baker, the marks of Judith Poynton and Mary Webb, Robert Thurston.

(*P. C. C. Wootton, 476.*)

Will of SARA TAYER of Keynton, Thornbury, widow. Dated 20 January 1670; proved 12 April 1673. To son John Tayer a clock. To son Thomas Tayer a silver bowl that was his grandmother's. To 2 eldest daughters Sara and Mary £250 each to make up their portions left them by their grandmother. To daughter Elizabeth a lease of certain grounds called Bann-Marsh and 2 acres in Deep More in Ham, parish of Berkeley, under lease granted by George, Lord Berkeley. To 2 youngest daughters Ann and Judith lease of messuage and land at Rockhampton, held from Nathaniel Mallett, my brother. To said 3 daughters Elizabeth, Anne and Judith £50 apiece. To daughter in law 20s. To grandchild Elizabeth Tayer £5. To Elizabeth Jayne 40s. To son John Tayer all residue and he sole Executor. Overseers: brothers Nathaniel and Samuel Mallett and son Thomas Tayer, and to them 10s for their trouble. To Walter Webb 10s. Witnesses: Nathaniel Mallett, Samuel Mallett and Robert Thurstan. (*Consistory of Gloucester.*)

Administration of goods of JUDITH TAYER, deceased intestate, granted 5 March 1683 to John Tayer, etc. Value of Estate 39s 2d.

(*Consistory of Gloucester.*)

Will of ABELL WHELER* of Thornbury, tiller. Dated 26 February 1613; proved 24 January 1614. To son William Wheller 6d. To daughter Elizabeth Wheller a brass pot, etc. To daughter Margery Wheller sheets, etc. To son Giles Wheller goods. To daughters sheep and lambs to be divided by John Champneys and Thomas Barton. To wife Jane Wheller residue of goods and she sole Executrix. Overseers: Thomas Barton and John Champneys. Witnesses: Thomas Harborn and John Champneys. (*Consistory of Gloucester.*

Will of JANE WHELLER† of Thornbury. Dated 30 March 1629; proved 1629, no date. To son Giles Wheller various goods that are in his possession. To son William Wheller 10s. To William Ogborne son of John Ogborne 10s. To Thomas Tayer and Ferdinando Tayer sons of Thomas Tayer her son in law 10s. To daughter Elizabeth Ogborn 12d. To daughters Elizabeth Ogborn and Margery Tayer all wearing apparel. To Thomas Tayer son of Thomas Tayer, her cosen, all residue of goods and he sole Executor. Overseers: son Giles Wheller and son in law Thomas Tayer. Witnesses: Thomas Tayer, John Champneys and Giles Wheller. (*Consistory of Gloucester.*)

*Father of Margery who married, 13 Apr. 1618, Thomas Tayer the emigrant to New England.

†Mother of Margery who married Thomas Tayer.

Will of GILES WHEELER, of Morton, Thornbury, husbandman. Dated 24 May 1650; proved October 1650. To wife Susanna £10 and various goods. To Ann wife of Guy Lawrence 20s. To Alice Wither daughter of Peter Wither 20s. To Agnes Gough 10s. To kinsman William Ogborn of Thornbury, baker, all residue of goods and he sole Executor. Overseers: Guy Lawrence and William Demey. Debts owing to testator—Robert Barton 40s, Edward Long 40s, John Windon 40s, Robert Godfrey 20s, Richard Butcher 3s 2d. Witnesses: Timothy Hacker and John Morris. (*Consistory of Gloucester.*)

Will of JOHN MORTIMER of Morton, Thornbury, yeoman. Dated 19 July 1615; proved November 1615. To be buried in the Churchyard of Thornbury. To 2 sons William and Francis £10 a piece. To daughter Johane £10. To wife Johane all residue of goods and she sole Executrix. Overseer: Brother in law John Searche. Witnesses: Richard Warner, John Longe and John Searche with others. Debts owing by testator: John Mallett of Bevington £4, William Webb of Shepperdine £5, John Pegler of Tortworth £8, Richard Warner of Faulfield 20s. (*Consistory of Gloucester.*)

Will of WILLIAM MORTIMER* of Thornbury. Dated 31 August 1626; proved 9 September 1626. To be buried in Thornbury Churchyard near body of late wife Margaret. To Richard Tayer £5 and various articles. To grandchild Richard Tayer bed, etc. To daughter Dorothy 12d. To youngest daughter Agnes Mortimer all residue of goods and she sole Executrix. Overseers: Thomas Croome [or Broome] and Agnes Croome [or Broome] and for their pains 12d. Witnesses: Ric: Brafeild, William Jones and Francis Ogborne. (*Consistory of Gloucester.*)

Will of FRANCIS MORTIMER of Thornbury, shoemaker. Nuncupative will, no date; proved 29 January 1647. To Andrew Butler his brother in law (the husband of Joan Butler alias Mortimer, his sister) and his children, he gave his free land in Thornbury, paying out of it unto his brother William 20s per annum during his life. All the rest of his goods he gave unto Maria his wife and she to be sole Executrix. Witnesses: Henry Marsh, Andrew Butler and Maria Mortimer. (*Consistory of Gloucester.*)

THOMAS TREADWELL OF IPSWICH, MASS., AND SOME OF HIS DESCENDANTS.

By WILLIAM A. ROBBINS, LL.B., of Brooklyn, N. Y.

[Concluded from page 198.]

29. NATHANIEL[5] TREADWELL (*Charles,[4] Nathaniel,[3] Nathaniel,[2] Thomas[1]*), born in Portsmouth, N. H., 6 Dec., 1730, died testate, in Portsmouth, 7 Feb., 1817, married in Portsmouth, about 1760, Sarah, born in 1743, died in Portsmouth, 10 Sept., 1815, daughter of Capt. Thomas and Anna (Treadwell) Walden of Portsmouth. He was a merchant, and resided in Portsmouth and Newmarket, N. H.

* Father of Dorothy who married, 5 Apr. 1624, Richard Tayer the emigrant to New England.

Children:

i. LYDIA,[6] bapt. in North Church, Portsmouth, 16 June, 1765; d. on her 10th birthday.

ii. NATHANIEL, b. Mch., 1765; probably living 19 July, 1817; m. in Portsmouth, 25 Nov., 1804, Abigail, probably living in 1817, probably the dau. of Richard Tucker of Portsmouth. He was a trader, designated "3rd" in 1804, and probably "Sr." in 1817, and resided in Portsmouth. No child.

iii. CHARLES, b. in Portsmouth, 10 Dec., 1767; d. in Newmarket, N. H., 3 June, 1843; m. in Portsmouth, 26 Feb., 1799, Elizabeth, b. in Portsmouth, 23 Dec., 1777, d. testate, in Newmarket, N. H., 1 Apr., 1862, dau. of Samuel and Mary (Pickering) Drowne of Portsmouth. He was a sea-captain, residing in Portsmouth and Newmarket, N. H. Children: 1. *Lydia Drowne.*[7] 2. *Elizabeth.* 3. *Charles.* 4. *Thomas Drowne.* 5. *Ann Elizabeth.* 6. *(Benjamin) Franklin.* 7. *Caroline Matilda.* 8. *William Henry Harrison Montgomery.* 9. *Mary Frances.* 10. *William Cutter.* 11. *Sarah Walden.* 12. *Louisa Tewksbury.* 13. *Napoleon Bonaparte.*

iv. ———(?), buried 2 Nov., 1783, aged 2 years.

v. ———(?), buried 21 Sept., 1783, aged 7 months.

30. JACOB[5] TREADWELL (*Charles,*[4] *Nathaniel,*[3] *Nathaniel,*[2] *Thomas*[1]), born 15 July, 1736, died, intestate, 22 Aug., 1787, married Ann, who was buried in Portsmouth, N. H., 4 Apr., 1794, probably the daughter of Daniel and Mehitable (Rindge) Rogers. He was a merchant, designated "Jr." in 1769, and resided in Portsmouth, N. H.

Children:

i. ANN[6] (NANCY), b. in Portsmouth, 27 Mch., 1766; d. in Dorchester, Mass., 9 Feb., 1840; m. in Portsmouth, 9 Sept., 1784, Rev. John, of Boston, Mass., b. in Boston, 31 May, 1754, d. in Boston, 14 Feb., 1813, son of Rev. Andrew and Elizabeth (Langdon) Eliot. He resided in Boston, Mass., and his widow was residing in Charlestown, Mass., in 1814. Children: 1. *Andrew.* 2. *John.* 3. *Anna.* 4. *George.* 5. *Elizabeth Langdon.* 6. *Mary Henrietta.*

ii. MARY, bapt. in North Church, Portsmouth, 7 June, 1767; d. probably unmarried, in Portsmouth, 9 Aug., 1838, aged 72 yrs.; resided in Boston, Mass., and Portsmouth, N. H.

iii. CHARLOTTE ROGERS, bapt. in North Church, Portsmouth, 14 Aug., 1768.

iv. MEHITABLE RINDGE, bapt. in North Church, Portsmouth, 17 Sept., 1769; d. probably unmarried, before 10 June, 1814; resided in Portsmouth.

v. GEORGE ROGERS, bapt. in North Church, Portsmouth, 13 Mch., 1774; living 15 Apr., 1805; d. probably before 10 June, 1814. He was a mariner, residing in Portsmouth, N. H.

vi. JACOB CUTTER, bapt. in North Church, Portsmouth, 20 Aug., 1775; d. in Portsmouth, 8 May, 1852, aged 77 yrs. He was a mariner, and resided in Moscow, Russia, and Portsmouth, N. H.

vii. WILLIAM KELLEY, bapt. in North Church, Portsmouth, 24 Nov., 1776; d. in New York city, 4 Nov., 1820, aged 44 yrs; m. in Portsmouth, 18 Oct., 1813, Mary, living 24 Aug., 1822, probably dau. of John Jackson, of Portsmouth. He was a printer, and resided in Portsmouth, N. H., and New York city. Child: *Charles Samuel.*[7]

viii. CHARLES CUTTER, bapt. in North Church, Portsmouth, 19 Dec., 1779; d. in Portsmouth about 1820. He was a merchant, residing in Demarara, W. I., Moscow, Russia, and Portsmouth, N. H.

ix. DANIEL, bapt. in North Church, Portsmouth, 23 Sept., 1781; living 15 Apr., 1805; d. probably before 10 June, 1814. He was a printer, and resided in Portsmouth.

31. JABEZ[5] TREADWELL (*Jabez,*[4] *Nathaniel,*[3] *Nathaniel,*[2] *Thomas*[1]), baptized in Ipswich, Mass., 21 Oct., 1739, died intestate, in Ipswich, 13 Jan., 1803, aged 63 years, married first (intention published in

Ipswich, 13 Apr., 1765), Elizabeth, born 27 Nov., 1744, died, probably in Ipswich, 30 Aug., 1782, daughter of Thomas and Judith (Lord) Burnham; and married second, in Ipswich, 22 July, 1784, Elizabeth, born 23 July, 1759, died in Ipswich, 19 Oct., 1793, daughter of Isaac Dodge of Ipswich. He was a captain in the Massachusetts militia, and resided in Ipswich.

Children, by second wife:

i. ISAAC DODGE,[6] b. in Ipswich, 19 May, 1785; d. intestate, perishing in the great earthquake at Caracas, Venezuela; m. in Newburyport, Mass., 17 June, 1806, Sarah, b. probably in Newburyport, 15 Feb., 1790, the dau. of Abraham and Hannah Gallishan, Jr., of Newburyport. Did she m. (2) (int. published in Newburyport, 15 Dec., 1814) John Stocker of Boston, Mass.? He was a gold and silver smith, finally becoming a director of the Mint and of the Department of Mining at Caracas, Venezuela, and resided in Newburyport, Mass., New York city and Caracas, Venezuela. Children: 1. *Jabez.*[7] 2. *Abraham G.*

ii. JABEZ, b. in Ipswich, 28 July, 1787; d. intestate, in Havana, Cuba, in 1806. He was a mariner.

iii. DANIEL, b. in Ipswich, 10 Oct., 1791; d. testate, in Cambridge, Mass., 27 Feb., 1872; m. in Boston, Mass., 6 Oct., 1831, Adeline, b. in Hingham, Mass., 24 May, 1804, d. in Boston, 27 May, 1885, dau. of Levi and Desire (Thaxter) Lincoln. He was a silversmith, engineer, inventor of note, and professor at Harvard College, residing in Boston and Cambridge, Mass. He probably had no issue.

32. SAMUEL[5] TREADWELL (*Jabez,*[4] *Nathaniel,*[3] *Nathaniel,*[2] *Thomas*[1]), baptized in Ipswich, Mass., 11 Oct., 1747, married in Ipswich, 7 Oct., 1784, Mary, baptized 4 July, 1762, daughter of Ammi and Martha (Foster) Burnham of Ipswich. He was a yeoman in 1784, and a mariner in 1786, residing in Ipswich (Chebacco Parish), probably removing elsewhere.

Children:

i. MARY,[6] bapt. in Ipswich, 2 Aug., 1789.

ii. SARAH, bapt. in Ipswich, 2 Aug., 1789.

iii. MARTHA, bapt. in Ipswich, 17 Jan. (? Dec.), 1790.

33. MAJ. WILLIAM[5] TREADWELL (*Jabez,*[4] *Nathahiel,*[3] *Nathaniel,*[2] *Thomas*[1]), baptized in Ipswich, Mass., 14 Jan., 1749–50, died intestate, in Worcester, Mass., 10 Apr., 1795, "of a broken heart," married, before Dec., 1777, Mary ———, born in 1747, and living in Worcester, 16 Mch., 1809. Did she die in Brewer, Me., between 10 Dec., 1822, and 22 Aug., 1833? Enlisting in 1775, he served heroically in the American army throughout the Revolution. At home on the battle field, he was unable or unfitted to fight the struggles of civil life, and, through poverty, he pathetically fell "a lingering victim to Despair" (Thomas's Massachusetts Spy; or the Worcester Gazette, vol. xxiv, Wednesday, 15 Apr., 1795), and on 14 Apr., 1795, he was buried with military honors in the Old Cemetery (now the Commons) in Worcester, a few feet to the northwest of the present monument to Timothy Bigelow, the grave stone once marking his grave having been levelled in 1853 and buried twelve inches beneath the surface. He was an original member of the Society of the Cincinnati. He resided in Worcester, Mass.

Children, born in Worcester:

i. LUCY,[6] b. 9 Dec., 1777; d. probably before 22 Aug., 1833, without leaving issue; m. in Worcester, 13 June, 1804, Nathaniel Lefavor of Lansingburg.

ii. MARY, b. 11 Oct., 1780; d. before 1812, without leaving issue; m. in Worcester, 6 Apr., 1809, Alpheus, b. (? Heath, Mass.) 26 Nov., 1783, d. 12 Sept., 1825, son of Jonah and Agnes (Cannon) Thayer. He was a merchant tailor, residing in Brattleboro', Vt.

iii. ELIZABETH, b. 22 Nov., 1786; living unmarried, in Boston, Mass., 22 Aug., 1833.

iv. THOMAS, b. 10 Jan., 1789; d. intestate, in Brewer, Me., 1 Nov., 1851; m. in Portland, Me., 15 (or 16) July, 1817, Mary Connell, b. 20 (or 24) July, 1796. d. intestate, 12 (or 13) Mch., 1839, probably dau. of Abraham Greenleaf of Brewer. He was a merchant and innkeeper, residing in Brewer, Me. Children: 1. *William Connell.*[7] 2. *Thomas Jackson.* 3. *Elizabeth Ann.*

v. SAMUEL, b. 22 Apr., 1791; d. intestate, in Brewer, Me., 11 Apr., 1826, probably unmarried. He was a farmer and trader, residing in Brewer.

vi. ABIGAIL, b. 9 Jan., 1793; living unmarried, in Boston, Mass., 22 Aug., 1833. Was she the Abigail who d. at the "Home for Aged Women," in Boston, 19 June, 1871?

vii. ANN (NANCY), b. 9 Jan., 1793; d. 21 May, 1824; m. (certificate dated 15 June, 1821) Capt. Jacob (a widower), b. 27 Mch., 1783; probably son of John and Elizabeth Holyoke.

34. NATHANIEL[5] TREADWELL (*Jabez,*[4] *Nathaniel,*[3] *Nathaniel,*[2] *Thomas*[1]), baptized in Ipswich, 28 Oct., 1753, died intestate, in Ipswich, 2 Jan., 1822, married in Ipswich, 17 July, 1786, Mary Hovey of Ipswich, who died in Ipswich, 10 (Ipswich records, 15 according to the grave stone) Jan., 1832, aged 81 years. He served in the Revolution, was a yeoman, designated "Jr." from 1784 to his death. He resided in Ipswich.

Children, born in Ipswich:

i. NATHANIEL,[6] b. 23 (28 according to the family Bible) Apr., 1787; lost at sea, Jan. or Feb., 1821; m. in Ipswich, 21 Sept., 1809, Elizabeth, b. in Ipswich, 27 Nov., 1786, d. in Ipswich, 11 Aug., 1872, dau. of Daniel and Mary (? Hannah) Smith. He was a prisoner in "Dartmoor Prison" in the War of 1812. He was designated "4th" in 1809. His widow resided in Ipswich and Salem, Mass. Children: 1. *Nathaniel.*[7] 2. *Thomas.* 3. *Susan.* 4. *Samuel.* 5. *Elizabeth.* 6. *Nathaniel William.*

ii. JABEZ, b. 17 Oct., 1788; d. in Salem, Mass., 4 Nov., 1840; m. in Salem, 17 Nov., 1811, Elizabeth G., b. in Marblehead, Mass., d. in Salem, in 1875, dau. of Thomas Homan of Marblehead. She m. (2) in Lynn, Mass., 10 June, 1849, John Russell (a widower) of Lynn. Jabez[6] was a carpenter and builder, residing in Salem, Mass. Children: 1. *Eliza Ann.*[7] 2. *Malvina H.* 3. *Mary Hovey.* 4. *Jabez.* 5. *Sarah Ellen.* 6. *Caroline F.* 7. *William H.*

iii. JOHN, b. 20 Nov., 1790: d. in Charlestown, Mass., 24 Sept., 1867; m. in Boston, Mass., 4 Dec., 1818, Clarinda R. F., b. in Eden, Me., 2 Nov., 1798, d. intestate, in Charlestown, 3 Apr., 1886, dau. of Thomas and Laura R. Newmarch of Boston. He was a cabinet maker, residing in Boston and Charlestown. Children: 1. *Clarinda R. F.*[7] 2. *John William.* 3. *Amelia E. N.* 4. *Laura Ann R.* 5. *John Thomas.* 6. *Andrew J.* 7. *Mary Louisa.* 8. *Ellen Maria S.* 9. *George W.* (?) 10. *Ason.* 11. *Georgianna F.* 12. *Angelia F.* (?)

iv. SAMUEL, b. 24 Apr., 1793; d. in Ipswich, probably before 14 Aug., 1833.

v. WILLIAM, b. 16 Jan., 1797. Did he die in Boston, Mass.? Was he the one who m. in Boston, 29 Dec., 1819, Dorothy W. Jackman? He was a tin-plate worker, and resided in Boston in 1827, and Worcester, Mass., in 1833, where he may have died.

35. NATHANIEL[5] TREADWELL (*Samuel,*[4] *Samuel,*[3] *Nathaniel,*[2] *Thomas*[1]), born in Wells, Me., 12 Sept., 1747, died in Kennebunk, Me., 20

Mch., 1828, married in Wells, 23 Dec., 1772, Phebe (Wells town records say Hannah, which is undoubtedly wrong) Ricker of Wells, who was living 3 Feb., 1816. He served in the Revolution, was a yeoman, and resided in Wells and Kennebunk.

Children:

i. LYDIA,[6] bapt. in Wells, Me., 31 May, 1778; d. probably in Kennebunk, Me., 19 Sept., 1800. Did she m. (int. pub. in Wells, 17 May, 1800) John Pope?

ii. SAMUEL, bapt. in Wells, 14 Oct., 1781.

iii. NATHANIEL, living 30 Sept., 1854; m. in Wells, Me., 4 Mch., 1802, Sally Jones of Alfred, Me., who d. in Kennebunk, Me., 30 Sept., 1854, aged 80 yrs. He resided in Kennebunk, Me. Children: 1. *Mehitable.*[7] 2. *Charles.* 3. *Samuel.* 4. *Dominicus.* 5. *Cyrus(?).*

iv. PHEBE, m. in Wells (that part now Kennebunk), Me., 17 Feb., 1805, John Wormwood of Wells. Child: 1. *A son.*

v. HAMMOND, living 1820; m. in Wells (that part now Kennebunk), Me., 9 Oct., 1809, Phebe Chick of Wells. Did she m. (2) (int. pub. in Kennebunk, 10 Feb., 1821) Wentworth Treadwell, of Kennebunk? He was a yeoman, residing in Wells and Shapleigh, Me. Children: 1. *Mary.*[7] 2. *Harriet (?).* 3. *Eldridge.* 4. *Brackett G.* 5. *James Munroe.* 6. *William P.*

vi. DANIEL, d. in Kennebunk, Me., 24 May, 1870; m. (int. pub. in Wells, Me., 7 June, 1817) Betsey Abbott, who d. in Kennebunk, 5 July, 1850, aged 71 yrs. He probably m. (2) (int. pub. in Kennebunk, 11 Sept., 1850) Mrs. Sarah Lord of Lyman, Me. He resided in Kennebunk, Me. Child: 1. *Hammond.*[7]

vii.(?) ISABELLA, living, 31 Oct., 1831, d. in Waterford, Me.; m. in Wells, 10 Nov., 1808, Stephen Pitcher, who d. in Waterford. He was a yeoman, and resided in Wells and Waterford, Me.

36. JAMES[5] TREADWELL (*Samuel,*[4] *Samuel,*[3] *Nathaniel,*[2] *Thomas*[1]), born in Wells, Me., 1 Sept., 1749, died intestate, before 12 Dec., 1811, married first (intention published 12 July, 1777) Shuah, who died after 12 May, 1791, daughter of Nehemiah and Tabitha (Littlefield) Littlefield of Wells; and married second, in Wells, 3 Jan., 1802, Huldah (Winn) Brock (a widow) of Wells, who died testate, after 24 Nov., 1806. He served in the Revolution, was a farmer, had the title "Capt.," and resided in Wells, Me.

Children:

i. HANNAH,[6] bapt. in Wells, 6 Sept., 1778; d. (? 4 Apr., 1799).

ii. MARY, bapt. in Wells, 10 Sept., 1779; d. probably before 27 Oct., 1790.

iii. ELIZABETH, bapt. in Wells, 10 Sept., 1779; d. probably before 1791.

iv. ASA, bapt. in Wells, 4 Aug., 1782; living in Wells, 27 Oct., 1804. He was a yeoman.

v. JAMES, bapt. in Wells, 13 Mch., 1785; living 24 Nov., 1806.

vi. BENJAMIN, d. testate, in Wells, 9 Aug., 1815, aged 28 yrs.; m. in Wells (that part now Kennebunk), 30 Nov., 1809, Eleanor, who d. in Wells, 7 May, 1820, aged 39 yrs., dau. of Israel and Eleanor (Dennett) Kimball of Wells.

vii. MARY, b. before 27 Oct., 1790; probably living 2 Dec., 1850; m. in Wells, 16 Dec., 1811, Benjamin Bourne, of Arundell, who d. probably in 1838. He was probably a mariner, and resided in Wells.

viii. ELIZABETH, bapt. in Wells, 12 May, 1791; d. in Wells, 19 Nov., 1815, aged 24 yrs., unmarried.

ix. ALPHEUS, d. in Wells, 24 (? 29) Jan., 1816, aged 20 yrs.

37. MARSTRESS[5] TREADWELL (*Samuel,*[4] *Samuel,*[3] *Nathaniel,*[2] *Thomas*[1]), born in Wells, Me., 18 Mch., 1750, died in Cornish, Me., 20 June, 1820, married in Wells, 20 Dec., 1781, Mary, born in Wells, 31

Oct., 1760, died in Cornish, 7 May, 1810, probably the daughter of Col. Nathaniel and Susannah (Jacquis) Littlefield. He served in the Revolution, and resided in Wells, and afterwards on Towle's Hill, Cornish, Me. It remains a problem just what his first name was intended to be, but the best source indicates it as above given, from which several variations in spelling can be found. At this day, Masters would probably be the accepted form.

Children:

i. NATHAN,[6] b. in Wells, Feb., 1783; d. in Wells, 29 Feb., 1783.

ii. JONATHAN, b. in Wells, 13 May, 1784; d. in Hiram, Me., 16 May, 1866; m. (1) in Wells, 20 Oct., 1808, Ruth, b. in Wells, 24 Nov., 1791, d. in Cornish, Me., 22 Apr., 1817, dau. of Elijah and (? Eunice) (Hatch) Stuart of Wells; m. (2) in Cornish, Me., 8 June, 1818, Lydia, b. in York, Me., 7 Sept., 1784, d. in Hiram, Me., 28 May, 1866, dau. of James Hill of Cornish, Me. He served in the War of 1812, and resided in Cornish and Hiram, Me. Children: 1. *Mark.*[7] 2. *Jonathan.* 3. *Nathan.* 4. *Hannah Jane.* 5. *Ruth Stuart.* 6. *Mary Littlefield.* 7. *Mastress.* 8. *Levi.* 9. *Charles Hill.* 10. *Enoch Merrill.* 11. *Eunice W.* 12. *Albert.*

iii. SUSAN M., b. in Wells, 26 Mch., 1786; d. unmarried, in Hiram, Me., 29 Nov., 1875.

iv. RICHARD, b. in Wells, 1 Oct., 1788; d. in Cornish, Me., Sept.. 1797.

v. MARY, b. in Cornish. Me., 25 Sept., 1792; d. (probably in Hiram), 25 Aug., 1858, unmarried.

vi. LYDIA, b. in Cornish, Me., 25 Sept., 1792; d. (? 18) June, 1847, unmarried.

vii. SAMUEL, b. in Cornish. Me., 12 Sept., 1794; d. in Naples, Me., Feb., 1882; m. Susan Thompson of Windham, Me., who was living 15 Oct., 1856. He resided in Hiram and Standish, Me. Probably no issue.

viii. TIMOTHY WENTWORTH, b. in Cornish, Me., 14 June, 1796; d. in Hiram, Me., 10 Oct., 1884; m. in Hiram, 26 Mch., 1823, Mary Berry (? Polly York) of Hiram, who d. shortly after marriage. He resided in Hiram, Me. Child: 1. ——— (?).

ix. RICHARD, b. in Cornish, Me., 26 Mch., 1798; d. in Lincoln, Me., 10 Jan., 1843; m. in Lincoln, Mary Blaisdell. He was a yeoman, and resided probably in Enfield and Springfield, Me. Children(?): 1. *Jonathan.*[7] 2. *Jacob.* 3. *Hannah.*

x. HANNAH, b. in Cornish, Me., 10 June, 1800; d. probably in Hiram, Me., 9 Oct., 1845 (? in Rumford, Me., 20 Nov., 1844); m. in Cornish, Me., 3 Oct., 1833 (? in Hiram, 7 Nov., 1839), Henry McGrath (a widower) of Hiram, b. in the North of Ireland, 1802; d. in Hiram, Sept., 1854, who m. (3) Mrs. Angelina H. Phinney of Baldwin, Me. He resided in Hiram, Me. Child: 1. *Dora Steele.*[7]

xi. JACOB, b. in Cornish, Me., 10 Apr., 1802; d. testate, in Buxton, Me., 23 Aug., 1854; m. in Buxton, 7 Apr., 1824, Melinda, b. in Buxton, 24 Nov., 1806, d. in Buxton, 3 Nov., 1861, dau. of Benjamin and Susanna Leavett of Buxton. He was a yeoman, residing in Buxton. Children: 1. *Albion Keath Paris.*[7] 2. *Charles Augustus.* 3. *Isabella Pitcher.* 4. *Susan Leavitt.* 5. *Mark T.* 6. *Jesse Appleton.* 7. *Joseph Appleton.* 8. *Elvira Pike.* 9. *Granville Switzer.* 10. *Mary Ann Frost.* 11. *Horace Ervin Pike.* 12. *Edwin Clarence.* 13. *Benjamin Franklin.*

38. SAMUEL[5] TREADWELL (*Samuel,*[4] *Samuel,*[3] *Nathaniel,*[2] *Thomas*[1]), born in Wells, Me., 19 Apr., 1752, died probably in West Kennebunk, Me., 29 Jan., 1835, married in Wells, 5 Dec., 1780, Susanna, born 14 Jan., 1757, died probably in West Kennebunk, 9 May, 1846, probably the daughter of Joshua and Joanna (Young) Edwards of Wells. He served in the Revolution, and was a yeoman, residing in West Kennebunk, Me.

Children :

i. Hannah[6] b. 17 Oct., 1781; d. 4 Apr., 1799.
ii. Hamons (Jonathan Hammond), b. 13 Oct., 1784; d. 10 Nov., 1785.
iii. Olive T., b. 7 Oct., 1786; d. 4 July, 1867; m. in Wells, Me., 18 Apr., 1805, John Jones, Jr., of Wells. Did he die at Kennebunk Landing, Me., 10 (or 20) Aug., 1855, aged 75 yrs.?
iv. Betsey W., b. 27 May, 1789; d. 23 May, 1819.
v. Martha, b. 15 Mch., 1791; d. 8 July, 1827.
vi. Joshua E., b. in Kennebunk, Me., 20 June, 1794; d. testate, in Kennebunk, 20 Aug., 1878; m. in Salem, Mass., 22 Aug., 1819 (? 1818), Frances Ingalls of Salem, who was b. in Salem, 3 Apr., 1796, and d. 12 June, 1879. He served in War of 1812, commissioned Capt. in the Maine militia, was a farmer, and resided in Salem, Mass., for a short time, and afterwards in West Kennebunk, Me. Children: 1. *Mary I.*[7] 2. *John William.* 3. *Joshua E.* 4. *Frances N.* 5. *Susan E.* 6. *Hannah.* 7. *Edwin.*
vii. Susanna, b. in Kennebunk, Me., 28 Feb., 1797; d. in Kennebunk, 26 Aug., 1826; m. in Kennebunk, 13 Dec., 1819, Oliver, of Wells (that part now Kennebunk), who d. in Kennebunk, 22 July, 1856, aged 57 yrs., son of Joseph and Ruth (Wakefield) Perkins of Kennebunk. He probably m. (2) Sally Littlefield. Children: 1. *Betsey A.* 2. *Celestine M.* 3. *Susan Alitha.*
viii. Samuel, b. 22 Nov., 1799; d. 10 Mch., 1825.
ix. John W., b. 26 Oct., 1801; d. 25 Dec., 1820.

39. Jacob[5] Treadwell (*Samuel,*[4] *Samuel,*[3] *Nathaniel,*[2] *Thomas*[1]), baptized in Wells, Me., 7 Oct., 1765, died on his farm in Frankfort, Me., probably after 1835, married ———. He was a farmer, and resided in Frankfort, Me.

Children:

i. Joseph,[6] b. (? 20) June, 1797; d. (? 20) Nov., 1882; m. Jemima Curtis. He was a farmer, and resided in Prentiss, Me. Children: 1. *Phebe Jane.*[7] 2. *Sarah Ann.* 3. *Amos.* 4. *John.* 5. *Uriah H.* 6. *Maria.* 7. *Edmund.*
ii. Samuel, d. before 1890; m. ———. He resided in Frankfort, Me. Children: 1. *Joseph.*[7] 2. *Theodore.* 3. *Elizabeth.* 4. *Jacob.*
iii. James, d. probably before May, 1858; probably m. Hannah N. ———, who m. (2) D. Storey (or Shorey) of Burlington (? Me.). He resided in Lowell(?), Penobscot Co., Me. Probably had a child: 1. *Nathaniel.*[7]
iv. Sally.

40. Joseph[5] Treadwell (*Joseph,*[4] *Thomas,*[3] *Nathaniel,*[2] *Thomas*[1]), baptized in Ipswich, Mass., 5 Mch., 1748–9, died after Mch., 1773, and probably before 1785, married, probably before 26 May, 1769, Susanna ———. Did she marry second, in Newburyport, Mass., 26 July, 1785, Michael Smith, probably the "Captain" who died in Newburyport, intestate, 11 May, 1828? Joseph[5] Treadwell was a mariner.

Children:

i. Joseph,[6] b. in Newburyport, Mass., 12 Aug., 1771; d. testate, in Bangor, Me., 8 June, 1842; m. in New Gloucester, Me., 18 Dec., 1792, Mary, b. 22 Feb., 1766 (? 1767), d. intestate, in Exeter, Me., 3 Feb., 1854, dau. of John and Ruth (Herrick) Tyler of New Gloucester, Me. He was a trader and builder, the first town clerk of Garland, Me., and resided in New Gloucester, Lewiston, Garland, and Bangor, Me. At the time of his marriage, he was residing at "Baker's Town so called." Children: 1. *Susanna.*[7] 2. *Ruth.* 3. *Mary (Polly).* 4. *John.* 5. *Joseph Tyler.* 6. *Sally.* 7. *Anna.* 8. *Benjamin.* 9. *Thomas Herrick.* 10. *Simeon.*
ii. Benjamin, b. in Newburyport, Mass., 19 Jan., 1774.

41. NATHANIEL[5] TREADWELL (*Thomas,*[4] *Thomas,*[3] *Nathaniel,*[2] *Thomas*[1]), born in Ipswich, Mass., 20 Dec., 1752 (? 1749), died in Ipswich, 20 Nov., 1834, aged 82 years, married first, in Ipswich, 4 May, 1775, Elizabeth, born 2 Nov., 1755, died in Ipswich, 25 Dec., 1808, daughter of (? Samuel) Stone of Ipswich; and married second, in Ipswich, 19 Mch., 1810, Elizabeth Fuller (probably a widow), who died intestate, in Ipswich, 26 Sept., 1828. This Elizabeth Fuller was a sister of William McNeal. Nathaniel[5] was a sea-captain and was designated "Jr." 1775. His vessel, the "Lucy," was captured by the French, and formed one of the "Spoilation Claims." He resided in Ipswich, Mass.

Children, born in Ipswich:

i. NATHANIEL,[6] b. 13 May, 1776; d. intestate, in the West Indies, 14 Nov., 1808; m. in Ipswich, 4 May, 1800, Mary, probably b. in Ipswich 29 Feb. (or 9 July), 1784, d. in Ipswich, 9 June, 1800, dau. of Lieut. Enoch and Eunice (Marshall) Pearson. Did she m. (2) in Ipswich, 20 Nov., 1818, William Manning of Ipswich? He was probably a mariner, and designated "4th" in 1800. He resided probably in Newburyport, Mass. Children: 1. *Mary.*[7] 2. *Sarah.* 3. *Thomas Warren.*

ii. THOMAS, b. 1 Oct., 1779; d. testate, in Portsmouth, N. H., 30 Mch., 1860; m. in Portsmouth, 13 Nov., 1800, Anna, b. in Portsmouth, 28 Feb., 1779, d. 3 Nov., 1855, dau. of Thomas and Mary (Whittemore) Passmore. He was a hatter and felt maker, residing in Portsmouth, N. H. Children: 1. *Thomas Passmore.*[7] 2. *Elizabeth.* 3. *Thomas Passmore.* 4. *Mary Ann.* 5. *Olive.* 6. *William Pepperrell.* 7. *Samuel Passmore.* 8. *Catherine Simpson.* 9. *Frances Dearborn.*

iii. SAMUEL, b. in 1781: d. in Portsmouth, N. H., in 1817; m. in Portsmouth, 9 Jan., 1809, Abigail Petergro, who was living 1 Jan., 1817. He was a carpenter, residing in Portsmouth, N. H. Children: 1. *Lucy Ann.*[7] 2. *Susan.* 3. *Elizabeth.*

iv. ELIZABETH, b. 18 Nov., 1783; d. in Ipswich, 28 Apr. (? 29 Mch.), 1853; m. in Ipswich, 30 Sept., 1804, John, Jr., b. in Ipswich, 15 Jan., 1781, d. in Ipswich, 9 Apr., 1857, son of John and Mary (? Woodbury) Chapman of Ipswich. He was a shoemaker, and resided in Ipswich. Children: 1. *Sally Treadwell.*[7] 2. *Elizabeth.* 3. *Hannah.* 4. *Mary Ann.* 5. *Susan.* 6. *John.* 7. *Mehitable.* 8. *Lucy.* 9. *William.* 10. *Warren.* 11. *Thomas Treadwell.*

v. JOHN, b. 27 Feb., 1786; d. intestate, in Boston, 19 Dec., 1853; m. in Portsmouth, N. H., 28 June, 1808, Hannah, b. in Kittery, Me., 24 Apr., 1785, d. (? San Francisco, Cal.) 24 Apr., 1864, probably the dau. of Joseph Jenkins. He was a hatter and resided in Boston, Mass. Children: 1. *Joseph Jenkins.*[7] 2. *Sarah Elizabeth.* 3. *Charles Thomas.*

vi. MEHITABLE(?), d. in Ipswich, 19 Jan., 1789.

vii. WILLIAM, b. 10 Mch., 1791; d. testate, in Ipswich, 30 Sept., 1870; m. in Ipswich, 23 Aug., 1814, Welcome, b. in Ipswich, 10 Dec., 1792, d. in Ipswich, 2 June, 1883, dau. of John and Rebecca (Swett) Seward of Ipswich. He was a mariner, residing in Ipswich. Children: 1. *William Francis.*[7] 2. *Abigail.* 3. *John Seward.* 4. *Elizabeth Stone.* 5. *Rebecca H.* 6. *Lucy Jane.* 7. *Isaac Cushing.* 8. *Frances Susan.* 9. *Charles Thomas.*

viii. HANNAH, b. 1 Sept., 1793; d. in Newton Highlands, Mass., 18 July, 1888; m. (1) in Ipswich, Mass., 12 Nov., 1812, Joshua Burnham, who d. probably in California, in 1851; m. (2) Samuel Albert Lake, who d. before his wife. Children by first husband: 1. *Elizabeth.* 2. *Mary Elizabeth.* 3. *George William.* 4. *Sarah.* 5. *John.*

ix. ROBERT, b. 2 Aug., 1795; d. (probably killed) in Europe, in 1819. On account of his early death, he probably never married, although engaged (m. int. pub. in Newburyport, Mass., 7 Nov., 1819) to Elizabeth Creasey of Newburyport, who was probably the dau. of William and Esther Creasey.

BECK FAMILY RECORDS.

Communicated by OTIS G. HAMMOND, Esq., of Concord, N. H.

THESE records were taken from an old account book kept by Henry Beck, and now in the possession of his descendant John A. Beck of Canterbury, N. H.

Melinda Beck Was Born May the 6 Day of a wensda In the year 1807
Polly Beck Was born July the 18 Day of a tusday In year 1787
Catherrine Beck was born Jenuary the 9 Day of a tusda In year 1810
Albert H Beck Was born may the 6 Day of a Wensda In Year 1812
John Beck Was Born Jenuary the 31 Day of a friday In Year 1817
Thompson Beck Was born the 6 Day of a Sunday In year 1819
Abiel Beck was born In March the 19 Day of a monday In Year 1821
Margaret Beck was born may the 20 Day of a tusday In Year 1823
Lowel Beck Was born August the 27 of a Saturday in year 1825
Diantha Beck Was born December the 15 Day of a monday in year 1828
Alvin Beck was born Novnber the 28 Day of a Sunday in year 1831
Eles [Alice] Beck was Born December 15th 1742 —
Henry Beck was Married to Eles Thompson January the 20 in the year 1762
Canterb[ur]y. Henry Beck Deceased January the 30 day in 1811 —
Abiel Beck Deceasd September the 28th in 1829 —
Diantha Beck Deceasd September the 18th in 1829 —
Albert Beck Decesed January the 23d in 1840 of a Thursday
Alice Beck Decesed January the 20 in 1841 of a Wednsday
Mary Ann Beck Deceased March the 18 of a friday 1842
John Beck Decesed October the 13 day 1843 of a friday
Mary Beck Died Sept 26 1851 Aged 69 yers
My father dyed ye 7 of november In the year 1734
Henry Beck born november the 14 In the year 1695
Mary Beck born febary ye 4 of a thosday In the yeare 1719/20
Margret Beck born November ye 20 of a monday In the yeare 1721
John Beck born august ye 16 of a Sabath day In the yeare 1724
Nathaniel Beck born June ye 17 of a tusday In the yeare 1729 —
Hannah Beck born July ye 20 1734 of a Saterday november ye 16 dessed
Elizabeth Beck born July ye 27 of a tusday In the year 1736 —
Henry Beck born January 27 1738/9 of a Saterday
My granfather Henry Beck was born In the Paresh of geywareck in warickshear In old england
Sarah Beck was Born December the 28 1763 of a wensday
Hanah Beck was Born Augt the first 1767 of a Saturday
Moley Beck was Born Aprill 18 of a tusday 1769 Deceasd July the 25—1781
Anne Beck was Born Aprill the 13 of a Saturday In 1771
John Beck was Born June th 4 of a thursday 1773
Margret Beck Born June th 4 of a thursday 1773
Charls Beck was Born maye the 29 of a monday 1775
Clement Beck was Born November the 3 Day of tusday In the year 1780
Henry Beck was Born October the 2 Day of a tusday In the year 1783
Poly Beck was Born Aprill the 8 Day of a tusday In the year 1785

ANDREW BENTON OF MILFORD AND HARTFORD, CONN., AND HIS DESCENDANTS.

By JOHN H. BENTON, Esq., of Washington, D. C.

1. JOHN[1] BENTON, of the parish of Epping, co. Essex, England, and Mary Southernwood, were married at Epping, May 25, 1618. (For an account of the family in England, see Charles E. Benton's "Caleb Benton and Sarah Bishop, their Ancestors and their Descendants," Poughkeepsie, N. Y., 1906.)

Their children were:

2. Andrew, bapt. Oct. 15, 1620.
   Thomas, bapt. Aug. 25, 1622.
   Marie, bapt. June 29, 1625.
   Elizabeth, bapt. Aug. 31, 1628.
   [Here occurs a register hiatus of 8 years.]
   John, bapt. Mar. 10, 1639.

The register shows the burial of a John Benton, Feb. 12, 1662, and of "the widdow Benton," June 5, 1665, but there is uncertainty as to their identity.

That the above record of Andrew, baptized Oct. 15, 1620, relates to Andrew Benton the emigrant is deduced from the facts that his tombstone in Hartford (whither he removed from Milford) shows he was "aged 63 yrs." at his death, July 31, 1683, thus agreeing with the probable time of birth, and that the name of John (his father) was given to three of his children, two of whom died in infancy, and the name of Mary (his mother) was given his second daughter.

That he was nearly related to Edward Benton the emigrant may be inferred from their coming together to America; and a coincidence of Christian names and other data suggests that John the father of Andrew the emigrant was probably a son of Andrew and Maria Benton, parents of Edward the emigrant; and if so, he was an older son whose birth failed of registration in the Epping parish records, or, possibly he was a son of the John Benton, baptized Apr. 14, 1588, whose father, Andrew Benton, born in 1548, inherited by will, in 1569, the manor of Shingle Hall, at Epping, of which his father, John Benton, became the owner in 1552.

In view, therfore, of the uncertainty as to an earlier ancestry, I choose to begin the ancestral line with John and Mary (Southernwood.)

2. ANDREW[2] BENTON (*John*[1]) was allotted parcel No. 64 at the apportionment in Nov., 1639, of the land at Milford, Conn., bought from the Indians in Feb. of that year. It contained three acres, and was situated on the west side of Half Mile Brook, near the crossing of what is now Spring and Hill streets, and to this were added several other parcels of ground. He married first, probably in 1649, Hannah, daughter of George Stocking of Hartford, a first settler there in 1636. They united with the church at Milford, he on Mar. 5, 1648, and she on Oct. 13, 1650, and were dismissed to Hartford, Mar., 1666, whither they had removed as early as 1662. Here he was a fenceviewer in 1663 and '64, a juror in 1664 and '67, was a freeman in May, 1665, and a suppressor of "disorders during public worship" (during the Hartford Controversy) and collector of minister's rates in 1667. He separated to the Second Church in Feb., 1670,

with his wife, daughter Hannah, and his fathers-in-law, Stocking and Cole. He married second, probably in 1673, Anne, daughter of John Cole, "a godly man of some public trust." She was the "bewitched maid" on whose account, mainly, Nathaniel Greensmith and his wife were hanged for witchcraft, Jan. 25, 1663. Goffe, the regicide, then in hiding at Milford, writes in his diary, Feb. 24, that after the hanging "the maid was well"; and Cotton Mather's Magnalia, in 1684, says of her that "she is restored to health, united with the church, and living in good repute." She died testate, Apr. 19, 1685, leaving an estate of £60.12.6, to be divided among her three surviving children, of whom Ebenezer was given a double portion because of "impotency." Hannah, his first wife, died probably in 1672. He was buried in Center Church Cemetery, and his gravestone, near the rear wall of the church, reads: "ANDREW BENTON AGED 63 YEARS. HE DYED IVLY 31 ANO 1683." His estate, appraised at £345.17.19, was administered by his son Joseph, and distributed, Dec. 18, 1683, to his widow, and children, Andrew Samuel, Joseph, Mary, and Dorothy, by his first wife, and Ebenezer, Lydia, and Hannah, by his second wife.

The homestead, formerly owned by Nathaniel Greensmith, was at the junction of the roads leading to Wethersfield and Farmington, and on the west side of the present Wethersfield Avenue. At the death of the widow, it became the property of his son Joseph Benton, who sold it in June, 1693. He owned several other parcels of land, one of which in the "Five Mile Lay Out," in East Hartford, was distributed to his eight surviving children, Mar. 24, 1689.

Children by first wife, all, except the last, born in Milford:

- i. JOHN,[3] b. Apr. 9, bapt. Apr. 14, 1650. "He died May [24] following in ye bed in ye night."
- ii. HANNAH, bapt. Nov. 23, 1651; m. John Camp, Jr.; mentioned in her grandfather Stocking's will, July 15, 1673; had a dau. *Hannah*, bapt. Nov. 24, 1672; d. prior to 1675, the year of her husband's second marriage.
- 3. iii. ANDREW, bapt. Aug. 12, 1653; d. Feb. 5, 1704.
- iv. MARY, b. Apr. 14, bapt. Apr. 15, 1655; m. (1) Nathaniel, son of John Cole, who d. testate Apr. 20, 1708, naming *Nathaniel*, his only child, executor; m. (2) Jonathan Bigelow, who d. testate Jan. 9, 1711, his wife and son Joseph being executors; m. (3) Mar. 19, 1713, Dea. John Shepard; buried Dec. 23, 1752, in First Church Cemetery, Hartford, "æ 90 yrs.", which should be 97 yrs. 10 mos. 8 ds.
- v. JOHN, b. Oct. 7, 1656; mentioned in his grandfather Stocking's will, July 15, 1673; d. prior to May 30, 1680.
- 4. vi. SAMUEL, b. Aug. 15, 1658; d. Apr. 10, 1746.
- 5. vii. JOSEPH, b. 1660; d. Aug. 12, 1753, "in 93 yr."
- viii. DOROTHY, b. probably in 1662; the only record of her is in the distribution of her father's estate, Dec. 18, 1683, and Mar. 24, 1689.

Children by second wife, born in Hartford:

- ix. EBENEZER, bapt. Jan. 4, 1674; "an impotent," living Apr. 20, 1708, at the death of his uncle, N. Cole.
- x. LYDIA, bapt. Feb. 13, 1676; united with the Second Church, Apr. 25, 1697.
- xi. HANNAH, bapt. Jan. 26, 1679.
- xii. JOHN, bapt. May 30, 1680; d. young, prior to Sept. 4, 1683.

3. ANDREW[3] BENTON (*Andrew*,[3] *Andrew*,[2] *John*[1]), who lived in Milford and Hartford, Conn., married Martha, daughter of Sergt. Thomas

Spencer, who mentions her in his will, proved Sept., 1687. He "owned y[e] covenant," Jan. 6, 1677, and both united with the Second Church, Dec. 10, 1694, prior to which time they presumably belonged to the First Church. As the eldest son, he received a double portion of his father's estate. His own estate of £94. 3. 4. was administered by his brother Samuel.

Children, all born in Hartford:

i. HANNAH,[4] bapt. Jan. 6, 1677; m. (1) Feb. 20, 1700, Edward Scofell of Haddam, who d. May, 1703, and had *Susannah* and *Hannah*; m. (2), in 1706, Benjamin Smith.
ii. MARTHA, bapt. Aug. 1, 1679.
iii. ANDREW, bapt. July 31, 1681; the only Benton to whom the following death is applicable: "July y[e] last 1704, One Benton and Wm. Omstead Sold[r] Slain by y[e] Indians; and 2 of y[e] Enemy Slain."—(See REGISTER, vol. ix, p. 161.)
iv. MERCY, bapt. Sept. 7, 1683.
v. JOHN, bapt. Feb. 22, 1685.
vi. DOROTHY, bapt. Apr. 22, 1688; m. May 3, 1716, John Gridley of Farmington, Conn.
vii. MARY, bapt. Nov. 2, 1690.
viii. EBENEZER, bapt. Oct. 18, 1696; chose his uncle Samuel Benton to be his guardian, Sept. 5, 1709, and Jonathen Bigelow, Sr. (his uncle by marriage), Nov. 6, 1710, and the latter having died, the court, Mar. 5, 1711, "allowed" Joseph Benton, his uncle, to be his guardian; d. Dec. 1770; m. Elizabeth, bapt. June 11, 1698, buried Mar. 9, 1791, dau. of John White of Middletown, Conn., of whom the Second Church record says, "The mother of John Benton [widow of Ebenezer Benton] aged 96" [she was in her 93d year]; his son *John*,[5] bapt. Nov. 15, 1724, was "buried," the same record says, "Nov. 9, 1805, æ. 81 years."
ix. ELIZABETH, bapt. Feb. 12, 1698.

4. SAMUEL[3] BENTON (*Andrew*,[2] *John*[1]) lived in Milford and Hartford, and for awhile in the town of Tolland, Conn., where he and his son Samuel were first proprietors, in 1716. He married, probably in 1679, Sarah, daughter of William and Sarah Chatterton of New Haven, Conn., who was born there, July 19, 1661. He died testate in Hartford, Apr. 10, 1746, making ample provision for his "beloved wife Sarah," and appointing Moses and Lydia, his two youngest children, to be executors.

Children, all born in Hartford:

6. i. SAMUEL,[4] b. Aug. 8, 1680.
ii. SARAH, b. Sept. 28, 1685.
iii. HANNAH, b. Mar. 14, bapt. Mar. 19, 1688; m. (1) May 11, 1711, Samuel Kellogg, Jr., who d. in 1712, and had *Sarah*, the only child, b. 1712; m. (2) Joseph Root.
iv. ABIGAIL, b. Dec. 9, 1691: m. (1) Joseph, of Wethersfield, son of John Camp of Hartford, who d. Dec., 1713, and had *Hannah*, only child, bapt. Sept. 25, 1712; m. (2) July 28, 1715, Richard Montague of Wethersfield. She d. in Wethersfield, May 9, 1753, "in 62d yr."
7. v. CALEB, b. Mar. 1, 1694.
8. vi. DANIEL, b. June 25, 1696.
9. vii. JACOB, b. Sept. 21, bapt. Sept. 26, 1698.
viii. MOSES, b. Apr. 26, bapt. May 3, 1702; m. Miriam ——, who d. Sept. 30, 1776, "age 61 yrs."; d. testate, May 11, 1755, his "Beloved Wiffe Merriam" being one of the executors. Children: 1. *Moses*.[5] 2. *Samuel*. 3. *Martha*. 4. *Miriam*. 5. *Lydia*.
ix. LYDIA, b. and bapt. Apr. 26, 1705.

5. JOSEPH[3] BENTON (*Andrew,*[2] *John*[1]), is first mentioned in his grandfather George Stocking's will, dated July 15, 1673. He married first, [Martha?] a daughter of Dea. Paul Peck of Hartford, who left him a legacy of £5 in his will, dated June 25, 1695; and married second, Feb. 10, 1698, Sarah, daughter of Bevil Waters of Hartford, "a man of good estate," who died Mar., 1729, leaving his "eldest daughter, Sarah Benton wife of Joseph Benton, £500."

He united with the church, Mar. 8, 1696, and she, Mar. 15, 1713. In 1714, probably, he removed from Hartford to the town of Tolland, Conn., where he and his son Joseph, and his brother Samuel and his son Samuel, appear as "inhabitants" and first proprietors, May 14, 1716. He was its first town clerk, from Dec., 1717, to Dec., 1720, a selectman in 1721 and '22, a first deacon of the church, and largely "intrusted with public affairs." At a survey of the line between the towns of Tolland and Coventry, in 1722, his house and three acres of land fell within the latter, but by agreement he was "still accounted an inhabitant" of Tolland. He was at Newington, Conn., Nov. 23, 1739, and in 1742 he removed, probably with his son Jehiel, to the town of Kent, in Litchfield Co., Conn. His gravestone, at the west side of Good Hill Cemetery, near the village of Kent, is inscribed: HEAR LIES THE BODY OF DEC:N IOSEPH BENTON WHO DIED AVGVST 12th 1753 in THE 93 Y'R OF HIS AGE.

Child by first wife:

i. JOSEPH,[4] m. Dec. 11, 1718, Sarah Pynchon; was a first proprietor of the town of Tolland, 1716; d. testate at Farmington, Conn., 1667, his will, dated June 25, 1666, giving "all my estate both real and personal to my beloved wife Sarah, to be at her disposal forever." Children: 1. *Andrew,*[5] bapt. Aug. 23, 1719. 2. *Martha,* bapt. Nov. 30, 1720.

Children by second wife, all born in Hartford:

ii. RUTH, b. Feb. 9, bapt. Feb. 10, 1699; d. Oct. 6, 1712.
iii. SARAH, b. Jan. 28, bapt. May 26, 1701; d. Oct. 7, 1712.
10. iv. ISAAC, b. Feb. 8, bapt. Feb. 14, 1703.
v. AARON, b. Mar. 24, 1705.
vi. JEMIMA, b. Mar. 21, 1708; m. Jan. 24, 1731, Benjamin Strong.
11. vii. JEHIEL, b. Jan. 27, bapt. Jan. 28, 1710.
viii. KEZIA, bapt. Sept. 19, 1714.

6. SAMUEL[4] BENTON (*Samuel,*[3] *Andrew,*[2] *John*[1]) lived in Hartford and Tolland, Conn., of which latter town he was a first proprietor, in 1716. He married, Jan. 2, 1705, Mary, daughter of Medad Pomroy of Northampton, Mass.

Children, perhaps all born in Hartford:

i. MEDAD,[5] bapt. Oct. 22, 1705.
12. ii. JONATHAN, bapt. Sept. 7, 1707.
13. iii. TIMOTHY, bapt. Mar. 9, 1710.
iv. EUNICE, bapt. June 22, 1712.
v. MARY, bapt. May 29, 1715.
14. vi. SAMUEL, bapt. Aug. 11, 1717.
vii. SARAI, bapt. Aug. 16, 1719.

7. CALEB[4] BENTON (*Samuel,*[3] *Andrew,*[2] *John*[1]), who lived in Hartford, married Hannah, daughter of Thomas (son of David) Ensign of Hartford. She united with the Second Church, Feb. 20, 1725, and he, June 27, 1725. He died July 25, 1725, his wife surviving him.

Children, all born in Hartford:

i. HANNAH,[5] bapt. July 31, 1720.
15. ii. CALEB, b. Jan. 28, bapt. Feb. 4, 1722.
iii. VIOLET, bapt. Dec. 8, 1723.
16. iv. ABRAHAM, bapt. Apr. 11, 1725.
v. THOMAS, m. July 3, 1761, Anne Stanley; d. 1815; lived at Windsor, Conn.
vi. SARAH, b. Feb. 23, 1729.
vii. SUSANNAH, b. Feb. 23, 1729.

8. DANIEL[4] BENTON (*Samuel,[3] Andrew,[2] John[1]*) lived in Hartford and Tolland, Conn. He united with the Second Church, Sept. 21, 1718, and married, Jan. 3, 1722, Mary, daughter of John Skinner of Hartford. He died in Tolland.

Children, all born in Tolland:

i. MARY,[5] b. Oct. 17, 1722; d. Mar. 16, 1723.
17. ii. DANIEL, b. Jan. 6, 1724.
18. iii. WILLIAM, b. Nov. 12, 1725.
iv. MARY, b. Apr. 9, 1727; d. Oct. 4, 1745.
19. v. ELIJAH, b. June 30, 1728.
vi. SARAH, b. May 8, 1730; d. young.
vii. HANNAH, b. July 12, 1731; d. young.
viii. JOHN, b. June 17, 1732; d. young.
ix. SILOAM, b. Dec. 11, 1733; d. young.
x. LYDIA, b. May 2, 1735.
xi. ABIGAIL, b. Nov. 25, 1736; m. July 19, 1757, Benjamin Davis.

9. JACOB[4] BENTON (*Samuel,[3] Andrew,[2] John[1]*) lived in Hartford, where he joined the Second Church, June 23, 1723. He removed to Harwinton, Conn., in 1736, and the first town meeting was held at his house, Dec. 20, 1737. He was the first town clerk, a deacon in the church, and several times a selectman. He married first, June 6, 1724, Abigail, daughter of Joshua and Mary Carter, who died Sept. 27, 1725; and married second, Apr. 4, 1728, Elizabeth, daughter of Barnabas and Martha Hinsdale of Hartford, who was born Jan. 9, 1703. He died Nov. 23, 1761.

Child by first wife, born in Hartford:

i. ABIGAIL,[5] b. Sept. 18, bapt. Sept. 19, 1725; d. Mar. 4, 1764; m. Timothy Dodd, who was bapt. Aug. 17, 1724, and d. Feb. 21, 1774.

Children by second wife, all, except the last, born in Hartford:

ii. JACOB, b. Jan. 2, bapt. Jan. 12, 1729; m. Hannah Slade of Harwinton, Conn., d. Jan. 13, 1807, at Alstead, N. H.
iii. PHINEAS, b. Jan. 10, bapt. Jan. 17, 1731; d. Aug. 16, 1739.
iv. AMOS, b. Nov. 10, bapt. Nov. 12, 1732.
v. BARNABAS, bapt. Jan. 3, 1735.
vi. ELIZABETH, bapt. June 17, 1738; d. Aug. 16, 1749.

10. ISAAC[4] BENTON (*Joseph,[3] Andrew,[2] John[1]*), who lived in Hartford, Tolland, Kent, and Salisbury, Conn., married Mar. 16, 1730, Ruth Norton of Edgartown, Mass. He was in Tolland, as early as 1716, removed from there to Kent in 1743, where he and his wife joined the church, Mar. 14, 1744, and from there went to Salisbury in 1746. He became a freeman April 8, 1751; was a sealer of weights and measures in 1753 and '55; a tither in 1754; and a lister and grand-juror in 1756. His gravestone in the Old Cemetery at Salisbury is inscribed: "Here Lies Interred The Body of Mr Ifsaac Benton He Died September 17th A.D. 1757 [æ 54]."

His son Isaac was executor of his will, and his estate of seventy-nine acres in the southwest corner of the town, near Ore Hill, and personal property of £43–19–8, was distributed, Aug. 16, 1760, to his widow, Ruth, and his eight surviving children.

Children, except the last three, born in Tolland:

i. SARAH,[5] b. June 14, 1731; m. John Towsley.
20. ii. ISAAC, b. Nov. 13, 1732.
21. iii. DAVID, b. Jan. 23, 1734.
22. iv. STEPHEN, b. July 10, 1737.
v. JOSEPH, b. Sept. 3, 1740; d. about 1761 or '62.
23. vi. NATHAN, b. Feb. 28, 1743.
24. vii. LEVI, b. Mar. 20, 1746, in Kent, Conn.
viii. RUTH, b. July 23, 1748, "in Oblong."
ix. JEHIEL, b. Aug. 9, 1752; d. June 3, 1753.

11. CAPT. JEHIEL[4] BENTON (*Joseph,[3] Andrew,[2] John[1]*) was a child when his father removed from Hartford to Tolland, Conn., in 1716. He married, Oct., 1731, Sarah Berry of Tolland, and removed to Kent, Conn., in 1742, where he and his wife joined the church, July 18, 1742. They both died in Kent, she, Sept. 16, 1784, "æ 78," and he, Oct. 30, 1789, "æ 79." Their gravestones are in Good Hill Cemetery, near Kent.

Children, all, except the last, born in Tolland:

i. JOSEPH,[5] b. Dec. 15, 1732; d. July 8, 1736.
ii. MIRIAM, b. July 8, 1734.
iii. KEZIAH, b. Mar. 25, 1736.
iv. NATHANIEL, b. Apr. 17, 1741.
v. ANNE, b. July 23, 1747.

[To be concluded.]

INSCRIPTIONS FROM OLD CEMETERIES IN CONNECTICUT.

Communicated by LOUIS MARINUS DEWEY, Esq., of Westfield, Mass.

[Continued from page 141.]

Suffield.

Mr. James Bagg, aged 19 years, and Mr. Jonathan Bagg aged 17 years, sons of Mr. James Bagg, late of Springfield deceased, and of Mrs. Bathsheba, now wife of Capt. Asaph Leavit, killed by lightning May 20, 1766.

John Burbank died 12 Mar., 1793, in 93d year.

Thomas Copley died 30 Aug., 1751, aged 75.

Mary his wife died 15 Aug., 1751, in 72d year.

John Crary died 4 Dec,, 1854, aged 79.

Deborah (Prentice) his wife died 5 Apr., 1853, aged 73.

Sandford Crary (son of John) died 29 Sept. 1840, aged 41.

Mrs. Mary Denslow died 18 June, 1784, in 55th year.

Rev. Ebenezer Devotion died 11 Apr., 1741, aged 57.

Mrs. Hannah his wife died 23 Mar., 1719, in 33d year.

Mrs. Navini (Taylor of Westfield), his wife died 6 Aug., 1739, aged 45.

John Dewey died 17 Jan., 1807, in 63d year.

Two children of John and Olive Dewey, Olive died 6 Nov., 1800, aged 10 mon. 10 days, John died 11 Aug., 1805, aged 4 years.

Lieut. Bildad Fowler, a soldier of the Revolution, died 19 Nov., 1814, aged 76.

Mercy Sikes his wife died 25 Apr., 1800, aged 43.

Rachel Hopkins his 2d wife died 5 Nov., 1855, aged 96.

Gideon Granger, Esq., died suddenly 30 Oct., 1800, in 66th year (father of Gideon Granger, postmaster general under President Jefferson).

Tryphosa (Kent) his wife died 21 July, 1796, in 58th year.

Anna wife of John Hall died 23 Aug., 1794, aged 49.

Nathaniel Harmon died 2 May, 1712, aged 57.

Daniel Hubbard died 27 July, 1748, in 60th year.

Capt. Joseph King died 6 Mar., 1756, in 67th year.

Hannah his relict died 4 May, 1805, aged 109.

John Lawton died 17 Dec., 1690, aged 60.

Benedick wife of John Lawton died 18 Nov., 1692, aged 57.

Capt. Asaph Leavitt died 14 Apr., 1774, in 82d year.

Hannah his wife died 24 Nov., 1726, in 35th year.

John Lewis died 3 Feb., 1828, aged 74.

Mary his widow died 9 Mar., 1840, aged 78.

Caroline daughter of John and Betsy Lewis died 24 Nov., 1827, aged 21.

Hannah daughter of John and Mary Lewis died 28 Oct., 1827, aged 21.

Rachel wife of Zebulon Mygatt died 14 May, 1721, aged 20.

Benjamin son of Benjamin and Mary Remington died 28 Apr., 1776, aged 10 mos. 22 days.

John Rowe died 23 Sept., 1795, in 92d year.

Posthumous Sikes died 16 Mar., 1756, in 45th year.

Victory Sikes died 13 Dec., 1793, in 83d year.

Helen Talcot wife of Wm. Mather died 6 Dec., 1770, aged 40.

Consider Williston died 14 Feb., 1794, in 55th year.

Rhoda his widow died 16 May, 1828, aged 87.

Elizabeth wife of Doctor David Willkoks died 19 Mar., 1760, in 42d year.

West Suffield.

Calvin Gillett died 26 Jan., 1844, aged 78.

Thankful his wife died 25 June, 1851, aged 82.

John Warner died 10 May, 1809, aged 84.

Anah his wife died 24 Feb., 1820, aged 95.

Enfield.

John Booth died 7 May, 1778, in 82d year.

Revd. Mr. Nath[ll] Collins, first pastor of the Church of Christ in Enfield, died 31 Dec., 1756, in 80th year.

Mrs. Alice Collins, wife of the Rev[d]. Mr. Nathaniel Collins, first Pastor of the Church of Christ in Enfield, died 19 Feb., 1735, in 53rd year (a great-grand-daughter of Gov. William Bradford of Plymouth Colony).

Susannah wife of John Hale died 17 Nov., 1757, aged about 67.

Lieut. Thomas Jones died 4 Nov., 1763, in 84th year.

Mary his wife died 8 Nov., 1744, in 60th year.

Abel King died 2 Aug., 1822, aged 38.

Benjamin Meacham died 14 Oct., 1776, aged 53.

Elizabeth his wife died 2 Aug., 1811, aged 85.
Lieut. Benjamin Meacham died 12 Oct., 1770, in 68th year.
Abner Meacham died 16 Dec., 1831, aged 74.
Lovicy his consort died 13 Jan., 1823, aged 59.
Benjamin Meacham died 2 Oct., 1817, aged 69.
Mehetable his wife died 17 June, 1790, aged 38.
Nathaniel Pierce died—Jan., 1755, in 84th year.
John Pierce died 28 Sept., 1713, aged 61 yrs. 11 days.
Ebenezer Prior died 12 Jan., 1841, aged 96.
Mary his relict died 17 July, 1846, aged 91.
Harriet Prior died 11 Dec., 1848, aged 63.
Thomas Sabin died 9 Oct., 1810, aged 75.
Capt. Joseph Sexton died 3 May, 1742' aged 76.
Hannah (Wright) his relict died 26 Nov., 1742, aged 73 (see *ante*, vol. 35, page 75).
Dr. Ebenezer Terry died 2 Aug., 1780, in 85th year.
Mary his wife died 5 Apr., 1762, aged 61.
Capt. Ephraim Terry, Esq., born 24 Oct., 1701, died 14 Oct., 1783.
Ann his wife born 20 Dec., 1702, died 10 Sept., 1778.
Col. Nathaniel Terry, son of Ephraim and Anne, born 3 June, 1730, died 20 Feb., 1792.
Capt. Samuel Terry died 2 Jan., 1730/1, in 70th year.
Martha, his relict, died 29 May, 1743, page 76.
Samuel Terry died 8 May, 1798, aged 72.
Mary his relict died 11 Feb., 1801, aged 70.
John Warner born 9 Oct., 1748, died 2 Jan., 1813.

Somers.

Ebenezer and Abigail Buckley had three children die in each year, 1740 and 1757.
Abigail Clark daughter of Simon and Abigail died 9 Apr., 1794, aged 18, of smallpox.
Edward Collins at Cambridge, 1630; Nathaniel Collins first minister at Middletown; Nathaniel Collins, Jr., first minister at Enfield, died in 1757; Alice his wife, a great-grand-daughter of William Bradford of the Mayflower and 31 years governor of Plymouth Colony.
Elijah Felt died 24 Jan., 1789, in 23d year, from an accidental gun-shot wound in the legs and knees.
Samuel Gowdy died 17 Nov., 1811, aged 74.
Abiah his wife died 20 Mar., 1818, aged 81.
Benjamin Jones died 5 Feb., 1754, in 72d year (the first settler).
Benjamin Jones died 13 Oct., 1794, in 85th year.
Elizabeth his wife died 28 June, 1800, in 82d year.
Daniel Jones died 23 Mar., 1792, in 46th year.
Jemima his wife died 13 Apr., 1782, in 38th year.
Eleazer Jones died 20 Apr., 1755, aged 62.
Capt. Charles Kibbe died 8 Dec., 1805, aged 59.
Mary his wife died 27 Jan., 1790, aged 53.
Edward Kibbe died 22 Aug., 1756, in 88th year.
Rebecca wife of Edward Kibbe died 16 Dec., 1769, in 76th year.
Grace wife of Jacob Kibbe died 15 Feb., 1734, in 30th year.
Nathaniel Mighells died 20 Aug., 1750, in 34th year.
George Gilbert Mixter born 15 Feb., 1821, died 1 Jan., 1904.

Maria Annunciate Gowdy his wife (daughter of Tudor Gowdy) born 27 Apr., 1823, died 8 Aug., 1893.
Ezra Parsons died 19 Dec., 1815, in 72d year.
Abigail his wife died 13 Aug., 1810, aged 66.
Daniel Sexton died 8 Oct., 1792, aged 90.
Mary his relict died 27 Apr., 1806, aged 90.
Daniel Sexton died 10 Mar., 1826, aged 89.
Catherine his relict died 7 July, 1834, aged 89.
Hannah wife of Daniel Sexton died 11 June, 1785, aged 33.
Joseph Sexton died 3 Mar., 1807, aged 63.
Rachel his consort died 27 Apr., 1796, aged 48.
Stephen Sexton died 14 Aug., 1792, aged 50.
Mehitable, his widow, died 10 Aug., 1825, aged 82.
Lydia wife of Benjamin Sitton died ——— 1729, aged 64.
Ebenezer Spencer died 20 Nov., 1787, aged 80.
Experience his wife, and daughter of Josiah Cooley of Springfield, died 19 June, 1771, aged 32.
Jacob Ward died 18 Sept., 1748, aged 51.

[To be continued.]

ENGLISH ORIGIN OF THE AMERICAN DEARBORNS.

Communicated by VICTOR CHANNING SANBORN, Esq., of Chicago, Ill.

PERHAPS misled by "Tradition," the investigators of families originating with Wheelwright and his Exeter Combination have turned from the blazed trail which leads into Lincolnshire, as indicated by the late Col. Chester and by "Long John" Wentworth. Thus the Towles are said to be Irish, and the Dearborns to have come from Devonshire.

The volumes of Lincoln Wills, in course of publication by the British Record Society, give ample clues to local families, as do always the documents of diocesan registries of probate, whose records mainly deal with families of small possessions, distinguished from those whose wealth or ambition inclined them to register their wills in the Prerogative Courts of Canterbury or York. In these Lincoln volumes appear many Towle wills, showing a family of that name residing in North Lincolnshire, and there are also a few Dearborn wills which I think show conclusively the origin of our American Dearborns to have been next door to the English home of their religious leader, John Wheelwright.

The following abstracts of Dearborn wills show a family of that name originating in Hogsthorpe, Lincolnshire (a parish next to Mumby where the Wheelwrights came from, and the very place where Wheelwright bought land from one Francis Levet), and branching into Binbrooke, Sibsey, Spilsby, and Hannay, thus leading the genealogist into five Lincoln parishes whose registers, extending as they do to the early 16th century, will undoubtedly furnish forth the Dearborn ancestry.

The Dearborns were of yeoman stock, and the name does not appear in any ancient records or pedigrees which I have found. It will be seen that these wills mention Christian names identical with our early Dearborns, except for the emigrant Godfrey, whom I surmise to have been a son of Thomas, the cousin of Henry of Hannay in 1635. The earliest name, Michael (uncommon in New England families), appears in the third American generation as the son of Ebenezer, who was the grandson of Godfrey.

My interest in the Dearborns being purely collateral, and I have not traced the family farther than the clues here printed. I found these in searching for the English origin of my ancestor Thomas Levet, who, like Godfrey Dearborn, followed Wheelwright to Exeter and moved to Hampton, where he established a home and left many descendants. I hope to print in the REGISTER, ere long, what I have discovered as to Levet's Lincoln and Yorkshire origin.

Will of MICHAEL DEREBARNE of Hoggestrope. Dated 24 April 1573; proved at Lincoln, 8 June 1573. To Agnes my wife iij of my best Kyen, xv Ewes, x hogges & wethers, one black mare, one gray mare and one "danded" mare; ij matris beds with all things thereto belonging; x pewter dublers; one table, one form, one pair of malt quernes and one "dishbinck" ij chairs, 5 acres of barley, 5 acres of beans, one wain and one plough. To John, my son, ij Kyen, x Ewes, iij wethers, vi hogges, one black "feley" one gray "feley," one plough etc. To Thomas, my son, when at the age of xx years, one matris bed, ij lining sheets; ij harden sheets; ij pyllows, one coverlet, and £ viij in ready money. To Agnes, my wife, the lease of my house that I have of the Queen's majesty with one lease I have of Thomas Herdman of Cumberworth for ij years after my death and then to John, my son. To evrie poor householder in Hoggestrope that hath no kye iiij d, to evrie house. To Jenet, my sister, dwelling at Partney one "Shedder burling." To every one of my brethren and sistern children. To John my brother one pair russet hose and my best black dublet. To Francis Massare my black dublet with the russet sleeves. To the Mother Church at Lincoln. Residue to wife Agnes and son John, equally. To Hoggesthorpe Church iii s. iii d. Wife Anne, Executrix. Supervisor: John Markby. Witnesses: Thomas Brgert, Water Edwards, John Markby. (*Lincoln Wills, 1574, vol. i, fo. 288.*)

Will of THOMAS DEARBORNE of Spilsby, mercer. Dated 12 December, 1568; proved at Louth, 8 April 1589. To be buried in Church of Binbrook. To the poor of Spilsby x li for the buying of them yearly iij chalder of coles. To my cozen John Burwell. To the poor of Hoggesthrope. To every one of my poor kinsfolks. To Mr. Thomas Atkinson v s, desiring him to be Supervisor. Residue to brother John Dearborne, full Executor. Witness: Thomas Atkinson, Clerk.

(*Lincoln Wills, 1589, fo. 224.*)

Will of JOHN DEARBEARN of Sibsey. Dated 11 October 1608; proved at Boston, 11 April 1611. To my wife. My son to be Executor. To every one of my cosins children xii d, to wit: Thomas Dearborn, William and Harry. To ten of the poorest householders in Sibsey x groats. To ten of the poorest householders in Hoggesthrope x groats. Residue to son John. My brother John Kettle, Supervisor. Witness: John Watson, Nicholas Stocks, Thomas Parker. (*Lincoln Wills, 1611, vol, i, fo. 179.*)

Will of HENRY DEAREBORNE of Hanney. Dated 12 Oct. 1635; proved at Louth, 23 October 1635. To be buried in churchyard of Hanney. To eldest daughter Tomazin Deareborne. To daughter Sarai. To son John Deareborne. If it shall please God to call Anne my wife out of this world before expiration of my lease, remaining years to son John. Residue to wife Anne, she sole Executrix. Witnesses: Thomas Paine, Clerk, Theophilus Drury. (*Lincoln Wills, 1635, vol. i, fo. 128.*)

PROCEEDINGS OF THE NEW ENGLAND HISTORIC GENEALOGICAL SOCIETY.

By GEO. A. GORDON, A.M., Recording Secretary.

Boston, Massachusetts, 4 April, 1906. The New England Historic Genealogical Society held a stated meeting at half past two o'clock this afternoon in Marshall P. Wilder hall, Society's building, 18 Somerset street, which was called to order by the Recording Secretary, the President being absent in Europe. Charles Sidney Ensign, LL.B., of Newton, was invited to preside. He accepted and served as chairman, *pro tempore*.

After the reading and confirmation of the minutes of the March stated meeting, Henry Leland Chapman, D.D., Professor of English in Bowdoin college, Brunswick, Me., was introduced as the essayist of the meeting. Mr. Chapman read a deeply interesting and discriminating paper on *Old Flud Ireson*, unfolding the history of the event on which the tradition is founded, and citing contemporary statements and documents. The thanks of the meeting were cordially voted, and a copy requested for deposit in the archives of the Society and, also, for a contribution to the REGISTER.

The executive officers, severally, presented reports, which were received, read, accepted and ordered on file.

Twenty-two new members were elected.

On motion, it was

Voted, That the By-laws be amended by substituting the word "last" for the word "second" in the second line of article 1, chapter III., so that the first paragraph of that article shall read:

Art. 1. The Annual Meeting of the Corporation shall be held on the last Wednesday in January of each year in Boston, notice of which shall be sent to Resident and Life Members by the Recording Secretary, one week in advance.

The Treasurer was authorized to sell and make title to house No. 4 Westmoreland street, Dorchester.

The meeting then dissolved.

2 May. The President being still absent, a stated meeting was held to-day at the usual time and place, Mr. Ensign acting as chairman.

The ordinary routine exercises were observed, and seven new members elected.

Walter Kendall Watkins, esq., of Malden, read a valuable paper on *Lemuel Cox, Boston's Bridge Builder and Inventor*, evidencing wide research and competent acquaintance with public events A.D. 1770–1800. A vote of thanks was passed, and a copy of the paper solicited for deposit in the archives of the Society.

No further business being presented, the meeting was dissolved.

NOTES AND QUERIES.

NOTES.

GENERAL ENOCH POOR was born in Andover, Mass., 21 June, 1736, but early became a citizen of Exeter, N. H. He was colonel in the 2d Regiment of New Hampshire troops in the Revolutionary army, and died near Hackensack, N. J., 9 Sept., 1780. The Report of the Adjutant General of New Hampshire for 1866, vol. ii, p. 339 note, says: "He was killed in a duel with a French Officer." This story passed until the Hon. Ellis Ames of Canton, Mass., communicated a paper to the Massachusetts Historical Society, stating that Gen. Poor was killed in a duel with Maj. John Porter, a Massachusetts officer. (1 Proceedings xix. 256-261.)

Both of these statements, however, are incorrect, according to the following deposition which was made shortly after Gen. Poor's death.

Brookline, Mass. ALBERT A. FOLSOM.

"THE NEW-HAMPSHIRE GAZETTE; or,
STATE JOURNAL, and GENERAL ADVERTISER.
[Vol. XXIV.] MONDAY, January 15, 1781. [No. 1264.]

Meffi'rs PRINTERS,

AS a Report has been spread thro' this State that the late Brigadier-General POOR died of a Wound received in a DUEL, the following Depofition may ferve to prove the Falfehood of said Report, and undeceive thofe whofe Credulity has thereby been impofed upon and misled; and by inferting it you will oblige many of his Friends.

I JEREMIAH FOGG, late Aid-du-Camp to Brigadier-Gen. POOR, deceafed, teftify that for fome Months before his Death I lived with him, attended him conftantly during his laft Sicknefs, until his Death, which I think was folely occafioned by a Bilious Fever, after thirteen Days Illnefs; that I affifted in laying out his Corps, and did not perceive that he had ever been wounded, and never knew or fufpected he had ever been engaged in any Duel; nor heard any fuch Report till fome Weeks after his Death, it was mentioned to me in a Letter from New-Hampfhire. JEREMIAH FOGG*

Rockingham ſs. January 13th, 1781.

Capt. JEREMIAH FOGG *made ſolemn Oath to the Truth of the above Depoſition by him ſubscribed, before* WM. PARKER,† Justice Peace."

EARLY AMERICAN EMIGRANTS.—The late Mr. Hotten in his introduction to the "Original List of Emigrants to America" tells us that the early settlers left the old country because of persecution—political and religious. The proceedings against the remonstrants were taken in the Courts of Star Chamber and High Commission. All the decree books of the first named jurisdiction are lost, and many of those of the latter, and so all interested in American ancestry have been prevented from using the records of the fines and punishments as a means of genealogical information. This hindrance has now been removed by the important discovery that two sets of fines imposed by the Star Chamber and High Commission exist in the Public Record Office, one series for both Courts appears to be perfect, but some of the other set have been lost. As they, in each case, give residence of the delinquent, and in some instances name the wife and children, the importance of this find to the descendants of

* Major Jeremiah Fogg, the son of Rev. Jeremiah and Elizabeth (Parsons) Fogg, was born in Kensington, N. H., in 1749. He was graduated from Harvard College in 1768, and was an Adjutant in Col. Poor's regiment in May, 1775, and a Brigade Major in 1782. He died 26 May, 1808.

† William Parker, the son of Hon. William and Elizabeth (Grafton) Parker, was born in Portsmouth, N. H., in 1731. He was graduated from Harvard College in 1751, and began the practice of law in Exeter in 1765. He was Register of Probate for many years, and 1 Jan., 1790, he received the appointment of Judge of Common Pleas for Rockingham Co., which office he held until his resignation in 1807. He married Elizabeth Fogg, a sister of Maj. Jeremiah Fogg, and had six children. He died 5 June, 1813.

early New England settlers cannot be over rated. I intend to at once copy and index those fines, as they will form a very useful addition to my other lists of emigrants.

NOTES FROM ENGLISH RECORDS.—Fowler *v.* Vaughan. 8 Dec. 1656, the answer of George Vaughan to a bill of complaint of Roger Fowler. "George Yeomans and Edward Yeomans are sons of Rachell Yeomans dec'd and if they be living are in parts beyond the seas, and as this deft. beleeveth, know now nothing of this bill exhibited in this Court in their names." Admon of Rachell Yeoman was granted to Sussanna Close, by the Court of Probate, the sister and next of kyn in the absence of said George and Edward. Debt due by the deft. Edward Yeoman and Rachell his wife father and mother of George and Edward. It is reported they are in Jamaica. (Chancery Bills and Answers, before 1714, Collins 152.)

Court Rolls of Warfield, co Salop. 23 Apl 1657. The jury present the death of Roger Crudington seised of a messuage and yard land in Newton, and that Ann his wife was living and held a moiety of the premisses for her life. George Crudgington, eldest son is abroad. Robert, second son, is admitted. (British Museum Ad. MS. 28832.)

Hanbury *v.* Ivory. 31 Oct. 1654, orator Peter Hanbury of London, gent., son of Edward Hanbury of Eling, co. Middx., gent, decd. At the time of the death of Edward Hanbury your orator was in remote parts beyond the seas, Viz. in New England, and sometime after returned home. Discovery of a lease. Deft. Luke Ivory. Answer sworn 10 Nov. 1654. The deft. Luke Ivory, tallow chandler, says that Edward was his father in law. Compt. is youngest son of Edward Hanbury. (Chancery Bills and Answers before 1714, C. 125.)

GERALD FOTHERGILL.

11 Brussels Road, New Wandsworth, London, Eng.

ANDREWS.—The following note shows the participation of minors in the land purchases in the Old Colony:

Under the heading "Henry Andrews of Taunton," Hon. Josiah H. Drummond published an account of the earliest generations of the Andrews family of Taunton, Mass., in the REGISTER, vol. 51, page 453, and I published a supplementary article in the REGISTER, vol. 52, page 16. Concerning the data in these two articles, Mr. Drummond and I were in substantial accord except as to the dates of birth and death of Henry[3] Andrews (Henry,[2] Henry[1]). We had a long discussion on these points, but were unable to come to an agreement. The matter is now definitely settled by statements found in an old Bible, the property of the Old Colony Historical Society, formerly belonging to Josiah[4] Andrews (son of Henry[3]) who recorded therein the deaths of his parents. This Bible was printed in Edinburgh in 1726. On the inside of the front cover is written: "Josiah Andrews his Book god give him grace their into Look that when the Bel Begin to toal the Lord have Marcy on this Sovl." On the inside of the back cover is written: "this book bot in ye year 1729 price——0-11-0." And on a blank page is inscribed the following:

"ianuary ye 25: 1734-5 henry andrews senyer desest being in ye seuenty
"forth year of his eage
"March ye 20 1736 Mary andrews died being in ye seventy^th^ year of her eage"

Hence, Henry[3] Andrews was born in 1661; or, more exactly, between Jan. 25, 1660-1, and Jan. 25, 1661-2.

The importance of definitely settling this birth-date—the reason for the long discussion and extended search among the records by Mr. Drummond and others—lies in the light it sheds on the rules and customs of the early settlers in the admission of associates in the land purchases.

In the list of Taunton South Purchase Proprietors, Nov. 26, 1672, occur the names of Henry Andrews and Henry Andrews Junior. The unanimous agreement of all the genealogists who have searched over and over again all the known records, is that these were Henry[2] Andrews and his son Henry[3] Andrews. Not the slightest trace of any other possible Henry Andrews has been found. Hence in the beginning it was assumed that Henry[3] Andrews, his father being alive, was an adult on this last-named date; but this assumption was soon found to be erroneous. Then Mr. Drummond studied the records for the laws on the subject, and, as a result, informed me that he could find nothing forbidding the admission of a minor, whose father was living, to purchase rights. If Henry the father had more than one purchase right, he wrote, there was no reason why he should not turn over one of these rights to his minor son.

In this same list there is one other parallel case. Peter[1] Pitts and his minor son Samuel[2] Pitts were both recorded as purchasers. I have been unable to find any record of the birth of Samuel[2] Pitts and therefore am unable to state *beyond peradventure* that he was a minor on this date. Yet I am quite sure that he was born in the year 1655.

REV. THOMAS CLAP'S MARRIAGES IN TAUNTON, MASS.—Among these is the following:

"Aprill 24 1737 Then Married William Cobb & Anne Will[*worn*] together both of Taunton."

In the copy made years ago by Rev. Charles H. Brigham, the woman's name is given as Anne Willis, but it should be Anne Williams, as shown by Bristol Co., Mass., Deeds, xlii:17, which has: April 13, 1756.—William Cobb of Norton and Ann his wife, for £19:19:0, to Richard Williams of Raynham, all our interest in the real estate which Mr. Ebenezer Williams of Taunton dec'd gave by his will to one Eb. Williams, a minor, who is also since dec'd, and in the homestead where grantee now dwells, and in all other real estate formerly belonging to the said Ebenezer Williams, the testator, that now or hereafter may come to said Ann, as she is one of the sisters of the said Eb. Williams, minor, deceased.

A. D. HODGES, JR.

Boston, Mass.

BRAINTREE GRAVESTONES.—There are several gravestones in the Braintree Cemetery on Elm Street, Braintree, Mass., some rough field stones, others irregular pieces of slate, all rudely inscribed and nearly all of them requiring considerable excavation to get at the inscriptions. Mr. William S. Pattee, in his History of Old Braintree and Quincy, omits these inscriptions, which are as follows:

MARY | THAYER | WIFE To | CHRIS^{T} THA^{yr} | AGED 45 1761 | (*footstone*) MT DYED | MAY 14 1761.

WIL'M THAYER | DYED IA^{y}. 27 | 1756 AG^{D} 19.

E T

Here lyes ye bdy oF | DELIVERE[ ] THAYER [ ]Ho [ ]ESE[ ]T IA^{oRy} 17 | 1723 AGED 78.

E T | June 30 1731.

Sarah Thayer Dyed march 21 | 1736

E T | dye^{d} MAY 21 | 1720

AMEy | HADen | AG 4 Mo.

Esther | HAd | en . W[ ] | of Saml. HAD | en . died feb. | 14 . 1758 | (*footstone*) E H | A 45

Samuel | Haden | Child died | Ap^{l}. 13 . 1754

Se^{P} 25 Ieru[ ] PrAR die[ ] | 1769

E H | 1734.

John Webb | died Oct^{r} | 18 . 1749.

D B | 1716 | AD

S + W | a + 23 | 1802.

Sarah Colling | Dyed july | 10 | 1770 | Aged 32.

noah | Haden.

Boston, Mass. EDW. H. WHORF.

TRESCOTT-ROGERS.—Samuel Trescott, of Milton, Mass., and Margaret his wife, one of the daughters of Jeremiah Rogers, late of Lancaster, deceased, convey to Edward Phelps of Andover, Mass., interest in the estate of said Jeremiah Rogers, in Lancaster, as well by right of said Mary as by purchase made by said Trescott of Abiah Warren of Boston, widow, one other daughter of said Jeremiah Rogers, May 31, 1710. (Middlesex Co. Deeds, vol. xv, p. 261.)

Ichabod Rogers of Lancaster, cordwainer, Jeremiah Rogers of Salem, wheelwright, and Jehosaphat Rogers of Topsfield, tailor, sons of Jeremiah Rogers of Lancaster, also convey their interest in their father's estate to Edward Phelps of Andover, May 12, 1710. (Middlesex Co. Deeds, vol. xv, pp. 261, 262.)

PARRISH—WATTELL.—John Parrish, of Preston, Conn., and William Wattell alias Wadell of Lebanon, Conn., appoint our brother John Bruce, of Woburn, our attorney to take care of the timber growing upon the land formerly belonging to our father John Wattell in Chelmsford, Mass., Nov. 24, 1709. (Middlesex Co. Deeds, vol. xv, p. 262.)

John Parise, of Groton, and Mary daughter of John Wattell, of Chelmsford, married at Chelmsford, Dec. 29, 1685. (REGISTER, vol. 51, p. 448.)

John Parish and wife Mary admitted by letter from Ipswich, Nov. 15, 1704. (Preston, Conn., Church Records, p. 130.)

10 Humboldt St., Cambridge, Mass. VIRGINIA HALL.

ALLYN-GILBERT.—Capt. Thomas Allyn, the second son of Matthew and Margaret (Wyatt), was with his father an early settler in Windsor, Conn. He married, Oct. 21, 1658, Abigail, the eldest child of the Rev. John Warham of Dorchester, Mass., and Windsor, Conn. Their youngest child, Hester or Esther, born Oct., 1679, married Ebenezer Gilbert of Hartford, Conn., son of Jonathan (the Colony Marshal and Indian Commissioner) and his second wife Mary Welles the neice of Gov. Thomas Welles. Ebenezer was own cousin to Jonathan Belcher the Colonial governor of Massachusetts and, later, of New Jersey. His father by his will, dated Sept. 10, 1774, among other provisions gave him 300 acres and upwards of land situated in what is now Berlin, New Britain, and possibly Meriden, and gave Hester £100. His estate, inventoried Feb. 12, 1682, was, £2484 17s 09d. After his mother's death on July 3, 1700, they removed to Great Swamp Parish (Kensington—Worthington—Berlin), where he built, before 1717, a brick house on Christian Lane, made from clay taken from his own land, not far from old Wethersfield bounds. The house is standing and has always been in the ownership of a Gilbert by direct descent from Ebenezer. He died in 1736, leaving an estate inventoried at £3824 12s 8d. His wife died Oct. 4, 1750, leaving an estate inventoried at £326 5s 11d. The writer is a descendant in the fifth generation. CHARLES S. ENSIGN.

Newton, Mass.

MUNCY.—In a communication to the REGISTER, vol. 50, page 488, it is stated that Hannah², daughter of William¹ Adams of Ipswich, Mass., married Francis Muncy, in 1659, and second, John Kimball; and the same statement appears in the Maine Historical Register, vol. 9, page 360, and in the Essex Antiquarian, vol. 2, page 87.

The facts are that Francis Muncy moved to Brookhaven, Long Island, where he had Lot 22 in 1664, and where he died in 1675, administration of his estate being granted his widow on 10 Sept. 1675. She married, that same year, John Ramsden (see New York Marriages; and Town Records of Brookhaven, L. I., page 80), which is also proved by a record in which the two sons [John and Samuel] of Francis and Hannah (Adams) Muncy are called "sons in law" [step sons] of John Ramsden of Newtown, and agree to live with him and help him.

John Muncy, son of Francis and Hannah, married Hannah², daughter of Rev. Nathaniel¹ Brewster, and died 19 Feb. 1690-1. It was probably his widow, Hannah, who married John Kimball. WILLIAM LINCOLN PALMER.

Cambridge, Mass.

A SYMBOL OF TERMINAL CONTRACTION.—There has often been observed by expert copyists of old manuscripts a flourish or quirk at the end of certain words, which has not been reproduced or adequately indicated in transcription. It is frequently found; and as common instances may be given the words "Secr3," "Resp3," "Dra3" for Draper, etc. We have in general use today the abbreviations "oz." and "viz."; and the character "3" was, according to the lexicographers, "anciently used as a sign of terminal contraction." Now that attention is called to this identity of the flourish at the end and the symbol "3," it is hoped that its use in that way may be adopted by copyists and editors of early manuscripts. ALFRED B. PAGE.

CARY PEDIGREE.—(See Waters's *Gleanings*, vol. 2, page 1058.) One of the daughters of Richard Cary (the elder) of Bristol, by his second wife Johan, was Anne who married Nicholas Balle of Totnes in Devonshire, merchant, and by him had several children. The sons all died unmarried, the daughters married and had children. Mr. G. E. Cokayne* of the Heralds College is descended from one of the daughters. Another of the daughters married Sir Ralph Winwood, Secretary of State. Their mother, Anne Balle, widow, married Sir Thomas Bodley, founder of the Bodleian Library.

TALCOTT PEDIGREE.—(See Waters's *Gleanings*, vol. 2, page 1126.) The wife of Thomas Talcott of Horkesley, 1634, was Thomas Ball, *not* Bull. The Balls were located in that neighborhood at the end of the 15th century, and continued there, though in humble circumstances, till the beginning of the 19th century.
21 Wimborne Gardens, Ealing, London, W., Eng. H. HOUSTON BALL.

QUERIES.

Information wanted of the ancestry of the following:

CARPENTER.—Caleb Carpenter, born probably in R. I., Nov. 16, 1775; died Aug. 13, 1847, in Attica, Ohio; married (1) Rhoda Dyer, probably in R. I., about 1795-1800, and (2) Rebecca (Greene) Olds, probably in western N. Y.; went from R. I. to western New York—Geneva, Batavia, or Genesseo; said to have had a brother John, and a sister Sophronia who married a Stephen Andrews.

DYER.—Rhoda Dyer, born in R. I., whose father's name was perhaps John; tradition says her father "was an Indian fighter, was not killed in the massacre but singly afterwards."

GREENE.—Rebecca Greene, who married an Olds, and had two children, Horace and Arvilla, probably in western New York.

OLDS.—The Olds who married Rebecca Greene.

TITUS.—James Titus, said to have been a Vermonter, who married Philura, daughter of John White of Black Rock, N. Y., soldier in the war of 1812, whose wife was Mary Risley or Wrisley. The ancestry of this John White and Mary Risley is also wanted. DR. W. A. DEWEY.
Ann Arbor, Mich.

BAILEY-EMERY.—What was the ancestry of Andrew Bailey and Ruth Emery who were married, presumably in Boston or Cambridge, Mass., about 1775-6? Andrew Bailey (or Bayley) was a corporal in Capt. Scott's Co. of Col. Sargent's Regt. in the Revolution, said to have been of Peterborough, N. H. (See Mass. Soldiers and Sailors in the Revolution.) CORA EASTON.
Tecumseh, Neb.

COOK.—In the Middletown, Conn., Town Vital Records, vol. 2, page 244, are the following entries:

Elizabeth, daughter to Jacob Cook & Marcy his wife, born Nov. 11, 1743.
Mary, daughter to same two, born Nov. 15, 1745.
Josiah, son to same two, born Nov. 15, 1747.
Rebeckah, daughter to same two, born Sept. 26, 1749.
Elisha, son to same two, born Aug. 1, 1751.

The third child mentioned above, Josiah, born Nov. 15, 1747, was my great-grandfather, a record of whose family appears in the Strong Genealogy, vol. 2, page 1378, where the date of his birth is given as Nov. 26, 1746. I am unable to trace Jacob Cook or his wife Marcy, above named, and any assistance in this direction will be greatly appreciated. FRANK GAYLORD COOK.
10 Tremont St., Boston, Mass.

TAYLOR.—Parentage and ancestry wanted of Rowland Taylor who was born in Yarmouth, Mass., about 1720 or '21, went to Providence, R. I., where he married, Mar. 14, 1744-5, Sarah, daughter of Benjamin and Bethiah (Carey) Gorham, and removed to Barnstable, Mass., where all his children were born. In the fall of 1755, his widow, with five children, settled in Providence, where she married William Whipple in 1758, dying in 1810. F. C. CLARK, M.D.
161 Benefit St., Providence, R. I.

* Mr. Cokayne is a Corresponding Member of this Society.

MUNSEY.—The parentage and English ancestry is wanted of William Munsey, who first appears in Kittery, Me., in 1686, and then in Dover, N. H., from 1695 until his death in 1698, when his body was found, June 10th, in the Piscataqua river on the Maine side, the records saying that he was "By mischance or accidentally drowned"; also, of Francis Munsey, who was at Ipswich, Mass., as early as 1657, and then at Long Island, N. Y., from 1665 until his death in 1675, his widow, Hannah, daughter of William Adams of Ipswich, marrying John Ramsden of Newtown, Long Island, the year her husband died.

Cambridge, Mass. WILLIAM LINCOLN PALMER.

WATSON.—Joel Watson, of Nantucket, Mass., married there, in 1794, Elizabeth Skinner. He is said to have been born in Rhode Island. Can anybody give his parentage and ancestry? W. W.

Boston, Mass.

NEWTON.—John[3] Newton (John,[2] Rev. Roger[1]), born 1697, of Milford, Conn., married Martha, daughter of Samuel and Rachel (Lambert) Smith. She is said to have been his only wife, but there is evidence to the contrary. Of his six children, Elizabeth, Sibyl, and John, all baptized June 4, 1738, are presumed to have been by a first wife Elizabeth ——— ; the other three, Rachel, Susanna, and Martha, are known to have been by his wife Martha (Smith).

A gravestone in the Milford cemetery bears the inscription: "Mrs. Elizabeth Newton, wife to Mr. John Newton, Died July the 5 1734, In the 31st Year of Her Age"; and another is: "Mrs Martha Newton, wife to Mr John Newton, who died July ye 10th AD 1750 in ye 37th year of her age."

Can anybody give any information concerning Elizabeth, wife of John Newton?

90 Howe St., New Haven, Conn. J. T. NEWTON.

WILLIS-BROMLEY.—What was the parentage and ancestry of William Willis, born about 1725, possibly in Berkshire Co., Mass., and of his wife Bathsheba Bromley? MRS. H. H. CUMINGS.

Tidioute, Penn.

HISTORICAL INTELLIGENCE.

ENGLISH RESEARCH.—The Committee on English Research, of the New England Historic Genealogical Society, begs to call attention to the desirability of reviving investigation concerning the English ancestry of the pioneers of New England. From 1883 to 1899, former Committees secured funds by which valuable researches among the wills of the Prerogative Court of Canterbury in London were carried on by Henry F. Waters, Esq., the results of which were published in the REGISTER, giving clues which lead to determining the ancestry of many of the early settlers of New England; but since Mr. Waters's work was relinquished, comparatively little has been accomplished by the Society in that direction.

The Committee now solicits funds for continuing research in England, on the ancestry of the early New England colonists, the results to appear in the REGISTER, and it would be glad to receive suggestions and information on this subject.

Clues, not generally known, as to the origin of several early emigrants, have come into the Committee's hands, and the Secretary of the Committee will be glad to give information to anyone who may desire to make investigations.

CHARLES SHERBURNE PENHALLOW, *Chairman*,
FRANCIS APTHORP FOSTER,
JEROME CARTER HOSMER,
WILLIAM EBEN STONE,
JOSEPH GARDNER BARTLETT, *Secretary*,
} Committee on English Research.

KALENDER OF WILLS AT CAMBRIDGE.—The Cambridge Antiquarian Society, of Cambridge, England, will shortly publish a "Kalendar of Wills Proved in the Vice Chancellor's Court at Cambridge, from 1501–1757." These wills were until 1858 preserved at Cambridge, and in that year were removed to Peterboro' on the formation of the district probate offices. Here they remain. The object of the Society in undertaking this work is to render accessible the names of the testators of such wills. Orders for this valuable book should be addressed to the Society, 10 Trinity Street, Cambridge.

HOPKINS GENEALOGY.—It will be deeply regretted that the material of the Hopkins Genealogy was destroyed by fire in the late calamity at San Francisco. The following letter has been received from the compiler:—

"A large part of the Hopkins Genealogy which I was preparing was in press and would soon have been published. Our fire has totally destroyed the labor of years, and it is with regret that I announce that I shall not again attempt to take up its compilation.

I trust, however, that some one else may undertake the work, and such assistance as I may be able to furnish from memory is always at command. In order that such compilers may not be deterred from taking up the work, by the belief that I still have it in hand, I should appreciate the favor of a notice in the REGISTER to the effect that I have discontinued its compilation.

1860 Webster St., San Francisco, Cal. TIMOTHY HOPKINS."

BOOK NOTICES.*

[THE editor requests persons sending books for notice to state, for the information of readers, the price of each book, with the amount to be added for postage when sent by mail.]

A Branch of the Caldwell Family Tree. Being a record of Thompson Baxter Caldwell and his wife, Mary Ann (Ames) Caldwell, of West Bridgewater, Massachusetts, their ancestors and descendants. By CHARLES T. CALDWELL, M.D. The Olympia, Washington, D. C. 1906. 4to. pp. 18.

The line of Caldwells here given is traced to Robert Caldwell, of Warwickshire, Eng., who in 1653 is found on records at Providence, R. I. A "Numerical Chart—Complete Back to 1700" occupies six pages, and is followed, as a kind of appendix, by notes on the Leonard and Harvey families, Robert Cushman, John Alden, and others.

The Cary Family in England. By HENRY GROSVENOR CARY, Boston. Published by Rev. Seth Cooley Cary, Dorchester Centre, Boston. 1906. 4to. pp. 105. Ill.

The English family of Cary is in this volume traced to Adam de Kari, lord of Castle Kari in 1198. Besides the main line, itself displaying chiefly the names of knights, three branches of Cary nobles are included in the genealogy, those of Baron Hunsdon, the Earl of Monmouth, and Viscount Falkland, and in addition to these, the Clovelly, Cockington and Torre Abbe, and Somersetshire lines of Carys. The history of these families is presented in an interesting manner, and the author says that it is "an absolute certainty that they were our ancestors." The volume is a fine one in appearance, with clear print, wide margins, attractive illustrations, and good binding. There is no index.

The Chamberlain Association of America. Report of Annual Meetings, held in Boston, Mass., Aug. 19, 1904, and Sept. 13, 1905. Portland: Smith & Sale, Printers. 1905. 8vo. pp. 96. Price 50 cts. Address Sophia A. Caswell, 27 River St., Cambridge, Mass.

Rather more than half of this publication is occupied by "Personal Records," and the criticism which Gen. Chamberlain offered on the sketch of himself as originally prepared, as to its regrettable "breadth of statement and its length," is not inapplicable to some of the other sketches in the collection.

The Bristol Branch of the Finney Family. By FRANKLIN C. CLARK, M.D. Boston: New-Eng. Hist. Gen. Soc. 1906. Large 8vo. pp. 13.

This is a reprint from the REGISTER for January and April, 1906.

* All of the unsigned reviews are written by Mr. FREDERICK WILLARD PARKE of Boston.

The Descendants of Adam Mott of Hempstead, Long Island, N. Y. A Genealogical Study. Revised edition. By EDW. DOUBLEDAY HARRIS. The New Era Printing Co., Lancaster, Pa. 1906. 8vo. pp. 8.

In this new edition certain errors in the first edition have been corrected, and since the issue of the first, other lines of descent have been discovered, and questions then unresolved have been answered.

Ancestry and Descendants of Lieutendent Jonathan and Tamesin (Barker) Norris, of Maine. By their Great-grandson, HENRY MCCOY NORRIS, of Cincinnati, Ohio. The Grafton Press: Genealogical Publishers. New York. 1906. Large 8vo. pp. 60. Portrait.

Besides the above description, the title-page says: "In which are given the names, and more or less complete records, from 1550 to 1905, of about twelve hundred persons, among whom are sixty-nine of their ancestors, nine of their children, forty-eight of their grandchildren, one hundred and nine of their great-grandchildren, and one hundred and fifteen of their great-great-grandchildren." An unusual use of numbers is made in this work, to which allusion is thus made in the publishers' note: "The numbers in the index of this genealogy refer to sections in which the names indexed are treated . . . The pages of the book are not numbered, the numerals at the top of each page simply indicating the sections found on that page." This system was devised by the author. The volume is a fine example of the work of the Grafton Press.

Ancestry of John Prescott, Condensed. (*From Boston Evening Transcript, Aug. 14, 1995.*) [By MYRA LARKIN WHITE.] n. p.; n. d. Large 8vo. pp. 6.

The John Prescott to whom these pages refer is the "founder of Lancaster, Mass."

Fourteenth Annual Reunion of the Reynolds Family Association held at Mohican Hotel, New London, Conn., Thursday, Aug. 17th, 1905. Middletown, Conn.: Pelton & King, Printers and Bookbinders. 1906. 8vo. pp. 48.

Richardson-De Priest Family. By the Rev. ROBT. DOUGLAS ROLLER, D.D. Charleston, W. Va. n. d. 8vo. pp. 50.

This genealogy is a record of descendants of John Richardson whose father, coming from England, "settled in Virginia," and whose wife, Martha De Priest, inherited the estate "Westonville," in Hanover county, Virginia.

Richard Scott and his Wife Catharine Marbury, and some of their Descendants. By STEPHEN F. PECKHAM. Boston: Press of David Clapp & Son. 1906. Large 8vo. pp. 10. Facsimile.

This is a reprint from the REGISTER for April, 1906.

The Swift Family in Philadelphia. By THOMAS WILLING BALCH, Member of the Council of the Historical Society of Pennsylvania. From the Pennsylvania Magazine of History and Biography, April, 1906. Phila., 1906. Large 8vo. pp. 32. Portrait.

A large portion of this pamphlet consists of letters of John Swift who in 1762 was appointed by the Crown Collector of the Port of Philadelphia; they relate to his efforts to foil the illegal attempts of smugglers. It was this John Swift who originated the dancing parties which have been continued to the present day and are known as "The Philadelphia Assemblies." An interesting account of these "Assemblies" is included in this sketch of family history.

Wardwell. A brief Sketch of the Antecedents of Solomon Wardwell, with the Descendants of his two Sons, Ezra and Amos, who died in Sullivan, N. H. By ELIZABETH WARDWELL STAY. Greenfield, Mass.: Press of E. A. Hall & Co. 1906. Large 8vo. pp. 22. Price $1.00.

The first section of this genealogy consists of records of the Revolutionary services of the four sons of Thomas Wardwell, who was of the fourth generation from the Thomas Wardwell to whom, as the first of the name in America, the family is traced, and a portion of whose descendants is recorded in the second section.

Welch Genealogy. n. p.; n. d. 12mo. pp. 69+4.

The Welch line here given is traced to John Welch, of Boston. The last twenty-eight pages of the genealogy contain the records of the Stackpole family which is descended from James Stackpole, of Dover, N. H. Following the genealogy are two articles by way of appendix, "Kirk Boott and his Experience in the British Army," and "Recollections of the old 'Stackpole House.'"

Francis West of Duxbury, Mass., and Some of his Descendants. By EDWARD E. CORNWALL, M.D. Boston: New-Eng. Hist. Gen. Society. 1906. Large 8vo. pp. 14.

This is a reprint from the REGISTER for April, 1906, with additions.

Historical and Biographical Sketch. One Branch of the Williamson Family, from 1745 to 1906. Prepared and published by Rev. ROBERT DUNCAN WILLIAMSON, 1622 Seventh Avenue, Troy, N. Y. [1906.] 8vo. pp. 71. Portrait.

The branch of the Williamsons here recorded consists of the ancestors and descendants of David Williamson, born in 1786 and reared in York County, Pa. The contents of this sketch are largely biographical and of a specially personal nature. The book is excellently printed, but there is no index.

Ancestry of Bridget Yonge, Daughter of William Yonge of Caynton, Co. Salop, Esq., and Wife of George Willys of Fenny Compton, Co. Warwick, Esq., Governor of the Colony of Connecticut in 1642. n. d.; n. p. 8vo. pp. 25.

The first eight pages of this pamphlet are reprinted from the REGISTER for April, 1899. The remainder is prefaced by a note saying that it comprises "more facts relating to Bridget Yonge's connection with the Combe family of Stratford on Avon, and additional information concerning the Yonges of Kenton, Co. Salop."

Vital Records of Beverly, Massachusetts, to the end of the Year 1849. Volume I. —Births. Published by the Topsfield Historical Society, Topsfield, Mass. 1906. 8vo. Cloth. pp. 400.

Systematic History Fund. Vital Records of Grafton, Massachusetts, to the end of the Year 1849. Worcester, Mass.: Published by Franklin P. Rice, Trustee of the Fund. 1906. 8vo. Cloth. pp. 377.

Systematic History Fund. Vital Records of Phillipston, Massachusetts, to the end of the year 1849. Worcester, Mass.: Published by Franklin P. Rice, Trustee of the Fund. 1906. 8vo. Cloth. pp. 121.

Vital Records of Sturbridge, Massachusetts, to the year 1850. Published by the New England Historic Genealogical Society, at the charge of the Eddy Town-Record Fund. Boston, Mass. 1906. 8vo. Cloth. pp. 393.

Genealogy in the Library. By OTIS G. HAMMOND, of the New Hampshire State Library. Manchester, N. H.: John B. Clark Co. 1906. 12mo. pp. 18.

These lively and humorous pages abound in sensible remarks on the manner in which the librarian should deal with the genealogist, as also on the characteristics of patriotic societies, and will be appreciated by those who are brought into contact with such as the woman he mentions who remarked that "she should not feel a bit proud even if she found out that she was descended from Queen Elizabeth."

Rev. Asa McFarland, D.D., Third Pastor of the First Congregational Church, Concord, New-Hampshire. 1798–1824. A Sketch by Henry McFarland, (his Grandson,) read by Annie A. McFarland, (his Granddaughter,) at the 175th Anniversary of that Church, Nov. 19, 1905. [Concord.] n. d. Large 8vo. pp. 13. Ill.

The story of Dr. McFarland's pastorate of twenty-seven years is here pleasantly told, and leaves the impression of a life marked by goodness, tolerance, and diligence.

American Antiquarian Society. Salisbury Memorial. A Tribute from Yucatan. Worcester, Mass.: The Davis Press, Printers. 1906. 8vo. pp. 22. Portrait.

Mr. Stephen Salisbury was for eighteen years President of the American Antiquarian Society. His interest in Central America, made prominent by his visits to Yucatan, is recalled in the "Tribute" by Senor Olegario Molina and others.

Life of Rev. Jeremiah Shepard, Third Minister of Lynn, 1680–1720. By JOHN J. MANGAN, A.M., M.D. Privately printed. Lynn, Mass., U. S. A. 1905. Large 8vo. pp. 61.

This biography was written to correct the misrepresentations of its subject in Newhall's "Lin, or Jewels of the Third Plantation," which is largely fiction but so interspersed with fact that the reader is unable to distinguish between the two. A worthy task has been performed in setting right so admirable a character as that of Mr. Shepard, who was an associate of the Mathers, the Sewalls and the Saltonstalls, and who was distinguished for his patriotism. His eminence as a preacher is evident from the fact that he was invited to deliver the annual election sermon, May 25, 1715. A list of his works follows the memoir.

Memoir of Benjamin Barstow Torrey. By WILLIAM CARVER BATES. Boston: New-Eng. Hist. Gen. Soc. 1906. Large 8vo. pp. 9.

This is a reprint from the REGISTER for April, 1906.

Governor William Bradford's Letter Book. Reprinted from The Mayflower Descendant. Published by the Massachusetts Society of Mayflower Descendants. Boston, Massachusetts. 1906. 8vo. pp. VI.+62.

The re-publication of this fragment of Governor Bradford's Letter Book. at this time when interest in Pilgrim history is so widespread, is amply justified by the rarity of both editions of the third volume of the first series of the Collections of the Massachusetts Historical Society, in which it was first published in 1794 and reprinted in 1810. Through Prince's Chronology it is known that many of the letters used in Bradford's History of Plymouth Plantation were from this letter book. A list of these, and the few other known letters to and from Governor Bradford, would have added much to the usefulness of this reprint. * * *

Ballintubber Abbey, Co. Mayo: Notes on its History. By MARTIN J. BLAKE. From the Journal of the Galway Archæological Society. Vol. III. (1903–4). No. ii. Large 8vo. pp. 65–88. Ill.

This Irish Monastery was one of the Order of Canons Regular of St. Augustine, and was founded in the year 1216. It is still used as a place of worship.

Boston Town Records. A Volume of Records relating to the Early History of Boston, containing Boston Town Records, 1796 to 1813. Boston: Municipal Printing Office. 1905. 8vo. pp. 377.

This is the thirty-fifth volume in the series formerly called Record Commissioners' Reports, and consists of the ninth book of the original records of the town of Boston, with an index.

Old Dartmouth Sketches. No. 13. Being the Proceedings of the Third Annual Meeting of the Old Dartmouth Historical Society, held at the Rooms of the Society, New Bedford, Mass., on March 30, 1906, and containing, besides the usual reports, a Memoir of Thomas R. Rodman. [New Bedford. 1906.] 8vo. pp. 12.

The Great Swamp Fight in Fairfield. A Paper read at a Meeting of the Colonial Dames. By Hon. JOHN H. PERRY, on Oct. 12, 1905. New York. 1905. 8vo. pp. 12. Ill.

This fine paper consists largely, so far as its narrative portion is concerned, of a letter of Gov. John Winthrop, and is a complete account of the fight that ended the Pequot War, July 13, 1637.

The History of the Town of Lyndeborough, New Hampshire. 1735–1905. By Rev. D. DONOVAN and JACOB A. WOODWARD. Published by the Town,

Andy Holt, J. H. Goodrich, Luther Cram, Rev. D. Donovan, Jacob A. Woodward, History Committee. The Tufts College Press: H. W. Whittemore & Co. 1906. 2 vols. 8vo. pp. xvi+932. Ill. Plan.

There is nothing of interest or importance pertaining to Lyndeborough which has not received due attention in these volumes. The abundant information furnished is arranged under the captions usually found in town histories. "Old Cellar Holes" and "Town Fairs," however, are subjects not so often introduced in works of this kind, and illustrate, together with such literature as the poem on small-pox, the successful manner in which, from beginning to end, the authors have enlivened their undertaking. From the "Summary View" to the "Mortuary Record," the historical portion of the work, including ample biographical sketches, is thoroughly treated. The Genealogies, occupying two hundred and eighty pages, are a most valuable addition to the history. There is an "Index of names, places and subjects." The volumes are well printed and substantially bound.

History of Plymouth, New Hampshire. Volume I., Narrative. Volume II., Genealogies. By EZRA S. STEARNS, A.M., Member of New Hampshire Historical, New England Historic Genealogical and American Antiquarian Societies. Printed for the Town, by the University Press, Cambridge, Mass. 1906. 8vo. pp. 632, 801. Ill.

This history of Plymouth, N. H., was prepared under direction of a Committee of the town, and not the least of their wisdom was the selection of Mr. Stearns as the historian. Mr. Stearns, by an ample knowledge of sources, methodical preparation of chapters, and possessing a sense for detecting vital information, has produced a history of which Plymouth may well be proud. Volume I. treats of the proprietors and settlers, the affairs of state, militia, school and church, and vividly portrays the society of the town to date. The Revolutionary war period is finely and fully treated. Volume II. embraces genealogies, keeping close to the resident families, who were from the older towns, and of the fourth and fifth generations from the Puritan settlers. The genealogical annotation is the form recommended by the REGISTER. The two volumes make above 1400 pages, of which 800 are genealogies.

(Rev.) ANSON TITUS.

Inscriptions from the Long-Society Burying Ground, Preston, Conn. By GEORGE S. PORTER. Boston: Press of David Clapp & Son. 1906. Large 8vo. pp. 6.

This is a reprint from the REGISTER for April, 1906.

Publications of the Sharon Historical Society of Sharon, Massachusetts. No. 3—April, 1906. Boston: Press of H. M. Hight, 76 Summer Street. 1906. 8vo. pp. 32. Ill.

Besides the President's address, this issue contains interesting articles on "Massapoag Pond Bank" and "A Fire-proof Historical Society Building," both with illustrations.

Inaugural Address of Hon. Charles A. Grimmons, Mayor of Somerville, Massachusetts, to the Board of Aldermen, Jan. 1, 1906. [Somerville. 1906.] 8vo. pp. 18.

The Value of Colonial Influence. A Paper prepared and read at a Meeting of the Colonial Dames, by MABEL OSGOOD WRIGHT, *on Oct. 12, 1905.* New York. 1905. 8vo. pp. 28.

Furniture, architecture, manners, religion, literature, and legislation are here represented as sources of "Colonial influence," to which so much importance is ascribed by Miss Wright that she says that "without it the Constitution itself would be but as a sieve of shifting sand."

Senate. 58th Congress, 2d Session. Document No. 77. Les Combattants Français de la Guerre Américaine. 1778–1783. Listes établies d' après les documents authentiques déposés aux Archives Nationales et aux Archives du Ministère de la Guerre. Publiées par les soins du Ministère des Affairs Etrangères. Washington: Imprimerie Nationale. 1905. 4to. pp. 453. Ill.

This work was noticed in the REGISTER for Jan., 1904; but in this re-issue, for the use of the U. S. Senate, it is provided with a complete index which vastly increases its value.

Library of Congress. Journals of the Continental Congress, 1774–1789. Edited from the Original Records in the Library of Congress by WORTHINGTON CHAUNCEY FORD, Chief, Division of Manuscripts. Vol. iv. 1776, Jan. 1–June 4; vol. v. 1776, June 5–Oct. 6. Washington, Government Printing Office. 1906. 2 vols. 4to. pp. 416; 440.

The Two Hundred and Fiftieth Anniversary of the Settlement of the Jews in the United States. 1655–1905. Addresses delivered at Carnegie Hall, New York, on Thanksgiving Day, 1905. Together with other select addresses and proceedings. [New York. 1906.] 8vo. pp. xiii+262.

The special event commemorated in this volume is the grant by the Dutch West India Company, April 26, 1655, to the Jews to establish a settlement in "New Netherland." The celebration attracted the sympathy of Gentile as well as Jew, as is shown by such names among its participants as President Roosevelt, Ex-President Cleveland, Governor Higgins, Bishops Greer and Lawrence, President Eliot, and Lieut.-Governor Guild. These were among the speakers at Carnegie Hall, and at Faneuil Hall, Boston. The "Selected Addresses" were delivered the same day in various other cities. There is an appendix consisting principally of "Selected Editorial Utterances from the Newspaper Press," and correspondence. A frontispiece represents a "Commemoratory Medal" designed by Isidore Konti.

Massachusetts Soldiers and Sailors of the Revolutionary War. A Compilation from the Archives, prepared and published by the Secretary of the Commonwealth in accordance with Chapter 100, Resolves of 1891. Boston: Wright & Potter Printing Co., State Printers, 18 Post Office Square. 1906. 4to. pp. 1008.

The contents of this volume extend from SHA to STH.

Eighteenth Report of the Custody and Condition of the Public Records of Parishes, Towns, and Counties. Public Document No. 52. By ROBERT T. SWAN, Commissioner. Boston: Wright & Potter Printing Co., State Printers, 18 Post Office Square. 1906. 8vo. pp. 36.

Perhaps the most important part of this report is the series of "Don'ts," which has been sent as a circular to every city and town clerk. In the section relating to New Hampshire records, the paper by Mr. A. S. Batchellor, Editor of State Papers, treating of those documents, is quoted in full. The mistake of those who think that there is no further need of State supervision of public records is clearly shown by Mr. Swan in the portion of the report explaining the "Need of the Commission."

State of Rhode Island and Providence Plantations. Report of the Jamestown Ter-Centennial Commission made to the General Assembly at its January Session, 1906. Providence, R. I. E. L. Freeman & Sons, State Printers. 1906. 8vo. pp. 18.

Vital Record of Rhode Island. 1630–1850. First Series. Births, Marriages and Deaths. A Family Register for the People. By JAMES N. ARNOLD. Vol. xv. Providence Gazette—Marriages D to Z. United States Chronicle—A to Z. Published under the auspices of the General Assembly. Providence, R. I.: Narragansett Historical Publishing Company. 1906. 4to. pp. lxxv +577.

Mr. Arnold's expectation that "the reader will find pleasure as well as instruction in the perusal of this volume" will be fully realized, as it has been in its predecessors.

Library of Congress. List of Works on the Tariffs of Foreign Countries. General; Continental Tariff Union; France; Germany; Switzerland; Italy; Russia; Canada. Compiled under the direction of APPLETON PRENTISS CLARK GRIFFIN. Washington: Government Printing Office. 1906. 4to. pp. 42.

Library of Congress. An Introduction to the Records of the Virginia Company of London. With a Bibliographical List of the Extant Documents. By SUSAN

M. KINGSBURY, A.M., Ph.D., Instructor in History, Vassar College. Washington: Government Printing Office. 1905. 4to. pp. 214.

This volume, which is the outcome of research both in this country and abroad, contains a complete history of the Records of the Virginia Company, arranged in the following divisions: "Character of the Virginia Company," "Records of the Company under Sir Thomas Smythe," "Collections of Documents, 1616-1624," "Records of the Company under the Sandys-Southampton Administration," and "The Fate of the Original Records of the Company."

Chicago Historical Society. Charter, Constitution, By-Laws. Membership List. Annual Report. [Chicago.] 1905. 8vo. pp. 299-370. Ill.

Library of Congress Publications. Spring, 1906. [Washington, D. C.] 1906. 12mo. pp. 32.

This is a list of publications that have appeared since the removal of the Library to the new building, in 1897, and of others now in press.

Federal Fire Society of Portsmouth, N. H. Organized March 6, 1789. Published by the Society. 1905. 8vo. pp. 90.

The name "Federal" was chosen as the designation of this society simply for its patriotic associations. This volume contains the "Articles of Agreement, with Fac Simile of Signatures of the Founders," "Biographical Notes," "Observations," and a list of members.

Proceedings of the Twenty-Third Annual Meeting of the Lake Mohonk Conference of Friends of the Indian and Other Dependent Peoples. 1905. Reported by Miss LILIAN D. POWERS. Published by the Lake Mohonk Conference. 1905. 8vo. pp. 228.

Lowell Historical Society. By-Laws. [Lowell. 1906.] 32mo. pp. 15.

Society of Mayflower Descendants in the District of Columbia. Chartered March 22, 1898. Constitution and By-Laws with a List of Officers and Members. Washington, D. C. April 1, 1906. C. F. Sudwarth, Printer. 8vo. pp. 39. Ill.

Proceedings of the Most Worshipful Grand Lodge of Ancient Free and Accepted Masons of the Commonwealth of Massachusetts, in union with the Most Ancient and Honorable Grand Lodges in Europe and America, according to the Old Constitutions. Quarterly Communication: Dec. 13, 1905. Stated Communication: Dec. 27, 1905, being its One Hundred and Seventy-second Anniversary. M. W. JOHN ALBERT BLAKE, *Grand Master. R. W.* SERENO D. NICKERSON, *Recording Grand Secretary. Ordered to be read in all the Lodges.* Boston: The Rockwell and Churchill Press. 1906. 8vo. pp. iv+158-280+civ. Ill.

The Beginnings of the Massachusetts Charitable Mechanic Association. 1795-1808. [By JEROME CARTER HOSMER.] Boston, Mass. 1906. 8vo. pp. 18. Ill.

The initial movement in the formation of the Association was an announcement in the "Columbian Centinel" for Dec. 31, 1794. The establishing of the organization is described in the first of the four articles contained in this volume. The other three are sketches of the first three Presidents of the Association.

Publications of the Genealogical Society of Pennsylvania. Jan. 1906. 1300 Locust. Vol. III. No. 1. Phila.: Printed for the Society by the Wickersham Printing Co., Lancaster, Pa. 4to. pp. 104. Portrait.

The principal articles in this number are "Abstract of Wills at Philadelphia," "Memoranda from the Diary of John Dyer, of Plumstead, Bucks Co., Pa.," and "Some Genealogical Obstacles Considered." Besides these, there are the twelfth and thirteenth annual reports of the board of directors of the Society.

Charter, Constitution and By-Laws of the Descendants of Richard Risley, (Incorporated.) Hartford, Conn. The Deming Printing Co. 1905. 32mo. pp. 8.

DEATHS.

Samuel Adams Drake, long a member of this Society, and the son of one of its chief founders, died of Bright's disease, at his home in Kennebunkport, Me., Dec. 4, 1905. He had nearly reached the age of 72 years, having been born in Boston, Dec. 20, 1833. His father, Samuel Gardner Drake, needs no more than the merest word of passing honor and gratitude from this Society, so well are his fidelity and efficiency in the founding of this organization and in the real science of genealogy, known. His ancestry went back through the founders of Hampton, N. H., to the red hills of Devonshire and the clan which gave the world the renowned navigator, Sir Francis Drake; the English connections were not completely traced out, though the family group was ascertained. But the subject of this sketch depended neither on his remote ancestors nor his celebrated father for the honor of his name. As a young man, he made his way to California, and did his part as a gold-hunter. At a later time, he betook himself to Kansas, and threw his energies into the development of that state. There he was living when the Civil War broke out; and so strongly did he feel the error of Disunion that he became a leader in organizing Union forces. The state of Missouri appointed him a Brigadier-General for this work; and when he had performed that special task, he was commissioned Colonel of a regiment in Kansas, and led his troops to active and heroic service in the strife which waged over Missouri and the border regions.

When he took up the line of authorship he naturally saw events in a broad way, which no man not familiar with war could see; and his writings show remarkable comprehension of the strategic and the ultimate effects of the epochs he described. All the time he was a lover of the beautiful, delighting to paint the quiet homes and attractive resting places of the people no less than the arenas of strife. He lacked none of his father's historic sense, and was fond of the study of antiquity and the biography of notable persons. Withal he dreamed by times, and gave legends and tales with cleverness. Year by year he won friends by his frankness, blended well with rare courtesy in listening and great helpfulness in communicating. Among the members of Melrose and Kennebunkport parishes, of the Roundabout Club, U. S. Grant Post, G. A. R., the Loyal Legion, this Society and other associations, he held a high place for his witty and valuable communications and his companionability.

The summer sojourners of Kennebunk and Kennebunkport, many of them gifted and reputed, loved to linger in his simple library, see his nuggets of book and manuscript, and get in touch with his refreshing, unconventional currents of thought. When occasion called for it, he had a power of timely public speech which made his words memorable. The writer recalls how well he showed, in a local celebration of the centennial of the organization of our government, the wisdom of the Maker of History in raising up the leaders of the Revolution and of the establishment of our republic.

A list of his published writings may be made without order of composition or in exact statement of titles, to close this glimpse of the man and his life:—Old Landmarks of Boston, Around the Hub, Old Boston Taverns, New England Legends, Historic Mansions Around Boston, Our Colonial Homes, History of Middlesex County, Historic Fields and Mansions of Middlesex, Old Landmarks of Middlesex, On Plymouth Rock, Watchfires of '76, Myths and Fables of To-day, Border Wars, Captain Nelson, General Israel Putnam, The White Mountains, Nooks and Corners of the New England Coast, The Taking of Louisburg, Burgoyne's Invasion, Campaign of Trenton, The Making of Virginia and the Middle Colonies, The Making of the Ohio Valley States, The Making of the Great West, The Making of New England, The Battle of Gettysburg, The Young Vigilantes.

At the time of his death, he was engaged on an uncompleted History of the United States which his father had begun. General Drake also wrote many magazine articles of merit. He married, Oct. 5, 1866, Olive Nowell, born Oct. 5, 1837, daughter of David and Esther (Jones) Grant of Kennebunkport, who died Dec. 12, 1885, leaving him two daughters, Louise Isabel, wife of Arthur Harry Woodman of Melrose, and Alice Gardner, a teacher in Melrose Public Schools, who has been the especial delight and companion of his later years. From his home by the sea the body was brought to his former residence, Melrose, and laid in Wyoming Cemetery.

(Rev.) Charles Henry Pope.

Cambridge, Mass.

Stephen Salisbury

NEW ENGLAND
HISTORICAL AND GENEALOGICAL
REGISTER.

OCTOBER, 1906.

STEPHEN SALISBURY, A.M.

By Waldo Lincoln, A.B.

Stephen Salisbury, who was born March 31, 1835, at Worcester, and died there November 16, 1905, was descended from John Salisbury, a "mariner" of Boston, whose name first appears in a tax list for 1689, and who was twice married, first to Annabel, who died September 7, 1694, by whom he had three children: John, born January 5, 1690, died December 15, 1704, and Nicholas and James, twins, born August 20, 1694, both of whom probably died with their mother; second to Bridget Williams, to whom he was published September 25, 1695, and by whom he had two children: Nicholas, born October 28, 1697, and Benjamin, born November 7, 1699; the latter married Deborah Stearns of Watertown, and had a daughter, Deborah, who was buried beside her parents in Granary Burying Ground, Boston, but there is no record of their having other children.

Nicholas Salisbury was a "small merchant" at Boston, but through his children became connected with rising and socially prominent families. He died December 11, 1748, at Boston. His wife was Martha, daughter of Josiah and Rebecca (Elbridge) Saunders of Boston, who was born April 22, 1704, at Boston and died there February 18, 1792. They had seven sons, four of whom died in childhood and one never married. The sixth son, Samuel, was twice married and had four sons, of whom one died in infancy, one died unmarried, and a third, the oldest, Stephen, married twice, having by his first wife, Maria Morgan, one son who recently died in the West without male heirs; and by his second wife, Nancy Gardner, three sons, of whom one died in infancy, one never married, and the third, Stephen, died in 1875, leaving one son now living and married but without children. Samuel's fourth son, Josiah, had one son, the late Edward Elbridge Salisbury of New Haven, who left no children.

The seventh son and youngest child of Nicholas and Martha (Saunders) Salisbury was Stephen, born September 25, 1746, at Boston, died May 11, 1829, at Worcester. He married, January 31, 1797, at the age of fifty-one years, Elizabeth, daughter of Edward and Elizabeth (Harris) Tuckerman of Boston, who was born January 30, 1768, at Boston and died there October 19, 1851. They had three children, of whom but one, Stephen, lived to adolescence. Stephen, Jr., who was born March 8, 1798, at Worcester, and died there August 24, 1884, was three times married: first, November 7, 1833, to Rebekah Scott, daughter of Aaron and Phila (Walker) Dean of Charlestown, N. H., who was born December 21, 1812, and died July 24, 1843; second, June 25, 1850, to Mrs. Nancy (Hoard) Lincoln, widow of Captain George Lincoln of Worcester who was killed, February 23, 1847, at the battle of Buena Vista and was the son of the late Governor Levi Lincoln, she was daughter of Silvius and Nancy Mary (DeVillers) Hoard of Ogdensburg, N. Y., was born October 26, 1820, at Antwerp, N. Y., and died September 4, 1852, at Worcester, having had a daughter by Mr. Lincoln but no child by Mr. Salisbury; third, June 2, 1856, to Mrs. Mary Grosvenor Bangs, widow of Edward Dillingham Bangs of Worcester who died April 21, 1838, and daughter of Moses and Mary (Sykes) Grosvenor, she was born January 14, 1800, at North Wilbraham, and died September 25, 1864, at Worcester, without children. By his first wife, Rebekah Scott Dean, Mr. Salisbury had one child, Stephen, the subject of this memoir, who was, as has been shown, the last but one of the surviving descendants of John Salisbury, the founder of the family so far as it has been traced, to bear the name of Salisbury, and actually the last of the Worcester branch, and, he dying unmarried, this old and honorable New England family, associated for over two hundred years with all that is highest and best in New England life, connected by marriage with many names eminent in colonial and national history, and for one hundred and thirty years representing the aristocracy and wealth of what is now the second city of Massachusetts, has thus become practically extinct.

The first Stephen Salisbury associated himself in business with his eldest brother, Samuel, under the name of S. and S. Salisbury, as merchants in Boston, and came to Worcester in 1767, at the age of twenty-one, to establish a branch of the parent house, while his brother remained in Boston to manage the business there. The business was large and lucrative, and he left to his son, the second Stephen, a fortune which by the natural growth of the town and by wise management and judicious investment made him one of the wealthiest men in Worcester County. He in turn left a large estate to his son, Stephen, who treated it as his father had done, more as a trust for the benefit of his townsmen than for his own gratification. Simple in tastes and unostentations in manner and appearance, not caring for display and unassuming in deportment, both father and son, though born to the purple, if that expression may be applied to American life, present a vivid contrast to the garishness of to-day, when dollars seem to count for more than birth and to displace, in the vulgar mind, the refinements of education and breeding. It is difficult to think of Worcester without a Stephen Salisbury, for although none of those who have borne the name have been prominent in the government of the town, their influence has been felt in every enterprise, and their assistance has been sought and freely given in all worthy charitable and educational undertakings and in many of the varied business ventures of that busy place.

Stephen Salisbury, the third, was left motherless at the age of eight years, and from that time until his father's death, in 1884, his character was moulded more by his father, "whose sole constant companion he was," as he himself says, "for more than thirty years," than by any other influence. He first attended, at the age of six, a private infant school kept by Mrs. Levi Heywood, but was taken by his parents, during the following winter, 1841–2, to Savannah, Ga. Upon his return he was placed in the private school of Mrs. Jonathan Wood, and, in 1844, was sent to Boston to attend Miss Bradford's school for boys, where he remained a year, when he returned to Worcester and entered the public schools, ending with the Worcester High School, from which he entered Harvard College in the class of 1856, and received the degrees of A.B. and A.M. in due course. After graduation he studied for a winter at the Frederick William University in Berlin, and attended lectures at the Ecole de Droit in Paris, and, in the summer of 1857, travelled extensively in Europe, extending his trip to Turkey, Greece and Asia Minor. During the following winter he resumed his studies in Berlin, and, in the spring, in company with his father's family, visited Great Britain. Returning to Worcester in 1858, after an absence of more than two years, he became a student of law in the Harvard Law School, where he received the degree of LL.B. in 1861. In the following winter he visited his classmate David Casares, in Yucatan, and there laid the foundation for his interest in American archæology which persisted during his life. He, later, furnished means for extensive exploration of existing ruins in Central America, and contributed many articles concerning them to the American Antiquarian Society, which he afterwards published in three books on Maya antiquities, namely, in 1877, "The Mayas and the Source of their History," in 1879, "Maya Archæology and Notes on Yucatan," and in 1880, "Maya History and Mexican Copper Tools." In these books he gave the results of his own observations and translations of the reports of the men who, under his encouragement, carried on the exploration.

Returning to Worcester he entered the law office of Dewey and Williams, and was admitted to the Worcester County Bar in October, 1863, but he never actively practiced his profession, which he had studied to prepare himself for the care of the large estate of his father which he was to inherit and through which he was called to many positions of trust and responsibility which fully occupied his time. With the exception of a second visit to Yucatan and Mexico in 1885, and a trip to Europe in 1888, and another in 1890, he passed the remainder of his life in Worcester. After his father's death in 1884 he lived alone, a simple bachelor's life, not given much to entertainment though hospitable and fond of company, especially of that of the young.

Though of strong patriotic feelings he did not serve in the war of the Rebellion, his father requiring his services at home. He was drafted in 1863, but furnished a substitute. In December, 1863, he was elected to the Worcester Common Council, and served for three years, being president of the board in 1866. In 1892 he was elected to the Massachusetts Senate, and was twice re-elected, serving in 1893, '94 and '95. He was chairman of the committees on education, on banks and banking, and on the treasury, and a member of the committee on libraries. He was a member of the sinking fund commission of Worcester, from 1889 until his death, and a trustee of Worcester City Hospital from 1871 to 1889, and secretary of the board for all but one year of that time. Aside from these he held no public offices, declining a nomination for alderman after his service in the Council, and frequently refusing to be nominated for mayor; but he always took an interest in public affairs, and was, by general consent, the most public spirited citizen of Worcester. He was always a republican in politics, and was chief marshal of the republican parade in Worcester in the presidential campaign of 1896. His financial interests occupied much of his time, and he was connected as director or trustee with many corporations of a semi-public nature and served them all faithfully and well. He succeeded his father, in 1884, as president of the Worcester National Bank, which office he held at his death. He became president of the Worcester County Institution for Savings in 1882, and retained that office until 1905, when he was obliged to resign by the law prohibiting one man from serving as president of a national and a savings bank. He succeeded his father as trustee of the Worcester Polytechnic Institute, and became president of the trustees in 1895, and held that office until October, 1905, when he refused a re-election as the condition of his health required a release from some of his active duties. At the same time and for the same reason he resigned as vice-president of the trustees of Clark University, where he had been serving as virtual president since the death of the late Senator Hoar.

He was by no means a brilliant man, being rather slow of thought and hesitating in speech, but he generally said the right thing at the right time and was frequently felicitous in his use of the right words to express his ideas. Though always interested in historical studies he wrote but little; his books on the Mayas, already mentioned, and a memorial volume on his father, which was largely a compilation, being all that he published. He was a member of the Massachusetts Historical Society, the American Antiquarian Society, of which he was president from 1887 until his death, the American Geographical Society, the Archæological Institute of America, the Worcester Society of Antiquity, the Sociedad Mexicana de Geografia y Estadistica, the Conservatorio Yucatano, and the New England Historic Genealogical Society, which last he joined, as a life member, April 3, 1889.

To Mr. Salisbury's public spirit Worcester owes the deepest gratitude. He was liberal and bounteous in his public and private charities, and his support of public institutions was almost unlimited both in the money and time which he gave to them. He gave much to the Worcester Polytechnic Institute, as had his father before him, and presented a large tract of land to the city for a public park upon which he expended much for its development. He laid out with great wisdom the greater portion of his home estate, which with its unoccupied acreage had hitherto been rather a hindrance to the growth of the city in that direction, and succeeded, by liberal gifts of land and money and by his wise and liberal policy of development, in making it, with its group of public and semi-public buildings and pleasant homes, a most attractive residence quarter. His crowning work was the Worcester Art Museum which he was instrumental in having established, to which he contributed lavishly during his life and which, by his munificent bequest at his death, should eventually make Worcester the possessor of one of the finest and most important art collections in the country.

Some have criticised his gifts of land as being but a means to the increase of his own wealth, and, undoubtedly, it did enhance the value of his remaining real estate, but wealth was not what he cared for. His own life was most simple and unobtrusive and his personal wants but few. He had no sympathy for display, no taste for ostentation. He was thoroughly old-fashioned in his ideas, and modern manners and methods made him, in late life, rather pessimistic. His whole life was a protest against the present vulgarity of riches. His sense of duty was extreme and governed all his actions, so much so that he often sacrificed his comfort to it, and his generosity was but the expression of this sense of duty, of the feeling that his wealth was a public trust which he should administer for the public good.

UDALL FAMILY RECORD.

Communicated by JOHN DENISON CHAMPLIN, Esq., of New York City.

THE following record of two generations of the Udall family is from an account book of Dr. Lionel Udall, a practising physician at Stonington, Conn., in the first half of the eighteenth century. Dr. Udall, who is ignored by Wheeler in his history of the town, was a man of considerable prominence, and appears to have had a large practice in eastern Connecticut and throughout Rhode Island, extending from New London to Newport. He is said to have been born in England about 1690, to have come early to this country, and to have married in Stonington, where all his children were born, and where he died in 1767. The accounts in his book range from 1750 to 1767. Besides medical charges and credits on the opposite page to patients, the volume contains a few private memoranda and the genealogical record. The first half of the latter is in the handwriting of Dr. Lionel Udall himself, the last in that of his grandson James, born Sept. 19, 1779, son of Samuel Udall.

Anna Udall was Born ye 17th of July 1728
Abigail Udall was Born ye 28th of January 1729/30
Mary Udall was Born ye 5th of March 1731/2
Lionel Udall was Born ye 19th of Feb^{r} 1733/4
Dorothy Udall was Born ye 17 of Octob^{r} 1736
Samuel Udall was Born ye 17th of April 1739
William Udall was Born ye 13th of May 1741
Mary Udall was Born ye 25th of Octob^{r} 1743
Oliver Udall was Born ye 19th of March 1745/6
John Udall was Born ye 10th of Feb^{r} 1748/9
Hester Udall was Born ye 2nd of Novemb^{r} 1751

Copy of Samuel Udall's Family Record.

Samuel Udall was Born April 17th 1739
Lydia Chapman was Born Feby 16th 1744
Samuel Udall & Lydia Chapman was Married November 14th 1765
Lydia Udall was Born January 26th 1767
Abigail Udall was Born September 11th 1769
Samuel Udall was Born September 20th 1771
Fawnia Udall was Born May 2nd 1774
Sally Udall was Born May 6th 1777
James Udall was Born September 19th 1779
Marcy Udall was Born July 15th 1781

In the records of the First Congregational Church at Stonington is the following:

Nov. 17, 1734, Mr. Lionel Udall and his wife Abigail owned the covenant, and subjected themselves to ye discipline of the church, and the same day their children Anne, Abigail and Lionel, baptized.

The baptisms also of Samuel, William, the second Mary, and John are recorded.

The entire family removed about 1772 to Vermont, where many of the name have occupied prominent positions.

A CONNECTICUT REVOLUTIONARY ROLL.

Communicated by HENRY AUSTIN CLARK, Esq., of New York City.

THE following list of Connecticut men in the Revolution, with time of service, is taken from a "Pay Abftract of a Detachment from Col° Bardsley's Reg^{t} commanded by Capt Joseph Stebbins for the term of One Month as a Guard for Stamford Begining 24th Octr. 81 with Nov. 26th 81," now in the possession of the contributor. The list is not included in the published Record of Connecticut Men in the War of the Revolution.

Mens Names.	Commencement of Pay.	Time of Discharge.	In service months.	days.
Joseph Stebbins, Capt.	Oc^{t}. 24th	Novr 26	1	2
Jeremiah Patchin Lieu^{t}.	D°	D°	1	2
Theophilus Benedict Ens^{n}	D°	D°	1	2
Eli Taylor Serg^{t}	D°	D°	1	2
Nathan Hoyt D°	Oc^{t}. 28th	N^{r}. 4th		27
Daniel Phelps D°	D° 30th	D° 26		27
Joseph Thomas Corp	D° 27th	D°		29
James Platt D°	D° 29th	D° 25th		27
John Sherwood D°	Novr. 4th	D°		21
Aaron Chamberlin Pro^{t}.	Oc^{t}. 24th	D° 26	1	2
Edon Stevens	D° 25th	D°	1	1
Joseph Northrup	D° 26th	D°	1	
Joseph Stebbins	D° 24th	D° 25	1	1
Ezra Brunson	D° 29th	D°		27
Joshua Olmsted	D° 28th	D°		28
James Allen	D° 29th	D°		27
Stephen Bennitt	D°	D°		27
Francis Broughton	D°	D°		27
Gamaliel Smith	D°	D°		27
James Gutter	Novr. 1st	D° 26		26
Seth Gorham	D°	D°		26
Hugh Osborn	D° 2nd	D° 25		24
Abel Lampshire	D°	D°		24
John Leach	D°	D°		24
Abel Pullin[g]	D° 4th	D°		22
Matthew Lindsley	D° 5th	D° 26		21
Nathaniel Eastman	D° 8th	D° 25		17
Ethiel Bebee	D° 10th	D°		15
David Sturgis	D° 16th	D°		9
Zechariah Clerk	Oc^{t}. 18th	D°		28

ROBERT SHELLEY, OR SHELLY, OF SCITUATE AND BARNSTABLE, MASS., AND HIS DESCENDANTS.

Compiled by Hon. RALPH D. SMYTH and communicated by Dr. BERNARD C. STEINER.

1. ROBERT[1] SHELLY emigrated from England to Boston, coming in the *Lion* in 1632. He soon removed to Scituate, where he married Judith Garnett of Boston, on Sept. 26, 1636, and joined the church May 14, 1637 (see *ante*, vol. 14, page 300). He later removed to Barnstable, Mass.

Children:

i. HANNAH,[2] bapt. July 2, 1637; m. Mch. 9, 1662, David Linnell.
ii. MARY, bapt. Nov. 2, 1639; m. (1) Jan. 25, 1665-6, William Harlow; m. (2) Ephraim Morton.
2. iii. ROBERT.
iv. JOHN, bapt. July 31, 1642.

2. ROBERT[2] SHELLY (*Robert*[1]), of Barnstable, Mass., married ———.

Children:

i. JOSEPH,[3] b. Jan. 24, 1668-9.
3. ii. SHUBAL, b. Apr. 25, 1674; d. Apr., 1727.
4. iii. BENJAMIN, b. Mch. 12, 1679.
iv. TIMOTHY, d. at Branford, Conn., Sept. 27, 1738.

3. SHUBAL[3] SHELLY (*Robert*,[2] *Robert*[1]) married, Feb. 17, 1704, Mary Evarts, and removed to Guilford, Conn. She died Apr., 1738. His list in 1716 was £22.

Children:

5. i. EBENEZER,[4] b. Jan. 12, 1705; d. May 9, 1797.
6. ii. ROBERT, b. Nov. 18, 1706; d. Jan. 11, 1788.
7. iii. JOHN, b. Feb. 4, 1710; d. Oct. 21, 1751.
8. iv. SAMUEL, b. Dec. 10, 1712; d. May, 1746.
9. v. REUBEN, b. July 13, 1720; d. Sept. 15, 1794.

4. BENJAMIN[3] SHELLY (*Robert*,[2] *Robert*[1]), of Barnstable, Mass., married, Aug. 8, 1705, Alice, daughter of Ebenezer Goodspeed of Barnstable.

Children:

i. JOSEPH,[4] b. July 29, 1706.
ii. THANKFUL, b. Dec., 1707.
iii. LYDIA, b. May 8, 1713.

5. EBENEZER[4] SHELLY (*Shubal*,[3] *Robert*,[2] *Robert*[1]), of Guilford, Conn., married first, Aug. 5, 1730, Comfort Everest, who died Sept. 26, 1743.; and married second, May 8, 1746, Esther, daughter of Benajah Stone, Jr., and widow of Isaac Hill, who died Mch. 11, 1797.

Children by first wife:

i. CHLOE,[5] b. Mch. 24, 1732; m. Oct. 9, 1750, John Johnson of North Branford, who d. Nov. 8, 1796.
ii. ZERVIA, b. Mch. 23, 1736.
10. iii. TIMOTHY, d. Sept. 11, 1810.

Child by second wife:

iv. EBENEZER, b. Apr. 13, 1747; m. May 20, 1766, Sarah Pierson, and was living in Stratford in that year.

6. ROBERT[4] SHELLY (*Shubal*,[3] *Robert*,[2] *Robert*[1]), of Guilford, Conn., married, in 1736, Sarah, daughter of Daniel Bartlett. She died Feb. 14, 1790.

Children:

i. SARAH,[6] b. July 23, 1738; d. Feb., 1823; m. Mch. 6, 1776, Thelus Ward, who d. Apr. 24, 1804.
ii. PHINEHAS, b. June 29, 1748; d. at sea, Nov. 19, 1769.
iii. BEATA, b. Oct. 27, 1754; d. Aug. 26, 1756.

7. JOHN[4] SHELLY (*Shubal,*[3] *Robert,*[2] *Robert*[1]), of Guilford and North Bristol (now North Madison, Conn.), married, Jan. 16, 1731, Jerusha, daughter of Joshua Leete. She died July 8, 1763.

Children:

11. i. SHUBAEL,[5] b. 1732; d. Sept. 30, 1819.
ii. MARY, b. Dec. 31, 1734; d. Nov. 16, 1764; m. Oct. 22, 1761, Eber Hall of Guilford, who d. Jan. 10, 1782.
iii. LUCY, b. 1735; d. unmarried, Dec. 14, 1813.
iv. SAMUEL, b. 1737.
12. v. JOHN, b. 1744; d. May 14, 1804.

8. SAMUEL[4] SHELLY (*Shubal,*[3] *Robert,*[2] *Robert*[1]), of Guilford, Conn., married, Oct. 19, 1737, at Branford, Sarah Hitt of that town.

Children:

i. ZILLAH,[5] b. Oct. 25, 1739; m. Nov. 26, 1759, David Whedon of Branford.
ii. SAMUEL, b. July 25, 1742, removed to Goshen, Conn.
iii. TIMOTHY, b. Oct. 3, 1746; d. Sept. 27, 1748.

9. REUBEN[4] SHELLY (*Shubal,*[3] *Robert,*[2] *Robert*[1]) married, Mch. 24, 1752, Submit Johnson.

Children:

13. i. REUBEN,[5] b. Dec. 30, 1752; d. Feb. 4, 1800.
ii. BEULAH, b. Oct. 27, 1754.
iii. MEDAD, b. Apr. 2, 1759; m. (1) Jan. 22, 1789, Mary Griffing; m. (2) Feb. 27, 1791, Abigail Wakely of Durham.

10. TIMOTHY[5] SHELLY (*Ebenezer,*[4] *Shubal,*[3] *Robert,*[2] *Robert*[1]), of Guilford, married first, Oct. 28, 1761, Amy Bristol, who died Aug. 1, 1800; and married second, Feb. 21, 1808, Mindwell Stone, who died Dec. 28, 1830.

Children, all by first wife:

i. EDMUND,[6] b. Oct. 28, 1762; d. July 3, 1814; m. Zerviah Stone, who d. Nov. 21, 1828. Children: 1. *William,*[7] d. Nov. 10, 1815; m. Julia, dau. of Noadiah Norton, who was b. Feb. 15, 1779, and d. at New Haven, Mch. 18, 1861. 2. *Edmund*, b. Apr. 23, 1785; lived at Durham; d. Apr. 2, 1844; m. May 12, 1809, Mary, dau. of Capt. Jabez Chalker, who d. Apr. 7, 1857. 3. *Joy*, b. 1794; d. Mch. 13, 1852; lived in New Haven; m. Oct. 3, 1816, Margaret, dau. of Nathan Redfield, who d. Dec. 11, 1836. 4. *Russell*, b. 1791; d. of consumption, May 7, 1812. 5. *Ruth*, m. (1) Aug. 18, 1808, Seth Hubbard of Middletown; m. (2) ——— Seymour. 6. *Curtiss*, b. Aug. 23, 1795; d. Feb. 22, 1857; m. Martha, dau. of Asa Dowd, who d. Nov. 23, 1858. 7. *Orrin*, d. 1850; m. Elizabeth Palmer who was b. in England.
ii. ANNA, b. Feb. 29, 1764; m. John Hall.
iii. JOEL, b. Mch. 23, 1768; lived in Guilford; d. Aug. 3, 1833; m. Ruth Ramsay, who d. Nov. 20, 1845. Children: 1. *Joel Ward,*[7] b. 1790; d. Apr. 12, 1850; m. Eliza Lee of New London, who d. Apr. 5, 1850. 2. *Harvey O.*, b. 1795; lived in Guilford; d. Dec. 29, 1855; m. Oct. 23, 1834, Lois, dau. of Solomon Dowd; had no children. 3. *Harry*, d. Apr. 6, 1853; m. Roxana Johnson, who was b. Aug. 9, 1798. 4. *Anne*, b. Mar. 30, 1799; m. (1) William Richards; m. (2) May 15, 1828, Lyman Hotchkiss of North Guilford. 5. *Frederic*, b. 1803; d. unmarried, Nov. 22, 1831. 6. *Ruth*,

b. 1807; d. Nov. 28, 1831; m. June 24, 1828, William Truxton Stone, who d. Nov. 22, 1831. 7. *Joel*, lived in Guilford; d. Nov. 21, 1831; m. Apr. 25, 1825, Charlotte, dau. of Henry Griffing. After his death, she m. —— Bryan of New Haven. 8. *Lucinda*, m. Philander Cathcart. 9. *William*, b. Feb., 1815; lived in Guilford; d. Apr. 10, 1853; m. Sarah Ann Palmer, who d. in 1847.

iv. WILLIAM, b. 1780; d. Nov. 11, 1815.

v. POLLY, b. 1782; d. Mch. 24, 1836; m. Gideon P. Bassett of Guilford, who d. June 3, 1852.

vi. CLARISSA, b. 1784; m. Oct. 17, 1804, Zephaniah Buell.

vii. SARAH, b. 1786; m. Joel P. Hotchkiss.

11. SHUBAEL[5] SHELLY (*John,[4] Shubal,[3] Robert,[2] Robert[1]*), of Guilford, married, Jan. 31, 1764, widow Abigail Rice of Wallingford, who died June 13, 1819.

Children:

i. JERUSHA,[6] b. Aug. 1, 1765.

ii. SHUBAEL, b. Aug. 26, 1766; d. Nov. 13, 1766.

iii. MARY, b. Apr. 18, 1768; m. Samuel Bently of Stockbridge, Mass.

iv. ASA, b. May 20, 1769; m. Betsey Fox; lived in Genessee, N. Y.

v. ESTHER, b. July 3, 1770; m. Thomas Walstone.

vi. LUCY, b. Aug. 12, 1771; m. —— Shaner of Lansingburgh, N. Y.

vii. PHINEHAS, b. Mch. 11, 1773; lived in Guilford; d. Mch. 24, 1847; m. Dec. 14, 1798, Hannah, dau. of Charles Collins, who d. Dec. 20, 1861. Children: 1. *John Collins,[7]* b. Mch. 11, 1801; d. unmarried, April 1, 1869. 2. *Cynthia*, b. Jan. 15, 1803; m. Oct. 20, 1822, Guernsey Camp of Durham. 3. *Huldah*, b. Jan. 9, 1805: m. July 3, 1836, David Tibbals of Durham. 4. *Eveline*, b. Nov. 3, 1806. 5. *Peggy*, b. Aug. 15, 1809. 6. *Eli*, b. July 16, 1812. 7. *Samuel*, b. Mch. 16, 1816.

viii. SALMON, b. May 31, 1774; lived in Guilford; d. Oct. 27, 1849; m. Chloe Alcock of Wolcott, who d. June 3, 1818, aged 37. Children: 1. *Seymour,[7]* b. June 28, 1808; d. Nov. 8, 1810. 2. *Irwin*, b. June 8, 1811; lived in New Haven. 3. *George*, b. June 17, 1817; d. Mch., 1818.

ix. HAYNES, b. 1776; d. Aug. 12, 1795.

12. JOHN[5] SHELLY (*John,[4] Shubal,[3] Robert,[2] Robert[1]*), of Guilford, married, Nov. 30, 1768, Elizabeth Stone, who died Oct. 18, 1831, aged 82.

Children:

i. ANNE,[6] b. Aug. 2, 1769; d. July 16, 1801; m. Apr. 18, 1798, Amos Dudley of Guilford, who d. Sept. 13, 1843.

ii. ELIZABETH, b. Dec. 7, 1771; d. Oct. 19, 1772.

iii. ELIZABETH, b. Oct. 7, 1773; d. Feb. 21, 1798; m. 1792, Pierson Evarts, who d. Mch. 21, 1822.

iv. THOMAS, b. Mch. 31, 1777; lived in Guilford; d. Mch. 11, 1848; m. Feb. 5, 1797, Irene Meigs. Children: 1. *Julius,[7]* b. Aug. 31, 1798; lived in Madison; m. Sept. 10, 1820, Eliza Maria, dau. of Nathan Bradley, of Hammonassett, who d. June 26, 1858. 2. *Sylvanus*, b. Apr. 8, 1800; lived in Madison; m. June 21, 1824, Harriet, dau. of John Loveland, who was b. Aug. 1, 1805. 3. *William*, b. July 7, 1801; lived in Madison; m. June 2, 1824, Sarah Isbell. 4. *Chauncey*, b. Jan. 10, 1806; lived in Madison, Ohio; m. Alpha, widow of Abraham Foster. 5. *Elizabeth Ann*, b. Jan. 10, 1811; m. Marvin Foster. 6. *Rhoda*, b. Aug. 25, 1812; m. Alanson Foster. 7. *Rachel*, b. Apr. 26, 1815; m. John Kellogg of Madison, Ohio. 8. *Betsey*, b. Aug. 7, 1817; m. Gilson Leach. 9. *Charlotte*, b. Sept., 1821; m. Horace Foster of Madison, Ohio.

13. REUBEN[5] SHELLY (*Reuben,[4] Shubal,[3] Robert,[2] Robert[1]*), of Guilford, married, Mch. 8, 1785, Tabitha Saxton, who died Dec. 18, 1824,

aged 67. After his death, she married second, Samuel Dudley of Guilford, who died Dec. 17, 1819.

Children :

i. SHERMAN,[6] b. June 18, 1785; m. Temperance Bassett. Children: 1. *Eliza.* 2. *Julia.* 3. *Susan.* 4. *Ralph.* 5. *Sherman.*
ii. HARVEY, b. Nov. 25, 1788.
iii. MANSFIELD, b. Nov. 24, 1797.
iv. AMANDA, b. Nov. 24, 1797; m. Mch., 1817, Joel Alvah Lee.

RECORDS OF THE SECOND CHURCH OF SCITUATE, NOW THE FIRST UNITARIAN CHURCH OF NORWELL, MASS.

Communicated by WILFORD JACOB LITCHFIELD, M.S., of Southbridge, Mass.

[Continued from page 274.]

[The following records, on four loose sheets badly worn and broken, were found in Norwell since the appearance of the instalment on pages 271–274, *ante*, and belong to the pastorate of Rev. David Barnes.]

(Sheet No. 1, one side)

A Liſt of thoſe who Joined to the C^{hh} in 1786

July 21	1786	Elijah Whitman was received to Communion with the Church
July 6	1788	Charles Turner Junr.
Augst 3	1788	Eunice The Wife of Nath^{ll} Jordan
Octo^{br} 5	1788	Hannah Otis Daughter of Dr Otis
Octob^{r} 4	1789	Joſhua Clapp was admitted
May 2	1790	Nath^{ll} Winſlow and wife were admitted
Augst 7	1791	Hannah Turner wife to Charles Turner Eſq^{r}
Sep^{t} 4	1791	Thos Jenkins and wife were admitted to Communion
Nov^{br} 6	1791	Abiel Turner Junr
July 1	1792	Betſy Otis was admitted
Sept 2	1792	Foſter Waterman W^{r} And the widdow Sarah Neal
Sept 1	1793	The Wife of Luther Barrell belonging to The firſt Chh in Hingham beng diſmiſsed from y^{t} C^{hh} and recommended was received into this C^{hh}
		Elijah Whitman was diſmiſsed and recommended to ye firſt C^{hh} in Pembroke
June 1	1794	Polly Turner Daughter to Hon^{bl} Charles Turner was admitted to full communion
Sep^{t} 28		Mrs Hannah Stone wife to the Revd Mr Stone of Yarmouth
June 7	1795	Bethiah Winſlow of Scituate was admitted
July 5		Hannah Tolman
Auguſt: 2		John Briggs
Octob^{r} 4		The Wife of John Foſter Junr
Nov^{br} 5;	1797	Nath^{ll} Winſlow Junr and Wife
May 6	1798	Eben^{r} Copeland & Wife
		Hannah Copeland

June 3 — Sally Southworth wife to Thos Southworth
Cloe Sylveſter
July 1: — Joſhua Bryant and wife
Nabby Cuſhing Daughter to Nathaniel Cuſhing
Ruth Cuſhing wife to Pickles Cuſhing
Sally Turner
Lucy Sylveſter

(Sheet No. 1, other side.)

Augt 5 1798 — Joſhua Jacobs Junr And Wife
James Sparrel and wife
Deborah Waterman Junr was baptized and rec^{d} into ye C^{hh}
Bathſheba Houſe was alſo admitted
Nov^{br} 4 — Deborah Waterman
July 1799 — Polly Simons was admitted to communion
Octo^{br} 5 1800 — Samuel Waterman was admitted to communion
May 3 1801 — John Foſter admitted to communion
Sept. 6 — Thos Cuſhing & Wife
Octob^{r} 4 — William Barrel
Sept 4 1803 — John Hatch and his wife
Nov^{br} 11 — The Wife of Deacon John Ruggles
May 12 1805 — Ruth, the wife of Deacon Eliſh James
Mary The Wife John Foſter Senr
Ruſha Tower, D to Mathew Tower
Bathſheba Jones
June 2 — Baſhua Tower wife to Mathew Tower
May 4 1806 — John Jones was received into Communion
July 6 1806 — James Curtiſs Junr & Wife
The Widdow Prudence Turner
Emelia Sprague, Cynthia Nicols
July 27 — At a meeting of the Church regularly Notified The C^{hh} made choice of Thos Cuſhing for a Deacon. He accepted ye Office
May 10 1807 — Nabby Foſter wife to Capt Seth Foſter
Eunice Torry Daug^{ter} to James Torry
June 7 — James Barril
Sept 6 — Hitte Curtice wife To Sam^{ll} Curtice was received into the C^{hh} tho' not preſent She being confined by sickneſs
The same day Hitte Curtice Junr and Sophia Curtice Daughters of Sam^{ll} Curtice w^{r} Admitted to communion

(Sheet No. 2, one side.)

Deaths for the Year 1786.

Jany 1786 — Abraham a Negro Aged about 70 of Old age The Palſy and the relicks of the Omerial Diſeaſe
Jany 29 1786 — The Widdow Anna Soper aged about 60, of a Motification
March 28 1786 — Paul Curtice, Etat: 19: Suddenly by the overſetting of a loaded Carte
May 2 — —— Elms aged 9, of a Nervous Fever in the begin[n]ing which ended in a Conſumption
May 10 — Jemima Hatch aged 70 of a Dropſie

May 30	An infant belonging to Elijah Turner & wife w^{h} lived a few momints
June 8	Capt Benj^{a} Randall aged 62 of a Mortification as was ſupposed in his Bowells
June 27	An infant belonging to Eliſha Young and wife Aged about 3 Months of Convulſion fits
July 17	The wife of Joſhua Clapp Aged [*blank*] of a Conſumption
[*torn*]ugst 9	The Widdow Stockbridge Aged 78 of a Complication of diſorders
[*torn*]tob^{r}	The Widdow Perry aged 61 of a complication of diſorders
[*torn*]cem^{br} 15	Eliſha Foſter's Daughter aged 4^{rs} of a Diſsentery
[*torn*]n^{y} 2	Dr Ephraim Otis's Son aged 3 ^{yrs} of a Quinſy
[*worn*]an^{y} 13	John Stetson aged 92 of old age
Feby 19	Mercy Turner Widdow aged 83 of old age
March	A Child of Nath^{ll} Brooks Junr aged 18 month of a Conſumption
March	Mercy Clapp Aged [*blank*] of a billious Cholick
April	The widdow Hannah Hatch aged 78 of old age
Augst 31	Hannah Collmore wife to Benj^{a} Collmore aged 64, of a billious Diſorder
Octo^{br} 17	A Child of Calvin Daman and Wife aged 7 months of the Canker
Octo^{br} 18	Lazarus Bowkers Junr wife aged 41 of a Canker Fever
Octo^{br} 23	An Infant of Nath Jordan and Wife 14 Day old Diſorder Unknown
Decmb^{r} 16	Hannah Vinal aged 84 of old age
[*worn*]an^{y} 7 1788	—— Cole Wife to James Cole aged 68 of a billious diſorder
[*worn*]eb^{y}/5	A Daughter of Dea^{n} James aged 6^{yrs} of a billious diſorder & [*worn*]
[*torn*]^{y} 6	—— Stoddard wife to Benj^{a} Stoddard aged 72 of a [*worn*]
[*torn*]	a child of Thos Church Junr aged half an hour [*worn*]
[*torn*]	Jacob Vinal aged 88 of old age [*worn*]
[*torn*]	[B]arrell Daughter to James Barrell aged 26 of a [*worn*] of [*worn*]

(Sheet No. 2, other side.)

Feby 7 1794	Revd Nathan Stone of Yarmouth & Miſs Hannah Clapp, Scituate
March 6	Joſhua Herſy Junr of Hingham & Lucy Jacobs, Scituate
	Nathan Hunt of Quincy & Polly Turner of Scituate
May 18	Lazarus Bowker and Sarah Turner both of Scituate
July 6	Bartlett Barrell & Relief Naſh both of Scituate
July 9	Thomas Ford of Duxborough & Hannah Church of Scituate
Sep^{t} 1	Sam^{ll} Lewis of Falmouth and Nabby Turner Tolman, Scituate
Nov^{br} 26	Edmond Whitemore & Jane Cortherill both of Scituate
Jany 1 1795	John Turner and Cloa Clapp both of Scituate
March 22	Abijah Otis & Mary Turner both of Scituate
May 28	Fruitfull Sylveſter & Patty Clapp Negroes both of Scituate
June 7	David Whitcomb [in pencil] of Cohaſset and Prudence Dorithy of Scituate

June 18 Charles Lapham & Temperance Clapp both of Scituate
Augst 4 David Prouty and Lydia Stoddard both of Scituate [*worn*]
Sept 30 1795 Paul Otis and Lucy Bailey both of Scituate
Octobr 4 1795 John Cudworth Junr & Patty Litchfield both of Scit[*worn*]
Novbr 29 Thomas Cuſhing and Ruth Turner both of Scituate
Charles Whiting Cuſhing of Hingham & Deborah Jacobs of Scituate
December 2 1795 Elijah Randal and Ruth Woodward both of Scituate
January 1 1796 Nathll Stevens of Marſhfield and Lydia Church of Scituate
March 27 Conſider Howland of Marſhfield and Ruth Church of Scituate
Octo:br 26 Cato Negro man of scituate & Joanna Negro woman reſident in Scituate
[*worn*]br 13 Willam Cuſhing of Pembroke & Ruth Briggs of Scituate
[*worn*] Nathll Tnrner and Rachell Turner both of Scitua[*worn*]
[*worn*] Ebenezer Copeland & Sarah Waterman both of Scituate
[*worn*]is Whiting of Hingham & Abigail Bowker of Scituate
[*worn*] Naſh and Debby Cuſhing both of Scituate
[*worn*] Keen of Marſhfield & Suſannah Church of Scit[*worn*]

(Sheet No. 3, one side.)

Decemher 20 1787 Mr Jonathan Cuſhing of Hingham & Miſs Sarah Simmons [*worn*] Scituate.
March [*worn*] (20?) 1788 Perez Jacobs of Hanover & Relief Bowker Scituate
March 25 Elijah Bowker & Anna Sylveſter both of Scituate
April 17 Bela Mann of Hanover & Anne Bryant of Scituate
May 24 Wilm Jackſon of Plymouth & Nancy Barnes of Scituate
June 8 John James and Patience Clapp both of Scituate
Dcemb 25 Samuel Sprague and Lydia Mayhew, ditto
April 9 1789 Capt James Shaw of Abington and the Widdow Mary Turner of Scituate
April 9 Samll McChane of briſtol in the County of Lincoln & Phebe Cudworth in ye County of plymouth
April 30 Stephen Bowker and Lucy Cuſhing both of Scituate [*torn*]
June 12 Benja Hayden of Scituate & Ruth Lincoln of Cohaſset
Sept 21 Charles Turner Jur Eſquire & Hannah Jacobs both of Sci[*worn*]
Octobr 14. Eliſh Groſs and Deborah Sylveſter both of Scitu[*worn*]
Novbr 19 Mr Joſiah Cotton of Plymouth Clerk of the Court, To Rachell Barnes of Scituate
Novbr 26 Thos Waterman and Sally Winſlow b[*worn*] of Scituate
Decembr 17. Calvin Damon and Mercy Eelles both of Scituate
March 11 1790 Mical Clapp and Eunice Sylveſter bot[*worn*] of Scituate
[Dates of the following are worn off]
Samll Griffin of Fitswilliam and Hannah Bowker of Scitua[*worn*]
Joſeph Cuſhing and Deſire Bowker of Scitu[*worn*]
Elijah Lewis of Hingham & Sarah Stockbridge of Scit[*worn*]
[*worn*]l Tylden of Marſhfield and Peggy Foſter of Scit[*worn*]
[*worn*] Turner Lane and Lucy Stetson both of Scituate
[*worn*] Daman of Scituate to Hannah Dam[*worn*]

(Sheet No. 3, other side.)

[*worn*]an^y 27 1791 Benjamin Brooker [or Brookes] of Roxbury and Harriot Grandifon of Scituate
April 27 James Ewell of Marfhfield & Elifabeth Crague of Scituate
May 22 Gad Levet of Pembroke and Huldah Perry of Scituate
June 2 (?) 1791 Bille Corlew And Sarah Bourn both of Scituate
June 30 1791 Benjamin Bowker Junr and Cloa Stetson both of Scituate
Octob^r 2 (?) Elifha Briggs and Abigail Fofter both of Scituate.
Octob^r 13 Elijah Sylvefter of Hanover & Elifabeth Briggs of Scituate
Nov^br 17 Paul Otis & Penelopie Nichols both of Scituate
John Cafwell & Chriftiana Perry of Hanover.
Nov^vr 24 Jefse Curtis of Hanover & the widdow Lucy Morton of Scituate
Nov^br 21 Abner Crooker of Marfhfield & Deborah Stutson, Scituate
[*torn*] Decem^br 22 Thatcher Tilden of Marf[h]field & Lucy Turner of Scituate
Decem^br 25 Amos Litchfield and Afenath Stockbridge both of Scituate
[*torn*]an^y 1 1792. Jofeph Gannett & Ruth Gannett both of Scituate
Jany 19 1792 Pickles Cufhing & Ruth Cufhing both of Scituate
Feby 5 1792 Jofeph Battles and Sarah Turner both of Scituate.
March 9 1792 Nath^ll Eelles & Elifabeth Randall both of Scituate

Carried to the Town Clerk.

April 3. 1792 Sam^ll Fofter of Kingfton and Mary Otis, Scituate
June 10 Caleb Torry & Sufannah Litchfield both of Scituate
June 17 : 1792 Capt: Willm Church and the Widdow Jael Henderfon both of Scituate
[*torn*]g^st 12 Ward Jackfon & Lucy Nafh both of Scituate
Octo^br 22 Pollicarpus Jacobs & Lydia Clapp both of Bofton
Octo^br 25 Thos Carlow of Springfield & Abigail Carlow of Scituate
Octo^br 28 Elifha Turner & Lydia Briggs both of Scituate
Nov^br 4 Hawke Cufhing and Abigail Clapp both of [*torn*]
[*worn*]^br 8 Seth Stoddard and Martha Stockbridge both of [*worn*]
[*worn*]^br 24 James Wright and Lucy Brown both of Scituate
[*worn*] 1793 Isaac Thomas of Marfhfield, & Temperance Turn[*worn*]
Simion Litchfield and Lucy Hatch Both of Sci[*worn*]
[*worn*] 13 Henry Joflyn of Pembroke and Lou[*worn*]
[*worn*] Micah Lapham and Sarah Cufhin[*worn*]
[*worn*] Zacheus Lambart & Zipporah Cu[*worn*]
[*worn*] Samuel Donnely (?) [*the rest indistinct*]

(Sheet No. 4, written only on one side.)

[No year date appears]
[*worn*]arch 10 Sarah Fofter wife of John Fofter aged 46 of a Confumption
Afhur Spragues wife Aged 43 Diforder unknown
June 1 Nath^ll Eells wife aged 39 of a putrid fever
A Child of Willm Studly and Wife aged one Yea[r] of a Confumption
July The widow Damon aged 52 of a Languifhment
July The wife of Hawke Cufhing aged 41 of a Confumption

Octob 1	The Widdow Standley Aged 83 of old age
Octob^r 30	The Wife of James Colman aged 49 of a Dropſy

[The following records are a continuation of those appearing on pages 271–274, *ante*.]

Jany 5 1800	Elizabeth D to Sam^ll Tolman and wife in private
July 13	Mary D to Joſhua Jacobs Ju^r & wife
Sept 14	Eliza D to John Ewell and wife
14	Sarah Cuſhing D to Sam^ll Waterman and Wife
21	Margaret D to Willm Gallow and Wife in private
Octob^r 26	Caroline D to Thomas Cuſhing & wife
	Lydia D to Micah Lapham and Wife
	Hannah Cuſhing D to Perez Turner & Wife
Nov^br 2	Charlotte Appleton D to Sam^ll Kent and Wife
	Hannah wife to Sam^ll Kent at ye same time
	John Son to Nath^ll Cuſhing and Wife
Decm^r	Mary D to Pickles Cuſhing Junr & wife in private

[To be continued.]

ANDREW BENTON OF MILFORD AND HARTFORD, CONN., AND HIS DESCENDANTS.

By JOHN H. BENTON, Esq., of Washington, D. C.

[Concluded from page 305.]

12. JONATHAN[5] BENTON (*Samuel*,[4] *Samuel*,[3] *Andrew*,[2] *John*[1]) lived and died in Tolland, Conn., where he married, Apr. 26, 1730, Martha Skinner.

Children:

- i. MEDAD,[6] b. Mar. 19, 1733.
- ii. GIDEON, b. Apr. 19, 1735; d. May 26, 1741, "killed by falling into a water trough and being carried under a water wheel at iron works."
- iii. SARAH, b. Mar. 29, 1737.
- iv. EXPERIENCE, b. June 12, 1739.
- v. MARY, b. Sept. 4, 1741.

13. TIMOTHY[5] BENTON (*Samuel*,[4] *Samuel*,[3] *Andrew*,[2] *John*[1]) lived and died in Tolland, Conn., where he married, June 29, 1738, Abigail Scott.

Children:

- i. ABIGAIL,[6] b. Nov. 1, 1740.
- ii. ELANOR, b. Aug. 12, 1742.
- iii. MEHETABEL, b. Apr. 21, 1745.
- iv. ELIZABETH, b. Feb. 21, 1747.
- v. PRUDENCE, b. Mar. 12, 1749.
- vi. HULDA, b. July 15, 1751.
- vii. JERUSHA, b. Mar. 22, 1753.
- viii. TIMOTHY, b. Aug. 2, 1755; a Revolutionary soldier; m. Nov. 9, 1780, Sarah, dau. of Joseph West; "an educated man, a schoolmaster and captain of artillery."
- ix. EUNICE, b. June 18, 1757.

14. SAMUEL[5] BENTON (*Samuel,*[4] *Samuel,*[3] *Andrew,*[2] *John*[1]) lived in Tolland, Conn. He married, Dec. 22, 1743, Jane Bradley.
Children:

i. ELISHA,[6] b. Dec. 26, 1744.
ii. JONATHAN, b. Sept. 9, 1746; pensioned in 1832 as a Revolutionary soldier; "saw the battle of Bunker Hill from Roxbury st., Boston."
25. iii. OZIAS, b. Feb. 25, 1748.
iv. THANKFUL, b. Apr., d. Nov., 1751, "being burned in house."
v. THANKFUL, b. Aug. 22, 1752.
vi. DOROTHY, b. Feb. 23, 1755.
vii. SAMUEL, b. May 9, 1757; a Revolutionary soldier.
viii. ZADOC, b. Mar. 7, 1761; a Revolutionary soldier.
ix. SARAH, b. Dec. 21, 1764.
x. JACOB, b. Sept. 30, 1768.

15. CALEB[5] BENTON (*Caleb,*[4] *Samuel,*[3] *Andrew,*[2] *John*[1]) lived in Hartford, Conn., and later in Sandisfield, Mass., where he died in 1783, leaving a will dated July 23, 1777, but disproved June 3, 1783, as it had only two witnesses. He married Lydia ———, who survived him and married second, John Landon. (*Berkshire Co. Probate Records,* Pittsfield, Mass.)
Children named in will:

i. CALEB,[6] a Revolutionary soldier from Canaan, Conn.; "went southward with La Fayette in 1781"; d. Dec. 26, 1781.
ii. LYDIA, "oldest daughter"; executrix of her father's will.
iii. EZEKIEL, "oldest son" surviving.
iv. HANNAH, m. ——— Manly.
v. DANIEL, b. Aug. 5, 1773; m. 1793, Rhoda ———; d. May 24, 1825.
vi. MARTHA, m. ——— Dickinson.
vii. MARY, m. ——— Reed.

16. ABRAHAM[5] BENTON (*Caleb,*[4] *Samuel,*[3] *Andrew,*[2] *John*[1]) lived in Hartford, Conn., and later in Sandisfield, Mass., where he married, May 14, 1759, Martha Cook, "the first marriage in the county."
Children:

i. ABRAHAM,[6] b. June 10, 1760; d. young.
ii. MARTHA, b. Apr. 15, 1763; d. young.
iii. JOSEPH, b. Dec. 12, 1764; d. young.
iv. ABRAHAM, b. Feb. 25, 1766.
v. JOSEPH, b. Apr. 12, 1767.
vi. ELIJAH, b. June 13, 1769.
vii. ISAAC, b. Jan. 6, 1773.
viii. MELTIAH, b. June 5, 1775.
ix. STEPHEN, b. Sept. 11, 1777.
x. SAMUEL, b. June 13, 1779; d. young.
xi. MARTHA, b. Oct. 18, 1782.
xii. SAMUEL, b. Mar. 1, 1785.

17. DANIEL[5] BENTON (*Daniel,*[4] *Samuel,*[3] *Andrew,*[2] *John*[1]) lived and died in Tolland, Conn., where he married, Nov. 3, 1747, Mary Wheeler.
Children:

i. ELISHA,[6] b. Aug. 9, 1748; a Revolutionary soldier.
ii. MARY, b. Aug. 31, 1750.
26. iii. DANIEL, b. Apr. 29, 1752.
iv. AZARIAH, b. Mar. 29, 1754; a Revolutionary soldier; "died in prison ship, Long Island Sound, Dec. 29, 1776."
v. HANNAH, b. May 3, 1756; d. Oct. 18, 1757.
vi. HANNAH, b. Feb. 18, 1758.
27. vii. JACOB, b. Apr. 22, 1760: d. 1843.
viii. NATHAN, b. May 3, 1764.
ix. SILAS, b. June 6, 1766.

18. WILLIAM[5] BENTON (*Daniel,[4] Samuel,[3] Andrew,[2] John[1]*) lived in Tolland, Conn., and married, Dec. 14, 1750, Sarah Burroughs. He was a soldier in the French and Indian War, and "died at Oswego, N. Y., 1760."

Children:

i. SARAH,[6] b. Mar. 17, 1751.
ii. "A SON," b. and d. May 5, 1753.
iii. JOHN, b. Mar. 2, 1754.
iv. RUTH, b. Dec. 3, 1756.
v. ABIGAIL, b. Oct. 22, 1759.

19. ELIJAH[5] BENTON (*Daniel,[4] Samuel,[3] Andrew,[2] John[1]*) lived in Tolland, Conn. He married, Apr. 25, 1751, Mehetabel Chamberlain.

Children:

i. ABIJAH,[6] b. Feb. 25, 1752.
ii. LYDIA, b. June 6, 1753.
iii. LOIS, b. Apr. 4, 1755.
iv. MEHETABEL, b. Aug. 14, 1756.
v. ADONIRAM, b. Mar. 27, 1758; d. Oct. 29, 1760.
vi. ELIJAH, b. Apr. 17, 1760; pensioned in 1818 as a Revolutionary soldier (5 ft. 9 in. high, blue eyes, light brown hair); m. at Stewartstown, Coos Co., N. H., Oct. 20, 1793, Sally Sellingham; d. at Stewartstown, Aug. 14, 1841, his widow and seven children surviving.
vii. ADONIRAM, b. 1763; pensioned in 1818 as a Revolutionary soldier; d. at Surrey, Cheshire Co., N. H., Aug. 29, 1842; m. (1) ——; m. (2) at Surrey, N. H., June 5, 1816, Betsey Griffin, who was b. in 1770. Children by first wife, born prior to Jan. 1, 1794: 1. *Sarah.* 2. *Hiram.* 3. *Franklin.* 4. *Ruth.*

20. ISAAC[5] BENTON (*Isaac,[4] Joseph,[3] Andrew,[2] John[1]*) lived in Salisbury, Sharon, and Canaan, Conn. He married, at Sharon, Conn., Oct. 30, 1755, Jemima, daughter of Ezra and Anne (St. John) St. John, who was born Aug. 4, and baptized Sept. 9, 1739, at Wilton, Conn. He died "suddenly," Jan., 1812, "æ 79" (Salisbury Church Records).

Children:

i. ANNA,[6] b. Sept. 14, 1756.
28. ii. ISAAC, b. Dec. 28, 1758; m. Annar Allen.
iii. MARY, m. James Gates; d. Dec. 1, 1782, at Salisbury, Conn.
iv. EZRA, m. Apr. 4, 1792, Phebe White of Sharon, Conn.
v. JAMES, b. about 1768; d. at Salisbury, Conn., Jan. 22, 1849; m. (1) Mary Chapman, who was b. in 1769, and d. Feb. 20, 1800, "in the 31st year of her age"; m. (2) Dec. 2, 1800, Jerusha Bushnell, widow of R. W. Lee, who was b. Oct. 19, 1766, and d. May 15, 1850, aged 83 yrs., at Salisbury, Conn.

21. DAVID[5] BENTON (*Isaac,[4] Joseph,[3] Andrew,[2] John[1]*) was twelve years old when his father removed from Tolland and Kent to Salisbury, Conn. He was admitted a freeman, Apr. 11, 1763. From 1746 until 1777 his home was in the southwest corner of the town of Salisbury. In Feb. of the latter year he leased for fifty years a lot of ground, adjacent to the village, supposed to contain a sulphur mine, for one-fifth of the product, without cost to him; and disposed of his farm of 106 acres, leasing for 960 years the 55 acres "formerly laid out for parsonage lands," and "selling forever" the other 51 acres. In June, 1777, he bought land in and removed to Sheffield, Mass. His gravestone, in a family burying ground, a

half-mile from the state line, reads: "IN memory of Mr David Benton who died August 6th 1797 in the 63d year of his age." His will, dated July 14, probated Sept. 5, 1797, makes his sons Caleb and Stephen executors, and divides two-thirds of his estate equally among his seven surviving children, giving one-third to his wife Sarah. The surname of his wife, to whom he was married probably in 1758, has not been ascertained. The births of their children appear in Salisbury town records.

Children:

i. CALEB,[6] b. Jan. 2, 1759; d. at Catskill, N. Y., July 28, 1825.
ii. LYDIA, b. Mar. 26, 1761; m. Samuel Taylor; removed to Palatine District, Montgomery Co., N. Y., prior to her father's death.
29. iii. DAVID, b. Dec. 2, 1763.
iv. MARY, b. Nov. 9, 1765; unmarried at time of her father's death.
v. SARAH, b. Mar. 22, 1768; d. Apr. 4, 1772.
vi. STEPHEN, b. July 22, 1770; became owner of the homestead, which he sold June 13, 1803, and removed to Montgomery Co., N. Y.; a captain in N. Y. State Militia.
vii. SARAH, b. Apr. 30, 1773; unmarried at time of her father's death.
viii. RUTH, b. Feb. 29, 1776; m. ——— Plumb, prior to her father's death.

22. STEPHEN[5] BENTON (*Isaac,*[4] *Joseph,*[3] *Andrew,*[2] *John*[1]), a Revolutionary soldier, married, May 4, 1759, Prudence Reynolds "of Oblong," who was born at Westerfield, Conn., in 1740. He died Nov. 10, 1820, in Richmond, Mass.

Children:

i. LYDIA,[6] b. June 19, 1760. (Salisbury records.)
ii. JOSEPH, b. July 23, 1762. (Salisbury records.)
iii. PRUDENCE, b. June 9, 1764. (Salisbury records.)
iv. STEPHEN, b. Sept. 9, 1766.
v. SUSAN, b. Dec. 31, 1768.
vi. RUTH, b. Apr. 24, 1771.
vii. ELIZABETH, b. Sept. 4, 1773.
viii. ZILPA, b. Jan. 31, 1778.
ix. DARIUS, b. Oct. 31, 1781, in Richmond, Mass.; d. Dec. 13, 1827; m. Oct. 1, 1811, Fanny Fowler, who was b. Mar. 19, 1782, at Guilford, Conn., and d. Apr. 16, 1862.
x. POLLY, b. June 1, 1784.

23. NATHAN[5] BENTON (*Isaac,*[4] *Joseph,*[3] *Andrew,*[2] *John*[1]) was "accepted as a freeman" at Salisbury, Conn., Apr. 9, 1770. He married Esther ———.

Children, on Salisbury records:

i. ESTHER,[6] b. Nov. 13, 1766.
ii. BETTY, b. Dec. 22, 1768.
iii. LUCY, b. Feb. 9, 1771.
iv. ANNA, b. Aug. 9, 1773.
v. NATHAN, b. Apr. 13, 1776.

24. LEVI[5] BENTON (*Isaac,*[4] *Joseph,*[3] *Andrew,*[2] *John*[1]) was "accepted as a freeman" at Salisbury, Conn., Sept. 19, 1775. He removed to Sheffield, Mass., in 1777, and to Canaan, Conn., in 1780; and was a first settler of Yates Co., N. Y., in 1789, its town of Benton being named in his honor. In 1816, he and his wife removed to Franklin Co., Ind., where they died at "an advanced age." He married, Oct. 30, 1769, Mary, daughter of Abner and Hannah (Dyer) Woodworth of Salisbury, Conn.

Children, the first three on Salisbury records:

i. MARY,[6] b. July 14, 1770; m. Feb. 2, 1792, Thomas Barden.
ii. OLIVE, b. Jan. 29, 1772; m. (1) in 1791 (the first marriage in Yates Co.), Ezekiel Crocker; m. (2) Ezra Rice.
iii. LEVI, b. Feb. 26, 1774; m. Jan. 24, 1796, Nancy, dau. of James Parker.
iv. LUTHER, b. 1776; d. May 23, 1803, "lost at sea."
v. HANNAH, b. 1778; d. Sept. 17, 1780.
vi. CALVIN, b. 1781; d. July 24, 1856; m. Lois Barden.
vii. JOSEPH, b. June 27, 1783; m. in 1807, Aney Reynolds; lived in Franklin Co., Ind.; d. June 9, 1872.
viii. NANCY, b. 1785; m. (1) John Riggs; m. (2) Ezra Rice.
ix. HANNAH, b. 1788; m. Robert Havens.
x. RUBY, b. July 30, 1796; d. July 26, 1817; m. Dr. Erastus Webb.

25. OZIAS[6] BENTON (*Samuel,[5] Samuel,[4] Samuel,[3] Andrew,[2] John[1]*) lived in Tolland, Conn. He married, Nov. 19, 1772, Sarah Day of Ellington, Conn., who died Mar. 24, 1816. He died Mar. 21, 1816. "The father, mother and four sons died in a few days of each other of an epidemic called by the physicians congestive pneumonia."

Children:

i. SOLOMON,[7] b. May 1, 1775.
ii. ADONIJAH, b. May 25, 1777; d. Mar. 24, 1816; m. Nov., 1803, Ann Post of Tolland.
iii. OZIAS, b. Jan. 1, 1781; d. Mar. 26, 1816.
iv. IRA, b. Sept. 16, 1783.
v. ALVIN, b. May 21, 1786; m. Mar. 24, 1813, Ruth Kingsbury.
vi. ALFRED, b. Jan. 6, 1789.
vii. BENJAMIN, b. June 14, 1791; d. Mar. 21, 1816.
viii. LEVI, b. Feb. 6, 1794.

26. DANIEL[6] BENTON (*Daniel,[5] Daniel,[4] Samuel,[3] Andrew,[2] John[1]*) lived in Tolland, Conn. He married, Feb. 18, 1779, Betty Richards.

Children, on Tolland records:

i. ELISHA,[7] b. May 20, 1780.
ii. BETTY, b. Mar. 20, 1782.
iii. EUNICE, b. July 23, 1784.
iv. AGNES, b. Feb. 12, 1787.
v. PHEBE, b. Aug. 12, 1791.

27. JACOB[6] BENTON (*Daniel,[5] Daniel,[4] Samuel,[3] Andrew,[2] John[1]*) was pensioned in 1818 as a Revolutionary soldier, having had four years service, and was at Burgoyne's surrender, Oct., 1777. The witnesses in his pension papers say: "A man of veracity, a fine, honorable, honest man." He lived all his life in Tolland, Conn. He married first, Mar. 14, 1782, Sarah Weston of Willington, Conn., who died Sept. 23, 1787; and married second, July 1, 1789, Sarah Ladd of Tolland, who survived him. He died July 9, 1843.

Children by first wife:

i. ANN,[7] b. Feb. 1, 1783.
ii. WILLIAM, b. Aug. 29, 1785.

Children by second wife:

iii. AZARIAH, b. June 8, 1790.
iv. RUTH, b. Dec. 8, 1791.
v. DANIEL, b. May 3, 1794.
vi. SUSALLA, b. Feb. 19, 1796.
vii. CHESTER, b. Feb. 5, 1798.
viii. JACOB, b. June 1, 1802.

28. ISAAC[6] BENTON (*Isaac,*[5] *Isaac,*[4] *Joseph,*[3] *Andrew,*[2] *John*[1]) was born Dec. 28, 1758, in Salisbury, Conn., and died in Steuben, Oneida Co., N. Y. His occupation, as indicated, was probably that of his father, who is mentioned as "a very ingenious mechanic and millright," in allusion to his constructing at Canaan, Conn., during the Revolutionary war, "a slitting mill" for the manufacture of nail rods. (*Litchfield Co. Centennial Celebration*, 1851.) He married Annar Allen. The pension papers of her brother Gideon Allen, a Revolutionary soldier, show that his father removed in 1750 from East Haven, Conn., to Woodbury, from which he afterward removed to Salisbury and thence to N. Y. She died near Brighton, Canada, about 1846.

Children:

i. ANNA,[7] m. Reuben Myers; d. in Oneida Co., N. Y.
ii. AURELIA, d. young.
iii. CLARISSA, m. Peter Crouter, who removed from New York, and d. near Brighton, Canada.
iv. HEMAN, d. in Greenville, N. Y., aged 21 yrs.
v. ISAAC, m. Olive Crouter; d. at Gooderich, Canada.
vi. ALLEN, b. June 9, 1792, at Greenville, N. Y.; m. 22 July, 1819, Deborah, b. Feb. 1, 1798, at East Haddam, Conn., d. Aug. 23, 1867, at Cato, N. Y., dau. of Abraham Willey, a Revolutionary soldier; was a physician; d. at Cato, Cayuga Co., N. Y., Sept. 12, 1879.

29. DAVID[6] BENTON (*David,*[5] *Isaac,*[4] *Joseph,*[3] *Andrew,*[2] *John*[1]) at the age of thirteen years, in 1777, removed with his father from Salisbury, Conn., to Sheffield, Mass., and in Feb., 1788, bought land adjoining his father's. In 1789 he removed with his brother Caleb and his uncle Levi Benton to New York, and was a first settler of the present town of Seneca, Ontario Co., as was his uncle Levi, a first settler of the adjoining town of Benton in Yates Co. In May, 1819, he removed to Brownstown, Jackson Co., Ind. In 1832 he was pensioned as a Revolutionary soldier, having served from July to Nov., 1780, in Capt. Warner's company of Col. John Brown's regiment, from Berkshire Co., Mass. He was present at an engagement with Tories and Indians under Sir John Johnson, Oct. 19, near Fort Plank, Montgomery Co., N. Y., in which Col. Brown and about forty of the command were killed. Shortly thereafter the regiment returned home and was disbanded. In July, 1781, he enlisted at New London, Conn., as a marine on the Brig *Favorite* of 16 guns, and when at sea about twelve days it captured a brig with a cargo of wine, bound from Madeira to New York, and he and others were put on board the prize, but before reaching port, it was recaptured by the British Frigate *Alpheus*, and "all kept at sea 30 days as prisoners," during which the British and French fleets "had the battle [Sept. 5.] off the capes of Virginia." After this, they were taken to New York and confined in the prison ship *Jersey* till exchanged in Jan., 1782. His headstone in Fairview Cemetery, at Brownstown, is inscribed: "IN memory of DAVID BENTON who died March the 7th 1845. aged 82 years." He married first, Mar. 17, 1784, Sarah, born June 9, 1765, at Salisbury, Conn., died Nov. 25, 1825, at Bath, N. Y., daughter of Benjamin and Sarah (Stewart) Bingham; and married second, Oct. 17, 1826, Thankful (Reynolds) McKane, who was born Jan. 6, 1796, and died in 1874,

at Hamilton, Ohio. His family Bible, printed in Cambridge, England, in 1769, shows the following children.

Children, by first wife:

i. HENRY,[7] b. Dec. 20, 1784; d. May 23, 1872, at Waterville, Wis.; m. (1) Feb. 5, 1807, Betsey Woolley; m. (2) Apr. 9, 1812, Hannah Dickenson, who d. May 14, 1825; m. (3) Apr. 10, 1830, Sarah Hoyt Rose, who was b. Feb. 14, 1797, and d. Dec. 27, 1870. He had seven sons and three daughters.

ii. GEORGE, b. Dec. 29, 1786; d. Feb. 15, 1859, at Lyons, N. Y.; m. Susan ——, who was b. 1789, and d. 1852. They had two sons and three daughters.

iii. SARAH, b. Nov. 27, 1790; d. Sept. 7, 1876, at Bath, N. Y.; m. Sept. 27, 1814, Moses H. Lyon, who was b. Nov. 18, 1789, and d. Apr. 21, 1763, at Bath, N. Y. Children: 1. *William B.*,[8] b. Feb. 1, 1817; d. June 1, 1835. 2. *David W.*, b. 1821; d. 1893. 3. *James*, b. 1823, now living at Bath, N. Y. 4. *Robert M.*, b. 1825; d. 1903.

iv. MARY, b. Nov. 5, 1795; d. Mar. 7, 1883, at Bath, N. Y.; m. Aug. 12, 1819, at Brownstown, Ind., William B. Ruggles. Only child: *William Benjamin*, b. 1827; d. 1892.

v. WALTER, b. May 7, 1799; d. Apr. 3, 1890, at Brownstown, Ind.; m. (1) Jan. 9, 1821, Elizabeth Coe, who was b. Aug. 11, 1800, and d. Sept. 18, 1823; m. (2) Mar. 31, 1824, Hetty (Vermilya) Banks, who was b. May 1, 1805, and d. Nov. 6, 1875;* m. (3) Mary Jane (Freeze) Daly, who was b. Apr. 16, 1830, and d. Sept. 2, 1887. He had seven sons and four daughters.

vi. WILLIAM DAVID, b. July 9, 1803; d. July 17, 1893, at Brownstown, Ind.; m. July 3, 1823, Malinda Johnson, who was b. Jan. 10, 1806, and d. July 16, 1897. They had three sons and two daughters.

vii. NORMAN, b. Mar. 5, 1807; d. Jan. 13, 1875, at Bath, N. Y.; m. (1) Hannah Wright, who was b. Sept. 26, 1811, and d. June 16, 18—; m. (2) June 15, 1842, Mary Diana Daniels, who d. Apr. 2, 1866. He had one son and four daughters.

Child by second wife:

viii. ELIZABETH, b. Jan. 18, 1828, at Brownstown, Ind.; d. Oct. 28, 1880, at Brownstown; m. Feb. 13, 1848, John Q. A. McPherson, who was b. 1824, and d. Aug. 17, 1863, at Courtland, Ind. They had one son and five daughters.

PASSENGER LISTS TO AMERICA.

Communicated by GERALD FOTHERGILL, Esq., of New Wandsworth, London, England.

[Continued from page 243.]

A Report of Passengers on board the American Ship *Active*, whereof Robert McKown is Master, burthen 138 tons, bound for Philadelphia, sworn at Newry, 6 May, 1803.

James Moore	aged 21	Clerk	Martha Parnell	aged 18	———
James Rendles	" 40	Labourer	Robert Mills	" 40	Labourer
John Rendles	" 38	"	Eliza Barnett	" 16	———
Eliza "	" 16	———	Jane "	" 12	———
Thomas "	" 12	Labourer	William Stewart	" 50	Labourer
John Barnett	" 38	"	Margaret "	" 38	
Margaret "	" 34	———	Ann "	" 24	

* John Hogan Benton, the compiler, of Washington, D. C., was born of this marriage, at Brownstown, Ind., June 10, 1829.

Eliza Laverty	" 20	———	Agness Stewart	aged 20		
Andrew Barnett	" 24	Labourer	Susannah "	" 18		This one is crossed out
Annabella "	" 20	———				

A Report of Passengers on board the American Ship *Diana* of New Bedford, Burthen 223 Tons, whereof Henry Hurter is Master, bound for New York, sworn at Newry, 18 May, 1803.

Isabella Allen	aged 32		of Market-hill
John Collins	" 36	Labourer	" "
Patk Crowley	" 39	"	" "
Mary "	" 39	———	" "
Richd Burden	" 28	Labourer	Fentona
James Farrel	" 40	"	Stewartstown
Patrick Philips	" 24	"	Stralane
Thomas Rooney	" 40	"	Banbridge
Mary Martin	" 20		"
Charlotte Brothers	" 26		"
Isaac Collins	" 30	Labourer	Monaghan
John Martin	" 36	"	"
John Brothers	" 30	"	"
Thomas Lewis	" 30	"	"
John Michael	" 30	"	Dundalk
William Sleith	" 23	"	"
Henry Ells	" 30	"	Newry
Thos Fure	" 39	"	"
Thos Smith	" 37	"	Bathfriland
Rebecca Brothers	" 45	———	Newry
Benjamin Philips	" 30	Labourer	Dundalk
Hanna Mytrood	" 25	———	Newry
James Downs	" 30	Labourer	Coatehill
Samuel Crawley	" 35	"	"
John Burden	" 32	"	Ballybery
Sarah Barder	" 31	———	"
Rebecca Deblois	" 24	———	Ballyconnell
Eliza Whithom	" 23		Killyshandon
Mary Cahoone	" 22		Cavan
Mary Overing	" 25		"

A List of Passengers intended to go from this Port by the Ship *Hopewell* of and for New York, burthen 125 tons, sworn at Newry, 6 June, 1803.

Peter Downey	aged 22	Labourer	Joseph Humphies	aged 26	Labourer
William Thornbury	" 40	"	Robert Humphries	" 40	"
Wm Daly	" 30	"	Moses "	" 17	"
Geo Ferrigan	" 32	"	James Couser	" 18	"
Wm Martin	" 36	"	Robert Humphies	" 19	"
Sam Smyley	" 35	"	James Reed	" 20	"
John McCeaverell	" 35	"	Thos Mcleherry	" 21	"
Pat Cullager	" 20	"	John Anderson	" 25	"
David Humphies	" 52	"			

A List of Passengers intending to go from Belfast to New York in the Ship *Wilmington*, Thomas Woodward, Master, 360 Tons, sworn 9 July, 1803.

John Houston	aged	30	Farmer
Mrs Houston	"	27	
Houston	"	7	Children
"	"	5	"
"	"	2	"
Robert Stewart	"	27	Farmer
Mrs "	"	24	
—— "	"	2	Child
James Galway	"	18	Farmer
Thomas Allen	"	25	"
Willm Erskin	"	32	"
Isabella Dick	"	16	——
John Cross	"	35	Farmer
Wm Crozier	"	26	"
Henry McHenry	"	40	gentn
Hen Read	"	30	"
Jane Curry	"	36	——
Mary "	"	14	——
Eliza "	"	12	——
John Curry	aged	9	——
Robt Warwick	"	30	gent
Hen Garrett	"	33	Farmer
S Ann "	"	27	——
Mary Maucally	"	23	——
John Browne	"	45	gent
Robt Jackson	"	30	"
John Murphy	"	28	"
John Thompson	"	26	"
Thos McCrellos	"	34	Farmer
Thos McConaghy	"	27	"
John Cameron	"	39	"
Lavinia "	"	20	——
Agnus "	"	17	——
Martha "	"	14	——
Elinor "	"	9	——
Saml Chestnut	"	30	gent
Mary Cameron	"	36	——

List of Passengers engaged to sail on board the American Ship *Margaret*, Wm. M. Boyd, Master, for Wiscasset in the United States, sworn (indorsed from Dublin) 12 July, 1803.

Edwd Irwin	aged	50	Labourer	Wexford
Geo Phillips	"	30	"	"
Thos Maguire	"	32	"	"
Patrick Irwin	"	31	"	"
Jos Cavaneagh	"	34	"	"
Tho Best	"	22	"	"
Mary Irwin	"	40	——	"
Ann Irwin	"	9	——	"

A List of Passengers intending to go in the Brig *Sally*, Timy Clifton, Master, for New York, burthen 147 Tons, now lying in the Harbour of Dublin, sworn 5 Aug., 1803.

Alice Flood	aged	22	spinster	Dublin
Margaret Kelly	"	45	"	"
Elizabeth Flood	"	24	"	"
Alicia Purfield	"	18	"	"
Ann Eagle	"	10	"	"
George Eagle	"	9	——	"
Mary Bennett	"	30	spinster	"
Nich Campbell	"	24	Labourer	"
Nancy Fallis	"	20	spinster	"
James Grant	"	17	Scotch Labourer	——
Hugh Kelly	"	24	Labourer	Dublin
Bernard Fitzpatrick	"	38	Farmer	Tullamore
Ellen "	"	28	his wife	"
Mary "			a child	"
John Lyons	"	30	Farmer	
& an infant				

A List of Passengers engaged to sail on board the Brig *George* of New Bedford, burden 172 tons, Jacob Taber, Master, for New York, sworn 16 Aug., 1803.

John OBrien	aged 28	Clerk	Dublin
Michael Brannon	" 23	Farmer	Mayo
John Lyons	" 30	Farmer	Tullamore
Mark Evans	" 30	"	Queens Co.
Mary Evans		his wife	
James Henney	" 25	Farmer	Dublin County
Pat[k] Doyle	" 20	"	Mayo
Bern[d] Fitzpatrick	" 36	"	Tullamore
his wife & child			
Henry OHara	" 23	"	Clare

A List of persons who have engaged their passage in the Ship *Eagle*, Andrew Riker, Master, of and for New York, sworn 27 Aug., 1803.

Robert Small	aged 27	height 5– 5	Labourer	Ballymony
W[m] Conoy	40	5–10	Farmer	Pensilvania
Alex[r] McKeown	18	5– 5	Labourer	Belfast
W[m] Williamson	25	6– 1	"	Killinchy
Owen Miskelly	25	5–10	"	"
Kitty "			spinster	"
W[m] Magill	23	5–11	Labourer	"
Roger Welsh	24	6– 1	"	"
James Reid	22	5– 7	"	Saintfield
Thomas Armstrong	31	5– 9	Farmer	Clonfeakle
Mary ———			spinster	
John Treanor	25	5– 9	Farmer	Killinchy
John Murphy	24	5– 9	Labourer	"
Alex[r] Orr	21	5– 9	gentleman	Ballymoney
Jas Boyd	30	5– 9	merchant	N[r] Ballameane
Sam[l] B Wiley	30	5–10	clergyman	Philadelphia
John Moorhead	24	5– 7½	merchant	Antrim
Marcus Heyland	22	5– 3	"	Coleraine
W[m] Freeland	20	5– 8	farmer	co Armargh
W[m] Deyrman	25	5–10	labourer	Drumbo
Ja[s] Mild	25	5–10	farmer	Aughaloo
Jo[s] Caldwell	22	5– 8	merchant	Ballymony
M[rs] Orr				Tobermore
John Breene	15	5– 7	farmer	Killenely
Sam[l] M[c]Neill	20	5– 8	grocer	Ballymeana
Jas Campbell	30	5– 5	labourer	Carmoney
Sam[l] Miniss	21	5– 7	"	Saintfield
James Mcauley	22	5–11	"	"
W[m] Dixin	22	5– 7	"	"
Sam[l] Moore	18	6–	gentleman	Portglenone
Alexr Graham	34	5– 8	M.D.	last residence Glasgow
Tho[s] Neilson	24	5– 5	merchant	Ballinderry
Sam[l] "	11	5– 8	none	"
Rob[t] "	28	5– 7	merchant	"
James Grant	28	5– 7	"	Armahilt

[To be continued.]

PETER CRARY OF GROTON, CONN., AND SOME OF HIS DESCENDANTS.

By LOUIS MARINUS DEWEY, Esq., of Westfield, Mass.

1. PETER[1] CRARY died in 1708 at Groton, Conn., where he was an early settler in 1663. He married, in 1677, Christobel, daughter of John Gallop of New London, Conn.

Children:

- i. CHRISTOBEL,[2] b. Feb., 1678-9; m. Ebenezer Harris.
- ii. PETER, bapt. Apr. 30, 1682; d. unmarried, before May 18, 1720.
- iii. MARGARET, bapt. Aug. 20, 1682; m. Ebenezer Pierce of Groton.
- 2. iv. JOHN, bapt. Aug. 8, 1686.
- v. WILLIAM, bapt. Nov. 6, 1687.
- 3. vi. ROBERT, bapt. May 11, 1690.
- vii. ANN (Hannah), bapt. July 17, 1692; m. Nathan Bushnell of Norwich.

2. JOHN[2] CRARY (*Peter*[1]), who was styled "judge," died May 29, 1759, aged 74, at Plainfield, Conn. He married first, at Plainfield, Oct. 12, 1715, Prudence White, who was born in 1688, and died Dec. 27, 1736, aged 48 years; and married second, Anna ———, who died Sept. 21, 1754, aged 61 years.

Children:

- 4. i. JOHN,[3] b. Aug. 13, 1716.
- ii. ELIZABETH, b. Dec. 26, 1717; m. at Plainfield, Jan. 15, 1738-9, Benedick Saterly.
- iii. HANNAH, b. Dec. 20, 1719; m. at Preston, Feb. 19, 1735-6, Daniel Woodward, Jr., and had *Asa*, b. Nov. 18, 1736.
- iv. PRUDENCE, b. Feb. 6, 1722.
- v. ANN, b. Dec. 10, 1723.
- vi. MARY, b. May, 1726.
- vii. LUCE, b. Aug., d. Dec. 15, 1728.
- viii. RACHEL, b. Jan. 9, 1730; m. at Plainfield, Jan. 29, 1756, Benjamin Spaulding.

3. ROBERT[2] CRARY (*Peter*[1]) lived at Groton, Conn., and married ——.

Children:

- 5. i. CHRISTOPHER,[3] b. about 1713.
- 6. ii. WILLIAM, b. about 1715.
- 7. iii. ROBERT, b. about 1717.
- iv. AARON, b. about 1719; d. before Dec. 4, 1781; a captain; m. at Griswold (Preston), Apr. 8, 1756, Mary Stanton.
- 8. v. BENJAMIN, b. about 1723.
- 9. vi. GEORGE, b. about 1725.
- vii. OLIVER.
- viii. CHRISTOBEL, m. at Plainfield, Aug. 21, 1751, Nathaniel Marsh.
- ix. LUCY.

4. JOHN[3] CRARY (*John*,[2] *Peter*[1]), lived at Plainfield, Conn., and there married, May 20, 1750, Mary Rayment (or Raymond) of Charlestown.

Children:

- i. ELIZABETH,[4] b. Aug. 6, 1751.
- ii. JOHN, b. Mch. 9, 1753.

5. CHRISTOPHER[3] CRARY (*Robert*,[2] *Peter*[1]), born about 1713, lived at Voluntown, Conn., and later settled at Clarendon, Vt., with his son Ezra. He married, at Voluntown, Mar. 7, 1737, Elizabeth Robins.

Child:

10\. i. EZRA,[4] b. 30 July, 1737.
And perhaps other children.

6\. WILLIAM[3] CRARY (*Robert,*[2] *Peter*[1]) lived at Voluntown, Conn., and there married, Nov. 12, 1741, Elizabeth Campbell.

Children:

i. ESTHER,[4] b. Sept. 20, 1742; m. March 25, 1773, John Wylie, Jr.
ii. SARAH, b. Mch. 1, 1744.
iii. PRUDENCE, b. Sept. 6, 1746.
iv. ARCHIBALD, b. Nov. 24, 1748.
v. JAMES, b. Oct. 30, 1751.
vi. WILLIAM, b. July 11, 1756.

7\. ROBERT[3] CRARY (*Robert,*[2] *Peter*[1]) died Jan. 30, 1790, aged 73, at Preston, Conn. He was a farmer, and lived at Voluntown as late as 1752, where his first five children were born. He married, June 3, 1742, Sarah, born Sept. 23, 1720, at Preston, died there Mar. 5, 1805, daughter of Dea. Jedediah Tracy.

Children:

i. HULDAH,[4] b. May 6, 1743; m. Feb. 25, 1762, as his second wife, Dr. Joshua Downer.
11\. ii. JOHN, b. Mar. 25, 1745.
12\. iii. EUNICE, b. Feb. 18, 1747; m. Apr. 17, 1768, John Morgan.
iv. LOIS, b. Apr. 10, 1750; m. June, 1770, Maj. Nathan Peters, afterwards of Gen. Washington's staff.
v. ELISHA, b. Mar. 7, 1752; d. unmarried, at Preston, Sept. 8, 1773.
vi. ROBERT, b. June 19, 1755; d. Mar. 14, 1757.
vii. SARAH, b. Feb. 19, 1758; d. unmarried, Nov. 6, 1775, at Preston.
13\. viii. ROBERT, b. Sept. 3, 1760.

8\. BENJAMIN[3] CRARY (*Robert,*[2] *Peter*[1]) lived at Plainfield, Conn. He married Amey ———.

Child:

14\. i. AARON,[4] b. Mar. 2, 1769; m. 1794, Harmony Averill.

9\. CAPT. GEORGE[3] CRARY (*Robert,*[2] *Peter*[1]) died Dec. 19, 1760, at Preston, Conn., where he married, May 18, 1756, Lucy Sterry.

Children:

i. MARY,[4] b. Oct. 15, 1756.
ii. ROBERT, b. Jan. 13, 1759.
iii. GEORGE, b. Sept. 19, 1760; perhaps m. Jan. 4, 1815, Betsey, dau. of Samuel and Amy Kinney, who was b. Sept. 5, 1790. Three children.

10\. EZRA[4] CRARY (*Christopher,*[3] *Robert,*[2] *Peter*[1]), born July 30, 1737, at Voluntown, settled at Clarendon, Vt., about 1768. He married at Voluntown, Dec. 29, 1756, Dorithy Randall.

Children*:

i. DESIRE,[5] b. Apr. 29, 1760; m. at Plainfield, Conn., Sept. 27, 1786, Nathan Glover.
15\. ii. NATHAN, b. Mar. 9, 1762.
16\. iii. ELIZA, b. Feb. 13, 1764.
iv. NATHANIEL, b. Nov. 13, 1766.
v. DOLLY.
vi. CYNTHIA.
vii. EUNICE.

* A letter from Mr. A. M. Crary, Herington, Kan., gives the last three children, and says that Nathan was born May 9, 1762, and died in 1852.

11. JOHN[4] CRARY (*Robert,[3] Robert,[2] Peter[1]*), born Mar. 25, 1745, at Voluntown, died Mar. 12, 1803, at Preston. He was a farmer, and married first, at Preston, Feb. 23, 1769, Ame, born Sept. 4, 1749, at Preston, died there Nov. 3, 1795, daughter of Samuel[4] Morgan (James,[3] Capt. John,[2] James[1]); and married second, Mar. 7, 1798, Mrs. Mary York of Stonington, who died in 1808 (?).

Children by first wife:

17. i. SAMUEL,[5] b. Sept. 13, 1770; m. E. Powell.
ii. ELISHA, b. Mar. 4, 1774; d. Oct. 22, 1775.
iii. SARAH, b. Jan. 7, 1776; d. Mar. 4, 1813; m. at Preston, Conn., Rev. Lemuel Tyler, a Congregational minister.
iv. AMY, b. Oct. 18, 1778; m. (1) —— Bingham; m. (2) —— Rix.
v. JOHN, b. Sept. 11, 1784; m. S. Witter.

Children by second wife:

vi. LUCY, b. Feb. 15, 1799; d. Oct. 4, 1802.
vii. FANNY, b. Apr. 1, 1801; d. May, 1842; m. William Palmer, and had *Jedediah*, who d. unmarried, and *William*.
viii. MARTHA, b. Dec. 19, 1803; m. Feb. 25, 1829, John F. Gardner of Montville, who was b. Nov. 5, 1808, at Norwich, Conn., and had *Henry*, who m. Mrs. Caroline (Beebe) Shaw, and *Mary*, who m. Alfred Beebe.

12. EUNICE[4] CRARY (*Robert,[3] Robert,[2] Peter[1]*), born Feb. 18, 1747, at Voluntown, Conn., married at Preston, Apr. 17, 1768, John Morgan (Samuel,[4] James,[3] Capt. John,[2] James[1]), who was born Mar. 21, 1742, at Preston, and died there July 9, 1816.

Children:

i. SANFORD MORGAN,[5] b. Jan. 5, 1769, at Preston; d. in early life, at Baltimore, Md.; m. Sylvia Prinderson, who d. at Ledyard, Conn., Dec. 1, 1826, aged 56 yrs.,
ii. AMY MORGAN, b. June 20, 1770; m. —— Leet.
iii. EUNICE MORGAN, b. Jan. 14, 1772; m. Mch. 27, 1791, Elijah Clark.
iv. SALLY MORGAN, b. Oct. 11, 1773; d. Oct. 24, 1775.
v. ELISHA MORGAN, b. Sept. 24, 1775; m. Aug. 5, 1798, Lydia Palmer.
vi. CAPT. JOHN MORGAN, b. Sept. 18, 1777; m. Nancy Palmer.
vii. SALLY MORGAN, b. Sept. 6, 1779; m. Jan. 1, 1804 (?), Rev. Joseph Prentice.
viii. ERASTUS MORGAN, b. Apr. 22, 1782; m. Oct. 12, 1806, Polly Meech.
ix. THISBE (PHEBE) MORGAN, b. Oct. 6, 1783; m. —— Andrus.
x. ROBERT CRARY MORGAN, b. June 4, 1786; said to have m. and settled near Utica, N. Y.
xi. CHARLES MORGAN, b. Jan. 4, 1792; d. unmarried, Mar. 11, 1822, at Preston.

13. ROBERT[4] CRARY (*Robert,[3] Robert,[2] Peter[1]*), died Mar. 24, 1805, aged 45 years, at Preston, Conn., where he married first, Dec. 7, 1780, Cynthia Lamb of Stonington, who died Feb. 10, 1792 (? 1782); and married second, Jan. 23, 1783, Margaret Kimball.

Child by first wife:

i. CYNTHIA,[5] b. June 22, 1782; m. Mar. 1, 1804, Capt. Charles Meech.

Children by second wife:

ii. AARON, b. Dec. 16, 1783.
iii. SALLY, b. about 1784; d. Apr. 9, 1794.
iv. MARY (POLLY), b. Oct. 22, 1787; d. Apr. 26, 1802.
v. GIDEON RAY, b. Mar. 16, 1793.

vi. NABBA, b. Sept. 18, 1796.
vii. EUNICE, b. July 21, 1802.

14. AARON[4] CRARY (*Benjamin,*[3] *Robert,*[2] *Peter*[1]) lived at Plainfield, Conn. He was a captain. He married, Apr. 17, 1794, Harmony Averill, who died Sept. 15, 1812, aged 40 yrs., 6 mos., 7 days.

Children:

i. LUCY,[5] b. Sept. 16, 1795.
ii. BENJAMIN, b. Aug. 5, 1797; m. (1) Abigail ——, who d. Jan. 30, 1822; m. (2) at Plainfield, Conn., Nov. 14, 1824, Nancy Palmer.
iii. JAMES, b. July 8, 1799; d. Oct. 26, 1844; m. Jan. 22, 1829, Elizabeth Wylie of Voluntown.
iv. SAMUEL, b. June 3, 1801; m. Sept. 9, 1835, Olive C. Kennedy of Voluntown.
v. AARON AVERILL, b. July 27, 1803.
vi. WILLIAM PEIRCE, b. Apr. 29, 1806.
vii. STEPHEN, b. June 6, 1808.

15. NATHAN[5] CRARY (*Ezra,*[4] *Christopher,*[3] *Robert,*[2] *Peter*[1]), born at Voluntown, Conn., was taken to Clarendon, Vt., by his father, in 1768, when about six years old. He lived for a time at Wallingford, Vt., was a Revolutionary soldier and Methodist minister, and moved to St. Lawrence Co., N. Y., about 1806, living in Potsdam, where he died in 1852, aged 90 years. He married, May 1, 1783, Lydia Arnold.

Children:

i. EZRA,[6] b. 1787.
ii. APPLETON, b. Sept. 23, 1789; d. Aug. 6, 1867, at Pierrepont, N. Y.; m. Roby, dau. of John Hopkins of Wallingford, Vt. A son, *A. M.*, is living in Herington, Kan., and others at Crary, N. D.
iii. NATHAN, b. 1790; d. 1861; a soldier in War of 1812.
iv. ORIN, b. 1796; d. 1878; a soldier in War of 1812.
v. ORANGE SMITH, b. 1803; d. 1889; known as a poet. A son, *George L.*, was living in 1904 at Crary Mills, N. Y.
vi. EDWARD, b. 1805; has descendants in Wisconsin.
vii. JOHN WESLEY, b. 1808; d. 1902.
viii. STEPHEN, b. 1812; d. 1880.

16. ELIAS[5] CRARY (*Ezra,*[4] *Christopher,*[3] *Robert,*[2] *Peter*[1]), born at Voluntown, Conn., was taken to Clarendon, Vt., in 1768, when about four years old. He married Betsey, daughter of David Palmer of Voluntown, and Vermont.

Children:*

i. SOLOMON,[6] b. about 1790; lived at Pottstown, St. Lawrence Co., N. Y.
ii. POLLY, m. Dr. John Fox of Wallingford, Vt., whose father came from Woodstock, Conn.
iii. ELIAS, lived in Illinois.
iv. SALLY, lived at Pottstown.
v. NATHAN.
vi. CYNTHIA.
vii. DAVID, a doctor; d. in 1851, at Hartford, Conn.
viii. GEORGE.

17. SAMUEL[5] CRARY (*John,*[4] *Robert,*[3] *Robert,*[2] *Peter*[1]), born Sept. 13, 1770, at Preston, Conn., died Oct. 16, 1810, at Binghamton, N. Y., married Aug. 4, 1793, Eliza Powel, who was born May 4, 1774.

* All married.

Children:

i. JULIA ANN,[6] b. June 27, 1794.
ii. AMELIA, b. Feb. 4, 1796.
iii. CAROLINE E., b. Dec. 27, 1798.
iv. ADALINE M., b. Sept. 4, 1800; m. —— Budlong.
v. WILLIAM S., b. July 4, 1802.
vi. CORNELIA E., b. June 16, 1805.
vii. SARAH A., b. Feb. 12, 1807.
viii. JANE H., b. Oct. 5, 1809.

GENEALOGIES IN PREPARATION.

[Concluded from page 281.]

APPENDIX.

BACON.—*The Maine branch of Michael of Dedham, Mass.*, by William L. Palmer, 22 Sacramento Place, Cambridge, Mass.

BANKS.—*Richard of York, Me.* (?), by Dr. Charles N. Banks, Vineyard Haven, Mass.

BARKER.—*All lines*, by John Herbert Barker, 53 Park St., Somerville, Mass.

BARNES.—*Thomas of Middletown, Conn.*, by Mrs. George Frederick Ralph, 5 Plant St., Utica, N. Y.

BICKFORD.—*Jeremiah of Truro, Mass.*, by Miss Ella F. Elliot, 59 Oxford St., Somerville, Mass.

BOOKSTABER, or BUCHSTABER.—*Jacobus of Orange Co., N. Y.*, by J. E. Bookstaver, 6 Lockwood St., Binghamton, N. Y.

BOURNE.—*Richard of Sandwich, Mass.*, by Mrs. Susan K. Bourne, Barrington, R. I.

BROWN.—*James of Middletown, Conn.*, by Edwin A. Hill, Room 348 U. S. Patent Office, Washington, D. C.

BROWNELL.—*Thomas of Portsmouth, R. I.*, by George Grant Brownell, Jamestown, N. Y.

BUFFUM.—*Robert of Salem, Mass.*, by F. S. Hammond, Oneida, N. Y.

BURDAKIN.—*James of Boston, Mass., and all other lines*, by John Herbert Barker, 53 Park St., Somerville, Mass.

CAMPBELL.—*Douglas Neal of South Carolina*, by Mrs. C. M. Atkinson, Pine Village, Warren Co., Ind.

CAMPBELL.—*John of Wayesville, Ohio*, by Mrs. L. D. Temple, 5 Winter St., Watertown, Mass.

CAREW.—*All families*, by W. G. Richards, 59 Hill Park, Crescent, Plymouth, England.

CASS.—*John of Hampton, N. H.*, by Alfred C. Cass, 271 West Rittenhouse St., Germantown, Philadelphia, Pa.

CHAFFE.—*All families*, by W. G. Richards, 59 Hill Park Crescent, Plymouth, England.

CHASE.—*Aquilla, Thomas, and William*, by Mary L. C. Smith, 24 Preston St., Hartford, Conn.

CLUTTERBUCK.—*Various branches of Gloucestershire, Eng.*, by W. P. W. Phillimore, 124 Chancery Lane, London, W. C., England.

COOKE.—*Maj. Aaron of Dorchester, Northampton and Westfield, Mass., and Windsor, Conn.*, by Lyndon P. Smith, 27 Charter Oak Place, Hartford, Conn.

COPELAND.—*Lawrence of Braintree, Mass.*, by Warren T. Copeland, Lock Box 875, Campello, Mass.

DAY.—*Robert of Hartford, Conn.*, third edition (compiled by the late George E. Day, D.D.), Committee: Wilson M. Day, Willoughby, Ohio; Jeremiah Day, Catskill, N. Y.; Edward L. Day, Cleveland, Ohio.

DOLBEAR.—*All families of Co. Devon, Eng.*, by W. G. Richards, 59 Hill Park Crescent, Plymouth, England.

EASTCOTT, or ESTCOTT.—*All families*, by W. G. Richards, 59 Hill Park Crescent, Plymouth, England.

FAUNCE.—*John of Plymouth, Mass.*, by Mrs. Herbert W. Pinkham, 109 Grand View Ave., Wollaston, Mass.

FOOTE.—*Nathaniel of Wethersfield, Conn.*, by Abram W. Foote, Middlebury, Vt.

FRANCIS.—*William of Virginia*, by W. W. Stockberger, U. S. Dept. of Agriculture, Bureau of Plant Industry, Washington, D. C.

FRANKLIN.—*All families*, by W. G. Richards, 59 Hill Park Crescent, Plymouth, England.

GLANVILLE.—*All families*, by W. G. Richards, 59 Hill Park Crescent, Plymouth, England.

GRIFFEN.—*Edward of Maryland, Flushing and New Amsterdam, N. Y.*, by Robert B. Miller, 41 Van Buren St., Brooklyn, N. Y.

GRINNELL.—*Daniel of Saybrook, Conn.*, by Edwin A. Hill, Room 348 U. S. Patent Office, Washington, D. C.

HAZEN.—*Edward of Rowley, Mass.*, by Dr. Tracy E. Hazen, Barnard College, Columbia University, New York City.

HOLLAND.—*Nathaniel of Watertown, Mass.*, by E. W. E. Holland, 56 Clarendon St., Boston, Mass.

HULL.—*George of Dorchester, Mass., Windsor and Fairfield, Conn., Rev. Joseph of Weymouth, Mass., and Richard of New Haven, Conn.*, by Hull Family Association, c/o Herbert G. Hull, 3 Broad St., New York City.

KILBURN.—*Thomas of Wethersfield, Conn.*, by Elvira Adams Atwood, 322 Prospect Road, South Haven, Mich.

KNIGHT.—*All lines*, by John Herbert Barker, 53 Park St., Somerville, Mass.

LEE.—*Benjamin of Manchester, Mass.*, by Joseph L. Edmiston, 533 Grand Ave., Riverside, Cal.

MOFFAT.—*All lines of Scotland, Ireland and England*, by George West Maffet, Lawrence, Kas.

NEWBOULD.—*Michael of Mansfield Township, Burlington Co., N. J.*, by William Romaine Newbold, University of Penn., Philadelphia, Pa.

NUTTING.—*John of Groton, Mass.*, by John Herbert Barker, 53 Park St., Somerville, Mass.

PALMER.—*William of Hampton, N. H.*, by William L. Palmer, 22 Sacramento Place, Cambridge, Mass.

POPPLETON.—*Samuel of Richland Co., Ohio*, by W. W. Stockberger, U. S. Dept. of Agriculture, Bureau of Plant Industry, Washington, D. C.

STONE.—*John, Jr., of Guilford and Milford, Conn.*, by Charles S. Smith, Terryville, Conn.

A BIT OF ATHOL, MASS., HISTORY.

Communicated by WILLIAM BLAKE TRASK, A.M., of Dorchester, Mass.

THE following return, filed in Massachusetts State Archives, *Towns, etc., 1742–1751*, vol. 115, page 834, with supplement on page 836, relates to settlers of the plantation called Payquage, which was incorporated Mar. 6, 1762, as the town of Athol.

"In Obedience to the Order of The Great and General Court . . .

I the Subſcriber being Choſen by the Proprietors of the Townſhip of Poquiog on the 16th of May AD: 1750 their Clerk—hereby Return the Names of thoſe that have Done their Duty on their Rights according to the Beſt of my Knowledge but the former Clerk Mr Joseph Lord Refuſing to Give up the Books I have Not a Liſt of the Names of the Firſt Proprietors that Drew their Lotts. And Therefore all I Can Say is that there is but fifteen Familys in the Place Excepting Two Sons of Said M^{r}. Lords one is a Singleman Near Twenty one years of age and the other is a Lad and may be about Fifteen years old the Names of the heads of the Fifteen Familys are Richard Morton, Nathaniel Graves, Eleazer Graves, William Oliver Nathan Wait James Straten John Oliver Robert Marble Hugh Holland Ephraim Smith Samuel Morton Abraham Nutt Aaron Smith Abner Lee James Fays Right & Robert Young—Gad Wait Lived there Near Fifteen years Cleared about Ten acres of Land and was Killed and and was a Singleman John Smead Lived there Several years Did his Duty Well and was Captivated once and Then Killed by the Indians—Ezekiel Wallingford fully Complied with the Duty and was Killed by the Indians—Benjamin Townsend Lived on James Holdins houſe Lott and Did the Duty & Died—Jeremiah Wood fully Complied with the Courts Grant—I was an Original proprietor my Self and the Duty was Done by Stephen Farr on the home Lott—

Capt Joseph Harrington Complied with his Duty and alſo the Duty on a Right he bought of one Goddard as I apprehend.

There were Several others that have worked but they are gone and who the owners are I Cant Tell—

There was one Dexter Did the Duty on the fourth home Lott West Poquiog Weſt. Aaron Smith alſo Did the Duty on the Seventh home Lott West Poquiog Eaſt

March 23^{d}: 1750 Att^{t}: ABNER LEE Prop^{t}: Clarke

Worcester ſs March 23^{d}: 1751

Mr Abner Lee ye above Subſcriber under oath to the Truth of ye Aforegoing and of the Settlement made in ye New Township Called Poquiog So far as he could then Recollect the Same.

Coram J. CHANDLER Jus pa."

"March ye 25th 1750

Hon^{o} Sr theſe few Lines are to Deſire You that You would Put into that Paper that I Left with You that m^{r} Joseph Lord Liued on His one Lot N° 3 East Paquiog East meney Yeares and m^{r} Smead Dec^{d}. Liued on His one Lot N°. 4 west Pequiog west ſom yeares and m^{r} Badcock Had Part of ſeuerell Rights as I think and Bult two Littel Houſes and was taken Captiue: If You will Put it in will oblidge Your moſt Humble ſarvent

ABNER LEE"

GRANTEES AND SETTLERS OF SUDBURY, MASS.

By GEORGE WALTER CHAMBERLAIN, M.S., of Weymouth, Mass.

FROM a critical examination of the fifty-six heads of families who were first granted land in Sudbury, about one half are known to have immigrated from the south of England.

Name	*Where from*	*County*	*First appears*
Belcher, Andrew	London		1639.
Bent, John	Penton-Weyhill	Hampshire	1638.
Betts (Beast) Robert			1636.
Bildcome, Richard	Sutton-Mandeville	Wiltshire	1638.
Blandford, John	Sutton-Mandeville	Wiltshire	1638.
Browne, Mr. Edmund*			1637.
Brown, Thomas	Bury St. Edmunds	Co. Suffolk	1637.
Browne, William†			1639.
Buffumthyte, "Wyddow"			1639.
Curtis, Henry‡			1635
Daniell, Robert			1636.
Davis, Robert	Penton-Weyhill	Hampshire	1638.
Flynn, Thomas			1639.
Fordham, (Rev.) Robert			1639.
Freeman, John§			1635.
Goodnowe, Edmund	Dunhead	Wiltshire	1638.
Goodnowe, John	Semley	Wiltshire	1638.
Goodnowe, Thomas	Shaftsbury	Dorsetshire	1638.
Griffin, Hugh			1639.
Hayne, John‖	Sutton-Mandeville	Wiltshire	1638.
Hayne, Walter	Sutton-Mandeville	Wiltshire	1638.
Howe, John			1639.
Hoyte, Thomas¶			1639.
Hunt, Robert			1638.
Hunt, Widow			1638.
Johnson, Solomon			1639.
Joslyn, Thomas**	London		1635.
Kerley, William	Ashmore	Dorsetshire	1638.
Knight, John			1636.
Loker, Henry††			1639.
Loker, John			1639.
Maynard, John			1639.
Munnings, George	Rattlesden	Co. Suffolk	1634.
Newton, Richard			1639.
Noyse, (Mr.) Peter	Penton-Weyhill	Hampshire	1639.
Noyse, Thomas	Penton-Weyhill	Hampshire	1639.

* Probably came from Bury St. Edmunds, Co. Suffolk.
† His wife came from Hetcorne and Frittingden, Co. Kent.
‡ Joan Parker of St. Saviour's, Southwark, Surrey, was his sister.
§ He came in the ship *Abigail*, in July, 1635.
‖ Son of Walter Hayne.
¶ Not mentioned in Savage's Genealogical Dictionary nor in Pope's "Pioneers.
** He came in the ship *Increase*, in April, 1635.
†† Brother to Robert Davis.

Parker, William			1635.
Parmenter, John Sr.			1639.
Parmenter, John Jr.*			1639.
Pelham, (Mr.) William†			1630.
Pendleton, Bryan			1634.
Prentiss, Henry			1639.
Reddock (Ruddock) John			1639.
Rice, Edmond	Barkhamstead	Hertfordshire	1639.
Rice, Henry	"	"	1639.
Rutter, John	Penton-Weyhill	Hampshire	1638
Sanger, Richard	Dunhead	Wiltshire	1639.
Stone, John	Great Bromley	Co. Essex	1635.
Taintor, Joseph	Upton-Gray	Hampshire	1639.
Toll (Towle) John			1639.
Treadway, Nathaniel			1639.
Ward, William			1639.
White, Anthony	Ipswich(?)	Co. Suffolk	1639.
White, Thomas			1636.
Wood, John			1639.
Wright, Widow‡			1639.

THE BELCHER FAMILIES IN NEW ENGLAND.

By Joseph Gardner Bartlett, Esq.

[Concluded from page 256.]

15. Jeremiah[4] Belcher (*Ens. Edward,*[3] *Jeremiah,*[2] *Jeremiah*[1]), born in Lynn, Mar. 23, 1702-3, removed to Milton with his parents when about seventeen years of age, and about 1730 settled in that part of Stoughton which was later Stoughtonham (now Sharon), where he afterwards resided until his death, Aug. 7, 1775. He married, June 13, 1726, Mary, born June 5, 1701, daughter of Jonathan and Hannah (Hobart) Hayward of Braintree, who died July 21, 1775.

Children:

i. Jeremiah,[5] b. in Milton, June 26, 1727; resided in Stoughtonham; served in the French and Indian War in 1757, and performed protracted service during the Revolution; m. Feb. 26, 1756, Amy, b. in 1734, dau. of Jonathan and Sarah (Field) Howard of Bridgewater. Twelve children.

ii. Jonathan, b. in Braintree, May 22, 1730; m. Apr. 16, 1761, Sarah,[5] b. May 7, 1739, dau. of Daniel[4] and Mary (Harkness) Richards of Stoughton; lived in Stoughtonham. Several children.

iii. Susanna, b. May 14, 1734; m. Sept. 9, 1755, Benjamin Savil, Jr., of Stoughton.

iv. Hannah, b. Nov. 25, 1736; m. (1) as his second wife, Nov. 25, 1756, Dea. Stephen Badlam of Stoughton; m. (2) (int. recorded Mar. 25, 1769) Lieut. John[5] Holmes of Stoughton.

v. Sarah, b. June 11, 1739; d. Aug. 20, 1756.

vi. Mary, b. Aug. 21, 1742; m. Nov. 29, 1763, Benjamin Richards of Stoughton.

* Son of John Parmenter, Sr.

† He came with Winthrop, but returned in 1652.

‡ She married John Blandford in 1642; her name was Dorothy.

16. SAMUEL[4] BELCHER (*Ens. Edward,[3] Jeremiah,[2] Jeremiah[1]*), born in Lynn, Mar. 8, 1704-5, settled in Stoughton, where he was a farmer and housewright, and died Mar. 8, 1740-1, administration on his estate being given to his widow, Apr. 14, 1741. In Oct., 1759, his property was divided among his widow and surviving children. (Suffolk Co. Probate, vol. 55, pp. 263, 338.) He married, Jan. 26, 1726-7, Mary, born Nov. 3, 1706, daughter of John and Mary (Holbrook) Puffer of Stoughton, who survived her husband, and died Mar. 12, 1782.

Children:

i. MIRIAM,[5] b. Sept. 13, d. Oct. 5, 1728.
ii. BELA, b. Dec. 28, 1730; chose Benjamin Crane of Milton for his guardian, Aug. 2, 1745; died a few years later, unmarried.
iii. MARY, b. Nov. 4, 1732; m. May 30, 1756, Adam Blackman of Stoughton.
iv. MIRIAM, b. May 19, 1735; m. Nov. 16, 1752, Philip Liscomb, Jr., of Stoughton.
v. REBECCA, b. June 6, 1738; m. Nov. 10, 1757, Elhanan Lyon of Stoughton, who d. in 1770.
vi. ABIGAIL, b. Oct. 8, 1740; m. Sept. 13, 1759, David, son of Elhanan and Hannah (Tilden) Lyon of Stoughton, who was b. April 11, 1739, and was a Lieut. in the Revolution.

17. EDWARD[4] BELCHER (*Ens. Edward,[3] Jeremiah,[2] Jeremiah[1]*), born in Lynn, Jan. 16, 1706-7, lived in Dorchester, and later in Stoughton where he died. Administration on his estate was granted Oct. 8, 1756. He married, Nov. 12, 1730, Anna, born May 3, 1710, daughter of Humphrey and Elizabeth (Withington) Atherton of Dorchester, who died about 1761, administration on her estate being given on Oct. 23 of that year. (Suffolk Co. Probate.)

Children:

i. ATHERTON,[5] b. Sept. 26, 1731.
ii. SARAH, b. Dec. 6, 1734; d. June 9, 1766; m. Dec. 13, 1753, Ezekiel Tilestone of Dorchester, who was b. Apr. 6, 1731, and d. in 1812.
iii. ANNA, bapt. June 5, 1737; m. Aug. 11, 1757, John Lloyd of Stoughton.
iv. JOHN, b. Sept. 26, 1740; settled in Stoughton; marched on the Lexington alarm, Apr. 19, 1775; m. Mar. 27, 1763, Abigail Bracket. Nine children.
v. SAMUEL, b. Sept. 12, 1744; resided in Dorchester, where he d. Aug. 6, 1812; m. Sept. 29, 1772, Rachel, b. Jan. 5, 1750-1, dau. of Ebenezer and Abigail (Billings) Pope of Dorchester, who d. Jan. 3, 1801. Ten children.
vi. ELIZABETH, b. about 1747; on Oct. 8, 1762, Consider Atherton was appointed her guardian. (Suffolk Co. Probate.)

18. CLIFFORD[4] BELCHER (*Ens. Edward,[3] Jeremiah,[2] Jeremiah[1]*), born in Lynn, Oct. 12, 1710, settled in Stoughton, where he owned over 300 acres of land, and where he lived until his death, Apr. 26, 1773. Besides farming, he also engaged in business as a blacksmith and as a carpenter. He married, June 24, 1740, Mehitable,[4] born Dec. 8, 1706, daughter of Samuel[3] and Sarah (Clapp) Bird of Stoughton, who died Feb. 20, 1779.

Children:

i. SAMUEL,[5] b. June 28, d. July 16, 1741.
ii. PRESERVED, b. Oct. 6, d. Oct. 26, 1744.
iii. CLIFFORD, b. Oct. 7, 1745; m. Nov. 22, 1770, Betty, b. Sept. 23, 1750, dau. of Jonathan and Betty (Snell) Copeland of Bridgewater;

lived in Stoughtonham; had three children; the parents and all the children d. between Aug. 12 and 26, 1775. He marched on the Lexington Alarm, April 19, 1775.

iv. LOVE, b. July 11, d. Sept. 25, 1747.

v. JOSEPH, b. May 13, 1749; d. May 27, 1814; was a carpenter and resided in Stoughton (now Canton); m. (int. recorded Oct. 28, 1775) Mary,[5] b. Dec. 26, 1754, dau. of Elijah[4] and Hannah (Puffer) Baker of Stoughton, who d. Feb. 26, 1839. Ten children.

vi. CAPT. SUPPLY, b. Mar. 29, 1751; served as private in the Revolution; in 1778 he bought a farm in what is now South Canton where he opened a tavern, but sold the place and moved to Maine in 1785, locating first at Hallowell (now Augusta), where he remained some six years, and then, in 1791, settled on the Sandy River, in what is now the town of Farmington, Me., where he became the leading man in the community, holding the offices of selectman, town clerk, captain, and justice of the peace, and serving as representative to the General Court in 1798, 1801, and 1809; also taught school and practiced medicine; died in Farmington, June 9, 1836; m. May 2, 1775, Margaret, b. May 13, 1756, d. May 14, 1839, dau. of William More, of Boston, and his wife Margaret, dau. of John and Abigail (Parsons) Johnson, of Boston, and widow of Richard Francis. Ten children.

vii. MEHITABLE, b. Oct. 10, 1752; m. Dec. 15, 1774, Josiah Harris of Stoughton; lived in Fitchburg in 1792, where their dau. *Mehitable* m. Mar. 4, 1798, Sewall Fullam.

19. JOSEPH[4] BELCHER (*Ens. Joseph,*[3] *Jeremiah,*[2] *Jeremiah*[1]), born Oct. 25, 1698, inherited lands in Chelsea from his father, and also acquired houses in North street in Boston, where he resided and carried on the business of housewright. He died in 1744, administration on his estate being given on Aug. 24 of that year. He married, Nov. 14, 1726, Elizabeth, born Jan. 30, 1700-1, daughter of James and Love English of Boston, who died Apr. or Aug. 23, 1762, aged 61, and is buried in Copp's Hill cemetery.

Children

i. ELIZABETH,[5] b. Oct. 13, 1727; m. Oct. 26, 1749, Nathaniel Green Moody.

ii. COL. JOSEPH, b. Apr. 13, 1729; was a brazier and pewter manufacturer; settled in Newport, R. I., where he became a prominent man; in 1756 he was captain of a company on an expedition against Crown Point; during the Revolution he was colonel of a regiment of Newport militia; served in the Rhode Island Assembly in 1776 and 1777; when Newport was occupied by the British troops, he retired with his family to Brookline, Mass., where he died, Sept. 27, 1778; after the war was over, his family returned to Newport; m. in Newport, Feb. 14, 1750-1, Hannah Gladding, who d. in Newport, Oct. 4, 1813, aged 83. Fourteen children.

iii. MARTHA, b. July 20, 1730.

iv. JAMES, bapt. July 29, 1733.

v. WILLIAM, bapt. Oct. 26, 1735.

20. NATHANIEL[4] BELCHER (*Ens. Joseph,*[3] *Jeremiah,*[2] *Jeremiah*[1]), born Oct. 5, 1703, lived in Boston, and later in Chelsea, where he died Dec. 31, 1781. He married, Feb. 22, 1727-8, Deborah,[4] born Jan. 10, 1707-8, daughter of John[3] and Persis (Holbrook) Farrow of Hingham, who died Nov. 18, 1784.

Children:

i. NATHANIEL,[5] b. about 1729; lived in Chelsea; m. Apr. 24, 1755, Anna, b. Mar. 30, 1727, dau. of Ebenezer and Mary Dowse of Billerica. Five children.

ii. John, b. about 1732.
iii. Hannah, bapt. Aug. 25, 1734.
iv. Priscilla, bapt. Feb. 13, 1736-7.

21. Jonathan[4] Belcher (*Ens. Joseph,*[3] *Jeremiah,*[2] *Jeremiah*[1]), born Feb. 27, 1717-18, lived in Chelsea, where he died Oct. 17, 1785. He married, May 13, 1742, Elizabeth, born Oct. 23, 1718, daughter of Samuel and Abigail (Floyd) Tuttle of Chelsea, who died Dec. 5, 1796.

Children:

i. Jonathan,[5] b. Apr. 8, 1743.
ii. Elizabeth, b. Sept. 30, 1744; m. (1) June 1, 1786, Ezra Glover of Dorchester; m. (2) Mar. 27, 1797, William Barrows of Boston.
iii. David, b. Mar. 28, 1747; lived in Chelsea; was drowned Sept. 8, 1794; m. Feb. 20, 1787, Elizabeth, b. Oct. 18, 1754, dau. of John and Susanna (Chamberlain) Sargent, who d. July 12, 1817. Four children.
iv. Mary, b. July 25, 1749.
v. Joseph, b. May 10, 1751; lived at Pullin Point, now Winthrop; was a soldier in the Revolution; m. Dec. 18, 1781, Rachel, b. Oct. 16, 1756, dau. of Richard and Mary (Green) Shute of Malden. They had at least six children, one of whom was *Joseph,*[6] b. in 1782, d. Feb. 25, 1850, who m. Nancy, b. in 1786, d. in 1849, dau. of Joseph and Sally (Belcher) Burrill. They had ten children, the youngest of whom, Warren,[7] b. in 1825, has always resided at Winthrop, Mass., where he was appointed Postmaster in 1853, and continuously held the office for 53 years, resigning May 28, 1906. Mr. Belcher has in his possession a large number of interesting family papers, pertaining to every generation of his ancestral line in New England,—among them several original deeds of Jeremiah Belcher of Ipswich.
vi. Martha, b. Mar. 12, 1754; m. May 3, 1787, Ebenezer Burrill, perhaps son of Samuel and Anna (Alden) Burrill of Lynn.
vii. Abigail b. Mar. 7, 1758.

22. Joseph[4] Belcher, Jr. (*Joseph,*[3] *David* [?],[2] *Jeremiah*[1]), born probably about 1708, lived in Chebacco parish, Ipswich, until his marriage, when he settled in Manchester, Mass. He was a mariner, and died about 1745. He married, Dec. 8, 1730, Mary, born Mar. 22, 1708-9, daughter of George and Jane Cross of Manchester, who married second, Oct. 3, 1750, Thomas Murphy, and died Feb. 21, 1776.

Children:

i. Mary,[5] bapt. Oct. 3, 1731; d. young.
ii. Mary, b. June 6, 1733; m. Jan. 27, 1755, John Sinnet of Marblehead.
iii. Ruth, b. Sept. 26, 1735; m. Nov. 10, 1763, Daniel Rust of Ipswich.
iv. Joseph, b. Dec. 8, 1737; was a fisherman, and lived in Manchester; lost at sea, in the autumn of 1763; m. Mar. 8, 1759, Elizabeth, bapt. Mar. 16, 1737-8, dau. of John and Sarah (Pearce) Tuck of Manchester, who m. (2) (int. rec. Feb. 2, 1766) Anthony de Myng. Three children.
v. Abigail (probably), b. about 1740; m. May 1, 1762, John Bowls.
vi. Jane, bapt. Mar. 21, 1741-2; m. Feb. 12, 1762, William Camp.

23. Andrew[4] Belcher (*Samuel,*[3] *Richard,*[2] *Jeremiah*[1]), born in Cambridge, Sept. 10, 1740, was taken to Wrentham in infancy by his parents, and is mentioned in his father's will as living in Sept., 1773. It seems likely he was the Andrew who was enrolled as private in Capt. Samuel Miller's company, on Aug. 8, 1757. Also, he was

probably the Andrew who married, in Canterbury, Conn., May 18, 1769, Abigail Burt. No further information of him has been secured.

24. JOHN[4] BELCHER (*Samuel,[3] Richard,[2] Jeremiah[1]*), born in Wrentham, June 20, 1744, was a husbandman, and passed his life in his native town, inheriting his father's homestead. He was a soldier in the Revolution. He married first, Dec. 18, 1777, Hannah,[6] born June 22, 1751, daughter of Edward[4] and Deborah (Green) Rawson of Mendon, who died about 1785; and married second, Oct. 9, 1787, Susanna, daughter of Abner and Martha (Robbins) Hazeltine of Upton. His will, dated Aug. 15, 1815, probated Apr. 5, 1825, names wife Susanna, sons Harvey and Rawson to have the property of their mother, sons Manning, Samuel, Abner, Daniel and Caleb, and daughters Hannah and Susanna.

Children by first wife:

i. JOHN,[5] b. Aug. 13, 1779; no further record; probably d. unmarried.
ii. RAWSON, b. Jan. 6, 1781.
iii. HARVEY, b. July 12, 1784; settled in North Brookfield, where he m. Jan. 3, 1813, Nancy, b. Sept. 26, 1791, d. June 12, 1874, dau. of Eli and Elizabeth (Smith) How of North Brookfield; d. July 19, 1858. Eleven children.

Children by second wife:

iv. HANNAH, b. July 25, 1788.
v. MANNING, b. July 13, 1790; graduated at Brown University in 1814; settled in South Carolina, where he taught school most of his life, and d. Sept. 13, 1868; m. in 1817, Susanna, b. June 23, 1790, dau. of Judge Samuel Day of Wrentham.
vi. SAMUEL, b. July 25, 1792.
vii. ABNER, b. Sept. 6, 1794; inherited his father's homestead.
viii. DANIEL, b. July 5, 1797; settled in Illinois.
ix. DR. CALEB, b. Feb. 2, 1800; graduated from Brown University in 1823, and the Harvard Medical School in 1827; practiced his profession in Falmouth, Mass., from 1827 to 1847, and in Cumberland, R. I., from 1848 to 1875; d. in Cumberland, Apr. 7, 1875.
x. SUSANNA.

25. DAVID[4] BELCHER (*Samuel,[3] Richard,[2] Jeremiah[1]*), born in Wrentham, Aug. 14, 1746, went to Bellingham about 1775, where he resided until 1783, when he removed to Thompson, Conn., where he lived until 1798, and then finally located in Stafford, Conn., where he died in 1811. He served in the Revolution. He married, Apr. 22, 1778, Rachel,[4] born Apr. 10, 1748, daughter of Elisha[3] and Sarah (Bates) Burr of Hingham.

Children:

i. COL. SAMUEL,[5] b. in Bellingham, June 14, 1779; lived in Hartford, Conn., where he d. in 1849, leaving a large estate for the times; m. Apr., 1805, Pamelia, dau. of Eleazer Pinney of Ellington. Two children, who d. unmarried, before their father.
ii. SARAH, b. Nov. 4, 1781; m. John Perry of South Brimfield.
iii. DAVID, b. 1785.
iv. JOHN, b. 1787; d. 1789.
v. RHODA, b. 1789.

26. WOODBRIDGE[4] BELCHER (*Samuel,[3] Richard,[2] Jeremiah[1]*), born in Wrentham, Oct. 10, 1749, lived in Palmer, Mass., during the Revolution, later in Rowley, Mass., and finally in Weare, N. H.,

where he died. He served in the Revolution. He married first, in Palmer, Mass., Sept. 24, 1778, Rebecca Chase; and married second, in 1790, Mehitable, born Nov. 6, 1752, daughter of Oliver and Elizabeth (Jewett) Tenney of Rowley.

Child by first wife:

i. SAMUEL,[5] m. Anna, dau. of William and Polly (Walker) Caldwell; removed to Stockbridge, Vt.

Children by second wife:

ii. OLIVE TENNEY, b. Dec. 21, 1792; d. July 29, 1802.
iii. HARRIET YOUNG, b. Oct. 14, 1794.
iv. OLIVER TENNEY, b. Jan. 1, 1797; settled in Stockbridge, Vt.

27. JONATHAN[4] BELCHER (*Jonathan,[3] Richard,[2] Jeremiah*[1]), born about 1734, lived in Framingham, and later in East Hartford, Conn. He served as private in Capt. John Nixon's company, from April 10 to May 25, 1758; was private in Capt. Moses Maynard's company, on Apr. 25, 1757; and marched to Springfield from Framingham, on Aug. 16, 1757, as private under Capt. Samuel Curtis, when the latter started for the relief of Fort William Henry.

He married, in Providence, R. I., Mar. 2, 1760, Sarah, born Apr. 22, 1741, daughter of Jacob and Martha Hartshorn of Providence, who was buried there, at St. John's Church, July 11, 1769.

Children:

i. JACOB,[5] b. about 1761; lived in Framingham; served in the Continental army in the Revolution; d. Aug. 11, 1840; m. Mar., 1782, Anne, b. Oct. 8, 1759, dau. of Ezekiel and Hannah (Edmands) Rice of Framingham, who d. June 13, 1838. Four children.
ii. MOLLY.
iii. JOHN, b. about 1766; lived in Framingham, where he d. Oct. 7, 1843; m. in 1787, Sally, b. in 1771, probably dau. of William and Sarah Williams of Reading, who d. Feb. 26, 1853. Seven children.
iv. HANNAH, m. June, 1788, Ephraim Pratt.

28. DANIEL[4] BELCHER (*Jonathan,[3] Richard,[2] Jeremiah*[1]), born June 14, 1736, lived in Framingham, where he was enrolled in Capt. Jeremiah Belknap's company, Apr. 26, 1757. He died in Nov., 1787. He married Hannah, baptized Oct. 15, 1749, daughter of Thomas and Elizabeth (Drury) Winch of Framingham.

Children:

i. DANIEL.[5]
ii. JASON, lived in Framingham; m. Nov. 9, 1800, Anna, b. Nov. 24, 1780, dau. of Silas and Elizabeth (Jones) Winch of Framingham. Five children. She m. (2) in 1826, Benjamin Dudley of Framingham, and d. Jan. 3, 1838, aged 57.
iii. BETSEY, d. young.

29. EZRA[4] BELCHER (*Jonathan,[3] Richard,[2] Jeremiah*[1]), born in 1751, inherited his father's homestead, and was a noted singing master. He died June 29, 1826. He married, Mar. 18, 1794, Susanna, baptized Feb. 5, 1769, daughter of Samuel and Lois (Pratt) Dadmun of Framingham, who died May 17, 1854.

Children:

i. RUTH,[5] b. Nov. 14, 1794.
ii. LUCY, b. Apr. 23, 1797.
iii. LUTHER, b. Apr. 23, 1797.
iv. EZRA, b. Feb. 24, 1799.
v. SUSANNA, b. July 21, 1801.

30. JOSEPH[4] BELCHER (*Jonathan,[3] Richard,[2] Jeremiah[1]*), baptized in July, 1755, passed his life in Framingham, where he died June 29, 1833. In the Revolution, he served as corporal in Capt. Moses Harrington's company, from Dec. 20, 1776, to March 1, 1777. He married, in May, 1782, Hannah, born Sept. 9, 1756, daughter of Thomas and Hannah (Rice) Kendall, who died May 18, 1854, aged nearly 98.

Children:

i. MARY,[5] b. Feb. 6, 1783; m. Stephen Lord of Sullivan, N. H.
ii. PATTY, b. Dec. 20, 1785; m. ——— Harrington; d. Feb. 25, 1845.
iii. JOSEPH, b. June 21, 1788; lived on his father's farm; d. Nov. 16, 1828; m. Jan. 11, 1814, Abigail Hunt of Sudbury, who m. (2) Oct. 17, 1830, John Moore of Framingham, and d. Oct. 4, 1833. Six children.
iv. HANNAH, b. Mar. 28, 1791; d. Dec. 15, 1849.
v. THOMAS, b. Sept. 3, 1793; d. Oct. 30, 1821.
vi. CURTIS, b. June 1, 1796; d. Nov. 16, 1815.
vii. BETSEY, b. Apr. 11, 1800; m. Nov. 30, 1828, Amos White of Waltham; d. Nov. 4, 1873.

A BARRINGTON, NOVA SCOTIA, PETITION.

Communicated by Mrs. HELEN WRIGHT BROWN, of Boston.

THE following petition of Massachusetts settlers at Barrington, N. S., filed in the Massachusetts State Archives, *Revolutionary Resolves*, 1776–1777, seems worthy of publication.

"Barrington Nova Scotia, October 19th 1776—

Gentlemen

We the Subscribers Inhabitants of Barrington in ye Province of Nova Scotia, Haveing hired and partly Loaded the schooner Hop[*illegible*] with Fish and Liver Oyl bound for Salem or Newbray In the Province of the Masſachusetts bay—Earnestly Pray and Request of you the Honble Congreſs or those whose busineſs it may be to see to it. To permit and Suffer the said Loading to be Disposed of by Heman Kenney and part of the amount to be lay'd out in proviſsions for the Support of us the Subscribers which are Intirely Destitute of any for the Support of them or their Children and it is Impoſsible to get any Elsewhere And a long Winter Approaching God only knows what will become of us;

We look on ourselves as Unhappyly situated as any People in the world, being Settlelers from the Maſsachusetts bay for whose wellfare we Earnestly pray haveing Fathers Brothers and Children liveing there; And we have in the Course of these unhappy Times done everything in our power to Aſsist those unfortunate people that have been Taken and come into this place from Halifax to help them over the bay on their way home. And have not at any Time done anything Eigher by Supplys or men to Injure our native place and Country:— In the above veſsell are Three Families with their Effects which have left this place and gone to the places in your province where they formerly came from, And we the Subscribers don't see but that we must follow them for we don't think we can Live Quietly here for our Imployment is such for the Support of our families to

Viz[t] Fishing as you look upon as a Disservice to the great cause you are Imbarked in and we cannot but follow it while we are thus Situated; Therefore we Earnestly pray and Request of you in your great Goodneſs and Wisdom to Aſsist us with Proviſsions as we the Subscribers shall want for this winter and till such time as we can remove ourselves from this place to our former homes Unleſs the Tremendus Times are Settled, Which God grant may be soon; We have Authorised and Appointed our Friend M[r] Heman Kenney to Answer and Reply to any Questions and to represent our Deplorable Scituation to you the Hon[ble] Congreſs or others who he may be call'd before: And we are ready to keep up a Correspondence with the Inhabitants of your province to Exchange fish for other proviſsions if you should see fit to Incourrage such a Trade untill such Time as we can Remove ourselves from this place provided you are Determin'd to Prevent our fishing on this Shore. For the Privaters have taken Severall of our Schooners from us and the fish caught in them to the great Distreſs of the fishermen which have not done any Thing but fishing to Injure you which they could not help being the only way they have to maintain their families. For all which causes and Reasons we cannot but flatter ourselves that you will Receive this Memoriall from us And Answer our Request which will Enable us to Support our Wifes And Children and we cannot think the Request being Granted any Damage to you. We mean not to offend you in anything but should be glad to know our Destiney if any of us should tarry at this place dureing these times for we have not seen nor heard from you anything who are in Authority but only from some of the men on board the privaters that have made this a place of Rendevous who tell us all the Dreadfull Things that can befall any People, to Viz[t] That the Indians are Commission'd to come on the back of us to kill burn and Distroy A Picture, this drawn by them, that we the Descendants from America Cannot think ever Enter'd into the breasts of the free and Generous sons of America. We are Gentlemen, your most humble petitioners and very humble Servants—

Solomon Smith	David Crowell
Isaac King	Elisha Smith
Ths. Doane	William Granwood
Reuben Cohoon	Solomon Smith Juner
Theodore Smith	Benjamin Kirby
Stephen Nickerson	Samuel Batman
Elkanah Smith	Joseph Smith
Jonathan Smith	Jonathan Smith J[r]
Isaac Kenney	Joseph Atwood.
Gamaliel Kenney	Timothy Corell.
Marcy Kenney	Joshua Attwood
Isaac King Juner	John Reynolds
Sam[l] Osborn Doanes	Joseph Kenwrick
Thomas Crowell	Solomon Kenwrick Juner
Edmand Doane.	

[*In the margin.*] N. B. We hope and desire you will not give this a place in your News papers, tho you should think it worthy which may be of Damage to us if we should remain at this place."

The following is written on back of the last page of the foregoing letter.

"In the House of Representatives
Nov 15th 1776.

Resolv' Whereas it appears to this Court that the within petitioners inhabitants of Barrington in Nova Scotia have proved themselves firm friends of the united States of America; and on that account are determined as soon as may be to transport themselves & their families from that province to this state in order to get out of the reach of British tyranny. And it being represented that the said inhabitants of Barrington from a determined refusal of trade with the enemies of America have exposed themselves to great hardships thro' want of such provisions as are necessary to support them until they be removed;

therefore

Resolved that the prayer of the within petition be so far granted as that the within named Heman Kenny be and he hereby is permitted to purchase and export from any town or place in the state to said Barrington, solely for the purpose of enabling the said inhabitants thereof to transport themselves from thence to this state 250 bushels of corn 30 barrels of pork 2 hogsheads of Molasses 2 d° of rum 200 lbs of coffee

Sent up for Concurrence
J. Warren Spkr

In Council Nov. 16th 1776

Read and Concurr'd
John Avery Dpty

Consented to

Jer Powell	Benj Austin
Caleb Cutting	Wm Phillips
R. Derby Jnr	Dl Hopkins
J. Winthrop	Eldad Taylor
S. Holton	Moses Gill
John Whitcomb	Danl Davis
Jabez Fisher	D. Sewall
B. White.	

(Resolve of the House granting Permifsion to the Inhabitants of Barrington in Nova Scotia to purchase Provifsions and transport themselves from thence Nov. 16th 1776)"

JOHN SOLENDINE OF DUNSTABLE, MASS., AND HIS DESCENDANTS.

By Ethel Stanwood Bolton, B.A., of Shirley, Mass.

1. John[1] Solendine, a carpenter by trade, was a settler at Dunstable, Mass., about 1674. No definite facts are known of his former residence, either in this country or in England, but he seems to have associated upon terms of equality with the Tyngs, Ushers, and other prominent families of Dunstable. In 1682, he "was engaged to complete the unfinished meeting-house, which was probably but little more than a log shanty;*" he also built the first bridge across Salmon Brook. The first marriage entered upon the records of the town was that of John Solendine and Elizabeth

* History of Dunstable.

Usher, on August 2, 1680.* Elizabeth Usher was the daughter of Robert Usher of Stamford, Conn., and his wife Elizabeth the widow of Jeremy Jaggers,† and a niece of Hezekiah Usher of Dunstable. Robert Usher had died when Elizabeth was still a young girl, and had left her in charge of her uncle. John Solendine and his wife settled in Dunstable, where his four children were born. He lived in a fortified house. In 1692, Maj. Thomas Hinchman, who commanded all the troops in that part of the Province, sent a petition to the General Court, in which he states that "all ye Inhabitants of Dunstable excepting 2 familys desire to draw. off. viz Jno Sollendine & Thos Luff whose Garrisons are nere to each other, these seem willing to ——— themselves with 10 or 12 sould^rs." John Solendine stayed, and as late as 1711 resided in one of the seven fortified houses in Dunstable, with four soldiers regularly quartered there. About the time of his marriage, his wife's uncle, Hezekiah Usher, bought of Major Simon Willard three fourths of "Nonacoicus Farm," now a part of the town of Ayer, Mass. At that time "Nonacoicus" was partly in Groton and partly in Harvard, its northern boundary being the brook still called Nonacoicus. Willard had built a blockhouse on the farm, and the Ushers took possession of it, and lived there. This farm bore a rather prominent part in the fortunes of the Solendines.

Children:

i. SARAH,[2] b. Apr. 15, 1682 (1680, in Middlesex Co. Records).
2. ii. JOHN, b. May 8, 1683.
iii. ELIZABETH, b. June 3, 1685; m. in Charlestown, July 20, 1710, William Farr, also of Dunstable.
iv. ALICE, b. Jan. 16, 1687.

2. JOHN[2] SOLENDINE (*John*[1]) was born in Dunstable, May 8, 1683. Of his early life little is known, but he evidently followed the Ushers to Groton, for, some time before 1718, he married Susanna Woods.‡ According to a deed§ she was the daughter of Samuel Woods of Groton, and a sister of Samuel Woods, Jr., of Alice Woods, of Rachel wife of Jonathan Whitcomb, and Mary wife of John Goss. The Ushers had left Groton some time before John Solendine went there, for after the death of his great-uncle Hezekiah, Hezekiah Usher, Jr., his son and executor, had sold Nonacoicus to Jonathan Tyng of Dunstable. The younger Usher was a prosperous merchant of Boston. The indenture relating to the sale was signed on May 11, 1687, "between Hezekiah Usher, of Boston, Merchant, Heir and Executor of Hezeziah Usher late of Boston, deceased," and Jonathan Tyng of Dunstable guardian of John Tyng "his son & Heir apparent & intrust to & for ye s^d Jno Tyng one of the Grandchildren of ye said Hezekiah Usher deceased."‖

In 1713, John Solendine, and Henry Farwell of Dunstable, bought from Jonathan Tyng the part of "Nonacoicus Farm" which had formerly belonged to his great-uncle¶ Hezekiah Usher. To this

* Recorded as Apr. 2, 1679, in the marriages returned to Middlesex County, and as Apr. 4, 1679, in the records of Chelmsford, Mass.

† Robert Usher married first, May 13, 1659, Elizabeth Jaggers, and had *Elizabeth*, b. Feb. 25, 1659-60, *Robert*, *Mehitable*, and *Sarah*; and married second, Elizabeth Symms. He was a member of the General Court in 1665,1667.

‡ She was born about 1686, the daughter of Samuel[2] (Samuel[1]) and Hannah (Farwell) Woods of Groton.—EDITOR.

§ Middlesex County Deeds, Vol. 39, p. 266.

‖ Middlesex Co. Deeds, Vol. 10, p. 49. Sarah Usher married Jonathan Tyng, and John was their fourth child.

¶ Middlesex Co. Deeds, Vol. 18, p. 519.

they added seventy acres south-east of the farm, which would be in the town of Harvard. He apparently, at the time or soon after, settled on his farm, where he remained for the rest of his life. He was a very active real estate operator, his holdings being in at least four towns—Groton, Shirley, Harvard and Lancaster.

In 1738, John Solendine died intestate, aged 55 years, and on Mar. 12, 1739, his widow Susanna was granted letters of administration.* The total property was valued at £1523 : 18 : 4. The land "adjoining Bartlett" still bears his name, and is known in Shirley as "the Solendine Meadows," or "Cellendine" as some deeds have it. The widow Susanna married, in 1739, John Haughton of Bolton, Mass.

Children:

i. SUSANNA,[3] b. Feb. 11, 1718; m. June 19, 1740, Manassah Divol of Lancaster.
ii. WILLIAM, b. Apr. 23, 1721; d. young.
iii. JOHN, b. Apr. 28, 1725; d. young.
iv. SARAH, b. May 8, 1727; d. Feb. 24, 1754, according to the Town records, but alive in 1757, when her brothers agreed to pay her some £27, according to the Probate records.
3. v. JOHN, b. Nov. 10, 1729.
4. vi. ISAAC, b. Apr. 18, 1732.

3. JOHN[3] SOLENDINE (*John,*[2] *John*[1]) was born in Groton, Nov. 10, 1729. In 1738, when their father's estate was administered, he and his brother Isaac were both called of Lancaster, where they probably resided with their mother and step-father, John Haughton. Just after John[3] came of age, his father's estate was finally distributed, and he received two pieces of land in Shirley, on one of which was the "Solendine Meadows." He built a house in Shirley, after his marriage in Groton, on June 17, 1752, with Dorcas Whipple, but they had a short married life. The following year Mrs. Solendine gave birth to twins, and died almost immediately after. The daughter Dorcas died the same year; and not long after, John[3] and his young son moved to Lancaster. In 1761, John Solendine was serving on the western frontier of the colonies, under Capt. Richard Saltonstall, with many other Lancaster men. He died Apr. 17, 1766, in Lancaster.

Children:

i. DORCAS,[4] b. May 23, 1753, in Shirley; d. Aug. 18, 1753.
5. ii. JOHN, b. May 22, 1753, in Shirley.

4. ISAAC[3] SOLENDINE (*John,*[2] *John*[1]) was born in Groton, Apr. 18, 1732. He was only six years old when his father died, and at least until 1744 he was allowed to live with his mother. In the latter year, Manassah Divol, his oldest sister's husband, petitioned the Court and obtained the guardianship of Isaac and his sister Sarah.† No sooner had Isaac reached his majority, however, than the speculative spirit of his father seized him, and he began to buy real estate. He bought and sold land in Lancaster, Leominster, Rutland and other towns until 1804. In that year Jacob Fisher, William Wilder and John Prentiss, Selectmen of Lancaster, petitioned the Court to

* Middlesex Co. Probate, 15645½.
† Worcester Co. Probate, 51784.

appoint a guardian for Isaac, that he "does by excessive drinking, Idleness &c. so spend, waste and lesson his Estate, as thereby to expose himself to want & suffering circumstances."*

Isaac Solendine never married, so far as is known. He bought a farm near his brother John, in 1758,† but in 1762 he sold it again, and followed his brother to Lancaster, where he lived the remainder of his life. He died in Lancaster, of consumption, Sept. 16, 1806, aged 75 years.

5. JOHN[4] SOLENDINE (*John*,[3] *John*,[2] *John*[1]) was born in Shirley, Mass., May 22, 1753. As a young boy, after the death of his mother, he was taken to Lancaster by his father, and there he spent the rest of his life. His intention of marriage with Susanna Farwell was published May 8, 1773. He died of pleurisy, Feb. 25, 1807, aged 55 years. On Mar. 4, 1808, his widow committed suicide, at the house of her son-in-law, Calvin Wilder.

Children:

- i. JOHN,[4] 1774; d. Nov. 2 or 4, 1825, of consumption, in the Poor House at Lancaster, aged 51 yrs.
- ii. SUSANNA, m. Dec. 17, 1795, Calvin Wilder of Lancaster.
- 6. iii. MANASSAH, b. 1780.
- iv. MARY ANNE, b. 1795; d. Feb. 25, 1807, aged 12 yrs. 9 mos.

6. MANASSAH[5] SOLENDINE (*John*,[4] *John*,[3] *John*,[2] *John*[1]) was born about 1780, in Lancaster. He married, Jan. 1, 1804, Deborah Fairbanks of Bolton. His six children were all born in Lancaster, where he lived until 1823. On Feb. 11 of that year, James Parker, Jr., of Shirley, wrote in his diary, "Manassah Soulendine moved into the Frost Farm." This farm was on the banks of the Nashua, in "Pine Plain," lying north of the Catecoonemaug in Shirley. Two years later, Adeline, his second daughter, went to James Parker, Jr.'s, to live and work, and on June 10, 1825, Mr. Parker wrote, "Abraham Durant and Adeline Solendine were married at my house and went off: moved to Westford same day."

On Nov. 8, 1827, Deborah, wife of Manassah Solendine, died of consumption, aged 46 years, and two years later her daughter Celinda died. Manassah wrote to the Hon. Nathaniel Paine, Judge of Probate, that it was "inconvenient" for him to administer the estate, and requested that Jacob Foster be appointed. He is called then of Lancaster, and it is probable that he moved to his native town after the death of his wife.

On Aug. 16, 1832, Manassah Solendine died of consumption. His wife's gravestone is the only one remaining in Lancaster which bears the Solendine name.

Children:

- i. CELINDA,[6] d. intestate, 1829.
- ii. ADELINE, b. Mch. 27, 1806; m. June 10, 1825, Abraham Durant of Westford.
- iii. SUSAN WILDER, b. Jan. 2, 1808.
- iv. ELVIRA, b. May 10, 1820.
- v. MARY, b. May 10, 1822.
- vi. JULIA ANNE, b. Jan. 1824; d. Sept. or Oct., 1825.

* Worcester Co. Probate, 51785.
† Middlesex Co. Deeds, Vol. 59, p. 479.

INSCRIPTIONS FROM OLD CEMETERIES IN CONNECTICUT.

Communicated by Louis Marinus Dewey, Esq., of Westfield, Mass.

[Concluded from page 308.]

Lebanon.

Abigail wife of Caleb Abel died 11 Nov., 1748, aged 69.
Caleb Abel died 26 May, 1814, aged 82.
Mrs. Elizabeth Abel died 2 Aug., 1814, aged 84.
Lydia wife of Ebenezer Bacon died 2 Jan., 1791, aged 76.
Timothy Bailey died 4 July, 1833, aged 62.
Ruth Hutchinson, wife of T. Bailey, died 4 May, 1810, aged 31. (Next to Joseph and Ruth Hutchinson.)
Mrs. Ann, relict of Benjamin Bissel, died 5 Nov., 1778, aged 52.
Col. James Clark died 29 Dec., 1826, aged 96 years 5 mos. "He was a soldier of the Revolution and dared to lead where any dared to follow. The Battles of Bunker Hill, Harlem Heights and White Plains, witnessed his personal bravery and his devotion to the cause of his country. He here in death rests from his labours For 'there is no discharge in that war.'"
Capt. Simon Cross died 23 Feb., 1796, aged 86.
Thomas Hunt, Jr., died 24 Apr., 1735.
John Huntington died 20 Feb., 1777, aged 71.
Mehitable (Metcalf), wife of Ensign John Huntington, died 2 Apr., 1750, aged 52.
Ruth, consort of Joseph Hutchinson, died 24 Apr., 1782, aged 68.
Abigail, wife of William Metcalf, died 24 Sept., 1764, aged 56.
Daniel Metcalf died 28 Feb., 1831, aged 83.
Elizabeth, his wife, died 29 Mch., 1824, aged 73.
David Metcalf died 7 Sept., 1823, aged 65.
Anna, his relict, died 13 Oct., 1834, aged 79.
Hannah (Avery) relict of Jonathan Metcalf, died 9 Nov., 1755, aged 76.
William Metcalf (son of Jonathan) died 13 June, 1773, aged 64.
Jerusha, consort of John Mory, died 24 Apr., 1736, aged 25.
Samuel Seabury died 16 Mch., 1800, aged 82.
Lieut. Jedediah Strong died 1 Mch. 1737.
Mary, wife of Benjamin Sprague, died 10 July, 1723, aged 42.
Prudence, second wife of Benjamin Sprague, died in Stonington, 18 May, 1726, aged 38; formerly wife of Joseph Denison and daughter of Joseph Minor of Stonington.
John Webster died 10 April, 1731 (?), aged 45.
Hannah, his wife, died 12 June 1773, aged 63.
Capt. Jonathan White died 2 Mch., 1788, aged 86.
Nathaniel Williams died 15 Feb., 1814, aged 71.

Columbia.

Julia S., wife of Rev. F. D. Avery, born 22 Feb., 1823, died 24 June, 1855; lived at East Hartford.

Sophia, wife of Paul W. Avery, died 13 Feb., 1840, aged 26, buried at Andover, Conn.

Hinchman Bennet died 1 Feb., 1809, aged 81.

Lydia, his wife, died 31 Mch., 1791, aged 45.

Hannah, relict of Robert Bennett of the Island of Newport, died 8 Mch., 1789, aged 83.

Nathaniel Brown died 8 June, 1828, aged 70.

Lydia, his wife, died 27 Dec., 1814, aged 49.

Rev. Thomas Brockway, A.M., died 5 July, 1807, aged 62, in the 36th year of his ministry.

Capt. Samuel Buckingham died 31 July, 1756, aged 61.

Carey Clark, a lieutenant of the Revolution, died 15 May, 1842, aged 86.

Martha, his wife, died 17 April, 1824, aged 66.

Capt. Joseph Clark died 10 Sept., 1769, aged 77.

Rebecca, his wife, died 1 June 1759, aged 61.

David Cole died 18 March, 1809, aged 69.

Capt. Nathaniel Cushman died 14 April, 1753, aged 41.

Gershom Dorrence, Esq., died 26 Nov., 1848, aged 79.

Mary, his wife, died 30 Aug., 1854, aged 86.

Samuel Dunham died 9 Dec., 1779, aged 61.

Richard English died 15 Apr., 1748, aged 61.

Mary, his wife, died 17 June, 1748, aged 58.

Elisha Fitch, died 25 Dec., 1791, aged 77.

Noah Foot died 27 Feb., 1809, aged 71.

Tabathy, his wife, died 1 Aug.. 1815, aged 63.

Joshua Fuller died 23 Mch., 1771, aged 70.

Elizabeth, wife of Capt. Samuel Fuller, died 13 Apr., 1774, aged 47.

Samuel Guile died Jan. 29 (?), 1750, aged 74.

Mrs. Sarah Guile died 8 Aug., 1750, aged 72.

Capt. Joseph Hills died 11 Sept., 1786, aged 58.

Capt. Joseph Hills died 5 Mch., 1815, aged 92.

Elijah and Abigail Hunt's children.

Stephen Hunt died 7 Apr., 1784, aged 82.

Esther, his wife, died 17 Feb., 1795, aged 83.

John Hutchinson died 9 Feb., 1725, aged 43.

Dr. Timothy Hutchinson died 29 July, 1758, aged 44.

Capt. Nathaniel Hyde.

Abijah Lincoln, Lieut., died 20 June, 1812, aged 74.

Phebe, his relict, died 22 Mch., 1820, aged 81.

Consider Little died 3 Aug., 1831, aged 85.

Rebecca, his wife, died 25 Oct., 1825, aged 75.

John Little died 1 July, 1833, aged 83.

Rebecca, wife of John Little, Jr., died 14 Dec., 1787, aged 35.

Submit, relict, died 31 Mch., 1842, aged 70.

Josiah Lyman died 6 Feb., 1760, aged 70.

Sylvester Manley died 28 Apr., 1850, aged 65.

Sally (Phelps of Hebron), his wife, died 29 Apr., 1875, aged 83.

Stephen Peirce died 7 Oct., 1766, aged 85.

James Pinneo died 14 June, 1821, aged 90.

Ebenezer Richardson died 18 May, 1756, aged 68.

Elizabeth, his wife, died 25 Apr., 1783, aged 92.

Capt. Eleazer Richardson died 28 Feb., 1798, aged 33.

Eleazur Richardson died 31 Aug., 1787, aged 51.
Hannah, his wife, died 14 Mch., 1814, aged 72.
Abigail, his daughter, died 28 Oct., 1786, aged 20.
Asabel, his son, died 31 Dec., 1813, aged 38.
William Sprague died 9 April, 1795, aged 79.
Elizabeth, his wife, died 26 May, 1789, aged 72.
Abel Webster died 10 Dec., 1853, aged 79.
Jerusha, his wife, died 23 May, 1814, aged 44.
Miriam, his 2[d] wife, died 21 Jan., 1864, aged 88.

Mrs. Rebecca Welch, who has been the widow of Daniel Huntington of Norwich and Joseph Bingham and Thomas Welch of Windham, died 12 Aug., 1780, aged 88.

Capt. Samuel West died 10 Jan., 1835, aged 91.
Sarah, his wife, died 12 Aug., 1815, aged 75.
Sally, his wife, died 18 Nov., 1851, aged 84.
Eliphalet Woodward died 16 Oct., 1826, aged 75.
Priscilla, his wife, died 12 Oct., 1838, aged 81.
Deacon Israel Woodward died 30 July, 1797, aged 89.
Mary, his wife, died 7 Jan., 1790, aged 77.

Israel, Esther, Sarah and William, children of Israel Woodward, Jr., died in 1770, 1771, 1775, 1782.

Josiah B. Woodward died 1 April, 1793, aged 20.

Samuel Wright, deacon in the 2[d] Cong. church in Lebanon, died 18 Apr., 1734, aged 61.

Rebecca, his wife, died 7 Oct., 1760, aged 83.
Capt. Seth Wright died 20 Oct., 1775, aged 48.
Mrs. Elizabeth Wright died 7 Dec., 1771, aged 83.

[Other epitaphs are to Buel, Dewey, and Woodward. See also REGISTER, *ante*, vol. 12, page 55.]

Farmington.

Mr. John Cowles died 9 Oct., 1748, in 79th year.
Capt. Isaac Cowles died 7 Feb., 1756, in 82d year.
S. H[art] died 18 Sept., 1689, aged 55.
Capt. John Hart, 2d, died 11 Nov., 1714, in 50th year.
Mary, wife of Capt. John Hart, died 12 Sept., 1738, in 74th year.

J[ohn] L[ee] died 8 Oct., 1690, aged 70; born in Essex Co., Eng., 1620; settled in Farmington, 1641; married Mary Hart, 1658.

Mrs. Mary, wife of Ens. Samuel Newell, died 25 Apr., 1752, in 86th year.

Thomas Portter died 11 Feb., 1726.
Mrs. Martha, wife of Mr. John Porter, died 11 July, 1749, in 85th year.
I. S[cott?] died 10 Oct., 1706.
A. S[cott] died 1688.
Mr. Thomas Stanly died 14 Apr., 1713, aged 63.
Mr. Asahel Strong died 7 Oct., 1739, in 71st year.
Stephen Tuttle died 23 June, 1735, aged 32.
A. W. died 24 June, 1707.
Lieut. Samuel Wadsworth died 29 May, 1731, in 72d year.
Capt. Joseph Woodruff died 23 Jan., 1737, in 49th year.
Mr. Mathew Woodruff, Sen., died 23 Apr., 1751, in 84th year.

BLANCHARD FAMILY RECORDS.

The following items were copied by the late George Dana Boardman Blanchard of Malden, Mass., a Life Member of this Society, from an old manuscript book, once the property of Abel Blanchard of Andover, Mass., now at the Bible Society, Astor Place, New York City. The book was evidently commenced by the first Samuel Blanchard, of Andover, Mass., and continued by members of the family.

Samuel Blanchard was maried to hes wif Mary in the year 1654 upon the 3 day of ienury.

My sonn Samuel was boren upon the 29 day of septembar 1656.

My daughtar Sarah was boren upon the 15 day of febrary 1657.

My daughtar Mary was boren upon the 18 day of aprel 1659.

My son Jonathan was boren upon the 25 day of may 1664.

My son Joshuah was boren upon the 6 day of agust 1661.

My daughtar Abigal was boren upon the 5 day of March 1668

My wife died upon the 20 febrary 1669.

I Samuel Blanchard was marred to my wif hanah upon the 24 day of juen in the yer 1673.

My son Thomas was boren upon the 28 day of Aprel 1674.

My son John was boren upon the 3 day of July 1677.

My son Samuel of my wif hanah was boren upon the 4 day of Jun 1680.

My daughtar hanah was boren upon the 26 day of Septembar 1681.

Samuel Blanchard sennar was boren in the year 1629 Agust the 6 day.

I Samuel Blanchard landed in New ingland on the 23 day of Jun in the year 1639.

I Samuel Blanchard cam to Andovar with my famaly upon the tenth day of iun in the yer 1686.

I bought my horce of John whelar upon the 18 day of march 1691.

The following records are by Thomas[2] Blanchard (Samuel[1]).

My son Thomas was born in the year 1700 and one the 15:th day of Jenaivery

My son Joseph was born one the 19:th day of febrery in the year 1701

My son Isaac was born Septemb the 20th in the year 1702

My son Josiah was born upon the 16th day of Agust in the year 1704

My daughtar Elisabeth was born upon the 25:th day of march in the year 1706.

My daughtar Hannah was born on the 6: day of may in the year 1708

My daughtar Roas was boarn upon 12: day of Jenauery in the year 1709

My daughtar Deborah was born upon the 18: day of Apriel and in the year 1712

My daughtar Lida was born one the 22: day of Agust in the year 1714

My wife departed this life Agust the 27: in the year 1714

I was maried to my wife Hannah upon the 21 day of Septembar in year 1715

My daughtar Mahittabel was born upon the 3 day of Octobar 1716

My son Nathaniel was born upon the 2: day of febrery in the year 1719

My son Isaac departed this life Jenawery the 25: in the year 1722.

My Grand daughtar Sarah Blanchard was born July the 25 in the year 1723

My son Thomas entred upon his sarvis with Mr John Bradish of Cambridg upon the 24: day of Novembar in year 1711.

May the 15: 1723 My son Thomas Blanchard then returned from dwelling at Bildreca and becam a bordar in my houce.

My wife Hannah departed this life June the :25: 1724

My daughtar Roas departed this life Novembar the: 22 in the year :1724:

My Mothar Hannah Blanchard departed this life July the :10:th: 1725 and as wee reseve it in the 79:th year of har age

My Grandson Joseph Blanchard departed this life upon the 3: day of desembar in the year 1758 in the 5 year of his age.

My daughter Elisabeth Chandler departed this Life upon the first day of July and in the year 1735.

My daughtar Deborah entred upon har sarvice with Lift Dean upon the 18 day of July in the year 1723.

My son Isaac the 2: was born upon the 23: day of Octobar in the year 1723.

My daughtar Elisabeth was maried upon the 22: day of Novembar

I was maried to my third wife Jude Hill upon the 21 day of februry in the year 1726.

My wifs daughtar Abiah Hill came to dwell with mee upon the 10:th day of Desembar in the year 1729

THE FOLLOWING RECORDS APPEAR TO HAVE BEEN WRITTEN BY JOSIAH[3] BLANCHARD (THOMAS,[2] SAMUEL[1]).

March the 17 in the year 1759 my father Thomas Blanchard Departed this life being in the 85 year of his age and he was Buried the 19th

I was Married unto my Wife Sarah upon the 23 day of December 1730

My Daughter Abigal was maried to Samuel Holt february 14 1760

October 18: 1765 my son Josiah was married to Lydea Tienkins

October 29: 1765 Joshua & Ben went off to wilton with 20 sheep to winter there

my Barn at Wilton was set up in May 1765 and Joshua enterd his saruice October 30 the same year on my place their

My Daughter Sarah was Born on Sabbath Eavining the 27 febrvary 1732

my Daughter Abigail was Born on Munday morn the 23 Day of September 1734

my Daughter Elisebeth was Born on Munday the 3 Day of April 1738

my Son Josiah was Born on fryday the 10 Day of October 1740

My Daughter Unice was Born on Saterday the 30 Day of October 1742

In the year 1749 October ye 5 my Daughter Vnice Departed this Life

my Daughter Elisebeth Departed this Life April 13: 1752

my aged father Thomas Blanchard Departed this Life March 17: 1759 being in the 85 year of his age

my one mother Rose Blanchard Departed this Life augest 24: 1714

my wife Sarah Departed this Life September 11: 1778

my Daughter Sarah Departed this Life March 27: 1782

July 23: 1773 my Sister Deborah Departed this Life being the wife of Joseph Abbot

My wife Sarah Departed this life September 11: 1778 being in the 67 year of her age.

my Son Joshua was Born thirdsday the 13 Day of november 1746
my Son Benjamen was Born on Tusday the 3 Day of July: 1750

The account of the Birth of my grandchildren my Daughter Abbigals Children

Samuel Holt was Born munday on the 7 Day of September 1761
Isaac Holt was Born Satter Day January 21 in the year 1764
abigal and Elisebeth Holt were Born on Tusday the 19 Day of may 1767 These were Twins
November 20: 1775 pircy Hholt was Born
augest 22 pircy Holt Departed this Life

my Son Josiah his child Lydea was born on Sabbath Day ye 3 Day of augest 1766
his Daughter Hannah was Born on Thurdiday ye 19: Day of October (1769)
his son Josiah was Born on Tusday Septembor 3: 1771
December 14: 1775 his son Isaac was Born
September 2: 1778 my grandson Isaac Departed this Life
October 9: 1779 my second granson Isaac was born

my Son Joshua his son Joshua was Born on munday ye 8 Day of July 1771.
Joshuas Second son Amos was born Thirds Day ye 14 of January 1773
his Daughter Elizebeth was Born on Sabath Day morn 16 Day of October 1774
Joshuas Daughter Vnice was born Augest 3: 1776
September 24 his child vnice Departed this Life
Augest 3: 1778 vinice y^{e} 2 was Born
Ezra was born March 23: 1780
Abel was born October 10: 1782

my son Benjamins Children. his child Sarah was Born $Septem^{r}$: 10th: 1775
June 11: 1777 his child Abigal was Born
September 9: 1777 his child Sarah Departed this Life

RECORDS BY JOSHUA^{4} BLANCHARD (JOSIAH,^{3} THOMAS,^{2} SAMUEL^{1}).

My Father Josiah Blanchard Departed this life April 10: 1783.
My brother Josiah Blanchard Departed this life April 30th 1790 In the 50 eth year of his age
My Daughter Lydia dyed August 8: 1801

[ACCOUNT IN ANOTHER HANDWRITING.]

Joshua Blanchard married his wife Elizabeth Keyes Jan'y 30, 1770.

Their childrens names

	Joshua	was	born	July 8, 1771
	Amos	"	"	January 14, 1773
	Elizabeth	"	"	October 16, 1774
1st	Eunice	"	"	August 8, 1776
2nd	Eunice	"	"	June 6, 1778
	Ezra	"	"	March 23, 1780
	Abel	"	"	October 10, 1782
	Rhoda	"	"	November 7, 1784
	Lydia	"	"	November 5, 1786

1st Eunice	died	September 24	1777
Lydia	"	August 28	1801
Ezra	"	June 4	1805
Joshua		July 23	1810
Abel	"	March 15	1818
Amos	"	August 17	1847
2nd Eunice	"	January 4	1850
Elizabeth	"	November 20	1857
Rhoda	"	June 30	1857

The Father and Mother of this family—
Mother died July 14 1817 monday eve ½ past 11
Father " Octo 10. 1818 Saturday eve ½ past 10

RECORDS OF THE CHURCH IN EASTBURY, CONN.

Communicated by Miss Mary Kingsbury Talcott, of Hartford, Conn.

From the manuscript copy owned by the Connecticut Society of Colonial Dames.

Eastbury Society, in Glastenbury, was incorporated by the General Assembly of Connecticut in May, 1731. The church record of baptisms, marriages, etc., from that date to 1768 is lost.

On Apr. 20, 1769, Rev. James Eells was called to the pastorate, and remained there until his death, Jan. 20, 1805. He was born Mar. 11, 1742-3, in Middletown Upper Houses, Conn., a son of Rev. Edward and Martha (Pitkin) Eells, was graduated at Yale College in 1763, studied theology, and was licensed to preach by the Hartford South Association of Ministers, Oct., 1768. He was a cousin of his neighbour Rev. John Eells of Glastenbury, both being grandsons of Rev. Nathaniel Eells of Scituate, Mass.

This parish is now called Buckingham. (See Glastenbury Centennial, 1853; Dexter's Yale Graduates, III., 18.)

An Account of Baptisms.

Collected from those that Baptized them whilst Destitute of a Settled Minister.

Octr 1767 Elisha, Son of Elisha & Penelophe Holester was Baptized by the Revd Edward Eells.

Feb 1768. William, Son of Elizur & Cloe Burnham was Baptized by the Revd Joshua Belding.

Apll 23 1769. Penelophe, Daughter of Elisha & Penelophe Holester Baptized.
Elihu, Son of James & —— Rice was Baptized.
Samuel, Son of Solomon & —— Andrews was Baptized.

Apll 30 1769 Rhoda, Daughter of Isaac & —— Talcott was Baptized
Onnor, Daughter of Elizur & —— Hubbard " "
Hannah, Daughter of Elijah & —— Loveland " "

Naoma, Daughter of Peter & —— Pease was Baptized.
Penelophe, Daughter of Aaron & —— Hubbard " "
These were Baptized by the Rev[d] John Eells.

The following is an Account of Those Baptized Since the 23[d] of August AD. 1769.

Aug[t] 27th Roswell, Son of Hezekiah & Mary Hubbard was Baptized.
Sept[r] 3 Christopher Vansant, Son of Lot & Mabel Loveland was Baptized
Sept 17. Lucy, Daughter of Isaac & —— Hale was Baptized.
Sep[tr] 24. Sarah, Daughter of Dea[n] Hezekiah & —— Wickham was Baptized.
Thomas, Son of Ruben & Mary Sparks was Baptized.
Sarah, Daughter of Ruben & Mary Sparks was Baptized.
Oct[r] 1 Unice, Daughter of Joseph Goodall Jun[r] & —— his Wife was Baptized
Oct. 29 Elisha, Son of Abraham Fox Jun[r] & Martha Fox was Baptized.
Nov. 5. Elizabeth, Daughter of Benjamin & Elizabeth Fox was Baptized.
Dec[er] 11th Erastus, Son of Robart & —— Loveland was Baptized.
Lydia, Daughter of William & Joannah Heldreth was Baptized.
Dec[br] 18. Zadok, Son of Benjamin & Anna Andrews was Baptized.
Dec[br] 31. Elijah, Son of Elijah & —— Loveland " "

1770.

Jan[y] 21. John, Son of John & —— Goodale was Baptized.
Feby 11th Elizas, Son of Charles Andrews, Jun[r] & his Wife was Baptized by the Rev[d] M[r] Robbins.
Feby 18th Lucy, Daughter of Elisha Loveland Jun[r] & his Wife was Baptized
March Abigail, Daughter of James & Hannah Wise was Baptized
Ap[ll] 1. Joseph, Son of Banona & —— Wolf was Baptized.
Ap[ll] 8th Francis, Son of Elizur & —— Loveland was Baptized.
Ap[ll] 15 Gilbert, Son of John & —— Wier was Baptized.
Ruth, Daughter of Joseph & —— Goodale was Baptized by the Rev[d] John Eells.
Ap[ll] 22. John, Son of John & —— West was Baptized.
Abigail, Daughter of Solomon & —— Andrews was Baptized by M[r] Lathrop.
May 6th Lucy, Daughter of Simon & —— Kenney was Baptized.
Betty, Daughter of Samuel & Elizabeth Delings was Baptized
May 27th John, Son of John & —— Holden and Baptized.
John, Son of Jeremiah & —— Hurlburt was Baptized.
June 3 Elisha, Son of Nehemiah & —— Strickland was Baptized.
August 4. Johanna, Daughter Benj[n] & —— Strickland was Baptized.
James, Son of Timothy & ——Goslee was Baptized.
Aug[st] 26. Calvin, Son of Lemuel & —— Pease was Baptized.
Merriam, Daughter of Jonah & —— Fox was Baptized.
Sep[br] 9 Edith, Daughter of Nathaniel & —— Holester, was Baptized by Rev[d] M[r] Dunning.
Sep[br] 16. Jonathan, Son of Charles —— Wiley was Baptized.
Sep[br] 30 Elizabeth, Daughter of William House, Jun[r], & —— His Wife was Baptized

Oct^{br} 4.	Peter, Son of Widow Huldy Riley was Baptized
Nov 18.	Joel, Son of James & —— Wright " "
Novr 25	Ephraim, Son of Ruben & Jemima Kenney was Baptized.
Decr 30	'Jemima, Daughter of Thomas Holester, Junr., & his Wife was Baptized
1771.	
Jany 6th	Obediah, Son of Timothy & —— Wood was Baptized
Jany 20th	Martha, Daughter of Ephraim & Martha Baker was Baptized.
Jany 27th	Dorcas, Daughter of —— Kenne & Wife was Baptized.
Feby 13th	Elinah, Marchent was Baptized Privately at the House of Sam^{ll} Pease.
Feby 17th	Leonard, son of Elizur & —— Hubbard was Baptized.
Feby 24th	Mille, Son of Aaron & Dolly Hubbard was Baptized.
	Samuel, Son of Jonathan & Rachel Holding was Baptized.
	William, Son of William & Johanna Heldreth was Baptized.
	Lazarus, Son of Lazarus & Rebecca House was Baptized.
	William, Son of David & Mehitable Loveland was Baptized.
March 3	Joseph, Son of Joseph & —— Tryal (Tryon?) was Baptized Privately.
March 24	Sarah, Daughter of William & Sarah Fox was Baptized.
May 12th	Mary, Daughter of Thomas & —— Hunt was Baptized
	Mehitibel, Daughter of Isaac & —— Smith was Baptized.
May 26th	Roger, Son of Elisha & Penelope Holester " "
	Moses, Son of Timothy & —— Morley " "
June 2nd	Ruth, Daughter of Peleg & —— Welding " "
	Naomai, Daughter of Elizabeth & —— Delings was Baptized.
	Sarah, Daughter of Jeremiah & Sarah Write " "
June 9th	Fredrick, Son of Isaac & —— Fox was Baptized
July 28th	George, Son of Hezekiah & —— Hubbard was Baptized.
August 4	David, Son of John & —— Goodale " ".
Sepr 29.	John, Son of Noah & Sarah Bartlett . " "
	William, Son of Lemuel & —— Tubbs " "
	Hepsebeth, Daughter of Benjn & —— Fox " "
Octr 20	Eliezer, Son of Charles Andrews, Junr & Wife was Baptized
Octr 27	Easter, Daughter of Gideon Holester Junr & his Wife "
	George, Son of Joseph Simons & Wife was Baptized.
Nov^{br} 17th	Rhodea, Daughter of Isaac & —— Talcott "
1772	
Jany 12th	Francis, Son of Ichabod & Easter Holester "
	Asenath, Daughter of Amos & Mahitibel Smith was Baptized.
Jany 19	Milley, Daughter of Elizur & —— Loveland was Baptized.
	Martha, Daughter of Abraham & —— Fox " "
Jany 21.	John, Son of John & Dorathy Wier " "
March 1	Anne, Daughter of John & —— West
March	Sarah, Daughter of Israel & Sarah Holester " "
Ap^{ll} 19	Isaac, Son of Ruben & Mary Sparks "
May 3	Nathaniel, son of Nathaniel & —— Holester " "
	Russel, Son of Jonah & —— Fox "
	Molle, Daughter of Phinehas & —— Grover " "
June 14th	Lovice, Daughter of Phineas & —— Grover " "
June 21st	Mary Anne, Daughter of Lott Loveland Junr and Mabel Loveland was Baptized.

June 28th	Nehemiah, Son of Nehemiah & Elizabeth Wier was Baptized.
July 19th	Olle (?) Daughter of Solomon & —— Andrews
	Martain, Son of Martain & Freelove Woodruff was Baptized.
July 26th	Jonathan, Son of Anna Holester was Baptized.
	Prudence, Daughter of Ephraim & Martha Baker was Baptized.
Augt 16	Jeremiah, Son of James & Hannah Wier was Baptized.
Septr 6	William, Son of Lemuel & —— Pease was Baptized.
	Jeremiah, Son of Jeremiah & Sarah Write was Baptized.
	Elizabeth, Daughter of Benonah & —— Dewolf "
	Abigail, Daughter of Tediah Smith was Baptized.
Septr 27.	Sarah, Daughter of Elijah & —— Loveland was Baptized.
	Unice, Daughter of Timothy & —— Morley " "
Octr 4	Sarah, Daughter of Sarah Goff was Baptized.
Octr 11	Asa, Son of Richard & —— Fox was Baptized.
	Thomas, Son of Timothy & —— Goslee was Baptized by the Revd John Eells.
Octr 19th	Unice, Daughter of Timothy & —— Wood was Baptized.
Octr 26.	Reuben, Son of Reuben & Jemimah Kenne "
Novr 15th	Gillet, Daughter of Joseph Goodale Jnr & his Wife was Baptized.
Novr 22	Jonathan, Son of Jonathan & —— Loveland was Baptized.
Decbr 22	Asa, Son of Asa & —— Woodruff was Baptized.
1773.	
Jany 10th	Hannah, Daughter of Nehemiah & —— Andrews was Baptized.
Jany 17	Elizur, Son of Elisha & —— Andrews was Baptized.
Jany 31st	Daniel, Son of Benjamin & Morna (?) Andrews was Baptized.
Feby 7	Sarah, Daughter of Peleg & —— Welden was Baptized.
Feby 14	George, Son of Isaac & —— Hale " "
March 8	Ruth, Daughter of Isaac & Ruth Fox " " Privately.
Marh 14	Susannah, Daughter of Ruben & —— Wrisley was Baptized.
March 28	Sarah, Daughter of Elizur & —— Hubbard " "
Apll 4	William, Son of John & —— Goodale was Baptized.
Apll 26	Elizebeth, Daughter of Samuel & Elizibeth Nowland was Baptized.
May 30th	Anna, Daughter of Amos & Mehitebel Smith was Baptized.
June 6th	Anna, Daughter of John & Doratha Wier " "
June 13	Elizebeth, Daughter of Benjmn & —— Strickland " "
	Samuel, Son of Samuel & —— Dealines " "
	Sarah, Daughter of David & —— Loveland " "
June 28	Lemuel Tubbs was Baptized.
	Nehemiah Tubbs " "
	Ruth Tubbs " "
	Unice Tubbs " "
	Three Persons were Baptized upon their Mothers Account.
July	Aaron, Son of Aaron & —— Hubbard was Baptized.
Augut	Betty, Daughter of Edward & Sarah Potter was Baptized upon her Account.
Sepbr 3d (?)	Jeremiah, Son of Jeremiah & —— Hurlbert was Baptized.
	Hannah, Daughter of John & Hannah Willis was Baptized.
	Jubal, Son of David & —— Dickerson was Baptized.
	Joseph, Son of Noah & Sarah Bartlett " "

Septh 16th	Peres Graves, Son of Elisha & Penelope Holister was Baptized.
	Elijah, Son of James & —— Wright was Baptized.
	Joshua, Son of Samuel & Elizabeth Nowland was Baptized.
Octr 10	Samuel, Son of Gideon Holester, Junr & Wife " "
	Samuel, Son of Samuel Covill & Wife " "
	William, Son of Kenny & Wife
	Lucy, Daughter of Abraham & —— Fox " "
	Anna, Daughter of Elizur Loveland & Wife " "
Nobr 6	Hannah, Daughter of —— Demon & Wife " "
Novr 13	Daniel, Son of Samll & —— Smith was Baptized.
	Milla, Daughter of William House Jur and Wife was Baptized.
Novr 20th	Ezekiel, Son of Lemuel & —— Tubbs was Baptized.
Novr 27th	Benjamin, Son of Joseph Simons & Wife was Baptized.
Decbr 12	Onnor, Daughter of Jeremiah & Sarah Write " "
1774	
Jany 23	Hapsabeth, Daughter of Peter and Ann Pease was Baptized Privately.
Feby 20th	Jemima Doolittle was Baptized—she being Adult.
Feby 20th	Abraham, Son of Peter & Ann Pease was Baptized.
	Anna, Daughter of Charles Andrews Jur & Wife was Baptized.
	Lucretia, Daughter of Ephriam & Martha Baker " "
Marh 28th	Betty, Daughter of Jonah & —— Fox " "
	Rebeccah, Daughter of Phineas & —— Grover " "
Apll 3	Delight, Daughter of Solomon & —— Andrews " "
Apll 10th	Phebe, Daughter of Nathaniel & —— Holester " "
	Enos, Son of Thoder [Theodore] & Anner Holister " "
	John, Son of Charity Pease was Baptized.
Apll 23	Betty, Daughter of Nehemiah Andrews " "
	Dennis Daughter of Edward & Sarah Potter was Baptized upon her Account.
May	Stalita, Daughter of Thomas & —— Hunt was Baptized.
	Sally, Daughter of Isaac & Rhoda Talcott " "
May 29th	Uniss [Eunice] Daughter of Ichabod & Holester was Baptized.
June 21st	Israel, Son of Nehemiah & Elizabeth Wier was Baptized by Mr. Robert Robbins.
July 3d	Timothy, Son of Timothy & —— Woods was Baptized.
July 17th	Sarah, Daughter of Israel & Sarah Holester was Baptized.
July 24th	Aaron, Son of Timothy & —— Morley was Baptized.
Augut 28	Bethuel, Son of Aaron & S Goff was Baptized
Sepb 10th	Isaac, Son of Isaac & Fox " "
Octr 9th	Anna, Daughter of Joseph & Tryon was Baptized.
Octr 22	Rosinah, Daughter of Rebecca Hills was Baptized Privately.
Novbr 3	Sarah Nevels was Baptized.
Nov 27	Samuel Pease " "
Decr 4th	Nathan, Son of Ruben & Mary Sparks was Baptized.
1775.	
Jany 15th	Mary, Daughter of Ebenezer & Mary Fox was Baptized.
Jany 22	Jeremiah, Son of Jeremiah & Sarah Write " "
Feby 9th	Hope, Daughter of Amos & Mehitable Smith " "
Apll 23rd	Samuel, Son of Sarah Willard was Baptized.
	Eunice, Daughter of Robert & —— Kenney was Baptized.
Apll 30th	Wright, Son of Ruben and —— Risley " "

May 6th James, Son of James & Hannah Wier was Baptized.
Morris, Son of Lazarus & —— House " "
June 4th Gerah, Son of Joseph Goodale Junr & his Wife "
Hapsebeth, Daughter of Peter & Ann Pease was "
June 11th Isaac, Son of Isaac & Kenney " "
Molly, Daughter of Aaron & —— Hubbard was Baptized by the Revd John Eells.
June 18th Jemimah, Daughter of Isaac & —— Smith was Baptized.
July 11th Wright, Son of Isaac & —— Hale " "
Nathaniel, Son of Nathaniel Hill & Wife " "
July 30th Stephen, Son of William & Joannah Heldrith was Baptized.
Penelope, Daughter of Timothy & —— Goslee " "
Mary, Daughter of Samll & Elizebeth Noulding " "
Augst 11th Timothy, Son, Abigail, Daughter, of Gideon Hollister Junr & his Wife (twin Children) were Baptized.
Augst 27 Hannah Dwight. Daughter of Elisha & Penelope Holister was Baptized.
Bershabah, Daughter of Ephraim & Martha Baker was Baptized upon her Account.
Septbr 30 Benjn Son of Benjn & Mary Strickland was Baptized.
David, Son of David & Jemimah Hubbard " "
Doratha, Daughter of Thomas Smith Sterns & Mary Sterns was Baptized upon her Account.
Hannah, Daughter of Levi & Easter Loveland was Baptized.
Octbr 8 Mary, Daughter of Elisha & Rebeccah Hills was Baptized.
Jabez, Son of Samuel & Elizebeth Deling " "
Octbr 13 Ezekiel, Son of Ezekiel & —— Skinner " "
Decbr 3 Savory, Daughter of Lemuel & —— Tubbs was Baptized.
Decbr 10th Jonathan, Son of Solomon & Sarah Andrews " "
Decbr Jonathan, Son of Elizur & Cloe Burnham " "

1776

Jany 14th Charles, Son of Benoni Dewolf & Wife " "
Jany 27th George, Son of Nathaniel & —— Holester " "
Feby 4th Penelope, Daughter of Thomas Holester Junr & Wife was Baptized.
Elizebeth, Daughter of Abraham Fox & Wife was Baptized.
March 3 Joseph, Son of Joseph & —— Wares " "
Roxanna, Daughter of Appleton Holmes & Wife " "
Elizur & Walter Hale, Sons of Elizur & —— Hale " " privately by the Revd Joseph Huntington of Coventry.
March 10 Edward, Son of Edward & Sarah Potter was Baptized upon her Account.
March 17th Anna, Daughter of Deacon Hezekiah Wickham & —— his Wife was Baptized.
Elizebeth, Daughter of Elizur Loveland & —— his Wife was Baptized.
James, Son of Peleg Welding & —— his Wife was Baptized.
March 24th Roger, Son of Charles Andrew Junr and —— his Wife.
March 31 Wright, Son of John & Hannah Welles was Baptized.
Apll 15th John, Son of Mr —— at Orford, the name of the Persons forgotten.
Olle, Daughter of Joseph Simons & ——Wife was Baptized.
Philomathy, Daughter of Israel and Sarah Holester "

Ap^{ll} 22	Josiah, Son of Jonathan and Holden was Baptized.
Ap^{ll} 29	Aaron, Son of Phineas and Grover " "
May 5th	John, Son of John & Doratha Wier " "
May 19th	Elizur, Son of Elizur & —— Kenney '
May 26	Sarah, Daughter of David and —— Dickerson " "
	Rhoda, Daughter of William House, Junr & Wife " "
June 9th	Benjamin, Son of Samuel & Abigail Smith " "
	Charity, Daughter of Peletiah & Mary Loveland " "
Jan 16	Margerett, Daughter of Samuel and Margerett Webster was Baptized.
June 30th	Jesse, Son of Hurlburt Wife was Baptized.
	Onnour, Daughter of Kenney & —— Wife "
June 30th	Juilliania, Daughter of Timothy & Sarah Briant was Baptized.
Augst 4th	Betty, daughter of Hezekiah & Mary Hubbard " "
Aug 18th	Rhoda, Daughter of Israel & Sarah Fox " "
Sep^{t} 7th	Anna, Daughter of Nehemiah & —— Strickland " "
Octr 3	Roger and Ruth Twin Children of Isaac and Ruth Fox was Baptized Privately.
Octr 6th	Elijah, Son of Isaac & Elizebeth Tryon was Baptized.
Octr 7th	Sarah Daniels was Baptized privately.
Octr 20	Mary Ann, Daughter of Aaron & Sarah Goff was Baptized.
	Hope, Daughter of Timothy & Wood " "
Nov^{br} 3	Charity, Daughter of Ruben & Kenney " "
Nov^{br} 10	Mary, Daughter of Hugh & Mary Cally " "
	Leonard, Son of Mathew & Martha Grover " "
Dec^{br} 1st	Nehemiah, Son of Nehemiah & Elizebeth Wier " "
	Electe, Daughter of Thomas Hunt & Wife was Baptized.
	Mary, Daughter of Nehemiah & Abigail Holster was Baptized.
Dec^{br} 8th	Josiah, S^{on} of Jeremiah & —— Wright " "
1777	George, Son of Lemuel & Jones " "
Ap^{ll} 5	William, Son of William & Sarah Smithers " "
Ap^{ll} 6	Gedidah Pease, Daughter of Peter and Ann Pease " "
" 7th	George, Son of James & Wright was baptized privately.
May 13	David, Son of David & Hapsabeth Fox "
	Zehira, Daughter of Ebenezer & Mary Fox was baptized.
May 18th	Molly, Daughter of Benonah & Dewolf " "
	Easter, Daughter of Ichabod & Easter Hollester " "
June 1st	Hannah, Daughter of —— Hills & Wife was Baptized by the Revd John Eells—he living in Orford his Christian name is not remembered.
June 7th	Solomon, Son of the Widow Sarah Andrews was Baptized privately.
June 8th	Hennery, Son of Hennery & Esther Huxford was Baptized upon her Account.
July 20th	Prue, Daughter of Joseph and Tryon was Baptized.
July 28th	Samuel Daniels was Baptized.
July 28th	Jemimah, Daughter of Ruben & —— Risley was Baptized.
July 29th	David, Son of Isaac & —— Tubbs was Baptized Privately.
Augt 21	Solomon, Son of Appleton & —— Holmes was Baptized.
	Ezekiel, Son of Ezekiel & —— Skinner " "
Septr 7th	Molly, Daughter of Belden & Mabel Skeel " "
Sep^{t} 23^{d}	Lorana, Daughter of Samuel and Elizebeth Nowland was Baptized by the Revd John Eells.

Octr 12th Elisha, Son of Elisha & Rebecca Hills was Baptized.
Jebial, Son of Lazarus & —— House " "
Nov^br 17th Benjn, Son of William & Hannah (Johannah?) Heldreth was Baptized.
John, Son of Stephen and Sarah Fox was Baptized.
Seth, Son of Lemuel Jones & Wife " "
Dolly, Daughter of Aaron & Dolly Hubbard was Baptized.
Anna, Daughter of Isaac Tubbs & Zilphiah his Wife was Baptized.
Nov^br 27th Walter, Son of Edward & Sarah Potter was Baptized privately on her account.
Decr 14th Joseph, Son of Belden & Mable Skeel was Baptized—they belonging to Orford.

[To be continued.]

JOHN RUSSELL OF CAMBRIDGE, MASS., AND HARTFORD, CONN., AND HIS DESCENDANTS.

Compiled by Hon. RALPH D. SMYTH, and communicated by Dr. BERNARD C. STEINER.

1. JOHN[1] RUSSELL, the emigrant, of Cambridge, Mass., and Hartford, Conn., died May 8, 1680. He married twice. The name of his first wife is unknown, but his second wife was Dorothy, widow of Rev. Henry Smith of Wethersfield.

Children by first wife:

2. i. JOHN,[2] b. 1626; d. Dec. 10, 1692.
ii. PHILIP, a glazier; lived at Hatfield, Mass.; d. May 19, 1693; m. (1) Feb. 4, 1664, Joanna, dau. of Rev. Henry Smith, who d. Dec. 29, 1664; m. (2) Jan. 10, 1666, Elizabeth, dau. of Stephen Tenney, who d. Sept. 19, 1677; and m. (3) Dec. 25, 1679, Mary, dau. of Edward Church, who d. May 1, 1743.

2. REV. JOHN[2] RUSSELL, JR. (*John*[1]), of Wethersfield, Conn., and Hadley, Mass., graduated at Harvard College in 1645. He married first, June 28, 1649, Mary, daughter of John Talcott of Hartford; married second, Rebecca, daughter of Thomas Newberry, who died Nov. 21, 1688; and married third, Phebe, widow of Col. John Whiting, who died Sept. 19, 1730.

Children by first wife:

i. JOHN,[3] b. Sept. 23, 1650; d. Jan. 29, 1669-70.
3. ii. JONATHAN, b. Sept. 18, 1655; d. Feb. 20, 1710-11.

Children by second wife:

4. iii. SAMUEL, b. Nov. 4, 1660; d. Jan. 25, 1731.
iv. ELEAZER, b. Nov. 8, 1663; alive in 1687.
v. DANIEL, b. Feb. 8, 1666-7; d. Dec. 17, 1667.

3. REV. JONATHAN[3] RUSSELL (*John*,[2] *John*[1]), of Barnstable, Mass., graduated at Harvard College in 1675, and married Martha, daugh-

ter of Rev. Joshua Moody, who died Sept. 28, 1729. He was settled at Barnstable, Sept. 18, 1683, and all his children were born there but the eldest, who was born at Hadley, Mass.

Children:

i. REBECCA,[4] b. July 7, 1681.
ii. MARTHA, b. Aug. 29, 1683; d. 1686.
iii. JOHN, b. Nov. 3, 1685; d. Aug. 25, 1759; graduated at Harvard College, 1704.
iv. ABIGAIL, b. Oct. 2, 1687; d. Mch. 20, 1774; m. Dec. 21, 1710, Nathaniel Otis of Barnstable.
v. JONATHAN, b. Feb. 24, 1689–90; d. Sept. 10, 1759; graduated at Yale College, 1708; m. Dec. 26, 1715, Mary, dau. of Col. John Otis of Barnstable; was a clergyman at Barnstable, succeeding his father in the pulpit of that church.
vi. ELEAZER, b. Apr. 12, 1692; m. Margaret Otis of Barnstable.
vii. MOODY, b. Aug. 30, 1694.
viii. MARTHA, b. Jan. 27, 1696; m. Dec. 26, 1717, Thomas Sturgis of Barnstable.
ix. SAMUEL, b. May 1, 1699; was a physician; m. 1737, Bethia, dau. of James Paine of Eastham.
x. JOSEPH, b. Oct. 11, 1702; d. Feb. 12, 1712–13.
xi. BENJAMIN, b. Oct. 11, 1702; d. Feb. 12, 1712–13.
xii. HANNAH, b. Sept. 12, 1707.

4. REV. SAMUEL[3] RUSSELL (*John,*[2] *John*[1]) married Abigail, born in 1665, daughter of Rev. John Whiting of Hartford. He graduated from Harvard College in 1681, and was pastor of the church in Branford, Conn., to the membership of which he was admitted Mar. 7, 1687–8, and his wife was admitted in the next month. In his house was held the famous meeting of clergymen at which the Collegiate School of Connecticut (now Yale University) was founded.

Children:

5. i. JOHN,[4] b. Jan. 24, 1686; d. July 7, 1757.
ii. ABIGAIL, b. Aug. 16, 1690; admitted to the church, 1709; m. (1) Mch. 4, 1716, as his third wife, Rev. Joseph Moss of Derby, who d. 1731; and m. (2) Aug. 6, 1733, Rev. Samuel Cook of New Haven.
6. iii. SAMUEL, b. Sept. 27, 1693; d. Jan. 19, 1746.
7. iv. TIMOTHY, b. Nov. 18, 1695; d. Sept., 1794.
v. DANIEL, b. June 19, 1698.
8. vi. JONATHAN, b. Aug. 21, 1700; d. Aug., 1774.
vii. EBENEZER, b. May 4, 1703; d. May 22, 1731; graduated at Yale College, 1722; was admitted to the Branford Church Nov. 10, 1726; was pastor of the church at North Stonington; m. June 14, 1727, Content, dau. of Benjamin and Mary (Fanning) Hewitt.
9. viii. ITHIEL, b. 1705; d. Mch. 25, 1772.
ix. MARY, b. 1707; m. Apr. 5, 1727, Benjamin Fenn, a merchant, of Branford.

5. COL. JOHN[4] RUSSELL (*Samuel,*[3] *John,*[2] *John*[1]), of Branford, married, Dec. 17, 1707, Sarah Trowbridge of New Haven. She was admitted to the Branford Church in 1709, and died Jan. 23, 1761, aged 74. He was admitted to the Branford Church Nov. 5, 1714.

Children:

i. JOHN,[5] b. Sept. 13, 1710; admitted to the church July, 1736; m. Oct. 11, 1732, Mary Barker; d. Mch. 12, 1750. Children: 1. *Edward.*[6] 2. *John.* 3. *Mary.* 4. *Thomas.* 5. *Joseph.* 6. *Ebenezer.* 7. *Orphanna.*

ii. THOMAS, b. Sept. 15, 1712; admitted to the church Apr. 28, 1734; m. Abigail ———, and had *Lydia*[6] and *Esther*.
iii. SARAH, b. Dec. 24, 1715; admitted to the church July 1, 1736; m. John Barker.
iv. ABIGAIL, b. Dec. 24, 1717; m. June 11, 1739, James Hall of Cheshire.
v. MARY, b. Sept. 12, 1720; admitted to the church July 1, 1736; m. Oct. 24, 1744, Rev. Thomas Canfield of Roxbury, who probably studied for the ministry with the Rev. Philemon Robbins of Branford, and joined the church there Dec. 28, 1740; d. Jan. 16, 1794.
vi. REBECCA, b. Feb. 6, 1723; admitted to the church Oct. 29, 1738; m. Dec. 26, 1749, Ezekiel Hayes.
vii. LYDIA, b. Jan. 31, d. Oct. 2, 1724.
viii. SAMUEL, b. Sept. 23, 1726; d. Dec. 13, 1804; m. Dec. 22, 1748, Elizabeth, dau. of John Linsley, and had *Sarah*,[6] *Samuel*, *Bethiah* and *Timothy*.

6. REV. SAMUEL[4] RUSSELL (*Samuel*,[3] *John*,[2] *John*[1]), of North Guilford, married, Dec. 10, 1718, Dorothy, daughter of Samuel Smithson of Guilford, who died May 11, 1755. He graduated at Yale College in 1712; studied theology with his father; was tutor at Yale, in Saybrook, from 1714 to 1716; declined a call to the church in Stratford, in 1719, and accepted one to North Guilford in 1723; was the first pastor there, and had preached there at intervals since 1722. He remained in office until his death, and left an estate of £5000, nearly one-fourth of it in books.

Children:

i. ELIZABETH,[5] b. Dec. 22, 1720.
ii. HANNAH, b. Sept. 26, 1722; m. (1) Nov. 24, 1741, Samuel Stevens; m. (2) Daniel Crane.
iii. SAMUEL, b. 1724; of North Guilford; d. Feb. 21, 1790; m. Mch. 8, 1753, Deborah, dau. of Timothy Baldwin, who. d. Apr. 18, 1811. Children: 1 *Samuel*[6]. 2. *Abigail*. 3. *Elizabeth*. 4. *Deborah*. 5. *Samuel*. 6. *Samuel Smithson*. 7. *Timothy*. 8. *Sarah*.
iv. THOMAS, b. Oct. 16, 1727; d. 1803; graduated at Yale College, 1749; was a physician; resided at Cornwall, Conn., and Piermont, N. H.; m. Mary, dau. of John Patterson of Stratford. Children: 1. *Thomas*.[6] 2. *Mary*. 3. *Cynthia*. 4. *Hannah Esther*.
v. DOROTHEA, b. Jan. 7, 1731; m. Aug. 1, 1749, Rev. John Richards of North Guilford and Piermont, N. H., who d. in 1811, aged 85.
vi. AMANDA, b. May 1, 1733; d. Mch. 22, 1783; m. June 8, 1758, John Redfield, a physician of Guilford, who d. May 14, 1813.
vii. LUCRETIA, b. June 23, 1735; d. June 14, 1813; m. Jan. 1, 1760, Jared Scranton of North Guilford, who d. Nov. 12, 1816.

7. TIMOTHY[4] RUSSELL (*Samuel*,[3] *John*,[2] *John*[1]), of Derby, married, Nov. 2, 1721, Mary, daughter of Capt. Joseph Hull of Derby.

Children:

i. ABIGAIL,[5] b. Sept. 29, 1722; m. Rev. Jonathan Lyman of Oxford.
ii. MARY, b. Oct. 10, 1726.
iii. SAMUEL, b. Dec. 3, 1733.
iv. JOSEPH.
v. SIBYL.

8. JONATHAN[4] RUSSELL (*Samuel*,[3] *John*,[2] *John*[1]), of Branford, married, Dec. 12, 1722, Eunice Barker.

Children:

i. EUNICE,[5] b. Nov. 6, 1725; d. young.
ii. EBENEZER, b. Mch. 21, 1728; d. 1802; m. Apr. 30, 1754, Mabel, dau. of Dea. William Dudley. Children: 1. *William*.[6] 2. *Sarah*. 3. *Ebenezer*. 4. *Lucy*. 5. *Tempe*. 6. *Philemon*.

iii. Jonathan, b. July 25, 1731; m. Oct., 1753, Lydia Barker. Children: 1. *Eunice.*[6] 2. *Lois.* 3. *Irena.* 4. *David.* 5. *Jonathan.* 6. *Esther.* 7. *Lucretia.* 8. *Augustus.*
iv. Abigail, b. Nov. 5, 1734; m. Miner Merrick.
v. Lydia, b. 1736; m. Justus Rose.
vi. Timothy, b. Apr. 8, 1738; m. Nov. 24, 1764, Chloe Merrick. Children: 1. *Clarissa.*[6] 2. *Mary.*
vii. Mary, b. 1740; m. Lemuel Sanford of Durham.
viii. Eunice, b. July 25, 1744; m. Rev. Nathaniel Bartlett of Reading, Conn., who d. 1809.

9. Ithiel[4] Russell (*Samuel,*[3] *John,*[2] *John*[1]), of North Branford, married, Jan. 23, 1728, Jerusha Harrison, who died May 7, 1738.
Children:
i. Jerusha,[5] b. Aug. 23, 1729; m. —— Benedict.
ii. Ebenezer, b. Nov. 23, 1731.
iii. Submit, b. Apr. 17, 1735; d. Aug., 1799; m. Rev. Noah Wetmore of Bethel, Conn., and Brookhaven, N. Y., who d. Mch. 9, 1796.
iv. Ithiel, d. 1828; m. Nov. 20, 1771, Eunice Harrison. Children: 1. *Ithiel.*[6] 2. *Anne.* 3. *Samuel Ithiel.* 4. *Erastus.* 5. *Eunice.* 6. *Jerusha.* 7. *Thomas.*

THOMAS TREADWELL OF IPSWICH, MASS., AND SOME OF HIS DESCENDANTS.

By William A. Robbins, LL.B., of Brooklyn, N. Y.

[Concluded from page 298.]

Addenda.

12. Jacob[4] Treadwell (*ante*, page 54). The order of his children should be: i. Anna.[5] ii. William Earl. iii. Nathaniel. iv. Daniel. v. Elizabeth. vi. Sarah. vii. Samuel. viii. John. ix. George.

ii. Elizabeth[5] Treadwell (*Jacob,*[4] 12) (*ante*, page 54) died probably in Truro, Nova Scotia, 5 Jan., 1811, aged 72 years; married in Middleton, Mass., 10 Nov., 1766, Jotham Blanchard, who died in Truro, Nova Scotia, 18 Mch., 1807, aged 62 years, a merchant, styled "Colonel," who lived in Portsmouth and Peterborough, N. H., moving to Truro, Nova Scotia in 1785, presumably because of his royalist proclivities. Children: 1. *John.* 2. *Sarah.* 3. *Elizabeth.* 4. *Rebecca.* 5. *Hannah.* 6. *Jonathan.* 7. *Edward Sherburne.* 8. *Nancy.*

14. Charles[4] Treadwell (*ante*, page 55) married second, 2 Jan., 1787 (*not* 1786), Mrs. Phebe Dennett, she then being aged 67 years. (New Hampshire Gazette.)

iv. Mary[6] Treadwell (*Jacob,*[5] 26) (*ante*, page 197) married Joseph Knight, who died probably 20 Nov., 1798 (*not* 1778).

x. Leverett[6] Treadwell (*Jacob,*[5] 26) (*ante*, page 197) married Martha Tredwell (*not* Treadwell).

STRANGERS IN DORCHESTER, MASS.

THE following records of strangers in Dorchester, Mass., appear in a memorandum book kept by Noah Clapp, Town Clerk of Dorchester, now in the possession of this Society.

In a preface it says: "In this Book is inſerted the Names of a number of Perſons, who came into the Town of Dorchester to live, ſundry of them with their Families, between April 10th. 1767 & June 23d. 1789, but have not obtained the Approbation of the Town for their Dwelling there, at a General Meeting of the Inhabitants of sd. Town of Dorchester, as the Law Required."

William Allen & his Family removed into the Town of Dorchester in the latter End of the year 1777, or the beginiug of the year 1778, from Boſton.

Docr. Joseph Gardner Andrews removed from Boſton into this Town in the year 1788.

Samuel Allen came into this Town in the year, from Braintree.

Thomas Annis came into this Town in the year from Milton.

Robert Aiers came into this Town in the year from

Annabel Allen a negro came into this Town in the year 1789 in the Spring from Braintree.

Nathaniel Arnold & his Family came into this Town in the year 1785 or 1786, from Milton.

John Armſtrong came into the Town to live in the year from Boſton.

Henry aiers came into this Town to live, in the year from Boſton.

Capt. Samuel Avery came into this Town to live with his Family, in the year from

Seth Adams came into this Town to live with his Family, in the year from

Thomas Allen came into this Town to live, in the year from

Samuel Allen came into this Town to live, in the year from

Capt. Samuel Avery came into this Town to live, with his Family, in the year from

Stephen Adams came into this Town to live, in the year from

David Barrow & Mary his Wife, & their Children David Mary & Elisabeth, and her Mother ——— Sutton; came to live in this Town, in April 1787 last from Milton:—taken in by Mr. Luke Trott.

Elisabeth Baker came to live in this Town in March 1788, last from Milton; taken in by Mr. Saml. B. Lyon.

James Boies removed from Milton into the Town of Dorchester in the year

Benjamin Beal & his Family removed from England into the Town of Dorchester, in the year

Joseph Beal removed from Braintree into the Town of Dorchester in the year

Reuben Blake removed into this Town in the year last from Boſton.

John Biſby removed from Sharon into this Town in the year

James Baker tertius from Stoughton, removed into this Town in the year

James Bowdoin Efq[r]. removed from Bofton with his Family in the year into the Town of Dorchester.

James Blake Jun[r]. removed from into this Town, in the year

[*torn*] Willard Baxter came into this Town [*torn*]ar from Braintree.

Ezekiel Blake came into this Town from Milton, in the year

Ezra Badlam came into this Town from Dedham, in the year

Stephen Badlam came into this Town from Dedham, in the year

Shepard Bent came into this Town from in year

Enos Blake came into this Town from Milton, in the year

John Bufsey removed from Milton into this Town to live, in the year

Francis Blanchard came into this Town to live, in the year from Roxbury.

Francis Blanchard Jun[r]. came into this Town to live, in the year from Brookline.

James Brazier came into this Town to live, in the year 1768 or 1769, from

Brown & her three Children came into this Town to live, in the year 1768 or 1769, from

Samuel Bowman came into this Town to live, in the year 1669 [*sic*] or 1770, from

Hepzibah Blackman came into this Town to live in the year 1770 or 1771, from

Eliza. Bennet came into this Town to live, in the year 1786, from Bofton.

John Burke with his Family came into this Town to live, [*torn*] year 1786 or 1787, from Bofton.

Elizabeth Billings came into this Town to live in the year 1783 or 1784, from

Nancy Bates came into this Town to live in the year 1783 or 1784, from

Nancy Bailey came into this Town to live in the year 1784 or 1785, from

John Bufsey & his Family came into this Town to live, in the year 1785 or 1786, from Milton

Afa Bird came into this Town to live, in the year 1785 or 1786, from

Jemima Bailey the Widow of Samuel Bailey of Bofton came into this Town to live, July 20th. 1786.

David Butler came into this Town to live, in the year from

John Barry came into this Town to live, in the year from

Jacob Hafey Bootman came into this Town to live with his Family, in the year from

David Burns came into this Town to live, in the year from

Francis Le Barron a Foreigner came into this Town to live, in the year

William Cleaveland Baker came into this Town to live, in the year from

William Bartlett came into this Town to live, in the year from

George Blackman came into this Town to live in the year from

William Bartlett came into this Town to live with his Family, in the year from Bofton

Isaac Crane last from Milton, came to Dorchester Oct[r]. 1788. Taken in by

Samuel Coolidge Efq[r]. came into the Town of Dorchester in August 1769, from Watertown.

William Chambers came into this Town in the year 1785, from Milton.

Jeremiah Crane came into this Town in the year 1785, from Milton.

Richard Clark came into this Town in the year from

Thomas Clap tertius came into this Town in the year 1789 in the Spring from

Thomas Collock came into this Town in the year 1789 in the Spring from

Elifha Crane came into this Town in the year from Stoughton.

Samuel Capen came into this Town in the year from Stoughton.

Ephraim Capen came into this Town in the year from Stoughton.

Jacob Cooper came into this Town in the year 1785, from Bofton.

Ifaac Crane came into this Town in the year from Milton.

Samuel Crehore came into this Town in the year from

John Crehore came into this Town in the year from

Lemuel Crane came into this Town in the year from Stoughton.

George Clark came into this Town from Milton, in the year

William Chambers came into this Town to live in the year 1785 or 1786 from Milton.

Thomas Carnes his Wife & Children & Nurfe came into this Town to live in the year 1768 or 1769, from Bofton.

David Crane came into this Town to live, in the year 1770, from Milton.

Thomas Cheney & his Family came into this Town to live in the year 1781 or the begining of the year 1782, from

William Cox & his Family came into this Town to live in the year 1782 or the begining of the year 1783, from

Sarah Clark came into this Town to live, in the year 1782 or 1783, from

Sufanna Campbell came to live in this Town in the year 1783 or 1784 from

Thomas Collier his Wife & Children came into this Town to live in the year 1784 or 1785, from

Nathaniel Crane came into this Town to live, in the year 1785 or 1786, from

Cowper a Foreigner, came into this Town to live in the year 1787, with his Family, from Bofton.

Ralph Crane came into this Town to live, in the year from

Jonathan Clark came into this Town to live, in the year from

Jofeph Chadwick & his Family came into this Town to live, in the year from Bofton.

James Calder came into this Town to live, in the year from

Benjamin Cox came into this Town to live, in the year from

John Curtis came into this Town to live, in the year from Roxbury.

John Dier came to live in this Town, in the year from Weymouth.

John Dolbeare came to live in this Town from Bofton, in the year

Charles Daniels came into this Town to live in the year from Milton

Joseph Doll came into this Town to live, in the year from

Dinah a Negro came into this Town to live, in the year 1784 or 1785 from

Benjamin Darling & Mary his Wife came into this Town to live, in the year 1784 or 1785, from

Mary Everenden came to live in the Town of Dorchester, in the Fall 1783, last from Stow.

Jefse Ellis came to live in this Town, in the year from Dedham.

John Eafty came into this Town to live in the year from Sharon.

Abel Ellis came into this Town with his Family in the year from Dedham.

Pearfon Eaton came into this Town to live, in the year from Lunengburg.

Edward Everett his Wife & three Children came into this Town to live in the year 1669 [*sic*] or 1770, from

Benjamin Eaton came into this Town to live in the year 1783 or 1784, from

Lewis Edwards a Child came to live in this Town in the year 1783 or 1784, from

John Farrington came to live in the Town of Dorchester, in the year 1782. Last from Stoughton.

Enoch Fenno came into this Town from Stoughton, in the year

Ifaac Fenno came into this Town from Stoughton, in the year .

Jefse Fenno came into this Town from Stoughton in the year

Edward Fairbanks came into this Town from Dedham, in the year

John Fling & his Mother came into this to live in the year from Milton.

Simon Fuller a negro came into this Town to live, in the year from Bofton.

Fulfom came into this Town to live, in the year 1785, or 1786, from

Chloe Fifk came into this Town to live in the Spring of the year 1789, last from Dedham.

Louis Gray came to live in this Town in last from Roxbury, taken in by Mr. John Goff.

Andrew Gillefpie & his Family came to live in the Town of Dorchester, in the year 1772. Last from Bofton.

Abraham Gould came to live in the Town of Dorchester, in the year 1782. Last from East Sudbury.

James Gourley came to live in the Town from in the year

James Green & his Family came to live in the Town from in the year 1782 or the begining of 1783.

John Green came to live in the Town from Nova Scotia, in the year

Jonas Green came to live in the Town from in the year

Gould come into this Town to live in the year 1788, from Milton.

Samuel Glover came into this Town to live, in the year from Milton.

Edmund Griffin came into this Town to live, in the year 1669 [*sic*] or 1770, from

Michael Grout & his Wife came into this Town to live, in the year 1770, from

Jacob Green came into this Town to live, in the year from

Thomas Gulliver came into this Town to live, in the year from

James Green came into this Town to live, in the year from

1787 Jacob How and Abigail his Wife; and their Child Polly, came to live in this Town; last from Milton; taken in by Mr. Henry Vose.

Ebenezer Holmes, last from came to live in this Town, in March 1787. taken in by Ebenezer Wales Esqr.

John Stiffon Homanman, Mary his Wife, & their Son Thomas, last from St. George's (at the Eastward) came to live in this Town in 1789, taken in by Mr. Js. Boies,

Rufus Harrington last from came to live in this Town in the year 1789. Taken in by Mr. Samuel Harrington.

Anna Holmes from Stoughton came into the Town in the year 1789, taken in by Mr. Alexander Glover.

Samuel Harrington came into this Town in year from

Shepard Bent came into this Town in the year from Milton.

Peter Hubbart came into this Town in the year from Braintree.

John Roufe Hutchings came into this Town, in the year from

Benjamin Hitchbour Efqr. came into this Town from Bofton, in the year 1788.

Jacob How came into this Town from Milton, in the year

Joseph Hunt came into this Town in the year from

John Hill came into this Town in the year from

Robert Hall & Foreigner came into this Town to live in the year 1786 or 1787.

John Hackelton & his Wife came into this Town to live in the later End of the year 1767 or in the year 1768, from

Martha Hayden came into this Town to live, in the year 1669 or 1770, from

Elijah Hayden his Wife & five Children came into this Town to live, in the year 1669 [*sic*] or 1770, from

Nathaniel Hubbard came into this Town to live, in the year 1770, from

Zena Hayden came into this Town to live, in the year 1770, from

Holbrook & his Family came into this Town to live, in the year from Weymouth.

The Widow Hayden came into this Town to live in the year 1783 or 1784, from

William Harden came into this Town to live, in the year 1785 or 1786, from

Job Hayward came into this Town to live, in the year from

Ifaac Horton came into this Town to live with his Family, in the year from

Francis Howe came in this Town to live in the year 1824 From Boston

Lucy Howe came in this Town

Tristam Jones came to live in Town in October 1787 last from Boston, taken in by Mifs Atherton.

Benjamin Jacobs came into this Town to live, in the year from Scituate.

Ruth Jones came to live in this Town, in the year from Braintree.

Edward Jones came into this Town with his Family to live, in the year from Braintree.

Samuel Jennerfon & his Family came into this Town to live, in the later end of the year 1767 or in the year 1768, from

Jonathan Joy his wife & two Children came into this Town to live in the year 1669 or 1770, from

Jane Jennerſon came into this Town to live in the year 1669 [*sic*] or 1770, from

Seth Johnſon came into this Town to live in the year 1784 or 1785, from

Jupiter a Negro man came to live in this Town, in the year 1784 or 1785, from

Obadiah Johnſon came into this Town to live with his Family, in the year from

Windſor Jones came into this Town to live, in the year from

Seth Johnſon came into this Town to live, in the year from

[To be concluded.]

HARTLAND, CONN., CHURCH RECORDS.

Communicated by HELEN ELIZABETH KEEP, of Detroit, Mich.

THE first church at Hartland, Conn., was organized May 1, 1768, with the following eleven members:

Simeon Crosby.	William Porter.
Benjamin Hutchins.	Elenora Banning.
Phineas Kingsley.	Mary Giddings.
Benjamin Ackley.	Ruth Porter.
Eleazer Ensign.	Hannah Ackley.
Cornelius Merry.	

The following have been ministers at Hartland:

Starling Graves, ordained June 29, 1768; died 1772.* (The Society records say: "deceased abroad summer or autumn of 1773 from ill health taken leave of his people in the spring of 1773.")

Aaron Church, ordained Oct. 20, 1773; deceased Apr. 19, 1823.

Ammi Linsley, ordained July 19, 1815; dismissed Dec., 1835.

Aaron Gates, from 1836 to 1841.

James Clay Houghton, "1843"–1845.

Nelson Scott, ordained Sept. 24, 1846, after having supplied one year; dismissed June 4, 1857.

July 17 AD 1768 Deodate Johnson Ensign y[e] son of Mr Eleazer & Mrs Lydia Ensign was baptized July 17 1768

Mrs Hannah Andrews the wife of Mr Nehemiah Andrews & Mrs Elizabeth Gates wife of Mr Jesse Gates, were both received into the Church of Christ at Hart Land by letters of recommendations from y[e] 2 Church of Christ at East Haddam Aug 5th Day AD 1768

Mrs. Lidia Crosby wife of Mr Simion Crosby was reced into the Church of Christ at Hartland by a letter of recommendation from the 3rd Church of Christ in East Haddam August AD 1768

Philota Prat Daughter of Mr Jared Prat and Dorcas his wife of Granville was baptized Sept[r] 4 AD 1768 (at Granville when I was there)

Mrs Eunice Ensign the wife of Mr Daniel Ensign was reci[d] into the Church of Christ at Hart Land by a letter of recommendation from the Church of Christ at Salmon Brook October 2 1768

* His will was probated Oct. 15, 1772.

Mrs Susanna Merry the wife of Mr. Cornelius Merry was received into full communion with the Ch of Chr in this place Oct 2 day AD 1768

Sarah Wilder daughter of Mr Joseph Wilder of East Haddam was baptized Nov 14 1768

Joel Persons son of Mr David Persons & Rebekah his wife of Granville was baptized Nov 20 1768 at Granville when I was there

Jesse Gates Jun son to Mr Jesse Gates & Elizabeth his wife was baptized Dec 11 1768

Mrs Sarah Tiffiny wife of Mr Conseder Tiffiny was reced into full communion with the Ch of Ch in this place & was baptized Dec 25 1768

Mr William Chamberland was received into full communion with the Ch of Ch in this place Jan 22 1769

Mr Joshua Giddings was admitted into full Communion with the Ch of Ch in this place Feb 5 1769

Mr Nehemiah Andrews was admitted into full communion with the Ch of Ch in this place Feb 5 1769

Ruth Kingsbury daughter of Mr Phe^has^ Kingsbury & Hannah his wife was baptized (by the Rev Mr Strong) Feb 12 1769

Mr Barzellai Willey and Joanna his wife were both admitted into the Ch of Ch at Hart Land by a letter of recommendation from the 3rd Ch of Ch in East Haddam Mar 19 1769

Mr Jonathan Bill was admitted into full communion with the Ch of Ch in this place March 19 AD 1769

William Chamberland Junr son to Mr William Chamberland was baptized April AD 1769

Mrs Abigail Ackley wife of Mr Hezekiah Ackley was rece^d^ into full communion with this Ch & was batiz'd May 17 1769

Elijah & Hannah Bill son & daughter of Mr Jonathan Bill & Mary his wife were baptized May 7 1769

Baptized a child for Mr Buel (?) of Simsbury Augt 1769

Calvin Ackley Son of Mr Hez^ah^ Ackley & Abegail his wife was baptized May 8 1769

Mr Urial Holms & Mr Samuel Crosby were both taken into full communion with the Ch of Ch in this place May 21 1769

Mr John Hudson & his wife & sister viz Hannah & Mary were rec^d^ into the Ch of Ch at Hart Land by letters of recommendation from the 3rd Ch of Ch at East Haddam June 2 1769

Mr John Bordan was rec^d^ into the Ch of Ch at Hart Land by a letter of recommendation from the 2nd Ch of Ch at East Haddam June 2 1769

Mrs Abigail Banning wife to Mr Saml Banning Jur was rec^d^ into the Ch of Ch of Lime June 4 1769

Seba daughter of Mr Samuel Banning Jur & Abigail his wife was baptized June 4 1769

Urial Holms Jr son to Mr Urial Holms & Statiry his wife was baptized by ye Rev^d^ Mr. Smith of Granville June 11 1769

Elijah Willey son to Mr Barzillai Willey & Joanna his wife was baptized June 18 1769

Lydia, Elihu, Abigail, Hezekiah Elephalet Zilpha & Benjamin Children of Mr Hezekiah Ackley & Abigail his wife were baptized June 18 1769

Mrs Hannah Kingsbury wife of Dea^n^ Phinehas Kingsbury were into full commnn with the Ch of Ch in this place July 23 1769

Benjamin, John, Sarah, Jane, Niles & Cloah children of Mr Joshua Gidding & Jane his wife were baptized July 23 1769

Mr Thomas Giddings was rece[d] into the Ch of Ch at Hartland by a letter of reccomndatn from the 3rd Ch of Lyme Aug 4 1769

Joshua Giddings Jr son of Joshua Giddings & Jane his wife was baptized Aug 6 1769

Eunice Phelps daughter of Mr Charles Phelps & Eunice his wife was baptized Aug 6 1769

Ebenezer Crosby son of Mr Simion Crosby & Lydia his wife was baptized Sep 3 1769

Lovisa Borden Daughter of Mr John Borden & Mary his wife was baptized Sept 10 1769

Normon Merry son of Mr Cornetious Merry & Susanah his wife was baptized Oct 1 1769

Martha Bushnell wife of Mr. Josiah Bushnell was rece[d] into the Ch at Hartland by a letter from the ch at Seybrook Dec 1 1769

Marvin Brace son to Mr. Abel Brace & Keziah his wife was baptized July 29 1770

Mr. Joel Ackley & Lois his wife were received into the church at Hartland by letter recommended from the church at East Haddam Aug 2 1770

Huldah Ensign Daughter of Eleazer Ensign & Lydia his wife was baptized Aug 12 1770

Mr Alexander Bushnell was received into the Church of Christ at Hartland by a letter from 3rd Church of Christ of Lyme Dec 2 1770

Israel Doñe Ackley son to Mr. Hezekiah Ackley & Abigail his wife was baptised Jan 6 1771

Lydia Ensign wife of Eleazer Ensign was received into full communion with the Church of Christ in this place Jan 13 1771

Jediathan Brace son to Abel Brace & Keziah his wife was baptized Feb 16, 1771.

Alexander Bushnell son to Alexander Bushnell & Cloa his wife was baptised Feb 24 1771

Mr Moses Cowdrey was received into full communion with the church at this place March 10 1771

Asa Anne Ambros Mehitabel Martha Dimmis & Elizabeth children of Mr Moses Cowdrey & Martha his wife were baptized March 10 1771

Mrs Ruth Bushnell wife to Stephen Bushnell was baptized & received into full communion with the church in this place March 24 1771

Electa Porter daughter of Mr William Porter & Ruth his wife were baptized March 24 1771

Solomon Case son of Solomon Case was baptised June 23 1771

Ruth & Stephen Bushnell, children born to Steven Bushnel and Ruth his wife were baptized Apr 14, 1771

Jonathan Emmons was received into the Church of Christ at Hart Land by a letter of recommendation from the first Church of Christ in East Haddam July 7, 1771. (On another record, May 22.)

Mary Cowdry wife to Mr Jacob Cowdry was received into full communion with the Church of Christ in this place July 14, 1771.

Thos Treadway Phelps son to Mr Charles Phelps & Eunice his wife was baptized Aug 4 1771

Rachel Emmons daughter to Mr Jonathan Emmons & his wife was baptized Aug 4 1771

Joel Brace Son of Joseph Brace & Gemimah his wife was baptized by the Rev. Jededdiah Smith of Granville Aug 18 1771

Mrs Rebekah Adams y[e] wife of Mr Daniel Adams was taken into the

Ch of Ch in this place by a letter of reccommedation from the 1st Ch of Ch in Suffield Aug 25 1771

Louvisa Hutchens daughter of Mr Benjamin Hutchens & Ruth his wife was baptized by the Rev Mr Strong of Salmon Brook Sep 22 1771

I baptized a child at Salmon brook Sep 22 1771

Lydia Crosby daughter of Mr Simon Crosby & Lydia his wife was baptised Oct 6 1771

Lydia & Bitty Cowdry children of Mr Jacob Cowdry and Mary his wife were baptised Oct 6 1771

John Willey son to Mr Barzellai Willey & Joanna his wife was baptized by the Rev Mr Smith of Granville Oct 27 1771

Clary Bushnell daughter to Mr Steven Bushnell & Ruth his wife was baptized Nov 14 1771

Eunice Phelps wife of Mr Charles Phelps was received into the Church at Hartland by a letter from the Church at Litchfield December 1st 1769.

Experience Brainard the wife of Mr Ashel Brainard was received into full Communion from the church of Christ in this place Dec 3 1769

Eunice & Juda children of Mr Thomas Goos of Barkhamstead was baptised Jan 22 1770 at his house at Backhamstead.

Temperance daughter of Thomas Giddings & Mary his wife was baptised Feb 18 1770

Mr Abel Brace was received into full membership in this place May 6 1770

Mary, Amasa & Statira Children of Mr Asahal Branard & Experience his wife were baptized Mar 3 1772

Joel Cowdrey son to Mr Jacob Cowdrey & Mary his wife was baptized April 5 1772

Almirah Brace Daughter to Mr Abel Brace & Kaziah his wife was baptized May 3 1772

Anna Merry daughter to Mr Cornelious Merry & Susanah his wife was baptized May 17 1772

Daniel Adams son of Daniel Adams & Rebekah his wife was baptized May 24 1772

Baptized Sarah Bancroft at Granville daughter of William Bancroft Jr of Granville May 31 1772

Mrs Kaziah Brace wife of Mr Abel Brace was taken into full communion with the Ch of Ch in this June 7 1772

Anna Shephard daughter to Mr Eldad Shephard & his wife was baptized June 7 1772

Lidia & Lucy Bill children to Mr Jonathan Bill & his wife was Baptized July 7 1772

Mr Theodore Woodbridge was recd into the Ch of Ch at Hartland by a letter of recommendation from the first Ch of Ch at Gasonbury Jan 24 1773

Baptisms by me Aaron Church

1773

Oct	31	Aaron son of Joel & Louis Ackley Sep 16
Nov	7	Lydia Curtis daut Abel & Kezeah Brace Nov 7
Nov	3	Ruben son Ruben & Cloe Burnham

1774

Jan	2	Anna, Ezekel } Ch. Ezekeel & Anna Kellogg

	Olevir son Seth & Martha Roberts
Feb 7	Harris son Jonathan & D'fire Emmons
27	Cephas son David Holcomb (Salmon Brook)
May 26	Silas son Dⁿ Thos & Mary Giddings
June 5	Eunice Gilbert wife of Joseph Gilbert
June 5	Tryphena dau. Ruben & Lydia Hale } By Mr Strong
June 12	Lucinda dau. Jonathan & Mary Bill } By Mr Strong
" 19	Thoder son Remembrance & Mary Shelden
"	Trueman son Cornelius & Susannah Merry
" 6	Whitemore son Ebenezer Baldcone Granville
	Deneson son Deaⁿ Phenehas & Hannah Kingsbury by Mr Smith
July 10	Aholebamah, Sarah, John ch. John & Cloe Bates
17	Hannah, Esther, Daniel, Charity, Norman, Trueman, ch. Daniel & Hannah Bushnel (by Rev Mr. Smith of Granville)
24	David son Jesse & Eliz Gates
31	Abegail, Theodosia, Aseneth, Experience, Asa ch. Asa Smith
Aug 7	Ruth dau. Hezekiah & Abegail Ackley
Sep 11	Candace dau. Asahel & Experience Brainard
18	Mary-Green, Benjamin, Joseph, Hannah, Samuel, Violet ch. Benjamin & Hannah Reed
Oct 16	Nathaniel, Lydia ch. Nathaniel & Lydia Butter
	Levi son Noah & Lydia Chapel
Nov 27	Ephraim Wilder
Dec 25	James son Eldad & Rebeckah Sepherd (by Mr Smith)
1775	
Jan 13	Cloe dau. John & Cloe Bates
Jan 29	Amasa son Daniel & Hannah Bushnel
Apr 9	Elizabeth dau. Joseph & Jemimah Brace
April 14	Caleb Burnham son W^m & Ann Selby
30	Aaron, Levi, David, Benjamin, Rufus Eleanor, Hannah, ch. Josiah & Hannah Meeker
May 7	Enos, Seth, Mary, Augustin, ch. Enos & Mary Lane
28	Josiah son Josiah & Hannah Meeker
June 4	Hannah dau. Nathaniel & Lydia Butler
July 16	Rhoda dau. Capt Abel & Keziah Brace
Aug 20	Wm Selby
Sep 24	John son John & —— Kingsbury by Mr. Torward
Oct 1	Theodore son Eleazer & Lydia Ensign
22	Mary dau. Alexander & Chloe Bushnell
30	William Clement
Nov 12	Samuel son Josiah & Hannah Meeker
19	Persis dau. Joel & —— Meachom
1776	
Jan 7	Abegail dau. Seth & Martha Roberts
Feb 4	Anne dau. W^m & Anne Selby
18	Israel son Thomas & Susanna Jones of Barkhamsted
Mar 16	Nathan Hatch of Barkhamsted
Mar 17	Ruth widow of Jonathan Couch
April 21	William son Isaac & —— Penfield
28	Benjamin son Noah & Lydia Chapel by Mr Sage
May 12	Joel Miner
	Lois dau. Leu't Thos & Lydia Beman
	Henry, Lydia, Mary Williams, ch. to Dr. Jeremiah & Lydia Emmons

Eli son Eli & Abigail Andrews
Samuel son Samuel & Ruth Andrews
May 26 Lois dau. Joel & Lois Ackley
Christopher son Joel & Temperance Miner
June 2 Calvin son Ruben & Chloe Burnham
Anne dau. Israel & Bulah William
Sibil dau. Samuel & Lydia Crosby
" 16 Jonathan, Ruth, Delilah ch. Widow Ruth Couch
30 Theodosia dau. William & Caroline Williams
July 7 Jeduthan son Simion & Lydia Crosby
14 Nehemiah, Hephzebah, Asahel, ch. Nehemiah & Hephzebah Andrews Jr
Aug 4 James, Sarah, Phebe, ch. James & Sarah Hungerford
Aug 15 Erastus Lyman.
Aug 11 Sarah dau. Dea^n Phinehas & Hannah Kingsbury
18 Thomas, Rhoda, ch. James & Sarah Hungerford
Sep 19 Ebenezer son Ebenz & Phebe Hale
Oct 13 Sebra dau. Joel & Temperance Miner
27 Eliphalet son Eliphalet & Jael Parker
Nov 3 Joanna dau. Daniel & Hannah Bushnel
Esther dau. Joseph & Jeremiah Bruce
Sarah dau. Uriah & Mahitable Hyde
17 Frederic son —— Mercy Sheldon.

Members.

1774 July 3. Hez^h Atkins & wife by a letter from Goshen.
Martha wife of Daniel Seward by Letter from Darham
Augt. 14. Benjamin Reed & his wife Hannah.
Sept 11. Nathaniel Butler & his wife Lydia
Statira wife to Uriel Holmes
Sept 25. Rebekah wife of Eldad Shepherd.
Oct 2. Noah Chapel & his wife Lidia
Reuben Hale was admitted by letter from the church at Oxford.
Oct 30. Ruth wife to Samuel Phelps.
Nov. 6. Lydia Waters by a letter from Gilead.
Nov. 27. Jacob Cowdry
Ephraim Wilder.
1775. Jan 15. Josiah Meeker & his wife Hannah.
Jan. 22 Enos Lañe & his wife.
Mar 12. Benjamin. Letter from Simsbury.
Apr 2. William Williams.
May 7. Joseph Wilder by a letter from East Haddam.
July 9. Ann, wife to William Selby.
Aug. 20. William Selby
Israel Williams & Bulah his wife.
Thankful wife to Aaron Bush.
Dec 24. Dr Jeremiah Emmons.
1776. Jan. 7. Thomas Jones of Barkhamstead admitted to the church.
Hannah Kingsbery
Feb. 4. John Kingsbery.
Elishema Porter
Mar 3. Ruth wife of Capt Benjamin Hutchins.

		Abigail wife of Eli Andrews.
	Mar 10.	Isaac Penfield by a letter from 4th church in Guilford.
	Mar. 17.	Hephzibah wife of Nehemiah Andrews, Jun'r.
		Ruth widow to Jona. Couch.
	May 5.	Eli Andrews.
	" 12.	Samuel Benjamin & his wife by letter from Granville.
		Joel Miner
		Samuel Andrews & his wife Ruth
		Mary wife to John Borden.
	June 30.	Daniel Kingsbery & his wife.
	July 28.	James Hungerford.
	Sept 22	Sarah wife of James Hungerford
	" 29.	Susanna wife of Elisha Giddings.
1776.	Oct. 13.	Eliphalet Parker & his wife Jael.
	Oct 13.	Mary wife to Jonathan Bill
		Chloe, wife to Alexander Bushnell.
	Nov 10.	Ebenezer Hall & his wife Phoebe.
	Nov 24	Oliver Hitchcock by a letter from Wallingford.
	Dec 3.	Mercy wife to Oliver Hitchcock.
1777.	Jan. 12.	Lydia wife to ye Rev^{d}. Aaron Church by letter from Wilbraham.
		Rebecka Adams.
		Martha Haize
		Felix Leavit.
	Mar 16.	Mary wife to Daniel Fox by letter from Millington.
	Mar 30	Prince Taylor Jun'r.
	Apr 6.	Temperance, wife to Joel Miner.
	May 4.	Thankful wife to Thos. Spencer.
	Sept 1.	Abigail wife of Jona. Shipman by letter from Walpole.
1778.	Jany 4.	Ephraim Wright & his wife Olive.
	Feb. 1.	Jesse Gates
		John Chandler & his wife.
	Feb 3.	Daniel Ensign.
	Mar 1.	Phinhas Kingsbery Junr.
	23.	Ephraim Fox.
	Apr. 26.	Deborah wife to Lt. Uriah Church.
	June 14.	Wid^{w} Caroline Ensign.
	Sept 6.	Anne Cowdry.
	13.	James Markom & his wife Jane.
	Sept. 27	Benoni Beach & his wife Mary Ann.
1779.	June 12.	Mary wife to Micah Scovil.
	July 4.	Wm Chapman & wife Rebecka Hawk
1778	Oct. 25.	Jacob Sawer & his wife
1779	Sept 26	John Wilder
	Oct 3.	Abner Banning & his wife Timothy Morley & his wife recommended to 1st Windsor.
		Wid^{w} Sarah Mack.
1780.	June 25	—— Rothbone
	Oct 8.	Lydia Kellogg.
1781.	Jan 7.	Janna Griswold
	Sept 23.	Venus
	Nov 4.	—— wife to Samuel Miller Jun'r.
	Dec. 30.	Timothy Tiffany & his wife.

1782	Mar 3.	Edward Brockway.
	Aug 2.	Elnathan Norton & his wife
		Elijah Coe & his wife Margaret.
	Oct 6.	Thomas Bushnell & his wife Rebecka.
	Nov 3.	Oliver Emmons & his wife Annah
	" "	Rebecka wife of David Adams.
1783.	May 4.	Asahel Borden & his wife Jemima.
	June 29.	Isaac Flowers & his wife —— of Granville.
	Aug 31.	Isaac Meachom & his wife
	Aug 31.	Eunice the wife of Isaiah Clark.
	Sept 21.	Ruth wife to Aaron Warner
	Oct 12.	Joshua Giddings Jr. & his wife Submit.

[To be concluded.]

NOTES AND QUERIES.

Notes.

List of Emigrant Liverymen of London.—The following list is of some value as, besides the fact of a man having emigrated, we get the name of the Livery to which he belonged, and from this the record of apprenticeship can be obtained, giving age, parentage and place of birth.

The book from which this information is taken has no title page nor is it dated, but it was made about 1801-2, Sir John Eamer, knt., being Lord Mayor.

The names in the body of the book are under wards and streets, then follows that part of London outside the city, next the near counties, then the distant counties, Wales and Scotland, and finally a list of the Liverymen whose addresses are unknown or are abroad.

Those who are stated to be in America or abroad are here printed, but some of the others may have been in America, unknown to the Clerk of the Company, so the list might repay a search for any individual in America thought to have come from England.

Bakers.
William Lovell in America.

Barbers.
James Sparks abroad.

Blacksmiths.
John Batchelor in America.
William Batchelor in America.

Brewers.
James Harvey in America.

Broderers.
John Davidson abroad.
John Greenfield in America.

Clock-makers.
James Upjohn in America.

Cooks.
John Davis in America.
Henry Pace in America.

Coopers.
Isaac Patching in America.
John Toulmon abroad.

Cordwainers.
James Gautier abroad.

Curriers.
David Compigre in America.
John Cooke Pettit in Philadelphia.

Distillers.
John Field in America.

Drapers.
Zachariah Clark abroad.

Dyers.
George Cooke abroad.
Thomas Mitchell abroad.

Felt Makers.
James Bliss in America.

Fishmongers.
Stephen Addington in America.
Thomas Horne abroad.
William Price, supposed in America.

Framework Knitters.
Arthur Lee abroad.
Robert Mason abroad.
Stephen Tayre abroad.

Girdlers.
William Carnaly abroad.

George Illman abroad.
Robert Ledlee abroad.
John Tayleure abroad.

Glass Sellers.
Samuel Anderson abroad.
James Ansell abroad
Joseph Fielder abroad

Goldsmiths.
Philip F. Fatio East Flordia.

Grocers.
John Parker Church abroad.
John Fox.

Innholders.
John Banks in America.

Joiners.
Peter Banner abroad.

Leathersellers.
James Lapins abroad.
Richard Oakes abroad.
James Spiring abroad.

Mercers.
John Chamberlain Robson abroad.
Stevens Direly Totton esq abroad.

Musicians.
Thomas Knott in America.
Thomas Wilkinson in America.

Pewterers.
Thomas Giffen Jamaica.

Stationers.
Daniel T. Eaton in America.
William Harryman New York.
John Miller America.
John Martin in America.
James Rivington in New York.
Robert Wilson in Philadelphia.
Samuel Wakeling in America.

Tinplate Workers.
William Falkner in America.

Tylers and Bricklayers.
John Bell in America
Benjamin Chamberlain in America.
John May Evans in America.
James Fullick in America.

Vintners.
Samuel Durham jun abroad.
John Rider abroad.
Richard Waller abroad.

Gerald Fothergill.

11 Brussells Road, New Wandsworth, London, Eng.

Thomas Mallet, of Newport, R. I., "came from Great Marlow in y° county of Buckingham, Old England, and departed this life in the year of our Lord 1704 on on ye 16 day of January and in ye 56 year of his age," as his gravestone in Trinity Church graveyard, Newport, tells us. He left *no children*, but was survived by his widow Mary, who was born in 1664, married first, probably in 1682, Samuel Wilcox of Dartmouth, who died before June 9, 1702,* married second, Thomas Mallet, married third, John Sanford of Newport, and died at Newport, Dec. 15, 1721, in the 57th year of her age according to her gravestone inscription, on Jan. 15, 1722, according to the petition below. Her gravestone in the Common Buring Ground on Farewell Street, Newport, bears an armorial design and is described in *The Heraldic Journal*, vol. iii.

William[2] Wood (*John*[1]) of Portsmouth, R. I., married Martha[2] Earle (Ralph[1]) of Portsmouth, as shown by Ralph[1] Earle's will, dated Nov. 19, 1673. William[2] Wood moved to Dartmouth, Mass., and there died in 1697. The inventory of his estate was taken in July of that year, and the estate divided among his ten children, viz.: i. William Wood; ii. George Wood; iii. Josiah Wood; iv. Daniel Wood; v. John Wood; vi. Joseph Wood; vii. *Mr. Mallet's wife*; viii. Sarah Wood; ix. Margaret Wood; x. Rebecca Wood. (Austin's Gen. Dict. of R. I., p. 231.)

Hence the name of Thomas Mallet's wife Mary was Mary Wood. By her first husband, Samuel Wilcox (son of Daniel and Elizabeth (Cook) Wilcox*) she had three children, whose births, as children "of Samuel Willcocks," are recorded at Dartmouth, Mass. They were: *Jeremiah*, born Sept. 24, 1683; *William*, born Feb. 2, 1685; and *Mary*, born Feb. 14, 1688.† William evidently died young. Jeremiah and Mary appear at various dates in Newport Land Evidences;‡ and in Oct., 1723, Jeremiah Wilcox, the only son of Mary Sandford dec'd, late wife of John Sanford of Newport, butcher, and Capt. Thomas Brooks, whose dec'd wife Mary (formerly Mary Wilcox) was the only daughter of said Mary Sanford, petitioned the Town Council for a settlement of said Mary Sanford's estate.§

A. D. Hodges, Jr.

Boston, Mass.

* Austin's Gen. Dict. of R. I.
† Register, xxii: 67.
‡ Newport Land Evidences, iv: 16, v. 102, vi. 464, vii: 12, 75, 76. 206.
§ Newport Town Council Records, 1719-1724, pp. 198-9.

WILSON.—The following family record is from an old Bible now in the possession of Mrs. L. Melville French, Manchester, N. H.:—

Marriages.

Thomas Wilson * Maried to Esther Spaldin Nov. 24th A.D. 1774.

Births.

Thomas Wilson B. May 31st A. D. 1745
Esther Wilson B. May 30th A. D. 1744

Deaths.

Thomas Wilson Died May 31 A. D. 1815
Esther Wilson Died April 13 A. D. 1819
Lois Spaldin Died January 18th A. D. 1790
John Jr. Wilson Died March 29th A. D. 1792
John Wilson Died October 8th A. D. 1792
Mary Wilson Died August 3d A. D. 1794
Eleazer Spaldin Died December 4th A. D. 1805
Mary Blood Died Oct. 7th A. D. 1813 In the 51 year of her age
Sewall Blood Died Dec. 17th A. D. 1814 In the 49th y of his Age
Aretas Blood Son of S. & M. Blood Died June 6th A. D. 1816 In the 25th y of his age.

BETHUNE.—In the article on George Bethune, *ante*, page 238, Mr. Noyes states that Bethune came to Boston about 1710, and was a member of the Scots Charitable Society. He was indeed a member of that Society, joining in 1705, and was in Boston earlier than that year, having been a witness on 11 Oct., 1703, to a document signed by William Gibbins.

Mr. Noyes does not mention the parish in Scotland from whence Bethune came, neither is it mentioned by Mrs. John A. Weisse in her history of the Bethune family. William Bethune, advocate, had the estate of Craigfoodie in a parish of Fifeshire called Dairsie. It is two miles north-east of Cupar. In Dairsie Castle lived Archbishop Spottiswood, and there he wrote his Church History of Scotland. In the parish are also two hills of moderate height, Foodie and Craigfoodie, both being remarkable for bearing crops nearly to their summits. That of Craigfoodie is 554 feet high, parts of it being known as Easter and Wester Craigfoodie. Five miles north-west of Cupar is Creich, of which the Bethunes were lairds.

William Bethune, advocate, of Craigfoodie, made his will in 1703, and died in 1706. In the "Inquisitionum Retornatarum Abbreviatio" we find under date of 10 May, 1680, "Magister Gulielmus Beathune de Craigfuidie advocatus, haeres Jacobi Beathune filii Roberti Beathune de Bandorie, fratris,—in annuoredditu 100 l. de villa et terris de Coull; in terris de Easter Leathrisk. in speciale warrantum dictae villae et terrarum de Coull."

George Bethune purchased the estate on the south corner of Washington and Summer streets, Boston, in 1724, and there erected a brick house which stood for over a century in the possession of the family, and was known as Bethune's Corner. A description of the house shows it to have been a fine example of the dwellings of that period. WALTER KENDALL WATKINS.

Malden, Mass.

QUERIES.

GILFORD.—William[3] Gilford (Paul,[2] John[1]), born in Hingham, Mass., in June, 1689, was taken in childhood to that part of Scituate, Mass., now Norwell, where he lived until about 1730, when he removed to Leicester, Mass. His wife was Elizabeth ———. What was her parentage and ancestry?

1820 Hawthorne Ave., Minneapolis, Minn. J. GUILFORD.

* Thomas Wilson, of Plainfield, Windham co., Conn., was a son of James Wilson, b. 1713, d. 1782, a native of the north of Ireland, who emigrated in 1722, with his mother, Jean Wilson (see Boston Selectmen's Minutes), and settled in the province of Connecticut, where he lived and died at Plainfield. There James Wilson married Hannah Spalding, b. 5 Mar. 1717, d. 30 Oct. 1802, a daughter of Jonathan and Judah (Billins) Spalding (see Spalding Memorial, 775).

Esther Spalding was a daughter of Eleazer Spalding, b. 1721, d. 1805, of Plainfield; and Lois Spalding, b. 1721, d. 1740, a sister of Mr. Wilson's mother. They resided at Windsor, Vt., at the Low Meadows, so called (Spalding Memorial, p. 113).—GEO. A. GORDON.

I am anxious to obtain information regarding either the antecedents or descendants of the following:

SAMUEL McILWRATH, born Dec. 25, 1718, who lived at Morristown and Mendham, N. J., and married, in 1755, Isabel Aikman.

PETER NORRIS, who lived in Morristown and Mendham, N. J., and married, in 1745, Mary Mahurin.

RICHARD PEARSE, born 1762, in Bristol, R. I., who married, in 1781, Candace Peck of Rehoboth, Mass. He lived at Bristol, R. I., Rehoboth, Mass., and Sudbury, Vt. MRS. GRACE PEARSE DIGGS.

1913 Brooklyn Ave., Los Angeles, Cal.

HERRICK.—What was the ancestry of Martha Herrick who married (1) Nov. 3, 1793, Amos Loomis, and (2) Belden Crane? Amos Loomis was born and married at Southampton, Mass., and moved to Portage Co., Ohio, where he died about 1820.

KINGSLEY.—Parentage and ancestry wanted of Tabitha Kingsley who was born about 1740, married, Apr. 10, 1762, Nathaniel Loomis of Southampton, Mass., and there died Sept. 19, 1815, aged 75.

DART.—Parentage and ancestry wanted of Mary Dart who married, Apr. 17, 1760, Solomon Loomis, born Nov. 14, 1734, died Apr. 17, 1760, at Bolton, Conn. He was an original member of the church in Vernon, Conn. When did Mary (Dart) Loomis die?

MORGAN.—Parentage and ancestry wanted of Susanna Morgan who was born at Wallingford, Conn., Oct. 19, 1720, and married, July 27, 1741, Benjamin Andrews of Wallingford. Was she a daughter of Joseph Morgan? If so, who was her mother? And when did she die? ELISHA S. LOOMIS.

Berea, Ohio.

WILLET.—Who were the parents of Francis Willett who married Martha Silver and lived in Newbury, Mass., in 1634? Who were the parents of Nathaniel Willet who was born in Hartford, Conn., in 1642, and who was his wife? Who were the parents of James Willet of Stoneham, Mass., about 1720, and who was his wife? J. E. BOOKSTAVER.

Binghamton, N. Y.

BAILEY.—Information is wanted of Meigs Bailey and his descendants. He was born about 1775, at Haddam, Conn., and is said to have migrated to New York State.

CRARY.—John Crary, brother of Peter of New London, Conn., is said to have settled near Boston. Has any one any records of his descendants?

John Crary of Suffield, Conn., was born 1775, it is supposed near Preston, Conn. Can any one tell me of his family and antecedents?

SHAPLEY.—Benjamin Shapley was early at New London, Conn. Where did his descendants locate?

Rufus Edmunds Shapley, born Dec. 22, 1786, emigrated to Dauphin Co., Penn., about 1799. He had a brother David. Their father died when they were very young. Who has their family records? LOUIS MARINUS DEWEY.

Westfield, Mass.

HISTORICAL INTELLIGENCE.

JOHN HAMPDEN.—It is proposed to build in Chalgrove, Oxfordshire, England, in memory of John Hampden, the patriot, one of the twelve grantees of land in Connecticut in 1632, who was mortally wounded in the skirmish of Chalgrove Field in 1643, a Village Hall for general purposes, on a plot of ground within the Vicarage Glebe. The Vicar has offered the site, and the Patrons (the Dean and Chapter of Christ Church, Oxford) have sanctioned the plan.

In Chalgrove itself little if any help can be obtained, and it is hoped that admirers of John Hampden elsewhere may wish to combine in promoting this useful work. Subscriptions will be gladly received, on behalf of the Committee, by the Rev. J. Howard Swinstead, Chalgrove Vicarage, Wallingford, Oxfordshire, Eng.

BOOK NOTICES.*

[The editor requests persons sending books for notice to state, for the information of readers, the price of each book, with the amount to be added for postage when sent by mail.]

Paternal Pedigree. Compiled by Joseph Whitman Bailey. Boston, Mass. 1906. Blue Print Chart. 4 ft. 8 in. by 1 ft. 10 in.

In a note Mr. Bailey says: "While there is some slight difference of authority as regards a few distant and unimportant lines, it is believed that no such difference exists in any of the more material descents."

Thomas Ferrier and Some of his Descendants. Compiled by Elizabeth Ferrier Lane. The Independent, Elkhorn, Wisconsin. 1906. 8vo. pp. 56.

Thomas Ferrier came from Ireland, probably in 1729, and in 1731 is found at Little Britain, in what is now Orange Co., N. Y. At the end of the record of his descendants are short sections bearing the titles "Vanderoef," "Wisner," "Ancestors of Hiram W. Lane," and "Goldin." The print of the pamphlet is fine, and the amount of matter put into its pages is considerable, and well indexed.

Freese Families. By John Wesley Freese. Published jointly by the Author and Benjamin Marsh Freese and Edwin Abraham Freese, all Great Grandsons of Abraham Freese. 1749–1800. [Cambridge. 1906.] 8vo. pp. 78. Ill.

The name of the immigrant Freese of New England has not been discovered. This genealogy begins with John Freese who settled on Freese's Island, incorporated as a part of Deer Isle, Maine. The record of the descendants of his sons, Abraham, Isaac and Jacob, constitutes the greater part of the work, with with the exception of the "Miscellaneous Data" which consist of "disconnected items concerning individual Freeses." The genealogy contains many biographical details. Print and binding are good, and there are fifteen full-page illustrations. There is no index.

The Hills Family in America. The Ancestry and Descendants of William Hills, the English Emigrant to New England in 1632; of Joseph Hills, the English Emigrant to New England in 1638, and of the Great-grandsons of Robert Hills, of the Parish of Wye, County of Kent, England, Emigrants to New England 1794–1806. Compiled by William Sanford Hills, and edited by Thomas Hills. The Grafton Press: Genealogical Publishers. New York. 1906. Large 8vo. pp. xx + 713. Ill. Plans. For sale by the publishers, 70 Fifth Ave., New York City.

The title pages indicate the contents of the greater part of the volume, the remainder consisting of "Partial Lines," "Recent Immigrants and their Families," "Supplementary Records connecting with the Connecticut Branch," and appendixes and indexes. The general accuracy of the work may be inferred from the statement of the editor that the compiler, though totally blind, being "blessed with a tenacious memory, was able to so arrange the results of his investigations that not in a single instance did the editor find confusion in his lines." It gives a careful and comprehensive record of more than five thousand individuals, and is a monumental work that every member of the family can regard with pride and satisfaction. The compiler and editor deserve great credit for the production of such an excellent genealogy, which is a finished example of good taste in the printer's art.

Genealogy of the Parke Families of Connecticut; including Robert Parke, of New London, Edward Parks, of Guilford, and others. Also a list of Parke, Park, Parks, etc., who fought in the Revolutionary War. Compiled by Frank Sylvester Parks. Washington, D. C. 1906. 8vo. pp. 333. Ill.

The principal contents of this volume, besides those indicated on the title page, are "Some English Parke Families," "Peter Park and Descendants," and "John Parks, of Emhurst, England." Peter Park was of Stonington, Conn.

* All of the unsigned reviews are written by Mr. Frederick Willard Parke of Boston.

Biography is abundant in these pages, and the genealogy itself, which is arranged according to the REGISTER system, comprises all that it has been possible to learn, during a search of six years, concerning the families which were the subject of the investigations. The work is thoroughly indexed.

A Genealogy of the Lineal Descendants of John Steevens who settled in Guilford, Conn., in 1645. Compiled by CHARLOTTE STEEVENS HOLMES, 1906. Edited by CLAY W. HOLMES, A.M., Elmira, N. Y. [Elmira, 1906.] Large 8vo. pp. 162.

In the chapter of this genealogy which relates to the emigrant ancestor, the author upsets the pedigree given to John Steevens in the genealogy recently issued by the Rev. C. Ellis Stevens, LL.D. Exception is also taken to Dr. Stevens's arrangement of the children of the emigrant. Of the American family, the descendants of Thomas,[2] son of John,[1] have been recorded with special care. There is an appendix containing "The Planters Covenant," wills, and miscellaneous matter. This well compiled and edited book is printed in clear type on exceptionally good and heavy paper, and is thoroughly indexed.

Tayer (Thayer) Family Entries in the Parish Register of Thornbury, Gloucestershire, England. Communicated by WALTER FAXON, Esq., and EDWARD HENRY WHORF, Esq. With Introduction and Notes by HENRY ERNEST WOODS, A.M.
Abstracts of Wills relating to the Tayer (Thayer) Family of Thornbury, Gloucestershire, England. Communicated by HENRY ERNEST WOODS, A.M. [Boston: Press of David Clapp & Son. 1906.] Large 8vo. pp. 11.

These two titles are combined in a single pamphlet, reprinted from the REGISTER for July, 1906.

In Memoriam. A Sketch of the Life of the Rev. Francis Bickford Hornbrooke, D.D. By his Wife. Together a Tribute by his Friend, James DeNormandie, D.D. Newton: Newton Graphic Publishing Co. 1905. 8vo. pp. 52. Ill.

Dr. Hornbrooke was ordained minister of the Union Congregational (Trinitarian) Church, East Hampton, Conn., in 1874, but afterwards embraced the Unitarian faith, finally becoming pastor of the Channing Church, Newton, Mass., from which he resigned in 1900. He died in 1903. Dr. Hornbrooke's breadth both of intellect and sympathy is finely indicated in this sketch. Dr. DeNormandie's tribute is the address which he delivered at the funeral.

Ralph's Scrap Book. Illustrated by his own Camera and Collection of Photographs, and compiled by his father, EDMUND BICKNELL. Dedicated to his friends and presented to them in his memory. Lawrence, Mass. 1905. Square 8vo. pp. 453.

This volume is the memorial of the talents of an only child whose literary abilities promised a life of success, but who died at the age of twenty-three. The book consists of reminiscences of his activities, extracts from his writings in prose and verse, and an account of his protracted struggle with the disease to which he finally succumbed.

Biographical Sketch of the Rev. Charles C. Kimball, D.D., LL.D. By J. H. E. n. p.; n. d. 12mo. pp. 8. Portrait.

Dr. Kimball was a Presbyterian minister, though several years of his life were devoted to educational work. He was born at Newport, New Hampshire, in 1834, and died in New York, in 1905.

An Address on the Character of General Seth Pomeroy, delivered on the Two Hundredth Anniversary of his Birth, by George Eltweed Pomeroy, at First Church of Christ, organized 1661, Northampton, Mass., Sunday, May 20, 1906, under the auspices of Seth Pomeroy Chapter, Sons of the American Revolution. [Toledo, Ohio. 1906.] 4to. pp. 19.

A Sketch of the Life of George Roberts, who fought under John Paul Jones. By CHARLES H. ROBERTS. 1905. Reprint with Corrections and Additional Memoranda. [Concord, N. H.] Large 8vo. pp. 8. Fac-simile.

George Roberts, the grandfather of the writer of this sketch, was born at Dover, N. H., in 1755. His family were Quakers. He was under Commodore Jones both in the *Ranger* and the *Bon Homme Richard*, and partook in the engagement with the *Serapis*.

Memoir of Robert Charles Winthrop, Jr. By HENRY HERBERT EDES. Reprinted from the Publications of the Colonial Society of Massachusetts, Vol. X. Cambridge: John Wilson and Son. University Press. 1906. Large 8vo. pp. 21. Portrait.

This interesting sketch closely follows in character one by the same author which appeared in the REGISTER for July, 1906.

Our Work. Vol. 2. No. 7. May 1, 1906. Published monthly under the auspices of the Winkley Guild, in the interests of the work at Bulfinch Place Church, [Boston, Mass.] 8vo. pp. 4. Ill.

The article in this number to which attention is particularly invited is "Bulfinch Place and the Bulfinch Family."

Historical Sketches of Bluehill, Maine, by R. G. F. CANDAGE, Brookline, Mass. Printed for the Bluehill Historical Society. Ellsworth, Maine: Hancock County Publishing Co., Printers. 1905. 8vo. pp. 83.

This volume is a collection of stories interspersed with genealogy, containing many anecdotes and personal reminiscences of members of the families of which accounts are given. The sketches consist of facts collected from history, tradition and memory respecting the homesteads of the Southern part of Blue Hill and their occupants. Some of the narrations are exceedingly humorous, as, for instance, that relating to the church meeting "to make enquiry concerning an alleged contradiction between the Rev. Mr. Fisher and Mrs. Fisher on the subject of some cherry rum thrown away between them."

Burlington, Connecticut. Historical Address delivered by Epaphroditus Peck at the Centennial Celebration, on June 16, 1906. Printed and published by the Bristol Press Publishing Co., Bristol, Conn. 8vo. pp. 36.

Vital Records of the Town of Dorchester from 1826 to 1849. Boston: Municipal Printing Office. 1905. 8vo. pp. 288.

This volume, arranged on the plan adopted for vital records issued under the the State act of 1902, is the thirty-sixth report in the series of Boston Records, and comprises, besides the contents denoted on the title-page, "additional deaths, copied from epitaphs of the First Burying Ground in Dorchester, which do not appear in the Dorchester Records."

Hills Family Genealogical and Historical Association. Incorporated July 6, 1894. Twelfth Annual Report of the Directors. Barnard Memorial Building, Boston, June 5, 1906.

This report calls particular attention to the publication of the Hills Genealogy, a notice of which will be found elsewhere in this issue of the REGISTER. After an appreciative recognition of the immense amount of work done by the compiler, the President of the Association, who was also the editor of the genealogy, gives a careful and exact description of the methods used in arranging and indexing the volume, which contains the record of more than five thousand names.

Proceedings of the Celebration of the Two Hundred and Seventy-fifth Anniversary of the Settlement of Medford, Massachusetts, June, 1905. Prefaced by a brief History of the Town and City from the day of settlement, by JOHN HOOPER. Published by the Executive Committee. [Boston. 1906.] Large 8vo. pp. xii+261. Ill. Maps.

Mr. Hooper's history occupies eighty-seven pages of this volume and is an excellent epitome of the development of the town. The five days of the anniversary celebration are completely recorded, all the addresses, which formed so large a part of the exercises, being given in full. The illustrations are numerous and of superior quality, the greater part being portraits.

History of the Marine Society of Newburyport, Massachusetts, from its incorporation in 1772 to the year 1906: Together with a complete Roster and a Narrative of Important Events in the Lives of its Members. Compiled by Captain

WILLIAM H. BAYLEY and Captain OLIVER O. JONES. [Newburyport.] 1906. 4to. pp. 506. Ill.

The objects of this Society, as stated in the preface, are "to improve the knowledge of the coast by the several members, upon their arrival from sea, communicating their observations, inwards and outwards, of the variation of the needle, soundings, courses, distances, and other remarkable things in writing, to be lodged with the society, for the greater security of navigation, and to raise a common fund for the relief of the members and their families in poverty, or other adverse circumstances." Interesting as the records of the society are, they are surpassed by the "Incidents in Lives of Members." A list of the curiosities in the Society's Museum appropriately follows this latter section of the work. There is an index of subjects and of members.

The Fifty-third Annual Report of the Directors of the American Congregational Association, presented on May the Twenty-eighth, 1906. Report of the Congregational Library. Boston: American Congregational Association, Congregational House. 1906. 8vo. pp. 22.

The French Blood in America. By LUCIAN J. FOSDICK. Illustrated. New York, Chicago, Toronto, London and Edinburgh: Fleming H. Revell Company. [1906.] 8vo. pp, 448.

This work consists of three books; the first, "The Rise of Protestantism in France"; the second, "Early Attempts at Colonization"; the third, "The French Protestants in America," the last book being divided into four parts entitled respectively, "New England," "The French in New York," "Pennsylvania and the Southern States," and "The French in Various Relations." From this outline of its contents its comprehensive character will be seen, justifying the author's assertion that no other single volume is its equal in this respect. From Joan of Arc, who is considered the forerunner of the Protestants, to the settlement of the Huguenots in America, the history of French Protestantism and of its connection with this country is given most fully. The letter-press and illustrations are in keeping with the general excellence of the volume, and there is a good index.

The Investments of Harvard College, 1776–1790: An Episode in the Finances of the Revolution. By ANDREW MCFARLAND DAVIS. Reprinted from the Quarterly Journal of Economics, Vol. XX., May, 1906. [Cambridge. 1906.] 8vo. pp. 399–418.

This pamphlet consists of what Mr. Davis calls a "brief inspection" of the accounts of Ebenezer Storer, treasurer of Harvard College at the period of the Revolution, and shows the admirable manner in which he and others who had charge of the college investments met the duties imposed upon them.

The John P. Branch Historical Papers of Randolph-Macon College. Published Annually by the Department of History. Vol. II. No. 2. June, 1906. Richmond: Taylor and Taylor Printing Co. 1906. 8vo. pp. 183. Price $1.00. Address Wm. E. Dodd, Editor, Ashland, Va.

The contents of this number consist of "R. M. T. Hunter," by D. R. Anderson, and "Virginia Opposition to Chief Justice Marshall,"—Reprints from the *Richmond Enquirer*, 1821.

Library of Congress. Journal of the Continental Congress. 1774–1789. Edited from the Original Records in the Library of Congress by WORTHINGTON CHAUNCEY FORD, Chief, Division of Manuscripts. Vol. VI. 1776, Oct. 9–Dec. 31. Washington: Government Printing Office. 1906. 4to. pp. 857–1173.

Library of Congress. List of Works relating to Government Regulation of Insurance. United States and Foreign Countries. Compiled under the direction of APPLETON PRENTISS CLARK GRIFFIN, Chief Bibliographer. Washington: Government Printing Office. 1906. 4to. pp. 46.

Library of Congress. Select List of Books on Municipal Affairs, with Special Reference to Municipal Ownership. With Appendix: Select List of State Documents. Compiled under the direction of APPLETON PRENTISS CLARK GRIFFIN, Chief Bibliographer. Washington: Government Printing Office. 1906. 4to. pp. 34.

Ecclesiastical Records. State of New York. Published by the State under the supervision of HUGH HASTINGS, State Historian. Volumes V., VI. Albany: J. B. Lyon Co., Printers. 1905. 2 vols. 8vo. pp. xlix+3148—3800; lix+3801—4413.

The documents published in these "Records" are arranged under the heads of the respective Governors, and in chronological order. In these volumes the dates are Jan. 3, 1751—Aug. 1810. A large proportion of the contents is correspondence. As to the work in general, its plan includes all denominations, furnishing therefore a complete ecclesiastical history of the State.

Official Records of the Union and Confederate Navies in the War of the Rebellion. Published under the direction of the Hon. CHARLES J. BONAPARTE, Secretary of the Navy, by Mr. CHARLES W. STEWART, Superintendent Library and Naval War Records. By authority of an Act of Congress approved July 31, 1894. Series I—Vol. 20. West Gulf Blockading Squadron. From March 15 to Dec. 31, 1863. Washington: Government Printing Office. 1905. 8vo. pp. xiv+960. Ill. Map.

Princeton Historical Association. Extra Publications, Number One. A Brief Narrative of the Ravages of the British and Hessians at Princeton, 1776-1777. Princeton, N. J.: The University Library. 1906. Large 8vo. pp. x+56. Price $1.00. Apply to Library of Princeton University.

This narrative was written by some person in his eighty-fifth year whose name it has been impossible to ascertain. Though including accounts of the battles of Trenton and Princeton, it affords no new information respecting either. Its importance consists in its relation of facts regarding the "twenty-six days tyranny" of the British and Hessian occupation of Princeton. The notes of the editor, Mr. V. L. Collins, Reference Librarian of Princeton University Library, furnish many confirmations of the sufferings inflicted by the hostile army on the people of New Jersey. In addition to the extensive annotation there is an index.

The Twentieth Regiment of Massachusetts Volunteer Infantry, 1861-1865. By Brevet Lt.-Colonel GEORGE A. BRUCE. *At the Request of the Officers' Association of the Regiment.* Boston and New York: Houghton, Mifflin and Co. The Riverside Press, Cambridge. 1906. 8vo. pp. viii+519. Ill. Maps.

This regiment, commanded by Col. William Raymond Lee, was known as the Harvard Regiment from the fact that a large proportion of its officers were young men from Harvard College. Its services were of the most notable character, and it is the fifth on the list of regiments that encountered the heaviest losses. The engagement at Ball's Bluff, in which this regiment partook and which was particularly fatal to Massachusetts men, is related with what the author considers undue prolixity, but which he says "is the only correct and complete history of it that he has ever seen." The record of the actions of the regiment, which is compiled from official reports, general and regimental histories, and newspapers, is supplemented by the Roster.

The Word Park in the United States. By ALBERT MATTHEWS. Reprinted from the Publications of the Colonial Society of Massachusetts, Vol. VIII. Cambridge: John Wilson and Son. University Press. 1906. Large 8vo. pp. 373-399.

This pamphlet is a collection of facts accumulated in the course of an investigation into the history of our National Parks.

Bulletin of the Society of Mayflower Descendants in the State of New York. No. 2. Printed for the Society. New York. April, 1906. 4to. pp. 39-87. Ill.

Besides various lists and reports of committees, this number contains articles on "The Pilgrim and His share in American Life" and "Governor John Carver."

Constitution and By-Laws, Officers and Members of the Ohio Society of the State of New York. 1906. [New York. 1906.] 12mo. pp. 47.

Library of Harvard University. Bibliographical Contributions. Edited by WILLIAM COOLIDGE LANE, Librarian. No. 57. Catalogue of the Molière Collection in Harvard College Library, acquired chiefly from the Library of the late Ferdinand Bôcher, A. M., Professor of Modern Languages. Compiled by THOMAS FRANKLIN CURRIER, Catalogue Department, and ERNEST LEWIS GAY. Cambridge, Mass. Issued by the Library of Harvard University. 1906. Large 8vo. pp. 148.

Proceedings of the Bostonian Society at the Annual Meeting, Jan. 9, 1906. Boston: Old State House. Published by Order of the Society. 1906. Large 8vo. pp. 105.

Besides various reports and lists, this publication contains papers on "Josiah Quincy, the Great Mayor" and "Boston when Ben. Franklin was a Boy."

Proceedings of the Maine Historical Society, Jan. 26, 1905, to Nov. 23, 1905. Portland: Smith & Sale, Printers. 1905. Large 8vo. pp. 25.

Proceedings of the Most Worshipful Grand Lodge of Ancient Free and Accepted Masons of the Commonwealth of Massachusetts, in union with the Most Ancient and Honorable Grand Lodges in Europe and America, according to the Old Constitutions. Quarterly Communications: March 14, 1906. Special Communications: Feb. 21, March 28, May 15, 16, 1906. M. W. John Albert Blake, Grand Master. R. W. Sereno D. Nickerson, Recording Grand Secretary. Boston: The Rockwell and Churchill Press. 1906. 8vo. pp. 37.

Proceedings of the New Jersey Historical Society. A Magazine of History, Biography and Genealogy. Published quarterly. Third Series. Vol. III. No. 2. April, 1906. Library of the Society, West Park St., Newark, N. J. Large 8vo. pp. 97-152.

Important articles in this number are "Life and Times of Rev. Jonathan Elmer," "Books and Pamphlets relating to New Jersey History and Biography, published in 1898-1900," and "Some Unpublished Revolutionary Manuscripts."

Proceedings and Transactions of the Royal Society of Canada. Second Series—Vol. XI. Meeting of May, 1905. For sale by James Hope & Son, Ottawa; The Copp-Clark Co. (Limited), Toronto; Bernard Quaritch, London, England. 1906. Large 8vo. Variously paged. Ill. Map.

The section of the Transactions relating to "English History, Literature," etc., consists of articles on "Brest on the Quebec Labrador," "The Late Arthur Harvey," "A Review of the Founding and Development of the University of Toronto as a Provincial Institution," and "Origin of the French Canadians." The section relating to "Littérature Française, Histoire," etc., contains a paper of importance on "Pierre Gaultier de Varennes, Sieur de la Vérendrye, Capitaine des troupes de la Marine, Chevalier de l'Ordre Militaire de Saint-Louis, Découvreur du Nord-Ouest, 1685-1749." The scientific portions show the usual variety of subjects.

Proceedings of the Worcester Society of Antiquity, for the year 1904. Vol. XX. Nos. 4, 5, 6. Worcester, Mass. Published by the Society. 1905, 1906. 4to. pp. 191-298. Ill.

The articles of special interest in these publications are "General Israel Putnam," in No. 4, "Treatment of the Indians by the Colonists," in No. 5, and the "Memorial of William Henry Bartlett," in No. 6. Besides these, there is also, in the last number, a short "Memorial Sketch of Rev. Carlton Albert Staples."

Report of the Officers to the Society of Middletown Upper Houses, with Lists of Life and Charter Members. Cromwell, Conn. May, 1906. 8vo. pp. 8. Ill.

Index to Obituary and Biographical Notices in Jackson's Oxford Journal, (Newspaper) 1753-1853. Compiled by EDWARD A. B. MORDAUNT. Vol. I. (1753, 1754, 1755.) London: Montagu St., Portman Square, West. 1905. Entered at Stationers' Hall. (Second Edition.) Large 8vo. pp. 34.

ERRATA.

Vol. 60, page 207, line 20, *for* 1642-43, *read* 1632-43.
Vol. 60, page 209, line 37, *for* David, *read* Daniel.
Vol. 60, page 278, line 30, *for* Eng., *read* Ire.
Vol. 60, page 305, last line, *for* Navini, *read* Naomi.
Vol. 60, page 315, line 10, *for* Thomas *read* Thamar.

INDEX OF PERSONS.

INDEX OF PLACES.

[371

THE NEW ENGLAND HISTORICAL AND GENEALOGIC REGISTER.

VOL. LX.—JANUARY, 1906.

WHOLE NUMBER, 237.

BOSTON:
PUBLISHED BY THE
NEW ENGLAND HISTORIC GENEALOGICAL SOCIETY.
1906.

Editor,
HENRY ERNEST WOODS, A.M.

CONTENTS—JANUARY, 1906.

*** *Illustrations:*

☞ Entered at the Post Office in Boston, Massachusetts, as second-class mail-matter.

New England Historic Genealogical Society.

The attention of all persons interested in historical and genealogical research is called to the following estimate of the financial needs of the Society:

For a new five-story fire-proof Library building in rear of Society's House, with a hall to seat 300 persons, stack room for 250,000 books, and a reading room to accommodate 80 readers (tentative plans can now be seen at the Society's rooms, and suggestions are invited)	$60,000	
Library fixtures, furniture, etc.	30,000	
Land, 5,000 square feet, purchased, but not yet paid for	30,000	$120,000
For addition to permanent fund, for purchase and binding of books, and increased expenses of a new building (calling for $3,000 additional income per annum)		75,000
For copying records of births, marriages and deaths from court files, church records, clergymen's and undertakers' private records, graveyard inscriptions and family bibles		10,000
For preparing and printing a catalogue of the 60,000 books and pamphlets belonging to the Society .		8,000
For Alphabetical Abstracts or Digest of personal items in the Boston News-Letter and other New England newspapers, from 1704 to 1815, estimated to be equal to 8000 printed pages		6,000
For Genealogical research in England, a permanent fund of		15,000
For printing Abstracts of Wills from the Prerogative Court of Canterbury, England (first volume now completed), a fund of		10,000
For printing an Index to the first 50 volumes of the New-England Historical and Genealogical Register (now complete in manuscript)		7,000
For estimated loss in printing Vital Records to 1850 of Massachusetts towns		5,000

The Treasurer, Nathaniel C. Nash, 18 Somerset St., Boston, and all other officers of the Society, will be glad to advise persons intending to give or bequeath money to the Society.

MEMORIAL BIOGRAPHIES, VOL. 6.

THE Sixth Volume of Memorial Biographies of deceased members of the New England Historic Genealogical Society has been published. It contains memoirs of 179 members of the Society, or of all who died between June 23, 1864, and September 5, 1871. The five previous volumes contain memoirs of 311 members, making a total of 409 memoirs in the six volumes.

Each volume contains over five hundred octavo pages, printed on superior paper, handsomely bound, and indexed. The price is $2.50 a volume, or $12.00 for the six volumes. When the books are sent by mail, the postage, 25 cents a volume, will be added.

This series of volumes is replete with historic and biographic lore, of constantly increasing value—great pains having been taken to make the memoirs complete and accurate. Only a small edition is printed.

Address: NATHANIEL C. NASH, TREASURER,
18 SOMERSET ST., BOSTON, MASS.

GENEALOGY OF THE DESCENDANTS OF EDWARD BATES OF WEYMOUTH, MASS. By SAMUEL A. BATES. 8vo. pp. 143. Price $1.25, delivery extra. Address, NATHANIEL C. NASH, Treasurer, 18 Somerset Street, Boston, Mass.

REGISTER RE-PRINTS, SERIES A.

The following re-prints of genealogies which have appeared in the NEW ENGLAND HISTORICAL AND GENEALOGICAL REGISTER may be obtained upon application to NATHANIEL C. NASH, *Treasurer*, 18 Somerset Street, Boston, Mass.

No. 1.	Descendants of Eltweed Pomeroy of Dorchester, Mass., and Windsor, Conn.	(16 pp.)	$0.50
No. 2.	" " John Moore of Sudbury, Mass. . . .	(22 pp.)	.50
No. 3.	" " Samuel Walker of Woburn, Mass. . .	(9 pp.)	.50
No. 4.	" " William Luddington of Malden, Mass., and East Haven, Conn.	(13 pp.)	.50
No. 5.	" " Henry Brooks of Woburn, Mass. . .	(20 pp.)	.50
No. 6.	" " John Hill of Dorchester, Mass. . . .	(22 pp.)	.50
No. 7.	" " Digory Sargent of Boston and Worcester, Mass.	(12 pp.)	.50
No. 8.	" " Henry and John Sherburne of Portsmouth, N. H.	(22 pp.)	.50
No. 9.	" " John Russell of Dartmouth, Mass. . .	(20 pp.)	.50
No. 10.	" " William Cotton of Portsmouth, N. H. .	(26 pp.)	.50
No. 11.	Research in England—An Essay to aid the Student .	(36 pp.)	1.00
No. 12.	Descendants of Benjamin Wilmot of New Haven, Conn.	(9 pp.)	.50

MASSACHUSETTS
VITAL RECORDS.

THE NEW ENGLAND HISTORIC GENEALOGICAL SOCIETY is publishing, by a Fund set apart from the bequest of ROBERT HENRY EDDY to the Society, the Vital Records (Births, Marriages and Deaths) of Towns in Massachusetts whose Records are not already printed, from their beginning to the year 1850, in books of 8vo size, in clear type, on good paper, and with cloth binding. The arrangement is alphabetical.

Subscription to these Records, if made in advance of publication, will be taken at the rate of one cent per page, which includes binding.

Only a limited number of copies are being printed. The type is then distributed, and the extra copies held on sale at a considerable advance on the subscription price.

Address all communications to HENRY ERNEST WOODS, *Editor*, 18 Somerset Street, Boston, Mass.

Vital Records Published:
Montgomery
Pelham
Walpole
Peru
Alford
Hinsdale
Medfield
Lee
Becket
Sudbury
Tyringham
Bedford
New Braintree
Washington
Gt. Barrington
Gill
Arlington
Waltham
Chilmark
Bellingham
Palmer
Medway
Newton

Vital Records in Preparation:
Edgartown
Norton
Sturbridge
Medford
Dracut
Middlefield
Heath
Scituate
W. Stockbridge
Billerica
Weymouth
Foxborough
Wayland
Dalton
Williamstown
Pembroke
Brookline
Tisbury
Holliston
Granville
Hingham
Hopkinton
Dover
Townsend
Carver
Duxbury
Taunton

(Others in prospect)

Editor,
HENRY ERNEST WOODS, A.M.

CONTENTS—APRIL, 1906.

*** *Illustrations:*

☞ Entered at the Post Office in Boston, Massachusetts, as second-class mail-matter.

Committee on Publication.

THE

NEW ENGLAND HISTORICAL AND GENEALOGICAL REGISTER.

SUPPLEMENT TO APRIL NUMBER, 1906.

PROCEEDINGS

OF THE

NEW ENGLAND HISTORIC GENEALOGICAL SOCIETY

AT THE

ANNUAL MEETING, 10 JANUARY, 1906,

WITH

MEMOIRS OF DECEASED MEMBERS, 1905.

THE

NEW ENGLAND

HISTORICAL AND GENEALOGICAL

REGISTER.

VOL. LX.—JULY, 1906.

WHOLE NUMBER, 239.

BOSTON:
PUBLISHED BY THE
NEW ENGLAND HISTORIC GENEALOGICAL SOCIETY.
1906.

CONTENTS—JULY, 1906.

*** *Illustration:*
Portrait of Robert Charles Winthrop, Jr. (to face page 223).

☞ Entered at the Post Office in Boston, Massachusetts, as second-class mail-matter.

MASSACHUSETTS
VITAL RECORDS.

DAVID CLAPP & SON, PRINTERS, 291 CONGRESS ST., BOSTON.

THE

NEW ENGLAND

HISTORICAL AND GENEALOGI

REGISTER.

VOL. LX.—OCTOBER, 1906.

WHOLE NUMBER, 240.

BOSTON:
PUBLISHED BY THE
NEW ENGLAND HISTORIC GENEALOGICAL SOCIE
1906.

Editor,

HENRY ERNEST WOODS, A.M.

CONTENTS—OCTOBER, 1906.

[OVER]

AMERICANA FOR THE SAN FRANCISCO FREE PUBLIC LIBRARY.

The Library Committee of the New England Historic Genealogica Society invites all persons interested in historical and genealogica work, who consider it a privilege to assist in replacing the book destroyed by earthquake and fire last April, to send their gifts o books to 18 Somerset St., Boston, for free shipment to San Francisco

Lightning Source UK Ltd.
Milton Keynes UK
UKHW012231070119
334942UK00010BA/1642/P